UNCENSORED RUSSIA

also edited by Peter Reddaway

UNCENSORED RUSSIA

PROTEST AND DISSENT IN
THE SOVIET UNION

The Unofficial Moscow Journal
A Chronicle of Current Events

Edited, translated and with a commentary by
PETER REDDAWAY

With a Foreword by Julius Telesin

AMERICAN HERITAGE PRESS
A DIVISION OF McGRAW-HILL BOOK COMPANY
New York   St. Louis   San Francisco   Toronto

Library of Congress Catalog Card Number 71-37760

07-051354-6

PRINTED IN GREAT BRITAIN

CONTENTS

5

PART VI: TRIBUTARIES

PART VII: DAMS

LIST OF ILLUSTRATIONS

Between pages 384 and 385

Figures in the text

A NOTE ON THE ILLUSTRATIONS

The illustrations in this book are a unique collection. Only half of them have appeared previously, and those often in obscure places. Most have reached the West at some risk to their carriers, but this last stage has involved the least of the difficulties. To draw or photograph prisoners in labour camps, for example, is fraught with danger. Even more tricky is getting the finished products out of the camps, as careful body searches are the norm for prisoners on their release. Doubtless, therefore, 'free workers' who live outside the camps, and even administrative personnel sometimes act as couriers. Also very difficult is the photographing of 'action shots' outside court-houses or during demonstrations. Here police of different hues are always present in large numbers, ready to pounce: many are the

1*

cameras they have threatened to break, the films that have been rudely exposed.

And yet despite all this we have photographs from the Mordovian and Siberian camps, from the Oryol prison, from places of exile on the Sino-Soviet border, and near Lake Baikal, from a civil disturbance in Central Asia, from the Crimea and the Caucasus, from Riga and Gorky, from Kiev and Kirov, and so on. I am grateful to the photographers and the couriers concerned, mostly unknown to me, and hope that the use of their material in this book will bring them satisfaction.

Copyright belongs as follows: on plates 5 and 6 to A.P., plate 7 to U.P.I., plates 31 and 33–9 to Europa Civiltà, Largo Brindisi 18/5, 00182 Rome, plates 2, 3, 16–19, 23, 27, 58 and 60 to Julius Telesin, plates 24 and 59 to Victor Fedosseyev, plates 14, 15, 42, 49 and 50 to Transworld Feature Syndicate, 52 High Holborn, London WC1, plate 22 to London Express News and Features, 41 Shoe Lane, London EC4, plates 9 and 13 to the Alexander Herzen Foundation, Amstel 268, Amsterdam-C, plate 10 to Kuratorium Geistige Freiheit, Postfach 1825, 3001 Bern, Switzerland, plates 12, 26, 28, 30, 40–41, 43–5, 56, 63–5, 70–74 to A.C.E.R., 91 rue Olivier de Serres, Paris 15, plate 11 to Possev-Verlag, D623 Frankfurt/M 80, Flurscheideweg 15, plates 4, 21 and 25 to Frank Starr, plates 29 and 54 to P.I.U.F., 3 rue du Sabot, Paris 6, plates 32 and 61 to David Khavkin, plate 55 to M. Davies, c/o Weidenfeld & Nicolson, London, plate 53 to Prolog, 875 West End Ave., New York, N.Y. 10025, plate 75 to the Latvian Social Democratic Party, Stockholm, plates 46–8 to Arts et Progrès, 37 Ave. Eugène Adam, 78 Maisons-Laffittes, France, plates 66 and 76 to Boris Tsukerman, plate 1 to Hélène Zamoyska, plates 51, 52, 68 and 69 to myself, and plates 8, 20, 57, 62 and 67 to no one whom it has been possible to identify. The map on p. 204 (fig. 2) is reproduced from *Ferment in the Ukraine*, edited by Michael Browne, © 1971 by Michael Browne, by kind permission of Macmillan & Co. Ltd, London and Basingstoke.

A NOTE ON SOVIET LAWS

Among the various Soviet laws mentioned in the *Chronicle*, the two which appear most frequently are articles 70 and 190–1 of the Russian (i.e. R.S.F.S.R.) Criminal Code. Article 70 reads:

'Agitation or propaganda carried on for the purpose of subverting or weakening Soviet power or of committing particular especially dangerous crimes against the state, or the [verbal] spreading for the same purpose of slanderous fabrications which defame the Soviet political and social system, or the circulation or preparation or keeping, for the same purpose, of literature of such content, shall be punished by deprivation of freedom for a term of six months to seven years, with or without additional exile for a term of two to five years, or by exile for a term of two to five years.'

Article 190–1 reads:

'The systematic dissemination by word of mouth of deliberate fabrications discrediting the Soviet political and social system, or the manufacture or dissemination in written, printed or other form of works of the same content, shall be punished by deprivation of freedom for a term not exceeding three years, or by corrective labour for a term not exceeding one year, or by a fine not exceeding one hundred roubles.'

The texts of other articles of the criminal law may be found in H. J. Berman, *Soviet Criminal Law and Procedure* (Oxford University Press, London, 1966).

A NOTE ON TRANSLITERATION
AND TRANSLATION

The transliteration system used here is eclectic, being designed primarily to give the lay reader some idea of how words and names are pronounced. But it follows a consistent pattern. The less obvious parts of this pattern are: (1) the Russian 'e' is transliterated 'ye' only after a preceding vowel; (2) the Russian 'ы' is transliterated 'i' (rather than 'y') only when preceding a Russian 'e'; (3) Ukrainian proper (but not place) names have been transliterated from their Ukrainian forms according to a separate system; (4) first names have been anglicized only when the Russian form is almost identical to the English; (5) for names like Beria, Khrushchev, Izvestia and Kiev, conventional forms have been used.

As for translation, these points should be noted: (1) the Communist League of Youth—a body for people aged from about 15–27—appears normally as 'Komsomol', the Russian acronym for its full title; (2) the words Procurator and Procuracy have been used: Soviet Procurators have a dual function, not only prosecuting in criminal cases, but also being responsible for the observation of legality throughout the Soviet legal system; (3) the R.S.F.S.R.—the Russian Soviet Federated Socialist Republic, by far the largest of the U.S.S.R.'s fifteen constituent republics—appears normally just as Russia; (4) although the terms *kandidat nauk* and *doktor nauk* appear as Master of Science and Doctor of Science, it should be noted that the former is nearly on the level of an average Western Ph.D. and the latter, not normally attained before the age of forty, is well above it.

Finally, (1) passages in parentheses in the *Chronicle* text belong to the *Chronicle*, whereas those in square brackets have been added by the editor; (2) all footnotes are by the editor except where the *Chronicle* is indicated; (3) editorial commentary is distinguished from the *Chronicle*'s text by the use of italics; (4) a row of dots within square brackets—[...]—indicates the omission of a passage or phrase which exactly repeats information given elsewhere in the book.

DATES OF ISSUE OF THE *CHRONICLE*

(a) Numbers translated in this book:

No. 1 : April 30th, 1968

No. 2 : June 30th, 1968

No. 3 : August 30th, 1968

No. 4 : October 31st, 1968

No. 5 : December 25th, 1968

No. 6 : February 28th, 1969

No. 7 : April 30th, 1969

No. 8 : June 30th, 1969

No. 9 : August 31st, 1969

No. 10 : October 31st, 1969

No. 11 : December 31st, 1969

(b) Subsequent numbers referred to in this book:

No. 12 : February 28th, 1970

No. 13 : April 30th, 1970

No. 14 : June, 30th, 1970

No. 15 : August 31st, 1970

No. 16 : October 31st, 1970

No. 17 : December 31st, 1970

No. 18 : March 5th, 1971

No. 19 : April 30th, 1971

No. 20 : July 2nd, 1971

No. 21 : September 11th, 1971

ACKNOWLEDGMENTS

Many people have helped in the preparation of this book, whether with translation, the provision of information, or their criticisms of different parts of it. Among others I would particularly like to thank: Bohdan Bociurkiw, Michael Bourdeaux, Gerald Brooke, Michael Browne, Abraham Brumberg, Martin Dewhirst, Peter Dornan, Cornelia Gerstenmaier, Max Hayward, Stuart Hood, Xenia Howard-Johnston, Nina Karsov, Roland Lajoie, the late William McAfee, Michael Nicholson, Leonard Schapiro, Hilary Sternberg, Victor Swoboda, Szymon Szechter, Julius Telesin, Boris Tsukerman and Karel van het Reve. I am also grateful to my agent Patrick Seale, who gave practical help and encouragement at a time of negative responses from publishers, my editor, Michael Petty, for his considerateness, and my secretary Joan Moyce, who, like the best *samizdat* typists, has invariably been quick, kind, accurate and patient. For the compilation of the index, no small task, I am indebted to a special friend, Kathy Tietgens.

P.R.

INTRODUCTION

Was there ever a country with a censorship and an arbitrary government where secret presses and the underground distribution of manuscripts did not exist, — once intellectual movements and the desire for liberty existed? This is just as natural a state of affairs as the publication of material abroad and emigration.

Alexander Herzen, January 1865[1]

From the five issues of the *Chronicle* to date one may form at least a partial impression of how the suppression of human rights and of the movement for them has been occurring in the Soviet Union. Not one participant in this movement can feel his task is ended with the end of Human Rights Year. The general aim of democratization, and the more particular aim pursued by the *Chronicle*, are still to be achieved.

Chronicle No. 5, December 1968[2]

Although at present the social base of the Democratic Movement is indeed very narrow, and the movement itself has been forced to operate in extremely difficult conditions, the ideas proclaimed by it have begun to spread widely throughout the country—and that is the beginning of an irreversible process of self-liberation.

Pyotr Yakir, March 1970[3]

The *Chronicle of Current Events* is one of the most important documents ever to come out of the Soviet Union. An unofficial Moscow journal, its significance can perhaps be compared, in recent years, only with Khrushchev's 'secret speech' of 1956 about Stalin's crimes, or Solzhenitsyn's story of 1962, *One Day in the Life of Ivan Denisovich*, about the Soviet concentration camps. For its first eleven issues (April 1968–December 1969) — whose texts make up this book—do no less than trace in fascinating detail the emergence of the first broad, if loosely organized, movement of dissent in the U.S.S.R. for almost half a century. They are the strongest proof that 'intellectual movements and the desire for liberty' — to use Herzen's phrase of 1865 — have reappeared and become active.

The *Chronicle* is in fact the 'organ' of these movements' mainstream, a mainstream called by its members either the Democratic Movement or, with a narrower application, the Civil (or Human) Rights Movement. Given such names, it is not surprising that the movement's general aim has been the

15

democratization of Soviet society, or that the Czechoslovak evolution of 1968 aroused its admiration.

The movement has already, as the *Chronicle* shows, suffered many reverses. It will certainly suffer many more — perhaps much worse — in the years ahead. Nevertheless, the evidence of this book suggests that the Soviet historian Pyotr Yakir may well be right in asserting that 'the ideas proclaimed by it have begun to spread widely throughout the country — and that is the beginning of an irreversible process of self-liberation.'

To assert this — it should at once be said — is in no way to prejudge how long any such liberation would last. After a long, perhaps irreversible process Russia liberated herself from the tsarist autocracy in March 1917: in less than a year her liberty had been snuffed out. History, indeed, never repeats itself exactly. In the second half of this century, however, a near-repetition of that winning and losing of liberty is — as another Moscow historian, Andrei Amalrik, has argued[4] — one of the possibilities, an ugly joker in the pack.

But the *Chronicle* does not record only the emergence of the Democratic Movement. It is also a document of the highest historical value for the dramatic way in which it lights up many other areas of Soviet life. The official press, of course, tells us a certain amount about the political, social and economic views of particular citizens and officials, about the practices of the courts, the Procuracy and even the secret police, about party policy towards the national and religious groups, and so on. But often we can have little or no idea how reliable this information is, for it has all passed through one of the world's most powerful censorship machines en route to the reader and has come out with a suspiciously low content of serious criticism of the system.

Thus the Soviet press is usually — especially in the many areas where politics enter — a primary source of inferior worth. It frequently reflects not what the writer believes, but rather what he knows the censor wants, or what the censor has turned his copy into. It is, moreover, usually written in turgid, stereo-typed language, choked with clichés of phrase and concept.[5] And certain subjects — not just military security but, for example, national frictions or practices in prisons, labour camps and mental hospitals — are virtually taboo.

The *Chronicle*, by contrast, focuses precisely on many of those aspects of Soviet life where the official press is most inadequate. It illuminates them, like the best primary sources, in precise, unemotive language. It is uninhibited by censorship, yet in taking advantage of this it is constrained by potent considerations to achieve a high level of accuracy. In brief, it both articulates the demands of aggrieved groups in Soviet society and throws fresh light on those institutions with which the groups conflict. Meanwhile almost nothing of all this is reflected — at least recognizably — in the official press.

The origins of SAMIZDAT

But what of the tradition which produced the *Chronicle*? And how has it evolved over the century and a half of its existence?

In the years around 1820 people like the poet Pushkin and the playwright Griboyedov developed the habit of distributing privately in manuscript those works which the censors disliked. The practice was boosted early in the reign of Alexander II both by the freer political atmosphere and by the circulation in Russia of Herzen's uncensored paper *The Bell* (1857–67), published mainly in London. Moreover, political manifestoes and tracts now began to appear in Russia itself, to circulate, with varying degrees of legality, alongside literary works and *The Bell*. This trend accelerated with the formation of the first illegal political groups in the 1860s and 1870s and of the first political parties round the turn of the century. As tsarism approached its end, the variety of the illegal and semi-legal literature being produced grew steadily: it covered a wide spectrum of political, national and religious views. At the same time the censorship fluctuated in severity, even collapsing altogether for a time in 1905.

In short, then, the persistence of arbitrary government and watchful censors — in a period when 'intellectual movements and the desire for liberty' began to flourish — naturally gave birth to 'secret presses and the underground distribution of manuscripts'.

March 1917 brought a brief spell of total, heady freedom. After the Bolshevik seizure of power in October, this was severely curtailed, and a new censorship — which came to be known as *Glavlit* — was set up. Until about 1930 literature of many sorts passed from hand to hand, and even as late as 1932 the Bolshevik Ryutin dared (foolhardily as it turned out) to circulate an anti-Stalin programme. But as the censorship tightened, so the terror grew. Circulation slowed to a trickle, and the owners of manuscripts, typescripts, books by Trotsky and other heretics or non-believers, consigned them with furtive prudence to the flames. By the years 1937–8, when the population of the concentration camps rocketed to 9–10 million, these graves for the living had, ironically, become the last notable refuge of free expression. A rich literature of songs developed in them, often with strong political overtones or words.

The situation did not change radically until after Stalin's death in 1953. At this stage the censorship eased, the camps gradually discharged most of their by now 10–15 million inmates, and, with Khrushchev's attack on Stalin in early 1956, a new era seemed possible. But soon Khrushchev was backtracking. Dismissed censors were re-engaged, Boris Pasternak's *Dr Zhivago* was rejected for publication, and the most creative writers were reduced to a 'conspiracy of silence' or—as time went on—to circulating their works in private. In the case of some writers—such as Pasternak, Alexander Esenin-Volpin, Andrei Sinyavsky, Yuly Daniel, Valery Tarsis, Mikhail Naritsa, Anna Akhmatova and others—they opted for publishing abroad. At the same time unofficial journals like *Syntax* (1958–60), *Phoenix* (1961 and 1966) and *Sphinxes* (1965)[6]— edited by Alexander Ginzburg, Yury Galanskov and Valery Tarsis respectively—appeared and in due course found their way abroad.

The fact that unsanctioned activity of this sort did not assume a large scale before the late 1960s may be explained mainly by Khrushchev's policies. Erratic though these were, he eased the censorship—especially in the period 1959–62, which culminated in Solzhenitsyn's explosive *One Day*—and, if we overlook the young poet Iosif Brodsky, he avoided putting any well-known intellectuals or writers on trial. In the autumn of 1965, however, arrests of such people began in Moscow and the Ukraine, and the censorship tightened. Liberals' hopes of getting their stories and articles into print faded. The Khrushchev era of more or less peaceful coexistence between the party and the liberal intelligentsia[7] was at an end.

Symptoms of the new conditions were that serious criticism of Stalin was now forbidden, that two secret police generals were appointed to sit on the Supreme Court,[8] and that in 1966 Sinyavsky and Daniel received savage sentences of seven and five years' hard labour. This trial—and even more so that of Galanskov and Ginzburg in January 1968—gave an immense stimulus to unofficial literary life, provoking mass protests and turning people's attention in a remarkable degree towards politics.

Seemingly, in fact, it was the year 1966 which saw the birth of an expressive new Russian word—full of ominous overtones for the authorities—*samizdat*.[9] An acronym on the model *Gosizdat* (short for 'State Publishing-House'), *samizdat* means 'own publishing-house': if the state one won't publish me, I'll publish myself. Thus the U.S.S.R.'s only forum of free thought now had a name. Soon the *Chronicle* would supply a catalogue.

The whole institution clearly reeked to the authorities of another dread word—castigated by Bolshevik leaders from Lenin downwards—spontaneity. Worse still, the word *samizdat* caught on so spontaneously that mention of it in the press soon became unavoidable. Among the first people to use it here was General of the K.G.B., A. Malygin. Writing in McCarthy-like tones in January 1969, he declared: 'Lately all kinds of literature with harmful contents have been circulating in manuscript form. Advice on this activity comes from abroad. This so-called *samizdat* is composed at the direct instigation of western intelligence and is actively supported by it.'[10]

But how does a work get into *samizdat*? Usually the author, or a friend of his, or a publishing-house editor, types out some copies and passes them around. In this way popular items are typed and retyped indefinitely and often reach the outside world through the help of a Soviet or Western tourist. In that case they have a chance of second publication, this time in *tamizdat*, i.e. in the Western press or an émigré journal '*tam*' or 'over there'. Finally they may also then be broadcast back to the Soviet Union by Western radio stations, thus achieving a third 'publication'.[11]

In a famous letter to the fourth Congress of Soviet writers in 1967, Solzhenitsyn called for the abolition of 'the now intolerable oppression of the censorship': 'not provided for by the

Constitution, and therefore illegal, it is nowhere called by its proper name and goes under the mysterious label of *Glavlit*.' Because of this 'survival of the Middle Ages ... our writers are not trusted, not endowed with the right to express their cautionary judgments about the moral life of man and society, to interpret in their own way social problems or the historical experience which has been lived through with so much suffering in our country.'

Never a truer word — and never a stonier response. *Glavlit* waxed exceeding strong.

But so too — in reply — did *samizdat*. In the four years since Solzhenitsyn wrote his letter some seven hundred documents, articles, stories, plays and books have reached the West from mainstream *samizdat*. Though containing most of the heavy-weight items, these seven hundred represent but a small proportion of the whole.

The tradition of the Democratic Movement

Such was the situation into which, on April 30th, 1968, the *Chronicle* was born. A journal unique in form, it corresponded well to the needs of the time. With *samizdat* — especially its protest document division — in full bloom, different oppressed sectors of society felt an increasing desire for reliable information about each other. This was exactly what the *Chronicle* began to provide: regular, accurate, concrete information about a steadily widening variety of groups. Thus the most essential prerequisite for any even loosely co-ordinated activity above the local level now existed: a reliable news bulletin. The Democratic Movement was coming into existence. It was, moreover, no surprise when the *Chronicle* later became — in a semi-formal sense — the Movement's organ.

This book provides abundant evidence by which to judge what the term Democratic Movement really means in the Soviet Union today. But history provides further perspectives, and in view of the uncanny trends of continuity which, alongside those of change, run through Russian and Soviet history, these are of especial interest.

The anti-tsarist movement of the nineteenth century had various streams at various times, also different names: opposition movement, liberation movement, revolutionary movement. But, to generalize, we may say that the mainstream of the movement received its first big impulse, in the 1850s, from the government's disastrous handling of the Crimean War. With the authorities thus discredited, the movement's backbone, the intelligentsia, felt all the more justified in aspiring to the socio-political role which had, since its emergence several decades earlier, been denied it. At the same time, various foreign influences came into play, increasing the intelligentsia's confidence and widening its choice of tactics. The foreign press became available and foreign travel became easy. The émigré press and émigré political groups put down roots.

However, notwithstanding strenuous efforts from the 1870s on to politicize the largely indifferent, often hostile 'masses', the movement remained until the turn of the century essentially middle and upper class in composition. So its numbers understandably remained small, even in the 1890s totalling in the mainstream no more than a few thousand. This did not however mean that the authorities ignored it: from Herzen's *Bell* onwards the movement could on occasion frighten the government and, in certain spheres, affect its policies. In general, though, the movement was seen in the nineteenth century as a potential, long-term danger of much more serious proportions than any immediate trouble it might cause. As things turned out, this view was rather accurate.

Ideologically speaking, the movement was always widely diverse, the full spectrum of views first becoming clear in the late 1850s. True, in 1902-3 P. B. Struve tried to unify a broad range of opposition groups round the paper *Liberation*, but he failed. The *Chronicle* has, therefore, no forebears.

Most groups in the nineteenth-century movement called regularly for civil and economic freedoms for all sections of society. Significantly, however, law was not often regarded as one of the main ways of securing these freedoms. Indeed, the more 'left' groups tended to show considerable contempt for law and a corresponding readiness to use force in achieving their aims. Also, while some of the movement's leading members were broad-minded, considerate people, almost saintly in their self-sacrifice, others were the incarnation of dogmatism and intolerance. 'Under the flag of science, art and persecuted freedom of thought,' Chekhov once wrote, Russia would one day be ruled by 'toads and crocodiles the like of which were unknown even in Spain at the time of the Inquisition'.[12] He shared this pre-vision of Stalinism with another writer, Dostoyevsky.

The Movement's Aims and Structure

If we turn now to the roots of today's Democratic Movement, then Khrushchev's denunciation of Stalin in 1956 stands out as a turning-point in some ways equivalent to the tsarist régime's Crimean War. After that speech few open-minded people could continue to believe in Stalinism, an ideology which had led to the torture and execution of millions and the deportation of whole nations. Many knew these facts already, but Khrushchev's speech transformed them into legitimate subjects for reflection, discussion, written analysis. The feeling thus arose among the liberal intelligentsia that the Communist Party did not—contrary to its claims—know all the answers, moreover was capable of gross errors. The intelligentsia could thus claim back all the more legitimately at least the socio-political role it had possessed in the 1920s, if not a larger one.

Part of that role, it was felt, should be the task of curtailing arbitrariness and police terror by the development of some measure of the rule of law. In this way a repetition of Stalinism —which had cut down the intelligentsia as much as any other social group—might be prevented. Secondly, liberals thought, the intelligentsia should press for the maximum of compensation for those individuals, groups and nations who had, in their millions, populated the camps: in many cases, of course, it could only try to compensate surviving relatives and descendants. And thirdly, it should try to promote the country's material well-being by getting its scientific and economic expertise applied by the régime in the most rational ways.

These various aims have, in the last decade or so, proved more difficult to achieve than their nineteenth-century equivalents. This is not surprising, for independent action becomes almost impossible under a system which aspires with considerable success to the complete control of society. Moreover, the need to work always within the system often enforces a demoralizing number of compromises: not only one's job, but one's wife's job, one's flat and any privileges one may have are all instantly removable by the state. Hence the relief which many members of the Democratic Movement have felt in casting off the burden of excessive compromise and opting for *samizdat* and other essentially extra-system activities.

As for foreign links, all reformist elements—those fully within the system as well as those on the fringes—have, as in the last century, profited from their development. Especially under Khrushchev foreign books and periodicals became more accessible, travel abroad, even defection, was possible for some, Western radio stations broadcasting in Russian were in certain periods not jammed, and émigré material began to circulate.

Since Khrushchev's fall, however, reformism within the system has become increasingly difficult, and the birth of the Democratic Movement is one of the results. Those who fight for retrospective justice for Stalin's victims, for example, must now spend part of their energy opposing the rehabilitation of the executioner rather than promoting that of the executed.

Again as in the last century, the Democratic Movement is essentially middle and upper-middle class. Launched partly through the unification of groups in the natural sciences and the humanities, it has yet to make any serious appeal to 'the people' or '*narod*'. Not surprisingly, therefore, its adherents are few in number: only about two thousand mainstream members have so far dared to identify themselves deliberately by name. Clearly, however, these people receive support from many thousands of sympathizers who, while reading and circulating *samizdat*, prefer for various reasons to stop short of signing protests, forming groups or demonstrating.

The movement's class-structure becomes clearer if we analyse the identifiable mainstream members by occupation. We find then that nearly a half (with scientists strongly represented) have academic jobs, nearly a quarter are writers, artists and actors, one in eight is an engineer or technician, one in ten is in publishing, teaching, medicine or the law, one in twenty is a worker, a similar proportion are students, and one in a hundred is in the military.[13]

Ideologically speaking the Democratic Movement is—so far at least—less diverse than its nineteenth-century forerunner. The main explanation for this lies in the movement's remarkable unanimity on one vital point: the importance of law as a potential, even actual, instrument through which to promote democratization and secure civil rights. This sharp divergence from the nineteenth-century pattern helps to keep Leninists like General Grigorenko, neo-Marxists like Roy Medvedev, Christian socialists like Anatoly Levitin and liberal democrats like Andrei Amalrik—to use some over-simplified labels— surprisingly united. Such diverse tendencies do, in fact, take a common stand on the Soviet Constitution, all trying to liberalize both the content and application of various Soviet laws. How long their unity would last if the régime relaxed its pressure on them is of course hard to say.

In any case, along with their respect for law goes a remarkable mutual tolerance and lack of dogmatism. This holds true both in personal dealings and in ideas. The *Chronicle*, as will be seen, provides a platform for any views of generally democratic tendency. And the factionalism, splitting tactics and personal intolerance which marked much of the pre-1917 Liberation Movement—especially on the left, where Lenin surpassed all comers—have yet to appear in the Democratic Movement. This is so even though—to indulge in a moment's crude historicism—the Democratic Movement of today might be broadly compared with the Opposition Movement in the 1880s or, possibly, the 1890s. And by that period factionalism in the anti-autocracy ranks was already rife.

The CHRONICLE'*s editorial position*

But what about the ideological position of the *Chronicle* itself? As Chapter 1 shows, its origin was firmly tied to the designation of 1968 by the United Nations as International Human Rights Year. Thus above the title *A Chronicle of Current Events*, which has remained constant ever since, the first issue carried the masthead 'Human Rights Year in the Soviet Union'. Backing this up on the first page there appeared what was to prove a regular feature, the text of article 19 of the U.N.'s Universal Declaration of Human Rights:

> Everyone has the right to freedom of opinion and expression; this right includes freedom to hold opinions without interference and to seek, receive and impart information and ideas through any media and regardless of frontiers.

When 1968 ended, however, the *Chronicle* (in No. 6) changed its masthead, with characteristic spirit, to 'Human Rights Year in the Soviet Union Continues'. The next change, equally significant, came in early 1970 in No. 12. Here the new formulation—'The Movement in Defence of Human Rights in the Soviet Union *Continues*'—identified the *Chronicle* even more closely than before with the movement which its pages regularly describe.

These outer signs reflect accurately the *Chronicle*'s position. The political liberalism underlying article 19 of the U.N.'s Declaration does indeed also underlie the *Chronicle*'s editorial policy. Individuals with widely differing views are, for example, given an equal amount of space. Similarly with *samizdat* items. And the activities of almost all the known democratically inclined groups are at least on occasion recorded. An exception here has been the Baptists: prior to 1970 their extensive activity received minimal coverage, almost certainly for lack of links with the mainstream of the movement. In addition, militant Ukrainian nationalists had scarcely been mentioned before No. 17, perhaps for lack of links, or perhaps because the *Chronicle* was unsure how democratic they were in orientation. On the other hand, the editors have once or twice included illuminating accounts of chauvinist or fascist groups, notably that of the Moscow economist Fetisov (see p. 431), while at the same time strongly underlining the *Chronicle*'s opposition to them.

But the *Chronicle* contains little purely editorial material, so particular aspects of its editors' position must often be inferred. No. 5, however (see pp. 53-4), provides some broad guidelines. After discussing the movement for human rights and its 'general aim of democratization', the editors go on to describe 'the more particular aim pursued by the *Chronicle*' as: 'seeing that the Soviet public is informed about what goes on in the country' in the field of human rights. Thus 'the *Chronicle* is in no sense an illegal publication, and the difficult conditions in which it is produced are created by the peculiar notions about law and freedom of information which, in the course of long years, have become established in certain Soviet organizations. For this reason the *Chronicle* cannot, like any other journal, give its postal address on the last page.'

Two important points emerge. First, the *Chronicle*'s aim is openness, non-secretiveness, freedom of information and expression. All these notions are subsumed in the one Russian word *glasnost*. Second, the *Chronicle* is not the organ of any rival to the party, any political 'opposition'. Indeed the word opposition appears but rarely in its pages, mainly perhaps because the K.G.B. often affects, rightly or wrongly, to see no difference between opposition to a particular action or law and opposition to the whole Soviet system. The *Chronicle* regards itself as legal because it merely compiles an accurate record of events, and where there is truth there can—legally speaking—be no 'libel', 'anti-Soviet' or otherwise. It does not incite its readers to anti-Soviet acts, but urges them, usually implicitly, to defend Soviet legality. Certainly, in areas where this legality is ambiguous it adopts a liberal interpretation. Thus it believes in genuinely equal rights for all the nationalities of the U.S.S.R., in real religious freedom for believers (to be achieved by putting into practice the constitutional principle of separation of church and state), and in a foreign policy of sincerely peaceful coexistence, which would rule out the invasion of Czechoslovakia, and so on. It rejects in general the use of coercion, and notwithstanding the moral absolutism of particular individuals sometimes reflected in its pages, its own ideology is clearly reformist and gradualist in nature. One senses a sceptical view —grounded in Soviet experience—not only of Jacobinism but also of the very concept of revolutionary upheaval.

The *Chronicle*'s attitude to economic matters is harder to gauge. Clearly it sympathizes with the views of the physicist Andrei Sakharov, who in turn looked with admiration on the economic liberalization worked out in Czechoslovakia in 1968 by Professor Šik. However, like the Democratic Movement and the pressure group to which the movement gave birth in May 1969—the Action Group for the Defence of Civil Rights—the *Chronicle* has been much more concerned with law and politics than with economics. Composed mainly of professional people whose most cherished rights of free expression and communication have been under constant attack, the movement has so far said little about the economic rights of the workers and peasants. The same has therefore gone for its mirror, the *Chronicle*.

In sum, then, the *Chronicle*'s ideological position appears to be reformist, with liberal tendencies in politics and liberal socialist ones in economics. Certainly its editors' rationality and moderation mark them off sharply from emerging Slavophile and chauvinistic groups. We should also note that, while surveying a wide range of views in its first two years, it has increasingly seemed to be seeking a less defensive, more positive approach to its task of spreading information and enlightenment. This task is of course extremely difficult in a country whose political system has for half a century discouraged the growth of any popular belief in concepts like rationality, moderation or the rule of law.

The CHRONICLE's *themes*

As the complete text of the *Chronicle*'s first eleven issues — barring a few passages of repetition — form the core of this book, no detailed analysis of its contents is necessary here. A few generalizations may nevertheless be useful.

What broad trends, for example, have been reflected by the *Chronicle* since the spring of 1968? On the one hand we may conclude that the Democratic Movement has to a considerable extent overcome in its own ranks the Stalin-induced 'inertia of fear' and maintained its momentum. Set-backs have occurred, notably in mid-1968 when some of its members succumbed again to fear — partly because of the relative vigour of the authorities' reprisals against those who protested about the Galanskov–Ginzburg trial, and partly in view of the fairly decisive, if delayed, Soviet action in Czechoslovakia — but these set-backs were surmounted. On the other side of the equation the authorities have pursued what might be described as a policy of hesitant repression. They have gradually tightened the censorship, but have normally arrested only those civil rights activists who have most persistently refused to conform. The dialectic of the two sides' interaction has been interesting: a wave of repression provokes a wave of protest, which in turn provokes further repression, and so on, it seems, ad infinitum.

Statistically speaking, the *Chronicle*'s first eleven issues have reported in at least some detail on: the arrests of 37 people, the trials of 85 more, and the extra-judicial persecution of 250 more; the fate in forced-labour camps and prisons of

102* people, in prison 'mental hospitals' of 27;* and the self-immolation, successful or otherwise, of four people. In addition to this and other material these issues have also described the contents and authorship of some 160 items of *samizdat*.

In this book the content of the *Chronicles* has been divided according to theme into twenty chapters. These have their own brief introductions, and the number of the *Chronicle* from which each passage comes is shown in the margin. The chapters have then been grouped into the following sections: the *Chronicle's* editorial pronouncements; the most important mainstream events in chronological order; the struggle for survival in the camps, prisons and 'mental hospitals'; the vigorous campaigns of the national and religious groups—Crimean Tatars, Meskhetians, Ukrainians, Jews, Baptists, Orthodox and Uniates; the literary world of Alexander Solzhenitsyn and *samizdat*; the fight for civil rights throughout the country; and the problems posed by Stalin, censors, secret policemen and fascists. Reference is, incidentally, sometimes made in this book to *Chronicle* Nos. 12 to 20. These became available during the book's preparation.

The CHRONICLE's *production and distribution*

We have discussed the *Chronicle's* ideology and contents. Let us turn now to its editing and distribution. Its editors are anonymous: we have little clear idea of their identity. We know for sure only that they live in or near Moscow. It could even be that they change or rotate at intervals. Possible evidence for this hypothesis is both the uneven quality of some of the editing —No. 11, for example, falling below the usual high standard— and the great variations in size between, at the extremes, No. 3 with 2,000 words and No. 11 with 16,000.

The only person so far charged with being one of the editors is the poet Natalya Gorbanevskaya. As, however, the charge was made in her absence, at a brief, formal trial[14] which condemned her to indefinite detention in a prison 'mental hospital', its validity remains uncertain. In any case various indications suggest that scientists may be more involved than literary people. First, the *Chronicle's* plain, unemotional language is not notably literary. Second, the *Chronicle* carries relatively little

* Some of these people figure also among the 85 whose trials are reported.

material about the literary world. Third, very few of the *samizdat* items summarized by the *Chronicle* are the work of professional writers. And, fourth, the compiler of two 'White Books' on political trials produced in 1968(see pp. 66 and 73) — books which clearly helped to influence and establish the *Chronicle*'s style — was a physicist, Pavel Litvinov.

A final, vaguer point concerns the commonly held view that in the Soviet Union writers are the boldest and most numerous champions of freedom. This view must be designated a myth. Of the 6,500 members of the Writers' Union only a hundred or so can convincingly claim to be active liberals. Most of the others have been corrupted by the constant pressure to write what the censors want.

Anonymity, let us recall, has seemed to the *Chronicle*'s editors a regrettable necessity, forced on them by the authorities' disregard for legality. They have, however, triumphantly overcome the initial distrust which it engendered, thanks to the consistently high level of accuracy in their work. The cool tone, the paucity of value judgments, the designation of rumours and unconfirmed reports as such, the subsequent correction of minor errors, the willing exercise of self-criticism on one or two occasions — all this has inspired confidence. That confidence has grown still more when the maximum of cross-checking against the Soviet press, reports from Western correspondents in Moscow, and other *samizdat* documents has confirmed the *Chronicle*'s accuracy and revealed no serious errors at all. True, this may be partially explained by the *Chronicle*'s words (p. 320), 'in *samizdat* ... there is complete freedom of research'. And of course wariness of the charge of 'anti-Soviet libel' provides a strong incentive to accuracy. But on the other hand the editors have repeatedly published news within days of the event, leaving themselves little or no time for research and checking. Moreover, we should always remember that they operate in a society where the police control most of the means of communication — telephones, mail, foreign travel, etc. — and make daily use of elaborate means of surveillance and eavesdropping.

A major conclusion can be drawn from all this: the *Chronicle*'s editors and correspondents must be people of unusual calibre, deeply dedicated to the success of their enterprise.

But how do the correspondents pass information to the

editors? No. 5 answers this question directly: 'Simply tell it to
the person from whom you received the *Chronicle*, and he will
tell the person from whom he received the *Chronicle*, and so on.
But do not try to trace back the whole chain of communication
yourself, or else you will be taken for a police informer' (see
p. 54).

As for the correspondents' own sources, these vary widely. In
the compiling of trial accounts, for example, many people —
including defendants, witnesses and lawyers — who have been
present either at the original trial or at the appeal hearing, can
help. In addition, leaks of information and even of documents
(see pp. 176–83) sometimes provide material from official
institutions, just as they did a century ago for Herzen's *Bell*.

One of the most remarkable features of the *Chronicle*'s evolution has been the rapid spread of its correspondents' network.
Whereas No. 1 carried substantial material from only Moscow,
Leningrad, Kiev, Novosibirsk and the Mordovian camps, No.
11 added to these five places nineteen further ones: Gorky,
Ryazan, Vladimir and Obninsk in central Russia, Solikamsk in
the Urals, Krasnoyarsk Province in Siberia, Tallinn and Riga
on the Baltic, Dnepropetrovsk, Kharkov, the Crimea, Odessa
and Lvov in the Ukraine, Tashkent in Central Asia, and,
abroad, Germany, Czechoslovakia, Paris, Amsterdam and
London. Indeed, the only populated parts of the Soviet Union
from which little or nothing appeared in the first eleven
Chronicles were Lithuania, Moldavia, Armenia, Azerbaidzhan
and the Far East Province on the Pacific. By No. 17, only the
last two areas remained in this category.

The *Chronicle* is distributed in the standard *samizdat* ways.
Usually one copy becomes ten or more in the hands of a typist,
but sometimes it becomes an indefinite number in the dark-
room of a photographer. Duplicators and copying machines —
regarded by the K.G.B. as quasi-military objects — cannot be
bought by private citizens and so are not normally used (see
p. 168). The period before a copy reaches the West has so far
varied from about two weeks to two months.

The CHRONICLE *and Soviet society*

It has sometimes been suggested that the *Chronicle* exists in a
sort of vacuum, in the private world of — to use a phrase

ГОД   ПРАВ   ЧЕЛОВЕКА В СОВЕТСКОМ СОЮЗЕ

П Р О Д О Л Ж А Е Т С Я

Хроника текущих событий

> Каждый человек имеет право на
> свободу убеждений и на свободное вы-
> ражение их; это право включает сво-
> боду беспрепятственно придерживать-
> ся своих убеждений и свободу искать,
> получать и распространять информа-
> цию и идеи любыми средствами и не-
> зависимо от государственных границ.
>
> Всеобщая Декларация
> Прав Человека,статья 19

Выпуск I /6/, 28 февраля 1969 года

Содержание : Суд над Ириной БЕЛОГОРОДСКОЙ. — Дело Бориса
КОЧУБИЕВСКОГО. — Дело Ивана ЯХИМОВИЧА. — Уль-
тиматум политзаключенных. — Внесудебные полити-
ческие. репрессии 1968-1969 г.г. — Лысенковцы под-
нимают голову. — Раз"яснение национальной поли-
тики. — Новости самиздата. — Краткие сообщения. —
Поправка к 4 выпуску .

Fig. 1. The title page of *Chronicle* 6, February 28th, 1969

beloved of Western correspondents in Moscow—'a small and dwindling band of dissidents'. The most eloquent refutation of that view must be the pages of this book. Not only do the *Chronicle*'s contents tend to be overlooked, but the fact is also ignored that just as the journal has grown steadily in size, so too—despite all arrests—have the number of correspondents and their geographical distribution. Certainly the *Chronicle* has a small circulation—at a guess perhaps a few thousand copies. But many of its readers and correspondents, while politically on the fringes of society, are professionally at its core: physicists, chemists, biologists, geologists, economists, teachers, doctors, journalists—people without whom society cannot progress, nor missile programmes prosper.

True, the *Chronicle* offers little appeal to the workers and peasants—except to those who support in large numbers the different forms of national and religious dissent—and it has described only one workers' revolt (see p. 290). At the same time, though, the 'people' appear in the *Chronicle*'s pages more often as indifferent or even sympathetic to the Democratic Movement than as hostile to it. It may indeed be that the people's deep distrust of the highly paid intelligentsia is now moderating somewhat, if only with regard to its most liberal wing. Among other factors, the major foreign radio-stations broadcasting in Russian have audiences of many millions, and a worker who hears a protest document by General Grigorenko and then learns of his imprisonment might well sense, however vaguely, that this man came from the people, fought heroically in the war, and was now 'doing something useful'—for which he was prepared to suffer.

The régime, of course, fears nothing more than a link-up between dissident intellectuals and the working-class. Understanding full well that such a link spelt the beginning of the end for the tsarist autocracy, it tries at intervals to whip up popular feeling against the 'bespectacled haters of the people and traitors to the fatherland' whom it puts on trial.

More surprising, though, than the absence of worker-intellectual links outside the national and religious dissent, is the relatively small amount of student activity reflected in this book. Clearly student involvement could give a powerful boost to the Democratic Movement, and equally the lack of it could cause the movement to sag. It may therefore signal an important change that from No. 12 onwards the *Chronicle* has carried much more extensive material on student dissent. Perhaps Soviet students are now on the move.

In sum, then, the *Chronicle* seems more likely, with its compelling power of Truth in a public world of Newspeak, to flourish than to perish in a vacuum. If, that is, it survives the police.

The CHRONICLE *and the régime*

As yet not only the police but the Soviet authorities in general have maintained an almost total silence about the *Chronicle*. The charge against Gorbanevskaya—that she was an editor of a journal which depicted Soviet reality 'in a libellous light'— is in fact the sole official mention of it so far to become public. Yet nothing is more certain than that the K.G.B. has been working hard to learn everything possible about its editors and correspondents, both through infiltration and—where that fails—intensive observation. This, indeed, provides the most plausible explanation of the *Chronicle*'s continued existence: let the *Chronicle* decoy trouble-makers into our sight and save us the bother of ferreting them out ourselves. Then we can pick them off one by one in our own good time. Although several dozen prominent dissenters have been imprisoned who *may* have had links with the *Chronicle*, it is impossible to know how much success the K.G.B. has had with this tactic.

Another, less likely explanation of the *Chronicle*'s survival to date, is that the police simply cannot keep track of the perhaps constantly changing editors. Still more unlikely—though not quite impossible—is the theory that elements in the K.G.B. are actively protecting, even assisting the *Chronicle*, regarding it as a lesser evil than what would ensue if it were ruthlessly suppressed. The people associated with it and their friends might then, according to this view, take to the underground proper, which would not suit the K.G.B. at all.

The question arises here as to just how easily the police *could* suppress the *Chronicle*, assuming that they both opted for this course and succeeded in obtaining the go-ahead from the Politbureau. If, in other words, they arrested several hundred people in Moscow and Leningrad, might not the *Chronicle* resurface, perhaps a few days behind schedule, in Novosibirsk or Kiev? A scenario of roughly this sort was in fact sketched by the writer Georgy Vladimov, when he hypothesized — in a letter of 1967 defending Solzhenitsyn — about *samizdat*: 'Organize a massive search ... arrest the authors and circulators, and still at least one copy will be preserved; having survived, it will be copied, and all the more abundantly than before.'[15]

It is however doubtful whether the present collective leadership of Brezhnev, Kosygin and Podgorny could ever act decisively enough to order mass arrests. Indeed, Andrei Amalrik goes further, seeing weakness of this sort in the system as a whole: 'To put it simply, the régime is getting old and cannot now suppress everyone and everything with the same energy and vigour as before.'[16] Even, though, if a strong leader were to emerge, and were then somehow to redynamize the régime, he would surely hesitate to arrest certain prominent members of the Democratic Movement. For when the mathematician Esenin-Volpin was put in a 'mental hospital' in February 1968 a massive protest secured his release (see pp. 81–83), and similarly with the biologist Zhores Medvedev in June 1970. Clearly, therefore, a scientist as eminent as Andrei Sakharov could not be arrested without deeply alienating much of the scientific community. Thus, since large parts of this community staff the huge missile and space programmes, and also perform other functions essential to the Soviet economy, such a step could be taken only by desperate men. Yet if Sakharov and his colleagues remained free, the *Chronicle* might well — notwithstanding sweeping arrests in other professions — continue to appear.

A final consideration against the course of mass arrests is the effect these might have on the machinery of repression itself. Not least in importance among the *Chronicle*'s revelations is the information it gives on certain operators of this machine who have decided in various ways deliberately to put a spanner in the works.[17] It may well in fact be that K.G.B. investigator P. M. Goryachyov, Procuracy investigator Julian Vronsky, M.V.D. Captain Yury Fyodorov and top Moscow lawyer Boris Zolotukhin all decided to upset the machine as a result of their professional handling of political dissidents. Certainly something not so dissimilar led Procuracy investigator Nikolai Danilov to leave his job and move into the orbit of the Democratic Movement: 'From 1960 to 1963 he worked in the Sakhalin regional Procuracy, where he dealt with the rehabilitation of victims of Stalinism. According to his account, by 1963 they had managed to rehabilitate only a quarter of all those who had perished.' (See p. 382.) And not many people have been rehabilitated since 1963.

Of course the number of 'unreliable' operators of the machinery of repression roughly trebles if not just Zolotukhin but also a dozen or so of his defence lawyer colleagues are mentioned. For no longer do these people — in Stalin-era style — assist the prosecutor in blackening their clients: instead they defend them with persistence and courage, thereby winning the Democratic Movement's admiration.

Mass arrests, in fact, although they could always occur, might lead to some serious breakdowns in the machine. A continuation of the present 'salami' tactics on the other hand — 'wearing the bastards down' — seems a much more probable course for an ossifying régime. Given the moral strength of the Democratic Movement, it is unlikely to produce any dramatic success.

The CHRONICLE and the outside world

So much for the *Chronicle*'s relation to Soviet society and the régime. What about the outside world?

As the *Chronicle* has developed, its pages have carried an increasing amount of material connected with abroad: summaries of *samizdat* items translated from various languages, especially Czech; extracts from foreign articles and letters defending Solzhenitsyn; accounts of demonstrations in the U.S.S.R. by Westerners on behalf of Soviet political prisoners;[18] a list of foreign civil rights groups who supported the first appeal to the United Nations of the Action Group for the Defence of Civil Rights (see p. 153); and an account of the Alexander Herzen Foundation, set up in Amsterdam to publish *samizdat* manuscripts under scholarly auspices in Russian and other languages (see p. 374). In addition the *Chronicle* has printed material addressed to the outside world, such as the

Action Group's petitions to the U.N., Pavel Litvinov and Larissa Daniel's appreciation of some of the Western demonstrators, and one of the Crimean Tatar appeals 'to world public opinion' (see pp. 93, 150–53, 249–52).

World opinion, however, has so far proved remarkably indifferent both to the Tatars and to the *Chronicle*. The latter had been appearing for two whole years—packed with information available nowhere else—before it began on occasion to catch the attention of the world press. U Thant, moreover, has yet to show that he is concerned, or even knows, about the many desperate Soviet appeals addressed to him—if, that is, we discount his order to U.N. offices throughout the world not to forward to New York any such appeals. These, he said, apparently oblivious that some countries have a postal censorship, should be sent by their authors direct to New York. In this way he brought all U.N. offices into line with the Moscow one, which had refused even to accept the hand-delivered appeals of the Action Group (see p. 152.)

Of course Western news media face difficulties in dealing with the Soviet régime. An editor fears that news stories based on the *Chronicle* may lead to the expulsion of his Moscow correspondent, whether the stories are written by him or by a specialist in London or Paris. Only stronger collective action by newspapers and governments will change a still poor, though slightly improving situation. Certainly current practices give the world very little idea of the Democratic Movement's significance and strength.

The world's response to the *Chronicle*, and to *samizdat* in general, has however been less indifferent in two areas. The major Western radio-stations—of incalculable significance for the Democratic Movement—and the more responsible emigré groups have both made energetic (if vain) efforts to keep up with the massive flow of material, publishing and broadcasting as much of it as possible in the form received. Moreover, the few dubious documents—presumably circulated by the K.G.B.—have almost without exception been spotted by them at once and discarded. Finally, there have been no indications of the Democratic Movement being embarrassed by publicity in the outside world or support from responsible foreigners. On the contrary, the items relating to such matters carried by the *Chronicle* (listed above) suggest appreciation. Hints even appear—like that of Anatoly Marchenko (see p. 186)—that 'the humanists and progressive people of other countries' tend to pay more attention to the iniquities of, say, the Greek and Spanish régimes than to those of the Soviet régime, and that this—once the facts are known—is unjustified. Although Marchenko himself may never learn it if he dies in the camps, it should in fact be said that the more conscientious groups such as Amnesty International have in the last two years been digesting the facts which he and others have provided at such cost to themselves, and begun to adjust the balance of their activity accordingly.

As for the foreign radio-stations, their crucial significance has been publicly stressed by several dissenters, notably Yury Galanskov, Lev Kvachevsky and Vladimir Bukovsky.[19] The latter, for example, has explained that the Democratic Movement expands in proportion to the spread of *samizdat* throughout the country, and that 'That depends on the world outside, on the Western radio-stations.'

Turning points in Western understanding of Russia

Now, in the early 1970s, the world is—thanks to the writings of Marchenko, Solzhenitsyn, Litvinov, Sakharov, Grigorenko, Amalrik and the Ukrainians Chornovil and Moroz, among others—at least beginning to get the feel of the Soviet system in the post-Stalin era, and to do so from first-hand, non-academic sources. In this book the *Chronicle* is able to make its own unique contribution to these sources by showing for the first time the full breadth and depth of the Democratic Movement.

This book may thus fulfil a somewhat similar function to that of one of its ancestors, an ancestor of different character perhaps, but related none the less. This is a work called *Underground Russia*, by Sergei Kravchinsky (Stepniak), which in 1882 gave the world its first vivid account of the anti-tsarist movement and thereby stimulated the intensive Western study of Russia which followed. The introduction was written in London by the populist thinker and publicist Peter Lavrov, and it contains—if we discount the fact that the Democratic Movement of today is reformist rather than revolutionary—

some remarkable parallels with the present. After deploring Western ignorance of the Russian opposition Lavrov continues: 'In fact the publications of the revolutionists which have been issued during the last three years abroad and from the secret press of St Petersburg, present a rich source of information respecting the modern revolutionary movement. But all these materials, being in the Russian or Ukrainian language ... have remained for the most part unknown to Europe.' The Russian émigrés had done little and 'as for the few European scholars who know the Russian language the materials furnished by the revolutionary press [abroad] are quite insufficient for them, and do not preserve them from great blunders.' Alas, but a digression on the modern counterparts of these scholars would require more space than can be afforded here.

Stepniak's book made an enormous impact in its various translations, winning high praise from William Morris, Emile Zola, Alphonse Daudet and Mark Twain. In 1884 Stepniak settled in London and, devoting himself to intensive literary and lecturing activity, became in 1890 one of the founders of the Society of Friends of Russian Freedom. Organized and supported by eminent liberal and radical figures of the time, this society was for twenty-seven years, with its regular paper *Free Russia* and its support for the extensive Western publishing of *samizdat* which developed in that period, a sizable thorn in the tsarist government's flesh. It was guided by a formula of Stepniak's, which people like Marchenko, Litvinov and Larissa Daniel would no doubt endorse today, and which therefore provokes the thought that maybe the society ought now to be refounded: 'Every energetic manifestation of sympathy for our liberative movement from the people of the neighbouring countries is an event for Russia and has no less a moral effect on our people than a manifestation of opposition in Russia itself. That is the mode in which European countries can contribute to the strengthening of the liberal movement in our country.'[20]

The CHRONICLE's influence

But just how big is the *Chronicle*'s impact? Probably it exerts its greatest influence by being a central point which informs a large number of groups and individuals about each other's activity. This helps to create closer unity, both practically and spiritually. The *Chronicle* may well not exert much influence directly, through being read by the authorities, although it does remind them with its confident tone that the Stalinist atomization of society has gone for good, and it does inform them of the Democratic Movement's alarming scope. Doubtless much greater pressure is exerted on the authorities by the actual letters or lobbying of groups and individuals than by the recording of such activity in the *Chronicle*. But—and this is the vital point—the morale of the letter-writers and lobbiers is higher for the existence of the *Chronicle*. The extra morale may indeed make the difference between getting and not getting a colleague out of a 'mental hospital', between the Crimean Tatars organizing or failing to organize another mass lobby, and so on.

In this role the *Chronicle* has, within the Soviet Union, already received the supreme compliment, that of imitation. In 1970 the *Ukrainian Herald* and a Zionist journal, *Exodus*, both modelled on the *Chronicle*, began to circulate. Clearly, groups of Zionist Jews and nationally conscious Ukrainians found the *Chronicle* either too remote or too limited in the space it could devote to their special concerns, and accordingly branched out on their own. Clearly, too, the *Chronicle* has begun to feed in due measure on its offspring.

But apart from the *Chronicle*'s uniquely rich information, its co-ordinating role, and the pointers it provides for the Soviet Union's evolution, its deepest meaning probably lies elsewhere: in the moral qualities it reveals in a large number of individuals. These qualities, being of an unusual order, are partly what generates the Democratic Movement's self-confidence. They are also the guarantee that the movement is not an insignificant or passing phenomenon.

They belong, of course, not only to the people described in the *Chronicle*'s pages, but also to the *Chronicle*'s creators. For above the extravagant rhetoric of many of the world's persecuted groups, the *Chronicle*'s coolness, moderation and objectivity in the face of all adversity speak with a deeper resonance. The endless cycle of intimidation, arrest, interrogation, beatings and imprisonment merely provokes its editors into a fiercer determination than ever to perform their journalistic duty to the limit without flinching.

The other sort of heroism is actually to suffer the beatings and imprisonment without yielding an inch to the oppressors. Marchenko survives the appalling camp conditions so as to expose them in a book, and then, inevitably, returns to them; Grigorenko performs a similar cycle in the equally terrifying 'mental hospitals', inspiring in his interval of freedom the supporters of many causes; Litvinov and his comrades demonstrate on Red Square in the almost certain knowledge that they will be beaten up and then dispatched for years to Siberia; Daniel, Galanskov, Ginzburg and others continue to live out their values of integrity and compassion in the camps and thereby give fresh hope to their fellow-prisoners; Chornovil defends his Ukrainian colleagues in a remarkable book, pays the penalty, but bounces back and at once supports the Action Group for the Defence of Civil Rights; Anatoly Levitin, having joined the Action Group and defended some of the noblest spirits of his Orthodox faith, returns to prison with equanimity at the age of fifty-five; and Rollan Kadiyev fights for his Crimean Tatar people to the last moment of his month-long trial and doubtless beyond.

This small sample of the moral heroism revealed in the pages which follow gives some idea of the *Chronicle*'s deepest and most hopeful message. The plague of Stalinism is indeed no longer: such heroism can now become known. At the same time the *Chronicle* underlines the new relevance of some words penned by Stepniak in 1885, which bear repeating today: 'The plague kills indiscriminately, but the present régime chooses its victims from the flower of the nation.'[21]

London School of Economics
and Political Science
July 1970–*September* 1971

PETER REDDAWAY

UNCENSORED RUSSIA

Foreword of an Eyewitness*

The first eleven numbers of the *Chronicle* cover the period 1968–9, years when I still lived in Moscow. I therefore consider it my first duty to confirm the accuracy of the *Chronicle*'s reports on all those events which I personally witnessed or took part in. A few insignificant mistakes apart, I can say that everything is correct, everything reflects what happened, nothing has been fabricated or invented.

Naturally I did not witness much of what the *Chronicle* recounts. In most cases, however, my close friends saw or participated in what occurred, and I do not doubt their honesty or objectivity. I vouch for their reliability, and also for the fact that the information I received from a variety of independent sources coincided exactly with the reports of the *Chronicle*.

All this firmly convinced me that the *Chronicle*'s editors were going to enormous lengths to achieve objectivity. As for the few inaccuracies, usually corrected in subsequent issues, these are explained by the peculiar conditions under which the *Chronicle* is produced and also by the mistakes which inevitably occur when documents are repeatedly retyped. But none of this is significant enough to make us hesitate in regarding the *Chronicle* — by virtue of its truthfulness — as a unique Soviet journal.

The *Chronicle* inevitably reports the facts in brief, condensed form, and for this reason the Western reader may well not feel the whole drama of some event which is described in a few lines. Many vivid and important details remain untold.

What happened to me was trivial. I was put neither in prison, nor in a concentration camp, nor in a psychiatric hospital. None the less, as I am now readily accessible for the task, I can relate in more detail some of the episodes about myself which are briefly reported by the *Chronicle*.

In No. 7 a search of my apartment on December 23rd, 1968, is described (see p. 310). In fact, the search — in the strict sense of that word — was only one of several actions concerning

---

* Julius Telesin, the author, is a Jewish mathematician who lived in Moscow until 1970, when he left for Israel (see plate 60).

me undertaken by the chekists* (i.e. secret police) on that day. Two of them picked me up at home in the morning and carried me off to the K.G.B.'s Lefortovo for an interrogation. 'Carried me off' is really putting it too strongly: they only asked me to come, and I, because of my as yet underdeveloped character, concurred. A few months later, in a similar situation, I made no such concession, already well knowing that according to the law a 'witness' (and it was in this capacity that they needed me on both occasions) should be called to interrogation by a summons. However, on the first occasion I not only went with them, but also let them into my room beforehand (again, I was later not so friendly) and thus allowed them to estimate the potential value of the search which followed: on the table lay a pile of typescripts of the sort to arouse their deep suspicions.

The point is that without a warrant for a search or arrest no official person, however high his rank and however innocent his pretext, has the right to enter one's room without an invitation to do so. Otherwise an 'infringement of the inviolability of citizens' homes', indictable under article 136 of the Russian Criminal Code, occurs. It is quite another matter that it infringes Soviet tradition to bar one's home to a policeman who wants to check if anyone is living there illegally: authority must always be respected! But I was not thenceforth hospitable to uninvited guests, and they reconciled themselves to this.

Anyway, by now I was in the office, being interrogated 'in connection with the Burmistrovich case' by Major Gulyayev. In the course of the interrogation he invented various detective-story details and put them into the record in my name. When the record was given to me for signature I did not just sign it, but wrote above my signature that in such-and-such places this or that had been wrongly recorded, and that in reality this or that was the truth. All this very much displeased him. When, some ten days later at the next interrogation by the same major, I wrote in the record before signing it that the major had been coarse and threatening in various ways, the major read my note and expressed his displeasure with these words: 'My sincerest thanks to you for that!' This phrase was

---

* K.G.B. men like to call themselves chekists to underline their descent from the security police of Lenin's day, named the Cheka.

evidently designed to make me feel that I had done a decent fellow a bad turn.

But let us return to the first day. After the interrogation — as yet it was still afternoon — I was driven home for a search of my room. In all, five chekists came with me. We drove up to my house, got out of the car, but did not go to my room. Two of them waited with me on the street, while the others drove off 'for some witnesses'. 'We can't enter your room without witnesses,' Gulyayev explained. And then I escaped! I did not actually intend to escape, but merely wanted to get far enough away from them to give some reliable-looking passer by, without hindrance, my mother's phone-number, so that he could call her and tell her that my room was being searched.

But what happened then was like a Western. The two chekists chased after me, and then the car with the other chekists and the witnesses arrived to join in the pursuit. The next development was intriguing: the witnesses — two young men — took part in my detention, thus failing to show that 'impartiality' which the law demands of witnesses. I got the impression that the chekists were not thrilled by this extraordinary chase in the centre of a thickly populated city and in the absence of any ordinary policemen. Moreover, I did not juridically have the status even of a 'detainee'. It availed them little that they wanted to search my room. For that they needed to call when I was at home, and enter with witnesses and a search warrant — and then all would have been civilized. But on the street only ordinary police and, in certain cases, volunteer police (*druzhinniki*) can detain people. A year later, when some chekists wanted simply to inspect, on the street, the documents of a companion of mine (I no longer had the charm of novelty for them, but they did not know this person and their curiosity was understandable), they whistled long but in vain for a policeman. They evidently did not want to make a direct approach to us and get a humiliating rebuff.

But let us return to our story. We went up to my room, they showed me their search warrant signed by a Procurator, and then for several hours the seven of them (including the 'witnesses'!) turned my room upside down. From the nooks and crannies they brought almost everything written in manuscript or typescript and dumped it all on the table in the middle. They did not, however, take a typed copy of the U.N. 'Pacts on Human Rights', nor did they take typewritten poems by Pasternak, Mandelshtam, Tsvetayeva and Akhmatova. (And yet other people, and myself too a year later, had such items taken as well, so it is hard to detect any logic in the matter.) Captain Pustyakov, after reading a bit of Mandelshtam, wondered how such nonsense could please anyone. I asked him what literature he liked and he said useful literature. So I advised him to read something like 'The Book of Tasty and Healthy Food', and all the chekists promptly took offence. When I saw in the hands of one of them a folded sheet of paper with pressed flowers in it I said that these came from the grave of my grandfather and Major Gulyayev ordered him in great anger to 'put it back immediately'. But they were, by the way, bad actors, always over-acting. One of the chekists, on seeing my Czech tumblers, said that they must have been made before the troops were sent into Czechoslovakia, as tumblers were no longer being made there! In other words he realized what I probably thought about the Czech events, and here he was, mocking my incorrect attitude. A pity I did not think fast enough to ask him what he needed in life apart from tumblers.

Lieutenant Sergeyev discovered an Israeli medallion among my collection and began to ask me snidely what it was. I told him it was a Star of David, but when asked about other objects I replied that I was not an expert on them and that if they were making a search they must be looking for specific sorts of evidence: if this or that was not such evidence, then it should be put back in its place.

Great was Gulyayev's joy when they found a typescript of Sinyavsky's essay 'What is Socialist Realism?' He even phoned his boss immediately and reported that they had found 'Socialist Realism'! At first I thought his joy resulted only from the fact that this was a criminal object—as 'established' by a court! Gulyayev had stated with satisfaction that my copy contained precisely those phrases which 'rendered' this object criminal, in particular those about the prisons which we had destroyed so as to build new ones. These phrases he quoted aloud from my copy. Only later did I realize he had rejoiced in the belief that this copy was the very one which Burmistrovich had given someone to read, but which they had not found at his apartment, unlike the other works of Sinyavsky and Daniel, which all figured at his trial as material evidence (see pp. 68–70). Evidently the major seriously underestimated the 'productivity' of *samizdat* if he did not realize that several people could each have their own copy. I began to perceive then that the K.G.B. were far from being all-knowing and all-powerful, as they sometimes seem from a distance.

The 'legal' part of the search ended with them 'confiscating' from me Sinyavsky's essay, an appeal by Burmistrovich's wife to the Procurator-General about her husband's arrest, and my typewriter, and with the entering of these three objects in the search record. Overjoyed by the fact that the whole pile of *samizdat* which by the end had mounted up on my table had not been put in the record and therefore (o formal logic!) remained mine, I quickly signed the record and in the space for noting complaints boldly wrote 'No complaints', although it would have done no harm to note the diligent work of the 'witnesses' on the street and in my room, the anti-semitic episode with the medallion, and a few other trifles besides. But, to repeat, I was glad that almost all my treasured possessions remained mine.

But my happiness was premature. Folding the record and putting it away, they said: 'And all *that* we will examine at our place!' Here I should have prevented them taking it all, and generally behaved like any old woman being robbed, i.e. screamed and fought. However, I refrained from such boldness and only later, with everything already in my briefcase, did I make a weak attempt not to surrender it. The briefcase had now been taken from me, and I had recorded this robbery accompanied by force merely in speech. When later, in all statements and interrogations, I began to expound at the least opportunity how I had been 'robbed by a group of officials of the K.G.B. of the U.S.S.R. Council of Ministers', and how such-and-such officers of the K.G.B. had, with the witnesses, 'taken part in the robbery', I sensed from the reaction to my words that they felt in a very awkward position in regard to me. Was it a joke? The U.S.S.R. Council of Ministers! Robbery!

After I had been robbed I was driven off for the second time that day to the K.G.B. Once again I could have refrained from being so co-operative, and also from doing another stupid thing when I arrived: I signed my name on two pieces of paper with which, using official glue and some string threaded through the briefcase's handle and lock they had 'sealed' it. Naturally such a 'seal' in any case had no juridical value, partly because of the technical imperfection of the 'seal' but mainly because of the absence of witnesses at this operation. Nevertheless I need not have helped them to create even an illusion of legality.

They had one further aim: Major Gulyayev asked me to rewrite the record of the morning interrogation. I quickly refused, although it would have been wiser to find out first why he wanted me to do this. However, it was clear enough: with my 'corrective' remarks at the end, this record clearly revealed a crime against due process committed by the major, i.e. an investigation conducted 'with artificial manufacture of prosecution evidence' (indictable under article 176).

All day long I had scarcely eaten. Allowed home late in the evening, I was first handed a summons to appear the next morning. The next day they kept me likewise till evening, handing me again a summons for the morrow. In this way they put me on a sort of 'conveyor-belt'. Of course, it was not as inhuman as the 'conveyor-belt' of Stalin's time, when the investigators worked in shifts while the person under interrogation got no sleep for several nights; but the basic principle was the same. After two days on the conveyor-belt I fell ill, and two days running Gulyayev came to my room with doctors and tried to interrogate me in bed. Both times I sent them away. It is interesting to note that when, the first time, the major had been annoyed by my unfriendly welcome and my desire to discover at all costs the juridical basis of his visit, he at once began to consult on the phone, from the corridor of my communal apartment, with another chekist who had taken part in the robbery, Captain Solovyov. 'But what are *we* here for? He's only having a limited examination!' said Gulyayev, and the doctors sitting in my room heard this. That gave me the chance to explain to them that the major did not have the right to conduct this undertaking ('But what are *we* here for?', i.e. the K.G.B.), but had wanted to force his way in by bringing the doctors (the 'limited examination').

The whole cycle of 'investigative actions' in the Burmistrovich case did not end for me until the New Year of 1969. But my briefcase full of *samizdat*, stolen from me with the application of force by a group of officials of the K.G.B. of the U.S.S.R. Council of Ministers, is still lying in the offices of the K.G.B. of the U.S.S.R. Council of Ministers.

In *Chronicle* 6 there is a report of an incident in the Mendeleyev Institute concerning a lecture on official policy towards the Crimean Tatars (see pp. 253–4). Let me expand on how they 'checked our documents' on that occasion. When three people approached me while I was standing with a Tatar in the Institute corridor and asked us to show our documents, I, as usual, inquired first with whom I had the honour of speaking. At that time the habit of checking the documents of anyone forcing himself upon me began to enter my flesh and blood, although this was not good form: Soviet people respect the boss.

Two of the three announced themselves as lecturers at the Institute, but the third, after a certain show of mystery, presented the card of a K.G.B. lieutenant. I explained to him that his card made no impression on me, that we would show our identity cards only to representatives of the law, i.e. the ordinary police, and that what an organization called the K.G.B. might be I had the right not even to know. He did not try to insist, but we were then inveigled into a room with a telephone, where some lecturers — the original two plus others — voluntarily took upon themselves the function of our 'jailers', while the chekist phoned the police to ask for a policeman to come and check our documents. Two policemen arrived, and the comedy of checking our documents began. We handed our identity-cards to a policeman, he passed them to the chekist, who copied our names on to a piece of paper and returned the cards to the policeman, who then gave them to us. While all this was going on, a remarkable scene had occurred. My 'co-prisoner', seeing how the policeman passed his card to the chekist, wanted to grab it from him, and said to the policeman: 'But I'm giving my card only to you, I'm not giving it to him!' The chekist recoiled a bit, muttering: 'But it was given to me by *him*, it was given to me by *him*!' (i.e. the policeman). The scene was magnificent: the splendid scorn of the Tatar who refused to recognize the thought police, the brazenly self-righteous fumbling of the chekist, and the gaping mouths of the lecturers, who had evidently not hitherto imagined that one could behave so 'cheekily' towards such a mighty organization, which, moreover, at conduct of this sort, begins in an incomprehensible way to look so pitiful.

I have given two examples of how the condensed reports of the *Chronicle* can be filled out if one recalls everything that occurred. And perhaps, for the outside observer trying to grasp from the *Chronicle* exactly what is happening in the Soviet Union in the sphere of the struggle for human rights, it is precisely this non-existent 'context of detail' which is the greatest lack.

I would like also to express what the *Chronicle* represents for me. I am often asked when exactly I first conceived the desire to go and live in Israel. The question is quite understandable from a Western person spoiled by all his freedoms. He has merely to conceive the desire to live in another country and then to make certain technical arrangements. But what does it mean to 'conceive the desire' in a land where, in the words of Marx, 'freedom is the recognition of necessity'? How can I want what is, judging by the experience of others, impossible? I could not even dare to want so much all at once—to go and live in Israel! If this *was* what I wanted I could not grasp it, so unreal was the notion. My desires probably originated in nothing more than the desire not to harm my friends during an interrogation. When I succeeded in that, I became more 'aggressive', adding to the interrogation record evidence of the crime of the investigator who had tried to extract testimony from me by illegal means. I did not immediately understand that the experience of others, which suggested the impossibility of realizing various legal desires, by no means suggested an absolute impossibility, but only the impossibility of achieving them by traditional means, i.e. by remaining captive to the incapacitating force of fear.

Each step towards overcoming this fear was made with difficulty, but provided valuable experience for the next. There occurred what my close friend Vladimir Bukovsky spoke of in his TV interview (see p. 67). In line with what he said, an enormous role was played in this acquisition of experience by the personal example of my friends, friendship with whom is for me a matter of great pride. From such as Bukovsky, Litvinov, Grigorenko, Amalrik—there are too many to name them all—who had nothing in common with Zionism, I learned how to struggle for my legal right to live in my historic homeland. It is precisely the concrete stages of this 'learning' of inner freedom which I recall most vividly on re-reading the *Chronicle*. The events recorded in the *Chronicle* are for me landmarks on the road of the transformation of many people from apes into men.

Starting with the trial of Sinyavsky and Daniel, the increasing repressions and protests have progressively intensified the passing of time for us. Thus the period of the first eleven *Chronicles* presented here, ending with 1969, already feels for me like the Middle Ages (with its Renaissance—the torrent of protests around the Galanskov–Ginzburg trial). Since 1969 almost a year and a half has passed! Eight more issues of the *Chronicle* have appeared. May this 'contemporary history' become known to the inquiring Western reader without delay.

Jerusalem,   JULIUS TELESIN
June 1971

Part I · The Mirror of the Movement

1. THE *CHRONICLE* ABOUT ITSELF

The *Chronicle* is in no sense an illegal publication.

Chronicle No. 5

The Chronicle's *profile—its style, its operating principles, its relation to the law—has been sketched in the Introduction. This chapter throws the picture into sharper relief by presenting the sparse but illuminating editorial material from the journal's pages.*

The first words—at once ironic and serious—of the first issue (April 30th, 1968) were these:

On December 10th, 1968, twenty years will have elapsed since I the United Nations General Assembly adopted the Declaration of Human Rights.

On December 10th, 1967, Human Rights Year began all over the world.

On December 11th, the trial was due to begin in the case of Yury Galanskov, Alexander Ginzburg, Aleksei Dobrovolsky and Vera Lashkova. The trial was, however, postponed and did not begin till January 8th, 1968. [See Chapter 3.]

When Human Rights Year ended in December 1968, the Chronicle *continued the fight. It ran a revealing appeal to readers under the defiant title:*

HUMAN RIGHTS YEAR CONTINUES   5

Readers of the *Chronicle*! December 10th was observed as Human Rights Day all over the world. Human Rights Year, declared by the United Nations, has now come to an end. From the five issues of the *Chronicle* to date, one may form at least a partial impression of how the suppression of human rights and the movement for them has been taking place in the Soviet Union. Not one participant in this movement can feel his task is ended with the end of Human Rights Year. The general aim of democratization, and the more particular aim pursued by the *Chronicle*, are still to be achieved. The *Chronicle* will continue to come out in 1969.

The *Chronicle* is in no sense an illegal publication, and the difficult conditions in which it is produced are created by the peculiar notions about law and freedom of information which, in the course of long years, have become established in certain Soviet organizations. For this reason the *Chronicle* cannot, like any other journal, give its postal address on the last page. Nevertheless, anybody who is interested in seeing that the Soviet public is informed about what goes on in the country, may easily pass on information to the editors of the *Chronicle*. Simply tell it to the person from whom you received the *Chronicle*, and he will tell the person from whom *he* received the *Chronicle*, and so on. But do not try to trace back the whole chain of communication yourself, or else you will be taken for a police informer.

The Chronicle *almost never appeals directly for information. An exception occurred after it had listed some reprisals against certain unnamed students (see pp. 91 and 479):*

5 The *Chronicle* draws readers' attention to the need to establish the so far unknown names of the students who have been subjected to reprisals in Gorky and Moscow.

The tone and scope of the Chronicle—*matters of great importance—are clarified in the following 'Reply to a Reader':*

8 The *Chronicle* thanks the Leningrad reader for his letter analysing issues of the *Chronicle* in detail. Whilst agreeing with his evaluation of the *Chronicle*'s aims, and with many of his individual comments, the *Chronicle* would like to reply at greater length to two of his statements:

1. 'The *Chronicle* will carry conviction only if its tone is calm and restrained, thus precluding the possibility of its readers entertaining the slightest doubt as to its legal character. This too will be conducive to increasing its popularity.' So writes the reader, having informed us that, in the opinion of some of his friends, the *Chronicle* has a 'hysterical tone'. The reason for this, he thinks, lies in the abundance of value judgments.

The *Chronicle* makes every effort to achieve a calm, restrained tone. Unfortunately the materials with which the *Chronicle* is dealing evoke emotional reactions, and these automatically affect the tone of the text. The *Chronicle* does, and will do, its utmost to ensure that its strictly factual style is maintained to the greatest degree possible, but it cannot guarantee complete success. The *Chronicle* tries to refrain from making value judgments—either by not making them at all, or by referring to judgments made in *samizdat* documents. In certain cases one is obliged to give an appraisal of the facts, otherwise their true significance might escape the unsophisticated reader.

2. ' ... I am not sure if one can classify the whole of the rich content of the *Chronicle* (for instance, the reviews of *samizdat*) under the heading of "the Human Rights Movement", without stretching the definition. For this reason the title of the *Chronicle*, too, does not seem to me to be particularly apposite.'

The *Chronicle* disagrees sharply with this comment. On the contrary, the 'rich content of the *Chronicle*' represents only a few of the many aspects of the concept 'human rights movement'. To get an idea of just how much this movement can embrace, one has only to glance through the U.N. Declaration of Human Rights.

Samizdat has a dual right to figure in the *Chronicle*: first, in so far as a part of it is expressly devoted to the question of human rights; secondly, the whole of *samizdat* is an example of freedom of speech and the press, of creative freedom and freedom of conscience, put into practice.

The *Chronicle* has to admit that Soviet legal practice, for example, is given very narrow coverage in its pages—only those arrests, searches and legal proceedings which clearly represent acts of political repression, irrespective of which article of the Criminal Code is involved. But what is the record of juridical practice in 'purely criminal' cases? No one has yet systematically gathered information on the numerous violations of the human rights in this area which are set out in the Declaration of Human Rights and guaranteed by Soviet law.

Here is an example, as it happens from Leningrad. It has come to the attention of the *Chronicle*, because it does in fact have political overtones. But even if there were no such overtones, even if the criminal prosecution were justified, it would be no less striking an example.

On June 1st, 1969, Efim Slavinsky, a translator and graduate of Leningrad University, was arrested by organs of the MVD. He was charged under two articles of the Criminal Code—'drug-trafficking' and 'maintaining an establishment for the smoking of drugs', and a search was made on these grounds. Slavinsky himself was taken away soon after the search began, and his wife, upset and frightened, signed a record after the search without making any protest. Meanwhile, apart from taking away old medicine bottles and boxes, and a small quantity of powder which they named 'anasha', the investigators removed 65 books without making an inventory, stamped them and threw them into a sack, and took also a number of papers, notebooks, and a diary—also without an inventory—and put them in a similar sack. Who knows what might disappear from these sacks, and—more important—what might 'appear' in them? But this is a violation of the law with which readers of the *Chronicle* are already familiar. In Slavinsky's case there was an even more flagrant violation.

On June 5th, four days after his arrest, the newspaper *Evening Leningrad* carried a short report of the arrest, entitled: 'He will surely pay.' The editors and the author had both trampled on one of the basic human rights—the presumption of innocence. It was hardly surprising: the author of the article was a certain Lerner, who had earlier in his career directed the campaign against Iosif Brodsky [see also p. 431], a campaign that was initiated by the Leningrad press and led to the arrest, conviction and exile of the poet. Incidentally, one of the polemical articles on Brodsky dating from that time included a paragraph devoted to Slavinsky, and Lerner was one of the authors.[1]

Would you not say that this episode,[2] which was not included in the *Chronicle*, indicates that, far from overstepping the bounds of the title, the range of the *Chronicle* is far narrower than the title would suggest?

Tone and scope are also the subject of the following two items. The first concerns a section of the Chronicle *with the title, from No. 8 onwards, of 'Extra-judicial Political Persecution'. Previously the last word had been 'Repressions'.*

The *Chronicle* is changing the title of this regular section, since 8 the material it receives has a wider range than the term 'repression' suggests. Persecution of dissenters does not always go as far as direct repression such as dismissals, expulsions, reprimands and so on; it may take the form of discussions at meetings, talks with various authorities, etc. These kinds of persecution often form a basis for the creation of 'public opinion', and a springboard for future repressions. Therefore the *Chronicle* considers it impossible to disregard facts of this kind, and does not think it necessary to put them in a separate section, since all kinds of persecution are part of the same phenomenon.

Many readers of the *Chronicle* have expressed critical com- 10 ments on the section '*Samizdat* News' in No. 9, because of the part which talked about the 'Letter to Members of the Polit-bureau'. Readers were critical of the fact that the commentary to this document [see p. 319] abounded in value judgments.

The *Chronicle* agrees with these comments by readers, thanks them for their criticisms, and will try in future to keep to facts and avoid judgments.

Some readers have also expressed the opinion that the *Chronicle* carries on religious propaganda in its pages.

The *Chronicle* does not agree with this, and considers it necessary to clarify the matter thus: It is not the aim of the *Chronicle* to carry on either religious or anti-religious propaganda, since it considers that the question of religious belief is a matter for the conscience of the individual. However, in so far as there are in the Soviet Union various forms of persecution of believers, and restrictions on freedom of conscience, which are violations of the Universal Declaration of Human Rights, the *Chronicle* considers it necessary to publish these facts [see Chap. 16].

The Chronicle's *profile becomes clearer still from its description of a different sort of* samizdat *publication called* '*On Certain Current Events: a Short Bulletin*' :[3]

The *Chronicle* has in its possession one undated and un- 7 numbered copy of this bulletin, which relates to approximately January–February 1969. The issue consists of seven items:

1. Expulsions from the Party; 2. The attempt on the life of Brezhnev;* 3. The tightening-up in the publishing houses; 4. The article on Stalin in the tear-off calendar for 1969;† 5. About the film *Andrei Rublyov*;‡ 6. About the short story 'The Locust's Jaws';§ 7. From the biography of K. F. Katushev, a secretary of the Central Committee of the party. This bulletin, compared with the *Chronicle*, is more analytical and contains a number of judgments and speculations, in particular speculations and rumours from 'high political' circles, which the *Chronicle* prefers to refrain from printing. Despite the doubtfulness of some judgments, the *Chronicle* considers such an analytical publication very useful and welcomes it. In addition, the *Chronicle* will utilize material from the bulletin for its issues in the same way as it does with any other *samizdat* document.

On the crucial question of accuracy the Chronicle's *record is remarkable. Very few of the names, dates and facts which it prints are of the sort which can be checked by the editors in reference sources before publication, yet their mistakes are few. Moreover, when two copies of a given issue have reached the West the differences between them have not gone beyond points of spelling. So the standards of the typists are high too. It may of course be that copies reaching the West emanate from sources not far removed from the editors, and for this reason contain few mistakes resulting from retyping. In any case, the following appeal to readers — 'On the Reliability and Accuracy of Information in the* Chronicle' *— has evidently been heeded.*

7   The *Chronicle* aims at the utmost reliability in the information it publishes. In those instances when it is not absolutely certain that some event has taken place, the *Chronicle* indicates that the piece of information is based on rumour. But at the same time the *Chronicle* requests its readers to be careful and accurate in the information they provide for publication.

---

* In January 1969. Brezhnev is thought to have been the intended target of some shots fired at Soviet cosmonauts.
    † Part of the re-Stalinization campaign.
    ‡ Not released in the U.S.S.R. because of its unorthodox techniques and its equally unorthodox treatment of the icon-painter (1360–1430) who forms the subject of the film.
    § A scurrilous anti-intellectual story by Oles Benyukh, published in the journal *Oktyabr* (January 1969).

A number of inaccuracies occur during the process of duplicating copies of the *Chronicle*. These are mistakes in names and surnames, in dates and numbers. The quantity of them grows as the *Chronicle* is retyped again and again, and they cannot be corrected according to the context, as can other misprints.

Finally, the Chronicle *likes to keep up its readers' morale. These are the determined last words of No. 11 :*

HUMAN RIGHTS YEAR IN THE SOVIET UNION CONTINUES II

The *Chronicle* will continue to appear in 1970.

Part II · The Mainstream

2. THE CASE OF SINYAVSKY AND DANIEL

No *cause célèbre* in modern times has had a greater impact on the
intellectual world than that of the Soviet authors Andrei Sinyavsky
and Yuly Daniel.

> Günter Grass, Graham Greene, François Mauriac,
> Arthur Miller, Ignazio Silone, 1967[1]

Why, it may well be asked, should the Chronicle *concern itself with a
case which took place as far back as 1965–6? The answer probably lies
both in our epigraph and in the more specific fact that the case of
Sinyavsky, a brilliant critic and exponent of the grotesque, and Daniel,
a writer of powerful poems and stories, played a key role in the emergence
of the Democratic Movement. Since the death of Stalin in 1953 no
widely known writer or intellectual had been jailed. In September 1965,
however, at the same time that arrests of such people began in the
Ukraine, Sinyavsky and Daniel were rounded up. In February 1966
they faced charges of having pseudonymously published 'libellous works'
in the West since 1959, with deliberately subversive intent, and were
punished to the tune of seven and five years respectively in strict-régime
camps.*

*These sentences sparked off widespread protest: the defendants had
pleaded not guilty and the prosecution had manifestly failed to prove any
subversive intent. The injustice seemed so overwhelming, indeed, that
the young writer Alexander Ginzburg set to work and compiled an
impressive 'White Book' on the case, later published abroad in
Russian and other languages.[2]*

All this explains why the Chronicle *should have printed an item
entitled 'An addition to the collection of materials on the Sinyavsky–
Daniel case known as the 'White Book':*

In his introduction to the collection the editor, Alexander 4
Ginzburg, pointed to the possibility that the materials he had
collected were incomplete and expressed the hope that the
collection would be completed. Recently a letter has come to

light, written by Vitaly Potapenko[3] of Riga in January 1966, i.e. before the trial, and addressed to the editors of *Izvestia*:

Dear Sirs,

I am not in the habit of writing to newspapers. It is true that I write about once a year to some paper or another on a subject that interests me, but only once a year and sometimes even less frequently.

I always read your paper with pleasure, but not long ago I was deeply disturbed by an article by D. Eryomin, entitled 'The Turncoats'[4] and published on January 13th, 1966, in your No. 10/15098.

The tone of the article and the author's intentions reminded me of the articles that used to appear in *Pravda* and *Izvestia* between the years 1935 and 1939. It differed from them only in detail and in that it did not begin and end with the words 'for the dogs—a dog's death', 'crush the skunks', 'death to the traitors', and so on.

Many of you witnessed those times, and you well know and remember what they resulted in for us. I really cannot believe that you wish to resurrect those dark years of our history, when hundreds of thousands of innocent people were arrested. You must also remember the comments in the press which those articles evoked. Shivers ran up my spine and my hair stood on end when I [leafed through the old newspaper files and] read those comments. You probably did not experience such feelings at that time. That was another age. And I am very glad that this time five days passed before you were able to publish no more than three comments. This shows that many people, the majority, have not forgotten those terrible years.

But this is why I am writing to you: in his article D. Eryomin categorically states that the works of A. Sinyavsky and Yu. Daniel are 'anti-Soviet lampoons' and that the authors 'have sunk to crimes against the Soviet system'.

Who gave him the right to decide and state this? At the moment A. Sinyavsky and Yu. Daniel have been accused of this, but the trial has still not taken place and the court has not reached its verdict. And yet the comrades from Voronezh [the authors of one of the comments] echo him like parrots. Such statements are called 'contempt of court' and are an attempt to influence public opinion and the decision of the court.

D. Eryomin used further libellous expressions like 'anti-Soviet fanatic' and so on, and these are repeated by the comrades from Baku, Voronezh and Latvia.

Who gave them the right to refer to people in such libellous terms? They should be held responsible for their criminal actions under article 130, part 2, and article 131, part 2, of the Criminal Code.

Any objections by you in this particular case are futile because, according to the special section of *Soviet Criminal Law*, 'whether or not there was an element of truth in the offending phrase is irrelevant to the determination of libel ... Whether or not the victim took offence or knew of the libel is likewise irrelevant ... ' (*Soviet Criminal Law*, Special Section, p. 175).

And since the law applies to everyone, I request you to take appropriate measures to see that D. Eryomin is brought to justice, together with the authors of the comments and the editor responsible for the edition of your paper, No. 14/15102 of January 18th, 1966, who allowed the slanderous and libellous remarks to appear in the editorial introduction.

I hope that the editorial committee has sufficient courage to admit its blunder in passing an article with such contents, filled with the spirit of years gone by.

It was just this lack of responsibility for such slanderous and libellous expressions that led to the mass mistrust, slander and persecution of the years 1935–9.

And I don't want it all to start again: to stop this happening it is necessary to enforce the law and punish those who have broken it, so as to discourage others from doing the same.

I express no opinion on the works of A. Sinyavsky and Yu. Daniel because I myself have not read them and I cannot judge them from the words, the biased words, of D. Eryomin. In order to express one's opinion, even if unfavourable, on a literary work, one must read the work oneself; one should not judge from quoted extracts, because one does not know their original context. In our works of literary criticism people often say and write that one should not produce a critical article in the way that D. Eryomin has done.

My opinion is shared by many of my comrades, but they do not wish to become involved in this 'shady and risky' affair; but someone must try to see that the law is properly observed and thus prevent a repetition of the lawlessness of past years.

And EVERYONE must REMEMBER that until the court has pronounced its verdict NO ONE has the right to call anybody a criminal, an enemy, and so on. NO ONE!

I hope to receive an answer *from you* and I hope that justice will triumph.

All the best,
Sincerely yours,
V. POTAPENKO

I'm glad I was born in 1937, otherwise ...

Not surprisingly the Chronicle *has also shown interest in the fate of the two writers in their captivity. True, Sinyavsky has featured in its pages only as having refused to petition for clemency,[5] but Daniel has cropped up repeatedly in various contexts. No. 8 records that 'In the spring of 1969 a cycle of poems by Yuly Daniel was found during a search and confiscated as being "anti-Soviet"'. And No. 10 reports the circulation in* samizdat *of his moving work 'And at that Time',[6] 'a narrative poem written in 1968 and devoted to the era of mass repressions and the older generation of camp-prisoners.'*

Moreover, Daniel's literary activity in the camps has been matched by his vigour and courage in protesting, striking and rallying the morale of others, thereby combating the arbitrary acts of the camp administration. All this — in which his friend Ronkin took part too — is recorded at length in Chapter 10 and also in Anatoly Marchenko's book My Testimony.[7] *In the summer of 1969, however, it led to a drastic reprisal:*

9 At the beginning of July the writer Yuly Daniel and the engineer Valery Ronkin [see plates 30 and 31], who was convicted in the affair of *The Bell*,[8] were sent to Vladimir

prison to spend the rest of their terms there. Daniel's term expires on September 11th, 1970, Ronkin's on June 12th, 1972. After that, Ronkin still has to spend three years in exile. The address of the prison is: Vladimir-oblastnoi, p/ya OD/1 — st.2.

As Chapters 4 and 5 recount, Daniel's wife Larissa had exchanged her freedom for Siberian exile in 1968. Prior to this she had defended her husband to the utmost, visiting him in Mordovia and repeatedly protesting on his behalf.[9] This role was now assumed by their teenage son Alexander (see plate 7). His desperate 'Open letter to the writer Graham Greene',[10] written around the beginning of December 1969, is summarized by the Chronicle *in one of its reviews of samizdat:*

The author of the letter is the son of Yuly Daniel, the political [11] prisoner, and Larissa Bogoraz, who is now in exile. He expresses his concern for the fate of his father, the writer Yuly Daniel, and of V. Ronkin (sentenced for participation in an illegal Marxist circle, 'The Union of Communards'), both of whom have been accused of 'violating camp regulations' and sentenced to confinement under prison régime in Vladimir jail for the rest of their terms (which in Daniel's case means ten months and in Ronkin's almost three years). Alexander Daniel writes of the injustice of this sentence, and of the prison régime, which is especially harsh for Ronkin in view of the length of his sentence and his physical condition.

'And what do I want from you, Mr Greene? To tell the truth, I don't know. I don't know what you will be able to do, I have no idea what anyone can do in these circumstances. I, for one, can do no more. After all, I am not yet nineteen ... I just hope that you will think it possible and necessary to do something. I am hopeful that publicity will help us, at least a little.'

As for Alexander's own fate, the Chronicle *had earlier reported the following gloomy tale of victimization:*

Alexander Daniel ... finished school in 1968 and applied to the [8] physics faculty of Tartu University [in Estonia]. After he had beaten all the other applicants in the examinations, the number of places in the Department of Theoretical Physics was cut, and all the places available were taken by applicants who had not

3

sat the competitive examinations. In November 1968 Daniel began working at the Computer Centre of the Moscow Construction-Engineering Institute, but in May 1969 he was forced to leave 'at his own request'. At a meeting of party activists, where the Department of Applied Mathematics was condemned for having taken Daniel on the staff, the Rector of the Institute, Doctor of Technical Sciences Strelchuk, expressed particular dissatisfaction that there were many Jews in the department. 'Of course, I am not an anti-semite,' he said, 'but we must after all be internationalists' [i.e. employ fewer Jews]. The head of the personnel department, Feldsherova, who had given Daniel his job, received an official reprimand. Formally speaking, her guilt consisted in employing a minor without agreeing the matter with the trade union committee.

To return now to Ginzburg, on January 23rd, 1967 he was arrested for compiling the 'White Book'. *On January 17th–19th his friend Yury Galanskov and others had met a similar fate for producing the almanac* Phoenix 1966, *which contained two works by Sinyavsky, one of them judged 'criminal' at his trial. And on January 22nd some thirty people demonstrated in Moscow against the latter arrests, against article 70 of the Russian Criminal Code—used to sentence Sinyavsky and Daniel— and against the recently introduced articles 190–1 and 190–3, which had clearly been designed for use against dissenters and which had already provoked a powerful high-level protest.*[11]

This flurry of events led to trials for some of the demonstrators, which in turn gave birth to a new 'White Book'. *This one was compiled by a friend of Ginzburg's, the young physicist Pavel Litvinov, and its title was* The Case of the Demonstration in Pushkin Square on January 22nd, 1967. *The* Chronicle *wrote about it as follows:*

5 The documents on this case have been assembled by Pavel Litvinov. Included among them are verbatim records of the trial of Victor Khaustov and of that of Vladimir Bukovsky [see plate 4], Vadim Delone and Evgeny Kushev. A number of other documents are reproduced in this collection, which has been circulating in *samizdat* since the beginning of 1968. In the autumn it was also published [in Russian] in London,[12] but unfortunately this edition—for some unaccountable reason—

omits the letter of P. G. Grigorenko which forms the logical conclusion to the whole collection. [The letter is included in the English-language edition.[13]]

Regarding the two demonstrators given the longest terms — three years each — the Chronicle *reported:*

Khaustov and Bukovsky are serving their sentences in corrective-labour camps. Their addresses are as follows: V. A. Khaustov, Orenburgskaya oblast, Sol-Iletsky raion, st. Chashkan, p/ya YuK 25/7A; V. K. Bukovsky, Voronezhskaya oblast, st. Bor, p/ya OZh 118/4B. 2

The first camp is in the south Urals, the second in central Russia south of Moscow, where:

In October [1968] Vladimir Bukovsky was concussed when a pile of timber collapsed on him. He was unable to work as a result, but was accused of malingering and put in a punishment cell. He started a hunger strike in protest. Against the usual rule he was put in a communal cell and his cell-mates declared a ten-day hunger strike in support of him. Only after this was Bukovsky transferred to hospital for a while. 5

The release of Bukovsky and Khaustov — in January 1970 — was reported in Chronicle *No. 12.[14] At once Bukovsky, a talented prose-writer,[15] became one of the most prominent of the democrats. Among other things he sent an open letter to the Greek composer Mikis Theo-dorakis,[16] inviting him to intercede with the Soviet authorities on behalf of the U.S.S.R.'s political prisoners, and he denounced in a filmed interview[17] the practice of putting political dissenters in 'mental hospitals' — a practice to which he himself was earlier subjected. In March 1971, after appealing to Western psychiatrists urgently to investigate these matters, he was once again arrested.*

During the trial of Sinyavsky and Daniel the court — as we have mentioned — defined certain of their works as 'criminal'. To circulate these works thus became a criminal offence, and hence the charge in the sad but notable case of the mathematician Ilya Burmistrovich, about which the Chronicle *wrote at length:[18]*

8   THE TRIAL OF ILYA BURMISTROVICH

On May 21st, 1969, the Moscow City Court examined the case of Ilya Burmistrovich [see plates 2, 3, 26], accused under article 190–1 of the Russian Criminal Code. Burmistrovich was charged with circulating works by Yuly Daniel — *Moscow Speaking, Hands, Atonement* and *The Man from MINAP* — and the following works of Andrei Sinyavsky: *Lyubimov* and *What is Socialist Realism?*[19] The court, which consisted of Chairman L. I. Lavrova and Assessors Taldykin and Zazulin, found Burmistrovich guilty, and sentenced him to three years in an ordinary-régime camp. The Prosecutor was Babenko and the defence lawyer Yu. V. Pozdeyev.

Ilya Burmistrovich is a mathematician with a higher degree, author of nine scientific treatises and father of a two-year-old girl. He was arrested on May 16th, 1968, and spent more than a year in Lefortovo prison before being brought to trial. The investigation was conducted by K.G.B. organs.

When asked if he understood the charge, Ilya Burmistrovich replied in the negative, and said he would not answer the question of whether he would plead guilty until someone explained the essence of the charge to him. Burmistrovich referred to his right to know what he was accused of, and said that this was not clear from the bill of indictment.

Judge Lavrova refused to explain the charge further, justifying her refusal on the grounds that such explanations were usually reserved for poorly educated people, and not people with higher degrees.

Burmistrovich gave the following reasons for not understanding the charge:

> First, does the charge mean that I wished to deceive my friends about the Soviet social and political system? Secondly, there exist, as you know, certain assertions which are neither true nor false. Am I right in saying that the propagation of such assertions is not indictable under article 190–1? Thirdly, I am not clear which assertions defame and which do not defame the Soviet social and political system. I ask you to give me some indication of your criterion in deciding this. This request of mine caused

some embarrassment during the pre-trial investigation. Fourthly, the charge mentions some 'fabrications' contained in the works of Sinyavsky and Daniel. I would like you to explain to me what you mean by saying that this or that assertion is contained in a given work. There were plenty of assertions mentioned in the verdict on Sinyavsky and Daniel which are not contained in their writings ... Fifthly, I ask you to indicate, for each of the works I am charged with passing around, for each one separately, what the fabrications are which they contain. Furthermore, Sinyavsky and Daniel were accused under article 70 of the Criminal Code. In the sentence passed on them it was said that their works were written from an anti-Soviet position, but there is not a word about any 'fabrications'.

Ilya Burmistrovich received no explanation from the Judge, but his logical approach to the formulation of the charges is worth paying serious attention to. He was trying to direct attention not to the unimportant facts which served as grounds for the pre-trial and the court investigations—who gave what to whom to read or type—but to the essential point: did the content of the works he was distributing correspond to the formula set out in article 190–1? The court, of course, refused to take this line, and proceeded to have the facts on the handing around and typing of the literature corroborated, as if the 'deliberate falsehoods' and 'defamation of the Soviet system' contained in them required no proof. The Prosecutor plainly said that the content of Sinyavsky's and Daniel's works was not a subject for examination, since those works had already been condemned in the name of the Republic. But even here he gave no answer to the point Burmistrovich stressed, namely the difference between conviction under article 70 and conviction under article 190–1.

As with the trial of Kochubiyevsky [see pp. 303–6], the extremely aggressive behaviour of the Judge must be mentioned. The People's Assessors were silent for the whole of the trial, and the Prosecutor addressed the accused in reasonably mild language, restricting himself to concrete questions. But Judge Lavrova, according to the comments of those present, 'beat the soul' out of the accused, cut him short, made ironic remarks at his expense, and so on. During the adjournment she reproved him for misusing his rest period by looking at his relatives.

It was comparatively easy to get into the courtroom, although many of the seats had been occupied beforehand by K.G.B. men. But later on the approaches to the court were closed; people who went out when the court adjourned for a break were not allowed to go back in, and the Judge cleared the courtroom of several persons with whom the K.G.B. guards were already acquainted. For instance, she suggested that Natalya Gorbanevskaya, next to whom someone was chattering, should leave the room, and she suddenly addressed herself to Pyotr Yakir with: 'What are you smiling at? If you think it's funny, then get out.' She could not actually bring herself to have him turned out, but he didn't manage to get back into the courtroom after the break. A slightly condensed verbatim record of the trial of Ilya Burmistrovich has come out in *samizdat*,[20] and also a separate typescript of Burmistrovich's final plea.

10 On September 11th, the appeal was heard by the Russian Supreme Court. The composition of the court was as follows: Chairman Ostroukhova, members of the court Lukanov and Timofeyev. The Procurator was Babenko, and the defence lawyer Pozdeyev. The sentence was confirmed. In October Ilya Burmistrovich was sent off to Krasnoyarsk Province.

11 Ilya Burmistrovich ... is now [December] in a camp. His address is: Krasnoyarsky krai, st. N. Ingash, p/ya 288/1–5–3.

Subsequently, No. 17 showed again the Chronicle's *concern for Burmistrovich and his family by listing his daughter's name, birthday and address.*[21]

An equally sad episode, in its way, concerning the forty-year-old Elena Georgiyevna Krupko of Odessa,[22] *took place at the same time as Burmistrovich's trial, i.e. three whole years after the two writers had been sentenced:*

As a result of polio contracted in childhood, her arms and legs 11
are paralysed and she moves around on crutches only with the
greatest difficulty. She graduated from the Arts Faculty of
Odessa University and worked there for eighteen years as an
assistant in the Russian literature department. She was dismissed from her post in the spring of 1969 for letting friends
read copies of Alexander Solzhenitsyn's letter to the congress
[of the Writers' Union in 1967] and the final pleas of Andrei
Sinyavsky and Yuly Daniel at their trial.

But the trial also gave rise to a more constructive tradition than that of
persecuting people like Burmistrovich and Elena Krupko, as these two
items show:[23]

On December 5th, 1968, the traditional demonstration to mark 6
Constitution Day took place on Pushkin Square in Moscow. It
is well known that the first demonstration at the Pushkin
monument took place on December 5th, 1965, as a sign of
protest against the arrest of Sinyavsky and Daniel and was held
under the slogan 'Respect the Constitution!'[24] The demonstration in 1968 was a silent meeting: about twenty people stood
for ten minutes with heads bared around the monument. A
large number of volunteer police and K.G.B. men were also
present: they waited expectantly on the sidelines but did not
themselves attempt to organize any provocations.

On December 5th, 1969, the traditional silent demonstration 11
was held on Pushkin Square ... This time about fifty people
went to Pushkin Square to honour the memory of their
comrades in camps, prison and exile. At six o'clock in the
evening the demonstrators, surrounded by a crowd of plainclothes security men, bared their heads.

3. THE GALANSKOV-GINZBURG TRIAL

So intolerably unjust were the procedures of the court that even the official journal of the British Communist Party, normally a faithful spokesman for the Soviet Union, felt compelled to publish its criticisms.

Bertrand Russell (see p. 93)

The Galanskoven-Ginzburg trial of January 1968 was, in part, a direct follow-up to that of Sinyavsky and Daniel: Ginzburg had to be punished for his 'White Book'. But—the police mind doubtless thought—how much more convincing it would be to try him together with his friend Galanskov, long an active dissenter,[1] and their typist Lashkova. Moreover, by adding Galanskov's associate Dobrovolsky, who appears—unlike the others—to have had some genuine ties with the émigré Russian group N.T.S.,[2] the authorities could hope to induce a highly desirable atmosphere of conspiracy, subversion and foreign links. In such an atmosphere, proponents of a big trial must have argued, heavy sentences could be handed out and the liberal intelligentsia intimidated. The momentum of the new samizdat movement would be halted or even reversed. And the bothersome N.T.S. could, with skilful propaganda techniques, be portrayed in black colours, its influence curbed.

In the event things turned out otherwise. The N.T.S. was delighted at the publicity it received in the Soviet and foreign press,[3] and the samizdat movement, incensed at the mockery of a trial, expanded into a loose but recognizable civil rights movement with—from April 1968— its own de facto organ, the Chronicle. The latter's first number, indeed, dealt almost exclusively with the trial. It therefore forms the core of this chapter.

The material reveals the birth of a movement in two senses. First, groups and individuals in such far-flung places as Moscow, Leningrad, Novosibirsk, Latvia, the Ukraine and elsewhere, all—in unprecedented fashion—made simultaneous and similar protests against a single event in Moscow. Second, these protests then found their way to a central point, were 'processed' there, then redistributed as the Chronicle. The different groups thus got to know about each other and new links could more easily be established.

The trial also gave rise to a third 'White Book'. *First the* Chronicle *reported the circulation in* samizdat *of extensive trial materials,[4] then the superseding of these by Pavel Litvinov's vast compilation* The Trial of the Four.[5] *When this work of over 200,000 words later reached the West, it became clear that with its remarkable scholarship and comprehensiveness it far surpassed its forerunners. This chapter, in fact, serves merely as an introduction to it.[6]*

The Chronicle*'s No. 1, let us now recall, began by juxtaposing the trial of the young intellectuals with the start of Human Rights Year (see p. 53). It continued:*

All four were charged under article 70 of the Russian Criminal 1
Code (anti-Soviet agitation and propaganda), and Galanskov was additionally charged under article 88–1 (illicit currency transactions). All four were arrested in January 1967 and had spent nearly a year in [Moscow's] Lefortovo prison, in violation of article 97 of the Russian Criminal Code, according to which the maximum period of pre-trial detention may not exceed nine months.

Yury Galanskov, born in 1939, was employed before his arrest as a worker in the State Literary Museum and was also a second-year student attending evening courses at the Historical Archives Institute. He compiled and issued the typewritten literary collection *Phoenix 1966*.[7] Galanskov's poems were printed in the first *Phoenix* (1961)[8] and they also circulated separately in typescript.

Alexander Ginzburg, born in 1936, was also employed in the State Literary Museum and was a first-year student attending evening courses at the Historical Archives Institute. He compiled a collection of materials on the case of Sinyavsky and Daniel (the so-called 'White Book'), which he sent in November 1966 to certain Deputies of the U.S.S.R. Supreme Soviet and to the State Security Committee of the U.S.S.R. [the K.G.B.]. In 1960, he was prosecuted by the K.G.B. in connection with the publication of the poetry collections *Syntax*[9] (three issues) but was convicted under article 196 para. 1 of the Russian Criminal Code (forgery of documents), and given a sentence under that article of two years in corrective labour camps — the maximum term, in spite of the insignificance of the crime (forging a certificate in order to sit an exam on behalf of a

3*

friend) and the complete absence of mercenary motives in his actions. He served the sentence in camps in the Komi Autonomous Republic [in the north Urals].

In 1964 the K.G.B. again tried to institute proceedings against Ginzburg under article 70, charging him with possessing 'anti-Soviet' literature, but the case was dismissed for lack of any real evidence.

Aleksei Dobrovolsky, born in 1938, worked as a book-binder in the State Literary Museum and was a first-year student at the Moscow Institute of Culture. In 1957 he was sentenced under article 58–10 of the Russian Criminal Code (the present article 70) to six years' corrective labour.* He served the sentence in Potma in Mordovia. He was released from the camp in 1961. In 1964 he was again faced with criminal proceedings but, following a forensic psychiatric examination, was pronounced insane (schizophrenia was diagnosed) and sent to the special psychiatric prison hospital in Leningrad. The collection *Phoenix 1966* published an article by Dobrovolsky, 'Interrelationships between knowledge and faith'.[10]

Vera Lashkova [see plate 9], born in 1945, worked before her arrest as a typist at Moscow University and was a second-year student at the Institute of Culture.

The court proceedings lasted for five days (January 8th–12th), twenty-five witnesses were heard, the court was shown material evidence confiscated during searches (money, N.T.S. books and pamphlets, and a hectograph, all discovered in Dobrovolsky's flat, two copies of the collection *Phoenix*, found in Galanskov's and Ginzburg's flats), also an edition of the 'White Book' published abroad in March 1967, and several typewriters, on which the 'White Book' and *Phoenix* materials had been copied.[11]

The trial was formally public, but admission to it was by permit. In November 1967 a letter with 116 signatures[12] was sent to the Moscow City Court, the authors of which, referring to the current practice of refusing access to public trials, asked in advance that they should be given the opportunity to attend these proceedings. Not one of the signatories of the letter was

---

* This appears to be inaccurate. According to very interesting official documents he was sentenced to three years in 1958. See *Russkaya mysl*, Paris, March 7th, 1968, *Possev*, Frankfurt, October 6th, 1967.

given such an opportunity; the procedure used for allocating permits to attend the trial has still not become entirely clear. All that is known is that, apart from a large number of K.G.B. agents and members of Komsomol operational squads, and a few representatives of the legal profession (e.g. only two passes were issued to the Moscow Collegium of Lawyers), the remainder of the audience obtained their permits principally from district committees of the Communist Party.

The nearest relatives (Galanskov's parents, sister and wife, Ginzburg's fiancée, Dobrovolsky's mother, Lashkova's mother, and also, after the testimony of witnesses had been heard, i.e. towards the end of the third day of the hearing, Ginzburg's mother and Dobrovolsky's wife) were present in the courtroom. On the second day of the hearing Galanskov's sister Elena Galanskova was not readmitted to the court after going out for a few moments to get a breath of fresh air (she was pregnant) — allegedly because she had spoken to witnesses who had not yet been questioned.

In spite of the severe frost a large number of people gathered near the court building, more especially towards the end of each day's sessions. The largest number — some 100 people (not including foreign correspondents[13] and the huge number of informers) assembled on the last day to hear the verdict pronounced.

The court (the Procurator was Terekhov, the Judge Mironov) sentenced Yury Galanskov to seven years' imprisonment to be served in strict-régime camps, Alexander Ginzburg to five years, Aleksei Dobrovolsky to two years and Vera Lashkova to one year.

The lawyers of all four convicted entered appeals. The appeals were heard in the Russian Supreme Court on April 16th, 1968 (Procurator Terekhov, Judge Ostroukhova). The sentence of the Moscow City Court was upheld.

Lashkova was released on January 17th, 1968, having served her sentence in full. Right up to the appeal hearing the three remaining accused were held in Lefortovo prison (article 97 of the Russian Criminal Code thus being further infringed).

The Moscow trial provoked a widespread response among the Soviet public. The first of these was an appeal, written while the trial was still in progress by Larissa Bogoraz and Pavel Litvinov, and addressed 'To world public opinion';[14] it described the atmosphere of illegality attending the court hearing and called for public condemnation of this disgraceful trial, for the punishment of those responsible, the release of the accused from detention and a retrial which would fully conform with the legal regulations and be held in the presence of international observers.[15] After sentence was passed and the trial had ended, a series of collective and individual letters was addressed to Soviet judicial, government and party authorities as well as to organs of the press (mainly in reply to articles which had appeared in certain newspapers). The total number of people who have signed such letters amounts (up to the present) to about 700.

LIST OF THE PRINCIPAL SOVIET PRESS ARTICLES ON THE TRIAL[16]

1. 'From the court-room', *Vechernyaya Moskva* [*Evening Moscow*], January 14th, 1968.
2. T. Aleksandrov and V. Konstantinov, 'Bound by a single belt', *Izvestia*, January 16th, 1968.
3. F. Ovcharenko, 'The lackeys', *Komsomolskaya pravda*, January 18th, 1968.
4. 'No indulgence!' (a review of readers' letters), *Komsomolskaya pravda*, February 28th, 1968.
5. A. Chakovsky, 'Reply to a reader', *Literaturnaya gazeta* [*The Literary Gazette*], March 10th, 1968.*

DESCRIPTION OF THE MOST IMPORTANT LETTERS

1. A letter to the U.S.S.R. Procurator-General and to the Russian Supreme Court on the lack of publicity given to the trial, the interference of state security bodies in the conduct of the court hearing, and the question of whether the charge of links with the N.T.S. was not a cover-up for dealing with activities which, although legal, were disapproved of by the K.G.B. The letter calls for the case to be reheard by a differently constituted court, in full conformity with the rules of legal procedure, and with publicity completely assured. It also

* For strong reactions to this article see pp. 338, 474.

demands that those officials guilty of gross illegalities be called to account. 80 signatures.[17]

2. A letter to the U.S.S.R. Procurator-General and the Russian Supreme Court enclosing the appeal by Bogoraz and Litvinov, which the signatories fully endorse. The letter refers to the trial having been effectively held *in camera*, to the biased nature of the court and the verdict, and to the increasingly arbitrary conduct of political trials in general. The letter calls for the case to be retried in an atmosphere of genuine publicity and in full compliance with legal norms in the presence of representatives of the public chosen from the signatories, and for the punishment of the persons guilty of organizing the trial and bringing the Soviet legal system into disrepute. 224 signatures. (Known as the 'Letter of 170', from the original number of signatures collected.)[18]

3. Letter to L. I. Brezhnev, A. N. Kosygin, N. V. Podgorny, and the U.S.S.R. Procurator-General R. A. Rudenko concerning the lack of publicity during the trial and the obscurely worded and contradictory newspaper articles in *Izvestia* and *Komsomolskaya pravda*, pointing out that the 'open' trials of recent years call to mind the 'open' trials of the 1930s. The letter calls for a fresh, public and objective review of the case — in the interests of truth and legality and the prestige of the socialist state, and in the name of justice and humane behaviour. 24 signatures, mostly members of the Writers' Union.[19]

4. Letter from ten Leningraders to the editors of *Pravda*, *Izvestia*, the *Morning Star*, *L'Humanité* and *Unità*, supporting the appeal of Bogoraz and Litvinov and calling for the case to be retried. Simultaneously, the letter draws attention to the detention of a group of intellectuals in a Leningrad prison without trial for about a year, and expresses apprehension as to whether their imminent trial will be conducted legally [see pp. 376–80].[20]

5. Letter to L. I. Brezhnev, A. N. Kosygin, N. V. Podgorny, the President of the U.S.S.R. Supreme Court, A. F. Gorkin, and the U.S.S.R. Procurator-General R. A. Rudenko, concerning the injustice of the trial of Ginzburg, whose case is regarded as a direct continuation of the trial of Sinyavsky and Daniel, while the verdict and the charge of contacts with the N.T.S. are seen as an attempt to crush the compiler of the

collection of materials about their case. The letter calls for an immediate review of the case. 120 signatures.[21]

6. Letter to the U.S.S.R. Procurator-General and the Russian Supreme Court from a group of scientists, engineers and graduate students in Novosibirsk.* It expresses alarm at the violation of the principle of publicity and calls for the verdict to be rescinded and the case reheard, and for the prosecution of those guilty of violating the principles of publicity and legality. 46 signatures.[22]

7. Letter to L. I. Brezhnev, A. N. Kosygin, and N. V. Podgorny from a group of Ukrainian intellectuals and workers. The practice of infringing the principles of legality and publicity is condemned in the letter. 139 signatures.[23]

8. Letter from the relatives and friends of the accused to the chief editor of *Komsomolskaya pravda* and its party committee concerning the mendacity of F. Ovcharenko's article 'The lackeys' and demanding an open discussion of the article in the editorial office and in the Union of Journalists. 29 signatures.[24]

9. Open letter to the editors of *Komsomalskaya pravda* from O. Timofeyeva (Galanskov's wife [see plate 7]) with a detailed refutation of the false information given by F. Ovcharenko.[25]

10. Letter from L. I. Ginzburg (Ginzburg's mother) [see plate 9] to *Komsomolskaya pravda* about the libelling of A. Ginzburg by the author of the article 'The lackeys' and asking for a correction and refutation of the article.[26]

11. Letter from ten friends and acquaintances of Ginzburg to the chief editors of *Pravda*, *Izvestia* and *Komsomolskaya pravda*, refuting the articles in *Izvestia* and *Komsomolskaya pravda*.[27]

12. Letter from thirteen witnesses who appeared at the trial, concerning the contravention of article 283 of the Russian Code of Criminal Procedure, which requires the witnesses to be present in the courtroom until the end of the court hearing: the Judge and the 'court commandant' had summarily dismissed the witnesses immediately after they had testified. The letter is addressed to the President of the Moscow City Court, the President of the Russian Supreme Court, the President of the U.S.S.R. Supreme Court, the Procurator of the Russian Republic and the U.S.S.R. Procurator-General.[28]

* For reprisals see p. 396.

13–14. Letter to L. I. Brezhnev, A. F. Gorkin, R. A. Rudenko and the President of the U.S.S.R. Academy of Medical Sciences, Blokhin, written by Z. M. Grigorenko to protest against the refusal to summon her husband, P. G. Grigorenko, as a witness in the trial, on the basis of the false information that he was mentally ill.[29] P. G. Grigorenko's own letter to the Russian Supreme Court, setting forth the evidence which he was unable to give in court, concerning the origin of the money found in the possession of Dobrovolsky.[30]

[*15–16–17. The letters of the 116 (see p. 74), the 44*[31] *and the 31,*[32] *all written before the trial, and added to the list by* Chronicle *No. 2.*[33]]

The above is a list of the letters with the largest number of signatures and the letters of persons most closely connected with the trial and the accused and best acquainted with the facts of the case. In addition, there is a large number of personal and collective letters of protest (up to 8 signatures).

Among the most comprehensive of these may be mentioned: the appeal by I. Gabai [see Chap. 6], Yu. Kim [see pp. 88, 394] and P. Yakir [see Chap. 7], 'To those who work in science, culture and the arts', in which the political trials of recent years are directly linked with other symptoms of neo-Stalinism in our country;[34] a statement to the President of the Russian Supreme Court by A. E. Levitin (Krasnov) [see Chap. 16], who appeared as a witness at this trial and at the Bukovsky trial, in which he points to the encroachments on freedom of speech and conscience as a reason for the actions of Galanskov and Ginzburg and calls for both young men to be set free;[35] a letter sent to the Communist Party Central Committee by the chairman of the 'Jauna Gvarde' collective farm in Latvia, party member I. A. Yakhimovich [see Chap. 6], concerning the immense harm done to our country by such trials and by the persecution of dissenters;[36] a letter from L. Z. Kopelev [see p. 90], a member of the party and of the Union of Writers, addressed to the Secretariat of the party Central Committee, in which he says that the recent trial constitutes a fresh attempt to 'consolidate' the ideological struggle and the work of political education by repressive actions which damage our culture and prestige and, eventually, state security itself: he calls for a review of the damaging decisions reached by the court, the dismissal of the persons responsible for such trials, the publication of the materials pertaining to these trials, and the removal from the public order and state security organs, the Procuracy and the courts of the right to interfere in cultural life;[37] a letter from V. M. Voronin of Arzamas [in Gorky Region] to the chief editor of *Izvestia* concerning the immoral and unsubstantiated nature of the article by T. Aleksandrov and V. Konstantinov, in which some facts are distorted and others glossed over;[38] a letter from the translator A. Yakobson [see Chap. 7] demonstrating the falsity of the articles 'The lackeys' and 'Bound by a single belt': the letter contains no additional information but merely analyses in detail the actual wording of the articles;[39] a letter from L. Plyushch [see p. 157], a mathematician in Kiev, to *Komsomolskaya pravda* in which he explains why he believes the *samizdat* documents about the trial and not the official articles.[40]

Not one of these letters was answered.

The unprecedented extent of the movement of protest provoked a series of repressive measures.

(a) At the beginning of February 1968 Mrs L. I. Ginzburg, Irina Zholkovskaya (A. Ginzburg's fiancée) and Olga Timofeyeva (Galanskov's wife) were summoned to the Moscow Procuracy. Obedience being legally compulsory when a witness is summoned, but the notices making no mention either of the purpose of the summons or of the consequences of failure to appear, O. Timofeyeva did not answer the summons. Mrs Ginzburg and Miss Zholkovskaya were subjected to a 'prophylactic chat' for allegedly spreading false information about the trial.[41] The chat ended with a threat that article 190–1 of the Russian Criminal Code might be invoked.

Following this, L. Bogoraz, P. G. Grigorenko, P. Litvinov and P. Yakir were summoned for similar 'prophylactic chats', but this time to the K.G.B. offices (Litvinov did not obey either the first or the second summons, but later, in March, was called to the Moscow Procuracy).[42] The content of the chats was identical: all the persons summoned were warned that they should cease their 'public activities'. Pyotr Yakir, the son of Iona Yakir, the army commander *who was shot in 1937*, was told: '*You* aren't your father's spiritual heir! *We* are his spiritual heirs.' When Larissa Bogoraz said that she would not talk until she was allowed to make a statement about the grossly illegal methods of persecution practised in the case of former political prisoner Anatoly Marchenko [see Chap. 9], she was told that this statement was yet further evidence of her 'anti-social activities'. In a letter to Yu. V. Andropov, chairman of the K.G.B., P. G. Grigorenko described his own lengthy chat, which had been full of threats. He too received no reply to his letter.[43]

(b) On February 14th–15th, two of the most active participants in the protests, Alexander Volpin [see p. 358], Master of Physical-Mathematical Sciences, and Natalya Gorbanevskaya [see Chaps. 4, 5 and 7], a translator, were forcibly interned in psychiatric hospitals.

Without any warning and without her relations' knowledge, Gorbanevskaya was transferred on February 15th from maternity clinic No. 27, where she was being kept with a threatened miscarriage, to ward 27 of the Kashchenko hospital. The decision to transfer her was taken in consultation with the duty psychiatrist of the Timiryazev district, and the transfer was said to have been motivated by the patient's requests to be discharged. On February 23rd, Gorbanevskaya was discharged from the Kashchenko hospital as the psychiatrists admitted she was not in need of treatment.

On February 14th, A. S. Volpin was taken from his home by the police and the duty psychiatrist of the Leningrad district [of Moscow], Albert Matyukov. The reason given was that Volpin had not reported for a long time to the psychiatric out-patients' department where he was registered (and to which he had not once been summoned during the past four years). He was put in ward 3 of the Kashchenko hospital, where he was roughly handled by the ward supervisor, A. A. Kazarnovskaya, and the house doctor, Leon Khristoforovich (who did not give his surname). On February 16th, on an order signed by I. K. Yanushevsky, chief psychiatrist of Moscow, Volpin was transferred to No. 5 hospital at Stolbovaya Station, seventy kilometres from Moscow (this is a hospital mainly for chronically ill patients and also for petty criminals sent for compulsory treatment). Appeals made by his relatives to I. K. Yanushevsky remained unanswered. Only after an appeal addressed to the U.S.S.R. Minister of Health, Academician B. V. Petrovsky, initially by Academicians A. N. Kolmogorov and P. S. Aleksandrov and then by a further ninety-nine academics (including the most eminent Soviet mathematicians: academicians, professors and Lenin prize-winners),[44] was some improvement made in Volpin's situation. At the present moment he is back again in Kashchenko hospital, but in ward 32 which is quieter than ward 3.

The only official basis for such actions could be the instruction 'On the immediate hospitalization of mentally ill persons who constitute a danger to society' (see the collection *Health Legislation*,[45] vol. 6, Moscow, 1963). In the first place, however, this is only official and not legal, since the very fact of compulsory hospitalization conflicts with articles 58–60 of the Russian Criminal Code [see p. 234], according to which compulsory measures of a medical nature are prescribed by a court. Moreover, the hospitalization of 'socially dangerous' persons directly conflicts with a fundamental principle of legality— that of the presumption of innocence, since it is a person who has actually *committed* an offence who is recognized as socially dangerous and this can be decided only by a court verdict. Secondly, even this rather cruel and illegal instruction was flagrantly disregarded. A person sent to hospital must, within twenty-four hours after arrival, be examined by a commission of three people—this was not done in either Volpin's or Gorbanevskaya's case. Their relatives were not informed, which is also obligatory according to the instruction. Finally, a commission appointed after the letters from the mathematicians merely established that Volpin was in need of treatment, and to some extent improved the conditions of his internment. According to the instruction the commission is in any case bound to examine a patient once a month and, furthermore, to issue a finding not as to whether he is ill or not, but as to whether his illness is still of the 'socially dangerous' type—if it is not, the patient should be discharged into the care of relatives. The regular commission, which met on April 17th, also declared that Volpin needed to undergo another one and a half months of 'treatment'.

[Nevertheless] on May 12th, after three months in psychiatric 2 hospitals, Alexander Volpin was discharged.[46]

(c) The next, and so far the widest, wave of repressions 1 affected Communist Party members who had signed one or other of the letters. All the district party committees in Moscow were sent copies or photostats of the letters (including even those whose authors had addressed them to the court and the Procuracy, without even sending copies to the party Central Committee). The district committees went through the lists of signatories and hunted down 'their' party members. In almost all cases identical action was taken—expulsion from the party, regardless of the decision taken by local party cells and of whether the particular case had ever been considered at a meeting of the party organization. The following were expelled from the party:*

1. Lyudmila Alekseyeva, editor in the 'Nauka' publishing-house. She had signed the letter of the 80. On the district committee's recommendation she was dismissed from her job.[47]

2. Lyudmila Belova, Master of Philosophical Sciences, participant in the Great Patriotic War, decorated, a research officer at the Institute of the History of the Arts, signed the letter of the 80.

3. Boris Birger, artist, member of the Moscow branch of the Artists' Union, signed the letter of the 24 (the 'writers' letter').[48]

4. Piama Gaidenko, Master of Philosophical Sciences, research officer at the Institute of the International Workers' Movement, signed the letter of the 80.[49]

5. Alexander Ogurtsov, Master of Philosophical Sciences, research officer at the Institute of the International Workers' Movement, signed the letter of the 80.[50]

6. Leonid Pazhitnov, Master of Philosophical Sciences, research officer at the Institute of the History of the Arts, signed the letter of the 80. On the party district committee's recommendation he was dismissed from his job.[51]

7. Valentin Nepomnyashchy, critic, member of the Journalists'

* Later, however, No. 5 reported that 'A number of people have been re-admitted to the party on appeal, expulsion being replaced by the lesser sanction of a "severe reprimand". They include Fedot Suchkov, Yury Karyakin, Lyudmila Belova, Moisei Tulchinsky and Sergei Fomin.'

Union, head of the Soviet literature department in the magazine *Questions of Literature*, signed the 'writers' letter'. Removed from post of departmental head.[52]

8. V. M. Rodionov, Doctor of Biological Sciences (Institute of Medical Biochemistry[53]), signed the letter of the 120.

9. Fedot Suchkov, critic, member of the Writers' Union, subjected to repression in Stalin's time, signed the 'writers' letter'.[54]

10. Moisei Tulchinsky, Master of Historical Sciences, took part in the Great Patriotic War, decorated, works at Nauka publishing house, signed the letter of the 120.[55]

11. Isaak Filshtinsky, Master of Historical Sciences, senior research officer at the Institute of the Peoples of Asia, subjected to repression in Stalin's time, wrote a letter with his wife to A. N. Kosygin asking for a humane review of the case.[56]

12. Sergei Fomin, Doctor of Physical-Mathematical Sciences, professor at Moscow University, signed the letter of the 99 mathematicians on behalf of Volpin.

13. Aron Khanukov, chief engineer in a building materials plant, signed the letter of ten friends of Ginzburg sent to *Komsomolskaya pravda*. Removed from his job as chief engineer.[57]

14. Boris Shragin, Master of Philosophical Sciences, research officer at the Institute of the History of the Arts, signed the letter of the 80 and gave his address as sender of the letter; also signed appeal to the Budapest consultative meeting (more about this appeal later). On the party district committee's recommendation dismissed from his post.[58]

15. Grigory Yablonsky, physicist (Novosibirsk).[59]

16. Ivan Yakhimovich, chairman of 'Jauna Gvarde' collective farm, Kraslava District, Latvia. Wrote letter to the party Central Committee. Removed from chairmanship of collective farm.

17. Valery Pavlinchuk, physicist (Obninsk), signed letter of the 170. Deprived of his security pass and dismissed 'because of staff cuts'.*

At the same time as participants in the protest campaign began to be expelled from the party, the lawyer B. A. Zolotukhin, defence counsel for Ginzburg, was also expelled 'for

* See also pp. 96, 411–13

adopting a non-party, non-Soviet line in his defence'. In his defence speech the lawyer convincingly refuted all the prosecution's evidence and — for the first time in many years' experience of political trials — called for the complete acquittal of his client.[60] After his expulsion from the party B. A. Zolotukhin was removed from his post as head of a legal consultation office.[61]

Simultaneously with this party 'purge', two other persons were expelled for quite different reasons: Yury Karyakin, philosopher and literary critic, for an anti-Stalin speech made at an evening held in memory of [the writer] Andrei Platonov;[62] and Grigory Svirsky, writer and member of the Writers' Union, for a speech made at a meeting of the Moscow Writers' Party Organization devoted to the danger of a Stalinist revival and the problem of censorship.[63]

All the expulsions involved violations of the Party Statutes (to the extent that some members were expelled without being given a hearing).

In the case of many of the non-party members who had signed various letters, 'chats' were held at their place of employment and suggestions were frequently made that they should resign 'at their own request'.[64] Some persons were deprived of foreign assignments already scheduled for them. Fresh lists of 'undesirable' authors appeared in editorial and publishing offices. Some manuscripts already scheduled for publication were rejected.

Yury Aikhenvald and his wife Valeria Gerlin were dismissed from their teaching jobs for signing the letter of the 170 (both were victims of repression in Stalin's time).*

Yury Glazov, Master of Historical Sciences, who signed the

---

* No. 5 reports: 'Their dismissal was carried out in such a flagrantly illegal way that the school had to reinstate them after a court order. The record of a discussion of Gerlin's case at a trade union meeting at her school and in the education department of the local Soviet is circulating in *samizdat* [partial text in *Possev* 10 (1968), pp. 55–60 and in A. Brumberg, *In Quest of Justice* (Pall Mall, London, 1970) doc. 77]. Apart from its purely documentary value, which derives mainly from the light it throws on how little the concept of legality means to the mass of educated people, this record is one of the few documentary works of the past year which can be read for literary pleasure as well as for the information it provides.' No. 2 adds that the couple are both teachers 'of Russian language and literature', Aikhenvald also being 'a poet and translator', both were rehabilitated after the camps, and both dismissed 'under article 49 of the Labour Code'. See Aikhenvald's poems in *Grani*, Frankfurt, 65 (1967), pp. 38–50, and 70 (1969), p. 117.

letters of the 170 and the 80 and the appeal to the Budapest conference [see below], was dismissed from the Institute of the Peoples of Asia.[65] For 'staff reduction' reasons the following were dismissed from their jobs: Alexander Morozov and Dmitry Muravyov (letter of the 120), editors in the 'Iskusstvo' publishing-house,[66] Irina Kristi, junior research officer at the Institute of Theoretical and Experimental Physics (letters of the 170 and the 99),[67] and the head of a laboratory in the same Institute, Alexander Kronrod, Doctor of Mathematical Physics (letter of the 99).[68] Sergei Vorobyov, an editor in the 'Soviet Encyclopedia' publishing-house, was expelled from the Komsomol for having at a meeting expressed dissatisfaction with the methods of discussion: signatories of letters were being condemned, yet none of the persons present had read the letters.

This roll-call of people subject to extra-judicial reprisals is extended in Chronicle *No. 2 to make a list of 91. This list includes the people named in No. 1 — whose fate is recapitulated — but adds many more. Later No. 5 adds a further 63 names, although naturally only a small proportion of these had been persecuted in connection with protests against the Galanskov-Ginzburg trial. Most of the material in these two lists — with the exception of repetitive passages — has been inserted at relevant points in the book, often in the notes. Information on the thirty-odd individuals whose protests concern this chapter and who are not mentioned anywhere in the main text appears in notes 48, 62 and, especially, 69.[69] Details of reprisals against residents of Leningrad, Novosibirsk, the Ukraine, etc, are given mainly in Chapters 14 and 19.*

Meanwhile, No. 1 continues by presenting an episode of crucial importance, marking as it did the first time that a varied group of people got together to protest on a variety of issues:

1 On February 24th, 1968, an appeal was sent to the Budapest conference of Communist and Workers' Parties, the full text of which we quote here:

TO THE PRESIDIUM OF THE CONSULTATIVE CONFERENCE OF COMMUNIST PARTIES IN BUDAPEST

A series of political trials have been conducted in our country in recent years. The essence of these trials lies in the fact that people have been tried *for their convictions*, in violation of their fundamental civil rights. Precisely as a result of this, the trials have been conducted with gross violations of legality, the major one having been the absence of publicity.

Our society no longer wishes to submit to such illegality, and this has led to indignation and protests, which have been growing from trial to trial. A great number of individual and collective letters have been sent to various judicial, governmental and party organs, all the way up to the Central Committee of the Communist Party. These letters have gone unanswered. Instead, the reply to those who have protested most actively has been dismissal from their work, a summons from the K.G.B. and threats of arrest, or finally — the most shocking form of reprisal — forcible confinement in a mental hospital. These illegal and anti-human actions can produce no positive results; on the contrary, they increase tension and give rise to further indignation.

We believe it our duty to point out also that several thousands of political prisoners, of whom the rest of the world is virtually unaware, are in the camps and prisons. They are kept in inhuman conditions of forced labour, on a semi-starvation diet, exposed to the arbitrary actions of the administration. After they have completed their sentences, they are subjected to extra-judicial and frequently illegal persecution — restrictions on their choice of a place of residence and administrative surveillance, which places free men in the position of exiles.

We also call your attention to the fact of discrimination against small nations and the political persecution of people who are struggling for national equality, all this being particularly clear in the case of the Crimean Tatars.

We know that many communists abroad and in our country have repeatedly expressed their disapproval of the political repressions of recent years. We ask the participants in the consultative meeting fully to consider the peril caused by the trampling on the rights of man in our country.

The appeal was signed by:

Aleksei Kosterin	Writer; Moscow, Malaya Gruzinskaya 31, kv. 70 [see Chap. 6]
Larissa Bogoraz	Philologist; Moscow V–261, Leninsky prospekt 85, kv. 3
Pavel Litvinov	Physicist; Moscow K–1, ul. Alekseya Tolstogo 8, kv. 78
Zampira Asanova	Doctor; Uzbekskaya S.S.R., Ferganskaya oblast, Yangi-Kurgan [see Chap. 12]
Pyotr Yakir	Historian; Moscow Zh–280, Avtozavodskaya 5, kv. 75
Victor Krasin	Economist; Moscow, Belomorskaya ul. 24, kv. 25 [see Chap. 7]
Ilya Gabai	Teacher; Moscow A–55, Novolesnaya ul. 18, kor. 2, kv. 83
Boris Shragin	Philosopher; Moscow G–117, Pogodinka 2/3, kv. 91
Levitin-Krasnov	Religious writer; Moscow Zh–377, 3-ya Novokuzminskaya ul. 23
Yuly Kim	Teacher; Moscow Zh–456, Ryazansky prospekt 73, kv. 90
Yury Glazov	Linguist; Moscow V–421, Leninsky prospekt 101/164, kv. 4
Pyotr Grigorenko	Construction engineer, former Major-General; Moscow G–21, Komsomolsky prospekt 14/1, kv. 96

Only three or four dozen professional writers signed protests against the Galanskov-Ginzburg trial, but the way in which these liberals avoided serious reprisals — through mutual solidarity backed by other colleagues — is shown in this item:

2 It is said that after certain sentences had appeared in the press, especially in the *Literary Gazette*[70] and *Literary Russia*[71] on the incompatibility of signing letters about the trial and remaining a member of the Writers' Union, several writers (the names of Vasily Aksyonov, Evgeny Evtushenko and Vladimir Ten-

dryakov* have been mentioned) approached the Union secretariat and declared on behalf of 100 (according to other versions 120 or 150) members of the Union, that if even one signatory were expelled, then they too would leave the Union's ranks. It is also said that a similar statement was presented by Veniamin Kaverin [see pp. 336–7] in his own name and on behalf of Pavel Antokolsky,[72] Konstantin Paustovsky and Kornei Chukovsky.†

None the less, to bolster the illusion that their authority was more than minimal, the Union's officials acted like the pedantic, authoritarian, but basically weak schoolmaster who hands out subtly and almost infinitely graded reprimands to disobedient children:

To conclude the news of extra-judicial repressions the *Chronicle* 6 prints in full a report from the Information Bulletin of the Board Secretariat of the U.S.S.R. Union of Writers [1968, No. 6(18), p. 15]. Some of the writers mentioned here have been referred to in the *Chronicle*, but in terms of repression through party or professional channels. Here thirty-five writers have received various kinds of punishment from the Union of Writers.

REPORT FROM THE BOARD SECRETARIAT
OF THE MOSCOW ORGANIZATION

Information Bulletin No. 4 has already reported that on April 17th the Board Secretariat of the Moscow writers' organization discussed the question of men of letters who had signed a declaration defending Ginzburg, Galanskov and others.

The Secretariat's resolution stated in particular that the irresponsible actions of a few writers showed that they had infringed that part of the Statutes of the U.S.S.R. Union of Writers which obliges its members to engage in an ideological struggle against bourgeois and revisionist influences.

At its session of May 20th, 1968, the Board Secretariat

---

* Popular writers aged about forty, most of whose work can be freely published.
† Two grand old men of Soviet literature who died in 1968 and 1969 respectively.

of the Moscow writers' organization resolved to announce to Writers' Union members that in view of the political irresponsibility manifested in the signing of declarations and letters which, by their form and content, discredited Soviet laws and the authority of Soviet judicial organs, and for ignoring the fact that these documents might be exploited by bourgeois propaganda for purposes damaging to the Soviet Union and Soviet literature, the following measures had been taken:

A severe reprimand and warning, with an endorsement in his personal file, for L. Z. Kopelev.

A reprimand with endorsement in their personal files for: V. P. Aksyonov, D. S. Samoilov, B. I. Balter,[73] V. N. Voinovich,[74] L. K. Chukovskaya [see pp. 335, 420], A. A. Shteinberg.

It was decided to give a severe rebuke to the following members of the Writers' Union: B. A. Akhmadulina, N. M. Korzhavin, V. V. Shitovaya, B. M. Sarnov, F. A. Iskander, G. M. Pozhenyan, L. E. Pinsky, I. N. Solovyova, F. G. Svetov, K. A. Ikramov, Yu. D. Levitansky, E. G. Adamyan, E. M. Golysheva, N. D. Otten-Potashinsky.

The following members of the Writers' Union were given strong warnings: K. P. Bogatyryov, V. N. Kornilov, N. V. Naumov,[75] Yu. O. Dombrovsky, V. E. Maksimov, L. A. Levitsky.

The following members received a warning: V. A. Khinkis, K. L. Rudnitsky,[76] N. N. Matveyeva, V. A. Kaverin, M. F. Loriye, Yu. P. Kazakov, Yu. F. Edlis, and M. M. Roshchin.[77]

Finally, as regards Soviet opponents of the trial, the Chronicle *relates in some detail this university case:*

4 In the spring of this year, Kaidan, a student of the Language and Literature Faculty of Moscow University, wrote a letter to his wife, who was in another town, describing the circumstances surrounding the trial of Ginzburg, Galanskov and the others, giving extracts from the appeal of Bogoraz and Litvinov

'To World Public Opinion', and also describing the anti-semitic outbursts which he had witnessed at a Moscow railway station. This letter was 'accidentally' opened and fell into the hands of the K.G.B., who sent it to the Dean's office. Early in the academic year Kaidan was expelled from the Komsomol, excluded from the Department of Military Training, and finally expelled from the University. At present he is in a psychiatric hospital after attempting to commit suicide.

No. 5 takes further the sad story of 'V. Kaidan, student in the Depart-ment of Mathematical Linguistics' [of the Language and Literature Faculty]:

Subsequent information now enables a fuller picture of his case to be given. He was one of several third-year students who in the spring of 1968 refused to join in condemning the teaching record of Shikhanovich [see plate 60] when the latter was being expelled from the University[78] ... These students were themselves threatened with expulsion. At this time the letter from Kaidan to his wife was intercepted ... At the beginning of the academic year, in October, Kaidan was investigated three times — once at a general meeting of Komsomol activists, in the presence of representatives of the Faculty's party committee. A group of his fellow students condemned his 'activities', but spoke against his expulsion, asking that they be allowed to stand as surety for his good behaviour. Kaidan himself made a statement of regret in writing, but this state-ment was rejected as 'false' because he refused to name the person who had let him read the appeal by Bogoraz and Litvinov. At all the meetings on his case it was decided to expel Kaidan from the Komsomol and to recommend to the Rector that he be expelled from the University. It is said that Kaidan now suffers most of all on account of having written a statement of regret. He did in fact go into the Kashchenko Mental Hospital, but rumours that this happened after a suicide attempt cannot be confirmed.

Four students who, like Kaidan, refused to denounce Shikhanovich have been expelled from the University for 'lack of progress in military training'.

Foreigners, too, were involved in protests against the trial. On January 14th, for example, a group of fifteen people—including W. H. Auden, A. J. Ayer, Cecil Day-Lewis, Jacquetta Hawkes, Julian Huxley, Mary MacCarthy, Yehudi Menuhin, Henry Moore, Bertrand Russell, Paul Scofield, Stephen Spender, and Igor Stravinsky—sent a telegram in reply to Larissa Daniel's and Pavel Litvinov's appeal 'To world public opinion'. It read: 'We, a group of friends representing no organization, support your statement, admire your courage, think of you, and will help in any way possible to us.'

A few months later two demonstrations took place, recorded by the Chronicle *as follows:*

2   PAMPHLETS OF THE 'CHURCH' GROUP IN MAYAKOVSKY SQUARE[79]

In Moscow at 6 p.m. on June 17th, in Mayakovsky Square, three young English people attempted to distribute leaflets [see plate 8] demanding the liberation of Soviet political prisoners. The young people, 20-year-old Janette Hammond, 21-year-old John Careswell and 25-year-old Vivian Broughton, were detained by representatives of the state security organs and the next day deported from the Soviet Union. They are members of the youth organization 'Church', a union of Christian radicals, Marxists and anarchists founded a year ago. It is well known for its many street demonstrations against American aggression in Vietnam. In January,[80] after the Moscow trial, its members organized a six-hour demonstration outside the Soviet embassy in London.

In no way is the 'Church' leaflet of an anti-Soviet nature. In it both the words of the authors of the leaflet and the declaration by Bertrand Russell express only the regret and concern felt by many of the friends of our country about the repressive measures which have been taken in the Soviet Union against the freedoms of speech and conscience. The leaflet opens with pictures of Yury Galanskov and Lord Bertrand Russell, and the slogans FREEDOM FOR GALANSKOV, FREEDOM FOR THE BAPTISTS, FREEDOM FOR ALL POLITICAL PRISONERS IN THE U.S.S.R. The leaflet contains short informatory notes about five of the political prisoners: Andrei Sinyavsky, Yuly Daniel, Yury Galanskov, Alexander Ginzburg and Vladimir Bukovsky, and on the persecution of the Baptist Christians in the U.S.S.R. An excerpt from the appeal by Larissa Bogoraz and Pavel Litvinov, 'To World Public Opinion', is also printed in the leaflet, together with the declaration of Bertrand Russell, which is presented below in slightly abridged form [as in the leaflet]:

There is an influential body of people in the West which is always ready to condemn as wicked anything that happens in the Soviet Union, whilst at the same time boasting of the 'liberty' and 'democracy' enjoyed in the so-called Free World. Such people live in a black-and-white world and show no willingness to judge questions on their merits. Those of us in the West who have struggled over the years against these Cold Warriors have welcomed the enormous changes in the Soviet Union in the past fifteen years, changes which have undoubtedly led to greater human happiness and freedom. These admirable developments are endangered by the mock trial just held in Moscow. So intolerably unjust were the procedures of the court that even the official journal of the British Communist Party, normally a faithful spokesman for the Soviet Union, felt compelled to publish its criticisms. The Soviet writers should be retried before an open court and have the right to defend themselves fully.[81]

Earlier, on June 6th, a representative of the Flemish Committee for Co-operation with Eastern Europe, Roger de Bie, distributed near the Arbatskaya underground station copies of the committee's petition for the release of certain political prisoners, and also postcards bearing their pictures. He too was detained and deported.

On June 23rd, Larissa Bogoraz and Pavel Litvinov made the following statement:

We are deeply touched by the courageous action of the three young English people in openly demonstrating in defence of human rights in our country. We realized some months ago that our protest had found a response among leading men of culture in Europe and America. That was for us a tremendous moral support. Now we are happy to see, from the example of the Flemings and the English, that progressive young people in the West also understand the meaning of our struggle.

Meanwhile the young intellectuals sentenced at the trial had begun their terms in the severe conditions of the Mordovian strict-régime labour camps. We shall meet them there again in Chapter 10. The prospect must have been most fearful for the chronically ill Galanskov, but both he and Ginzburg were fortified by the knowledge that they had stood firm in their most testing hour and thereby helped to inspire the birth of the Democratic Movement.

2 Yury Galanskov and Alexander Ginzburg arrived at Mordovian camp No. 17 in May. Their address is: Mordovskaya A.S.S.R., st. Potma, p/o Ozerny, p/ya ZhKh 385/17a. From the very first day of their arrival they were set to work sewing mittens for specialized work-clothing. A short while later Yury Galanskov was sent to the hospital camp for the examination of a stomach ulcer. Aleksei Dobrovolsky is a member of the construction brigade now working at the same hospital camp. His address is: Mordovskaya A.S.S.R., st. Potma; p/o Yavas, p/ya ZhKh 385/3.

4. THE INVASION OF CZECHOSLOVAKIA AND THE RED SQUARE DEMONSTRATION

Since the Sinyavsky-Daniel trial, since 1966, not a single arbitrary or violent act by the authorities has passed without a public protest, without censure. This is a valuable tradition, the start of people's *self-liberation* from the humiliation of fear, from connivance in evil ... If Herzen a century ago, by speaking out in defence of Poland's freedom and against its great power suppressors, alone saved the honour of Russia's democrats, then the seven demonstrators [on Red Square] have undoubtedly saved the honour of the Soviet people. The significance of the demonstration of August 25th cannot be overestimated.[1]

Anatoly Yakobson,* September 1968

The dramatic Soviet invasion of Czechoslovakia on the night of August 20th–21st, 1968, introduced a new dimension into the Soviet civil rights movement. Previously the movement had been little if at all concerned with criticizing Soviet foreign policy, so preoccupied was it with its own problems vis-à-vis the authorities. But this particular aggressive act at once aroused many of its members to outraged protest. First, the Soviet government's action was so blatant, so crushing and so universally condemned that few liberally minded people could fail to be indignant, however passive or even approving many other Soviet citizens might be. More important still was the fascination which the democratization in Czechoslovakia had naturally held for Soviet liberals, giving them the hope that the same process might one day occur in the U.S.S.R. These hopes, as some had foreseen would happen, were now dashed.

The demonstration of August 25th and other acts of protest by Soviet citizens form the core of this chapter. Further such acts feature, for various reasons, in different chapters, while Chapter 5 records the trial of the demonstrators and the circumstances surrounding it. All this material gives a vivid preview of Natalya Gorbanevskaya's remarkable book Midday: the Case of the Demonstration of August 25th, 1968, on Red Square,[2] *which covers the same historic events in greater detail.*

* See pp. 80, 151, 424–6

95

No. 3 of the Chronicle *came out only ten days after the invasion and reported thus:*

3 On August 21st, 1968, the forces of five member-countries of the Warsaw Pact carried out a treacherous and unprovoked attack on Czechoslovakia.

The aggressive actions of the U.S.S.R. and her allies met with a sharp rebuff from world public opinion.

This issue of the *Chronicle* will deal with the events in our country which in one way or another are connected with the question of Czechoslovakia.

The facts show clearly that even in conditions which practically preclude the possibility of resistance, the struggle for the realization in practice of the principles of humanism and justice has not ceased ...

On July 29th a letter was handed in [by Grigorenko and Yakhimovich, see plate 22] to the Czechoslovak embassy, signed by five Soviet Communists. It approved the new course of the Czechoslovak Communist Party and condemned Soviet pressure on Czechoslovakia [see p. 110].

On July 30th, Valery Pavlinchuk [see pp. 411–13] died. A young physicist from Obninsk, one of the most active and public-spirited people and communists of the city, a talented scientist and teacher, he was expelled from the party and dismissed from his work for circulating *samizdat*. Shortly before his death he sent an open letter to Alexander Dubček, in which he directly expressed his solidarity with the new political course in Czechoslovakia, seeing it as an example of real socialist construction, free from dogmatism and excessive police control.

Even before the invasion, Czech newspapers had disappeared from the book-stalls, and with the invasion *L'Humanité*, *L'Unità*, the *Morning Star*, *Borba*, *Rinascita* and other publications ceased to arrive. Regular jamming of broadcasts from foreign radio stations began. The press and the ether were monopolized by our own propaganda.

On August 24th, in Moscow's October Square, a certain citizen shouted out a slogan against the invasion of Czechoslovakia and was roughly beaten up by some strangers in plain clothes. Two of them hustled him into a car and drove off; the third remained beside a second car. Indignant onlookers began to demand that

1. Andrei Sinyavsky (left) and Yuly Daniel (right), carrying the lid of the coffin at Pasternak's funeral, Peredelkino, 1960.

2. (*top left*) Ilya Burmistrovi
Moscow mathematician, bef
his arrest in 1968 (see pp. 67

3. (*above*) Burmistrovich in
Siberian camp, 1970.

4. (*left*) Vladimir Bukovs
Moscow, 1970.

5. (*top right*) Alexander Gin
burg before his arrest in 196

6. (*top far right*) Ginzburg ir
his Mordovian camp, 1969.

7. (*right*) Galanskov's inju
wife Olga is carried from
trial of her husband by Pa
Litvinov (left) and Alexand
Daniel (right), January 12
1968.

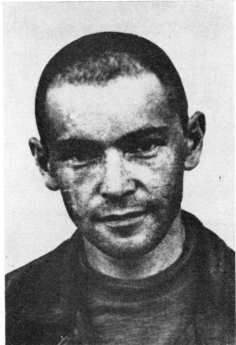

свободу галанскову!
свободу баптистам!
свободу всем полит-
заключенным СССР!

ЮРИЙ ГАЛАНСКОВ

28-илетний поэт и пацифист, отбывает семилетний срок за свою деятельность за мир и свободу.

БЕРТРАН РАССЕЛЛ

Британский философ мировой известности, выдающийся среди прогрессивных кругов Запада. Его комментарии суда над Галансковым приводятся на последней странице.

8. (*left*) Page 1 of the 'Churc[h] leaflet showing Galanskov an[d] Bertrand Russell (see p. 92).

9. (*above*) Valeria Novodvorskay[a] Moscow student (see p. 109).

10. (*below*) Vera Lashkova, Mo[s] cow student (left), with Ginzburg[']s mother Lyudmila, Moscow, 196[8]

the police should detain this participant in the assault. But the police only examined his papers.

Many incidents are known of non-attendance on principle at meetings held with the aim of achieving unanimous approval for the sending of troops into Czechoslovakia. There have also been cases where people have found the courage either to refrain from voting or to vote against giving such approval. This happened at the Institute of the International Workers' Movement, at the Institute of the Russian Language, in one of the departments of Moscow State University, at the Institute of World Economics and International Affairs, at the Institute of Philosophy and at the Institute of Radio Technology and Electronics.

Pamphlets containing protests against the occupation of Czechoslovakia have come to circulate widely in Moscow. The text of one of these documents is printed below.

LET US THINK FOR OURSELVES

The Central Committee and the majority of members of the Communist Party of China, also of the Communist Parties of Albania, Indonesia, North Korea and the so-called 'parallel Communist Parties'* of Japan, India and Australia declare that 'bourgeois revisionism' and open counter-revolution are triumphant in the U.S.S.R., that the Communist Party of the Soviet Union, having unmasked the cult of Stalin and his crimes and not having recognized the genius of Mao, 'has betrayed the ideals of proletarian dictatorship', that 'the Soviet press slanders China', and so on.

But supposing a few of our ardent successors of Stalin or Beria suddenly decided to call on our Chinese, Albanian and other brothers to come to their aid?

What if the tanks and parachutists of these brothers suddenly appeared during the night in the streets of our towns? And if their soldiers, in the name of rescuing and defending the ideals of communism — as they understand them — began to arrest the leaders of our party and state, to close the newspapers, shut down the radio stations, and shoot those who dared to resist?

---

* i.e. the pro-Chinese parties which exist alongside pro-Soviet parties and groups.

4

Not only the overwhelming majority of Czech and Slovak communists, but also all the Italian, French, English, Swedish and Norwegian communists, as well as Rumanian and Yugoslav communists, in short the huge majority of communists of the whole world — among them the leaders of the 78 (out of 90) parties which have so far supported the Soviet party in its quarrel with the Chinese party — are convinced that after January 1968 Czechoslovakia had for the first time really begun to implement the ideas of Marx, and that in all our writings about 'counter-revolutionary threats' and 'revisionist degeneration' in Czechoslovakia there was not a single word of truth.

What if these foreign communists — and with them the great many like-minded people in Hungary, Poland, the G.D.R. and Bulgaria — communists who are convinced that the Soviet party is committing serious political errors, that the consequences of the Stalin cult have not only not been eliminated in our country but have even been considerably strengthened, and that the unprovoked military invasion of a peaceful socialist country bears witness to just this; supposing they all decided to 'rescue' us, and to set up in our country the type of socialism that they considered correct, with the help of tanks, guns and parachutists?

What if there were to appear on the streets of our towns tanks and propagandists with machine-guns, from Yugoslavia, Rumania, Czechoslovakia and the G.D.R., and they were to begin to prove to us that this signified nothing other than brotherly help and an expression of proletarian solidarity?

Let us think about all this. Let us think whom all the events of August 21st have really helped, and whom they have harmed.

Two students of the Mechanics-Mathematics Faculty of Moscow State University were arrested after gathering signatures for a petition of protest. These students are now free.

The most outspoken protest against the aggression in Czechoslovakia was the sit-down demonstration which took place at 12 o'clock on August 25th, 1968, in Red Square. A letter from one of the participants in the demonstration, Natalya Gorbanevskaya, gives detailed information about this event:

To the chief editors of *Rude Pravo*, *L'Unità*, the *Morning Star*, *L'Humanité*, *The Times*, *Le Monde*, the *Washington Post*, *Neue Zürcher Zeitung*, the *New York Times*, and any other paper which will publish this letter.[3]

August 28th, 1968   *Moscow, A–352, Novopeschanaya ul.*
d. 13/3, kv. 34.

Dear Editor,

I ask you to print my letter about the demonstration in Red Square in Moscow on August 25th, 1968, since I am the sole participant of that demonstration still at liberty.

The following people took part in the demonstration: Konstantin Babitsky, a linguist [see plate 18]; Larissa Bogoraz, a philologist; Vladimir Dremlyuga, a worker [see plate 13]; Vadim Delone, a poet [see plate 11]; Pavel Litvinov, a physicist; Victor Fainberg, a fine arts specialist; and Natalya Gorbanevskaya, a poet. At midday we sat on the parapet at Execution Place [in front of St Basil's Cathedral] and unrolled banners with the slogans LONG LIVE FREE AND INDEPENDENT CZECHO-SLOVAKIA (written in Czech), SHAME ON THE OCCU-PIERS,* HANDS OFF CZECHOSLOVAKIA, FOR YOUR FREEDOM AND OURS. Almost immediately a whistle blew and plainclothes K.G.B. men rushed at us from all corners of the square. They were on duty in Red Square, waiting for the Czechoslovak delegation's departure from the Kremlin.[4] They ran up shouting 'They're all Jews!', 'Beat the anti-Sovietists!' We sat quietly and did not resist. They tore the banners from our hands. They beat Victor Fainberg in the face until he bled, and knocked his teeth out. They hit Pavel Litvinov about the face with a heavy bag, and they snatched away from me a Czechoslovak flag and smashed it. They shouted at us, 'Disperse, you scum!' But we remained sitting. After a few minutes cars arrived, and all except me were bundled into them. I was with my three-month-old son, and therefore they did not seize me straight away. I sat at Execution Place for about another ten minutes. In the car they beat me. Several people from

---

* Gorbanevskaya corrects this in *Midday* to DOWN WITH THE OCCUPIERS, and adds that a fifth slogan read FREEDOM FOR DUBČEK.

the crowd which had gathered, ones who had expressed their sympathy with us, were arrested along with us, and released only late in the evening. During the night searches were made of all those held, on the charge of 'group activities flagrantly violating public order'. One of us, Vadim Delone, had already been conditionally sentenced under this article earlier, for his part in the demonstration of January 22nd, 1967, on Pushkin Square. After the search I was released, probably because I had two children to look after. I am continually being summoned to give evidence. I refuse to give evidence on the organization and conduct of the demonstration, since it was a peaceful demonstration which did not disturb public order. But I did give evidence about the rough and illegal actions of the people who detained us: I am ready to testify to this before world public opinion.

My comrades and I are happy that we were able to take part in this demonstration, that we were able, if only for a moment, to interrupt the torrent of barefaced lies*and the cowardly silence, to show that not all the citizens of our country are in agreement with the violence which is being used in the name of the Soviet people. We hope that the people of Czechoslovakia have learned, or will learn about this. And the belief that the Czechs and the Slovaks, when thinking about the Soviet people, will think not only of the occupiers, but also of us, gives us strength and courage.

NATALYA GORBANEVSKAYA

A team of investigators of the Moscow City Procuracy is conducting the investigation into the demonstration. They are Akimova, Gnevkovskaya, Lopushenkov, Galakhov and Solovyov. Three of them worked on the investigation into the Pushkin Square demonstration of January 22nd, 1967. General supervision of the progress of the investigation is in the hands of the Moscow Procurator's assistant, Fyodorov. The participants in the demonstration have been charged under article 190–3, which specifies a sentence of up to three years for obstructing the flow of transport and the work of state institutions (?). It

* e.g. the Soviet press reports that the troops giving 'fraternal assistance' were being welcomed with flowers by the Czechoslovaks.

has been learned for certain that—as part of the pre-trial investigation—material of a purely personal nature is being collected and that untrue versions of events are being concocted, which provide opportunities for false and misleading interpretations.

Meanwhile the people who committed sadistic and hooligan acts in the square, in particular the beating up of Fainberg and Litvinov, have had no measures taken against them.

Reports have come in of incidents in other towns of the country. In Leningrad and the Baltic Republics leaflets condemning the invasion of Czechoslovakia have come to circulate widely.

In Tartu a student has been arrested for writing a protest on a cinema wall. The name of the student is not known.

In Leningrad on August 1st and 2nd four people were arrested: a legal adviser, Yury Gendler; a chemist, Lev Kvachevsky; an engineer, Evgeny Shashenkov; and a jurist, Nikolai Danilov. They were searched on an absurd pretext, and literature of allegedly anti-Soviet content was confiscated.

The real reason for their arrest was an attempt to write a letter about Czechoslovakia. The majority of those arrested had previously been subjected to repression [on their case see pp. 380–86].

More detailed information about pending trials in Moscow and Leningrad will be known later.

Subsequent issues reported more detail on the Tartu student, then further immediate protests:

The Estonian student who wrote CZECHS, WE ARE YOUR 4 BROTHERS on a cinema wall in Tartu on the night of August 21st–22nd was savagely beaten up while in detention. His kidneys were damaged and he is still in hospital. [No. 5 added:] Now he has been removed from hospital by K.G.B. men, and so far nothing is known about his fate.

LENINGRAD. On the night of August 21st–22nd, 1968, a 4 20-year-old Leningrader, Boguslavsky, wrote on the sculpture of three horses by Klodt: BREZHNEV — GET OUT OF CZECHO-SLOVAKIA. He was arrested immediately on Anichkov Bridge and two weeks later was sentenced under article 70 to five years in a strict-régime labour camp. In October the Russian Supreme Court, considering his appeal, reclassified his action under article 190–1, and consequently altered his sentence to three years in an ordinary-régime camp (the maximum penalty under this article).

7 MOSCOW. On one of the first days after the Czechoslovak invasion, Vladimir Karasev, a graduate of the Physics Faculty at Moscow University, hung a placard up in the hall of the main Moscow University building, and began collecting signatures in protest against the sending of troops into Czecho-slovakia. When not long afterwards some university security men came up, he had managed to collect no more than four signatures. As Karasev refused to go with the security men of his own accord, they threw him to the ground and dragged him off by his arms and legs. One of the postmen from post office V–234, who appeared at this point, hit Karasev in the face a few times, shouting abusive political slogans at him: 'Fascist, Bandera-ite'* and so on. At the Police headquarters they demanded that Karasev write an explanation of the motives for his action, and then sent him off to a mental hospital, where he then spent about three months. On his discharge from the hospital, Karasev fixed himself up with a job as a stoker in a factory near Moscow.

6 NOVOSIBIRSK. On the night of August 25th, 1968, slogans condemning the invasion of Czechoslovakia appeared on several public buildings in the Akademgorodok suburb of Novosibirsk. One of them read: BARBARIANS — GET OUT OF CZECHOSLOVAKIA. Dogs were used in the search for those who had written the slogans, but no one was found. From previous experience it was known that the slogans would not wash off easily and so they were covered with newspapers.

5 MOSCOW. Bopolov, a student of the Institute of Foreign Languages, wrote a letter to the 'Voice of America' condemn-ing the invasion of Czechoslovakia; he did not send the letter

---

* Stepan Bandera (1909–59), Ukrainian nationalist émigré leader, assassinated by the K.G.B. in Munich.

and lost it, but it was later found by somebody in the Institute; a meeting of his fellow students voted his expulsion from the Komsomol and recommended to the Rector that he be expelled from the Institute. Three hours later Bopolov threw himself into the Moscow river, but was saved and put into a mental hospital.

Marina Melikyan, a lecturer in the Department of Russian for Foreigners at Moscow University, voted against a resolution expressing approval of the invasion of Czechoslovakia and was dismissed 'at her own request'.

Aronov, a member of the Institute of Organic Element 7 Compounds, abstained at a meeting where Czechoslovakia was discussed. The Institute did not apply for an extension to his Moscow residence permit and he was dismissed from work when his permit expired.

But the colleagues of protesters were not always without a spirit of solidarity, as the next item (of 1969) — about the same institute as Aronov's — shows :

MOSCOW. In May of this year Rokhlin, a Master of Chemical 8 Sciences at the Institute of Organic Element Compounds, was considered along with other candidates for competitive re-election, at a meeting of the Academic Council. The Director of the Institute, Academician Nesmeyanov, called upon the members of the Academic Council to vote against the re-election of Rokhlin. 'I am a man who remembers certain sorts of things,' said this former President of the Academy of Sciences. 'Last year Rokhlin was one of those who spoke at a meeting in the Institute against the sending of Soviet troops to Czechoslovakia.' In spite of expectations to the contrary, this speech did not affect the result of the voting. Rokhlin was elected Senior Research Officer, with an average ratio of votes for and against.

Thus the critical spirit did not disappear with the passage of time. Moreover, the distorted Soviet press reporting from Czechoslovakia also came in for attack : [5]

8 LENINGRAD. In February 1969 V. M. Lavrov, Doctor of Geology and Head of the Coal Department at the All-Union Geological Research Institute (V.S.E.G.E.I.), sent an unsigned letter to the offices of the paper *Pravda*, addressed to the journalist Sergei Borzenko. The letter contained sharp criticism of Borzenko's articles on the situation in Czechoslovakia, and the writer expressed the hope that 'all honourable Leningraders would subscribe' to his opinion. The letter was posted in a different district of the city from that of the Institute, but within three days Lavrov was faced with the charge of having written an anonymous political letter. Several closed party meetings were held in the Institute, with K.G.B. participation. Lavrov was demoted to rank-and-file geological work, and the Coal Department was purged.

Not surprisingly, the suicide of the Czech student Jan Palach in Prague on January 16th, 1969, struck a chord in the willingness for self-sacrifice of the Soviet civil rights activists, as shown in the attempt to imitate him by Ilya Rips of Riga (see pp. 243–4) and in the next two items. The second one—an appeal by Grigorenko and Yakhimovich[6]— was a logical follow-up to their visit to the Czechoslovak embassy on July 29th, 1968.

6 MOSCOW. On January 25th, 1969, the day of Jan Palach's funeral, two girl students of Moscow University appeared on Mayakovsky Square with a placard on which were written two slogans: ETERNAL MEMORY TO JAN PALACH and FREEDOM FOR CZECHOSLOVAKIA. They stood in the square behind the statue of Mayakovsky for about twelve minutes. A silent crowd gradually began to gather round them. Then a group of young people, calling themselves volunteer police but without any armbands, came up to the girls. They took away the placard and tore it up, but, after a consultation, let the students go.

6 TO THE CITIZENS OF THE SOVIET UNION:

The series of self-immolations begun on January 16th, 1969, by the Prague student Jan Palach in protest against the interference in the internal affairs of the Czechoslovak Socialist Republic continues. Yet another (for the time being, the last) human torch burst into flames in Wenceslas Square in Prague on February 21st.

This protest, taking such a terrible form, is aimed above all at US, THE SOVIET PEOPLE. It is the unasked-for and in no way justified presence of OUR armies which causes such anger and despair among the Czechoslovak people. It is not for nothing that the death of Jan Palach has stirred the entire working population of Czechoslovakia.

WE all carry our share of the blame for his loss, as for that of our other Czechoslovak brothers who have committed suicide. By our approval of the intervention of our armies, by our justification of it, or simply by our silence, we are helping to ensure that human torches will continue to burn in the squares of Prague and other cities.

The Czechs and Slovaks have always considered us their brothers. Can we really allow the word 'Soviet' to become for them a synonym for the word 'enemy'?!

Citizens of our great country!

The greatness of a country lies not in the might of its armies brought down upon a small freedom-loving people but in its MORAL strength.

Can we really go on watching in silence as our brothers perish?!

By now it is already clear to all that the presence of our armies on the territory of the Czechoslovak Socialist Republic is serving neither the defence interests of our motherland nor the interests of the countries of the socialist commonwealth.

Do we really not have the courage to admit that we have made a tragic mistake and to do everything in our power to correct it?

That is our right and our duty!

We call upon all Soviet people who do not approve of this rash and hasty act to use all legal means to achieve the withdrawal of Soviet troops from Czechoslovakia and a renunciation of interference in that country's internal affairs! Only in this way can the friendship between our peoples be renewed.

Long live the heroic Czechoslovak people!

Long live Soviet–Czechoslovak friendship!

February 28th, 1969   PYOTR GRIGORENKO
                                         IVAN YAKHIMOVICH

4*

*A year after the invasion, No. 9 produced for the occasion the following
evidence, revealing that opposition and protest had far exceeded what was
known to the outside world and even — so spontaneous had it been — some
of the best informed people in Moscow :*

9 Recently yet more expressions of protest against the sending of
troops into Czechoslovakia have become known. There are
grounds for supposing that the number of such incidents is far
greater than it has been possible to discover. For instance, in
October 1968 it was reported to Leningrad district party
committees that there had by that time been seventeen acts of
protest in Leningrad. The *Chronicle* has reported only one of
them — the inscriptions made by the 20-year-old Boguslavsky.
One more incident has become known: a car drove at high
speed across Palace Square, and two packets of leaflets were
thrown out of the windows. One of the packets burst, scattering
leaflets in all directions; the second fell to the ground without
coming open. The car managed to get away. Next day, this
request was made in a Leningrad radio programme of announcements: if anyone had noticed the number of a car out of which
'a parcel of valuable documents' fell on to Palace Square, would
he please inform the authorities of that number.

In the town of Roshal, in Moscow Region, the 23-year-old
Valery Lukanin displayed a poster in his window this spring
protesting against the continuing presence of Soviet troops in
Czechoslovakia. He was dispatched to a psychiatric hospital,
and, without being informed of the fact, was declared insane,
with the diagnosis 'a serious form of schizophrenia'. The fact
that his case was being investigated was concealed from him:
Lukanin's actions were classified under article 70 of the Russian
Criminal Code.[7] Nor was he informed that on June 23rd there
had been a trial at which compulsory treatment in a special
psychiatric hospital was ordered. Lukanin's mother was
threatened that if she told her son about the trial when she
visited him, she would in future not be allowed visits. On
July 18th Valery Lukanin was sent to the special psychiatric
hospital in Kazan.

At the beginning of July, a Doctor of Biological Sciences,
Sher, was brought to trial in Rostov-on-Don. He was charged
under articles 65 (espionage) and 70 of the Russian Criminal

Code. In practical terms the charge related to a letter Sher had written to the Central Committee of the party, in which he protested at the sending of troops into Czechoslovakia, and at the revival of Stalinism: Sher demanded in particular that all those who had worked with Stalin—and especially A. N. Kosygin—should resign their posts. On the grounds that Sher was charged with 'industrial espionage', the trial was declared a closed one at the request of the Procurator. The judicial investigation failed to confirm the charges and the defence demanded a verdict of not guilty. The court reclassified Sher's actions under article 190–1 of the Russian Criminal Code, and sentenced him to two years in an ordinary-régime camp.

In one of his articles Anatoly Kuznetsov* has reported that soon after the demonstration of August 25th, 1968, he found a letter in his Tula letterbox supporting the demonstrators' action.[8]

One ironical comment on the sending of troops into Czechoslovakia was made by students of the Estonian Agricultural Academy at the traditional student carnival last autumn in Tartu. The students held up placards with slogans, the following of which are known: LONG LIVE THE WISE AND FLEXIBLE FOREIGN POLICY OF THE SOVIET UNION; WELCOME, TOURISTS IN YOUR TANKS; YANKEES, GET BACK BEHIND LAKE CHUDSKOYE [where Alexander Nevsky threw back the Teutonic Knights in 1242]; WELCOME TO THAT UNSWERVING LENINIST, COMRADE LENTSMAN [Lentsman is the secretary of the Estonian Communist Party's Central Committee responsible for ideological work].

The Chronicle *also carried these items under the heading:*

THE ANNIVERSARY OF THE INVASION OF CZECHOSLOVAKIA 9

On August 20th, 1969, a group of Soviet citizens issued the following declaration:

On August 21st last year a tragic event took place: Czechoslovakia, a friendly country, was invaded by Warsaw Pact troops.

* The popular writer who defected to Britain in July 1969. See pp. 436–7.

The aim of this action was to put a stop to the process of democratization which had begun in that country. The whole world had been following the post-January developments in Czechoslovakia with hope. It seemed that the idea of socialism, which had been discredited during the Stalin period, would now be rehabilitated. The Warsaw Pact tanks destroyed this hope. On this sad anniversary we declare that we disagree, as before, with the decision to invade, which has endangered the future of socialism.

We declare our solidarity with the Czechoslovak people, who wanted to prove that socialism with a human face was possible.

These lines are prompted by the pain we feel for our homeland, which we wish to see truly great, free and happy.

And we are firmly convinced that a people which oppresses other peoples cannot be free or happy.

T. BAYEVA,* J. VISHNEVSKAYA,† I. GABAI, N. GORBANEV-SKAYA, Z. M. GRIGORENKO, M. DZHEMILEV,‡ N. EMEL-KINA, V. KRASIN, S. KOVALYOV, A. LEVITIN-KRASNOV, L. PETROVSKY,§ L. PLYUSHCH, G. PODYAPOLSKY, L. TERNOVSKY, I. YAKIR, ‖ P. YAKIR, A. YAKOBSON.

On August 21st, leaflets appeared in the housing-blocks where Moscow writers live, near the 'Airport' underground station and at Zyuzino, and also in the Moscow University hostel on the Lenin Hills, protesting at the continued presence of allied troops in Czechoslovakia. One of the three texts of these leaflets is signed 'Union of Communards'.[9]

On the anniversary of the sending of troops into Czechoslovakia, the mathematician Alexander Volpin, well known for his regular writings in defence of human rights, sent the following proposals to the U.S.S.R. Supreme Soviet:

    1. To withdraw the Soviet troops from Czechoslovakia immediately.

    2. To implement this withdrawal in such a way as to

* See p. 114.　† See p. 325.　‡ See pp. 160–61.　§ See pp. 120, 421–2
‖ See. pp. 122, 255–7.

restore to the Czechoslovak people in the greatest possible degree their national rights, and to liquidate all the undesirable consequences of the presence of foreign troops on Czechoslovak territory.

3. In memory of the sacrifices made by the Czechoslovak people, the most famous of which is the life of Jan Palach, one of the Moscow streets or squares to be renamed after him, for example Istorichesky Passage. The choice of a suitable street or square for renaming to be agreed with representatives of the Czechoslovak people.

4. Czechoslovakia to receive compensation for all material losses incurred due to the presence of Soviet troops on its territory.

Hardly expecting his proposals to be speedily accepted, Volpin nevertheless reminds the Supreme Soviet that 'any measures it may take to implement these proposals would be in accordance with the principles of international law, which the Soviet Union has many times supported, and would help to restore its reputation as a country which faithfully follows these principles'.

A few months later, on Soviet Constitution Day, another incident took place in Moscow: the arrest of a girl who tried to distribute copies of a poem she had written. The girl concerned was later sentenced to indefinite detention in the prison psychiatric hospital in Kazan, the Procurator comparing her act to the attempt on the cosmonauts' lives of January 1969. The Chronicle *printed her poem.*[10] *This was its first report:*

11

On December 5th, 1969, Valeria Novodvorskaya [see plate 10] was arrested in the Palace of Congresses, where she was scattering and handing out leaflets before the start of a performance of the opera *October*. Novodvorskaya made no attempt to escape, and continued to hand out leaflets until she was approached by K.G.B. men. The leaflets were written in verse form, and the theme was our tanks in Czechoslovakia. There was probably also something in them about the constitution. After Novodvorskaya's arrest, several copies of three manuscript booklets of her own poetry were removed from her flat.

Valeria Novodvorskaya is nineteen. She finished school in 1968 with a medal, and gained a place with honours in the French Department of the Foreign Languages Institute. At the time of her arrest she was in her second year there.

The Chronicle*'s regular samizdat section has carried two categories of material on Czechoslovakia. That devoted to the country's 'experiment' and the course of events there is — since it would interrupt the narrative here — presented in Chapter 18. The second category is summarized in No. 5 under the heading:*

5   OPEN LETTERS AND ARTICLES BY SOVIET AUTHORS
         ON THE QUESTION OF CZECHOSLOVAKIA

Before the Soviet invasion of Czechoslovakia, at the end of July 1968, when the Soviet press was conducting a particularly violent campaign against the democratization in Czechoslovakia and when the threat of intervention seemed more real than at any time before or after, there had already appeared two documents expressing sympathy for Czechoslovakia and indignation at the propaganda campaign: a letter to all members of the Czechoslovak Communist Party and the whole Czechoslovak people [see p. 96] signed by five communists, P. Grigorenko, A. Kosterin, V. Pavlinchuk, S. Pisarev and I. Yakhmovich; and an open letter by Anatoly Marchenko [see pp. 191–3] to the newspapers *Rude pravo*, *Prace* and *Literarni listy*.

The sending of Soviet troops to Czechoslovakia under the guise of 'fraternal help', unanimously approved in the pages of the Soviet press,[11] met with various forms of protest from individual Soviet citizens. Among the *samizdat* reactions to these tragic events may be mentioned: the letter of Ivan Yakhimovich;[12] 'September 1969' by Valentin Komarov;[13] 'The Logic of Tanks', an article by an anonymous author; 'An appeal to Communists' signed 'Communist'; a letter by P. Grigorenko and A. Kosterin;[14] and also a letter to the Party's Central Committee[15] from A. Kosterin, resigning from the party 'which has become the gendarme of Europe'.[16]

All these documents, though differing in style and form, make the same points: (a) the intervention in Czechoslovakia is the result of a revival of Stalinism; (b) the real reason for it was a wish to suppress democratization, freedom and the rule of law, and to destroy a dangerous experiment in combining socialism with democracy; (c) the invasion was a moral defeat for the occupiers; (d) our people and intelligentsia are collectively responsible for what has happened, and all honest, thinking people in our country must unite.

5. THE TRIAL OF THE DEMONSTRATORS

A hundred drunk women were brought. A thousand might have been. They confined themselves to jeering, but, given the order, they could have killed ... Many complained that they hadn't been allowed to shoot, or, at least, to run people down with a bulldozer ... People were showered with curses, of the choicest and foulest sort. The drunken women seemed to compete against each other in their filthiness and dirty threats ... 'I'm a worker,' cried one woman, 'and if I'm drunk, then it's on my own money.' An oldish man replied: 'You're lying. You're not a worker. You've got no honour. You're simply a hired thug.' ...
On those three days the cage doors were opened only a crack; the animals sitting inside merely showed their claws. One day the whole zoo might be unleashed onto the street.

Ilya Gabai, 'At the Closed Doors of an Open Trial'[1]

This atmosphere of scarcely suppressed mob violence — a device often used by the régime to try to intimidate dissenters — was one of the few things to distinguish the trial of the Red Square demonstrators from that of Galanskov and Ginzburg. Otherwise the two trials had much in common. Except for a few relatives it was held in camera, *the Judge and the Prosecutor clearly had their instructions from the start, several prosecution witnesses perjured themselves by giving false evidence, all the defendants firmly pleaded not guilty, their lawyers backed them up with spirit, and they were duly sentenced. After the trial the convicts were blackened and libelled in the press. All this, while clear enough in the* Chronicle, *is established beyond doubt in Gorbanevskaya's massive* Midday.

Gorbanevskaya (b. 1936), Larissa Bogoraz-Daniel (b. 1929), Pavel Litvinov (b. 1940) and Vadim Delone (b. 1947) we have already met several times in this book. As for their fellow-demonstrators, Konstantin Babitsky (b. 1929) had been a prolific linguistics scholar who had already experienced trouble: 'because he signed letters about the Galanskov-Ginzburg trial, the examination of his dissertation has been postponed indefinitely' (No. 5); Victor Fainberg (b. 1931) was a metal-worker in a factory who graduated in English from Leningrad University in 1968 and became a historic buildings guide; and Vladimir Dremlyuga (b. 1940) was a worker who had spent most of his life in Leningrad.

Once again the trial provoked foreign as well as domestic protests.

Among the former was one from the same group of eminent people that had sent a telegram to Litvinov and Larissa Bogoraz after the earlier trial (see p. 92). This time their telegram preceded the trial. It read:

> *We are gravely disturbed at press reports regarding the impending trial ... Surely a publicly conducted protest by young people who are patriots ought not to be treated as a criminal act. Remembering that the absence of impartial observers at the trial of Galanskov and Ginzburg gave rise to disquieting reports, we beg you to uphold the defendants' right to a free trial and unhampered defence by the lawyers of their choice.*[2]

This last point followed information — later confirmed in Gorbanev-skaya's book — that the lawyers S. L. Ariya and L. M. Popov had been intimidated by the authorities into refusing to take defence briefs in the case. No. 4 wrote about the trial as follows:

As reported in the third issue of the *Chronicle*, seven people staged **4** a sit-down demonstration at Execution Place in Red Square on August 25th, 1968, at 12 noon, as a protest against the sending of Soviet troops into Czechoslovakia. Six of them — Konstantin Babitsky, Larissa Bogoraz, Vadim Delone, Vladimir Dreml-yuga, Victor Fainberg and Pavel Litvinov — were arrested. The seventh, Natalya Gorbanevskaya, was not arrested, as she is the mother of two small children. She gave details of the demonstration in her letter of August 28th, sent to several Western newspapers.

On September 5th a forensic-psychiatric examination of Natalya Gorbanevskaya, under the direction of Professor Daniil Lunts, pronounced her of unsound mind. The Moscow Procuracy closed the case that had been initiated against her and entrusted her to the care of her mother.

The demonstrators were accused under article 190-3 of the Russian Criminal Code, which covers group activities disturbing public order, and article 190-1, which deals with deliberate fabrications that discredit the Soviet social and political system. The reason for this last accusation was the wording of the placards displayed by the demonstrators: FOR YOUR FREEDOM AND OURS, DOWN WITH THE OCCUPIERS, FREEDOM FOR DUBČEK, HANDS OFF CZECHOSLOVAKIA, and LONG LIVE FREE AND INDEPENDENT CZECHOSLOVAKIA.

From October 9th to 11th the Moscow City Court examined the cases of Konstantin Babitsky, Larissa Bogoraz, Vadim Delone, Vladimir Dremlyuga and Pavel Litvinov in the building of the Proletarsky District people's court. Judge Lubentsova presided over the court proceedings and the other members of the court were Bulgakov and Popov; the State Prosecutor was the Moscow Assistant Procurator, Drel, and the accused were defended as follows: Konstantin Babitsky by the lawyer Pozdeyev, Vadim Delone by Kallistratova, Vladimir Dremlyuga by Monakhov, and Pavel Litvinov by Kaminskaya. Larissa Bogoraz refused counsel and conducted her own defence.

The defendants and their lawyers filed a number of petitions:

1. For the calling of additional witnesses, because the court had called only those witnesses presented by the prosecution, and there were scarcely any among them whose evidence at the pre-trial investigation had coincided with the explanations of the accused. The court agreed to the representations as regards the calling of three [additional] witnesses out of seven. Tatyana Bayeva, for example, was not called; she had been detained in Red Square on August 25th, together with the demonstrators.[3] Bayeva had been searched and called previously many times for interrogation as a witness. It was made clear in court, although she herself knew nothing about it, that a criminal charge had been brought against her and then dropped. Nevertheless the court did not consider her an eye-witness of the events under consideration.

2. For the postponement of the case for further investigation, which would be aimed at establishing the identity of the people who snatched the placards and beat and detained the demonstrators, i.e. the identity of those people who had really disturbed public order in Red Square on August 25th. The accused had made this request at the time of the pre-trial investigation, but the investigating organs claimed then that they had no information about these people. The court also rejected the request. Meanwhile, on the very first day of the hearing, when these requests were made, the person who had knocked out Fainberg's teeth was seen near the court building, and evidence to this effect was presented to the court.

3. For the postponement of the case until the completion of the forensic-psychiatric examination of Victor Fainberg. In the

petition it was stated that there was no reason to separate his case and trial from the others; this request was also rejected.

4. For the admission to the courtroom of relatives and friends of the defendants. Only relatives (and then only some) had been allowed into the courtroom; some, allowed in on the first day, were told by the police on the second day, 'Yesterday it was your turn, but today some other relatives have come.' Pavel Litvinov's wife was detained near the court building on October 10th until it was almost evening, and then she was only allowed in after repeated requests from Litvinov himself and his lawyer.

All the circumstances of the formally open trial differed little from those well known through previous 'open' trials. The friends and sympathizers who were not allowed into the courtroom froze in the street in the rain and early autumn snow. State security agents in plain clothes, members of the security groups of the Young Communist League, young members of the Likhachyov factory volunteer police (both the last two groups without their armbands), eavesdropping on conversations, the photographing of those present—all this created an atmosphere of provocation. But not one of the provocations succeeded, despite the fact that even the local population had been dragged into their organization: the inhabitants of the nearest houses had been informed beforehand that currency offenders were being tried, a clever manoeuvre to instil into simple people hostility to the friends of the accused. And on October 10th, a large number of drunken louts, amongst them an unusually high proportion of drunken women, began to arrive at the court building. It transpired that numerous bottles of vodka had been placed on a table in a nearby yard and free 'refreshments' were being served.

About fifteen relatives of the accused were allowed into the court building through the main entrance, but then those outside were informed that the courtroom was full to bursting. All the other people present in the courtroom—journalists from several Soviet papers, representatives of the party's Central Committee, its Moscow City Committee, the K.G.B., the Procuracy, and the security group members, i.e. around sixty people—had reached the courtroom through the yard, by the back entrance, preferring not to enter the building under the gaze of the assembled crowd. The relatives of the defendants were later not permitted to leave the building during the adjournment, under the threat that their seats would then be occupied.

Later, No. 6 added:

6 This account by one of those present at the trial of the Red Square demonstrators has become known. All those chosen to represent 'the public' at the trial turned up at the Proletarsky District's party committee building at 8 a.m. on October 9th; there they were informed that they would be present at a trial of 'anti-Sovietists'. Then they were taken to the court in a bus which drove straight into the yard and they entered the building by the back door. They whiled away the time before the trial sitting in an empty room, where they were given dominoes, draughts and other games. Then they were allowed into the courtroom. The process of transporting the audience from the district committee building to the court through the back door was repeated on the following two days. The source, in his own words, felt embarrassed when in the course of the trial he recognized the falsehood of the information he had been given, and ashamed when, with the rest of the audience, he walked through the saddened crowd — which sympathized with the defendants — after the verdict.[4]

No. 4 now takes up the story again:

4 In the course of the judicial investigation the groundlessness of the charges became even more obvious. A group of five men who had detained the demonstrators stood out among the principal prosecution witnesses. These five, serving in the same military unit 1164, happened to be in Red Square on August 25th simultaneously and without prior arrangement and helped to detain the demonstrators; at the pre-trial investigation they gave evidence that the activities of the demonstrators had disturbed public order. On the very first day, under cross-examination, these people became confused in their statements about their previous acquaintance with one another. Apparently for this reason, on the second day the three who had not been questioned the first day turned out to be 'absent on business' and the court decided not to question them, despite the protests of the defendants and their counsel. Another witness for the prosecution was Oleg Davidovich, an official of the notorious Mordovian strict-régime labour camps:* despite both the fact that the description of the demonstration in his statements differed from all the other evidence, and that he recalled the time as 12.30–12.40 p.m. and claimed to have entered Red Square from the G.U.M. department-store (which, as everyone knows, is closed on Sundays), his evidence served as one of the major planks in the prosecution's case.

The local traffic policeman who was called as a witness is also interesting: his evidence is important in clarifying the question of whether the working of public transport was disrupted. On August 25th this policeman submitted to his superiors a report on what had occurred, without any reference to a disruption of transport. On September 3rd he submitted a new report stating that there had been a disruption. As was proved in court, between August 25th and September 3rd he had been called to the K.G.B.[5]

The accused pleaded not guilty. The examination of the defendants, their closing speeches and the speeches of the defence counsel convincingly proved the absence of any criminality in the activities of the demonstrators.

Procurator Drel devoted the major part of his prosecution speech to the events in Czechoslovakia, while the defendants were interrupted every time they referred to these events in order to decribe the motives of their actions or explain the wording of their slogans.

The Procurator demanded three years' imprisonment for Vladimir Dremlyuga and two years' for Vadim Delone. To the two years for Delone should be added an earlier suspended sentence of one year, of which he had served more than seven months during the investigation (i.e. the total term of imprisonment would be 2 years 4½months). For the remaining defendants the Procurator proposed, in view of the fact that none of them had a previous record and that all three of them had

* Correction in No. 6: 'In fact he works in the equally well-known strict-régime camps in the Komi Autonomous Republic [in the north Urals], at Vetyu station (address: st. Vetyu, v/ch 6592).'

children dependent on them, to invoke article 43 of the General Section of the Russian Criminal Code and sentence them not to detention but to exile: five years for Pavel Litvinov, four years for Larissa Bogoraz and three years for Konstantin Babitsky.

The court found the defendants guilty on both charges. As far as punitive measures were concerned, the court more than satisfied the demands of the Procurator. Vadim Delone, who had said in his closing speech, 'I appeal to this court not for mercy, but for restraint,' received six months longer in the camps than the Procurator had proposed: 2 years 6 months plus 4 months of his unserved term, making a total of 2 years 10 months. The remaining defendants received terms in camp and exile in accordance with the demands of the Procurator.[6]

The defendants and their counsel lodged appeals.

EXILE FOR BABITSKY, BOGORAZ AND LITVINOV: A SHORT COMMENTARY

Articles 190-1 and 190-3 of the Russian Criminal Code provide for the following punitive measures: either imprisonment for up to three years, or corrective labour for up to one year, or a fine not exceeding 100 roubles.

Article 43 of the General Section of the Russian Criminal Code provides that 'the court, in consideration of the exceptional cricumstances of a case and the personality of the guilty person, and deeming it necessary either to punish him less severely than the minimum limits envisaged by the law for the given crime, or to apply another, less severe, form of punishment, may permit such a mitigation but must provide an explanation of its reasons for so doing'. Under the guise of applying article 43, the court did not impose a less severe form of punishment, but took an average of the punitive provisions of articles 190-1 and 190-3. Exile instead of imprisonment, as a result of the application of article 43, is possible in those cases where a less severe form of punishment than imprisonment is not envisaged by a specific article (e.g. articles 64-9, 71, 75, 76-81 et al.). In this particular case, if the court felt it possible not to sentence the three defendants to imprisonment, it would have been logical to punish them by corrective labour or a fine.

Article 319 of the Russian Code of Criminal Procedure states that 'on the acquittal of the defendant, or on his release or exemption from punishment, or in the case of his being sentenced to a punishment not involving imprisonment, the court must, if the defendant is being held in custody, release him immediately in the courtroom.'

The verdict of the Moscow City Court stated that Babitsky, Bogoraz and Litvinov would be released from custody on arrival at their places of exile.

While awaiting the outcome of their appeals, all five continue to be held in custody in the Lefortovo prison. Being kept in custody is the severest of the existing forms of restriction. Pavel Litvinov rightly remarked in his final speech that there was no need to apply this measure. After such an open act as the demonstration of August 25th, it was certain that the demonstrators would not try to escape from the court and the police.

THE SOVIET PRESS ON THE DEMONSTRATORS' TRIAL

On October 10th the following official announcement appeared in the papers *Moscow pravda* and *Evening Moscow*: 'IN THE MOSCOW CITY COURT: On October 9th the criminal trial began in Moscow of K. I. Babitsky, L. I. Bogoraz-Brukhman, V. N. Delone, V. A. Dremlyuga and P. M. Litvinov, accused of violating public order in Red Square, Moscow, on August 25th of this year.'

On October 12th two articles on the trial were published:[7] 'Aiming for a sensation' by N. Bardin in *Moscow pravda*, and 'They got their deserts' by A. Smirnov in *Evening Moscow*.

Just like the official announcement the articles mention, in the first place, only one charge, that of violating public order: i.e. the charge under article 190-3. Secondly, even this 'violation' is not described, and nowhere is there any reference to the fact that this was a protest demonstration against the intervention of Soviet troops in Czechoslovakia. Instead, the writers of these articles, not shrinking from direct libel, give 'character-sketches' of the accused aimed at compromising them in the eyes of the reader. It was precisely this kind of 'information' that Larissa Bogoraz had in mind when she said in her closing speech on October 11th, 'I have no doubt that public opinion will approve the verdict. Public opinion will approve of three years' exile for a talented scholar and three years in the camps for a young poet, first because we shall be depicted as parasites, renegades and purveyors of a hostile ideology, and second because, if people appear whose opinion differs from that of the "public" and who have the audacity to speak out, they will soon end up here.' (She points to the dock.)

According to unconfirmed rumours, the correspondents of two Soviet papers who were present at the trial refused to write the articles required of them.

As for Gorbanevskaya's Midday, *the* Chronicle *can be seen in retrospect to have been recording its evolution stage by stage. No. 4 listed the first documents to circulate in* samizdat:

4   1. The letter from Natalya Gorbanevskaya [...]

2. A letter from Anatoly Yakobson replying to accusations that the demonstration was 'useless'.[8]

3. A letter from P. G. Grigorenko and A. E. Kosterin, condemning the arrest of the demonstrators and the organization of the impending trial.[9]

4. A letter from seven people, including Pyotr Yakir, written on the eve of the trial and entitled 'Those who will be tried on Wednesday'; a series of documents are attached to the letter.[10]

5. A letter from Vladimir Lapin, Mrs Z. M. Grigorenko and Leonid Vasilev addressed to the Politbureau of the Communist Party Central Committee: citing the conditions at the court building and the anti-semitic and anti-intellectual mood of certain groups of young people, the letter points to serious defects in the ideological education system.[11]

5   In addition, there is now a letter addressed to the deputies of the Supreme Soviets of the U.S.S.R. and of the Russian Republic.[12] The main point made in this letter is that the sentence on the five demonstrators is an infringement of fundamental civil rights. It is signed by ninety-five people, including the leading actor Igor Kvasha, the writer on church affairs A. Krasnov (Levitin), Doctor of Biological Science A. Neifakh, the writer Victor Nekrasov, the historians Leonid Petrovsky and

Pyotr Yakir, Doctor of Philology L. Pinsky, and the pianist Professor M. V. Yudina.

Some of the most striking *samizdat* items of 1968 were the final pleas at their trial of Larissa Daniel,[13] Pavel Litvinov,[13] Vadim Delone,[14] Vladimir Dremlyuga[14] and Konstantin Babitsky,[14] and the speech made in her own defence by Larissa Daniel.[15]

In August [1969] Natalya Gorbanevskaya finished compiling her book *Midday: The Case of the Red Square Demonstration of August 25th, 1968*, and it appeared in *samizdat*. The book consists of a prologue and four parts: 'Red Square', 'A Case of a Breach of Public Order', 'Kangaroo Court' and 'The Fate of Victor Fainberg'. Most of the book is taken up with a complete verbatim record of the trial of the demonstrators. Included in the book are, among other things, two previously unknown documents: a sketch by Ilya Gabai, 'At the Closed Doors of an Open Trial', and an article by P. G. Grigorenko, 'About the Special Psychiatric Hospitals (or Loony-bins)'.[16] The epilogue, which is devoted to showing that the demonstration of August 25th was not an isolated case of protest against the invasion, makes extensive use of material from the *Chronicle*.

Extra-judicial, but always unpleasant reprisals followed hard on the protests about the trial:

Natalya Gorbanevskaya, the poet who participated in the demonstration of August 25th, has been dismissed 'at her own request' from the State Institute of Experimental Pattern Design and Technical Research (GIPROTIS), where she worked as an engineer and translator. When she applied in October 1968 for an unpaid extension of her maternity leave, the authorities told her that they had, of course, no right not to grant the extension, but asked her to resign before the end of her leave so that there should not be a 'stain' on the institute. At the same time the head of the Department of Technical Information, Kuranov, declared that in any case Gorbanevskaya could not be allowed to resume her former work — although the work is in no way secret and does not require a security clearance.

6 For signing the letter [of the 95] defending the demonstrators of August 25th, Leonid Petrovsky the historian, Neifakh, a Doctor of Biological Sciences, S. Pisarev, a member of the Communist Party since 1920, and the man of letters Solomon Bernshtein have been expelled from the party. The geologist Yury Dikov also signed this letter:[17] the oral examination of his dissertation has been postponed for an indefinite period. Vladimir Rokityansky, who worked under contract as a translator in the Psychology Faculty of Moscow University, did not have his contract renewed.

5 Vladimir Gershovich, mathematician and lecturer in the training department of the Likhachyov Automobile Works, was outside the courtroom in which the demonstrators were being tried, and argued with some of his students who were members of the works' volunteer police squad [see p.115]; after they had denounced him to his superiors, he was dismissed from his work.

   Irina Yakir, a student of the Institute of Historical Archives [and Pyotr's daughter, see also pp. 255–7], went and stood outside the courtroom on October 9th; on October 10th, after classes, she was summoned to the Komsomol Committee and told not to go there any more, whereupon she said: 'My friends are on trial there and if I had been in Moscow on August 25th, I should have been with them.' She was expelled from the Komsomol.

   Oleg Melnikov, a student of the Biology Faculty at Moscow University, was outside the courtroom and signed a petition demanding that those who had gathered there should be admitted to the proceedings. The dean's office of the faculty (it is headed by Professor N. P. Naumov) ordered his expulsion from the university—just two months before he was due to take his final examinations.

But the fate of the convicted demonstrators was of course much worse:

5 On November 19th the Russian Supreme Court heard the appeals [...]

   The sentence of the Moscow City Court on all the defendants was confirmed.[18] At the beginning of December they were all sent to their places of punishment. Their addresses are: Vadim Delone: Tyumen-14, p/ya 34/2"1". Vladimir Dremlyuga: Murmansk-9, p/ya 241/17. Konstantin Babitsky: Komi A.S.S.R., pos. Krasnozatonsky, pochta do vostrebovaniya. Larissa Bogoraz: Irkutskaya obl., st. Chuna, pochta do vostrebovaniya. Pavel Litvinov is still in transit. It is known only that he is being sent to the Chita region.

No. 6 filled out the picture somewhat:

The address of Pavel Litvinov is: do vostrebovaniya, Verkhniye 6 Usugli, Tungokochensky raion, Chitinskaya oblast. Litvinov is now working as an electrician and metal-worker at a mine. There is, incidentally, no physics teacher in the village school, but Litvinov has not been employed to work in his special subject.

Larissa Bogoraz is working as an apprentice joiner at the lumber works in Chuna.

Konstantin Babitsky is working at the ship-building factory in Krasnozatonsky as a joiner.

But from now on news of harassment and provocation became the norm:

At the start of her exile in Chuna, in Irkustk Region, Larissa 8 Bogoraz [see plate 15] worked as an auxiliary in a sawmill, dragging heavy planks. As a result of this work the gastritis which she had developed in prison and on the journey became acute and she was ill for a long time. When the local post office needed a postman, the police did not allow it to take her on but promised to get her transferred to some more suitable work at the same sawmill. As for a long time none of the police even went to the mill, Larissa Bogoraz was dismissed. Then the police announced that they would get her some work, but threatened her with article 209 of the Russian Criminal Code — 'vagrancy and begging' — if the work did not suit her. At the present time she is working at the same sawmill as a scaffolding worker.

At the end of March and the beginning of April 1969, illegal, 7 secret searches were carried out in their absence in the rooms of Larissa Bogoraz in Chuna and of Pavel Litvinov in Verkhniye Usugli, the places where they are exiled.

8 In May of this year the senior investigator of the Kharkov K.G.B., Starkov, presented Alexander Daniel* with a confiscation order for the manuscript 'Save Our Souls' by Fyodor Fyodorovich Klimenko.[19] Klimenko is at present under investigation on a charge relating to article 62 of the Ukrainian Criminal Code, equivalent to article 70 of the Russian Code. He stated that this manuscript was handed by him to Larissa Bogoraz in 1968, and was now in her Moscow flat. It is known that in August 1968 three searches were made of Larissa Bogoraz's flat: at the time of the Marchenko case, of the Belogorodskaya case, and on the evening of August 25th, the day of her arrest.

The investigator made a record that, according to Alexander Daniel, the manuscript was not in the flat.

In June the three participants in the demonstration of August 25th who were exiled – Larissa Bogoraz, Konstantin Babitsky and Pavel Litvinov – were interrogated in connection with the Klimenko case, for which purpose Litvinov was transported under escort to Chita. In spite of the fact that Klimenko's statements are not only untrue but obviously implausible – for example, according to him Litvinov said to him in Bogoraz's flat: 'Give me your manuscript, I will publish it abroad and pay you ten thousand roubles', yet neither Litvinov nor Bogoraz even remember ever seeing this person – disregarding these blatant lies the investigating organs are apparently treating them seriously. Evidently exile seems to certain people too light a measure, and Klimenko's statements – whether they be the ravings of a sick man or deliberate inventions – can if necessary serve as the basis for further judicial repression.

9 At the beginning of July Pavel Litvinov was transferred to a manual labour brigade – theoretically for missing work, but in fact for a clash with the mine director. His 'missing work' was prompted by the fact that a period of three days' unpaid holiday which was due to him coincided with the arrival of some

---

* Larissa's son. See pp. 65–6.

friends of his on a visit [see plates 17 and 19]. So as to prevent him from seeing them any more, Litvinov was summoned away to 'emergency work', of which there was none. Litvinov refused to appear for work. A commission on labour disputes which examined his complaint decided in favour of the administration.

For the exiles Babitsky, Litvinov and Larissa Bogoraz, thousands of miles from Moscow in the Urals, south-east Siberia and central Siberia respectively, life was thus tough enough. But for Delone and Dremlyuga it was probably even harsher in their camps. These lay in the south Urals, the extreme north-west and, after Dremlyuga's transfer, the far north-east:

Vadim Delone is now in a camp at Tyumen. His poem 'A Ballad of Unbelief'[20] was discovered during a search. For this poem Delone was given ten days in the 'shizo'—the punishment isolator or prison. He and another convict in the 'shizo' tried to protect themselves from the terrible cold—one afternoon they let down their bunks and climbed into them in the hope of finding some warmth. For this infringement of the camp régime Vadim Delone has been forbidden any parcels or visits for half a year.   8

Vladimir Dremlyuga is at present in a camp at Murmansk [in the Arctic Circle]. He was allowed a personal visit [i.e. a visit with cohabitation permitted] from his wife for three days, but this was cut short at the end of the first day. Dremlyuga expressed his indignation, and for this he was sent off to the 'shizo'.   8

No. 10 brought more bad news:

Vladimir Dremlyuga ... has been transferred to Yakutia [in NE Siberia]. He spent three months on the journey. The reason for his transfer: his demand that the camp administration observe the safety regulations relating to prisoners' working conditions. His address: Yakutskaya A.S.S.R., g. Lensk, p/ya YaD-40/3.   10

But worst situated of all was Fainberg, as Gorbanevskaya describes in Part Four of Midday. *For the charge of mental illness — necessary to prevent his appearance, toothless, at the trial — soon led to imprisonment in the terrifying conditions of a prison mental hospital (see Chapter 11):*

4 At the end of October 1968 a forensic psychiatric team under the direction of Professor Daniil Lunts found that Victor Fainberg was of unsound mind. In accordance with existing legislation he will be tried *in absentia* by a court which will decide the question of compulsory measures of a medical nature. As mentioned, Victor Fainberg's teeth were knocked out in Red Square.

5 On December 24th the Moscow City Court, under the chairmanship of Judge Monakhov, ordered compulsory medical treatment for Victor Fainberg and his confinement in a mental hospital 'of special type'. Fainberg is still held in the Lefortovo prison while awaiting the results of his appeal, and he is in a poor state of health because of a recurrence of Basedow's disease. According to reports received so far, he is going to be put in the Kazan hospital, not in Leningrad where his aged parents live and where there is a similar hospital. The reason for this is that the Leningrad hospital is supposedly for 'politicals'.

Nevertheless:

8 At present Victor Fainberg is being kept in the Leningrad hospital. The authorities decided against putting him on trial, evidently because after his beating up on Red Square on August 25th, 1968, he had lost all his front teeth and had concussion. Fainberg has been given the diagnosis — cynical even for institutions of this sort — of 'schizoheterodoxy'. He was informed of this by the doctors who are 'curing' him.

In 1970 Fainberg wrote a long appeal to world public opinion denouncing these doctors and the system to which they belonged.[21] *He followed this in the spring of 1971 by launching an almost unprecedentedly long hunger-strike.*[22]

6. GENERAL GRIGORENKO AND HIS FRIENDS

He is a general to his fingertips. He is a general even in civilian clothes, which cannot conceal his military bearing and which suit so ill his warrior's build ... But no, the army has not destroyed his mind or his heart. Gentle, understanding, tolerant of all human weaknesses, sensitive and attentive to everyone, the general is a model of the genuinely educated person. Where did a peasant's son get this delicacy, this feeling of tact and these elegant manners? I do not know. Probably from nowhere. He was born that way and has remained so to the age of sixty-two. I remember him now, in this very room, where I entertained him a month ago at Easter. And I cannot believe it: has he really been arrested, thrown into some stinking cell?

Anatoly Levitin, May 1969[1]

Pyotr Grigorevich Grigorenko was born in 1907 in the village of Borisovka in Zaporozhe Province [south Ukraine]. His father was one of the organizers of the collective farm there, and Pyotr Grigorevich himself was the first in his village to enrol in the Komsomol. From the age of fifteen he worked as a metal-worker in Donetsk, where he also completed a course at the workers' higher education college. In 1929 Grigorenko entered the Kharkov Polytechnic Institute, but in his third year he was transferred to the Kuibyshev Military Engineering Academy by party directive. After completing his studies at the academy, he served four years in military units, then studied in the Voroshilov General Staff Academy. Grigorenko participated in the battle of Khalkhin-Gol [on the Manchurian border in 1939 against the Japanese] and in the Second World War. As a result of a hip wound Grigorenko became a second-category War Invalid.

He was awarded the Order of Lenin, two Orders of the Red Flag, the Order of the Red Star, the Order of the Patriotic War, and six medals. After the war Grigorenko spent seventeen years working in [Moscow's] Frunze Military Academy, first as Head of the Research Department, and later Head of the Cybernetics Department. In 1948 he defended his thesis and was awarded the degree of Master of Military Sciences. In 1959 he was given the rank of Major-General.

In 1961 Grigorenko spoke at a Party Conference of the Lenin District in Moscow, calling for the restoration of Leninist principles. Following this, he received a party reprimand, was suspended from his job, and six months later was demoted and sent to Ussuriisk [near Vladivostok]. The defence of his doctoral dissertation, fixed for November 1961, was cancelled.

Even in Ussuriisk, Grigorenko did not cease his open protests against the erratic policies of the party leadership then in power, and in February 1964 he was arrested by the K.G.B. To prevent him opening his mouth at a trial Grigorenko was declared insane and put in a prison psychiatric hospital in Leningrad, from which he emerged only fifteen months later. Meanwhile he had been reduced to the ranks and expelled from the party, although a sick man should not be considered *legally* responsible for his actions, and he should not have to bear responsibility before party and administrative organs either. The taking of these repressive measures is just one more proof that the tale of Grigorenko's 'insanity' is pure fiction.

After coming out of hospital, the war invalid Grigorenko was reduced to working as a porter to earn his keep.[2] But despite this painful existence, and despite the threat of new internment in a hospital, General Grigorenko never ceased his struggle against arbitrary acts. He protested against the trials of Khaustov and Bukovsky, of Ginzburg and Galanskov, and of those who took part in the demonstration of August 25th, 1968. He was one of the twelve co-authors of the appeal to the Budapest meeting, and spoke out in support of Anatoly Marchenko when the latter was arrested. He protested at the arrest of Irina Belogorodskaya, and later compiled a record of her trial.* He also compiled a collection of materials on the funeral of A. E. Kosterin, a very close friend, who had been carrying on the struggle with him against all manifestations of arbitrariness, especially arbitrary policies towards national minorities. Together with Ivan Yakhimovich he sharply condemned the continuing occupation of Czechoslovakia [see p. 104].

As time passed, Grigorenko became increasingly occupied with the fate of the Crimean Tatars, a people deprived of their homeland [see Chap. 12]. His numerous actions in support of the Tatars earned him the respect of a large section of the

* On Marchenko and Belogorodskaya, see Chap. 9.

(*above*) Vadim Delone, Mos-poet (see Chapter 5).

(*right*) Natalya Gorbanevskaya her son Yasik, Moscow 1969.

(*below*) Vladimir Dremlyuga Chapter 5) outside the hoslovak Embassy, Moscow, 29th, 1968 (Yakhimovich and orenko in background — see).

14. (*above*) Larissa Bogoraz-Da[niel]
and Pavel Litvinov, Moscow, 1[

15. (*left*) Larissa Daniel in exil[e]
her Siberian saw-mill, 1970.

16. (*top right*) Larissa Daniel, w[ith]
Victor Krasin, in front of [
shack in Siberia, 1969.

17. (*right*) (From right to [left]
Pavel Litvinov, Pyotr Yakir, Vi[ctor]
Krasin, Litvinov's wife M[aya]
Rusakovskaya, and Yakir's w[ife]
Valentina Savenkova at Litvin[ov's]
place of exile near the Manchu[rian]
border (see p. 124).

18. Konstantin Babitsky.

19. Yakir and Krasin visiting Litvinov (centre) in exile, 1969.

Tatar people. Two thousand Tatars appealed to Grigorenko to act as public defence spokesman at the trial of ten activists of the Tatar movement which is shortly to take place in Tashkent [see pp. 257–62]. Grigorenko sent this letter, together with a declaration of his own, to the Uzbek Supreme Court, but got no reply.

Meanwhile Grigorenko was caught up in an ever-thickening web of slanderous gossip and provocations. The story was circulated at various meetings and discussions that Grigorenko had 'sold himself to the imperialists for the sake of fame'. Declarations were put out, calculated to appeal to people's baser feelings, to the effect that Grigorenko was a Jew but was registered as a Ukrainian when he joined the party. An anonymous letter was circulated, supposedly written by the Crimean Tatars, explaining to their fellow-Tatars that Grigorenko was a madman and an 'anti-Sovietist'. In April this year the K.G.B. tried to organize a provocation by arranging a meeting between Grigorenko and a complete stranger who telephoned him; they possibly hoped to catch him 'red-handed' at the moment when some material of a truly anti-Soviet nature would be handed to him. Grigorenko came to this 'meeting' accompanied by a large group of his friends; K.G.B. cars were parked all around, and the whole place was thick with K.G.B. men. But at the sight of undesirable witnesses the K.G.B. had to call off their provocation. The 'stranger' never approached the General, and only later, after Grigorenko's arrest, did he pay a visit to Grigorenko's wife and stage a crude provocation. The police watch on Grigorenko himself, and his house, went to extraordinary lengths; they followed him in their cars, making no secret of it and even trying to provoke him to an open clash. In April 1969 Grigorenko appealed to Yu. V. Andropov [the head of the K.G.B.] in a second letter,[3] but as with the first, sent in February 1968,[4] he received no reply.[5]

Even this very brief sketch of Grigorenko's life up to early 1969 should suffice to reveal an interesting point: if one person had to be singled out as having inspired the different groups within the Democratic Movement more than anyone else, then it would surely be he. Indeed he became, while free, in an informal way the movement's leader. And not surprisingly. A prolific scholar,[6] a champion of Dubček socialism, a legend among the Crimean Tatars, an exposer of the 'mental hospital' treatment of dissenters, an admirer of Anatoly Marchenko and his book My Testimony, *a writer and signer of cogent petitions, the forthright leader of the crowds barred from political trials, rebuffing provocations and once even dragging a K.G.B. ruffian off to the police-station to report him*[7] — *Grigorenko was all these things, and they all grew naturally out of his large and remarkable personality. It is hard, therefore, to see the K.G.B. ever releasing him, except perhaps to die.*

Grigorenko considered himself a communist, but was also — a rare combination in the Soviet Union — a humanist. As with many Czechoslovak communists in 1968, communism came to mean for him above all social and individual justice. This held true, however much it might mean sharing the party's power with other people. And it would mean a lot of this, for the Soviet system had become 'a bureaucratic machine … moved by our hands and heads, crushing us mercilessly, destroying the best people of our society, relieving everyone of guilt, of responsibility for the crimes it commits, freeing its servants from their consciences: a terrifying, cruel and heartless machine.' As for 'the work of breaking down this machine', 'that is a long task which … involves in the first place a revolution in people's minds, in their consciousness, all of which is unthinkable in the conditions of totalitarianism.'[8] In going about this task Grigorenko worked harmoniously with non-communists, Christians, Muslims and Jews, all of whom were his friends.

But his closest friend was Aleksei Kosterin: 'I have known Aleksei Kosterin for a very short time. Less than three years. Yet we have lived a whole life together. While Kosterin was still alive, a person extremely close to me said, "You were made by Kosterin." And I did not object. Yes, he made me: he turned a rebel into a fighter. I will be grateful to him for this to the end of my days.'[9]

Thus spake Grigorenko at Kosterin's funeral in November 1968. This remarkable occasion — for which Crimean Tatars, Chechens, even Volga Germans had journeyed thousands of miles, and which, prolonging an old tradition, also became a political demonstration — was recorded in a disappointingly laconic way by the Chronicle:

5   THE FUNERAL OF A. E. KOSTERIN

The writer Aleksei Evgrafovich Kosterin died on November 10th. He had been a member of the Soviet Communist Party since 1916; he was a former prisoner of Stalin's camps and an active fighter for the rights of men and justice for small nations.

He was buried on November 14th. Between 300 and 400 people were present at his funeral. The *samizdat* booklet on this event[10] consists of a preface by the chief compiler [Grigorenko]; a description of the funeral ('Yet another mockery of sacred feelings') written by P. G. Grigorenko;[11] an obituary written by a group of Kosterin's friends and read at the morgue of the Botkin hospital by Anatoly Yakobson; speeches at the morgue by Muarrem Martynov (Crimean Tatar poet), S. P. Pisarev (member of the Communist Party from 1920), Ablamit Borseitov (school-teacher) and [Reshat] Dzhemilev (engineer);* speeches at the crematorium by Professor Refik Muzafarov (Doctor of Philology) and P. G. Grigorenko (Master of Military Sciences); speeches at the subsequent memorial meeting by Pyotr Yakir (historian), Khalid Oshayev (Chechen writer), Andrei Grigorenko (technician),† Zampira Asanova (doctor), Leonid Petrovsky (historian), and an unknown man to whom the compilers of this collection of documents have given the pseudonym 'a Christian'.

We can only regret that the Chronicle *summarizes so briefly a booklet which, after the* Chronicle *itself, is one of the most astonishing* samizdat *documents we have. Nor does the* Chronicle *do any better as regards the first document to give the outside world details about Kosterin. This was Grigorenko's speech at a dinner in honour of his friend's 72nd birthday, held at the Altai restaurant in Moscow on March 17th, 1968: 'This speech is about Kosterin's life, the support which he has given to the cause of the Crimean Tatars, and the tasks which confront their movement' (No. 5).*[12] *One would scarcely guess from this that Grigorenko's fiery words—which urged the Tatars not to request but to demand their rights, and also to use the most militant legally permissible methods of lobbying—repeatedly roused his Tatar audience to a state of near ecstasy.*

Unfortunately, however, both the speech and the booklet are too long to discuss properly here, although a few details should be added about Kosterin. He spent three years in tsarist jails, then seventeen (1938–55) both in Soviet jails and in exile. After his release a few of his stories and essays appeared—often severely censored—in Novy Mir *and elsewhere. He was the father of Nina Kosterina, killed in the war, whose* Diary *is a Soviet equivalent of* The Diary of Anne Frank. *Just before his death*

---

* See pp. 254-7.   † Pyotr and Zinaida's son [see plate 60].

he resigned in disgust from the party,[13] *and was also surreptitiously—without his or even his friends' knowledge—expelled from the Writers' Union.*

This squalid episode provoked a memorable attack by Grigorenko on the Union's officials, who had been hounding Kosterin for some time: 'They have forgotten, or maybe don't even know, that neither Pushkin nor Tolstoy belonged to this organization. They believe so much in the power of their bureaucratic procedures that they even tried to take away the title of writer from such an outstandingly great poet of our country as Pasternak. Nor do they understand that without their Union Solzhenitsyn will remain a great writer and his works will live through the centuries, while their bureaucratic creation—without writers like Pasternak and Solzhenitsyn—is a hollow farce of no use to anyone.'[14]

Five days later:

5   On November 19th there was a new series of house searches [in Moscow]. This time they were carried out 'at the request of the Tashkent K.G.B.' and nominally in connection with one of the cases involving Crimean Tatars. There was a search at the home of Ilya Gabai—the second in recent months, and the second time it has been done in his absence. P. G. Grigorenko's home was searched and practically the whole of his files were seized—that is, everything in typescript or manuscript, although the search warrant gave permission to seize only materials 'defaming the Soviet social and political system'. According to Grigorenko, the materials confiscated include: The Declaration of the Rights of Man; all the works of A. E. Kosterin; Academician Sakharov's essay [see pp. 354–5]; 'The Russian Road to Socialism' by Academician Varga;* 'Notes of an Intelligence Officer' by Colonel V. A. Novobranets; *My Testimony* by Anatoly Marchenko; Akhmatova's 'Requiem'; verse by Tsvetayeva; a poem by Korzhavin; Hemingway's *For Whom the Bell Tolls*; various personal letters; materials on the Crimean Tatar and Volga German movements; translations of articles from Czechoslovak newspapers; notes for a work on military history by Grigorenko himself,[16] and many other items.[17]

A large part of these materials were not itemized in the record—they were simply dumped into a sack, sealed and taken away.

* In fact an anonymous essay wrongly attributed to Varga. See note 15.

On the same day, in the town of Zhukovsky in the Moscow Region, there was a search at the home of Simode Asanova, the sister of Zampira Asanova. In Simferopol there was a search at the house of the doctor Esma Ulanova—all her files, including a large number of documents relating to the Crimean Tatar movement, were seized.

All this happened a few days after the funeral of A. E. Kosterin, and one may assume that the true (and illegal) purpose of these searches was to confiscate the texts of the speeches made at his funeral.

Grigorenko's reply was simply to compile his booklet again from scratch, in which task, except as regards a few items, he succeeded. But the K.G.B., too, can be persistent, and certainly death does not necessarily remove someone from its purview:

ACTIVITIES AROUND THE FAMILY OF A. E. KOSTERIN

Members of the K.G.B. have paid much 'attention' to Vera Ivanovna Kosterina, the author's widow, since her husband's death. They keep ringing her up, asking about her health, visiting her at home and inviting her to see them—at the K.G.B. Only a little is known about the details of their conversations: under pressure from her new friends, V. I. Kosterina has signed some sort of statement against her husband's friends; she is undertaking certain actions to enable the K.G.B. not to return to P. G. Grigorenko the copies of A. E. Kosterin's works given him by the author during his life and confiscated during a search; Vera Ivanovna has come to believe the K.G.B. and now herself tells her friends that Grigorenko sent abroad half of Kosterin's work. The most important thing with which the K.G.B. officials want to help her is the careful compilation of an archive of the late writer. It is to be feared that A. E. Kosterin's literary work, covering many years, will fall into the hands of the organization which he most hated.

Simultaneously the K.G.B. has busied itself with the 'education' of Kosterin's grandson, Aleksei Smirnov, a student at the Mining Institute. On March 31st and April 1st this year [1969], members of the K.G.B. twice interviewed Alyosha's* father—a man who has never taken an interest in the upbringing of his

* Pet form of Aleksei.

son and who has never once seen him over the past two years. At the first interview he was told that his son was mixed up with the 'fanatical anti-Sovietist' Grigorenko, and that both of them would soon be arrested. Even if they were not arrested his son would be expelled from the Institute. The following day they changed their tactics: Grigorenko would not be arrested but would be left as a 'bait for young people' — a note would be made of all those who came to see him; and Alyosha's father, in league with the K.G.B., could save Alyosha from this fate.

They interviewed Aleksei Smirnov himself on April 2nd this year at the Institute's personnel section. Two members of the K.G.B., calling themselves Vladimir Ivanovich Volodin and Aleksei Mikhailovich, interviewed him in what was basically an illegal interrogation: they questioned him about all his friends and acquaintances, discovered his political convictions, and gave him slanderous information about A. E. Kosterin's friends. Finally they demanded that he cease all 'contact with Grigorenko' — with whom, by the way, he is only very slightly acquainted.

8   THE ARREST OF GRIGORENKO

On May 2nd this year the telephone rang in Grigorenko's apartment. The caller said he was speaking on Mustafa Dzhemilev's behalf [see pp. 160–61] and that the Tashkent trial was beginning on May 4th. Grigorenko flew out to Tashkent at once, and there he found that the date of the trial had not yet been fixed, and that Mustafa Dzhemilev had not asked anyone to ring him. On May 7th, Grigorenko was arrested with his return ticket in his pocket, and, ill as he was, with a temperature of 38°C [100·5°F] they put him in the Uzbek K.G.B. prison. He is charged under article 191–4 of the Uzbek Criminal Code, which corresponds to article 190–1 of the Russian Code.

On the same day, seven Moscow flats were searched in connection with the Grigorenko affair; that of Grigorenko himself, and those of Ilya Gabai, Victor Krasin, Lyudmila Alekseyeva, Andrei Amalrik [see pp. 352–4], Nadezhda Emelkina, and Zampira Asanova. The searches were conducted by investigators of the Moscow Procuracy, on the instructions of the Uzbek Procuracy. The searches were directed by L. S. Akimova, from her desk in the Procuracy. She is known as the investigator of the Irina Belogorodskaya case, and as director of the investigation into both the Pushkin Square demonstration of January 22nd, 1967, and the Red Square demonstration of August 25th, 1968. During these searches not only was all *samizdat* literature confiscated, with all typewriters, notebooks and scraps of paper with telephone messages and other jottings, but also all personal correspondence, photographs and valuables. From Lyudmila Alekseyeva's flat they took personal letters written by Anatoly Marchenko, letters from Yuly Daniel to his family, and photographs of Solzhenitsyn, Marchenko, Litvinov and Bogoraz. From Nadezhda Emelkina they removed two savings books belonging to her mother. Emelkina herself was subjected to a body search, and furthermore, in the absence of a woman investigator, her person was illegally examined by a woman witness of the search. Generally speaking, during these searches the witnesses did not behave like people obliged to ensure the observation of legality but like active helpers of those carrying out the search.

P. G. Grigorenko is still in Tashkent. The investigation of his case is headed by investigator Berezovsky, who headed the investigation of the ten Crimean Tatars in whose defence Grigorenko had wished to speak. It was Berezovsky too who conducted the search of Grigorenko's flat in November 1968. The main questions being put to witnesses are: have they received from Grigorenko documents containing 'deliberate fabrications', and have they noticed in Grigorenko any signs of mental derangement? So far only a few witnesses have been called: in Moscow, the wife, daughter and niece of A. E. Kosterin; in Tashkent, Pyotr Grigorevich's sister, also D. Ilyasov and Z. Ilyasova, at whose flat Grigorenko was arrested.

Grigorenko's arrest has aroused public indignation. At the gates of the Tashkent prison the Crimean Tatars set up pickets and demanded his release. The same demand was one of the slogans used at the [Tatar] demonstration in Moscow on June 6th this year [see p. 254]. In one day fifty-five signatures were collected for an appeal in support of Grigorenko.[18] And his wife, Zinaida Mikhailovna, wrote an open letter about her husband's life, his misfortunes and his latest arrest.[19]

Other *samizdat* publications to appear are two significant works about P. G. Grigorenko: 'Light in the Little Window' by A. Krasnov-Levitin[20] and 'The Arrest of General Grigorenko' by B. Tsukerman.[21] The author of the first, a well-known church writer, quoting the New Testament parable of the Good Samaritan, writes that today he sees more of the Christian spirit not in the representatives of the Orthodox Church, but in the Samaritans, 'people from outside'. One example of a 'Good Samaritan' seems to him to be P. G. Grigorenko, who for his bold criticism first 'paid with his career, condemning himself to journeys from one prison or lunatic asylum to another, to searches and arrests, to humiliations and insults', and who recently 'came to the aid of the Crimean Tatar people, not his own kin, and paid for this with his freedom.' Reflections on P. G. Grigorenko and the fortunes of the Crimean Tatars lead Krasnov to the wider problems of the struggle for democracy and a sense of humanity in our country. The second work contains short biographical notes on P. G. Grigorenko and reveals the objective character of those problems which Grigorenko has devoted his energies to trying to resolve in recent years. Despite the restrained character of the analysis, the author is unable to conceal his feeling of admiration for P. G. Grigorenko's sincerity and moral stature, and of reverence for his moral heroism.

8 THE ARREST OF ILYA GABAI

When Ilya Gabai's flat was searched on May 7th this year, his archive of documents relating to the Crimean Tatars was confiscated. On May 19th Ilya Gabai was arrested and sent to Tashkent to be investigated by the same Berezovsky.

Ilya Gabai [see plate 21] is a teacher, poet and scriptwriter, whose main work was as an editor. He was first arrested in January 1967 for participation in the demonstration on Pushkin Square. After four months in Lefortovo prison he was freed for want of a corpus delicti.

Following the appeal 'To those who work in science, culture and the arts',[22] which Gabai wrote with Yuly Kim and Pyotr Yakir after the trial of Galanskov and the others, he was dismissed from his job, found himself unable to get work anywhere, and tried to get by on casual earnings.[23] Although

Gabai was away from Moscow on August 25th, 1968, working as a labourer on a distant expedition, the investigating organs summoned him for interrogation in connection with the inquiry into the demonstration held on that day. The interrogation was to all intents and purposes about the aforementioned appeal. From October 1968 until his arrest, Gabai's flat was searched four times. On each occasion the appeal was taken away, together with copies of letters written by Soviet citizens addressed to governmental and judicial organs, and some poems of Gabai's. From his archive of Crimean Tatar documents they removed newspaper clippings relating to the brave exploits of the Tatars during the Great Patriotic War, copies of letters written by Tatar labourers demanding to return to their homeland, Academician Sakharov's brochure, the booklet 'The Funeral of A. E. Kosterin', information bulletins of the Crimean Tatars and so on.

Tarasov, a senior investigator of the Moscow Procuracy, arrested Gabai without production of a warrant, and had him flown immediately to Tashkent. In Tashkent, investigator Berezovsky refused to answer any of the enquiries of Gabai's friends there, and also to pass on to him in prison a message from them; he declared that he had never heard of him and that there was no one by the name of Gabai in Tashkent. A parcel of food, clothing and money sent by Gabai's wife never reached him. For a whole month it lay in the Tashkent post office; the remand prison administration, who should by law have collected it and given it to the prisoner, did not do so, but informed Gabai's wife that her parcels had not reached them. The post office sent the parcels and money back to her. Recently Galina Gabai travelled to Tashkent in order to hand over food, money and clothing to her husband in person.

Ilya Gabai's friends have written a letter in his defence and sent it to the Procurator-General of the U.S.S.R. They have also compiled a small anthology of Gabai's verse, which has appeared in *samizdat*.[24]

THE INVESTIGATION OF THE CASES OF ILYA GABAI   9
AND PYOTR GRIGOREVICH GRIGORENKO

When Galina Gabai, wife of Ilya Gabai, addressed a complaint to the Procurator-General, protesting not only against the unlawful arrest of her husband, but also against his being sent to Tashkent without the slightest reason — according to the law the investigation should be held in the place where the offence was committed, yet Gabai had never been to Tashkent — she was told in reply that the case had been put under the jurisdiction of the Tashkent Procuracy since the majority of the witnesses were in Tashkent. As for Pyotr Grigorevich Grigorenko, it is clear from the information given in the last issue of the *Chronicle* that he was decoyed to Tashkent so that he could be arrested there.

But in July the interrogation of witnesses began in Moscow — first by investigators of District Procuracies, on the instructions of the Tashkent Procuracy, and then by investigator B. I. Berezovsky, who came to Moscow for the purpose.

Berezovsky is in charge of the Gabai and Grigorenko cases. So far it is not clear whether they will be treated as one case or two separate ones.

During his visit to Moscow, Berezovsky interrogated a large number of witnesses, thus proving the untruth of his statement that most of the witnesses were in Tashkent.

The witnesses are being questioned about Grigorenko's and Gabai's part in the composition of a number of documents which bear their signatures: among the documents listed are the appeal to the Budapest conference; the appeal 'To those who work in science, culture and the arts' written by Kim, Yakir and Gabai; letters supporting the demonstrators [of August 25th], and in defence of Anatoly Marchenko [see p. 192] and Ivan Yakhimovich [p. 148]; a letter from citizens of Moscow — which was never sent — in support of the Crimean Tatars;[25] the collection of materials 'In Memory of A. E. Kosterin'; and others. Questions are being asked also about the preparation and distribution of particular documents, and especially about what part in their preparation and distribution was played by the witnesses. As far as is known, not one of the witnesses has answered the questions concerning the preparation and distribution of documents, on the grounds that the documents are not libellous, and do not come under article 190–1, on which the case is based, and therefore their preparation and distribution cannot be a matter for the evidence of witnesses. Replying to Berezovsky's provocative statements that 'you keep on saying that you do everything openly', the witnesses said that the punitive organs were of a different opinion as to the criminality of the documents, and therefore the witnesses could only confirm their signatures, and not reveal information about other persons, which could be used against those persons. All, or nearly all, the witnesses declared that they regarded the arrest of Grigorenko and Gabai, and the investigation of their case, as unlawful actions, and some of the witnesses refused completely to testify for that reason.

Incidentally, these were all witnesses who can be described, if not as friends and like-minded people, then at least as sympathizers with the accused. It is known that Berezovsky has also summoned witnesses of another kind. One of them is a K.G.B. official, the head of the central operations squad, known as 'Oleg Ivanovich Aleksandrov'. This was the name he gave on an earlier occasion—at the trial of the demonstrators—after he had snatched a letter from a crowd of people outside the courthouse who had not managed to get inside, and the indignant crowd had led him to the police station, where he named himself. People who were at the courthouse for the trials of the demonstrators and of Galanskov and Ginzburg, remember him well, with his black beard: on both occasions it was he who directed the activities of the 'volunteer police without armbands'.[26] And constantly with him there was a man in a black cap, evidently the chief's right-hand man—he too came in useful for Berezovsky.

Another witness Berezovsky summoned was the ill-famed Aleksei Dobrovolsky, who made slanderous statements about Ginzburg and Galanskov at their trial. Since coming out of his camp this January, Dobrovolsky has been living in Uglich [north of Moscow]. Unlike most political prisoners, who for months after their release are unable to obtain residence permits or find work anywhere, Dobrovolsky obtained a permit extremely quickly and is now the head of a technical library, even though his only higher educational qualification is half a year spent at an institute of librarianship. As a rule, political convicts with both higher education and post-graduate experience, e.g. Leonid Rendel [see p. 222], or even a higher degree, as in the case of Mykhaylo Osadchy [see p. 286], can only expect to be offered jobs of the most unskilled variety, and certainly not work with books and people. It is known that soon after his arrival Dobrovolsky was already claiming that he would soon be given a residence permit for Moscow. Perhaps his latest perjury will help him with this too.

At the present time, witnesses are still being summoned to investigators of the Moscow Procuracy in connection with the Grigorenko and Gabai case. Most of them are being seen by investigator Obraztsov.

Galina Gabai, who travelled to Tashkent in July and was received extremely rudely by Berezovsky, was later summoned as a witness in Moscow. Now she has written a short essay, 'Two Meetings with Berezovsky', which has appeared in *samizdat*.

The two demonstrations by foreigners in Moscow after the Galanskov–Ginzburg trial now had a successor. The leaflets scattered at these demonstrations have since spread quite widely in the Soviet Union: the physicist Lev Ubozhko, for example, was arrested in the west Siberian city of Sverdlovsk in January 1970 for passing copies around.[27]

10 SCANDINAVIAN STUDENTS' DEMONSTRATION IN DEFENCE OF P. G. GRIGORENKO

On October 6th, 1969, at five o'clock in the evening, Harald Bristol of Oslo and Elizabeth Lie from Uppsala staged a demonstration in defence of the arrested General P. G. Grigorenko in the largest store in Moscow, G.U.M.

The two young people chained themselves to the second floor guard-railings with handcuffs and threw their leaflets over the edge. The leaflets contained a biography of P. G. Grigorenko and the text of an appeal by the Norwegian, Swedish and Danish SMOG Committees to the Chairman of the U.S.S.R. Council of Ministers, A. N. Kosygin. Among other things, the appeal says:

We condemn equally much the use of arbitrary methods in any country. This is not interference in the affairs of another state, but the moral duty of progressive people. Only by observing legality and human rights *in all countries* is it possible to prevent a revival of fascism, which starts with illegal secret police activities. Mr Chairman of the Council of Ministers! Your government speaks out in support of those who fight for human rights in Greece, Vietnam, South Africa and other countries. Why then are those who fight for these rights in the U.S.S.R. being arrested?

At the end of the leaflet Harald Bristol and Elizabeth Lie appeal to Soviet citizens:

We have come to your country to serve the cause of legality and human rights. We are handing you our appeal to A. N. Kosygin concerning the case of Major-General Grigorenko, who has fallen victim to the arbitrary methods of the K.G.B. In support of our appeal we refuse to leave the scene of our demonstration, and we declare a hunger-strike. We will fast until MAJOR-GENERAL GRIGORENKO IS RELEASED OR UNTIL PRIME MINISTER KOSYGIN GIVES US A GUARANTEE THAT MAJOR-GENERAL GRIGORENKO WILL WITHOUT DELAY BE GIVEN AN OPEN AND LEGAL TRIAL.

The leaflets contain portraits of P. G. Grigorenko and A. N. Kosygin.

A large crowd of people gathered below round a fountain, reading the leaflets attentively and passing them around to each other with no comments but with unconcealed interest. Many of them went up to the second floor to get a closer look at the young people. Meanwhile two policemen had appeared on the scene. Seeing the chain of the handcuffs, one of them ran off to get reinforcements. Two workers were sent, and they sawed through the chain. By this time K.G.B. officials had already appeared at the scene of the demonstration. The young people were taken to the nearest police station, followed by most of the crowd which had gathered, but none of the crowd was allowed into the station.

On October 8th, Elizabeth Lie and Harald Bristol were deported from the Soviet Union.[28]

To resume the story:

10 At the end of October P. G. Grigorenko was transferred from Tashkent to Moscow, where he has been put in the Institute of Forensic Psychiatry for an in-patient examination.

11 On December 3rd the investigation into the case of P. G. Grigorenko was completed in Tashkent. In August a forensic-psychiatric examination by Tashkent doctors had judged Grigorenko to be of sound mind. The experts also pointed out that, in any case, to confine Grigorenko in a psychiatric hospital at his age and in his poor condition would be wrong. Among the experts were Detengof, Chief Psychiatrist of Tashkent, and Kogan, Chief Psychiatrist to the Turkestan Military District. Dissatisfied with the experts' findings, the investigation organs sent Grigorenko to Moscow in October for a second medical examination. The 62-year-old Grigorenko was transported there in an unheated railway carriage and, dressed as he was in a light summer suit, he was so affected by the cold that he was delivered to Lefortovo prison in a state of semi-consciousness.

The second examination took place in the Serbsky Institute, where Grigorenko was held in a cell. On October 22nd, he was adjudged of unsound mind. The examination was carried out by Professor D. R. Lunts and doctors G. Morozov and V. Morozov.

The immediate sequel in Grigorenko's case was intensely dramatic, but also tragic. It can only be briefly summarized here. Somehow or other Grigorenko managed to write a diary for the period May–December, also two analyses of his case, and then to smuggle the 9,000-word manuscript out of the K.G.B. prison in Tashkent. On March 3rd, 1970, his wife Zinaida wrote a desperate appeal and, with her husband's manuscript attached, circulated it. It ended: 'People! Pyotr Grigorevich Grigorenko is threatened by death! I appeal to all democratic organizations which defend human rights, and to all the freedom-loving citizens of the world! Help me save my husband! The freedom of each is the freedom of all!'[29]

The manuscript had revealed cruel physical beatings of Grigorenko, but, still worse, his total isolation from the outside world: he had not been allowed to receive a single visit, a single letter, a single parcel, a single telephone call. After honest psychiatrists had pronounced him sane, K.G.B. ones had labelled him insane. In this way his trial could take place — on February 26th–27th — in his absence[30] *and he could be consigned indefinitely to the company of degenerates and genuine*

*madmen. He was eventually dispatched to the prison psychiatric hospital
in Chernyakhovsk near the Polish border.*

*Grigorenko's manuscript—written with a remarkable detachment and
even humour in the most fearful circumstances—will be an enduring
example of man's capacity for courage.*

Meanwhile No. 10 had reported:

The investigation into the case of Ilya Gabai has been com- 10
pleted. Gabai has been charged with compiling various documents, including the appeal by himself, Kim and Yakir, 'To
those who work in science, culture and the arts in the U.S.S.R.',
the appeal of Moscow citizens in support of the Crimean Tatars,
and others. The lawyer D. I. Kaminskaya submitted a request
that the case against Gabai be quashed. The petition was
rejected.

*In January 1970 Gabai duly got his three years in the camps for anti-
Soviet 'libel'. He pleaded not guilty at his trial in Tashkent and put up
a characteristically spirited self-defence.*[31]
*Ever since his arrest his equally spirited wife Galina had defended
him with determination in his ordeal, despite the harassment she had also
suffered in her professional life. On this the* Chronicle *wrote:*

Galina Gabai, the wife of Ilya Gabai, is a speech therapist and 9
teacher of literature at the Moscow inter-regional high school
for the deaf and hard of hearing. The party committee of the
Sverdlov District of Moscow asked the school administration
to deprive Mrs Gabai of her teaching post at the school. The
school director Usachev submitted a report to the pedagogical
council, in which he said, among other things, that G. B. Gabai
committed political errors in her comments on pupils' essays:
she called Stalin a criminal, and said nothing about his services
to the revolution. Moreover, claimed the director, G. B. Gabai
appealed in her comments to bourgeois individualism: he was
referring to a comment which Mrs Gabai had written—in
answer to a pupil's argument that society alone should bear the
responsibility for the fate of Chekhov's Ionych[32]—about the
personal responsibility of every man for his actions. The

Director also expressed his dissatisfaction with a speech Mrs Gabai had made at a meeting of the pedagogical council. She had said that teachers ought to write their comments in literary language, and not descend to the speech level of their deaf-mute pupils. They should teach them to speak in literate, not 'deaf-mute' language. The Director added that Mrs Gabai was an erudite teacher, that her comments were abstruse, and that the pupils had great difficulty in understanding them; therefore (?) she should be transferred to junior teaching. A number of teachers at the meeting of the pedagogical council spoke against these proposals, and the resolution was not carried. The local trade-union committee also opposed the transfer of Mrs Gabai to junior teaching. But the party organization and the school administration, obedient to a phone-call from the district party committee, passed a resolution transferring Mrs Gabai to teaching the 6th class, which has only six pupils, and the 7th class, which in practice is non-existent. She was not allowed to take the top class, No. 11, through to the end of the school year, and so as to comply with the administration's decision another teacher lost her duties with the 6th and 7th classes and became partially redundant; this person is due to retire in a year's time, and a full teaching-load is very important to her as regards her pension.

GRIGORENKO'S FRIEND IVAN YAKHIMOVICH

Let us turn now to a specially close friend of Grigorenko, of whom the Chronicle *wrote in April 1969:*

7 Ivan Yakhimovich is thirty-eight. He was born into a family of Polish workers and graduated in the faculty of history and philology of the Latvian State University. After university he worked as a teacher and as an inspector of a District Department of Public Education. In 1960 he went to work as the chairman of the 'Jauna Gvarde' collective farm in Kraslava District. Whilst working on the farm he enrolled as an external student at the Latvian agricultural academy. A few years ago the paper *Komsomolskaya pravda* wrote about Ivan Yakhimovich in ecstatic terms.[33]

In January 1968 Yakhimovich wrote a letter to the Central

Committee of the party, addressing it to M. A. Suslov, and here he protested at the trial of Yury Galanskov, Alexander Ginzburg and the others.[34] In March 1968 Yakhimovich was expelled from the party[35] and in May 1968 dismissed from his post as chairman of the farm.[36] In violation of the statute on agricultural co-operatives he was dismissed by higher organs without a collective farm meeting being held. Recently he has worked as a stoker in the 'Belorussia' sanatorium in Jurmale.

We have already met Yakhimovich in Chapters 3 and 4, but before continuing let Grigorenko shed more light on his personality. In a long statement just after Yakhimovich's arrest his friend wrote about him:

> *One had to see how he spoke with people, how they behaved towards him, what a moving friendship he had with his wife, how his three daughters loved their father ... to understand what a pure, honest, warm-hearted person he is. I got to know Yakhimovich in March 1968. He had come to Moscow to seek out Pavel Litvinov and Larissa Bogoraz. He had heard their appeal 'To World Public Opinion' on the foreign radio. This had made an impression on him and he had written, as one communist to another, a comradely letter to Suslov ... The latter, as is normal in relations between high party functionaries and ordinary communists, did not answer. However the letter aroused great interest in samizdat circles, began to be passed around quickly, and soon found its way abroad. After it had been broadcast on the foreign radio Yakhimovich was called to the K.G.B. In the course of a long conversation it was stated to him among other things that Litvinov and Bogoraz had not signed any appeal, that the appeal was a fabrication, an invention of the B.B.C. To find out who was right—the K.G.B. or the B.B.C.—was why he had come to Moscow.[37]*

In his letter Yakhimovich had condemned the sentencing of 'the most energetic, brave and high-principled members of our young generation ... Too bad for us if we are not capable of reaching an understanding with these young people. They will create, inevitably they will create, a new party. Ideas cannot be murdered with bullets, prisons and exile.' Moreover, he continued,

> *I live in the provinces, where for every house with electricity there are ten without, where in winter the buses can't get through*

*and the mail takes weeks to arrive. If information [on the trials]
has reached us on the largest scale you can well imagine what you
have done, what sort of seeds you have sown throughout the country.
Have the courage to correct the mistakes that have been made before
the workers and peasants take a hand in the affair.*

*The first sign that Yakhimovich was in serious trouble came in an
item entitled:*

4   A 'NEW METHOD' OF CONDUCTING SEARCHES

On September 27th, 1968, Ivan Yakhimovich's apartment was
searched [...] He is at present living with his wife and their three
children in the Latvian town of Jurmale. He has been illegally
deprived of his residence permit—the police simply crossed out
the permit stamp in his passport—and so he is, naturally, unable
to find work.

The warrant for the search, signed by the Assistant Procurator of Jurmale, Kviešonis, authorized a search on suspicion of Yakhimovich's involvement in the theft of 19,654
roubles from the Jurmale branch of the State Bank. Of course,
the searchers found no money but they did remove a few
samizdat materials, also Yakhimovich's letter protesting about
the arrest of the demonstrators on August 25th,[38] the rough
draft of his unfinished essay on the post-January developments
in Czechoslovakia, his wife's personal diary, and so on.

*After discussing similar searches by the ordinary police concerning Yury
Gendler and Andrei Amalrik (see pp. 381, 352) the* Chronicle *then
continues:*

4 These are the three examples of the way in which the organs of
state security are conducting searches through intermediaries,
using false criminal allegations which are later conveniently
forgotten. It was also the ordinary police who conducted the
searches of both the demonstrators and several other people in
the case of the Red Square demonstration of August 25th.
The products of the searches, with a few exceptions, were not
used at the trial. As was learnt after the trial, the Moscow City
Procuracy, which had conducted the investigations into the
case, handed over these products of the searches to, once again,
the K.G.B.

In December 1968, the Procuracy of the Latvian Republic 6 sanctioned the conduct of an investigation into material removed during a search at the flat of Ivan Yakhimovich ... Yakhimovich is accused under article 183–1 of the Latvian Criminal Code, which corresponds to article 190–1 of the Russian Code, but the concrete substance of the charge is not clear. The investigation is being conducted by a Procuracy investigator of the Lenin district of Riga, Kakitis, although Yakhimovich lives and is registered not in Riga, but in Jurmale. The first, and so far the only, interrogation of Yakhimovich took place on February 5th, 1969. The investigator was mainly interested in the way in which various documents had been distributed: how had Yakhimovich got hold of P. G. Grigorenko's article on Nekrich's book?[39] To whom had Yakhimovich given his letter addressed to Suslov and the Central Committee of the Communist Party? Why had Yakhimovich been distributing the appeal of Larissa Bogoraz and Pavel Litvinov 'To World Public Opinion'? And so on. The investigator specifically asked Yakhimovich about an unsent letter to Pavel Litvinov that had been written after the demonstration of August 25th, 1968, and removed during the search: 'In your letter you wrote, "I feel pride and admiration and, if I had been in Moscow, I should have been in Red Square with you." Do you still think this?' 'Yes,' Yakhimovich replied.

It is well known that during the search Yakhimovich's unfinished study of post-January events in Czechoslovakia was removed. At the end of the interrogation the investigator warned that next time Yakhimovich should give a theoretical analysis of his views on the events in Czechoslovakia. This warning ignores the fact that Yakhimovich, as the accused, is in no way obliged to do anything: to provide an explanation is simply his right; ignoring this, the Riga investigator apparently forgot that neither views nor their theoretical foundation are a matter for criminal prosecution.

THE ARREST OF IVAN YAKHIMOVICH

Ivan Yakhimovich was arrested on March 24th in the town of Jurmale in the Latvian Republic ... Three times, on February 5th, March 19th and March 24th, Yakhimovich was called for questioning by investigator of the Riga Procuracy

E. Kakitis, and after the third time he was arrested. Before his arrest Ivan Yakhimovich wrote an open letter, 'Instead of a final speech',[40] in which he spoke about himself and about the investigation, which was based on negative character reports and false evidence. Then he appealed to a number of his friends, to certain public figures, to the workers and peasants, to Latvians and Poles, and to communists from all countries, not to reconcile themselves to injustice.

The end of the investigation in the Yakhimovich case is expected in the middle of May.

The family of Ivan Yakhimovich consists of his wife Irina, who graduated from the faculty of history and philology, for a long time worked as a school teacher,[41] and is now forced to work as a nanny in a kindergarten; and three daughters of five, six and seven years. People recount how during the search, before Yakhimovich's arrest, his three daughters stood in the garden below the window and sang the 'Internationale'.

A group of Yakhimovich's friends have written a protest letter about his illegal persecution.[42] Together with the letters written either by Ivan Yakhimovich himself or in collaboration with like-minded friends, this protest letter is included in a collection of materials relating to him now circulating in *samizdat*.

9 At the end of August 1969 the Latvian Supreme Court examined the case of Ivan Yakhimovich. Yakhimovich's activities had been classified under article 183–1 of the Latvian Criminal Code, equivalent to article 190–1 of the Russian Code. The substance of his activities was as follows: spreading Bogoraz's and Litvinov's letter 'To World Public Opinion', preparing and distributing a letter to the Central Committee of the party, writing a letter in defence of the demonstration of August 25th — the only copy of which had not been circulated and was taken away during a search — and also uttering statements against the sending of troops into Czechoslovakia.

Ivan Yakhimovich had never been on a psychiatrist's register before. The first conclusion that he was of unsound mind was made by an out-patient commission of experts, who diagnosed 'schizophrenia'. The diagnosis of the in-patient commission was completely different: 'paranoid development of a psychopathic personality, amounting to mental illness'—and they also pronounced him insane. Both commissions recommended that Yakhimovich should be sent to a psychiatric hospital of special type.

The court granted the requests submitted by the defence lawyer S. V. Kallistratova: that additional witnesses be summoned, that additional documents be added to the case, and that Ivan Yakhimovich be called to appear in court. The defence also submitted a request that Yakhimovich be sent to another commission of experts since the conclusion of the second commission was not supported by the evidence it had examined. The woman specialist doctor in court said that she could not argue with the conclusions of the in-patient commission, but that since, during the interrogation of witnesses closely acquainted with Yakhimovich and during the interrogation of Yakhimovich himself, new data had been collected which could help to define his psychological state, she considered it necessary that Yakhimovich be sent to a repeat commission. The Prosecutor supported the lawyer's request for a repeat commission. The court resolved to have Ivan Yakhimovich sent to a repeat commission of forensic psychiatry experts at the Serbsky Institute. Judge Lotko, who presided over the trial, conducted the whole of the two-day hearing with a full observance of procedural norms, and with respect for the accused's right to a defence. According to eyewitnesses, Ivan Yakhimovich aroused the sympathy of all present, not excluding the Prosecutor and the escort soldiers.

This rare example of a fair trial in a political case had, however, a more predictable sequel. No. 11 reported that Yakhimovich 'entered the Serbsky Institute in December', and No. 13 that in April 1970 the Institute's recommendation of compulsory treatment in a mental hospital of ordinary (but not prison) type had been adopted by the Riga court.[43]

So now Grigorenko and his closest friends were all either dead or safely in confinement. However, the seeds they had sown were already proving their fertility.

7. THE ACTION GROUP FOR THE DEFENCE OF CIVIL RIGHTS

We appeal to the United Nations because we have received no reply to the protests and complaints which we have been sending for a number of years to the top political and legal bodies in the Soviet Union. The hope that our voice may be heard, that the authorities will stop the lawless acts which we have continually pointed out— this hope has expired.

Action Group's first letter, May 1969

A fortnight after Pyotr Grigorenko's arrest the Action Group for the Defence of Civil Rights in the Soviet Union was formed. Maybe this was no coincidence. Deprived at last of their inspiring leader, Grigorenko's colleagues probably felt an extra need for at least a minimum of formal co-ordination to their civil rights activities.

From the start the terms 'civil rights' and 'human rights' were used interchangeably in the group's title and other such phrases. Both terms have a fairly modest ring. Perhaps because of the re-stalinization process which the group saw beginning, the more radical notion of 'political rights' was eschewed. Indeed, in such an atmosphere the very creation of the group required enormous courage, given the acute, almost paranoiac fear which the secret police in totalitarian states always feel for groups beyond their close control. As the fifteen people concerned represented not only Moscow but also Leningrad, Kiev, Kharkov and the exiled Crimean Tatars in Central Asia, violent K.G.B. antagonism was in fact certain. Nor were these people cranks, but intelligent, mostly professional men and women with an average age of somewhat under forty.

Their first collective act is described here.

8 APPEAL TO THE U.N. COMMISSION ON HUMAN RIGHTS

On May 20th, 1969, a letter was sent to the U.N. Commission on Human Rights with a request to look into the violation in the Soviet Union of one of the basic human rights—the right to hold independent convictions and to propagate them by any legal means.[1] The letter points out that in political trials in our country people are being tried 'on the charge of libelling the Soviet political and social system, either with intent (article 70 of the Russian Criminal Code) or without intent (article 190–1) to undermine the Soviet system', while in actual fact none of the accused have attempted to libel or, still less, to undermine the Soviet system. People are being condemned on fabricated charges, in reality for their convictions. 'You are not being tried for your convictions'—the letter unmasks this favourite phrase of the Judges by referring to a series of trials: those of Sinyavsky and Daniel, Ginzburg and Galanskov, Khaustov and Bukovsky, the participants in the demonstration of August 25th, Anatoly Marchenko, Irina Belogorodskaya, Yury Gendler and Lev Kvachevsky [see pp. 380–86], the series of Ukrainian trials, including that of Chornovil, the trials of the Crimean Tatars, the trials in the Baltic States, in particular that of Kalninš [see pp. 212–13] and others, the trials of Soviet Jews demanding permission to emigrate to Israel, for example the conviction of Kochubiyevsky, and the trials of believers. The letter mentions the recent arrest of Victor Kuznestov [see pp. 240–42], Ivan Yakhimovich, P. G. Grigorenko and Ilya Gabai. The letter also refers to 'a particularly inhuman form of persecution: the placing of normal people in psychiatric hospitals for their political convictions.'

This letter was signed by the Action Group for the Defence of Human Rights in the U.S.S.R.: G. Altunyan (engineer, Kharkov), V. Borisov (worker, Leningrad), T. Velikanova (mathematician), N. Gorbanevskaya (poet), M. Dzhemilev (worker, Tashkent), S. Kovalyov (biologist), V. Krasin (economist), A. Lavut (mathematician), A. Levitin-Krasnov (church writer), Yu. Maltsev (translator), L. Plyushch (mathematician, Kiev), G. Podyapolsky (scientific research worker), T. Khodorovich (linguist), P. Yakir (historian) and A. Yakobson (translator). Besides these, there are thirty-nine signatures of support beneath the appeal.

The employees of the U.N. office in Moscow refused to accept the letter, declaring that they did not accept anything from private individuals. The letter was sent by post and handed to foreign correspondents.

On June 30th the Action Group sent an additional letter with information on 'new, particularly painful facts about the violation of human rights, about the new case brought against Anatoly Marchenko, and about imminent trials, the aim of which is to put away dissenters within the walls of prison psychiatric hospitals.'[2]

At roughly this time two other collective letters were sent, not formally by the Action Group, but by different combinations of its members and supporters. One of these was the denunciation of the Czechoslovak occupation on its first anniversary (see pp. 107-8).

   As for the other:

8 Ten people[3] have sent a letter[4] to the World Conference of Communist and Workers' Parties [...] The letter speaks of the sinister facts of re-Stalinization in our country: the political trials, the general persecution of dissenters, the attempts to rehabilitate Stalin, the increasing influence in the party leadership of people whose aim is to return to the Stalinist past. Appealing to the representatives of the communist parties, the authors of the letter ask: 'Can it be that such an obvious restoration of Stalinism in our country, which is at the helm of the communist movement, fails to arouse your anxiety?'

   The letter was sent to the Presidium of the conference, and copies were handed personally to delegates of the Italian and British Communist Parties, and also to other parties represented at the conference.

The third letter from the Action Group proper — dated September 26th, 1969 — was signed by thirty-six supporters but only ten members.[5] Arrests had taken their toll. Attached to the letter were special appeals for three of the victims: Levitin, Altunyan and Dzhemilev.[6]

10 A new appeal by the Action Group was handed in to the United Nations Information Centre in Moscow, in connection with the persecution of members of the Group. However, the deputy-director of the U.N. Information Centre in Moscow, Evdokimov, did not accept the appeal, as acceptance of the document would be, according to his written statement, 'a violation of Point 7 in Article 2 of the U.N. Charter'.

This last point raised a small storm in the West. But although other U.N. centres around the world had been regularly forwarding analogous petitions to New York, Mr Evdokimov turned out to be right. On October

3rd the U.N.'s fifty centres were instructed by U Thant to refuse all petitions in future. They thus became as illiberal as the Moscow centre and a notable blow had been struck at human rights.

The next appeal, dispatched on November 26th and signed by nine Action Group members, was, predictably enough, intercepted by the censorship. The first copy of it reached the West over a year later. The Chronicle *wrote:*

NOVEMBER 1969. The Action Group for the Defence of Human Rights in the U.S.S.R. has sent its fourth letter to the United Nations. The letter tells of repressive measures against members of the Action Group and against citizens who have supported its appeals to the U.N. 11

The fifth appeal was sent on January 17th, 1970, and signed by seven members and thirty-nine supporters.[7] To reach the West it took almost a year. Meanwhile the U.N. Commission on Human Rights had shown no sign of investigating, as requested, the disturbing information in any of the group's letters.

Thus the Chronicle *appeared to be consoling itself and the Action Group for the U.N.'s callous indifference when it reported:*

A number of European public organizations have come out in support of the [first] appeal which the Action Group for the Defence of Human Rights in the Soviet Union sent to the United Nations. Among them are: the International Committee for the Defence of Human Rights (Paris), Europa Civiltà (Rome), Kuratorium Geistige Freiheit (Bern), the Danish, Norwegian and Swedish SMOG Committees, Arts et Progrès (Paris), and the Flemish Action Committee for Eastern Europe (Antwerp). 9

The remainder of the tale of the Action Group — apart from its sixth letter, spelling out its principles of operation[8] — concerns its harassment by the K.G.B. Not all its members, however, have their troubles covered in this chapter. For various reasons the fates of two of them — Anatoly Levitin and Vladimir Borisov — are unfolded elsewhere, in Chapters 16 and 11 respectively. And a third member, Sergei Kovalyov, drops from the Chronicle's *purview altogether.*

10   PERSECUTION OF THE ACTION GROUP FOR THE
      DEFENCE OF CIVIL RIGHTS IN THE U.S.S.R.

The act of a group of Soviet citizens in appealing to an international organization, the United Nations, and protesting
against violations in the Soviet Union of basic civil rights and
Soviet laws, has become the subject of investigations by the
K.G.B. and the Procuracy [...]

However, the K.G.B. and the Procuracy have not restricted
themselves to Altunyan [see p. 162]: at the beginning of September [1969] Velikanova, Krasnov-Levitin, Lavut, Maltsev,
Podyapolsky[9] and Khodorovich, all members of the Action
Group, were summoned to interrogations at the Moscow K.G.B.
headquarters.

The interrogations were conducted by investigator Mocha-
lov, who violated article 158 of the Russian Code of Criminal
Procedure by his refusal to inform the witnesses to what case
their summonses related. The investigator asked about the reasons for the creation of the Action Group, and its aims. All the
witnesses were subjected to abuse, shouts and threats during
their interrogations: 'Scum!' 'Rabble!' 'We've had enough of
playing at democracy with you!' 'It's time to squash you!'
'Prison has long been calling out for you!' 'So you're trying to
topple Soviet power!' 'Want to liquidate the party!' 'Break up
the collective farms!' 'Restore private property!' 'You've got
together with the fascists! Sold out to the White Guards!'
'People shed their blood for you!'

All those summoned to interrogations refused to answer
questions which were not related to a case, and declared that the
appeal to the United Nations could not and should not be the
subject of an investigation. The investigator refused to enter in
the records corrections and additional statements made by the
witnesses, thus violating the Russian Code of Criminal Procedure. Because of this the majority of those interrogated
refused to sign the records of the proceedings [...]

On October 17th, 1969, a member of the Action Group for
the Defence of Civil Rights in the U.S.S.R., Yury Maltsev,
received a written summons to a military recruitment centre.
There he was told that he had to undergo a medical examination, and was taken without further ado into the neuro-patho-

logist's consulting-room where there were two psychiatrists in attendance, one from the district health centre.

Maltsev was asked whether he had ever requested permission to leave the Soviet Union;[10] why he was thirty-seven years old and not married; and why, with a degree in philology, he was working as a telegram-deliverer at the Central Telegraph Office. Maltsev asked in his turn what was the relevance of all these circumstances to the state of his health. The psychiatrists remarked that these circumstances were signs of oddity. Then an officer took Maltsev to the military commissar, who stated that he would like to use Maltsev as a translator, but for this a medical examination was obligatory. Some orderlies came into the commissar's office and took Maltsev away to the 5th section of the Kashchenko psychiatric hospital. Once there, Maltsev refused to change his clothes. The doctor on duty took him aside and said: 'We have no authority to discharge you from here, since it was not we who demanded that you be brought here. Your resistance will oblige me to ask the orderlies to help, and they will undress you by force.' On October 21st all the samples for analysis were taken from Maltsev, including a blood sugar test. Evidently they now propose to give him insulin injections. He has been interned for a month-long diagnosis.[11] In the words of the doctor, there will be no treatment carried out during this month, because treatment is dangerous for the health.

On October 21st, 1969, searches were conducted by officials of the Moscow city Procuracy at the homes of members of the Action Group N. Gorbanevskaya, T. S. Khodorovich and A. Yakobson. The search warrants did not state in connection with what case the searches were being made. There was simply a reference to article 190–1 of the Russian Criminal Code.

During the search of T. S. Khodorovich's flat, some friends arrived, but the officials in charge of the search did not allow them to be present while it was being made. The police were called and the friends escorted out of the flat.

From A. Yakobson were taken manuscripts of his works of literary criticism,[12] the compilation *Midday*, which concerns the trial of the Red Square demonstrators, and some poems of Yuly Daniel.

From T. S. Khodorovich were taken the appeal of the foreign students who demonstrated in the department store G.U.M., [see pp. 140–41] and the first letter of the Action Group to the U.N.

From N. Gorbanevskaya were taken her personal correspondence, her poems, and issues of the *Chronicle*.

One of the members of the Action Group, P. I. Yakir, has received a letter signed: 'On behalf of all the inhabitants of the town of Sumy [in N.E. Ukraine]: Chairman of Sumy Town Council Executive Committee, Bondarenko, and secretary of the Executive Committee, Krapivnaya.' The letter says, among other things: 'You have chosen the road of betrayal of the interests of the Fatherland.' P. I. Yakir received a similar letter from the Director of school No. 37 in Kishinyov [Moldavia] and the history teacher of the same school, Feldman, who wrote: 'It turns out that you, Pyotr Ionovich, are giving the West food for malicious propaganda … Come to your senses, Pyotr Ionovich, before it is too late, and do not sully the radiant name of your father, which our class enemies are trying to turn into a symbol for their struggle against the Soviet Union.'

Copies of both letters were sent by their authors to the Presidium of the U.S.S.R. Academy of Sciences.

P. I. Yakir received a similar letter from a certain citizen Rozin, who said that he had also signed protests against violations of legality. The *Chronicle* hereby reports that amongst the signatures on protests sent from Kiev, where Rozin's letter came from, there is no mention of the name Rozin.

To the Sumy Town Council P. I. Yakir sent the following reply:

> If we are afraid of causing a stir in the West, then we ought once and for all to renounce all criticism, self-criticism and open discussion, to renounce argument; for it is through argument, as you know, that the truth is born. My father, like many other honourable and innocent Soviet citizens, was destroyed by Stalinism. And it is Stalinism I too am fighting against. Do you suggest that in doing this I am bringing shame on the name of my father? Unfortunately there is a tendency nowadays to confuse anti-Stalinism with anti-Sovietism. In this way Stalinism is equated with Soviet power, and this conflicts with the spirit of the 20th and 22nd party congresses and the resolutions they passed.

In Kiev a search was made of the flat of L. Plyushch,[13] a member of the Action Group, in connection with the case of Oleg Bakhtiyarov.[14] Bakhtiyarov has been arrested under article 62 of the Ukrainian Criminal Code (equivalent to article 70 of the Russian Code). During the search, manuscripts of L. Plyushch's philosophical writings were confiscated, and then Plyushch was summoned to an interrogation. The interrogation was in connection with the case of G. Altunyan. L. Plyushch refused to testify, since the letter to the United Nations about which Plyushch was questioned is not a matter for legal investigation. L. Plyushch was interrogated a second time in connection with the case of Bakhtiyarov, from whom some philosophical works by Berdyayev had been confiscated on his arrest. At this interrogation, too, L. Plyushch refused to testify.

DETENTION, ARREST AND TRIAL OF VICTOR KRASIN 11

Victor Krasin was born in 1929. He is a former inmate of Stalin's camps, an economist by training, and a member of the Action Group for the Defence of Civil Rights in the U.S.S.R. He is the father of three children.[15]

At a quarter to midnight on December 20th Krasin was detained at a friend's flat. Policemen and plainclothes agents broke into the flat, almost tearing the door from its hinges. Roughly pushing aside the lady of the house, and flinging open cupboards in the corridor as they passed, the men strode swiftly into the room where Victor Krasin was. They presented him with a warrant for his detention, signed by the Procurator of the Perovo District of Moscow. With Krasin in the flat were his wife and three children, and also seven children belonging to the owners of the flat. They were woken up as they slept.

Krasin's wife wanted to telephone her friends and tell them of her husband's detention, but the police did not allow her to do this, and called her a hooligan. The intruders wanted to search the flat without a search warrant. The owner tried to resist, but they took away some translation work from him, saying that they wished to examine it. After this Krasin was taken away.

Krasin's wife and friends spent the whole night searching for him in the police stations of Moscow, and only next day did they

succeed in discovering that he was being held in police station
No. 57. Neither his friends nor his wife were informed of the
reasons for his detention. On the morning of December 22nd
Krasin was transferred to police station No. 102, where he was
held for the next two days. The deputy head of the criminal
investigation department of station No. 102, Mikhailov, told
Krasin's wife, Anna Krasina, during a conversation with her:
'We'll do as ordered — we might release him, we might convict
him, it doesn't depend on us.' During the time that Krasin was
held in the police station, that is three days, access to it was
strictly controlled; every person who entered was questioned in
detail as to where he was going and to whom. In the evening
of December 22nd an ambulance was called for Krasin. The
diagnosis was spasm of the aorta. Notwithstanding this, Krasin
was left in the same cell in terrible conditions: no windows, no
ventilation, and in the company of drunkards, hooligans and
mental cases whom the hospital would not accept for treatment.

On December 23rd Krasin underwent a medical examination, and was found to be suffering from heart and stomach
trouble. The medical team which diagnosed him laid down
that he could not engage in heavy physical labour, and recommended that he work in the speciality for which he was trained.

On December 23rd Krasin was taken for an interview with
the Procurator of the Perovo District, at which he was finally
told the reasons for his detention and arrest: for one year and
three months he had done no work, he had not thought of his
children's welfare, he had not attended parents' meetings at
school, and he had not been present on his son's birthday.

Krasin is known as an active fighter against Stalinism. He
had recently been working on the completion of his Master's
thesis, and had been employed as a freelance technical translator for V.N.I.I.T.I. [The All-Union Scientific Research
Institute for Technical Information.]

At six o'clock on the evening of December 23rd, after the
interview with the Procurator, Krasin's trial was held. His
wife was not informed of the time or place of the trial, and
it was quite by chance that she was present and appeared as a
witness. Krasin was charged (according to the decree of the
Russian Supreme Soviet of May 4th, 1961) with leading an
anti-social, parasitic way of life. The charge was based on a

reference from a post at which Krasin had not been working for a year and three months. The reference was signed by V. Mikhalevsky, a laboratory head at the Central Economics and Mathematics Institute. The accusations that Krasin had failed to attend parents' meetings and had not been present on his son's birthday figured in the trial too.

The Judge put the following question to Krasin: why was his mother's surname Rozenberg? Krasin replied that his mother had kept her maiden name.

Anna Krasina stated that she had no complaints against her husband, that for many years the whole family had lived on her husband's wages alone and no one had ever expressed any interest in what her children were eating, that at the moment she was earning a particular sum by translation work, and that she was anxious to finish work on her thesis. She said that to condemn her husband as a parasite would be completely unlawful.

The Judge asked Krasin what he could tell the Court. Krasin replied that he did not consider himself a parasite, but that if the Court brought in a verdict of guilty he would appeal against it, invoking the supervisory powers of the Procuracy.

Krasin was sentenced to five years' exile, the maximum under this decree. On December 24th he was sent off in a convicts' train for Krasnoyarsk Province.

THE ARREST OF NATALYA GORBANEVSKAYA   11

On December 24th, 1969, Natalya Gorbanevskaya was arrested.

Natalya Gorbanevskaya was born in 1936, and graduated from the philological faculty of Leningrad State University in 1963. A talented poet, she is [...] the mother of two young children (the elder is eight years old, and the younger one year seven months).

On December 24th a search was made of Gorbanevskaya's flat. The search warrant was signed by L. S. Akimova, senior investigator of the Moscow Procuracy, and the search was carried out by Shilov, an investigator of the Procuracy. Confiscated during the search were items of *samizdat*, the manuscript *Free Medical Aid*[16] and a copy of *Requiem* with a handwritten dedication by Anna Akhmatova.[17]

A search was made of the persons of the friends who were present in Gorbanevskaya's flat during the search.

Natalya Gorbanevskaya has been charged under article 190–1 of the Russian Criminal Code. The investigation is being conducted by L. S. Akimova. Gorbanevskaya is at present in Butyrka prison.

As early as 1968 — after the demonstration of August 25th — Gorbanevskaya was declared to be of unsound mind, and now she is threatened with imprisonment in a hospital prison for an unlimited term.

Precisely this sentence was imposed on her — in her absence — on July 7th, 1970. The Moscow City Court accused her of anti-Soviet slander and also of being one of the compilers of the Chronicle.[18]

THE ACTION GROUP'S CRIMEAN TATAR: MUSTAFA DZHEMILEV

Mustafa Dzhemilev was born in 1944. In 1962 he was one of a group of young Crimean Tatars in Tashkent which took part in the growing Tatar campaign to be allowed to return home to the Crimea, from which the whole nation had been exiled in 1944. For this he was sacked from his job in an aircraft factory. Six years later he wrote — at Pyotr Grigorenko's request — a fascinating memoir about the group's activities.[19] In 1966–7 he spent a year and a half in prison. On June 6th, 1969, a Tatar demonstration took place in Moscow (see pp. 254–7) and after it various Tatars, apart from the demonstrators, were expelled from Moscow:

8 One of them, Mustafa Dzhemilev, was sent to Gulistan [Tashkent Region] and taken into custody.[20] In protest at this, he went on hunger-strike, and after that was offered his freedom if he would give a written undertaking not to leave the place. Mustafa refused, and undertook only to report to the authorities immediately they requested. After giving this undertaking he was released.

9 In Gulistan, in the Uzbek Republic, an investigation is being conducted into the case of Mustafa Dzhemilev, under article 191–4 of the Uzbek Criminal Code, equivalent to article 190–1 of the Russian Code. The charge is participation in Crimean Tatar protests against the ban on a return to the homeland.

Mustafa Dzhemilev has had to sign a statement that he will not leave the town.

On September 11th a member of the Action Group, Mustafa 10 Dzhemilev, was arrested in Gulistan by investigator Berezovsky. Mustafa Dzhemilev's case has been joined with the case of I. Ya. Gabai, which was reported in the last issue of the *Chronicle*. Dzhemilev refused to have a defence lawyer, explaining his refusal by saying that he did not wish another lawyer to share the fate of B. Zolotukhin.* M. Dzhemilev petitioned for the appointment of a defence lawyer for him from the International Committee for the Defence of Human Rights [see p. 153].

On December 10th, 1969, 386 Crimean Tatars signed a docu- 11 ment protesting against the arrest of Mustafa Dzhemilev, an active member of the movement for the return of the Crimean Tatars to their homeland. The letter was sent to Brezhnev, Rudenko[21] and the United Nations Commission on Human Rights.

In January 1970, however, Dzhemilev was duly sentenced to three years in strict-régime camps, as a co-defendant of Ilya Gabai.[22]

THE ACTION GROUP'S KHARKOV SUPPORTERS

The first Action Group appeal revealed that not only a group member, Genrikh Altunyan, but also eight supporters, all engineers, came from Kharkov. The police harassment to which these people had previously been subject now became more intense:

On June 12th, 1969, several organizations in Kharkov held 8 general staff meetings in working hours in connection with the signing of the letter addressed to the United Nations. All the meetings were preceded by closed party meetings, at which speakers were nominated and draft resolutions agreed on for the general meetings. It should be noted that the K.G.B. put at the disposal of district party committees and of the directors of the various enterprises the letter in support of P. G. Grigorenko: they alleged that this was the letter that had been sent

* Alexander Ginzburg's lawyer: see p. 84.

to the United Nations. In addition to this, there was an atmosphere of hysteria and chauvinism at the meetings, because none of the district party leaders or K.G.B. men present attempted to put a stop to the hysterical tirades of speakers about how the United Nations was an imperialist, fascist organization; how the people who had signed the letter were traitors, accomplices of imperialism, and slanderers; how all the Tatars should be wiped from the face of the earth, and so on. Especial mention should be made of the speeches of Kartsev, secretary of the Krasnozavodsk District Party Committee, Academician Ivanov, director of the Ukrainian Technical Physics Institute, and Dubrava, a K.G.B. man. Not one of the signatories of the letter was allowed to speak, apart from G. Altunyan. The letter itself was not read out. The very fact that such an appeal had been sent abroad was condemned ipso facto. At every meeting, resolutions were passed condemning the signatories of the letter. At meetings held at the technical and production plant *Ukrenergochermet* [Ukrainian Ferrous Metals Power Supply Trust], the Ukrainian Technical Physics Institute, and the State Institute of Transport Planning [Giprotrans], additional resolutions were passed demanding the dismissal of V. Ponomaryov, S. Karasik, A. Levin and A. Kalinovsky, and demanding also that the matter should be transferred to the jurisdiction of the Procuracy. A meeting in the design shop at *Teploenergomontazh* [Thermal Power Station Construction Trust] condemned V. Nedobora in his absence. Those few who were brave enough to vote against the resolution, or who abstained from voting, are now undergoing threats and blackmail from the plant management.

To sum up, those condemned at the meetings for signing the letter to the United Nations are: Genrikh Altunyan, Sofia Karasik, Lev Kornilov, Alexander Kalinovsky and V. Nedobora (all senior engineers); Vladimir Ponomaryov (engineer); and Arkady Levin (chief design engineer). A short record of the Kharkov meetings has appeared in *samizdat.*

9   THE ARREST OF GENRIKH ALTUNYAN

On July 11th, 1969, Genrikh Altunyan was arrested in Kharkov. He was charged under article 62 of the Ukrainian Criminal Code, equivalent to article 70 of the Russian Code. The police arrested Altunyan without producing a warrant for his arrest or detention.

Genrikh Altunyan, a radio-technician and engineer [see plate 26], was until recently a Major in the Soviet Army and taught at a military academy. He holds awards from the U.S.S.R. Supreme Soviet for his many years of irreproachable service in the army, and has been a party member since 1957. He has two children.

In July of last year the flats of a number of Kharkov citizens, including Altunyan's, were searched.[23] During the searches the police removed *samizdat* copies of [Solzhenitsyn's] *Cancer Ward*, Academician Sakharov's brochure, issues of the *Chronicle*, and other things. After that, Altunyan and others were summoned as 'witnesses' in connection with article 187–1 of the Ukrainian Criminal Code, without[24] being informed of the concrete substance of the case. At the same time Genrikh Altunyan was expelled from the party,[25] dismissed from his job, and then from the army altogether, on the orders of the K.G.B. Among the reasons for his expulsion from the party was 'links with Yakir and Grigorenko'.

Despite the repressive measures taken against him, Altunyan continued to play an active part in the movement for the democratization of Soviet society. His signature stands at the foot of letters in support of the convicted demonstrators of August 25th,[26] and also in defence of Ivan Yakhimovich[27] and P. G. Grigorenko. He is a member of the Action Group for the Defence of Human Rights in the Soviet Union, which sent a letter of appeal to the United Nations. As reported in the previous issue of the *Chronicle*, a number of organizations in Kharkov held meetings in June to condemn those who had signed the letter in Grigorenko's defence. One such meeting was held in the Kharkov branch of the testing and repair administration *Orgenergoavtomatika*, where Altunyan worked. It was the only one of these meetings at which the 'accused' was allowed to speak. Altunyan first of all explained that the letter in Grigorenko's defence had not been sent to the United Nations, as spokesmen from the party organization and the party district committee claimed. He gave an account of the contents of both letters, and talked about the Crimean Tatar movement, about Grigorenko and Kosterin, the political trials, the facts of the rebirth of Stalinism, about Yakir, Yakhimovich and Gabai, and the events in Czechoslovakia. The meeting passed a resolution condemning Altunyan for his 'apolitical behaviour, as expressed in the appeal to the United Nations', and decided to inform the Procuracy about the appeal letter.

Altunyan appealed successively to all higher authorities in his efforts to be reinstated in the party. On July 1st his appeal was considered by the Party Control Commission of the Central Committee of the Party. The Commission rejected the appeal. Genrikh Altunyan has compiled a complete record both of his preliminary interview with an official of the Commission, N. P. Mardasov, and of the Commission's discussion of his appeal under the chairmanship of [S.O.] Postovalov.[28] The record shows just how strong are the anti-democratic, neo-Stalinist tendencies of the officials in even such a high party organ as this, and just how reluctant they are to listen to any arguments which conflict with official propaganda.

After his arrest Altunyan was put into the criminal prison on Kholodnaya Hill in Kharkov. A few days later he was taken from there to an unknown destination, and his wife was not informed of his address. At the present time he is back again in Kharkov, in a K.G.B. investigation cell.

On the day of his arrest, searches were made at the homes of several of his friends, and once more *samizdat* material was taken away. Ten Kharkov citizens have written an appeal to the U.S.S.R. Procurator-General in Altunyan's defence.[29]

The investigation of Altunyan's case is being directed by Major N. E. Babusenko, head of the investigation department of the Kharkov K.G.B. The witnesses are being questioned solely about Altunyan's part in the composition and distribution of two documents: the Action Group's letter and the letter in Grigorenko's defence.

11   THE TRIAL OF GENRIKH ALTUNYAN

On November 26th the trial of Genrikh Altunyan was held in Kharkov [...] After the pre-trial investigation the charge under article 62 was replaced by one under article 187-1 of the Ukrainian Criminal Code (equivalent to article 190-1 of the Russian Code), covering the manufacture and circulation of documents which contain deliberate fabrications and discredit the Soviet political and social system.

Fifteen witnesses were questioned at the trial, including eight witnesses for the defence. The court was shown manuscripts, letters and rough notebooks confiscated from Altunyan during a search. The trial was open, but the courtroom, as is always the case at such trials, was filled before the start of the hearing with a specially chosen audience.

Trukhin was the Procurator, Klyuchko the Judge and Ariya the defence lawyer.

The following were cited as evidence incriminating Altunyan:

1. a conversation with one of the witnesses for the prosecution in which Altunyan condemned the invasion of Czechoslovakia by troops from the Warsaw Pact countries, and welcomed the Red Square demonstration of August 25th, 1968. He also said that the state practised anti-semitism in our country;

2. the unfinished rough draft of a letter from Altunyan to the Moscow conference of communist parties, in which he protested against the dismissal from their jobs of people who had signed the letter to the United Nations. As Altunyan explained at the trial, he had given up the idea of writing this letter after he had checked the facts. The Procurator referred in his prosecution speech to the fact that information from Altunyan's draft letter had been published in foreign newspapers, thereby implying that Altunyan had given this information to the Western press;

3. preparing the final page of the transcript of an address [on the crisis in the Soviet economy] given by Academician Aganbegyan to employees of the Mysl[30] publishing-house (written in Altunyan's handwriting). At the pre-trial investigation Aganbegyan, who had been called as a witness, had stated that he had never said anything of the sort, and that the document certainly constituted a libel against the Soviet political and social system. Aganbegyan did not appear in court, although he had been summoned as a witness for the prosecution. After deliberating without retiring, the court resolved that the trial could continue in his absence. Under questioning Altunyan explained that he had lost the last page of the transcript and had attempted to reconstruct it from memory;

4. composing and signing a letter in defence of P. G. Grigorenko;

5. signing the letter to the U.N.[...];

6. signing a letter to the conference of communist and workers' parties in Moscow in June 1969.[31]

The Procurator's prosecuting speech enumerated all the charges as falling under article 70, even going as far as to state that Altunyan had committed particularly dangerous crimes against the state (regardless of the fact that Altunyan had actually been charged under article 190–1 and not under article 70). Procurator Trukhin demanded that the accused be imprisoned for three years.

In his speech, the defence lawyer, Ariya, did not contest points 4, 5 and 6 of the indictment, but maintained that the documents were not deliberately false, since the defendant, Altunyan, genuinely believed the statements in them to be true. He rejected the first three charges as unfounded. Concluding his speech, he appealed to the court to punish the defendant, Altunyan, in some way not entailing imprisonment.

Altunyan pleaded not guilty. In his final plea he declared that he always had fought and always would fight against manifestations of Stalinism in our country.

In sentencing Altunyan to three years in an ordinary-régime camp, the court based its judgment on the fact that Altunyan, a man with a higher education, could not fail to appreciate the libellous nature of the incriminating documents, especially as he had been warned repeatedly by state and party organs about his illegal activities, as expressed in the composing and signing of the documents cited by the prosecution. The sentence repeated in full the indictment.

The court made a separate resolution concerning all the defence witnesses who, like Altunyan, had signed the letter in defence of Grigorenko and the appeal to the U.N.: Nedobora, Karasik, Ponomaryov, Levin, Lifshits, Kalinovsky, Podolsky and Kornilov. Their cases were assigned for separate legal treatment. At the same time Irkha, a prosecution witness and party worker at the military academy where Altunyan taught, actually stated in court that it was not yet certain whether the rehabilitation of Army Commander I. Yakir had been justified.

On December 23rd, in Kiev, the appeal hearing took place in

the case of Genrikh Altunyan. His friends were not allowed into the courtroom, and were told that the hearing would be held *in camera*. The third charge was struck from the sentence, together with the words 'Altunyan committed particularly dangerous crimes'. The term of imprisonment was left unchanged.

This was not the end of the troubles of the men of Kharkov. First:

In Kharkov Arkady Levin, born in 1933, and Vladimir 11 Ponomaryov, an engineer, were arrested on December 2nd and 6th respectively. They had signed a letter on the occasion of the arrest of Pyotr Grigorenko, as well as the first and third appeals to the United Nations Human Rights Commission.

These arrests were evidently made in accordance with the decision taken at the trial of Genrikh Altunyan in respect of individual witnesses.

And second:

In Kharkov on November 27th, the day after the trial of Gen- 11 rikh Altunyan, Gritsenko, the investigator from the Kharkov Procuracy who was in charge of the Altunyan case, made a search at the flat of Nedobora, but nothing was confiscated. Gritsenko behaved extremely rudely, shouting and uttering threats, as indeed Nedobora's wife noted in the record of the search. At the time of the search, Leonid Plyushch (from Kiev) and Irina Yakir (from Moscow) were at Nedobora's flat. They were detained and taken to the police station where, in the course of a search of their persons, transcripts of the trial of Genrikh Altunyan were confiscated. The police interrogation continued until three o'clock in the morning. A warrant for the detention of Nedobora was served; he was released three days later.

Soon, however, Nedobora was rearrested and in two trials in March and April 1970 he, Ponomaryov and Levin — all aged thirty-seven — were sentenced to three years each in ordinary-régime camps. All behaved with courage and defiance in court.[32]

We have now discussed the Kharkov supporters of the Action Group. But what of the other supporters? Who are they? What has been their fate?

Among those whom we have met earlier are the Gabais, Alexander Esenin-Volpin, Yuly Kim, Alexander Daniel, Zinaida and Andrei Grigorenko, Mrs Lyudmila Ginzburg, and the Crimean Tatars Zampira Asanova and Reshat Dzhemilev. Supporters to be met later include Julius Telesin, Irina Belogorodskaya and the Ukrainian Vyacheslav Chornovil.

Finally come people who appear little if at all in this book, like the poet Julia Vishnevskaya, the artist Yury Titov, and Pyotr Yakir's wife, Valentina Savenkova (see plate 17).[33]

Reprisals against the Action Group's supporters have run the whole gamut from mere threats to internment in a prison mental hospital. The latter was the fate of one of the two men discussed below, Vladimir Gershuni. But the engineer Boris Efimov has so far suffered only severe harassment. First No. 2 wrote of him: 'An editor and signatory to the letters of the 116 and the 170, he was dismissed "because of redundancy" but has since been reinstated.' And then came these two items:

7 On March 21st a search connected with the case of Kuznetsov [see pp. 240–42] was carried out at his friend Boris Efimov's flat. The following were confiscated: sixteen copies of Efimov's draft for a new constitution of the U.S.S.R.; a letter with eighty-six signatures, sent to the Supreme Soviet with the demand that the pacts on human rights and the Declaration of the Rights of Man be ratified more quickly; a statement signed by eight people concerning the establishment of a Society for the Defence of the Pacts on Human Rights and the Declaration of the Rights of Man; V. Turchin's work 'The Inertia of Fear' [see p. 473] and a whole trunk of papers whose description was not recorded.

9 Boris Efimov is a senior engineer in the Information Department of the Experimental Construction Bureau for power and technological processes in the chemicals industry. The Director of the Bureau, E. I. Shipov, asked Efimov to apply to be dismissed 'at his own request', and did not hide the fact that he was acting on the instructions of the K.G.B. 'We cannot keep you here as an employee, because of your political unreliability: after all, we have a duplicating machine in the next room,' he said, referring to an ERA machine. Efimov was threatened with dismissal

'because of personnel cuts' if he refused to leave 'at his own request'.

THE ARREST OF VLADIMIR GERSHUNI 11

Vladimir Lvovich Gershuni [see plate 43], born in 1930, is a nephew of the founder of the Socialist-Revolutionary Party,[34] G. A. Gershuni. In 1949 Vladimir Gershuni was arrested and sentenced by decision of the Special Conference [i.e. in effect by the security police] to ten years in special camps for his part in an anti-Stalin youth group. The 1949 case was conducted by M.G.B.[35] investigator Nikolsky, who is now a pensioner. Vladimir Gershuni was tortured during the investigation. He was in the same camp which Solzhenitsyn describes in his story *One Day in the Life of Ivan Denisovich*, at the same time as the author.

Gershuni is a man with an unusually highly developed instinct for justice. For him, the struggle against lies and violence is not a part of life, but the whole of it. He cannot reconcile himself with any manifestations of Stalinism. Gershuni signed, amongst other documents exposing injustice, the appeal to the United Nations Commission on Human Rights.

On October 17th Vladimir Gershuni, a bricklayer [...] was arrested in Moscow. 10

Three weeks before his arrest Gershuni was detained in the 11 underground. During a search supervised by men in plain clothes at the underground station's police office, Gershuni had removed from him some *samizdat*, including a letter from V. I. Lenin to members of the Politbureau dated February 1st, 1922 [see pp. 319–21], and the manuscript of a satirical story *Dyadya* [*Uncle*].[36]

The day after Gershuni's arrest, on October 18th, 1969, a search was carried out in his flat. The record of the search shows two items: 1. *Samizdat* material in manuscript and typescript 2. P. G. Grigorenko: Collection of materials *In Memory of Kosterin*,[37] text in typescript. On October 21st a second search was made of Gershuni's flat. On the same day searches were also made at the Moscow flats of Natalya Gorbanevskaya, Tatyana Khodorovich, and Anatoly Yakobson. It is very possible that these were connected with Gershuni's case [see p. 155].

The investigation of Gershuni's case is being headed by investigator N. V. Gnevkovskaya of the Moscow Procuracy. A charge has been brought under article 190–1 of the Russian Criminal Code.

10 Gnevkovskaya was one of the team of investigators who worked on the case of the Pushkin Square demonstration of January 22nd, 1967. Gershuni's relatives were told by Gnevkovskaya that he had been pasting up leaflets in the Bauman District of Moscow on the night of October 17th–18th, but another of his relatives was told that he had been drunk, and was guilty of rowdy behaviour on the street, stopping passing cars, and so had been detained: in his pockets 'there turned out to be provocative literature'.

11 After his arrest Gershuni was put in Butyrka prison, and a week later transferred to the Serbsky Institute for psychiatric examination and diagnosis. He was declared of unsound mind. Gershuni is now in Butyrka prison. The investigation is expected to be completed in January or February 1970.

On March 13th, 1970, Gershuni was sentenced — in his absence — by the Moscow City Court to indefinite detention in a prison psychiatric hospital.[38] *At the end of the year, after a hunger-strike, he was sent to a newly instituted prison hospital in Oryol [see plate 41,] an old Russian city almost half-way to Kiev on the road from Moscow.*

Finally, in December 1970 the Chonicle *showed its concern for the Action Group's families. It printed the names, addresses and birthdays of the children of these imprisoned members and supporters: Gorbanevskaya, Krasin, Altunyan, Nedobora and Ponomaryov. Among other family addresses given were those of Gabai, Ronkin, Litvinov and Burmistrovich.*[39]

8. THE CASE OF THE
BALTIC FLEET OFFICERS

The time has come for the party to look people in the eye and revise its ways. If, however, all our methods of struggle give no positive result, then time will present the task of creating a new party, which, after a prolonged ideological struggle, will lead a socialist society to the triumph of Reason, Justice and Humanism, and enable Intellectual Freedom to flourish in our country ... RUSSIA IS WAITING FOR NEW PEOPLE.

Gennady Gavrilov, September 1968[1]

Without doubt this chapter contains some of the most dramatic material in the Chronicle. *The material is also of the greatest importance for gaining a clear view of some of the Democratic Movement's more radical components. But, tantalizingly, there is not yet enough of it. While it conjures up vivid images, their edges are blurred and they have yet to come fully into focus.*

One thing, however, is clear: Grigorenko and Altunyan are not isolated cases of military involvement in the Democratic Movement. Baltic Fleet officers, linked with civilians and apparently operating mainly from Tallinn, the capital of Estonia, have injected a vigorous strain of their own constructive thought into the movement. Whether this will lead eventually to a top-level military involvement in politics, possibly one day a take-over, is too early to say. Such traditions are weak in Russia: the Decembrist officers were an exception in 1825. Nevertheless, the general phenomenon of army take-overs has spread through so much of the world in the last two decades that the eventual infection of the Soviet military can by no means be ruled out. Who knows, indeed, whether Lieutenant Ilin, who apparently tried to assassinate the top party leaders in January 1969, represented only himself? Or did he come, as rumour had it, from some army group prepared—unlike the naval officers—to use terrorism in the tradition of the People's Will, the group which killed Alexander II in 1881?

The first indication that things were brewing in Tallinn came when two documents reached the West at the end of 1968. The first[2] concerned the well-known essay by Academician Sakharov (see pp. 354–5), which he had circulated in final form in the summer. It was signed 'Numerous representatives of the technical intelligentsia of Estonia', a

171

formula which left open the possibility—a likely one—that both Estonians and non-Estonians, both civilians and military people, were involved. The Chronicle *reported:*

5 Sakharov's study has evoked a response from representatives of the technical intelligentsia of Estonia. In an article entitled 'To Hope or to Act?' they maintain that Sakharov 'puts too much faith in scientific and technical means, in economic measures, in the goodwill of those who control society, and in people's common sense', and that 'the root causes he sees and the remedies he advocates are external, material ones, while the inner, spiritual, political and organic ones are ignored'. The article says that what we need most of all is a moral revival of society, since, 'having destroyed Christian values, the materialist ideology has not created new ones'. This has given rise to a society in which solidarity is an external, mechanical thing, and one which is actually based on socially alienated individuals who are fearful of their neighbours and feel insignificant and lonely before the state machine. New moral values are essential. The authors of the article demand not only intellectual freedom, but also political freedom, real democracy and a renunciation of the doctrine of militant, aggressive communism in foreign policy. The authors of the article conclude that the 'leading minds of our society' should apply themselves to working out new social, political and economic ideals.

This was a call for a political programme. The document had, moreover, put forward ideas somewhat more radical than the Chronicle's *summary would suggest. Written soon after the Czechoslovak occupation, it warned: 'For twelve years already, since the 20th party congress, we have waited and asked our leadership for liberating reforms. We are prepared to ask and wait for a certain time longer. But eventually we will demand and act! And then tank divisions will have to be sent not into Prague and Bratislava, but rather into Moscow and Leningrad!'*

As for foreign policy, 'was it not our country which "joined" to itself, in the period 1939–49, 700,000 square kilometres of territory ... ? We must give up the senseless accumulation of territory, the expansion of our great-power might, and our aggressive policies ... Since not just half but the greater part of the responsibility for the tension in the world lies with us, it is we who must make the first and biggest moves towards reconciliation.'

The second document—an 'Open Letter to the Citizens of the Soviet Union' dated September 1968 and signed 'Gennady Alekseyev, communist'—made various similar points from a more Marxist position, and provides the epigraph to this chapter.

Then, in October 1969, the Chronicle *reported the appearance in* samizdat *of the 'Programme of the Democrats of Russia, the Ukraine and the Baltic Lands':*[3]

This document gives an exhaustive analysis of the world 10 revolutionary movement, the world national liberation movement, and the ideological state of the world. The positive programme set out in this document is extremely interesting.

Now written on this document is a second title: 'Programme of the Democratic Movement of the Soviet Union'. Maybe, therefore, in order to distance itself from this programme, and perhaps also to discourage particular groups from writing in the name of the movement as a whole, the Chronicle *quickly added this note:*

The tenth issue of the *Chronicle* gave a brief account of the 11 'Programme [of the Democrats of Russia, the Ukraine and the Baltic Lands]'. This account must be considered unsatisfactory. The analysis of the contemporary international situation and the socio-political picture of the world presented in the programme cannot of course be considered 'exhaustive', as the tenth issue of the *Chronicle* rashly stated. The words 'exhaustive analysis' smack of dogmatism. The problems of the modern world are *inexhaustible* in their variety and complexity, and they certainly cannot be exhausted by any one programme. The programme expresses the views only of a certain group of people.

Most likely, we may conclude, this perhaps small group wanted to circulate its programme under a rather presumptuous title precisely in order to stimulate debate and find out how acceptable it was to wider circles.

But which people made up this anonymous group, the only effectively underground one linked with the Democratic Movement? It seems likely that they were connected, either directly or indirectly, with the authors of the two earlier documents. For the programme — a long, 20,000-word work — develops in detail, often using similar terminology, the ideas of those documents. The mention of 'the Baltic lands' is also suggestive. It was, in any case, the asked-for programme.

The latter is, unfortunately, too long to analyse here. But let us just note a few points: first, its militancy. One example of this is its epigraph, an unusual quotation from Alexander Herzen. It reads: 'Socialism will give rise in all its phases to extreme consequences, to stupidities. Then once again a cry of renunciation will burst forth from the titanic breast of the revolutionary minority, and once again a deadly struggle will begin, in which socialism will occupy the place of today's conservatism and will be conquered by an advancing revolution of which we do not know.'[4] Secondly we should note the Programme's tendency to praise Western democracy, sometimes to the point of idealization. The authors — it appears to be the joint work of people who have specially researched different parts of it — come out clearly for a mixed economy not all that different in nature from the capitalist economies of Western Europe. This marks them off from almost all the other tendencies in the Democratic Movement, which, in the rare cases when they discuss economics in depth, usually prefer various forms of market socialism. What also mark the group off are its evident exaggeration of the Movement's strength and its advocacy of underground as well as legal methods of struggle. In reviewing its two substantial documents of 1970 the Chronicle criticized it severely on these points, waiving its usual ban on value judgments.[5]

Now, while bearing in mind that the Programme's authors quite possibly had no direct links with the Baltic Fleet officers arrested in 1969, we can pass to the Chronicle's coverage of their case. Despite the apparent inaccuracy of this coverage in one or two places, it is all presented here in the original sequence:

8 According to unconfirmed rumours, a number of officers of the Baltic Fleet have been arrested in Tallinn, Leningrad and Kaliningrad. Rumours suggest that the arrests were made in connection with the distribution of a letter by Alekseyev, addressed to the citizens of the Soviet Union, about the invasion of Czechoslovakia.

The report that the arrests of officers of the Baltic Fleet were 9
connected with the letter by Alekseyev has been confirmed. The
letter was a protest against the sending of troops into Czechoslovakia. According to information received, thirty-one people
have been arrested in Estonia, not all of them officers. For
example, in Tallinn an engineer, Sergei Soldatov, was arrested.*
About a quarter of those arrested are Estonians. Although
rumours, possibly spread by official circles, say that those
arrested are members of a nationalist movement, materials
circulating at present in Russian and Estonian *samizdat* are
convincing proof that the opinions of the arrested people are
generally democratic and anti-Stalinist, and that their demand
for equal national rights is a logical part of their general
system of thought. One of the arrested is a coastguard officer of
the Baltic Fleet, Alekseyev.

ARRESTS OF OFFICERS OF THE BALTIC FLEET   10

Following inexact and partially contradictory reports of
arrests of Baltic Fleet officers, the *Chronicle* is now publishing
accurate information.

In May 1969 the naval officers Gavrilov, Kosyrev and
Paramonov were arrested in Paldiski, a town near Tallinn, and
in Kaliningrad [on the Baltic coast near Poland]. They are
accused of founding a 'Union to Struggle for Political Rights',
the aim of which was the realization in the U.S.S.R. of the
democratic rights and freedoms guaranteed by the Universal
Declaration of Human Rights. It is reported that during
searches K.G.B. officials found a printing press intended for the
publication of uncensored literature.

The investigation is being conducted by the K.G.B. organs of
the Baltic Fleet. The investigators—Captain Bodunov, Major
Drach and Colonel Denisenko—are officials of the K.G.B. and
the Baltic Fleet Military Procuracy. The Procurator supervising the investigation is Kolesnikov.

The K.G.B. investigation organs are attributing the leading
role and the 'Open Letter to the Citizens of the Soviet Union',
signed by G. Alekseyev, a pseudonym, to Gavrilov. As far as

---

* Modification in No. 10: 'It turns out that Soldatov has been forcibly interned
in a psychiatric hospital.'

can be ascertained, Gavrilov is holding firmly to his principles during investigation. Thanks to the testimony of Kosyrev, the K.G.B. have evidently reached the conclusion that the arrested men have connections with Leningrad, Moscow, Tallinn, Riga, Baku, Perm and Khabarovsk. It appears that Paramonov too is giving the investigators helpful testimony. The investigators are intent on discovering whether the arrested men had any connection with Ilya Gabai, who was arrested in Moscow in May 1969, and also with those citizens who have signed protests against violations of human rights in the U.S.S.R. The arrested officers are at present in the K.G.B. prison in Tallinn.

The unique documents in the next item presumably reached the Chronicle *through either a leak or a blunder in the K.G.B.:*

11 THE INVESTIGATION INTO THE CASE OF NAVAL OFFICER G. V. GAVRILOV AND OTHERS CONTINUES

On June 20th, 1969, a K.G.B. detective squad searched the flat of S. I. Soldatov in Tallinn. The search warrant, signed by Captain Bodunov, a senior investigator, indicated that citizen Olga Bondarenko had testified that Soldatov had been meeting a stranger in her flat. Confiscated during the search were personal correspondence with the Soviet writer V. M. Pomerantsev,[6] the Declaration of Human Rights, poems called 'Dream of Freedom' and 'On the Death of Kennedy', extracts copied from the *Confessions* of J. Rousseau, and a *samizdat* philosophical manuscript, *Man and the World*.

FIRST INTERROGATION: June 24th, 1969. In the Estonian K.G.B. headquarters, Pagari Street 2 [Tallinn], senior investigator A. Nikitin.

INVESTIGATOR. We should like to question you ... *for the moment* as a witness.

SOLDATOV. In connection with which case am I being questioned?

INVESTIGATOR. You are being questioned in connection with the case of Gennady Vladimirovich Gavrilov and a group of Baltic Fleet officers charged with anti-Soviet activities. Are you often in Moscow?

SOLDATOV. That is irrelevant to the case under investigation.

INVESTIGATOR. Are you acquainted with Yakir?

SOLDATOV. I wish to state that I am not prepared to give you any information about my acquaintances or my spiritual life.
(There follows a lengthy explanation about how refusal to testify can be a criminal offence.)

SOLDATOV. If you have any material evidence against me, lock me up without my collaboration.

INVESTIGATOR. We have a lot of evidence against you, you have had connections with these officers. We know that for certain.

SOLDATOV. Then draw up an indictment on the basis of that evidence.
(Soldatov is taken into another office.)

COLONEL BARKOV. You aren't an enemy of Soviet power?

SOLDATOV. I am an enemy of lawlessness.

BARKOV. Then why don't you assist the investigation, and confirm what is obvious? We know for sure that the accused Gavrilov got your address from Yakir and has been meeting you. Your obstinate refusal only increases our suspicions. Evidently you have some anti-Soviet peccadilloes on your conscience and feel uncomfortable ...

SOLDATOV. I've already said 'Lock me up without my help.'

BARKOV. We once interrogated and released a young man who had written an anti-Soviet poem. Later he started asking us to lock him up, if only for a year. Your vanity evidently makes you, too, aspire to appear a martyr.

SOLDATOV. I simply want to live my life as an honest man.

BARKOV. Then how are we to understand your attitude to Soviet law?

SOLDATOV. Those laws are themselves imperfect and frequently conflict with human rights.

BARKOV. But Solon said: 'If laws are imperfect, then let the lawgiver's error be forgiven.' Think what sort of position you will put the worthy Captain Bondarenko in. After all, his daughter confirms that you have met the officers in her flat.

SOLDATOV. That's a matter for her conscience. I know what I myself am talking about.

BARKOV. Think of the fate of these young officers. One of them is already completely beyond your help, but you could ease the position of another of them ...

SOLDATOV. I can't ease anyone's fate by going against my conscience.

BARKOV. Now that's simply cruel. How can you talk about human rights and struggle for them after saying that ...

SOLDATOV. Well, then. I will confirm just the evidence of Bondarenko's daughter and the officers—if that will save someone.

(Soldatov confirms that he had met someone; he cannot remember the time, place, appearance or names; the conversation was on general topics and he had noticed nothing illegal.)

BARKOV. Why didn't you invite this person to your home?

SOLDATOV. My wife doesn't like having strangers in.

BARKOV. Did they give you any documents? Did they discuss with you the foundation of a 'Union of Fighters for Political Freedom' and the publication of a newspaper called the *Democrat*? Did you promise to get hold of type-metal? Do you know a document called 'To hope or to act?'?

(Soldatov answers each question in the negative.)

BARKOV. What is your political credo?

SOLDATOV. The government is obliged to listen to the opinions of dissenters, of the democratic intelligentsia, and to implement democratic freedoms, which it is not doing.

(Signs record of interrogation.)

BARKOV. Whether you like it or not, the question of your relations with Yakir will inevitably be brought into the open.

SOLDATOV. That won't change my position.

BARKOV. You're evidently dissatisfied with our policy in Czechoslovakia?

SOLDATOV. I'm not thrilled to bits by it.

BARKOV. You'd like West Germany to send its troops there?

SOLDATOV. I would prefer not to have this sort of argument in a K.G.B. office. Goodbye.

SECOND INTERROGATION: June 28th, 1969. In the Estonian K.G.B. headquarters, senior investigator A. Nikitin.

NIKITIN. What can you say about the letter to the party Central Committee signed by you and your comrades at the Leningrad Polytechnic Institute?

SOLDATOV. Only that the answer we got to it didn't satisfy us.

NIKITIN. Where did you get the exercise-book containing political notes?

SOLDATOV. I found it in a lecture-hall and kept it.

NIKITIN. Where did you get the *samizdat* philosophical manuscript?

SOLDATOV. I don't remember.

NIKITIN. Where did you get the poems 'Dread of Freedom' and 'On the Death of Kennedy'?

SOLDATOV. I refuse to answer.

NIKITIN. How did your correspondence with the writer Pomerantsev begin? Is he your friend?

SOLDATOV. Just an acquaintance. It was on my initiative. I have no other information to give. I protest against the illegal confiscation from me of materials not relevant to the case, including the Declaration of Human Rights.

NIKITIN. Address your protest to the Special Department of the Baltic Fleet.[7] It's their instructions we're carrying out.

SOLDATOV. I am a civilian. My documents are irrelevant to the case of these officers.

NIKITIN. We decide whether they are relevant or not.

SOLDATOV. That's where the arbitrariness starts. Article 140 of the Russian Code of Criminal Procedure has been violated.

NIKITIN. But that sort of thing happened in the past. Things are different now.

SOLDATOV. What about the arrest of people for their beliefs, the confinement of healthy people in psychiatric hospitals?

NIKITIN. That question is decided by medical experts, not by us. We even help ex-political prisoners to find work.

SOLDATOV. Your charitable activities stare us in the face.

NIKITIN. We sent a couple of b——s to prison, and you're up in arms, kicking up a fuss for all the world to hear. What about the country's prestige? (A reference to Daniel and Sinyavsky.)

SOLDATOV. It's a question not of the nation but of principle. It's a matter of freedom of speech and artistic expression. Besides, one person who fights boldly for freedom is worth more than a million cowardly nonentities.

NIKITIN. Well that's as may be. It's all very abstract. But I still hope that you'll change your negative attitude to the K.G.B.

SOLDATOV. Even if you managed to convince me that you are

observing legality at the moment, who will give a guarantee
for the future?

NIKITIN. Of course, if the international situation becomes
tenser, we will take steps against those who have been
shooting at us (??).[8]

(SOLDATOV signs an order forbidding him to leave Tallinn.)

THIRD INTERROGATION: September 3rd, 1969. In the
Special Department of the K.G.B. for the Baltic Fleet,
Toompea Street 8, senior investigator Captain Bodunov.

BODUNOV. We are not satisfied with your evidence to the
Estonian K.G.B. I hope you've seen sense.

(The records of the interrogation of the accused A. V.
Kosyrev are now quoted: 'I asked him (Soldatov) to assist
in the establishment of a "Union of Fighters for Political
Freedom" and in the publication of a paper, the *Democrat*,
to which he very willingly agreed ... He also agreed to get
hold of type-metal ... His telephone number was obtained
from Yakir ... ')

BODUNOV. What have you to say about that?

SOLDATOV. I can't remember any such conversation. We
talked about general subjects.

BODUNOV. Have you known Yakir long?

SOLDATOV. Why are you so persistently interested in Yakir?
As far as I know, he is a universally respected citizen who in
legal ways defends human rights.

BODUNOV. But his personal friend I. Gabai has been arrested.
I had a word with the investigator who interrogated him.*
So he's not involved only in legal affairs.

SOLDATOV. I have nothing to say on that score. It's not clear
why Kosyrev needed to meet me.

BODUNOV. He saw in you a fighter.

SOLDATOV. I hadn't deserved that.

BODUNOV. Right, wait in the next room.

(There follows a confrontation and an identification procedure, in the course of which Kosyrev identifies Soldatov
and confirms his evidence about their conversation.)

BODUNOV (to Soldatov). What have you to say to that?

* The investigation of Gabai's case was carried out by senior investigator
B. I. Berezovsky of the Uzbek Procuracy [*Chronicle*'s note— pp. 136–40]

SOLDATOV. I consider the base and cowardly conduct of Kosyrev unworthy of an officer.

BODUNOV (slapping his hand on the table). I will not stand for any insinuations. You're sitting on a powder-keg which may explode at any moment.

SOLDATOV (to Kosyrev). There exists the K.G.B.'s court, and also the court of your comrades and of history. To *that* court you will have to answer your whole life long.

BODUNOV. There's no 'K.G.B. court', only the Soviet People's Court.

SOLDATOV. There's also the court of conscience. It is important to remain honest in all circumstances.

BODUNOV. You and your honest conduct won't be strolling around freely much longer.

SOLDATOV. Experience shows that honest people have frequently lost their freedom and become political prisoners. Then they have been rehabilitated. I'd rather be rehabilitated than a swine and free ... I request the opportunity to speak at the trial.

BODUNOV. Why?

SOLDATOV. In order to express my opinion about this case.

BODUNOV. In whose name? Who has authorized you? A Komsomol or trade union organization?

SOLDATOV. In the name of the democratic intelligentsia.

FOURTH INTERROGATION: In the Special Department of the Baltic Fleet. September 4th, 1969. Senior investigator Bodunov. (Confrontation with G. V. Gavrilov, the chief accused. Gavrilov does not recognize Soldatov.)

SOLDATOV. I demand to be allowed to take part in the coming trial.

BODUNOV. There is nothing for you to do there. You aren't helping in the search for the truth.

SOLDATOV (to Gavrilov). My name is ... (gives his names). Remember that I shall always be glad to meet you. How can I help?

GAVRILOV. Perhaps we *will* meet. There's nothing I need.

FIFTH INTERROGATION: September 23rd, 1969. (Soldatov has been summoned to the Special Department of the Baltic

Fleet, where he is awaited by K.G.B. Major Tikhonov and three men in white coats, headed by military doctor Petrenko. They turn out to be doctors from the Republic Psychiatric Hospital. The examination proceeds as follows:

'Were your parents ever sick?' — 'No.'

'Are you an only child?' — 'Yes.'

'Did you start school at the normal age?' — 'Yes.'

'What were you keen on at school?' — 'Mathematics and sport.'

'Did you aspire to be a leader?' — 'No.'

'Why did you leave secondary school at the age of eighteen instead of nineteen?' — 'The war.'

'Why did you choose mechanical engineering?' — 'I liked it.'

'Did you do well in your examinations?' — 'Yes.'

'How did you choose your friends?' — 'For their honesty and intelligence.'

'Why did you move to a different factory?' — 'I changed my line.'

'Don't your work-mates envy you?' — 'No.'

'What are your relations with your work-group?' — 'Perfectly correct.'

'Ah, only "correct". Why not warm?' — 'One can't make friends to order.'

'Don't you think you could make a technical breakthrough?' — 'No.'

'Are your parents hard-hearted towards you?' — 'No.'

'What made you marry your wife?' — 'I liked her.'

'Have you ever had experience of unrequited love?' — 'Yes.'

'Do you confide your views to your wife?' — 'She judges me by what I do.'

'Is your wife content with you?' — 'Ask her. Pick your questions more carefully.'

'Do you feel that life is hard and people are hard on you?' — 'No.'

'Do you believe in the supernatural? In the hereafter?' — 'Those are controversial questions.'

'Your favourite authors are ... ?' — 'Zweig, Dickens, Tolstoy.'

'Have you ever been to church?' — 'I have.'

'When did you become interested in religious and moral problems?' — 'When I learned to think.'

'Why are you interested in them?' — 'Not everything in life is as it should be.'

'Why do you like Tolstoy?' — 'He explores problems of human existence.'

'Your attitude to military service?' — 'I haven't yet adopted a definite attitude to it, because it's peacetime.'

'What do you think of *Man and the World*, the manuscript found at your flat?' — 'There's a lot I can't understand.'

'Where did you get it from?' — 'From acquaintances.'

'What is your attitude to the sending of troops into Czechoslovakia?' — 'Negative.'

'How should the question be settled?' — 'Peacefully.'

'You wouldn't like to head a delegation at negotiations?' — 'I'm not qualified in politics.'

'What do you think of Soviet policy?' — 'To make an analysis you need information from both sides. I haven't got that.'

'Don't you consider yourself able to change the Soviet political system?' — 'History is made by the masses.'

'Why have we gathered here for this conversation?' — 'The K.G.B. is worried about my health.'

'Why is the K.G.B. interested in you?' — 'Because of my inconvenient views and undesirable acquaintanceships.'

'Don't summonses to the K.G.B. embitter you?' — 'I've got used to them.'

'Does the present situation embitter you?' — 'At the moment I feel ashamed for the medical profession.'

'Have you ever had bumps on your head?' — 'Yes, lots.'

'Why do you have that ironic smile all the time?' — 'I'm enjoying this solemn ritual. It reveals your powerlessness.'

In early 1970 Soldatov was, despite his attempted self-defence through the courts, dismissed from his job,[9] and two unnamed officers were arrested in Poland in connection with the Gavrilov case.[10] In June Gavrilov, aged thirty-one, was sentenced by a Leningrad military tribunal to six years in strict-régime camps, and Aleksei Vasilevich Kosyrev, twenty-eight, to two years. Georgy Konstantinovich Paramonov was consigned to the Chernyakhovsk prison hospital. The charges, under articles 70 and 72, concerned the formation by these naval engineer officers of a 'Union to Struggle for Political Rights'.[11]

Part III · The Movement in Captivity

9. THE CASE OF ANATOLY MARCHENKO

> I am certain that not one decent person will remain indifferent to the fate of Marchenko. If you have not yet read it, read his book *My Testimony*, read his open letters—it's all in *samizdat*. Read, and you will see for yourself that Anatoly Marchenko is not a rogue, not an adventurer, but a gifted, original writer and publicist, an uncompromising and courageous man. Courageous for the sake of all of us, of each one of us.
>
> Larissa Bogoraz (Daniel), August 1968[1]

A LETTER BY ANATOLY MARCHENKO
PORTER, EX-POLITICAL PRISONER, AUTHOR OF
My Testimony

April 17th, 1968

g. Aleksandrov,
Vladimirskaya obl.
ul. Novinskaya 27.

To:
the Chairman of the Red Cross Society, G. A. Mitiryov;
the Minister of Health of the U.S.S.R., B. V. Petrovsky;
the Director of the Food Institute at the Academy of Medical Sciences, A. A. Pokrovsky;
the Patriarch of All Russia, Aleksi;
the President of the Academy of Sciences, M. V. Keldysh;
the President of the Academy of Medical Sciences, V. D. Timakov;
the Director of the Institute of State and Law, Chkhikvadze;
the Rector of Moscow State University, I. G. Petrovsky;
the Chairman of the Board of the Journalists' Union, Zimyanin;
the Chairman of the Board of the U.S.S.R. Writers' Union, K. Fedin;
the writers K. Simonov, R. Gamzatov, R. Rozhdestvensky, E. Evtushenko.
(Copies to the U.N. Human Rights Commission and to the International Human Rights Conference of the U.N.O.[2])

Five months ago I completed a book, *My Testimony*,[3] about the six years (1960–6) which I spent in Vladimir prison and in camps for political prisoners. In the introduction I write that:

> contemporary Soviet camps for political prisoners are as horrible as were Stalin's. In some respects they are better, in some respects worse.
>
> Everybody should know about this.
>
> Both those who want to know the truth but instead get false, glossy newspaper articles lulling the reader's conscience.
>
> And those who don't want to know and who shut their eyes and stop their ears, in order to be able to justify themselves later and to show their clean record: 'Good Lord, and we never knew ... ' If they have even a scrap of social conscience and genuine love for their country they will take a stand in its defence, as Russia's true sons have always done.
>
> I should like my testimony on Soviet camps and prisons for political prisoners to become known to humanists and progressive people of other countries — those who raise their voice in defence of political prisoners in Greece and Portugal, in the South African Republic and in Spain. Let them ask their Soviet colleagues in the struggle against anti-humanism: 'What have you done in order that your political prisoners in your own country are at least not "educated" by hunger?'[4]

I have done my best to make my book known to the public. However, there has been no reaction at all so far (except for a conversation about my 'anti-social activities' to which I was invited by a K.G.B. officer). Conditions in the camps remain the same. Thus I have been forced to turn to certain personalities who through their social position are among those most responsible for the state of our society and its level of humanity and legality.

You should know the following:

In the camps and prisons of our country there are thousands of political prisoners. Most of them were sentenced behind closed doors; there have been virtually no really open trials (apart from those of war-criminals); in all cases a fundamental principle of legal procedure—publicity—has been violated. Thus society controlled, and controls, neither the observance of legality nor the extent of political repression.

The situation of the political prisoners is generally the same as that of the criminal convicts, and in some respects it is considerably worse: political prisoners are at best held in strict-régime conditions, while for the criminals there is an ordinary-régime and an even lighter one; criminals may be released after serving two-thirds or half of their time, while the political prisoners have to serve every single day of their sentence.

Thus the political prisoners are treated in all respects like the most dangerous criminals and recidivists. There is no juridical and legal distinction.

The political prisoners are as a rule people who before their arrest were engaged in socially useful labour: engineers, workers, literary men, artists, scientists. In the camp, by way of 're-educational measures', they have to do forced labour, whereby the camp administration uses work as a means of punishment: weakly persons are forced to perform heavy physical labour; intellectuals are compelled to do unskilled physical work. Failure to fulfil the norm is regarded as a violation of the régime and serves as a pretext for various administrative punishments—veto on visitors, punishment cell, solitary confinement.

The most powerful means of influencing the prisoners is hunger. The usual rations are such as to make a person feel perpetual want of food, perpetual malnutrition. The daily camp ration contains 2,400 calories (enough for a seven- to eleven-year-old child), and has to suffice for an adult doing physical work, day after day for many years, sometimes as many as fifteen or twenty-five years! Those calories are supplied mainly by black bread (700 gm. a day). The convicts never even set eyes on fresh vegetables, butter, and many other indispensable products; these products are even prohibited from sale at the camp stall (as also sugar).

Let me state right away: the camp food as well as the camp clothes are paid for by the prisoners themselves from the earnings accredited to them. (Fifty per cent is deducted at once for the upkeep of the camp: barracks, equipment, fences, watchtowers, etc.) Only five roubles* a month—out of the money that remains after all deductions—can be spent on goods (including tobacco) at the stall. But one may be deprived even of this right, to spend seventeen copecks a day, 'for violation of the régime'. For example, the imprisoned historian Rendel (ten years for participation in an illegal Marxist circle)[5] was banned from the stall for two months for bringing supper to sick comrades in the barracks; so was the imprisoned writer Sinyavsky, for exchanging a few words with his friend Daniel when the latter was in the camp prison.

To punish a prisoner for 'violating the camp régime', e.g. for failure to fulfil the work quota, he may be put on the 'severe' food ration—1,300 calories† (enough for an infant of one to three years). This was the case, for example, with the writer Daniel and the engineer Ronkin (seven years for illegal Marxist activity) at the end of the summer of 1967.

Food parcels from relatives are 'not authorized' for prisoners sentenced to the strict régime; only by way of encouragement for good behaviour (that is, repentance, denunciation, collaboration with the administration) do the camp authorities sometimes allow a prisoner to receive a food parcel—but not before he has served half his sentence, not more than four times a year, and not over five kilograms!

Thus the camp administration wields a powerful means of exerting physical pressure on the political prisoners—a whole system of escalation of hunger. The application of this system results in emaciation and avitaminosis.

Some prisoners are driven by permanent malnutrition to kill and eat crows, and, if they are lucky, dogs. In the autumn of

* Slightly over £2 at the official exchange rate.

† In a letter to A. Chakovsky [see note 12] Marchenko breaks down the normal ration as six cupfuls of thin gruel, two cupfuls of soup made with rotten cabbage, and a piece of boiled cod the size of a match-box, all this containing only 20 gm. of fat, plus 700 gm. of black bread and 15 gm. of sugar. The 'severe' ration contains 400 gm. of cabbage soup, two cupfuls of thin gruel, the same size piece of cod and 450 gm. of black bread. We may note here that the Japanese concentration camp at Tha Makham on the River Kwai in Thailand had in 1942–3 a daily ration norm of 700 gm. of rice, 600 of vegetables, 100 of meat, 20 of sugar, 20 of salt and 15 of oil (with similarly few chances of buying extra food), this amounting to about 3,400 calories. Even here, though, vitamin deficiency diseases were very common. See article by Ian Watt in the *Observer*, September 1st, 1968.

1967 one prisoner from camp 11 of Dubrovlag found a way of getting potatoes while he was in the hospital section; he overate and died. (The potatoes were raw.)

Hunger reigns even more harshly in Vladimir prison and in the 'special-régime camps', where there are also numerous political prisoners.

In comparison with the permanent malnutrition, other 'means of influence' look relatively harmless. One must, however, mention a few of them: prohibiting meetings with one's relatives; complete shaving of the head; prohibiting the wearing of one's own clothes (including warm underwear in winter); obstructing creative work and the performance of religious rites.

Prisoners' letters of complaint and petitions, addressed to the Procuracy, the Presidium of the Supreme Soviet of the U.S.S.R., or the Central Committee of the party are returned without fail to the camp administration: the highest organs send them to the Ministry for the Preservation of Public Order [M.O.O.P.] or to the Main Administration of Places of Confinement [G.U.M.Z.], and from there—after a multi-stage journey round the departments—they somehow or other always end up in the hands of those against whom the complaints were directed, 'so that they can be checked'. All complaints naturally end in the same way with the camp administration's answer that 'the assertions have not been confirmed', and that 'the punishment was justified', and the position of the petitioner becomes unbearable. Sometimes he is even transferred to the [camp] prison or to solitary confinement for his latest 'violation of the régime'. Therefore the 'educators-cum-officers' often maliciously say to the dissatisfied prisoner: 'Go on, lodge a complaint against us; go on, write, it's your right.' Others, more simple-minded, warn him: 'Well, why protest? You know yourself the administration can always find a reason to punish any prisoner. You'll only harm yourself; better put up with it ... '

And indeed, 'The Regulations for Camps and Prisons', passed by the Supreme Soviet in 1961, give the camp administration practically unlimited opportunities to apply physical and moral pressure. Prohibition of food parcels, a ban on purchases from the camp stall, starvation rations, banning of visits, punishment cell, handcuffs, solitary confinement—all this is legalized by the 'Regulations' and applied to political prisoners. The camp administration finds these measures much to its taste, all the more so as among the 'educators' are not a few officials of the Stalinist concentration camps, used to unlimited arbitrary power (which, incidentally, was quite in line with their instructions at that time).

As the prisoners lack all rights, they are driven to dreadful and disastrous forms of protest: hunger-strikes, self-mutilation, suicide—in broad daylight the prisoner goes out of bounds towards the barbed wire, and there the guard shoots him 'for attempted flight'.

Some among you bear direct responsibility for the existing situation; the responsibility of others is determined by their public position. But I turn to you as my fellow citizens: we are all equally responsible to our motherland, to the young generation, to the country's future. It suffices that the generation of the 'thirties and 'forties put up with crimes committed 'in the name of the people'; it is impossible and impermissible to display again the criminal indifference which then turned the whole nation into accomplices in bloody crimes.

I appeal to you to:

Demand a public investigation into the situation of political prisoners.

Demand the wide publication of the 'Regulations for Camps and Prisons'; try to have special rules made for political prisoners.

Demand the publication of the food rations for prisoners.[6]

Demand immediate dismissal from 'educational' work of the former staff of Stalinist concentration camps and of such camp officials as have more recently displayed cruelty and inhumanity towards prisoners. Demand a public trial for them.

It is our civic duty, the duty of our human conscience, to put a stop to crimes against humanity. For crime begins not with the smoking chimneys of crematoria, nor with the steamers packed with prisoners bound for Magadan. Crime begins with civic indifference.

A. MARCHENKO

REPLY BY THE RED CROSS TO THE LETTER FROM 2
ANATOLY MARCHENKO

April 29th, 1968   *U.S.S.R. Executive Committee of
the Union (Decorated with the
Order of Lenin) of Red Cross and
Red Crescent Societies* [U.R.C.
and R.C.S.], *Moskva V-36,
1-y Cheremushkinsky proyezd, 5.
No. 182/125 yur.*

To Citizen A. Marchenko,
g. Aleksandrov, Vladimirskaya obl.
ul. Novinskaya 27

The letter sent in your name to the Executive Committee of the
U.R.C. & R.C.S. of the U.S.S.R. has not, unfortunately, been
signed by anyone,* and this makes it impossible and unneces-
sary to give it detailed consideration in substance.

The committee nevertheless considers it necessary to point
out briefly that our legislation and our Soviet conception of law
look upon people who have attacked the conquests of the
October Revolution as having committed a most serious offence
against their people and as deserving severe punishment rather
than any kind of indulgence or forbearance.

In the light of the foregoing the entirely groundless nature of
all your other assertions becomes obvious.

F. ZAKHAROV
Deputy Chairman of the Executive
Committee of the U.R.C. & R.C.S. of the U.S.S.R.

On July 26th, 1968, a thirty-year-old loader, Anatoly Mar- 3
chenko, sent an open letter to the editors of the newspapers *Rude
pravo*, *Literarni listi* and *Prace*, voicing his protest against the
campaign of slander and insinuations against Czechoslovakia,
and speaking of the threat of intervention in that country.[7]

Two days later, on July 28th, 1968, Anatoly Marchenko was
arrested in the street and sent to Butyrka prison. He was

* Marchenko probably confined himself to a typewritten signature and forgot
to sign by hand [*Chronicle's* note].

charged under article 108—infringement of passport [i.e identity card] regulations.

From 1960 to 1966, Anatoly Marchenko had served a sentence in the Mordovian political camps on a trumped-up charge of high treason. On completing his prison sentence, Marchenko wrote a book, *My Testimony*—an uncompromising, factual document on conditions in contemporary Soviet political camps and prisons. The facts given in Marchenko's book could not be refuted by the punitive organs of the country. The author began to be subjected to administrative blackmail and arbitrary measures. After a short interval he received two warnings that he was infringing the passport regulations. The first warning he received after undergoing a serious operation, the second was simply illegal.

On August 21st, 1968, the People's Court of [Moscow's] Timiryazev District (under Judge Romanov) examined the case of Marchenko, accused under article 108 of the Russian Criminal Code.

A seriously ill man, suffering from progressive deafness and anaemia, who has spent a great part of his life in the unbearable conditions of strict-régime camps and corrective prisons, he received the maximum sentence under that article—one year of strict isolation from society.

A group of Anatoly Marchenko's friends—Lyudmila Alekseyeva, Larissa Bogoraz, Yury Gerchuk, Natalya Gorbanevskaya, Pyotr Grigorenko, Victor Krasin, Pavel Litvinov and Anatoly Yakobson—appealed to the citizens of our country in a letter revealing the true reason for Marchenko's arrest.[8]

During the night of August 7th–8th Irina Belogorodskaya was arrested on charges of circulating this letter. She was accused under article 190–1 of the Russian Criminal Code, which carries a sentence of up to three[9] years for spreading information which defames the Soviet social system. A search was carried out in Belogorodskaya's flat and in the flat of three of the letter's authors.

Irina Belogorodskaya is so far in Lefortovo prison.

We will return to Belogorodskaya and her trial at the end of the chapter. Meanwhile, let her cousin Larissa Bogoraz describe the conditions in which Marchenko had been living prior to his arrest:

His book ... aroused such hatred for him in the K.G.B. that they begin to bait him like a hare: K.G.B. agents followed on his heels for months on end—I've spotted them so often that I know many of them by sight. And not only in Moscow, where he worked, and Aleksandrov where he lived: he went to visit relatives in Ryazan but wasn't allowed to leave the train and had to return to Moscow. He was seized on the street almost as soon as he had been discharged from hospital; and they smashed his face in and shoved him into a car when he came to Moscow for a literary evening.[10]

In such circumstances Marchenko wrote his various open letters. Among these was one to the chairman of the International Committee of the Red Cross (I.C.R.C.), asking him 'to send to the U.S.S.R. an I.C.R.C. mission to examine the conditions of Soviet political prisoners in the Mordovian camps ... and the Vladimir prison, and to furnish them with essential aid.' This request, he pointed out, exactly resembled the appeal of the Soviet Red Cross to the I.C.R.C. concerning Indonesian political prisoners, as published in Izvestia two weeks earlier.[11]

That he could apply his gifts of cool analysis just as well to Czechoslovak as Mordovian affairs was revealed in the letter he wrote a month before the Soviet invasion, anticipating it. Here he put his finger on the main reason for Soviet aggression by discussing the Czechoslovak liberals' exposure of the crimes of their country's Stalinists, and concluding:

It is understandable why our leaders hasten to intercede for the likes of Urvalek and Novotny: the precedent of making party and government leaders personally responsible before the people is a dangerous and contagious one. What if our own leaders should suddenly be required to account for deeds that have shamefully been termed 'errors' and 'excesses' or, even more weakly and obscurely, 'difficulties experienced in the heroic past' (when it was a matter of millions of people being unjustly condemned and murdered, of torture in the K.G.B.'s dungeons, of entire peoples being declared enemies, of the collapse of the nation's agriculture, and similar trivia)?

In October 1968 Marchenko's open letters began to circulate in collected samizdat form, as an appendix to My Testimony[12], together with the documents about the book such as those already mentioned, and also a passionate endorsement of it by Father Sergei Zheludkov of Pskov (see p. 329). In December, however, as No. 5 recorded, 'Anatoly Marchenko arrived at his camp [in the north Urals]. His address is: Permskaya obl., Cherdynsky raion, p/o Nyrob, p/ya ShZ/20/16 T.'

But appeals for Marchenko continued. In January 1969 ten people, headed by Grigorenko, wrote a carefully argued letter to the Russian Procurator-General, enumerating the official bodies to which My Testi-mony had been sent,[13] and in June the Action Group called for the intervention of the U.N.[14]

No. 8 at the same time initiated a new series of disturbing reports:

8   ANATOLY MARCHENKO ONCE MORE UNDER INVESTIGATION

The fate of Anatoly Marchenko, author of the book *My Testi-mony*, is well known to readers of the *Chronicle*. On August 21st, 1968, he was sentenced to one year in a strict-régime camp, for 'infringing the passport regulations'. The statement made by Marchenko's friends, that the charge against him was trumped up, was borne out at every step of the legal proceedings. As additional proof, mention may be made of how the People's Assessors [the Judge's two assistants] were 'instructed'. They were told that they were dealing with a criminal so cunning and insidious that he had not broken the law, and that this article of the Criminal Code was the only way of getting him into jail.

Anatoly Marchenko is a very sick man. In the camps of Mordovia he had meningitis and became deaf. After he came out, he had a trephining operation on the skull. He also suffered from heavy internal bleeding in the stomach, and a dangerously high loss of haemoglobin, and was saved only by a series of blood transfusions. The court had access to Marchenko's medi-cal reports. But despite this they sent him to a camp in the extreme north of Perm region, with a severe climate. In the camp Marchenko worked in a construction gang. In April 1969 he was put in the punishment cell for fifteen days for refus-ing to work in a basement without the protective clothing authorized for that particular job.

Marchenko's term of imprisonment ends on July 29th, but in May the Perm Regional Procuracy instituted new proceedings against him under article 190–1. Marchenko was transferred to Solikamsk prison. By his book, in which he tells the truth about life in the prisons and camps for political prisoners, he aroused a personal hatred for himself in the K.G.B. and the Ministry of the Interior, and it cannot be excluded that the persons who ordered these new proceedings to be instituted are intent on physically destroying him. Three years in a strict-régime camp for a man in Marchenko's condition could kill him.

THE TRIAL OF ANATOLY MARCHENKO   10

The *Chronicle* has already reported that Anatoly Marchenko has been sentenced again, to two years' imprisonment in strict-régime camps, under article 190–1 of the Russian Criminal Code.[15] Marchenko's trial was held on August 22nd in the reading room of the camp zone at Nyrob, a settlement in Perm Region, and was formally considered open, although of course no one except prisoners and administrative personnel is ever allowed into the zone.

Anatoly Marchenko was charged with uttering these statements: 'the Soviet Union is violating the sovereignty of other countries, and Soviet troops were sent into Czechoslovakia to suppress freedom with tanks'; 'there is no democracy in the U.S.S.R., freedom of expression, of the press, of creativity does not exist'; 'it is the Soviet Union who is to blame' for the events on the Sino-Soviet border. Apart from these statements, Marchenko was charged with refusing to report for work, and with declaring while in the punishment cell: 'The communists have drunk all my blood.' This charge was based on the testimony of two overseers, i.e. punishment-cell warders, Lopanitsyn and Sobinin. Since they contradicted each other in their evidence as to the date on which Marchenko had uttered this statement, it was stated in the indictment, and later in the sentence, that he had uttered it twice—on May 14th and 15th. After the overseers had reported, K.G.B. security officer Antonov, to whom the overseers are subordinate in their job, began to collect further material on Marchenko, and on May 31st he instituted criminal proceedings.

The charge was corroborated at the pre-trial investigation by duty warders Sedov and Dmitriyenko, as well as by the overseers' testimonies. Sedov was not summoned to appear at the trial, but his testimony was read out, in violation of the law, and also incorporated in the verdict. Dmitriyenko declared at the trial that he had not known Marchenko before, and had 'decided' that the statement attributed to him in the charge had been uttered by him, but now that he had seen Marchenko at the trial and heard his voice, he was firmly convinced that Marchenko had not spoken these words. Moreover, Dmitriyenko declared that he knew who had spoken the words; and he could name the man and summon him to court. The court did not react to this declaration, and ignored Dmitriyenko's testimony in the verdict, although a court is obliged by law to explain why it has rejected any testimony which contradicts the conclusions reached in the verdict. Fellow-prisoners of Marchenko in the punishment cell, summoned to court at his request, stated that they had not heard the sentence he was charged with uttering.

Concerning the other statements he was charged with, Marchenko said that he had held conversations with prisoners on these subjects, but that his statements had been distorted beyond recognition in the witnesses' testimony. Marchenko said he had been annoyed by the words of witness Burtsev to the effect that 'Czechoslovakia ought to be crushed once and for all', since he considered the idea of crushing a man, a nation or a people to reveal hatred of mankind. During conversations about freedom of expression, the press and creativity, Marchenko had in fact replied to prisoners that no ideal freedom of expression, press or creativity existed anywhere, nor did pure democracy, including in the Soviet Union: every country had its limitations.

The prosecution witnesses recounted Marchenko's views in a primitive and arbitrary form; not one of them reproduced them accurately, and their testimony was contradictory. According to Marchenko, the case against him was a fabrication of Antonov, the camp K.G.B. security officer, who had pressurized the witnesses—all dependent on him—into giving suitable testimony. The court declared that 'there was no reason not to believe the witnesses questioned at the trial, all the more so since many of them had given explanations even before proceedings began—some in their own handwriting—which confirmed the facts brought to light in court and which had led to criminal proceedings being instituted.' It was precisely these 'explanations', on the basis of which criminal proceedings had been instituted, which were given at interrogations conducted by the K.G.B. chief Antonov.

The court's second argument, which it considered proof of the reliability of the witnesses' testimony, was the fact that the investigation had been headed by the Deputy-Procurator of the Perm Region and 'the court has no reason to doubt his objectivity'.

The composition of the court was as follows: Khrenovsky, Chairman; Rzhevin and Biryukova, People's Assessors; Baiborodina, Procurator. Marchenko conducted his own defence.

On September 30th the Russian Supreme Court considered Marchenko's appeal, and an additional appeal by the lawyer Monakhov, who spoke at the hearing. The composition of the court was: Ostroukhova, Chairman; Lukanov and Timofcyev, Members of the Court; Sorokina, Procurator. The verdict of the Perm Regional Court was upheld.

Three months later No. 11 wrote: 'For reasons unknown Anatoly Marchenko [...] is still Solikamsk prison. His address is; Permskaya obl., Solikamsk, p/ya IZ 57/2.' And finally No. 12 reported that he had been 'sent off to a camp. His address is Permskaya obl., Solikamskii raion, p/o Krasnyi Bereg, p/ya AM 244/7-8.'

In conclusion we return to the case of Marchenko's friend Belogorodskaya (see plate 60). In September 1968 her husband Ivan Rudakov (see plate 60) was dismissed from his job as an engineer 'at his own request' (No. 6) and in December No. 5 reported that the investigation into her case 'has been completed'. The stage was therefore set for:

THE TRIAL OF IRINA BELOGORODSKAYA   6

On February 19th Irina Belogorodskaya was tried in Moscow. As reported in the third issue of the *Chronicle*, Belogorodskaya, an engineer at the Scientific Research Institute of the State Committee for Inventions, was arrested on the night of August 7th–8th, 1968, in connection with the distribution of a letter defending Anatoly Marchenko. Belogorodskaya's arrest and the preceding searches of her flat and those of three of the other signatories to the letter—Larissa Bogoraz, Lyudmila Alekseyeva, and Victor Krasin—resulted from the fact that, on the night of August 6th–7th, Belogorodskaya left behind in a taxi a bag containing her documents and several dozen copies of the letter defending Marchenko. The bag was handed over to the

K.G.B., who also conducted the searches, arrested Belogorodskaya and started the investigation, after which the case was passed to the Moscow Procuracy. The investigation into Belogorodskaya's case was conducted by L. S. Akimova. At the end of August and during September L. S. Akimova led the team which investigated the demonstration on Red Square of August 25th, 1968, but this is only one of the reasons why the investigation was unjustifiably dragged out.

The Procuracy received a declaration[16] by the signatories to the letter defending Marchenko, to the effect that they bore full responsibility for the letter, which they had written to acquaint the public with Marchenko's fate. Almost all the signatories to the letter — except for P. G. Grigorenko and Pavel Litvinov — were interrogated as witnesses in connection with their letter and also with their declaration relating to the arrest of Belogorodskaya. It would be natural to suppose that if the indictment considered the documents in question to constitute the substance of a crime under article 190–1 of the Russian Criminal Code, i.e. to contain deliberately misleading fabrications which discredit the Soviet social and political system, then they would have brought to justice the signatories to the letter as well, particularly since none of them denied their part in distributing the letter.

Nevertheless, Irina Belogorodskaya was brought to trial for attempting to distribute these letters, and not one of the signatories to the letter was called as a witness and given the chance to refute the charge that the said documents contained deliberate lies and in their 'deliberately misleading contents' discredited the Soviet political and social system. This is a serious breach of article 20 of the Russian Code of Criminal Procedure, which states: 'The court, the Procurator, the investigator and the person conducting the inquiry are obliged to take all the measures laid down by law to ensure a full, thorough and objective investigation into the circumstances of the case, to examine the arguments both for and against the accused and also the circumstances which caused the crime to be committed.' The investigator, when he signed the indictment, had proposed that the court should call three witnesses: Ivan Rudakov, who had been travelling with Belogorodskaya in the taxi; the taxi-driver, Kudryavtsev; and Surkova, the controller of the taxi pool—thus limiting the scope of the trial to the discovery of copies of the letter in the bag, and leaving aside the document itself, the intentions of the signatories and their conviction of the truthfulness of all that they had written. The Procurator, on receiving the case from the investigator, sent it straight to court, likewise ignoring this flagrant breach of article 20 of the Russian Code of Criminal Procedure and associating himself with it. Moreover, the administrative session of the court, which had the opportunity of extending the list of witnesses to be called, did not do so. Thus the conduct of the court hearing precluded the possibility of a 'full, thorough and objective investigation of the circumstances of the case', and the right of the accused to defend herself was artificially limited.

One may suppose that all this served two purposes. The first is mentioned in the letter written not long before the trial by P. G. Grigorenko and Anatoly Yakobson.[17] This was the purpose of provocation: by arresting and sentencing someone who is doing what is possible to help those who actively defend human rights and civil liberties in our country, to frighten many people off from taking any part in the democratic movement. The second aim was to complicate the defence of Irina Belogorodskaya, to force *her* to judge the element of criminality in the document and to confuse her. Her clear position was that she wanted to distribute these documents to help Anatoly Marchenko, and had complete faith in the signatories to the letter and the truthfulness of the documents. A discussion of the content of the documents, and a judgment on their 'deliberate falsehood' could have been reliably obtained only by questioning the signatories to the letter; all this was replaced by the interrogation of the accused. Just the same, the interrogation failed to prove the deliberate falsehood of the document or that Belogorodskaya considered it to be false. Nevertheless the verdict stated that, in intending to distribute these documents, she had known them to be false.

The court, presided over by Judge Monakhov, found Irina Belogorodskaya guilty of 'an attempt, which failed for reasons beyond her control, to distribute deliberately misleading falsehoods defaming the Soviet social and political system'—i.e. under articles 190-1 and 15 of the Russian Criminal Code. 'Taking into account a good character report from her place of employment', it sentenced her to one year's confinement in an ordinary-régime camp.

The circumstances in the court building were familiar from all previous 'open' trials, but perhaps a little less severe. Despite the fact that, as usual, the courtroom was already crammed full when the court building opened, some of the defendant's friends managed to get in. Dozens of those who had assembled outside saw Irina Belogorodskaya and greeted her. When, after the verdict, she was led off to the Black Maria, bunches of flowers flew towards her from the crowd, who were standing behind a line of policemen and people in plain clothes. Her escort tore from her hands the only bunch which she caught and threw it away, and a guard in plain clothes promptly trampled on it with hatred.

There is already a summary record of the trial of Irina Belogorodskaya by P. G. Grigorenko in *samizdat*.[18] The compiler of the record adds his own comments. One of the most important conclusions of this commentary is the following:

> In our society it is forbidden to stand up for those people who are, rightly or wrongly, assaulted by the state machine. For a mere signature in defence of an innocent man who has been convicted, or in protest against national discrimination, e.g. against the Crimean Tatars, people are subjected to lawless repression. This too is a hangover from the Stalin era, except that then people were put in prison for such a 'crime', even if they had only expressed their opinion orally, whereas now the authorities have so far limited themselves to relieving people of their jobs, expelling them from the party or the Komsomol, or driving them out of higher educational institutions. I. Belogorodskaya is the first to have been brought to trial for this ... and we, her friends, must think things over thoroughly after her trial. It seems to me that the fight against unjust sentences must in present circumstances become more persistent ... To stop judicial tyranny such sentences must be fought against until they are actually revoked.

The Authorities had tried Irina Belogorodskaya in the Bauman District Court on February 19th, 1969, and in this connection the Chronicle *reported:*

On the same day the trial of the mathematician Ilya Burmistrovich [see pp. 68–70] was due to take place in the building of the Timiryazev District Court; he was arrested in May 1968 and also accused under article 190–1, with the difference that the investigation was carried out by the K.G.B. There can be no doubt that, by arranging two similar trials on the same day, the organizers were hoping to distract public attention from at least one of them. There was unrestricted entry into the court building on Pistsovaya Street, where Anatoly Marchenko had been tried in August, and the public was freely admitted to the courtroom; even foreign correspondents came and occupied the empty seats. Later it was announced that the Judge had fallen ill and the trial was being postponed. Ilya Burmistrovich was taken back to the Lefortovo prison. A new date for the trial has not yet been announced.

In the cases of Belogorodskaya and Burmistrovich the right of the accused as regards their defence has been flagrantly violated: at the time of the completion of the pre-trial investigation the K.G.B. and the Procuracy announced that only a lawyer with a 'permit' would be allowed to defend the accused.[19]

A permit is only required in cases involving state or military secrets, and so it is also illegal that only lawyers with a 'permit' are allowed for all cases brought under articles 64 and 70 and other articles in the section of the Code concerning 'Particularly dangerous crimes against the state'. There can therefore be no reason whatsoever for demanding a 'permit' for cases brought under article 190–1.

The notions 'permit' and 'withdrawal of permit' are becoming a means of exerting pressure on the conscience of lawyers.

On April 15th, 1969, the appeal hearing in the case of Irina Belogorodskaya took place in the Russian Supreme Court. The sentence was left unaltered. 7

At the beginning of May Irina Belogorodskaya was sent to 8 camp 2 of the Mordovian complex, address: Mordovskaya A.S.S.R, st. Potma, pos. Yavas, uchrezhdeniye ZhKh 385/2. Her term expires on August 7th this year.

7*

9 On August 8th Irina Belogorodskaya [...] was released from her
ordinary-régime camp.

In September she signed the Action Group's third appeal to U Thant to
investigate the Soviet treatment of dissenters.

10. THE CAMPS AND PRISONS

Russia is still criss-crossed by a network of camps where—despite all the international conventions signed by the Soviet government—forced labour and cruel exploitation are the norm, where people are systematically kept hungry and constantly humiliated, where their human dignity is debased. Through these camps passes an uninterrupted human flow, millions strong, which gives back to society physically and morally crippled people. This is the result of a deliberate penal policy, worked out by experts and presented by them in special handbooks with a cynicism worthy of the concentration-camp experts of the Third Reich.

Yury Galanskov, Alexander Ginzburg
and five friends, Mordovia, Autumn 1969[1]

The Russian Criminal Code states flatly the following basic principle of penal policy: 'Punishment does not have as one of its aims the incurring of physical suffering or the lowering of human dignity' (article 20).

This principle is, however, so much bluff. As Marchenko showed in the last chapter, the legal regulations are in reality—particularly as regards the strict- and special-régime camps—clearly designed to cause physical suffering and loss of dignity. Indeed Soviet theoretical writings effectively admit this. The appeal by Galanskov, Ginzburg and their five fellow-prisoners, quoted above, gives extracts from a recent text-book. One writer describes agricultural work as the least effective form of forced labour, partly because 'it is impossible to limit the consumption by the prisoners of many food items which are produced in this form of colony (milk, eggs, vegetables, fruit, etc.). In this way the food consumption levels which exist for prisoners, and also the regulations on parcels and what relatives may hand over to them at meetings, lose their purpose.'[2]

The purpose of such regulations becomes even clearer in this chapter than in the last. But two important aspects of Soviet penal practice remain unexplored and should be briefly discussed here. First, the truly terrible conditions of life in the prisons and special-régime camps (like No. 10 in Mordovia) are scarcely described: for details of these, readers with strong nerves are referred to Marchenko's My Testimony. *And second, attention focuses exclusively on Mordovia (see fig. 2) and Vladimir, so that the vast network of camps covering the rest of the country goes by default. These camps contain the mass of ordinary*

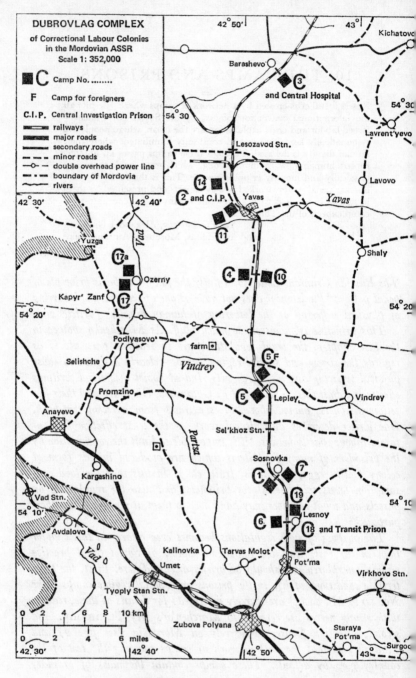

Fig. 2 The main Mordovian camp complex as it was in early 1969

criminals and also most of the politicals sentenced—like Marchenko (in 1968), Vladimir Bukovsky and Victor Khaustov—under either minor political articles, such as 190–1, or non-political articles (on trumped-up charges).

No close study has yet been made of this network. Thanks, however, in large part to the Soviet Baptists' assiduity in recording the fate of their imprisoned brethren[3] the following rough picture emerges.[4]

The exact addresses and locations of over two hundred Soviet labour camps are now known. These data indicate clearly that the total number is very much greater, perhaps around a thousand. Such an estimate derives from an apparent average of some seven or eight camps per region in a country of just over 130 regions. If each camp holds an average of about a thousand prisoners, as seems likely, then a total camp population of around a million at any one time would emerge. This can be compared to a 12–15 million figure at Stalin's death in 1953. To calculate the rough total of all people under some form of restraint, whether more or less severe than camp imprisonment, figures for the prison population and the number of people in exile would be needed. The former is probably relatively small, prison terms being much less usual than camp terms, but the latter may well be enormous. A third category to be added in are the politicals in 'mental hospitals'. No estimates, however, can yet be made of the size of these categories. Official penal statistics do not help: virtually all absolute—as opposed to percentage—figures are closely guarded state secrets.

Neither can the number of prisoners who are politicals—or 'prisoners of conscience'—yet be estimated. True, Marchenko uses the expression 'thousands',[5] and it is also certain that out of some 15,000 prisoners in the main Mordovian camp complex in 1969 about 2,000 were politicals. But political and religious prisoners—as well as exiles—are scattered throughout the country. Moreover, any close estimate becomes impossible because of the difficulty of knowing how many politicals have been sentenced on trumped-up charges under non-political articles, and indeed of defining, in Soviet conditions, the very concept of a political offence. It would be surprising, though, if the order of magnitude 'tens of thousands' were not valid for all prisoners of conscience, excluding exiles.

At least we may be sure of one thing: Khrushchev was indulging in a characteristic bluff when he claimed in 1959, 'We now have no prisoners in our jails for political reasons.'[6]

Such statements naturally caused deep bitterness among the great army of political prisoners, and not only, as Marchenko records, in some of the fifteen camps beside the M.V.D.'s thirty-mile railway line from camp 18 at Potma Station to camp 3 at Barashevo. For the camp addresses we now know, each indicating where political or religious prisoners are held, stretch from the Arctic Circle in the extreme north-west to Chita Region on the Manchurian border, from dark, icy Yakutia in northeast Siberia to warm and sunny Odessa on the Black Sea.

While some of these camps operate under the strict and special régimes, the majority have one of the two lighter varieties, 'ordinary' and 'hard'. The latter are never the lot of those sentenced in serious political cases, i.e. when—as under article 70—'specially dangerous state crimes' have been committed, and when the authorities almost invariably send the condemned men to the toughest camps in Mordovia or to Vladimir. The lighter régimes can, however, be assigned to minor political offenders, such as those sentenced under article 190–1.

As the material of this chapter shows, one of the few weapons available to prisoners in strict-régime camps is the hunger-strike. On February 20th, 1968, friends and relatives of some of the Potma prisoners sent this telegram to President Podgorny:

> *It has become known to us that in the Mordovian camps groups of political prisoners began a hunger-strike on February 12th, demanding: recognition of themselves as political prisoners and not ordinary criminals; an easing of the camp régime and an improvement in the food; an end to compulsory labour; and the removal of restrictions on correspondence. We support these demands. We also demand: regular reports to relatives about the health of those on strike, and meetings for them with members of their families.[7]*

This document records in a note that two of the political camps, 11 and 17a, then contained 2,500 and 350 prisoners respectively, and the Vladimir jail—which also holds non-politicals—1,000.

The strike was timed to catch the attention of the consultative meeting of world communist parties in Budapest, the meeting to which the famous 'letter of the 12' (see pp. 86–8) was sent. The Chronicle *reported on this and subsequent strikes:*

1 In February a hunger-strike was staged in camp 17[8] of the Mordovian camps (Mordovskaya A.S.S.R., st. Potma, p/o Ozerny, p/ya 385/17a). The following six persons[9] took part: Yuly Daniel, Boris Zdorovets, Victor Kalninš, Sergei Moshkov, Valery Ronkin and Yury Shukhevych. Between the eighth and

the tenth days artificial feeding was imposed on the strikers. After ten days the strike was called off. As a result several demands of the political prisoners were met: the administration now has no right to forbid meetings with relatives without the Procurator's approval; moreover, the Procurator's approval will also be required in future for the confiscation of personal papers and such actions must always be recorded in a legal document. It should be borne in mind that, in the past, whatever demands were made by strikers were not only not met, but frequently the mere fact of going on a hunger-strike was regarded as a 'breach of the regulations' and could serve as grounds for a spell in the camp prison, in the intensified-régime barrack or in Vladimir jail.

A POLITICAL PRISONERS' ULTIMATUM   6

At the end of February 1969 a group of political prisoners in camp 17 of the Mordovian labour camps, including Yuly Daniel, Yury Galanskov, Alexander Ginzburg, Valery Ronkin and Vyacheslav Platonov, presented an ultimatum to the camp administration: either the administration should respect the guarantees given when the hunger-strike was called off in February 1968 or the prisoners would start another hunger-strike. The hunger-strike would be aimed at the arbitrary actions of the administration of camp 17 and would be conducted only on its territory.

The immediate cause of the ultimatum was the withdrawal from Valery Ronkin of the right to a personal visit, due in May, on the grounds that he had described himself as a political prisoner in a conversation with a Major Golubyatnikov. In February 1968 a promise had been given that measures of punishment such as withdrawal of the right to visits would be applied only with the sanction of the Procurator. Other guarantees were also being ignored.

The strict régime at camp 17 is crueller than that at others. Camp 17 has become the place where those who, in the opinion of the administration, might exert an influence upon other prisoners are confined in isolation. It was for just this reason that Vyacheslav Platonov and Leonid Borodin found themselves in camp 17, having initially been put in camp 11, together with the other Leningrad 'Social Christians' [on their case see p. 376].

In camp 11 Vyacheslav Platonov landed up in the B.I.R. (barrack of intensified régime, i.e. the long-term punishment cells),[10] whereupon several dozen protest declarations were immediately sent to Moscow by the other prisoners. Platonov was released from the barracks but not returned to the camp zone; first, he and Leonid Borodin were transferred to the investigation prison at Saransk [capital of Mordovia], and then, at the beginning of February, they were both moved to camp 17.

7 The hunger-strike in labour camp 17 of the Mordovian complex did not take place as the camp authorities made concessions after prolonged discussions: the illegal decision, which deprived Valery Ronkin of a visit, was withdrawn.

8   ALEXANDER GINZBURG'S HUNGER-STRIKE

On May 16th Alexander Ginzburg went on hunger-strike in protest at being forbidden to have visits from his wife. He gave advance warning of this to the administration of camp 17 of the Mordovian camp complex, where he is being held, stressing that he would not enter into discussions with the administration, since the decision on this matter did not rest with them. He described his position in detail, and gave the reasons for his decision in a letter to I. G. Petrovsky, Deputy of the U.S.S.R. Supreme Soviet and Rector of Moscow University. Ginzburg has so far had no reply to this letter. Incidentally, the camp administration enclosed with the letter a favourable report on Ginzburg. Ginzburg has had no punishments, has never broken the camp rules, and has always fulfilled his work norm, although he is classified as disabled because of an injured hand, and as such is not obliged to fulfil the norm.

Alexander Ginzburg and Irina Zholkovskaya applied to register their marriage at a registry office at the end of 1966. This would have formalized a marriage which had already been in existence for a long time, as the testimony of neighbours, and certificates from the Housing Allocation Bureau, later confirmed. Six days before the registration date, Ginzburg was arrested. During the fifteen months which Ginzburg spent in Lefortovo prison, both he and Irina Zholkovskaya tried to obtain permission to register their marriage, but they were always told that registration in prison cells was prohibited.[11] In actual fact this prohibition is not laid down anywhere, and at least two instances have been recorded of marriages registered in a Leningrad cell, the prisoners having been charged, moreover, under the same article 70 of the Russian Criminal Code as Ginzburg: Valery Smolkin[12] in 1965, and quite recently Lev Kvachevsky [see pp. 380–86].

In Lefortovo prison the Procurator had told Ginzburg: 'When you get to the camp you will be able to register there.' When he got there, Ginzburg read in a camp instruction that 'the registration of marriages by prisoners interned in camps is not authorized'.

Nevertheless, during 1968 Ginzburg was allowed one personal and one ordinary visit from his wife, that is, respectively, 24 hours alone together, and 3 hours in the presence of a camp warder. In 1968 the long-established and generally accepted practice was still valid according to which visits were allowed if the parties could produce documentary proof of their marriage in common law. But in November 1968 the Ministry of the Interior issued a new order, stating that only registered couples could have personal visits. This order was a blow to an enormous number of families in which long-established marriages were unregistered, and which were now broken up by imprisonment. This is why it was promised that 'in exceptional cases' registration of marriage with a prisoner would be permitted.

The new order did not affect ordinary visits, but in spite of this, in 1969, Irina Zholkovskaya was refused even an ordinary visit, and her letters, petitions and countless visits to various authorities were fruitless. Apart from his wife, Ginzburg's only other relative is his mother, who is old and in ill health, and whose physical condition prevents her from making the journey to visit her son alone. And so his wife will always have to accompany her and spend the visiting time standing outside the barbed wire. In these conditions Alexander Ginzburg saw no other way of taking action than by hunger-strike. Ginzburg's psychological state prior to this decision is admirably described by Yuly Daniel in a letter to a friend.[13]

On May 16th Ginzburg began his hunger-strike. For four days he was sent out to work, although he was losing more and more strength. On the second day he received an official reprimand from a member of the camp administration, Ribchinsky, for leaving the workshop half an hour before the end of the shift. (He had, however, completed his norm.) Halfway through the fourth day Ginzburg was finally put in solitary confinement. This should be done on the first day of a hunger-strike. On the eleventh day they began to give him artificial feeding, but on May 31st, Doctor Lyubimov considered that he looked too well, and from June 1st to June 4th he was not fed.

On May 19th, 23rd and 26th a number of prisoners, including Yuly Daniel, Yury Galanskov, Valery Ronkin, Sergei Moshkov, Leonid Borodin, Vyacheslav Platonov, Valis Gajauskas,[14] Mykhaylo Soroka,[15] Dmytro Verkholyak and Victor Kalninš, sent a petition to the U.S.S.R. Procurator-General explaining the circumstances which made Ginzburg resort to a hunger-strike. On June 2nd the same group of prisoners appealed to the Presidium of the U.S.S.R. Supreme Soviet, and Ronkin and Galanskov announced that they too would strike in solidarity with Ginzburg. Valery Ronkin went on hunger-strike on June 2nd, Galanskov on June 3rd. On June 3rd Leonid Borodin and Vyacheslav Platonov [see p. 378 and plates 34, 35] joined them. On June 2nd Yuly Daniel sent a statement to the Procurator-General, with copies to the Minister of Health and the Red Cross, about the attitude of the doctor Lyubimov to the starving man. In his statement Daniel mentioned that Lyubimov was the doctor who at the time of the mass poisoning in the women's zone of camp 17 left a dying woman without giving her medical help.

On June 10th Alexander Ginzburg and his friends ended their hunger-strike.

All this time Irina Zholkovskaya was still appealing to the Ministry of the Interior, the K.G.B. and the Procurator-General's Office for permission for her next ordinary visit, which had been due to her since the end of April. She was also inquiring about registering her marriage, and, after she learned of the hunger-strike, about that too. Finally on June 6th V. Z. Samsonov, Deputy Director of the Camp Supervision Department of the Procurator-General's Office, confirmed to Ginzburg's wife and mother that the new regulation did not affect ordinary visits, and that if they had applied to his office earlier, they would have got permission for the visit. Samsonov suggested they make a fresh application for an ordinary visit when Ginzburg called off his strike. On June 11th Irina Zholkovskaya made her application to the Procurator-General's Office, and it forwarded the application to the Ministry of the Interior as before. Towards the end of June, that is, at the time the *Chronicle* was being prepared, she had had no reply.

Meanwhile her professional life also suffered:

Irina Zholkovskaya, wife of Alexander Ginzburg, and 8 teacher at Moscow University's Department of Russian for Foreign Students, has been suspended from teaching and transferred to purely technical work in one of the university's research libraries. The wording of the dismissal was 'unsuitability for the post occupied' and the reason given that Zholkovskaya had not renounced her husband, nor condemned him, and continued to believe in his innocence. Paradoxically, at the same time as both her department and the Academic Council of the Preparatory Faculty, and also the University's Academic Council, condemned and dismissed Zholkovskaya precisely because she was Ginzburg's wife, she herself was knocking at the doors of all possible authorities, trying to prove her married state and her consequent right to visit him.

In the end, however:

As a result of Alexander Ginzburg's hunger-strike, which 9 was supported by his friends, he has finally been granted permission to register his marriage with Irina Zholkovskaya. They were registered on August 21st in the camp zone.

HUNGER-STRIKES IN THE POLITICAL CAMPS 11
OF MORDOVIA

In the Potma camps for political prisoners (Dubrovlag, institution 385) in November–December 1969 there was a wave of hunger-strikes.

In the work area of camp 3 (not to be confused with the

hospital area which is also a part of camp 3) there was a hunger-strike in protest at the confinement of prisoner Berg in the cooler. Berg, who was convicted under article 70 of the Russian Criminal Code for setting up, with Vyacheslav Aidov [see plate 28], an illegal printing press, had been transferred to camp 3 from camp 19, being a specialist in non-standard equipment. However, in camp 3 he was put on unskilled labour and then sent to the cooler for attempting to protest. Participants in the hunger-strike were Vyacheslav Aidov and Nikolai Tarnavsky (convicted under article 70 of the Russian Code, also for attempting to set up an illegal press), Ivan Žukovskis (article 67 of the Lithuanian Code, equivalent to article 70 of the Russian, a journalist specializing in international affairs, convicted for conducting an interview which the authorities found objectionable), Valentyn Karpenko (article 70 of the Russian Code, term — eighteen months [see p. 289]), Valery Rumyantsev (article 64 of the Russian Code, term — fifteen years), and Lev Kvachevsky (article 70, term — three [in fact four] years).

After a collective hunger-strike which lasted several days, the administration released Berg from the cooler, decided his protest had been justified and the actions of Aleksandrov, the head of the camp section, who had put Berg on to unskilled labour, wrong. Vyacheslav Aidov, who refused to appear for an interview with the authorities when summoned, since he was too weak and could not walk after his hunger-strike, was put in the cooler without further ado. Berg, Tarnavsky, Žukovskis, Karpenko, Rumyantsev and Kvachevsky then went on hunger-strike in protest. This strike lasted several days and forced the camp administration to release Aidov too from the cooler.

In mid-November Berg was suddenly sent to Vladimir prison, and this provoked a third hunger-strike, which lasted three days, and in which Aidov, Tarnavsky, Žukovskis, Rumyantsev and Kvachevsky participated.[16]

In mid-November there was also a hunger-strike at camp 17a of Dubrovlag. One of the reasons for the strike was the camp administration's refusal to allow Victor Kalniņš [see plate 39] to receive a parcel from relatives. (Kalniņš is serving a ten-year sentence: he was arrested and convicted in 1962 under articles 66 and 67 of the Latvian Criminal Code, equivalent to articles

64 and 70 of the Russian, in a case about an 'anti-Soviet underground nationalist organization'; an objection was lodged against the sentence first by the Procurator of the Latvian Republic and then the Procurator-General of the U.S.S.R., but the sentence was confirmed.) One of those who went on hunger-strike, Yury Galanskov, was transferred during his strike to camp 3 (the hospital) and continued his fast there.

In December there were hunger-strikes in almost all the political camps of Dubrovlag. The strikes were in connection with International Human Rights Day—December 10th. In the first week of December at camp 17a there was a hunger-strike by Alexander Ginzburg, Victor Kalninš, Leonid Borodin and Vyacheslav Platonov [...] The strikers were protesting at the transfer of Yuly Daniel and Valery Ronkin to Vladimir prison. All four were put in the cooler. Yury Galanskov fasted in the hospital area of camp 3 from December 3rd to 10th for the same reason [see pp. 64–5].

In the work section of camp 3, Aidov, Tarnavsky, Žukovskis, Karpenko, Rumyantsev and Kvachevsky went on yet another hunger-strike in protest at the transfer of Berg to Vladimir prison.

In camp 19 P. M. Goryachyov went on hunger strike for two days—December 10th–11th. (He was sentenced under article 64 of the Russian Code. Until 1964 he was a detective in the K.G.B., then a lawyer. He was convicted for attempting to cross the border.) Goryachyov was put in the cooler.

In connection with the transfer of Daniel and Ronkin to Vladimir prison about seventy inquiries were made to various official authorities between July and November 1969, mainly from relatives of the two prisoners. These inquiries were sent to the Zubovo-Polyana district Procuracy in Mordovia, the Mordovian Republic Procuracy, the Procuracy of the Russian Republic, the U.S.S.R. Procuracy, the district people's court of Zubovo-Polyana District, the Mordovian Supreme Court, the administration of camp 17a, the central administration of Dubrovlag, the U.S.S.R. Ministry of the Interior, the Presidium of the Russian Republic Supreme Soviet, and the Central Committee of the Communist Party. So far, not one of these inquiries has received an answer of any substance.

Let us pass now to some of the Chronicle*'s items in which lives of great drama are often boiled down to a few paragraphs: those about individuals. Other such items — revealing the extent of the* Chronicle*'s information network — will be found in the notes.*[17]

In October 1968 a report appeared of the recent release of one of the strikers of February that year. He was:

4 Yury Shukhevych, who had served two terms: the first time he was sentenced to ten years at the age of fourteen because his father had been the underground leader of the Organization of Ukrainian Nationalists; on the day he completed his term in the prison at Vladimir he was rearrested on a false charge of anti-Soviet agitation, and sentenced to another ten years.

These grim facts were described in detail by Shukhevych in a remarkable document written in camp 17a in 1967.[18] *Here he also mentioned an even grimmer possibility, based on the knowledge that such things actually happened in Stalin's time: 'A mass crime could be committed against all the political prisoners in Mordovia (for this everything is already prepared): they would all be physically destroyed, after which those who had carried out the deed would themselves be destroyed.'*

An equally tragic and somewhat parallel case is the following:

7 In the spring of 1969 Kateryna Zarytska, Odarka Husyak and Halyna Dydyk, after twenty years in the Vladimir prison, were sent to a labour camp of strict régime to sit out the rest of their 25-year term. All of them took part in a post-war anti-Stalin partisan organization in the west Ukraine and organized the underground Red Cross. Their address is: Mordovskaya A.S.S.R., p/o Yavas, p/ya ZhKh 385/6.

Kateryna Zarytska was first in prison in Poland at the end of the 'thirties for her part in an attempt on the life of the Polish Minister of the Interior by a group of Ukrainian nationalists. Zarytska's husband, Mykhaylo Soroka, is in camp 17 of the same Mordovian complex of strict-régime camps — the same address, p/ya ZhKh 385/17a.[19]

The following three cases reveal further types of political prisoner:

9 It has become known that the 27-year-old Yury Belov[20] is in camp 10 of the Mordovian complex. Belov has already done a long term before in the same camps, when he was convicted

under article 70 of the Russian Code. After his release he wrote a book called *Report from Darkness*, and was sentenced to a new term of five years of special-régime for trying to send it abroad, under article 70 para. 2. Now he has been put in a special-régime camp, that is, a camp where the inmates are kept in cells. His address is: Mordovskaya A.S.S.R., st. Leplei, p/ya ZhKh 385/10.

In Moscow early in 1969 Erik Danne from Riga, who works for an international airline, was convicted under article 70 of the Russian Code for importing 'anti-Soviet' literature and having 'connections with the N.T.S.'[21] Erik Danne is now in Mordovia: address — st. Barashevo, uchrezhdeniye ZhKh 385/3.

THE FATE OF YURY IVANOV 10

After spending four months in the K.G.B. isolation prison at Saransk, where the attempt to 're-educate' him failed, the artist Yury Ivanov [see plate 33] has been sent to camp 17 of the Mordovian complex. Before Saransk, Ivanov was at camp 11, which has now been broken up and its inmates dispersed.[22]

Yury Evgenevich Ivanov is a Leningrader. Born in 1927, he is a son of the artist E. Sivers, who was arrested in February 1938, executed, and posthumously rehabilitated, and the grandson of a former Minister of Communications of the Russian Empire, who was arrested in November 1937, executed and posthumously rehabilitated.

Yury Ivanov was first arrested in 1947, with two other students of the Academy of Arts, for failing to attend lectures on Marxism-Leninism. All three were savagely beaten up during the investigation, and one of them died during it. Yury Ivanov and the second student were sentenced in absentia by the OSO or Special Board [a basically secret police institution of five people, set up in 1934 and abolished after Stalin's death] to ten years each in camps. After Ivanov had spent one year in a camp — administration 16 of the Kitoilag complex[23] — his relatives, who had been constantly campaigning for the case to be reviewed, achieved their aim — Ivanov was acquitted and released. After leaving the camp, Yury Ivanov graduated from the Academy of Arts and became a member of the Leningrad branch of the Artists' Union.

In 1955 Yury Ivanov was arrested and convicted under articles 58–3, 58–4, 58–10 and 58–11 for 'passing around anti-Soviet literature', and 'creating an organization', the members of which 'were not discovered'. He was sent off to work on the construction of the Kuibyshev[24] hydro-electric power-station; at that time about 8,000 prisoners convicted under article 58 [i.e. political prisoners] were working on the elevator and the sluice-gates.

In 1956 Ivanov's case, together with many others, was reviewed by a commission of the Supreme Soviet, but Ivanov was not released, since he refused to admit his guilt and did not repent. Soon after that he escaped, but was injured during his flight and picked up a week later. For his escape he was given a new sentence of a further ten years, to be reckoned from the time of his escape.

In 1956, after he had been sent to Dubrovlag, i.e. the Mordovian camps, Yury Ivanov led the strike committee of camp section 7–1 during a prisoners' strike in camp 7. He was convicted under articles 58–10 and 58–11 to a further ten years, to be reckoned from the time of his trial on the new charge. He spent a year in the Vladimir prison.

In 1959 there was an exhibition in London of sketches done by Yury Ivanov in the camps.

At the beginning of 1963 he was again convicted for 'anti-Soviet propaganda in the camp' under article 70 para. 2; once again it was ten years – 'the unexchangeable ten-rouble piece'[25] in camp slang. He spent three years of this term in Vladimir prison, then had two and a half years of special régime in camp 10 of Dubrovlag, and then in the summer of 1968 he was transferred to camp 11 with the strict régime. During the time Yury Ivanov spent at Saransk, efforts were made not only to persuade him to repent, but also to force him to hand over to the state his right to receive a legacy from abroad which was due to him.[26] On the first day of his stay in camp 17a his paints were taken away from him.

Nevertheless Ivanov soon managed to make a vivid series of charcoal drawings of his fellow-prisoners — Daniel, Ronkin, Galanskov, Ginzburg, Sado, Borodin, Platonov, Kalniņš, Soroka, himself and others — and these eventually found their way abroad.[27]

*A very special type of political prisoner is the subject of this revealing
article:*

CONCERNING SOME OF THE POLITICAL PRISONERS   4
SENTENCED FOR 'BETRAYING THE FATHERLAND'

Article 13 of the Declaration of Human Rights states:

1. Everyone has the right to freedom of movement and
   residence within the borders of each state.
2. Everyone has the right to leave any country, including
   his own, and to return to his country.

Article 64 of the Russian Criminal Code includes in the
concept of 'betrayal of the fatherland' 'flight abroad or refusal
to return to the U.S.S.R. from abroad'.

In practice any attempt to leave the Soviet Union and settle
in another country is defined as 'betrayal of the fatherland'.

It may be an attempt to cross the frontier illegally, although
article 83 of the Code makes provision for illegal crossing of the
frontier as such, and envisages the much less severe punishment
of imprisonment from one to three years. We must remember
that article 64 provides for terms of imprisonment from ten to
fifteen years and, in exceptional circumstances, execution (by
firing squad) and that anyone sentenced under this article is
bound to end up in a strict- or even special-régime camp.

Or it may be an attempt to obtain political asylum while
abroad. It must be stressed that such people who 'come back',
who have grown homesick for their native land and the families
they left behind and return to the Soviet Union, are usually put
on trial.

Here is the information available on some of the people
sentenced under article 64.

Andrei Novozhitsky served in the Soviet Army in East
Germany, went over to West Germany, and returned after a
year. He was sentenced to ten years and served part of his term
in the prison at Vladimir.[28]

Vladimir Pronin, a specialist in agricultural mechanics from
Cherkassy Region [in the central Ukraine], served in the Soviet
Army in East Germany, crossed to West Germany, returned,
and was sentenced to ten years.

Pyotr Varenkov, who also crossed over to West Germany

while serving in the army in East Germany, served twelve years in prison from 1953 to 1965.

Pyotr Tibilov, Yury Bessonov and a certain Budyonny,[29] who also served in the Soviet Army in East Germany and fled to the West, were given long sentences.

Not long before the end of his term of service Anatoly Gurov[30] fled from East to West Berlin, returned the same day to collect a colleague he had left behind, and as a result served a ten-year sentence.*

Anton Nakashidze, a dancer in the Georgian song and dance ensemble, remained in England while on tour and later returned: he was sentenced to ten years' imprisonment.[31]

Golub, a biologist, applied for political asylum while abroad and then returned to the Soviet Union and publicly recanted.[32] His return was reported in the press and he began work again, but six months later, when the fuss over his return had died down, he was arrested and sentenced.

Gennady Zamaratsky tried to flee across the Caucasian frontier into Turkey, served eight years' imprisonment including two stretches of three years each in the prison at Vladimir, and was freed in 1966.

Valery Zaitsev, a naval mechanic, tried to escape to America with the crew of his repair and rescue ship while working near the coast of Alaska in 1962. He was sentenced to ten years; the other members of the crew were tried with him but details of their names and sentences are not available.

Anatoly Rodygin, a naval officer, graduate of the Kronshtadt Naval Academy, poet, member of the Leningrad branch of the Writers' Union and captain of a fishing boat, tried to escape across the frontier by jumping into the Black Sea in 1962 and was sentenced to eight years' imprisonment. In 1966 he was dispatched to Vladimir prison because he 'was suspected of wanting to escape and had not embarked on the path of reform'.[33]

---

* This 'moving tale' has, however [No. 9], 'turned out to be nothing more than a camp legend invented by Gurov himself. Gurov spent quite a long time in West Berlin, where he worked as a radio-technician in an American "school for spies". He was arrested after being caught laying a microphone cable. And so crossing the border illegally was not the only act Gurov committed. It is just such people that the camp administration relies on: Gurov became notorious in his camp as a "custom-built informer" [*patentovannyi stukach*].'

Victor Samchevsky was sentenced for attempting to flee abroad.

In 1960 Anatoly Marchenko was arrested while trying to cross the frontier into Iran ... As is well known, Marchenko was recently sentenced again: this time a criminal charge of 'infringing the passport regulations' was fabricated against him—this is, incidentally, yet another article of the Criminal Code that directly contravenes article 13 of the Declaration of Human Rights, this time its first part.

The fate of yet another person condemned for 'betrayal of the fatherland', a stevedore from Archangel called Mikhail Konukhov, is described in detail in the book *My Testimony*.[34] Mikhail Konukhov made an official statement about his desire to adopt British citizenship. Afterwards he was for a long time subjected to various forms of illegal persecution and provocation by hooligans, then he was forcibly committed to a psychiatric hospital and in the end he was arrested and sentenced under article 64.[35]

Just as the most important prisoners are now sent for camp terms to unhealthy and swamp-infested Mordovia, so for their much rarer prison terms their lot is the tsarist jail — with its thousand-odd inmates — in the beautiful and historic city of Vladimir. Here, however, they live some six to a cell, on inhumanly low rations, and since 1966 the previous consolation of limitless time to read and think has been replaced by the obligation to work.

Marchenko's picture in My Testimony *of life in Vladimir in the early 1960s — all vivid greys and blacks — and Yury Ivanov's of the mid-1960s (see note 27) were updated by the* Chronicle *in late 1969 :*

POLITICAL PRISONERS IN VLADIMIR PRISON 11

The exact number of political prisoners in Vladimir prison (address: g. Vladimir, uchrezhdeniye OD–1, st.–2) at the present time is not known. There is no separate wing now for politicals, but there are several political cells in each of the four blocks of the prison: for example, there are two in the second [hospital] block, cells no. 72 and 79. As with the political prisoners in the Mordovian camps, a significant number here are Ukrainians and people from the Baltic states, who have been convicted in so-called nationalist cases. Here is a list, far from full, of the political prisoners in Vladimir:

1. Mykhaylo Masyutko from the town of Feodosia [in the Crimea], 45, sentenced in 1965 to six years for circulating Ukrainian *samizdat*, in particular his own stories about the camps of the Kalmyk Steppe [N.W. of the Caspian Sea], where he was a prisoner under the Stalin régime; he is in prison by court sentence, and is suffering from a severe stomach illness.[36]

2. Mykhaylo Horyn from Lvov [in W. Ukraine], 46, sentenced in 1965 to six years in camps for circulating Ukrainian *samizdat*, sent to prison for his complaints against the camp administration.[37]

3. Mykhaylo Lutsyk, convicted in a similar case.

4. Lev Lukyanenko, lawyer from Lvov, 42, sentenced in 1961 to fifteen years; the charge of 'betrayal of the fatherland' brought against him and a whole group[38] was based on the testimony of one of the accused, whom the Lvov K.G.B. promised to release—he was given ten years.

5. Ivan Kandyba, convicted either in the same case as Lukyanenko or for uttering statements in Lukyanenko's defence. Term—not less than ten years.[39]

6–8. Dmytro Kvetsko (fifteen years), Zynoviy Krasivsky (twelve years) and Mykhaylo Dyak (twelve years),[40] convicted in 1967 in the case of the 'Ukrainian National Front' (circulation of *samizdat* in printed form).

9. Justas Gembutas, a Lithuanian.

10. Varanavičius, a Lithuanian.

11. Vaivada, a Lithuanian.

12. Karl Šeffers, a Latvian.

13. Yusuf Aslanov, a Circassian.

14. Igor Ogurtsov, a translator and orientalist from Leningrad, 27, convicted in the case of the 'All-Russian Social-Christian Union' [see pp. 376–80]. In prison by court sentence.

15. Anatoly Samyshkin.

16. Georg Gladko, convicted, as the *Chronicle* has already reported,[41] for escaping from East to West Germany.

17–18. Yuly Daniel, writer from Moscow, Valery Ronkin, student from Leningrad.

19–21. Rodygin [see p. 218], Semenyuk and Vareta, transferred to Vladimir from the Mordovian camps in September–October 1969.

21. Berg, transferred to Vladimir in November, convicted in 1967 for an attempt to organize an underground printing-press [see pp. 212–13].

Earlier the Chronicle *had raised this specially tragic case:*

The Vladimir prison contains Svyatoslav Karavansky [see plate 29], sentenced in 1944 to twenty-five years for his role in a Ukrainian nationalist organization during the Rumanian occupation of Odessa; he was amnestied in 1960, but in 1965 was made to serve the remaining part of his 25-year sentence after writing an article on the subject of national discrimination against university entrants:[42] the Procurator-General of the U.S.S.R., Rudenko, protested the application of the amnesty in his case. Karavansky – at the same time as Valentyn Moroz, Mykhaylo Horyn and Mykhaylo Masyutko[43] – was transferred from camp 11 of the Mordovian complex to the Vladimir prison for a period of three years in the summer of 1967, on account of the complaints he had sent to official bodies and for reading material on the situation in the Ukraine. At the trial, when the question of altering his type of régime was to be decided, Karavansky demanded an interpreter. Trials inside a camp are always held without defence lawyers, the accused having no right to a defence; but at the same time, strange as it may seem, cases have been known when a sentence was revoked because an interpreter was not present at the trial. In answer to Karavansky's demand, the Judge, Mrs Ravenkova said, 'Give him a damned Ukrainian!' Karavansky objected to the Judge. The Prosecutor looked surprised and said, 'That was a slip of the tongue.' Karavansky's objection was not accepted.

The prison régime at Vladimir includes many more restrictions than a labour-camp régime. Only letters from immediate relatives are accepted, letters in Ukrainian are sent for translation before being handed over, parcels of books are banned, a prisoner's relatives have a right to only two half-hour visits a year, and everyone has to speak Russian during visits.

But even in these severe conditions, where every privation can be felt all the more keenly, Karavansky found the strength to stage a political protest. At the end of October 1968, he went on a hunger-strike, demanding the resignation of the government for their mistaken domestic and foreign policies. His hunger-strike lasted twenty-eight days. The circumstances surrounding the end of his hunger-strike are unknown. For his strike Karavansky was given fifteen days in the punishment cells.

Later No. 11 reported that 'in the autumn of 1969 a new charge was brought against Karavansky—"anti-Soviet propaganda"—and he was sent to the Ukrainian K.G.B. investigation prison in Kiev.'[44] This resulted, as No. 13 recounts,[45] in him receiving an additional five years in April 1970 for writing articles about the reconciliation of East and West, and—based on the accounts of eye-witnesses imprisoned in Vladimir ever since—the Soviet massacre of some 4,000 Polish officers in Katyn Forest in 1940.

The sufferings of Soviet political prisoners do not end on their release from camp or prison. Quite apart from the difficulty of finding anything but manual work, those sentenced on more serious charges like articles 64 and 70 are not allowed—according to a secret part of the 'Passport Regulations'—to settle in ports, border areas or big cities,[46] or within 100 or so kilometres of the latter, even if their wives or husbands live there. Larissa Bogoraz-Daniel has denounced these secret regulations as 'a left-over from eighteenth-century serfdom or Stalin's enslavement of the population' and attacked 'the hypocrisy of a government which— "for show"—demands throughout the world such a minimal human freedom as the right to choose one's place of residence, while at home it classifies the exercise of this right as a crime.'[47]

Similar attacks on both the 'Passport Regulations' and the 'Administrative Surveillance Regulations' of 1966 have been made[48] by Leonid Rendel, a Muscovite like his wife and friends, but forced to live far away from them:

1 In February 1968 the former political prisoner Leonid Rendel (article 58–10, case of Krasnopevtsev and others, essence of the case—'illegal Marxist circle', term ten years, served whole sentence in the Mordovian camps, released August 30th, 1967), at present residing in the village of Novo-Melkovo, Kalinin Region [north-west of Moscow], was placed under administrative

surveillance. The reason for this action was a recommendation by the camp administration that he be put under surveillance 'for repeated breaches of camp regulations and for maintaining his anti-Soviet convictions' (the breaches took the form of protests against the arbitrary actions of the camp authorities). The surveillance was imposed for six months and may be extended to up to three years. Under the surveillance order he is forbidden to leave the village without police permission (when he applied for permission it was refused) and he is obliged to report twice a month to the local police station.

The administrative surveillance of Leonid Rendel [...] was 4 ended in August [1968].

Finally, what of the overall penal policy and laws of the Soviet government? These were examined in part by Marchenko in the extracts quoted in Chapter 9, but the items below add much. The first, written in March 1969, is:

A LETTER FROM POLITICAL PRISONERS IN MORDOVIA TO 8 THE PRESIDIUM OF THE SUPREME SOVIET OF THE U.S.S.R.[49]

In connection with the envisaged discussion of a new Corrective Labour Code, a group of six political prisoners in camp 17 of Dubrovlag — Yury Galanskov, Alexander Ginzburg, Yuly Daniel, Victor Kalniņš, Sergei Moshkov and Valery Ronkin — suggest to the deputies of the U.S.S.R. Supreme Soviet that they acquaint themselves with the present situation of political prisoners. The authors show that the main forms of coercion used on political prisoners are: hunger, cold and humiliation. Their present situation is not regulated by any published laws, and so the deputies of the Supreme Soviet can either legalize or change this state of affairs.

This important document also points out that while current regulations formally came within the framework of the Corrective Labour Code of 1926, the latter 'not only fails to reflect life in prison today, but contains certain provisions which give the appearance of the wildest fantasy: work in one's speciality, no restrictions on correspondence or on receiving material aid from relatives, etc.' De facto it was 'supplanted by secret instructions during the tragic thirties'. Moreover, 'this tradition of putting a secret classification on the documents which determine our lot has survived to this very day.' The only one available to the authors is 'The Basic Rights and Duties of Prisoners', a generalized document which apparently summarizes parts of various secret laws and instructions such as the 1961 'Regulations on the Corrective-Labour Colonies and Prisons of the Ministry of the Interior'.[50] *The letter then analyses systematically what had been happening in practice in the authors' camp, giving illustrations such as this: 'We, the undersigned, have spent an aggregate of over twenty-two years in confinement and during this time not one of us has received a single food parcel in a camp.'*

But the deputies were deaf, frightened or unfeeling. Pravda *of July 12th, 1969, revealed no overall improvement in the situation, rather a slight deterioration. For example:*

10 Under the new corrective-labour legislation, prisoners are allowed only two parcels of printed matter per year. Although the new legislation comes into force only from November 1st, all parcels of books sent from the Ukraine and Moscow to camps 19 and 17a of the Mordovian complex in the summer of this year were returned.

Indeed the new 'Fundamentals of Corrective-Labour Legislation' provoked the document from which the epigraph to this chapter is taken:

11 LETTER FROM A GROUP OF PRISONERS,[51] written by Leonid Borodin, Yury Galanskov, Alexander Ginzburg, Yury Ivanov, Victor Kalninš, Vyacheslav Platonov and Mikhail Sado, and addressed to leading figures on the Soviet cultural scene: Irakly Abashidze, Chingiz Aitmatov, Rasul Gamzatov, Ernst Genri, Leonid Leonov, Alexander Tvardovsky and Georgy Tovstonogov.[52]

The authors show how the system of concentration camps established under Stalin and since condemned in words alone, continues to serve as the basis for penal policy in our country, though on a lesser scale.

The existing system of forced-labour camps (which has been preserved only in the Soviet Union and China) is the product of a deliberately fostered policy, which is formulated by experts on the subject and presented by them in special manuals. Extracts from these manuals quoted by the authors of the letter show only too well the mechanism for the physical and moral repression of prisoners.

20. (*left*) Major-General P. G. Grigorenko before his first arrest in 1964.

21. (*above*) Ilya Gabai, Moscow poet and teacher, before his arrest in 1969 (see p. 136).

22. (*below*) Grigorenko and Ivan Yakhimovich outside the Czechoslovak Embassy, July 29th, 1968 (see p. 96).

23. (*above*) Grigorenko with his wife Zinaida.

24. (*below*) Zinaida Grigorenko seeing off Boris and Alexandra Tsukerman, Moscow Airport, 1971 (see pp. 136 and 310).

25. (*top right*) Yakir (left) visiting Krasin in exile in Siberia, 1970.

26. (*bottom right*) Genrikh Altunyan, a Major from Kharkov (left—see pp. 161ff), and Ilya Burmistrovich (see plates 2 and 3) in their Siberian camp, 1970.

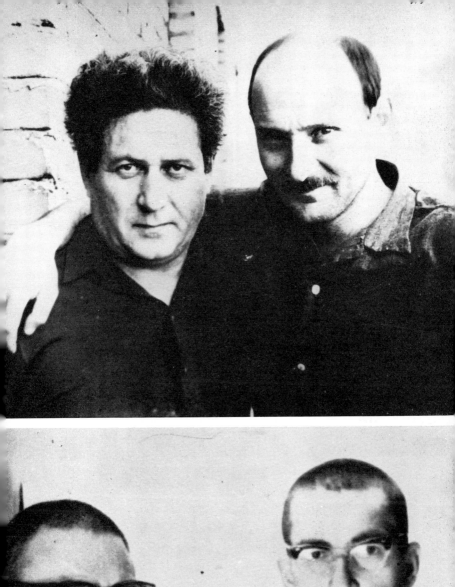

27. Anatoly Marchenko 1968.

28. (left) Vyacheslav Aidov before his arrest in 1968 (see p. 212).

29. (right) Svyatoslav Kara- vansky, Ukrainian writer (see p. 221).

30. (left) Valery Ronkin, Leningrad engineer, before his arrest in 1965.

31. (right) Ronkin drawn Yury Ivanov in Mordovia, 1969.

'Fear of looking into the underlying causes of criminal activity' means, of necessity, that the blame is shifted from society to the 'criminals', and particularly harsh retribution is exacted from them for the imperfections of that society.

The existence of camps for political prisoners ('the maintenance of criminals dangerous to the state in separate establishments') is a terrible disgrace to our contemporary penal policy. Apart from genuine war criminals (for the most part feeble old men, some of them mentally disturbed, living out the last years of their lives), the inmates of these camps are made up of participants in post-war nationalist movements who were given 20–25-year sentences in Stalin's camps, and some of whom went through German camps as well; young people sentenced for disseminating propaganda about national self-determination; preachers of various religious sects and denominations; and 'anti-Sovietists', sent to the camps for expressing and circulating ideas contrary to official doctrine.

The authors warn the creative intelligentsia, which shapes public opinion, of their responsibility for the policy of discrimination against national minorities as practised in the concentration camps, and of the sinister turn this policy has recently taken.

At about the same time, in the autumn of 1969, Yury Galanskov wrote a long, free-ranging essay of his own on Soviet penal policy.[53] *He appealed for support in reforming this policy to Western communists and the outside world at large, and proceeded from particular to general in this revealing fashion:*

> *Fortunately such events as the hunger-strike of February 1968 and the strike in support of Alexander Ginzburg sooner or later became known both in our country and abroad. The latter point is particularly important and valuable as regards our national interests. The Western press, and especially the Western radio-stations broadcasting in Russian, publicize arbitrariness and acts of crude coercion by Soviet official personnel, and thus force the state bodies and officials to take quick action. In this way the Western press and radio are fulfilling the tasks of what is at present lacking in Russia, an organized opposition, and thereby stimulating our national development.*

8

Unfortunately, though, Galanskov concludes, 'the West often devalues itself by a concern either for sensation or for temporary ideological compromise, and does not show the necessary persistence in its approach to matters which for us are of critical importance.'

11. THE PRISON MENTAL HOSPITALS

It is time to think clearly: the incarceration of free-thinking healthy
people in madhouses is *spiritual murder*, it is a variation of the *gas
chamber*, but even more cruel: the torture of the people being killed is
more malicious and more prolonged. Like the gas chambers these
crimes will *never* be forgotten, and all those involved in them will be
condemned for all time, during their life and after their death.

Alexander Solzhenitsyn, June 1970[1]

P. G. GRIGORENKO: ABOUT THE SPECIAL   11
PSYCHIATRIC HOSPITALS[2]

The idea of special psychiatric hospitals is not in itself uncom-
mendable, but as for the specific way this idea is implemented
in our country—there is nothing more criminal or inhuman.

The point is that the method of dealing with objectionable
persons by adjudging them insane and confining them to
psychiatric hospitals for lengthy periods or even for their whole
life is as old as the very idea of the 'madman'. Even taking
this into account, progressive people have long fought to
institute controls concerning the treatment of psychiatric
patients. They have also fought so that people who have committed crimes while of unsound mind should not be subject to
criminal punishment, but be sent for psychiatric treatment. The
distinguished Russian psychiatrists Bekhterev and Serbsky[3]
fought for this also. Soviet legislation went far towards meeting
the demands of progressive people. But the trouble is that the
whole thing has since been completely removed from public
scrutiny and placed under the control of a specially chosen
apparatus. Doctors for psychiatric hospitals are appointed by
special selection processes in which their medical qualifications
are of secondary importance and other qualities have precedence, the main one being the ability to knuckle under and
suppress their medical 'ego'.

We must start our discussion by asking whether the people
who find their way into the special hospitals are always real mental patients, or whether the prerequisites for repressive injustice
are built into the system. A person is sent to the notorious
Serbsky Institute of Forensic Psychiatry on the order of an

investigator. This institute nominally comes under the Soviet Ministry of Health, but I myself, on more than one occasion, have seen Professor Lunts, the head of the department diagnosing me, arrive at work in the uniform of a K.G.B. colonel. True, he always came into the department in his white coat. I have also seen other doctors of this institute in K.G.B. uniform. But the exact relation between the K.G.B. men and the Ministry of Health I have not managed to ascertain. People say that only one department is under K.G.B. control—the one which diagnoses political cases. I am inclined to think that the influence of the K.G.B.—and it is a decisive influence—extends over the whole of the institute's work. But even if what people say is true, the question arises: can the psychiatric diagnosis of political cases be objective if both the K.G.B. investigators and the medical experts are subordinate to one and the same person, and, what is more, are bound by military-style discipline?

I will recount what I have seen myself. I arrived in the second (political) department of the Serbsky Institute on March 12th, 1964. I had not previously even heard of such a method of repression existing in our time as the declaration of a healthy man to be of unsound mind; I was unaware that this 'Chaadayevan'* system existed in our country. I realized it only when I myself was presented with a committal order for a psychiatric investigation.

Having read the order, I looked at the investigator and asked: 'Well, so you've found a way out of your dilemma, have you?' The investigator, greatly embarrassed, started assuring me that the investigation would continue after the medical examination, and an indictment would be drawn up.[4] I felt there would be no more investigation, and that a mental hospital was my lot for the rest of my life.

In the department I was taken to there were eleven people. From what I imagined the examination to be like, I tried to predict what diagnosis awaited each of them. Even without medical training it was clear that the only one of us who was mentally abnormal was Tolya Edamenko, but he, according to my

---

* The noted Russian thinker Pyotr Chaadayev (1793–1856) was officially declared to be mad after the publication in 1836 of an essay in which he saw the only salvation for Russia's backwardness in the traditions of western Europe and of the Roman Catholic Church. He was not, however, put in a mental hospital.

prediction, would end up in an ordinary camp. The 'loony-bin', in my opinion, awaited three of us: myself, Pavel Borovik (an accountant from Kaliningrad) and Denis Grigorev (an electrician from Volgograd). The investigation against all three of us had yielded nothing and there was no foreseeable chance of finding anything.

All the others ought, in my opinion, to be found normal, although some of them were acting the idiot very skilfully, feigning pathological conditions. I had doubts about one, Yury Grimm, a Moscow crane-driver who had circulated leaflets bearing a caricature of Khrushchev. To him I said: 'If you don't recant, it'll be the loony-bin for you, if you do—a camp.' (An investigator was visiting him several times a week, trying to persuade him to recant and promising him all sorts of wonderful things.) Yury did 'recant' and got three years in a strict-régime camp.

Grimm's case testifies in the best possible way to the fact that the Serbsky Institute is simply a subordinate organ of the investigation authorities. Both the investigator and the doctor spoke to Yury about one thing only—recanting. Moreover the doctor was a worse bully than the investigator, painting a vivid picture of how Grimm would be shut away for ever among 'loonies' if he did not recant.

In Leningrad too I met people who had landed in a psychiatric hospital without being mentally ill. I was especially saddened by the tragic case of engineer Pyotr Alekseyevich Lysak. Because he had spoken at a student meeting against the expulsion for political reasons of a number of students, he had landed in a psychiatric hospital and, at the time of my arrival, had already been there for seven years. Bitter anger at this wild injustice, at his ruined life, had permeated his being, and he would write complaints daily, which, naturally, never reached their destination, but found their way into his hospital file and were used as an excuse for further 'treatment' (people who do not admit their illness are not usually discharged from special psychiatric hospitals). I tried to drum this truth into his head. During one such conversation, I said in irritation: 'Your reasoning is so unreal that I'm beginning to doubt your normality.' He stopped all of a sudden, looked at me with an expression I shall remember to the day of my death, and asked in a barely audible voice and a tone of bitter reproach: 'Do you really think that a man can spend seven years in here and still remain normal?'

Here is the very essence of the inhuman system of compulsory treatment. The whole horror of the position of a healthy man who finds himself in conditions like these lies in the fact that he himself begins to realize that in time he will become like those who surround him.

My military training, and maybe the iron constitution which my parents passed on to me, enabled me to learn quickly to insulate myself from my surroundings, and my internment in hospital passed without doing any particular harm to my psyche. The one thing I cannot forget, the thing that sometimes wakes me up at night, is a wild nocturnal cry mixed with the hollow sound of shattered glass. From that I could not insulate myself. Evidently during sleep one's nerves have no defence mechanism against such stimuli. But I can imagine what a man must go through who is receptive to everything around him through his highly strung nervous system, and whose defence mechanisms are not as well developed as mine.

Even if cases of people finding their way into these establishments were few and far between, even then every such case ought to be subject to the most thorough investigation with maximum publicity. But these cases are not accidents; they occur systematically. Moreover, the system is widely practised. I have said that within as little as one month, while I was being diagnosed, the Serbsky Institute promoted three healthy people to the ranks of madness and sent one undoubtedly abnormal man to a camp. The latter process is also part of the system. I only realized this after reading A. Marchenko's book *My Testimony*. Mentally sick people are necessary in the camps in order to make life even more unbearable for the healthy.[5]

In the Leningrad Special Hospital I met a young man who was interesting to talk to.[6] He had landed up there in the following way: he had been arrested for petty theft and would possibly have been released without being brought to trial if it had not suddenly occurred to the investigator that with this man's help he could round off a certain 'dead' case – a murder case which had never been cleared up. They did not require very much of the arrested man: he was to testify that at the moment when the murder was committed, one of his friends had been in the village where it took place. The man knew that this was untrue and refused to testify. The investigator then said: 'Aha, so you don't want to assist the investigation? ... Well then, I'll lock you up in a place where you'll remember me for the rest of your life.' And he sent him for a psychiatric examination. The diagnosis team declared him to be of unsound mind. The young man was lucky. In the hospital his doctor happened to be an honest man, who was able to get the findings of the diagnosis team annulled. But it took him *six years* to do it. As a rule it is impossible to have a diagnosis annulled, because the diagnosis is given on many occasions by repeated medical commissions, and can be revoked only with the consent of the doctor who gave the initial diagnosis.

For a healthy man, the atmosphere which surrounds him in a mental hospital is terrible, and no less terrible are his complete lack of rights and his helplessness. The 'patient' in a special psychiatric hospital does not even enjoy the miserable rights of the camp prisoner. He has no human rights at all. You can do anything you like to him, and no one will object. No one will defend him, and none of his complaints will ever reach the outside world. His only remaining hope is an honest doctor.

But I assert that *a system in which the only hope is someone's honesty is absolutely worthless.*

The atmosphere of the madhouse, the complete lack of rights and the absence of any real possibility of regaining one's freedom — these are the terrifying facts which everyone who lands in a special psychiatric hospital has to face.

Radical changes must be fought for in the diagnosis system and the conditions in which patients are kept in special psychiatric hospitals; the public must be given the right to exercise some real control over the conditions of confinement and the treatment of patients in these establishments.

That Grigorenko should write such an informative essay — combining personal experience with perspective, reflection and constructive proposals — will come as no surprise. He does not, however, deal with certain points. On history, for example, he omits to note that — notwithstanding the oft-quoted Chaadayev case and many generalized assertions by Soviet publicists — virtually no hard evidence exists of the tsarist régime imprisoning opponents in mental hospitals, and that the practice never became more than a passing, local phenomenon.

As for the Soviet period, Grigorenko did not have access to by far the most valuable source yet available: the testimony of a man who later became his friend, Sergei Pisarev. A communist and party worker, Pisarev spent two years in mental hospitals from 1953 to 1955 for criticizing the secret police's fabrication of the notorious 'Doctor's Plot' shortly before Stalin's death. In his letter of April 1970 to the Academy of Medical Sciences[7] he reports that such methods became systematic and widespread in 1936–8, when Andrei Vyshinsky established the first prison hospitals on behalf of his master Nikolai Ezhov, the head of the secret police.

Partly through Pisarev's efforts after his release, a high-powered commission of the party's Central Committee was set up in 1955 under A. I. Kuznetsov to investigate the whole practice. In Pisarev's words:

> The commission carried out many searching investigations in the Serbsky Institute, and also made trips to Kazan and Leningrad, where the two special hospitals were then situated. All the facts I had presented were completely corroborated by the evidence ... Among the ... 'Mentally ill' people sentenced to indefinite isolation, the commission discovered hundreds of absolutely healthy persons. It listed systematically the perversions of the truth in the diagnoses given by the Institute, in particular by D. R. Lunts (at that time a senior lecturer) and a number of other people. It was documentarily proved that — through the fault of the diagnostic institute under investigation — Soviet psychiatric hospitals throughout the country, and above all the two notorious special prisons for political prisoners in Kazan and Leningrad, had year after year been filled up mainly by sane persons ... who had been the innocent sufferers and victims of illegal repressive measures.

> The Kazan and Leningrad institutions 'operated under the inappropriate official description of "psychiatric prison hospitals", although no one ever even thought of giving any kind of treatment in them (for the really mentally ill people) ... The commission reached the unanimous conclusion that there was a need for a radical, fundamental reorganization in the field of psychiatric diagnosis.' As for the prison hospitals, the commission deemed it essential, 'while removing them unreservedly from the sole control of the administrative-investigation organs, to transfer them completely to the supervision of the U.S.S.R. Ministry of Health.'

Kuznetsov's immediate superior, however, to whom was submitted 'the whole of the immense and extremely valuable work done by the Commission, concealed it from the leaders of the Central Committee' and succeeded in suppressing it altogether. Kuznetsov and all those connected with the commission were removed from the Central Committee apparatus. Nevertheless certain improvements were stimulated by the very activity of the commission. For example :

a start was made in giving genuinely ill patients some kind of special treatment, and it is becoming increasingly frequent for the hospitals (which now have quite a few young, freshly trained specialists) to repudiate — *ultimately* — *some of the unfounded diagnoses of the Institute. But it is ... a frightening proof of the increase in the illegal political repressions collaborated in by the Serbsky Institute to find that — instead of the complete abolition of the two special hospitals outside the network of Health Ministry psychiatric establishments —* additional new hospitals of a similar type *have in recent years appeared in other cities.*

As regards the work of the Institute itself, even though it is now formally listed as administered by the Ministry of Health, it is a regrettable fact that no changes of direction have occurred in it. [Its main Stalin-period officials have been able] to stay on in their former *jobs and assiduously continue the evil practices of that era. Incidentally, not one of the people guilty of the crimes uncovered by the commission in 1955–6 has been* prosecuted under the law. *On the contrary, more and more fresh personnel have been trained and educated in the Institute precisely under the pernicious guidance of notorious criminals. [As before, therefore,] the Institute complaisantly utilizes pseudo-scientific phraseology to cover up the dishonest actions of officials in the investigation and procuracy organs.*

Finally, Pisarev calls for the Institute and all the special hospitals to be 'placed under the direct, continuous and exceptionally vigilant control and management of the Health Ministry, *with the participation in such control of the whole of our medical community.' The ministry and the Academy of Medical Sciences should, moreover, base their 'unavoidable close study' of the question 'on the materials and proposals of the 1955–6 commission ... which, in their essence, have in no way become obsolete.'*

That the prison hospitals are still directly under the Ministry of

8•

Internal Affairs (M.V.D.), and thus wide open to K.G.B. control, has recently been shown by the ministry's organ Towards a New Life.[8] *In 1970 this announced a ministry decision that in future the designation 'warder' would be changed to 'controller' in: 'investigation prisons, ordinary prisons, psychiatric hospitals of special type, educational-labour colonies and the juveniles' remand centre[9] of the Moscow soviet'.*

The two main legal procedures for forcibly committing people to mental hospitals are a complex matter. One comes within the framework of civil law, the other of criminal law. Civil cases are governed principally by an obscure Health Ministry 'instruction' of 1961, of doubtful legality, which reads: 'If there is a clear danger to those around him or to himself from a mentally ill person, the health organs have the right (by way of immediate psychiatric assistance) to place him in a psychiatric hospital without the consent of the person who is ill or his relatives or guardians.' This may be done by a single psychiatrist or ordinary doctor, and then the patient is detained or not, depending on the verdict of a panel of three psychiatrists. The panel decide, in fact, whether or not his condition in the present — and for the foreseeable future — is one of legal responsibility (deesposobnost). *If not, and he is considered potentially dangerous, he is normally kept in hospital indefinitely for obligatory treatment* (obyazatelnoye lecheniye). *This was the procedure used in the Esenin-Volpin case of 1968, analysed by the* Chronicle *with one slight inaccuracy in Chapter 3,[10] and also with the biologist Zhores Medvedev in 1970. Alternatively, the K.G.B. or the Procuracy can at this stage start a criminal case and apply the second procedure described below. This is what happened with Vladimir Borisov, as recounted later in this chapter. The 1961 instruction probably stemmed in part from Khrushchev's openly expressed equation of social deviation with insanity.[11]*

The second procedure, operative under criminal law (articles 58–60 of the Russian Code), is well illustrated in the pages which follow. First a man commits an act which the K.G.B., say, considers a crime: he is arrested and interrogated. Then, if the K.G.B. thinks he may have committed the crime in a state of legal non-accountability (nevmenyayemost), *or it wants to frame him and thus avoid an open trial which might involve his spirited self-defence and also provoke demonstrations, he is sent for psychiatric diagnosis to, normally, the Serbsky Institute. Professor Lunts and his colleagues then consult with the K.G.B. investigators as to what diagnosis would be politically most convenient, and duly produce it.*

This usually asserts that the crime was committed in a state of legal non-accountability. Then—even if the defendant is in general considered quite sane—a court which he has no right to attend normally endorses without question the Institute's recommendation of indefinite compulsory treatment (prinuditelnoye lecheniye). *Thus very few chances of challenging the machine exist in frame-up cases. The defence can do little but request a second, more objective psychiatric diagnosis. This has been tried in, for example, the cases of Yakhimovich, Grigorenko and Victor Kuznetsov.*[12]

All these practices have since 1968 become a hot issue between the régime and the Democratic Movement, partly because leading members of the movement have in increasing numbers fallen victim to them. The first extensive revelations—confirmed in all essentials by later evidence—were in fact made as early as 1963 by the writer Valery Tarsis. His Ward 7,[13] *describing in minimally fictionalized form his internment in Moscow's Kashchenko hospital, was published in the West in early 1965. But powerful confirmation did not come until February 1968, when the 'letter of the 12' to the Budapest conference called such methods 'the most shocking form of reprisal'.*[14] *In similar vein the Action Group's first appeal drew the U.N.'s attention to 'an especially inhuman form of persecution: the putting of normal people in psychiatric hospitals because of their beliefs.'*

Notable rebuffs to the régime in the cases of Esenin-Volpin and Medvedev[15]—*both released soon after their internment because of the weight of domestic and foreign protest—have also aroused attention in the outside world. So too has Vladimir Bukovsky's television interview of 1970, in in which he vividly described his stay in the Leningrad prison hospital in 1963–5.*[16]

The mental hospital procedures have, we should note, struck not just at political opponents but also at religious dissenters.[17] *So far, on the other hand, the Ukrainians, Jews and Crimean Tatars involved in national movements have only rarely been affected.*

In any case, opposition to the phenomenon has been gathering strength. As regards its victims, Esenin-Volpin could write in 1970: 'I sense that our society has not yet matured enough to make worthwhile a real campaign for the rights of those adjudged of unsound mind. However, particular cases are already reaching its consciousness and Grigorenko's case seems to me suitable as the starting-point for a broader struggle for these rights.'[18]

PROFESSOR DANIIL LUNTS

To date the Democractic Movement's most frequent target in this general field has been Professor D. R. Lunts:

8 [Lunts] is known to have headed the 'politicals' department of the Serbsky Institute as early as the beginning of the 'fifties. This department is now called the 'special diagnosis department', and Lunts has retained his post as director of all diagnoses connected with political cases. He was the expert who in 1963 declared Vladimir Bukovsky insane, and in 1967 sane. He once also declared Aleksei Dobrovolsky insane, but in 1967 Dobrovolsky, the only person whose testimony was used to build a case against Yury Galanskov, was pronounced psychologically normal (the charges against Alexander Ginzburg were not supported even by Dobrovolsky's testimony). Under the direction of this same Professor Lunts, P. G. Grigorenko was declared insane. It was Lunts, too, who was the expert who 'established' the insanity of Natalya Gorbanevskaya and Victor Fainberg, participants in the demonstration of August 25th. It is difficult to point to a single one of these cases in which the results of the diagnosis could be said to be justified on scientific and medical grounds. Experience makes it clear that each decision is taken at the K.G.B. level, and Professor Lunts has only to wrap it up in the form of a medical conclusion.

POLITICAL HOSPITALS AROUND THE COUNTRY

Political prisoners may find themselves in one of two main types of hospital. The first is more respectable: the hospitals appear in the telephone book, carry on plenty of normal psychiatric work, and only one wing comes under the greater or lesser control of the K.G.B.[19] The other type is directly subordinate, as we have seen, to the M.V.D. As regards the total number of de facto political prisoners in the two categories throughout the country, no estimate can yet be made. But it would be surprising if it did not run into the thousands.

The Chronicle writes of the second category thus:

8 The special psychiatric hospitals admit persons who have committed serious crimes (brutal murder, rape, thuggery), are not answerable for their actions, being in a mentally disturbed

state, and are therefore exempt from trial. Apart from this, it often happens that in order to isolate a person from society, he is declared insane, even if the investigators cannot prove him guilty of committing a serious crime but are nevertheless convinced of his guilt. His period of internment in the hospital is not determined by a court, and may last for any length of time at all.

Alongside those who are genuinely ill, perfectly healthy people are sent to these hospitals on account of their beliefs. In this way they are deprived of the right to defend themselves in court and are held in conditions considerably more severe than those existing in today's prisons and camps.

The first 'hospital' of this kind was already in existence before the war, in Kazan. There is still a special department for politicals dating from that time. After the war, a special colony was created in Sychyovka, in Smolensk Region, and chronically disturbed persons are even now being sent there, among them those politicals who, in the opinion of the K.G.B. and the management of the special hospitals, are the most dangerous. People who land in this colony are reduced to a condition of complete mental collapse. In 1952[20] a special hospital was opened in Leningrad, the address of which is Arsenalnaya ul. 9, p/ya US-20, st. 5.

In 1965 another one was opened in Chernyakhovsk,[21] in Kaliningrad Region, in the building which was formerly a German convict prison [see plate 42], address p/ya 216, st.2. In 1966 one was opened in Minsk [Belorussia], and in 1968 another in Dnepropetrovsk [Ukraine].

All these institutions have the following features in common: political prisoners, although of sound mind, are kept in the same wards as seriously disturbed psychiatric patients; if they will not renounce their convictions they are subjected, on the pretext of treatment, to physical torture, to injections of large doses of Aminazin and Sulfazin,[22] which cause depressive shock reaction and serious physical disorders; the régime is the same as for closed prisons, with one hour's exercise a day. Sometimes sodium aminate, a strong narcotic, is administered by injection, to weaken the patient, and after the injection he is interrogated. The staff consists of orderlies recruited from M.V.D. forces, their uniforms concealed by white overalls, male nurses chosen from among the criminal prisoners, also in white overalls (thieves and recidivist thugs), and lastly the senior and junior medical personnel, many with officers' shoulder-straps beneath their white overalls. The brick walls surrounding these prison hospitals are even more impressive than those of any other kinds of prison.

The most terrifyingly arbitrary régime prevails at the Sychyovka and Chernyakhovsk hospitals, where the sick patients, and the politicals with them, are the victims of daily beatings and sadistic humiliations on the part of the supervisory personnel and the nurses, whose rights are absolutely unlimited. For instance, in the spring of 1969 the patient Popov was beaten to death in the Chernyakhovsk hospital, and in the medical record it was stated that he had died of a brain haemorrhage.

From 1956 to the end of 1964 N. N. Samsonov,[23] a Stalin Prize-winner and a geophysicist who worked in the Arctic, was interned in the Leningrad hospital. He had written a letter to the Central Committee of the party criticizing some of Stalin's theoretical propositions.

The following politicals are at present in the same hospital: Nikolai Danilov and Evgeny Shashenkov of Leningrad,[24] the Moscow architect Oleg Smirnov,[25] and a good number of others.

Former teacher G. Forpostov is being kept in the Chernyakhovsk hospital for attempting to cross the Soviet-Polish border to live in his native Poland.

Until July 1968 the same hospital held the radio operator of the tanker *Tuapse*,[26] Ivankov, who asked for political asylum in the United States, and was later deceived into returning to the Soviet Union. From the moment he returned he has been shut up in prison psychiatric hospitals, and the doctors tell him quite openly that he is in for the rest of his life. The most remarkable thing about this case is that the repatriation department of the U.S. State Department has a letter from the Second Secretary of the Soviet Embassy in Washington, guaranteeing that when Ivankov returned to his homeland he would not be subjected to any repressive measures or persecution. While he was in Chernyakhovsk hospital Ivankov used to tell the other patients and politicals about his tragedy, and for this he was punished with Aminazin and Sulfazin injections in gigantic doses. In July

1968 he was transferred to the hospital of similar type in Dnepropetrovsk.

Prisoners in special or strict-régime camps who feel they can no longer bear the terrible conditions, sometimes try simulating madness—and some of them succeed. But when they get to a prison pyshciatric hospital they immediately realize that it is far worse than the severest camps. Some even beg the doctors on bended knee to 'let them out back to the camp'. People who manage to get out of these 'hospitals' are given a special type of identity card, like ex-prisoners. Those who persist in refusing to admit they are ill have, generally speaking, hardly any hope of getting out to freedom.

THE KAZAN SPECIAL PSYCHIATRIC HOSPITAL   10

The hospital has eleven sections; two of them house working patients. In the third the patients sew aprons, sheets and other articles, and in the fourth they are responsible for keeping the hospital in good repair. The working day is three and a half hours long; the monthly wage is two roubles, irrespective of productivity. Section 11 is designed for tubercular patients, but frequently healthy people are put into the cells with them, especially new arrivals. Patients are transported to the hospital in the usual way—in Stolypin prison trains* and *voronki* [black Marias.]

Treatment by Sulfazin injections is widely used in the hospital; this reduces the patient to a very serious condition: a temperature of 40 degrees Centigrade [104 Fahrenheit], weakness, rheumatism of the joints, headaches, and pains in the buttocks, where the injections are given. In normal psychiatric practice, as is well known, such injections are used as an extreme measure when violent fits occur. A less dangerous method of treatment is by intramuscular injections of Aminazin, but this is carried out in such a way that the injected Aminazin is not absorbed, but forms malignant tumours which have to be removed later by operation.

If the patients commit offences—refuse to take medicine, quarrel with the doctors, or fight, they are strapped into their beds for three days, sometimes more. With this form of punishment, the elementary rules of sanitation are ignored: the

* The Russian Prime Minister Stolypin (1906–11) introduced this type of train.

patients are not allowed to go to the lavatory, and bedpans are not provided.

The hospital library overflows with hack-writings from the Stalin period, but months pass without even these books being issued.

Into this hopsital people are put whose dissenting views are a 'crime' and a 'disease'. However, a case is known when a man was taken there who was really ill, and had not committed a crime. This man, whose name was Vladimir (the *Chronicle* does not know his surname), had an epileptic fit on the street. The police picked him up and took him to a sobering-up station. When he protested that he was not drunk, but ill, they beat him up savagely. His wife, who had written proof of the beating, wished to institute criminal proceedings against the policemen. However, the doctor who was treating the man, and his lawyer, persuaded him and his wife 'not to get involved in anything'. For one and a half years Vladimir was in an ordinary psychiatric hospital, and then he was sent to Kazan.

The *Chronicle* reminds its readers that according to the Russian Criminal Code [articles 58–60] internment in a special psychiatric hospital, like any other forcible treatment, can only be prescribed by a court.

The address of the hospital is: Kazan, UE 148/st. 6.

At the end of June 1969 the Chronicle *reported that 'in the course of July three court hearings are expected which will involve the ordering of compulsory measures of a medical character'. One of these concerned Yakhimovich, the other two Victor Kuznetsov and Ilya Rips. The latter two cases are described below, followed by that of Vladimir Borisov of Leningrad.*

7   THE ARREST OF VICTOR KUZNETSOV

On March 20th Victor Kuznetsov was arrested in the town of Pushkino in Moscow Region.

Victor Kuznetsov is thirty-three years old. His father was imprisoned and perished; his mother works as a shop-assistant, his wife as a laboratory assistant; he has two children—one of five and one of eight. In 1960 Kuznetsov completed a course in graphic arts at the Moscow State Pedagogical Institute and then up till 1966 worked for the Novosti Press Agency.

In March 1965, Kuznetsov spoke out during a debate on 'Cynicism in social life' at Moscow University; the debate was tape-recorded. After the debate K.G.B. agents grabbed Kuznetsov in the street and illegally searched him, whilst the papers found on him were handed over to the K.G.B.; after this he was summoned several times to the K.G.B. and at work an explanation was demanded.

In October 1966 Victor Kuznetsov spoke at a conference of the international student discussion club, 'Time and Thought', in the House of Friendship. 'The problem of freedom in the modern world' was the subject of discussion. Kuznetsov had only managed to recount the consequences of his last speech when, by closing the debate, the organizers prevented him from saying anything on the set subject. After this speech he was forcibly put in a mental hospital for investigation and spent two months there.[27]

After his return from hospital he worked as a design engineer at the experimental factory in Sofrino, as a painter and decorator for the management of the Yaroslavl railway line, and recently he was commissioned by 'Intourist' and 'Sovexport' to do some drawings.

Kuznetsov possessed a wide-ranging collection of *samizdat* works.

On March 20th, a search of his flat was carried out on the basis of a warrant signed by the chief investigator of the Ukrainian K.G.B., Captain Kolchik, the investigator in the Valentyn Moroz affair.[28] During the search a letter, 'Report from the Beria Reserve', was confiscated, also works by Sinyavsky, Daniel and others. After the search Kuznetsov was arrested. The next day a search was carried out at Kuznetsov's neighbours. Victor Kuznetsov's wife and friends were summoned to the K.G.B. for questioning, but no reasons for his arrest were divulged. The basic questions put by the investigator concerned the distribution of *samizdat* works.

THE TRIAL

On July 16th, 1969, the Moscow Regional Court, under the chairmanship of Judge Makarova, examined the case of Victor

Kuznetsov at a closed hearing. Kuznetsov's activities had been classified by the investigators under article 70 of the Russian Criminal Code. The substance of his activities was as follows: spreading the works of Sinyavsky, Daniel and Tarsis, and also Academician Varga's[29] work—'The Russian Road to Socialism' —and Moroz's letter 'Report from the Beria Reserve'. Kuznetsov was examined by an in-patient forensic psychiatric commission of experts, consisting of Lunts, Landau and Pechernikova, who pronounced him of unsound mind, gave a diagnosis of 'mild chronic schizophrenia', and recommended that he be sent to a psychiatric hospital of special type for treatment.[30]

Kuznetsov's defence lawyer, E. Kogan, pleaded for an open hearing, demanding that the accused's nearest relatives be allowed into the courtroom, and also that a new commission of experts be appointed. The Procurator Sorokin proposed that the appeal be rejected. The court rejected the appeal without giving reasons.

Several witnesses who appeared in court confirmed that they had read the works in question, and that they had been given them by Kuznetsov. But the 'anti-Soviet intent' necessary for conviction under article 70 was not indicated by the witnesses' testimony. A woman expert from the Serbsky Institute who appeared in court without ever having seen Kuznetsov, agreed with the opinion of the preliminary commission and stated that Kuznetsov was in need of a protracted course of treatment in a closed hospital.

The court resolved to send Victor Kuznetsov to a psychiatric hospital of special type.

On August 26th the Russian Supreme Court examined the case of Victor Kuznetsov after his defence lawyer had lodged an appeal. The decision of the court of first instance was left unaltered.

But earlier, on August 23rd, even before the appeal was heard, Kuznetsov had been sent to the Kazan special psychiatric hospital.

It should be noted that Victor Kuznetsov had never previously had any psychiatric treatment, and the only time he had been in a mental hospital before his arrest was in the autumn of 1966 when he was forcibly taken away by the K.G.B. and interned in the hospital after a speech he made at a debate.

THE CASE OF ILYA RIPS

In Riga Ivan Yakhimovich and Ilya Rips—who tried to burn 8
himself to death—have been declared insane. The *Chronicle* has
so far given only scanty and, in some respects, inaccurate
information on Rips.[31]

Ilya Rips [see plate 45] is twenty, and will not be twenty-one
until December [1968]. Before his fifteenth birthday he was one
of the winners of the International Schoolchildren's Mathematics Olympiad, and while still under sixteen he finished
school and became a student of the Faculty of Mechanics and
Mathematics at Riga University. For the whole of his studies he
was a holder of a Lenin scholarship, and was the pride of the
University. His graduation thesis, according to his teachers,[32]
could have served, as it stood, as the basis of a higher Doctoral
dissertation.[33] On April 10th he was assigned to a very good
post in the Physics Institute of the Latvian Academy of Sciences.
On April 13th he went and stood on Freedom Square with a
placard saying: I PROTEST AGAINST THE OCCUPATION OF
CZECHOSLOVAKIA, and set fire to his clothes, which he had
previously soaked in petrol. Some sailors who happened to be
passing quickly put out the flames, but beat up the young man
cruelly. Fortunately his burns were only slight. Rips's university friends came to the hospital where he had been taken and
offered themselves as blood donors. According to unconfirmed
rumours, repressive measures were taken by the university
against the students.

A charge was brought against Ilya Rips under article 65 of
the Latvian Criminal Code, equivalent to article 70 of the
Russian Code. It is extremely difficult to classify Rips's actions
under any article whatsoever of the Criminal Code. That is
probably why the article on 'anti-Soviet propaganda and
agitation' was chosen: in the first place, its formulation is the
most vaguely-worded, and in the second place, it ensures the
minimum publicity—for a start, it requires a defence lawyer
with a security pass. Apart from the fact that he attempted to
burn himself to death, Ilya Rips is not accused of anything.
Indeed the inquiry itself established that Rips's sole point of disagreement with Soviet policy was over a single action of the
government—the sending of troops into Czechoslovakia. In

these circumstances, to prove his guilt under article 65 of the Latvian Code—that is, to prove his intent to undermine the existing system—would be too difficult. It is far easier to have Ilya Rips isolated as 'insane', since the judges, following established practice, will regard the ordering of compulsory measures of a medical nature as a pure formality, without examining either the essence of the case or the essence of the diagnosis.

Following this model, the conclusion of the diagnostic team—'he must be considered insane and put in a psychiatric hospital of special type for compulsory treatment'—will almost certainly mean that Victor Kuznetsov, Ivan Yakhimovich and Ilya Rips will find their way into a prison psychiatric hospital.

10 On October 2nd in Riga the Latvian Supreme Court examined the case of Ilya Rips, for whom compulsory measures of a medical nature had been recommended [...] The court resolved to order compulsory treatment for Ilya Rips in a psychiatric hospital of ordinary type. Rips was defended at the trial by the lawyer S. L. Ariya.

Only in May 1971 was Rips released.

11   THE TRIAL OF VLADIMIR BORISOV
(OF LENINGRAD)

Borisov [see plate 44], born in 1943, is an electrician and a member of the Action Group for the Defence of Civil Rights in the U.S.S.R. From 1964 to 1968 he was in a psychiatric hospital prison in Leningrad (9 Arsenal Street), charged under article 70 of the Russian Criminal Code. In May 1969 he signed the [first] appeal to the United Nations and a letter in defence of P. G. Grigorenko. In June Borisov was summoned by the doctor in charge of the Vyborg District Out-Patients Clinic for Psychiatric and Neurological Diseases in Leningrad, where he had been registered since his discharge from the special hospital in the spring of 1968.

On June 12th, 1969, an ambulance and two doctors from the out-patients clinic were sent to fetch Borisov from work. The *samizdat* he was carrying was taken from him and he was driven to the clinic. No conversations were conducted with him. One of the doctors came up to him and said: 'Listen, Borisov, you're quite normal; you don't want to be sent to a lunatic asylum, do you? Better change your ideas about politics.' The other doctor began looking through the literature that had been taken away from Borisov: 'I've seen this and this, ah, now this is something new—must have a look at this.' His colleague called out to him: 'Leave that alone or you'll end up in the same place as him.'

Dzhemma Kvachevskaya,[34] Vladimir Borisov's wife, went to the clinic and asked to be given the literature confiscated from her husband. She was told: 'The literature will be appended to his medical record.'[35]

The doctor at the clinic told Borisov: 'I am hospitalizing you not on my own initiative, but in accordance with orders', and sent Borisov to Leningrad's Psychiatric Hospital No. 4 (the doctor in charge there, Vladimir Pavlovich Belyayev, is also the chief psychiatrist of Leningrad).

The following day V. P. Belyayev spoke with Borisov in the presence of doctors and orderlies. Borisov was questioned about his views and beliefs and about the reasons for his being admitted to hospital in 1964. At the end of the interview Belyayev said that what happened to Borisov would be decided by a commission, which would request that documents be sent from the hospitals in which he had previously been treated; Borisov would stay in this hospital for about ten days; he was permitted to read any literature published in the Soviet Union, but not to comment on it to the patients; he could have pencil and paper, but everything he wrote would have to be handed in for inspection and he was not entitled to correspond with people outside. In reply to Borisov's question, 'On what grounds have I been brought here?' Belyayev replied: 'It was reported to us that your behaviour had changed: you had become nervous and excitable.' Belyayev refused to say who made these 'reports'.

On June 23rd Borisov was called to the office of the head physician of the hospital, where the 'top-level' commission was in attendance. Its members were V. P. Belyayev, Chief Psychiatrist of Leningrad; Major-General Timofeyev, Chief Psychiatrist to the Leningrad Military District (who retired a few months ago, and who, in 1965, was a member of the commission which examined Borisov in the Leningrad hospital prison); a section head from Psychiatric Hospital No. 4; and a man in civilian clothes, who refused to give his name (it turned out later that this was Sluchevsky, Chief Physician of Leningrad Psychiatric Hospital No. 3). The conversation was mainly conducted by Timofeyev. Borisov's past and the reasons for his present confinement in hospital were discussed and Borisov was informed that he had been brought there because of the *samizdat* materials and because he had signed protest letters. These, as the man in civilian dress said, could only be regarded as evidence of mental disorder or hooliganism.

Timofeyev was interested in how Borisov had come to know P. G. Grigorenko. Borisov replied: 'At Arsenal Street', i.e. in the special hospital there. Then Timofeyev began questioning Borisov about his other Moscow acquaintances, and their views, and why Borisov did not like life in the Soviet Union. Borisov was asked how he intended to behave in the future, to which he replied that he had no intention of committing himself in any way; it would all depend on the circumstances. At this the meeting of the commission came to a close.

The commission's decision, that further treatment was essential, was announced not to Borisov but to his wife. Borisov was transferred to a hospital near where he lived (the Skvortsov-Stepanov Psychiatric Hospital No. 3, Section 15). In conversation with his wife, the section head, a woman, told her that Borisov needed treatment because he did not behave as a normal person should. To his wife's objection that this was not a symptom of illness, but a question of Borisov's personal opinions, the section head replied: 'Maybe, but he was unlucky; he is down on our register. What may be a system of opinions in a normal person is a sign of illness in your husband', and she recommended that Borisov's wife exert her influence on Borisov to make him see reason, since otherwise he would have to undergo constant treatment.[36]

Circulating in *samizdat* is a detailed account of how Borisov was sent to the psychiatric hospital entitled: 'A socially restive man.'[37]

10 At the end of September criminal proceedings were instituted under article 190-1 of the Russian Criminal Code against Vladimir Borisov of Leningrad, a member of the Action Group. He was charged with signing a letter to the United Nations and

a letter in defence of Grigorenko. Borisov had not been formally taken into custody, but had been taken to the department for violent patients at the city psychiatric hospital, where only his mother and wife were allowed to visit him. When Borisov found out that criminal proceedings had been instituted against him, he tried to escape from the hospital. After that, he was transferred to the prison psychiatric hospital on Arsenal Street, where people are [normally] admitted only if they have been convicted by a court. The investigation into Borisov's case is being conducted by the Leningrad Procuracy, under Senior Investigator Belov.

The trial of Vladimir Borisov, charged under article 190–1 of the Russian Criminal Code, took place on November 19th. V. E. Borisov was judged to be of unsound mind and the court decreed that he should undergo compulsory treatment in a psychiatric hospital of special type, i.e. a prison hospital.

The *Chronicle* does not yet know in which prison hospital Borisov will be confined.

Later the Chronicle *reported Borisov's return to the Leningrad prison hospital and also an odd conversation there between his wife and his doctor. The latter, having said he needed no medicines and having made him sound quite normal, then blandly stated that he would have to be interned 'for at least two more years'.*[38]

In the spring of 1971 he joined Fainberg in a hunger-strike lasting eighty-one days.

Finally, the Chronicle *reveals an official state of mind which affects to see not just social deviation but even individual protests and petitions as signs of insanity:*

A number of facts indicate that the reception rooms of the highest official bodies in Moscow either have an ambulance on permanent duty from the psychiatric first-aid service, or are in direct and speedy contact with this service. In many cases, people who have come to the reception rooms of the party Central Committee, the Council of Ministers, the Presidium of the Supreme Soviet, the All-Union Central Council of Trade

Unions, the K.G.B., and other organizations with complaints, generally of a non-political nature, have not been allowed to put their case, but have been forcibly driven off to Moscow psychiatric hospitals, and then, after a psychiatric diagnosis, to their local hospitals.[39]

In early 1971 an enormous quantity of material on the political manipulation of Soviet psychiatry was sent to Western psychiatrists by Vladimir Bukovsky.[40] He appealed to them to study the material, then discuss it in international forums. For 'there is', he wrote, 'no more fearful fate for a healthy person than indefinite confinement in a psychiatric hospital.' In September 1971, 44 psychiatrists provided the first solid response in a letter of support to The Times.[41]

Part IV · Individual Streams

12. THE CRIMEAN TATARS

Genocide was one of the terrible products of the two accursed Führers
of the twentieth century. But the frenzied Adolf fell at once upon
nations numbering hundreds of millions, while the 'Marxist' Stalin
preferred to 'get a little training' on the small nations. Among these
nations fate included the Crimean Tatars.

Pyotr Grigorenko, Spring 1969[1]

APPEAL BY REPRESENTATIVES OF THE CRIMEAN TATAR
PEOPLE TO THE WORLD PUBLIC   2

June 21st, 1968

In 1944 THE WHOLE OF OUR PEOPLE was slanderously
accused of betraying the Soviet motherland and was forcibly
deported from the Crimea.

All the adult men were at the front; able-bodied older men
and youngsters were in the labour corps. In one single day,
May 18th, about 200,000 defenceless women, children and
infirm persons were without warning driven out of their homes
by K.G.B. troops, loaded on to troop trains and removed under
escort to reservations. The operation was directed by Marshal
Voroshilov. For about three weeks they were transported in
closed trucks, almost without food or clothing, to Central Asia.
After the war was over the men who returned from the front
were sent to the same destination. As a result of the inhuman
deportation and the intolerable conditions in which we found
ourselves more than half of all our people[2] perished in these first
years. Simultaneously, our national autonomy was extinguished,
our national culture completely destroyed, our monuments
pulled down, and the graves of our ancestors defiled and wiped
off the face of the earth.

During the next twelve years we lived as exiles and were
discriminated against. Our children, even those born in exile,
were branded as 'traitors'; slanderous stories were published

about us and are to this day still being read by Soviet people.

Following the 20th party congress [1956] our people were relieved of the exile régime, but the accusation of having betrayed the fatherland was not dropped, and, as previously, we were not allowed to return to the Crimea. From 1957 until 1967 we sent to the party Central Committee and the Presidium of the U.S.S.R. Supreme Soviet hundreds of thousands of collective and individual letters calling for an end to be put to the injustice suffered. The representatives of our people in Moscow* were, after persistent requests, received on several occasions by the party and government leaders Mikoyan, Georgadze, Andropov and Shchelokov.[3] On each occasion we were promised a speedy solution of the Crimean Tatar problem, but instead there followed arrests, deportations, dismissals from employment and expulsions from the party.

Finally, on September 5th, 1967, there appeared a Decree of the Presidium of the U.S.S.R. Supreme Soviet which cleared us of the charge of treason but described us not as Crimean Tatars but as 'citizens of Tatar nationality formerly resident in the Crimea', thus legitimizing our banishment from our home country and liquidating us as a nation. We did not grasp the significance of the decree immediately. After it was published, several thousand people travelled to the Crimea but were once again forcibly expelled. The protest which our people sent to the party Central Committee was left unanswered, as were also the protests of representatives of the Soviet public who supported us.

The authorities replied to us only with persecution and court cases. Since 1959 more than 200 of the most active and courageous representatives have been sentenced to terms of up to seven years although they had always acted within the limits of the Soviet Constitution. Repressive action against us has been specially intensified recently. On April 21st, 1968, in the town of Chirchik, Crimean Tatars who had assembled to celebrate Lenin's birthday [see plates 49 and 50] were dispersed by troops

---

* The permanent unofficial delegation of the Crimean Tatar people in Moscow has been in existence since 1964. Representatives replace one another constantly and hold mandates signed by the residents of the towns and villages which have sent them to Moscow. They try to secure a solution to the national problem of their people, to obtain hearings with government and party leaders, and they publish an information bulletin [*Chronicle*'s note].

and policemen,* and more than 300 persons were arrested.⁴ In May 800 representatives of the people travelled to Moscow to hand the party Central Committee a letter calling for the people to be returned to the Crimea. On May 16th and 17th almost all the representatives were arrested and deported under escort to Tashkent.† At the same time four representatives of our intelligentsia were sentenced in Tashkent to various terms of imprisonment.⁵ Every day dozens of people are summoned to appear at their local K.G.B. offices and there pressured by blackmail and threats to renounce returning to our homeland.

The calumny is spread around that we want to return to the Crimea in order to expel those who are now living there. This is untrue. We are a peaceful people and have always lived and will live in friendship with the multi-racial population of the Crimea; we are not threatening anyone—it is we who are constantly being threatened with national extinction.

What people are doing to us has a quite specific name— GENOCIDE.

In the course of our struggle a total of more than 3 million signatures have been collected on the letters sent by our people to the Soviet Government. This means that each adult Crimean Tatar has affixed his signature to them at least ten times. But the appeal of 300,000 people, repeated ten times over, has re-echoed in vain. Not a single party or government body has ever given us a reply; not a single Soviet newspaper has ever once referred to our fight.

We appeal accordingly to the world public.

We appeal to all the peoples of the Soviet Union as a small independent people appeals to brother peoples.

* The persons directly responsible for the Chirchik excesses were the secretary of the party's city committee, Yakubov, who banned the peaceful Sunday outing, and Major-General Sheraliyev, who summoned the troops to Chirchik [*Chronicle*'s note].

† Stasenkov, Deputy Procurator of Moscow, declared: 'Your problem has been fully and finally settled and will be given no further consideration.' Demanding the departure of all the representatives, he threatened that force would be used. Force was used: Crimean Tatars were arrested in hotels, private apartments, on railway stations, squares and other points in Moscow, were bundled into a mail- and goods-train and sent under escort to Tashkent. A large group of representatives of the people was arrested at the building of the party Central Committee. Along with them the police arrested also those Muscovites who by their presence were expressing their sympathy for the Crimean Tatar people. The whole operation was led by General Volkov, head of the Moscow Public Order Administration [*Chronicle*'s note].

We appeal to all the peoples of the world and above all to those who have personally experienced the meaning of national inequality of rights and oppression.

We appeal to all people of goodwill in the hope that you will help us.

HELP US TO RETURN TO THE LAND OF OUR FATHERS!

The letter is signed by the following representatives of the Crimean Tatar people who hold a mandate authorizing them to fight on behalf of the people for the return to the homeland by all lawful methods:

1.	Zampira Asanova, doctor[6]	Bekabad [Uzbekistan]
2.	Rollan Kadiyev, theoretical physicist	Samarkand [Uzbekistan]
3.	Reshat Bairamov, electrician	Melitopol [S. Ukraine]
4.	Murat Voyenny, builder	Tashkent [Uzbekistan]
5.	Zera Khalilova, teacher	Namangan [Uzbekistan]
6.	Mustafa Ibrish, engineer	Tashkent
7.	Eldar Shabanov, driver	Bekabad
8.	Aishe Bekirova, teacher	Bekabad
9.	Ramazan Muratov, worker	Bekabad

(and so on—in all, 118 signatures:[7] doctors, engineers, workers of all specialities, pensioners, students, office-workers, housewives from Tashkent, Samarkand, Fergana, Chirchik, Margelan, Sovetabad, Andizhan, Angren, Begovat, Leninabad, etc., from the Kirghiz Republic, from the towns of Leninsk and Novorossiisk).

This document alone reveals that the Tatars have generated a mass movement unprecedented in Soviet history. Such a revelation can be confirmed many times over by those industrious enough to wade through all the documentary evidence from samizdat now available in the West. This already amounts in total to about five hundred pages, and grows steadily. Only some of it can be indicated here. For the historical back-

ground to the Tatars' deportation and subsequent fate, readers are referred to Robert Conquest's excellent book The Nation Killers,[8] *which also contains an analysis of the key events described in this chapter.*

The general nature of the problem and its relation to the Democratic Movement will already be clear from passages in earlier chapters about Grigorenko, Kosterin, Gabai and Mustafa Dzhemilev.[9] *This chapter fills out the picture.*

Not quite so clear are the Soviet authorities' reasons for their—in its effect—racist policy. Here one can only speculate. Fears doubtless exist that the Tatars could, under certain circumstances, be more loyal to their ethnic and cultural kin in Turkey than to the U.S.S.R. Such fears would cause worries about military security in the strategically placed Crimea, were the Tatars to return. Probably even more important, though, is the Soviet leadership's instinctive fear that if it yields to the demands of one aggrieved group, a hundred others will press their claims with renewed energy.

It was in early 1968 that the vital link-up—witness the 'letter of the 12' to the Budapest conference (pp. 86–8)—occurred between the Tatars and the radicals of the Democratic Movement in Moscow. An individual link had of course existed for a long time with Aleksei Kosterin. Indeed the growth of his friendship with Grigorenko in 1966–7 probably played a big role in the recruitment of the radicals to the Tatars' cause. But the Tatars' lobbying tactics must also take credit for the success, as this item shows:

A CLARIFICATION OF NATIONALITIES POLICY 6

In February 1968 Dmitry Motyl, a student of the physics and chemistry faculty of the Mendeleyev Chemico-Technological Institute in Moscow, showed his friends an appeal by the Crimean Tatars to people of good will. One of the students suggested to the Young Communist League committee that they should express their support for the demands of the Crimean Tatar people. In response to this a lecture on the position of the Crimean Tatars in the U.S.S.R. was arranged at the Institute on February 25th.

P. G. Grigorenko, who has for a long time been interested in this problem, the economist Julius Telesin,[10] and two Crimean Tatars, the engineer Kadyr Sarametov and Mustafa Murtaza-yev, a lathe-operator, came to hear the lecture. The lecture was

intended for students of the group in which Motyl was studying
and for members of the Young Communist League bureau.
P. G. Grigorenko had received permission to attend the lecture,
but when the lecturer came into the auditorium and saw
Grigorenko he immediately turned round and walked out
again. This can only be explained by the fact that the lecturer
must in reality have been a K.G.B. official who knew Grigorenko by sight. After this the lecture was transferred to another
auditorium and neither Grigorenko nor the student Motyl was
admitted. The doors to the auditorium were guarded by a
detachment of staff, headed by senior lecturer Chechin. The
secretary of the party committee of the Institute, K. M. Tyutina,
announced that the lecturer from the Central Committee of the
party was going to explain the party's policy on the nationalities
question and that the presence of 'outsiders' was undesirable.
J. Telesin and M. Murtazayev, who were in the Institute building, had their documents checked and were forced to leave,*
and K. Sarametov was held for four hours by the police.

The faculty bureau of the Young Communist League
decided to expel Dmitry Motyl from their organization.

*Grigorenko's arrest in May 1969, following soon after Kosterin's
death, was a heavy blow to the Tatars. Their reply was:*

8   THE CRIMEAN TATARS' DEMONSTRATION ON
          MAYAKOVSKY SQUARE, JUNE 6TH, 1969

On June 6th, 1969, the second day of the World Conference of
Communist and Workers' Parties, the Crimean Tatars staged a
demonstration on Mayakovsky Square. There were five
participants: Zampira Asanova, Enver Ametov, Reshat
Dzhemilev, Aider Zeitulayev, and Ibraim Kholopov. At a
quarter past twelve they unfurled banners at the foot of the
Mayakovsky memorial, with the slogans HAIL TO LENIN'S
NATIONALITIES POLICY!; COMMUNISTS, GIVE THE CRIMEA
BACK TO THE CRIMEAN TATARS!; STOP PERSECUTING THE
CRIMEAN TATARS!; and FREE GENERAL GRIGORENKO!
The last placard carried a photograph of Grigorenko.

A large crowd of about three hundred gathered round the
demonstrators, encircling them but not daring to approach

* See Telesin's detailed account of this episode, pp. 49-50.

really close. It was a silent crowd. There were two shouts of 'They shouldn't have betrayed Russia!' No one asked the demonstrators to disperse. The policemen on traffic duty left their posts and, after a short consultation, elbowed their way into the crowd and signalled to about ten of the bystanders, using some special signs. These people sprang into action, forced their way through the crowd to the demonstrators, and, supposedly expressing the 'anger of the people',[11] fell upon the demonstrators using physical violence. In a really professional manner they twisted their arms, and two women amongst them beat the demonstrators with their umbrellas. The demonstrators did not resist. Reshat and Aider shouted 'Long live Freedom!' 'So it's freedom you're after, eh? That's a good one!' said one of the policemen. Irina Yakir, who had been standing near the demonstrators, was detained with them.

Because the traffic police had left their posts, the flow of traffic slowed and a jam built up on [nearby] Pushkin Square. Half an hour later the crowds had still not left the scene, but people had split up into groups and were wandering up and down the square. Most of the conversations revealed attitudes of great-power chauvinism. Some students who tried to voice a different opinion were threatened and left hastily without starting an argument.

Those detained were driven off to 38 Petrovka Street [the Moscow Police Headquarters], where they were interrogated by investigators of the Ministry of the Interior. Irina Yakir was allowed to go later the same day, and the following day the participants in the demonstration were sent home. Very probably they escaped arrest because of the World Communist Conference which was then taking place.

Among the demonstrators the doctor Zampira Asanova from Uzbekistan should be singled out: she signed both the 'letter of the 12' and the above-quoted appeal, and also spoke at Kosterin's funeral.[12] But her fellows subsequently fared worse than she:

At present further repressive measures are being taken against 8 Reshat Dzhemilev. Dzhemilev is thirty-eight and a construction engineer. Every year since 1965 the Crimean Tatars have been sending him to Moscow as one of their representatives. He was one of the twenty Crimean Tatars who on June 21st, 1967, were received by the Chairman of the K.G.B., Andropov, the Secretary of the U.S.S.R. Supreme Soviet, Georgadze, the Attorney-General of the U.S.S.R., Rudenko, and the Minister of Public Order, Shchelokov. The reception of this delegation was an important step towards the political rehabilitation of the Crimean Tatar people.

On September 2nd, 1967, Reshat Dzhemilev was arrested as an 'organizer of the mass disturbances in Tashkent on August 27th and September 2nd, 1967'. On December 13th, 1967, the Tashkent City Court sentenced him to one year of corrective labour. By 'mass disturbances' were understood the numerous meetings held by Crimean Tatars in defence of their rights.

After the demonstration of June 6th, Reshat Dzhemilev was sent under escort to Nizhne-Bakanovka in Krasnodar Province [N. Caucasus] where his family recently came over to join him, and where he has now begun building a house. On arrival he was met by the police, who threatened him with prosecution under article 209 of the Russian Criminal Code, 'vagrancy and begging', if he did not immediately obtain a residence permit and a job. One might add that to get his residence permit Dzhemilev needs at least fourteen square metres of living space since his family consists of a wife and three children.

A few days after this, on June 15th, an incident was staged at the railway station, as a result of which Reshat Dzhemilev was given fifteen days for 'petty hooliganism'. Reshat was standing in the queue for tickets when an old man he did not know came up to him, squeezed in front of him, and dropped a glass of yoghourt on his feet. Reshat remained calm, but the police immediately rushed up and seized him; the old man vanished and no one tried to stop him; nor did the police approach any witnesses although Reshat demanded that they do so. Most probably Reshat was given his fifteen days 'for security reasons'; this had already happened to another Crimean Tatar activist in Gulistan. (A copy exists of an official police document which states quite openly that 'this man has been imprisoned for a period of fifteen days "for security reasons".')

Other participants in the demonstration were deprived of their residence permits for the places where they lived in Krasnodar Province.

32. David Khavkin (right, see p. 309) with a fellow-prisoner in Mordovia, 1960.
This is the first known photograph of the inside of a Soviet political camp to reach
the West.

33. A self-portrait
Leningrad   artist
Ivanov (see pp. 215 ff
drew the other portr
produced here in M
in 1969

34. Leonid Borodin, a
headmaster from Leningrad
Region (see pp. 207 ff and 376 ff).

35. Vyacheslav Platonov,
Leningrad orientalist (Cf.
Borodin).

36. Mikhail Sado, Leni
orientalist (see p. 376 ff

ry Titov, photographed in
'␣s Kashchenko Psychiatric
l, Spring 1971 (see pp.
472, also plate 60).

ry Galanskov (see also

38. Yuly Daniel (see also plate 1).

39. Victor Kalninš, Latvian journalist (see p. 212).

41. Outside the Oryol prison-hospital: prisoners being marched, 1971 (see p. 170).

42. Exterior of the Chernyakhovsk prison-hospital (see pp. 237 ff).

The Chronicle *then carried the following item, since when it has been silent on Dzhemilev:*

Criminal proceedings have been instituted against Reshat 9 Dzhemilev, one of the Crimean Tatar demonstrators on Mayakovsky Square in Moscow on June 6th. He has been charged under article 190–1 of the Russian Criminal Code with making a speech at the funeral of A. E. Kosterin, and with helping to compile the collection 'In Memory of A. E. Kosterin'.[13] Apart from that, he has evidently been charged for signing a letter in support of Ivan Yakhimovich.[14] The investigation is being conducted by the Krasnodar Procuracy, while in Moscow witnesses are being interrogated by Obraztsov, an investigator of the Moscow Procuracy.

In the period after the demonstration, ordinary Tatar delegates were — like the demonstrators — expelled from Moscow.[15] And one of their sympathizers also suffered a reprisal:

Irina Yakir, a student of the evening-course department at the 9 Historical Archives Institute, has been expelled from the Institute 'for failing to fulfil her study plan, and for conduct unworthy of a Soviet student'. As far as her study plan is concerned, Irina Yakir was in fact *ahead* of her year. The real reason for her expulsion was her presence on Mayakovsky Square at the time of the Crimean Tatars' demonstration on June 6th, 1969. She was only informed of her expulsion a month after the order was issued.

THE 'TASHKENT TEN'

With the Tatars' cause gaining ever wider support in 1968–9, and their literature circulating in steadily greater volume in samizdat,[16] *the authorities evidently felt the need for a decisive counter-attack. In autumn 1968 ten Tatar leaders were arrested:[17] by the end of the year the investigation had been concluded[18] and the ground prepared for a show trial. Then various delays ensued — evidently connected with political expediency — and the indictment was finally signed only in April 1969. Soon after this the* Chronicle *reported:*

9

There is in *samizdat* Grigorenko's last political pamphlet before his arrest—'Who are the Criminals?' [19] He wrote it after reading the charges brought against the ten Crimean Tatars.[20] In his pamphlet Grigorenko exposes the flimsiness of the charges; he deals with the question of the Crimean Tatars as a minority people, and the genocide of which they are the victims; with their national movement, which has the unanimous support of the whole people; and with the persecution of active participants in this movement. He refers to the decree of September 5th, 1967, which withdrew the treason charge brought against the Crimean Tatars but deprived them of their national name and of the right to return to their homeland. P. G. Grigorenko shows that the documents listed in the indictment[21] were based on facts, that these documents were sent to various high authorities, and that those authorities did not reply, nor did they attempt to refute the documents. The right to label them as libellous turned out to belong to the very same Uzbek authorities about whom the Crimean Tatars had complained in the above-mentioned documents. 'Not one of the facts set out in the documents', writes Grigorenko, 'was checked by anyone, and the investigating organs are not in possession of any proof that any of the facts used are unreliable. In consequence the investigators were forced to restrict themselves to unfounded abuse of the documents they examined.' As P. G. Grigorenko shows, the author of the indictment, Counsellor of Justice Berezovsky, makes use of the word 'alleged', and of inverted commas, as his main devices for proving a point: allegedly methods of force and arbitrariness are being applied, allegedly in exile, are allegedly in places of 'exile', and so on. But unsubstantiated allegations and lies are not the only things that Grigorenko discovers:

Sometimes Stalinism suddenly rears its ugly head. Here is what is written, for example, on page 10 of the indictment: 'This letter casts aspersions on the policy of the Communist Party and the Soviet government towards national minorities. The resettlement of the Crimean Tatars in 1944 is represented by the writers of the letter as "a barbarous crime". Well, this brutal deportation of 1944—that was part of the policy of the Communist Party and the Soviet

government towards national minorities, and those who call
it a "brutal crime" must be tried for slandering this policy.'

Grigorenko stresses that investigator Berezovsky and Procurator Ruzmetov, who countersigned the indictment, are revealed
as Stalinists not only through this casual slip, but by the very
nature of this whole trumped-up case.

THE TRIAL

From July 1st to August 5th a session of the Uzbek Supreme 9
Court took place in Tashkent. The Judge was Saifutdinov; the
People's Assessors, Samoilova and Isfandiarov; the Prosecutor,
Enkalov; and the defence lawyers, Monakhov, Zaslavsky and
Safonov. The accused were Reshat Bairamov, age 26, a fitter;
Aider Bariyev, age 31, a bulldozer-driver, father of two child-
ren; Svetlana Ametova, age 28, nurse and mother of a six-year-
old son; Munire Khalilova, age 24, a midwife; Riza Umerov,
age 49, an electro-welder, father of two; Ruslan Eminov, age
30, a foreman and father of two; Izzet Khairov, age 31, a
weights and measures engineer [see plate 48], a member of the
Communist Party and father of two children; Rollan Kadiyev,
a 32-year-old physicist [see plate 47], father of three; Ridvan
Gafarov, age 54, a pensioner and second-category invalid; and
Ismail Yazydzhiyev, age 49, father of two children, trained as a
teacher, fought in the Great Patriotic War, a bricklayer.

The accused had previously made the following requests:

1. that correspondents of *Pravda*, *Izvestia*, and the Crimean
Tatar paper *Lenin bairagi* be called to attend the trial;

2. that the trial be given full press coverage and be broadcast
live on television;

3. that a commission of experts be called to attend the trial,
to determine the facts about the questions raised in the documents to which the charges related;

4. that observers from the Central Committee of the party
and the Soviet government be called to attend the trial;

5. that the accused be given the necessary literature to
prepare for the trial;

6. that the conditions of their detention in prison be changed:
the accused were living in cells overflowing with criminals, and
could not make any preparations for their defence;

7. that they be given the medical help they needed;

8. that they receive a change of sheets and clothing.

Out of all the requests only the last two had been granted. In protest at the refusal of the prison and judicial authorities to make available the necessary legal and political literature, Rollan Kadiyev[22] had gone on a hunger-strike on June 20th, and he came into court in a condition testifying to this. He called off his strike only when threatened with a separate trial.

The accused declared their objection to the Prosecutor, a man well known from other Crimean Tatar trials, and refused to answer his questions. Rollan Kadiyev declared his objection to the Judge also. The objections were not upheld. The Prosecutor was notable for his ill-mannered behaviour, his disregard for the law, and his lack of respect for the accused as people. The Prosecutor declared that the accused were not political but criminal offenders, and that was why they were being held in the conditions prescribed for criminal offenders. The Prosecutor repeatedly brought pressure to bear on the defence: he told the lawyers how they ought to advise their clients, cut them short, and demanded that the court rebuke them.

During the whole of the proceedings neither the court nor the prosecution raised the question of having the facts which were described in the indictment as libellous fabrications either corroborated or refuted. The prosecution was concerned only with proving the fact that they were manufactured and distributed — while the accused did not deny many of these facts; on the other hand, they completely denied the libellous nature of the documents, and pleaded not guilty.

The Prosecutor demanded three years in camps for Bairamov, Bariyev, Khairov and Kadiyev; eighteen months each for Umerov and Gafarov; a year each for Ametova, Khalilova and Yazydzhiyev; and one year of corrective labour for Eminov. The defence demanded a verdict of not guilty.

The court passed a verdict of guilty, declaring the accused guilty under the articles brought against them, article 190–1 of the Russian Criminal Code and the equivalent articles [187–1 and 191–4] from the Ukrainian and Uzbek[23] Codes, and sentenced them as follows: Reshat Bairamov and Rollan Kadiyev to three years in ordinary-régime camps; Aider

Bariyev and Izzet Khairov to eighteen months; and Ridvan Gafarov and Ismail Yazydzhiyev to one year. The court decided that the term spent in pre-trial imprisonment (about ten months) was sufficient for Svetlana Ametova, Munire Khalilova and Riza Umerov. Ruslan Eminov was given six months' corrective labour. Yazydzhiyev's term expires in September, Gafarov's in October.

On August 5th, after the verdict of guilty had been passed, a crowd of about 500 to 700 Crimean Tatars who had gathered outside the courthouse marched in orderly fashion to the Procurator's office, and then to the Uzbek Communist Party Central Committee building. A sit-in demonstration was organized outside the Procuracy. But two blocks before they reached the Central Committee building, the demonstrators were met by a large force of police, who fell upon them. Some of the demonstrators were dispersed, some detained. After twenty-four hours' detention in police stations, almost all of them were released, except for four people who were given fifteen days' imprisonment.

Very soon the Chronicle *reported on the appearance in* samizdat *of 'Case No. 109':*[24]

Material from the trial, and part of the pre-trial investigation, 10 in the case of the ten Crimean Tatars. The *Chronicle* gave a brief report of the trial in the last issue. Among the materials from the pre-trial investigation, the most interesting is a whole series of denunciatory reports from official bodies and public organizations to which the Crimean Tatars had sent material about the tragedy of their people. Instead of replying to the letters from the Crimean Tatars, the heads and other representatives of these organizations passed the letters on to the K.G.B. Denunciations of the Crimean Tatars were written by Tikhonov, a rear-admiral of the Baltic Fleet, K. Voronkov, a secretary of the Board of the U.S.S.R. Writers' Union, A. Mukhtar and R. Faizi, Deputy Chairmen of the Uzbek Writers' Union, and Sh. Sagdulla, a literary consultant and secretary of the Uzbek Writers' Union Party Organization. The director of the Crimean Regional Museum, L. Zhuk, wrote a report about the comments written by Crimean Tatars in the museum's Visitors'

Book. In their comments they had said that the part played by the Crimean Tatars in the Great Patriotic War and in the struggle for a Soviet victory in the Crimea was not reflected in the museum's exhibits; on the stand labelled 'Heroes of the Soviet Union from our Crimean Homeland' there were no photographs of the Crimean Tatars who had been honoured with this high rank. The pages with their comments had been torn out of the Visitors' Book and added to the case-file.

The investigation into the case of the ten Crimean Tatars was conducted by the Uzbek Republican Procuracy and headed by senior Procuracy investigator B. I. Berezovsky. It became known that apart from him, the team of investigators included one other Procuracy investigator, B. N. Vorobyov, and eight K.G.B. investigators: B. N. Bobylyov, M. Nabiyev, V. M. Lysenko, K. M. Abushayev, D. R. Mustafayev, S. R. Mukanov, Ya. Shafeyev, and V. Ya. Manshetov.

In some of the Crimean Tatar documents which figured at the trial, the deportation of the Crimean Tatars from the Crimea in 1944 was described as genocide, the destruction of a nation. During the investigation, and at the trial, these assertions were contrasted with official K.G.B. reports, according to which: 'Of the people from the Crimea who were living under the "special settlement" régime, 13,592 died between May 1944 and January 1945, that is, 9·1 per cent', and 'for the period from January 1st, 1945, to January 1st, 1946, 13,183 people died, of which 2,562 were men, 4,525 women, and 6,096 children under 16.' These figures are certainly an underestimate – the people's statistics put the numbers who perished at 46 per cent. Moreover, they do not take into account all those who died during the journey. Nevertheless, as one of the defendants at the trial, Rollan Kadiyev, stated, even these figures are evidence of a terrible crime, and confirm the allegation of genocide. One of the basic accusations brought against the fascists at the Nuremberg trial, he said, was the great number of people who fell victims to the war – in four years the Soviet Union lost 20 million people, that is, about 2·5 per cent of the population each year, while according even to the K.G.B. statistics, approximately 10 per cent of the Crimean Tatar nation perished in the reservations of Uzbekistan in 1946 [or 1945?] alone.[25]

THE CRIMEAN HOMELAND ITSELF

In the Crimea itself the 1967 decree had led to much police brutality. Thousands of Tatars returned home full of expectation only to be severely disillusioned:

In the Crimea there are periodic police raids on Tatars who have returned home. On July 15th, 1968, eleven Crimean Tatar families were [see p. 265] brutally manhandled at the 'Bolshevik' state farm in the Krasnogvardeisky District. Since the publication of the decree of September 5th, 1967, only eighteen families and thirteen single persons have been given permits to reside in the Crimea. During the same period twelve thousand people have been expelled from the Crimea. Seventeen Crimean Tatars have been condemned to various prison sentences there, and two more are still being held under investigation.

The deputy head of the Crimean Region police, Lieutenant-Colonel Kosyakov, is reported to have said to the Crimean Tatars: 'The decree was published not for you, the Crimean Tatars, but for the newspapers, and the foreign ones at that ... Turkey — that's where you belong and that's where you should go!' In this he was backed up by Lieutenant-Colonel of the Police Pazin, who added: 'If tomorrow we get the order to shoot you, we will shoot you.'

These facts, together with others already known to readers of the *Chronicle*, are quoted in an appeal from the Crimean Tatars to all people of goodwill, to democrats and communists.[26] The Crimean Tatars ask that their rights be safeguarded, that they be protected from arbitrary and illegal treatment, and that they be helped to return home to the Crimea. Tens of thousands of people have already signed this appeal and signatures are still being collected. At the same time, signatures are being collected on an appeal from representatives of Soviet public opinion in support of the Crimean Tatars' demands.

As brutality and trials continued in the Crimea in 1968–9, the Chronicle *made regular reports. The following are the most notable:*[27]

7   THE 'RESETTLEMENT' OF THE CRIMEAN TATARS
IN THE CRIMEA

In 1968 the Uzbek authorities announced that Crimean Tatars would return to the Crimea in a planned way, making work contracts with representatives from the Crimea who had come to Uzbekistan. In this way they tried to avert the planned mass exit of Tatars to the Crimea. In the whole of 1968, through the system of labour recruitment, only 148 families were resettled; resettlement permits were issued only when the blessing of the K.G.B. was forthcoming — and to those who had not taken the slightest part in the national movement.

The *Chronicle* has already reported how the Crimean regional administration, obeying unwritten — most probably oral — instructions, greets the Crimean Tatars who return to their homeland without K.G.B. permits. In this issue a number of further incidents from 1968 are given, based on the recent protest of the Crimean Tatar people addressed to official bodies and Soviet public opinion.[28]

On May 26th, 1968, ninety-eight Crimean Tatars put up tents near the village of Marino outside the boundaries of Simferopol. On May 27th, at 4 p.m., the tents were surrounded by a ring of policemen, K.G.B. operatives and volunteer police — about two hundred and fifty men altogether. On an order from Lieutenant-Colonel Kosyakov, they began pulling down the tents and grabbing people, beating them up and shoving them into buses. Everyone who was at that moment standing near the tents — including women and children and war invalids — was transported in buses, guarded by police cars and motorcycles, to the Simferopol police headquarters. From there a group of thirty-eight Tatars was sent off to Baku without being given a chance to collect their belongings and clothes. They travelled for four days without bread or water. At Baku they were forcibly put on to the ferry *Soviet Turkestan* — even women were beaten. The crowd which had gathered were told that enemies of the people were being transported. On May 31st the ferry was met at Krasnovodsk by members of the police; the Tatars were put on to a train and sent off to Tashkent under K.G.B. guard.

On June 26th, 1968, a group of Crimean Tatars — twenty-one

people — came for an interview with Chemodurov, the president of the executive committee of the Crimean Regional Soviet, with a complaint about the administrators who had not given residence permits to Crimean Tatars. Chemodurov locked himself in his office and called up the police, who threw the Tatars out of the executive committee building and deposited them at the police station. Eleven of them were given fifteen days in prison, whereupon all of them, including the women, went on hunger-strike. The remaining ten were bought aeroplane tickets with the money taken from them when searched, and then sent to Dushanbe [in Tadzhikistan] where none of them had ever lived. Criminal proceedings were initiated against Mamedi Chobanov — one of those sentenced to fifteen days in prison — on a charge of resisting a representative of authority.

On August 26th, 1968, Mamedi Chobanov was sentenced to three years' imprisonment.

On August 27th, 1968, Mubein Yusupov and Fakhri Ismailov were sentenced to one year and to six months of imprisonment, respectively, for the same offence. They were arrested during a police attack similar to that staged against the Crimean Tatars at the executive committee building. Mustafa Nebi, Kadyr Sarametov and Muniver Abibullayeva, who tried to attend this trial and appear as witnesses, were detained and given fifteen days in prison.

On September 4th, 1968, Zekerya Asanov, arrested as the result of a police provocation, was sentenced to one year of imprisonment.

On July 10th, 1968, a group of Crimean Tatar families applied to the executive committee of the Crimean Regional Soviet for permission to settle in any part of the Crimea. Zubenko, an official of the committee, suggested they should move into empty houses on state farms. The Tatars moved into the houses in the first section of the 'Bolshevik' state farm in Krasnogvardeisky District. One night lorries were driven up to the houses by uniformed and volunteer police. They grabbed the Tatars' coats and blankets, threw them into the lorries, then wrenched the children away from their mothers and also threw them into the lorries. They dragged out the rest, twisting their arms and shouting: 'You sold the Crimea once and now you've

come to sell it again! Get out! Only Ukrainians are going to
live here!' The people who had gathered at the noise took the
Tatars' side. 'So you've found someone to take pity on! They
ought to be shot!' shouted the police bullies in reply to the
indignation of the local inhabitants. It all ended with the police
and the volunteers taking away with them various belongings
and four Tatars. The remaining Tatars were taken in for the
night by the local inhabitants. But at dawn the police and
volunteers returned, fell upon those who were asleep, beat them
up, tied their hands and shoved them all into lorries and drove
them to a waiting railway-truck in a siding. They were robbed
while being beaten up: eight wrist-watches and 1,000 roubles
were taken. At Novo-Alekseyevka station [Kherson region]
four more families, taken from the state farm 'Plenty' in
Dzhankoisky District, were in exactly the same way put into
the same truck. The Russian and Ukrainian workers of the first
section of the 'Bolshevik' state farm refused to go out to work
the day after this incident; also, seventeen Russian and
Ukrainian families demonstratively left the state farm, and four
immigrant families, recently brought from the Ukraine, refused
to settle there.

7   THE TRIAL OF GOMER BAYEV[29]

On April 23rd–24th and 28th–29th, 1969, the trial was held in
Simferopol of the Crimean Tatar Gomer Bayev, an engineer
[see plate 46] accused of distributing 'deliberate fabrications
defaming the Soviet political and social order' — article 187-1 of
the Ukrainian Criminal Code. The evidence for the prosecution
was: several letters from Crimean Tatars to official departments,
unsigned but allegedly distributed by Bayev; one of the Crimean
Tatar information bulletins, copied by Bayev into a notebook,
an action designated as 'distribution' because, according to a
witness's evidence, Bayev read out *something* from *some* notebook
at a meeting; and letters written by Bayev himself about the
position of the Crimean Tatars. In connection with the last
mentioned, it is extremely interesting how one of these letters
became involved in the trial. A senior research worker of the
Institute of Marxism-Leninism, Senichkina, a Party member,
published an article on the nationalities question in which she
wrote that the nationalities question in the U.S.S.R. had been

completely solved.[30] Gomer Bayev wrote a private letter to Senichkina in which he asked whether she considered the Crimean Tatar question solved as well, and if so, he asked her to explain why he, Gomer Bayev, had been sacked from his job, turned out of his hostel and told to leave the Crimea. Instead of replying, Senichkina sent the letter to the K.G.B., as it 'contained provocative questions'.

Judge A. A. Avramenko presided over the proceedings, the prosecution case was argued by Procurator Terentev, and the lawyer N. A. Monakhov defended the accused. The trial was conducted correctly: those who had in fact come to the trial were present in the courtroom instead of a specially chosen audience, as is common in Moscow.

Elkhov, the head of the Simferopol passport office, a witness, confirmed that it was virtually impossible for Crimean Tatars to be registered for residence in the Crimea. The same was said by the senior engineer of a state farm where a work-gang of Crimean Tatars (including Bayev) had been employed and immediately dismissed when their identity was discovered. The Procurator explained that this was so because they lacked specialized knowledge, but the engineer confirmed that the work-gang had the necessary qualifications, that the state farm was still in need of workers—up to a hundred—and that the state farm could provide them with accommodation. To the lawyer's question 'And if a similar work-gang were to come to you now, would you employ them?', the engineer quite frankly answered: 'But they wouldn't be given residence permits!'

The Procurator, having taken into account the defendant's hard-working way of life and the absence of any previous conviction, pointed out that the defendant had pleaded not guilty and had not recanted and therefore represented a danger to society. The Procurator demanded that Gomer Bayev be given three years in a labour camp, i.e. the maximum under the article concerned.

The defence lawyer made no reference to the contents of those documents which Bayev denied having helped to compile and distribute—and he convincingly showed that his client was speaking the truth. As regards the documents which Bayev had compiled, the defence lawyer adopted the following line: the facts set out in the documents are indisputable; strongly

worded phrases—the product of the emotions not the mind—
are to be found, but they cannot be called libellous. The defence
lawyer asked the court to acquit Bayev, there being no basis for
a criminal charge.

Gomer Bayev in his final speech[31] described the deportation
of his people from the Crimea, the way they had starved to
death in exile, and their struggle for the restoration of their
national rights.

The court found Gomer Bayev guilty under article 187-1 of
the Ukrainian Criminal Code and sentenced him to two years
in a labour camp.

Finally, the Chronicle *reports the beginning of an episode on which
several remarkable documents written by the participants are available :*[32]

8 In June 1969 four Crimean Tatar families who had come to the
Belogorsk District in the Crimean Region under the Organized
Labour Recruitment scheme and had bought houses with their
own money were forcibly ejected. The Tatars were turned out
at night into the rain; half-naked men and women were beaten,
wrapped in towels and bundled into the back of a lorry. Their
children were thrown in with them, and also a small part of
their belongings.

*After this they were put on a train, to be taken off it again when it
reached Ust-Labinsk in Krasnodar Province. From here, penniless, they
made their way back to the Crimea : they found their homes boarded up.
Two episodes in this wretched saga are recorded in plates 51 and 52.*

*Towards the end of 1969 the Tatars resorted to yet another tactic in
what had by now become one of history's most remarkable campaigns of
non-violent mass lobbying, one organized, moreover, on impeccably
democratic lines :*

11 Representatives of the Crimean Tatars have handed in to the
Central Committee documents which record the initial findings
of a referendum now being held among the Crimean Tatars.
They are asked to answer two questions: do they long to return
home to the Crimea and do they want to see the restoration of

the Crimean Autonomous Soviet Socialist Republic? The Crimean Tatars were rehabilitated as a people in a decree issued by the Presidium of the Supreme Soviet on September 5th, 1967, and officially cleared of the unfounded and libellous accusations which were originally used to justify their deportation. However, the decree also states that the 'Crimean Tatars have settled down in their present places of residence', and so, even though they have been rehabilitated, they are not being given an opportunity to return to their homeland. The referendum is an attempt to establish once and for all whether the Crimean Tatars really feel that they have 'settled down' outside the Crimea.

The initial findings have shown that a vast, indeed overwhelming, majority of those asked (with only a few isolated exceptions) yearn to return to their homeland and to see the restoration of their autonomy. The referendum is still going on, in Uzbekistan, Tadzhikistan, Kazakhstan, in Krasnodar Province—everywhere where Crimean Tatars are living. The poll will include the whole adult population, to a man, and the results of the referendum will be passed to the highest party and government authorities.

In 1970 the Tatars continued to have the full support of the Democratic Movement. In particular they must have rejoiced at a plea on their behalf by two Ukrainian scholars[33] *who argued like this: as an immigration target of 500,000 people had been officially planned for the Crimea—to eliminate the labour shortage—and as this was currently the size of the Crimean Tatar people, the latter should be allowed to provide the problem with a neat solution.*

13. THE MESKHETIANS

The nationalities question now looks especially disgraceful in our country. I have in mind the policy of genocide towards a number of small nations, begun under Stalin and continuing to this day. The Volga Germans and the Crimean Tatars still cannot return to the land of their fathers ... and are in fact condemned to forced assimilation ... But such things have been and are being experienced not only by the Germans and the Tatars. Just like them, a number of other small national groups are being subjected to genocide and discrimination ... Orally and in the press, slander is spread about these small nations. No struggle is conducted to counter the chauvinistic propaganda and discrimination ... All-Russian great-power policies are trampling underfoot the rights of the small nations to autonomy and and independent political, economic and cultural development.

Aleksei Kosterin, February 1968[1]

One of the small nations of whom Kosterin wrote are the Meskhetians, or Meskhi. As the Ukrainians and Jews belong to a different category, the Meskhi are the only small nation, apart from the Tatars, about whose national movement much is known. Such movements evidently exist also among the Volga Germans and the Soviet Greeks, but very little evidence about them has yet reached the outside world in documented form.[2]

As will be seen, remarkable parallels exist between the Meskhetians and the Tatars, regarding both their fates and their movements' tactics. In some ways the Meskhetians — with up to seven thousand people assembling for national conferences — have even outdone the numerically stronger Tatars. Indeed, how Stalin would turn in his grave if he heard of unauthorized meetings of this size: in his day — when order reigned! — three people chatting about the weather were a potential conspiracy to be quickly dispersed by the police.

The Meskhetians differ, however, from the Tatars in that they suffered deportation six months later, in November 1944, and moreover not as 'traitors', for the Germans had never occupied their lands. The explanation of their tragedy lies elsewhere. With the war nearly over, Stalin's eyes were already fixed covetously on north-east Turkey. That being so, and Stalin being Stalin, he evidently preferred to anticipate possible complications by removing from the frontier area people who, like the Meskhetians, might have had pro-Turkish sympathies. The Meskhetians' misfortune thus stemmed from the chance fact that their home lay along the Soviet-Turkish border, in an area not far from the Black Sea.

The Meskhetians also differ from the Tatars and almost all the other deported peoples in that their deportation was never reported. Indeed it remained totally unknown to the outside world for a quarter of a century. As Robert Conquest has written: 'It is as if, roughly speaking, the population of Iceland or Swaziland, of Kuwait or Alaska, should disappear without trace.'³

What, then, of the possibility of a restoration of justice to the Meskhetians? Presumably the Kremlin is inhibited here by the same considerations as in the case of the Tatars. The return home of the now embittered Meskhetians might, it may think, jeopardize military security. Second, and probably more important, to yield to one aggrieved lobby would risk encouraging a myriad others.

The Chronicle *brought the world its first detailed report on the Meskhetians' fate in 1969 with these two articles:*

THE MOVEMENT OF THE PEOPLE OF MESKHETIA 7 FOR A RETURN TO THE HOMELAND

On November 15th, 1944, the forcible deportation from Meskhetia (a southern part of Georgia) of the indigenous population took place. This population was mainly formed when, in the late sixteenth and early seventeenth centuries, the Meskhi Georgians gradually adopted the Turkish language and became converted to Islam. The all-union census of 1929 officially described them as Turks, and schools using Turkish were opened in the province.

In 1935–6 the people were suddenly renamed Azerbaidzhanis, and teaching was transferred to the Azerbaidzhani language. But on November 15th, 1944, they were once again stated to be Turks and deported to Central Asia and Kazakhstan. Apart from the Meskhi Georgians, the following were deported from Meskhetia: the Karapapakhi Azerbaidzhanis, the Islamicized Khemshinli Armenians, the Turkicized Kurds and the Meskhetian Turkmens, who also called themselves Turks. Common misfortune brought these varying ethnic groups together and welded them into one people.

The deportation took place on the pretext that evacuation to safe areas was necessary because of the supposedly advancing Germans. It was promised that the people would be returned to their homelands after the war. The tragic circumstances of this deportation are similar to those surrounding the history of

the Crimean Tatars and the peoples of the north Caucasus. A
few months after the deportation the régime for deported exiles
— the same as that for peoples accused of being 'traitors' — was
imposed upon all areas where the 'temporarily deported
peoples' had been put. The deported, who had left their homes,
property and livestock behind, perished in the alien climate
from starvation and cold. In Uzbekistan alone 50,000 people
died. A particularly large number of Turks died while transforming the Hungry Steppe [south of Tashkent] into the flower-
ing region of Gulistan. Those Meskhetians returning from the
front, including Heroes of the Soviet Union and those with
medals, were not allowed back to their homeland.

With the [unpublished] decrees of April 28th, 1956, and
October 31st, 1957,[4] promulgated by the Presidium of the
U.S.S.R. Supreme Soviet, the régime for deported exiles was
lifted, but the right to return home and compensation for confiscated property were not accorded to them. At the end of 1956
and beginning of 1957, delegates went to Moscow to obtain
permission for their people to return home. In answer the
Meskhi were announced to be Azerbaidzhani and were 'given
permission' to 'return' to Azerbaidzhan: they were recruited for
the cultivation of the Mugan Steppe [300 miles east of Mesk-
hetia]. Many went there, hoping to be nearer their homeland
and to return to it in the end.

A letter from the people as a whole, demanding permission to
return to their homeland and sent to the Presidium of the
U.S.S.R. Supreme Soviet, was handed over to the Presidium of
the Supreme Soviet of the Georgian Republic and from there to
the Georgian K.G.B. The K.G.B. is a body which in no way
has the right to decide this question; nevertheless, the head of
the K.G.B., [Aleksei] Inauri, wrote that, according to the
decrees of April 28th, 1956, and October 31st, 1957,[4] promulgated by the Presidium of the U.S.S.R. Supreme Soviet, the
people had not been granted permission to return to the area
from which they had been deported in 1944.

Over a period of a few years, the people's delegates, who had
formed a Temporary Committee for the Return of the People
to their Homeland, travelled to Moscow and Tbilisi [the capital
of Georgia] and obtained interviews with the highest party and
government authorities. In 1963 they encountered understand-

ing and humanity in the Second Secretary to the Central Committee of the Georgian Party, Zemlyansky, who said that he had known nothing about this terrible mistake and would immediately exert pressure to obtain permission for their people to return home. He also said that conditions should be created so as to make them forget their suffering. But this single defender of the Meskhi died a few months later.[5] Further visits by delegates to the reception rooms of Moscow and Tbilisi were fruitless, or indefinite answers were given to get rid of them, or they received an answer such as the following from Sklyarov, head of the reception room of the Presidium of the U.S.S.R. Supreme Soviet: 'I will not give your documents to Comrade Brezhnev, nor will he receive you; go home and get on with some work.' The Meskhi appealed to Georgian writers, journalists and cultural figures and found moral support, but none of them could give any real help; moreover, those who took up the cause of the persecuted people were frequently subjected to censure by official bodies.

On February 15th, 1964, the First Meeting of the People took place at the 'Leninist Path' collective farm in the Bukinsky District of Tashkent Region. Representatives of the all-union and republican Central Committees of the party, of the all-union and republican governments, and of regional and district party committees were invited to attend, but only some unidentified people in mufti appeared, who tried to prevent the delegates from assembling. Nevertheless, more than 600 delegates from Central Asia, Kazakhstan and the Caucasus, with mandates from the local assemblies of the people and representing the whole 200,000-strong people, took part in the meeting. Speeches were made on the early history of the people, on their present situation and on the organization of work. A petition to the party and government was drawn up. A Temporary Organizing Committee for the Return of the People to the Homeland was elected. The historian Enver Odabashev (Khozravanadze) was chosen as president. One hundred and twenty-five delegates were chosen to go to Moscow. A complete record of the meeting was sent to party and government leaders. Up to now, twenty-six meetings of representatives of the whole people have been held.

On the occasions when the people's delegates visited Moscow, they were informed that it would be far better to get the question settled in Tbilisi. In Tbilisi they were told that only the U.S.S.R. government could make the decision. In the autumn of 1964 the delegates were summoned to the Georgian K.G.B. building, and an unidentified lieutenant-colonel announced that the question would be decided at the beginning of 1965. The sole purpose of this announcement was to send the delegates back to Central Asia.

In the following period the K.G.B. organs of the Central Asian republics took their own measures: house arrests of delegates when they should have been leaving for meetings; talks with participants of the movement when alternately bribes were offered and threats made. In the offices of the party committee of the Kantsky District [in Kirgizia] Polikanov, the party district secretary, Kurmanov, deputy president of the Kirgiz K.G.B., and four unnamed men talked to Alles Izatov, a candidate member of the party and secretary of the Komsomol committee of the agricultural college in Frunze [the Kirgiz capital]. As a result of refusing to dissuade the people from writing to and visiting Moscow, Izatov was not made a party member. K.G.B. officials also tried every method of wrecking the people's regular meetings.

In March 1966 Alles Izatov and Enver Odabashev were about to fly to Tbilisi. After fruitless talks with them and attempts to prevent them reaching the airport, a provocation was organized. After they had checked in at the airport, some lieutenant-colonel or other advanced upon them and tore up their tickets and boarding cards, thus arousing the indignation of the surrounding people. The police detained a few members of the angry crowd as well as Izatov and Odabashev, who remained calm. On the following day all the rest were released, but these two were tried for 'petty hooliganism' and given fifteen days in prison: at the people's court of the Lenin District [of Frunze] the Judge was Turin, and the case was heard without assessors [of whom two are required by law].

In 1967 the people's delegates were promised that their question would be considered after the 50th anniversary of the October Revolution.

In April 1968 the 22nd national meeting, with over 6,000 delegates taking part, was held in Yangiyul [near Tashkent].

The meeting took place with army detachments, police with truncheons, and fire-engines surrounding it, but was conducted without any disorders. On the delegates' return journey, the police began detaining them and dispatching them to Tashkent. Thirty of them spent two to six months in preventive detention cells.

On May 30th, 1968, a resolution of the Presidium of the Supreme Soviet of the U.S.S.R. was promulgated to the effect that citizens of Turkish, Kurdish and Azerbaidzhani nationality who had been deported from the Akhaltsikhsky, Aspindzsky, Akhalkalaksky and Adigensky Districts and from the Adzhar Autonomous Republic [i.e. from Meskhetia] benefited from the same rights as all other citizens of the U.S.S.R.; but these people had by now put down roots in those republics where they now lived, and needed to have created for them there conditions which took into consideration their national peculiarities.[6]

After the promulgation of the resolution, the people once again sent their representatives to Moscow in order to gain permission for an organized resettlement in their home country. No one would receive them. On July 24th, 1968, 7,000 delegates converged on Tbilisi and gathered at Government House demanding an interview. They were met by volunteer police, by police with truncheons, and by army detachments. The delegates, including even women, were beaten up. They were searched for weapons. The delegates refused to be provoked: they did not get involved in fights but neither did they disperse. Finally, on July 26th, the first secretary of the Georgian Central Committee, Mzhavanadze, received a few of them and said that there was no room in Meskhetia for its indigenous population, that other districts in Georgia could accept them, but then only a hundred families per year; however, if they insisted on having their way, then they must apply to Moscow.

In August 1968 B. P. Yakovlev received delegates in the Moscow Central Committee reception room, saying that the leadership was at present engaged in more serious matters and would only be able to examine their question in two months' time; when this happened they would be informed. When they heard nothing, the delegates arrived in Moscow in November, and then once again they were sent from one reception room to another, while the following type of argument started being repeated more and more often: 'The Soviet Union is your homeland; the place where you live is your home; live and get on with some work.'

The exiled people cannot agree with this false argument. The people's movement for the restoration of historical justice continues.

9   NEW PERSECUTION OF THE MESKHI

'The people's movement for the restoration of historical justice continues' — those were the final words of the report in No. 7 of the *Chronicle* on the tragic fate of the small Meskhi people. Also continuing is the persecution of the Meskhi by the authorities.

The Meskhi are an ethnic mixture of Georgians, Azerbaidzhanis, Armenians, Kurds and Turkmenians. What they have in common has been created by their past experience of Turkish influence and their Muslim religion, and the persecutions they have suffered during the last twenty-five years have strengthened their unity as a nation. The unique culture of the Meskhi has attracted the attention of scholars. On May 23rd and 24th, 1968, the Georgian Academy of Sciences held a scholarly seminar on the history and ethnography of Meskhetia. At that time the indigenous population of Meskhetia was trying in vain to obtain permission to return to its homeland.

On November 18th, 1968, B. P. Yakovlev, an official of the Central Committee of the party, received [once again] a delegation of Meskhi representatives in Moscow — the twenty-fourth of its kind. During his talk with them, Yakovlev granted the Meskhi permission to settle in various regions of Georgia, and fifteen to thirty families were even allowed to settle in Meskhetia. Although this permission was not confirmed in writing, the Meskhi people decided at their meetings to trust this indefinite form of permission. However, those who were prepared to get up and go have met with persistent opposition: they are refused references from the places of work releasing them, they are not removed from the military service register, and no transport is provided for them.

Eight families from the kolkhoz 'Ady-Gyun' in the Saatly District of Azerbaidzhan left for Georgia, abandoning their homes and belongings because they had been refused transport.

They were given work at a state farm in the Makharadze District of Georgia, but were very soon dismissed, and deported back to Saatly District by the police. The Saatly District is in the Mugan steppe, and many Meskhi settled there after the decrees of April 28th, 1956 and October 31st, 1957,[7] which relieved them of the régime for deported exiles. Refusing to allow them to return to Georgia, the authorities tried to enthuse them with the idea of cultivating the Mugan steppe, an area with severe extremes of climate, and with almost no water fit for drinking—the water there is either bitter and salty or turbid and rather muddy. But the Meskhi moved there from Central Asia simply to be a little nearer their homeland.

The Meskhi from the kolkhoz '21st Congress of the Party', also in the Saatly District, managed to procure seven vehicles for their journey, but they were stopped by the police and forced to escape into Georgia on foot, leaving behind their belongings as trophies for the Saatly District police. There are many similar stories. Georgian railway stations and terminuses have become crowded with homeless people, deprived of their belongings and their work, with no roof over their heads, systematically driven out of their homeland the moment they set foot in it. Whole families with small children, old men and invalids are involved.

On April 19th, 1969, the President of the Temporary Organizing Committee for the Return of the Meskhi to their Homeland was arrested in Saatly. He is Enver Odabashev (Khozrevanadze),[8] an officer in the reserve, who took part in the Great Patriotic War. Odabashev was attending a teachers' conference, during which he was called outside. Waiting for him on the street was the district Procurator Kadirov, with two unknown men. The Procurator then lured Odabashev to the police station under false pretences, and left him there. Odabashev was held there until one o'clock in the morning, with no explanations and no food, and then summoned for interrogation by an investigator of the district Procuracy, Farzaliyev. The interrogation lasted until 3.30 in the morning, thus violating the statute of Soviet law which states that interrogations may not be held at night, except in urgent cases which cannot be delayed. Then Odabashev was put into an unheated room, where he soon caught a chill, dressed as he was in light clothing. In protest at his arrest by force and deception, and at the arbitrariness of the whole affair, Odabashev began a hunger-strike.

After Odabashev had been detained, a search was carried out in his house. Local police inspector Ummatov, Procuracy investigator Farzaliyev and others made the search, during which they took away from an archive copies of documents addressed to the party, the government and the people.

When they found out about Odabashev's arrest, on the morning of April 21st, the Meskhi left their work and came from all the village settlements in the area to gather in Saatly at the district party committee building, where they demanded the immediate release of their teacher of the people. When they met with refusal, the hard-working Meskhi sent express telegrams to L. I. Brezhnev and V. Yu. Akhundov.* The crowd did not disperse. Late in the evening of April 21st, the secretary of the district party committee, Babayev, who had been in Baku, returned in great haste, probably sent by the republican party organs. After lengthy deliberations with representatives of the Meskhi, the district committee secretary ordered Odabashev to be released.

Odabashev was brought in for interrogation, already prepared and photographed for deportation the next morning, and told: 'Sign here, we're releasing you.' The district police chief Mirzoyev, and the Procurator Kadirov, who had finally appeared, began shouting and threatening and demanding that Odabashev should not travel anywhere or participate in any meetings. That night, after his spell in a cold cell, and hungry from his strike, Odabashev signed a blank sheet of paper which the investigator, Farzaliyev, handed to him, as well as the record of his interrogation. No one can tell how this blank sheet will be used.

When the old teacher was let out into the street, he was met by the crowd of Meskhi, who had not dispersed although it was now late at night. They shouted: 'Freedom! Equality! Homeland or death! Our teacher lives!'

Reports began to circulate to the effect that Odabashev's arrest was to have been the first of a series of arrests of other activists. For the moment, however, the people's reaction has

* Then first party secretary of Azerbaidzhan.

put a stop to the unlawful actions of the authorities. Still, the threat of arrest has, as before, come to hang over active participants in the movement for a return to the homeland.

The Georgian government suggested earlier to the Meskhi that they settle in other areas of Georgia, in particular in Kolkhida [i.e. Colchis, in west Georgia]. By June 1969, 505 Meskhi families had arrived in Georgia. The Georgian population welcomed them as brothers, and helped them settle in. But on June 7th there was a round-up of Meskhi who had already arrived and found work, as a result of which they were sent off by train in various different directions. The fate of many of the victims of this round-up, or their whereabouts, are not known.

In 1970 the patience of the Meskhetians began to run out. As Chronicles *19 and 20 reported, they started to seek emigration to Turkey. In this they may well have been influenced by the success of several thousand Soviet Zionists in gaining permission to leave for Israel from 1968 on.*

14. THE UKRAINIANS

The present events in the Ukraine are a turning point: the glacier of terror which for many years has tightly fettered the spiritual life of the nation is breaking up. People are as ever thrown behind bars and as ever transported to the East. But this time they have not sunk into the unknown. To the great surprise of the K.G.B., *public opinion* has risen up for the first time in recent decades. For the first time a protest campaign has emerged; for the first time at a closed, illegal, trumped-up trial the journalist Chornovil has refused to testify; and for the first time the K.G.B. have felt powerless to suppress it all.

Valentyn Moroz, April 1967[1]

It was the sentencing of twenty intellectuals in 1965–6 which provoked the rebirth of a vigorous and independent Ukrainian public opinion. The famous book of Vyacheslav Chornovil—published in English as The Chornovil Papers—*recorded and analysed the fate of these people, while an equally notable work by the critic Ivan Dzyuba—*Internationalism or Russification?—*examined historically the issues which had so concerned them.*

These issues were by no means new. For the question of the political autonomy or independence of the Ukraine vis-à-vis Russia has existed—sometimes in acute form—for more than three centuries, and the emergence of a distinct and modern Ukrainian language and literary culture in the nineteenth century has evoked repressive Russian chauvinism in St Petersburg and Moscow ever since. Short respites have occurred. A temporary thaw in 1905–7 prepared the ground somewhat for the full but brief Ukrainian independence of 1917–19. Then, with Bolshevik political control firmly imposed, cultural and linguistic independence were, within limits, encouraged, until—in the 1930s—Stalin's ruthless Russification reduced the Ukraine's individuality to little more than its folk-costumes. A relaxation in the mid-1950s raised hopes. But it led only to the enunciation from about 1958 of Khrushchev's doctrine of the steady 'drawing together' of the fraternal Soviet nations, a process which would lead to their 'merging'. This programme clearly amounted to Russification in disguise, and since then the tone from Moscow has in general been one of increasingly militant Russian nationalism and even sometimes chauvinism.

Not surprisingly, nationally minded Ukrainians have reacted to this. The reduction of the use of Ukrainian in schools and colleges, and of publishing in Ukrainian, have been resisted, the rehabilitation of 'bourgeois nationalist' cultural figures and the defalsification of Ukrainian history doggedly persisted in. In its more political aspects the resistance has based itself on the wide measure of sovereignty given the Ukraine on paper by the Soviet and Ukrainian constitutions, and, in some cases, on the Ukraine's constitutional right to secede from the U.S.S.R.

This was the atmosphere which led in April 1968 to the writing of the 'letter of the 139', briefly described earlier (p. 78) because of its protest against the Galanskov–Ginzburg trial. Attacking also the conduct of Ukrainian trials, including Chornovil's, the letter stated: 'In the Ukraine, where violations of democracy are magnified and aggravated by distortions connected with the national question, the symptoms of Stalinism are being manifested even more overtly and grossly.'[2]

The strong challenge of this letter brought reprisals against a number of the signatories. No. 2's brief report on these[3] was followed by a large item in No. 5 entitled:

CASES OF PERSECUTION IN THE UKRAINE RESULTING 5
FROM THE LETTERS OF UKRAINIAN INTELLECTUALS AND
WORKERS TO THE SOVIET GOVERNMENT ABOUT THE
POLITICAL TRIALS IN THE UKRAINE AND IN MOSCOW

The Presidium of the Ukrainian Union of Soviet Artists described the letter [of the 139] as 'anti-Soviet' and issued a resolution expelling from the Union: A. A. Horska, L. N. Semykina, I. S. Lytovchenko, V. N. Lutsak, V. S. Dovhan, V. I. Zaretsky, H. Sevruk and A. Zakharchuk.

Zaretsky also received a 'strict reprimand' as a party member.

The leading role in this persecution of artists who had signed the letter was played by the sculptor Borodai. The accusations levelled against the signatories were openly anti-semitic in tone, full of abuse and loud allegations about 'enemies of the Soviet régime', 'Bandera-ites', etc.

The following people were, for having signed the letter, dismissed from various institutes of the Ukrainian Academy of Sciences (in accordance with decisions taken by their academic councils):

M. Yu. Braichevsky, well-known Ukrainian historian, Master of Historical Sciences, senior research officer of the Institute of History, and author of such studies as *When and How Kiev*

Arose, The Emergence of Ideas of the State among the Easter Slavs and *The Origins of Rus* [and eight other people].[4]

Among those in the Academy of Sciences of the Ukraine who distinguished themselves as ringleaders in this campaign of persecution were M. Shamota, the author of a negative review of O. Honchar's novel *The Cathedral* [see p. 291], and Skaba, the director of the Institute of History, who was once in charge of ideological work in the Central Committee of the Communist Party of the Ukraine. Shamota categorically demanded the dismissal of M. Kotsyubynska (see the second issue),* and Skaba, in denouncing Braichevsky, said 'I will not stand for this vermin'.

In Kiev University the lecturer V. A. Vyshensky was reprimanded for signing the letter. Master of Physical-Mathematical Sciences V. H. Bodnarchuk was dismissed from the university by an illegal order, without the sanction of the Academic Council, on grounds that have no basis in law: 'for actions incompatible with the high calling of a Soviet teacher'. The order was hurriedly signed by the Rector of Kiev University, I. T. Shvets, the subject of a celebrated newspaper feuilleton entitled 'Jack of All Trades'. This was done in spite of the fact that a teachers' meeting had voted only that Bodnarchuk be suspended from teaching work.

Shvets also distinguished himself as one of the organizers of the whole campaign at Kiev University. He denounced the Department of Applied Mathematics as a 'nest of opposition' that should be 'disbanded', demanded that 'party members who have spoken weakly must be investigated by the party bureau', and so on. He would not allow Bodnarchuk to finish his lecture course and conduct the examinations on it.

Symptomatic were the speeches by Corresponding Member of the Ukrainian Academy of Sciences, H. N. Polozhy. Polozhy is notorious among the mathematicians as the organizer of campaigns against Jews, and also of the campaign against two well-known mathematicians, B. V. Hnidenko and G. E. Shylov, in 1962. In his speeches, he kept saying that mathematicians should not go in for politics: 'Certain Moscow mathematicians were not doing very well in their work, so they

* No. 2: Mykhaylyna Kotsyubynska, a writer resident in Kiev and signatory to the Ukrainian letter, has been dismissed from her post.

decided to seek glory in another field.' Demanding drastic measures, he asked: 'Why do you waste so much time on them?' and said at one point: 'The University of Saint Vladimir' (the pre-revolutionary name of Kiev University) 'sounds just as good as "Shevchenko University".' Polozhy attacked a colleague in his own department, Didenko, simply because he abstained from voting at the meeting on Bodnarchuk, and rescinded a decision to recommend him for promotion to a senior lectureship.

The poet Ivan Drach[5] was expelled from the party.

While these and other reprisals[6] befell signatories of the 'letter of the 139' a campaign of intimidation was launched against the independent Ukrainian intelligentsia in general[7] and, as the following items show, certain signatories of the letter in particular:

In July 1968 the Lvov K.G.B. kept the [Kiev] literary critic 5 Ivan Svitlychny[8] under constant surveillance during his visit to the west Ukraine. In the end he was detained and searched. At about the same time, General of the K.G.B. Poluden, speaking at a meeting of party activists among the Lvov intelligentsia, denounced Ivan Svitlychny, Ivan Dzyuba and others. One of his accusations against them was that they maintained contact with Yuly Daniel through the latter's wife. 'What do they want with that Yid?,' Poluden asked for all to hear.

On March 28th, 1969, three searches were carried out in 7 Kiev: at the flat of the critic Ivan Svitlychny, at the place of work of his sister Nadiya Svitlychna[9] and at the flat of Natalya Karaziya. They visited Svitlychny without a search warrant and asked him to hand over a photocopy of a book by Avtorkhanov, *The Technology of Power*.[10] Svitlychny said that he had not got it, in fact thinking that it was not in his flat. But the K.G.B. had more exact information. They demanded a search warrant over the telephone, waited for it, carried out the search and with no difficulty found part of the photocopy. They found the second part of the photocopy in the library where Nadiya Svitlychna works. Natalya Karaziya had a typescript of Solzhenitsyn's novel *The First Circle* and a typewriter, on which she had begun retyping the novel, confiscated.

7 At the beginning of 1969 the critic Ivan Dzyuba [see plate 55] was summoned to the K.G.B. office at the Ukrainian Council of Ministers, where it was suggested to him that he wrote 'a reply to bourgeois propaganda' with reference to the publication abroad of his book *Internationalism or Russification?*.[11] Dzyuba stated that he considered his work to be Marxist, that he had had nothing to do with its publication and that the very idea of writing a 'reply' on receiving information from the hands of the K.G.B. made him indignant.

11 The Ukrainian critic and publicist Ivan Dzyuba has been expelled from the Writers' Union. His expulsion passed without a hitch at a meeting of a Ukrainian writers' section. Then the matter was discussed [in December 1969] at a writers' meeting chaired by Kozachenko.[12] Of the many speakers, only two demanded Dzyuba's expulsion, accusing him of disclosing state secrets. To Dzyuba's bewildered question—what secrets were they talking about, since his work did not give him access to any such secrets?—one of the speakers replied indignantly: 'Is not the disclosure of our party's nationalities policy the divulgence of a state secret?' The others present refused to vote for Dzyuba's expulsion and did not support these two in their speeches. The meeting lasted five hours. The chairman, Kozachenko, summing up the situation, postponed the vote for two weeks. The expulsion of Dzyuba did take place, but at a meeting restricted to certain writers. [It was soon revoked.[13]]

Meanwhile, one of the most vicious of the press attacks on the nationally minded Ukrainian democrats had received two stinging rebuffs. One of these[14]—by the young Kiev poet and critic Vasyl Stus—took the form of a 'Letter to the Board of the Ukrainian Writers' Union'. Its samizdat version[15] was summarized by the Chronicle *thus:*

8 The letter, in pamphlet form, concerns an article by O. Poltoratsky entitled 'Who is Protecting the Humanists?' in the paper *Literary Ukraine*.[16] Stus exposes Poltoratsky's slanders on Chornovil and Karavansky [see pp. 221–2], and unmasks his attitude, and that of 'the whole company of Poltoratskyites' who pass over the mass repressions in silence, and only rise up in arms 'with their talented pens ... when the West starts talking

about the massacres of the past'. In reply to the charge of mediocrity levelled at Chornovil and Karavansky, Stus encloses with his letter extracts from an article by Poltoratsky, 'Who is Ostap Vyshnya?', written in 1934, which describes Ostap Vyshnya as a 'fascist and counter-revolutionary', 'a kulak ideologist', 'a literary prostitute', 'a gutterpress profiteer' and 'a worthless pen-pusher'.*

While the battle raged between the régime and those democrats who remained free from arrest, the Chronicle *also reported on the fate of the imprisoned intellectuals and their first defender Chornovil. Items on Karavansky and others*[17] *— in Vladimir jail — have already featured in Chapter 10. Here is a further sample*[18] *of the* Chronicle's *coverage:*

Vyacheslav Chornovil [see plate 53], sentenced in 1967 for compiling a collection of materials on political trials in the Ukraine, went on hunger-strike in his camp from May 29th to July 16th [1968][19] as a protest against the confiscation of documents concerning his trial.[20] He ceased the hunger-strike when some of the documents were returned to him.

On February 3rd, 1969, the journalist Vyacheslav Chornovil was released; he was sentenced under article 187–1 of the Ukrainian Criminal Code in 1967 and served his sentence in a camp of ordinary régime. Two months before the end of his term he was put into solitary confinement in a cell of the Lvov K.G.B.; he was then presented with a warrant by Samayev, the Ukrainian Republic Deputy Procurator, for the investigation of new circumstances surrounding his case. This investigation was begun after Chornovil's collection of documents on the 1965–6 repressions against the Ukrainian intelligentsia, 'Woe from Wit', had been published abroad.[21] Chornovil had already been sentenced for compiling this collection, but nevertheless he was threatened with being recharged under article 62 of the code and given a longer sentence. Chornovil boycotted the investigation, calling it illegal. Before the end of his term the 'investigation' was closed.

* Vyshnya (1889–1956) was the most popular Soviet Ukrainian humorist. Imprisoned from 1933 to 1943, he conformed after his release and was praised by, among others, Poltoratsky.

7 Mykhaylo Osadchy, a man with a higher degree in literature, a teacher at Lvov University, a poet who had published a book, and an instructor of the Lvov regional party committee, was sentenced in 1965 under article 62 of the Ukrainian Criminal Code for distributing Ukrainian *samizdat* works; in 1967 he was released after serving his sentence, but until recently he was unable to obtain either a residence permit or work; he was detained for 'breaking identity-card regulations', being, in fact, detained at his own home in Lvov, among his family; finally, he was able recently to obtain a residence permit for the Lvov Region and is now a worker in the Lvov workshop for the deaf and dumb.[22]

7 At the beginning of April 1968 Valentyn Moroz [see plate 54] was sent back to the Vladimir prison, having spent over a year in the chief investigation prison of the Ukrainian K.G.B. He had been accused of writing the letter 'Report from the Beria Reserve',[23] which was sent to the Ukrainian Republic Supreme Soviet. It is definitely known that Moroz took no part in the investigation and gave no evidence. Probably the investigation was closed because the authorship of Moroz could not be proved. Valentyn Moroz still has four months of his sentence left; on September 1st [1969] he should be released.

10 On September 1st Valentyn Moroz was released from Vladimir prison on the expiry of his term. He has been sent to Ivano-Frankovsk with a recommendation that he be put under surveillance.

Moroz's freedom lasted for nine months. In June 1970 he was re-arrested[24] in Ivano-Frankovsk, after a house-search in April had revealed to the police new writings of his, including his essay — 'Chronicle of Resistance'[25] — about the vital need to preserve Ukrainian national traditions. These — subject to the constant state-sponsored erosion of Russification — survive in their purest form, Moroz writes, in the Hutsul area of the Carpathians.

But 'Report from the Beria Reserve' must have rankled most with the K.G.B., for it is intellectually and imaginatively the most brilliant of all the dissenters' writings on that organization. Justice cannot be done here to its deadly dissection of K.G.B. psychology, but it will quickly b clear that passages like this one could not fail to strike home: 'K.G.B. *Captain Kazakov, sent to check how far I had been* "re-educated" *(i.e. how far my individuality had been eroded), quite frankly admitted to me:* "Unfortunately we can't see what is in your head. If we could do this, and throw out (! ! !) everything that prevents you from being a normal Soviet man, there would be no need for so much talk".'

Also this one:

When Levko Lukyanenko[26] asked Captain Denisov, a Lvov K.G.B. investigator, 'For what purpose does article 17 of the Constitution, which gives each republic the right freely to secede from the U.S.S.R., exist?', the latter answered: 'For foreigners' (!). That's how it is! It transpires that the K.G.B. men are perfectly aware that they are defending not "socialist legality" but the right to violate it with impunity. They have no illusions about their organization and see it simply as a place where the pay is highest and there is no housing queue.'

And finally this one:

Rolling up their sleeves, the local Procurators join in and spare no efforts to help the K.G.B. men perpetrate their dirty deeds. During a conversation with the Deputy Procurator of the Dubrovlag camp administration I drew his attention to the fact that people seriously ill with stomach ulcers were kept on a starvation diet, contrary to law. He answered me with great calm: 'That's just what the punishment consists of—hitting the stomach.' ... Thus a continuous crime has been perpetrated for decades. No one should forget that the Nuremberg trials were not only for murder by steel, but also for murder by hunger.

In November 1970 Moroz received a new sentence, this time of fourteen years (five of them in exile).

Chornovil, meanwhile, was supporting the Moscow-based Action Group for the Defence of Civil Rights by signing its appeals to the U.N., and was also defending Karavansky, with Moroz and fourteen other former political prisoners, by writing an appeal in his defence.[27]

Among the signatories to the 'letter of the 139', students and workers featured in good numbers, alongside the scientists, writers and artists. As with the latter, a proportion of the former refused to be intimidated by the official pressures brought to bear on them for signing. The following *items[28] illustrate the mood among a section of young people and the symbolic force of the Ukrainian patriot and poet Shevchenko (1814–61), who had resisted Russification a century earlier:*

5   R. Motruk has been dismissed 'on account of redundancy' from the Kiev Radio Committee, because she disobeyed a warning from her superiors not to go to the Shevchenko monument on May 22nd [1968]. On that day, which is always observed by Ukrainians as the anniversary of Shevchenko's funeral, the Kiev authorities did everything possible to prevent a demonstration: they organized an official programme at the monument, with artistic performances by professionals and amateurs, and mobilized members of the Komsomol, the volunteer police and even the armed forces to watch. At the same time people for whom it is a natural tradition to go to the monument on this day were warned at their places of work that they should not do so.

8   May 22nd is the anniversary of the bearing of Taras Shevchenko's ashes home to his native land, and this year [1969], as last, an official festival was organized. After the festival had ended, late at night, a group of students singing Ukrainian songs stayed behind at the memorial statue and did not disperse for a long time. It later turned out that despite the darkness they had all been photographed, and all their songs and conversations had been tape-recorded. The university administration was called in to help identify the voices of those who could not be identified from the photographs. It is said that many of these students were deliberately failed in their examinations.

5   THE NAZARENKO CASE

In March 1968, in Kiev University and at the Agricultural Academy, leaflets were distributed calling for resistance to the Russification of Ukrainian culture. In connection with this a worker of the Kiev Hydro-electric Station O. Nazarenko [one of the 139], has been arrested. Nothing more is known of his fate at the moment.

8   In April 1968, after leaflets had begun circulating in Kiev, a pass system was introduced for almost all the city's higher

educational establishments, including the university, of which the only part one can enter without a pass is the Rector's office. External and internal students of the university have different passes, valid for different hours, and have been deprived of the chance to mix with one another in the university. The pass for visitors to the university has to have three official stamps.

In Kiev Nazarenko and two other employees of the hydro- 6 electric station, Kondryukov and Karpenko, were recently tried on a charge of engaging in anti-Soviet propaganda and agitation. The defendants distributed through the post leaflets protesting against the Russification of the Ukraine and describing the Shevchenko celebrations in Kiev. Nazarenko confessed his guilt, regretted his resort to improper forms of activity and took upon himself the entire responsibility for the actions incriminating all three defendants. The Procurator asked for six years in a strict-régime camp for Nazarenko and Kondryukov and two years for Karpenko. The defence demonstrated the necessity of redefining the charge under article 187–1 of the Ukrainian Criminal Code, which corresponds to article 190–1 of the Russian Code. The court confirmed the charge under article 62 of the Ukrainian Code and sentenced Nazarenko to five years in a strict-régime camp, Kondryukov to three years and Karpenko to one year six months.

Extra-judicial repressions are continuing in connection with 8 the case of [Oleksandr] Nazarenko, Vasyl Kondryukov and Valentyn Karpenko, who worked at the Kiev Hydro-electric Station, and were taking university evening classes. In January 1969 they were [...] charged with distributing leaflets, books published in the west Ukraine in the 'twenties and 'thirties, and samizdat works. Nazarenko and Karpenko were arrested in June 1968, and Kondryukov in September 1968. Their trial lasted from January 26th to 29th; the Judge was Matsko, the prosecutor Khriyenko.[29]

Lyudmyla Sheremetyeva was expelled from the Faculty of Journalism, where she was an external student, just before the defence of her graduation thesis. During the pre-trial investigation, Nazarenko testified that he had received, supposedly from Sheremetyeva, the book by Chornovil dealing with the political

10

trials of the 'sixties in the Ukraine. Searches made did not reveal any material to support this allegation, nor was it confirmed by any other testimonies. Sheremetyeva herself denied it during both the pre-trial and the court investigations. There were no other circumstances to 'incriminate' her, and so the reason given for her expulsion was friendship with 'a particularly dangerous state criminal' [i.e. Nazarenko], and, most important, her unwillingness to do a deal with the investigators. On March 1st Sheremetyeva began the authorized four-month period of leave from work to prepare and defend her thesis. But on April 7th she was expelled without any warning, and without any investigation in which she could take part, for 'actions incompatible with the title of Soviet student'. Later it was learned that the Dean and the Rector had received a letter from the K.G.B. informing them of Sheremetyeva's 'unprincipled behaviour' and of how she had been spreading 'hostile propaganda'. Even earlier, before the trial, in the autumn of 1968, Nadiya Kyryan had been expelled from the philological faculty, where she was a third-year external student. During a search, she was found to be in possession of some materials left for her by Nazarenko.

Later, No. 11 reported Karpenko's participation in some hunger-strikes (see p. 212) and his subsequent release on December 26th, 1969, from camp 3 in Mordovia. Other releases[30] *— and arrests*[31] *— of Ukrainians have been recorded in several issues of the* Chronicle.

INDUSTRIAL UNREST NEAR KIEV

It is possible that this item bears some relation to the case of Nazarenko and his friends, if only because they worked before their arrest at the industrial site concerned:

8 In mid-May 1969, workers at the Kiev Hydro-electric Station in the village of Beryozka met to discuss the housing problem many of them are still living in prefabricated huts and railway coaches despite the authorities' promises to provide housing The workers declared that they no longer believed the local authorities, and decided to write to the Central Committee of the Communist Party. After their meeting, the worker

marched off with banners carrying such slogans as ALL POWER TO THE SOVIETS! K.G.B. men drove up in veterinary vans and were greeted with shouts of 'What d'you think we are? Dogs?!' Remonstrating with the crowd, the K.G.B. men tried to whip up feelings of 'class hatred' towards one of the active participants in the affair, retired Major Ivan Oleksandrovych Hryshchuk, by pointing out that he was on a good pension, so what had he got to kick up a fuss about? Hryshchuk agreed that his pension really was undeservedly large—indeed he had already been donating it to a children's home for two years. Moreover, he earned his living by honest labour, unlike the K.G.B. men.

The next day there was an official meeting at which some of the speakers tried to blacken Hryshchuk, but by the time they left the platform they had been literally spat upon by the workers. The workers sent a delegation to Moscow with a letter signed by about six hundred people on their housing problem. At the end of June Ivan Hryshchuk was arrested in Moscow. The workers wrote a new letter, this time demanding his release as well.[32]

Just before his arrest there appeared on June 24th in the paper *Evening Kiev* a feuilleton entitled 'Khlestakov's Double',[33] by I. Pereyaslavsky. The usual type of libellous accusations are levelled at Hryshchuk—of course he's a drunkard, and he persistently refuses to pay alimony; then doubts are cast in a hinting way on his part in the Great Patriotic War and his behaviour in a fascist concentration camp. The feuilletonist writes that the delegation—which consists of some 'neighbours' (not a word about the hydro-electric workers)—is drinking in Moscow restaurants on the 900 roubles it has collected from certain gullible people.

GONCHAR'S 'THE CATHEDRAL' AND THE DNEPROPETROVSK PURGE

So far we have found Ukrainian national feeling asserting itself in, as could be expected, Kiev and the west Ukraine. But the storm which arose in cultural life in 1968 over the novel The Cathedral *by the Chairman of the Ukrainian Writers' Union, Oles Honchar, raged with special ferocity in Dnepropetrovsk in the south-east.*

First, though, the Chronicle *commented:*

7 Oles Honchar's novel expresses the idea of the historical continuity of the spiritual culture of the Ukrainian people. He has been criticized in the official press; 'letters from workers' indignant at 'the distortion of the life of the working class' have been printed in the newspapers. The novel was given a positive evaluation in the following *samizdat* works: a letter from a group in Dnepropetrovsk and a letter from the sculptor Ivan Honchar; a serious analysis of the novel is contained in the critic Yevhen Sverstyuk's work 'The Cathedral in Scaffolding'.[34]

Then, when publication in Russia was banned, the Chronicle *reported:*

10 This novel by the Lenin Prize-winner—which came out in Ukrainian in journal and book editions and was sharply criticized by officialdom—has appeared in *samizdat*, translated into Russian by Roman Rozental.

It was the Dnepropetrovsk letter mentioned above—the 'Appeal of the creative youth'[35]—which dramatically revealed the nature of the Dnepropetrovsk purge and which, clearly, provided the basis for the Chronicle's *summary of it. Part of this[36] follows here:*

7 S. Yu. Sheinin, from Dnepropetrovsk, one of the oldest journalists on the newspaper *Zorya*, has been expelled from the party and dismissed from work for a favourable review of Oles Honchar's novel *The Cathedral*.

M. T. Skoryk from Dnepropetrovsk,[37] employed by the newspaper *Zorya*, ridiculed 'I see life differently', an unfavourable article concocted by H. Dihtyarenko and others on the novel *The Cathedral*, and has been expelled from the party.

V. Zaremba, from Dnepropetrovsk, employed on the newspaper *Zorya*, has been expelled from the Komsomol and dismissed from work after he attacked an article in which the head of the *Zorya* information department, O. Z. Kyrylenko (a K.G.B. lieutenant), denounced the novel *The Cathedral*.

N. Dubinin, from Dnepropetrovsk, editor of the factory newspaper *Energetik*, was questioned frequently on party policy after publishing the favourable review of the novel *The Cathedral* by the workers D. Semenenko and V. Uniyat.

H. Prokopenko, from Dnepropetrovsk, teacher at an evening

school, has been given a severe reprimand by the party after insisting on the publication of an article answering the denouncers of the novel *The Cathedral*, H. Dihtyarenko and I. Moroz.

It soon became clear, however, in the following build-up of items, who had initiated the passionately anti-Russification 'Appeal':

I. Sokulsky, a poet from Dnepropetrovsk, has been dismissed 7 from work on the factory newspaper *Energetik*, produced for the Dnieper area.

In Dnepropetrovsk in mid-June of this year [1969] the poet 8 I. Sokulsky was arrested. He had previously been dismissed from his job for political reasons. It is not yet known what the charge is.

On June 13th the poet Ivan Sokulsky, who is about thirty years 10 old, was arrested in Dnepropetrovsk. He had earlier been dismissed from his job and expelled from Dnepropetrovsk University where he was in his fifth year. After this he worked as a fireman and then a sailor on the Kiev-Kherson river-steamer. It was on the steamer that he was arrested. Sokulsky is charged with circulating Ukrainian *samizdat*, and in particular with allowing his typewriter to be used by university students to type out several articles, including the famous letter from the creative youth of Dnepropetrovsk concerning the campaign of slander in connection with Oles Honchar's novel *The Cathedral*.

Ivan Sokulsky, aged twenty-seven, and [M.H.] Kulchynsky, 11 aged twenty-two, have been arrested in Dnepropetrovsk. A charge was brought against them under article 187–1 of the Ukrainian Criminal Code, equivalent to article 190–1 of the Russian Code, but this was later altered to article 62 of the Ukrainian Code (article 70 of the Russian). During a search, both were found to be in possession of the 'Appeal of Creative Youth', concerning the oppression of the free-thinking intelligentsia of Dnepropetrovsk. Sokulsky admitted that he was the author of the appeal. A large number of witnesses were summoned for interrogation and many confrontations of witnesses were held. The trial is expected to take place in January 1970.

It did, and No. 12 carried a detailed account.[38] *Sokulsky got four and a half years, Kulchynsky two and a half, and a third defendant, V. V. Savchenko, a two-year suspended sentence.*

Finally, a variety of individuals are recorded as having expressed their national feelings in different ways and with different aims. The results have varied from qualified triumph to tragedy. In Kolomiya of Ivano-Frankovsk Region, for example:

8 Anna Stadnychenko, a member of the Kolomiya Town Executive Committee's Department of Architecture, expressed her indignation at being forbidden to use the Ukrainian language in compiling technical documentation. When this new prohibition was introduced, the reason given was that the forms used for technical documentation were printed in Russian. Stadnychenko referred to article 17 of the law 'On guaranteeing the equality of languages and promoting the development of Ukrainian culture', passed by the Central Executive Committee of the Ukrainian Congress of Soviets and the Ukrainian Council of People's Commissars on July 6th, 1927. She received a severe reprimand from the party and in September 1968 was dismissed from her job under article 47g of the Labour Code. Later Stadnychenko was reinstated in her job, but the strict reprimand was not withdrawn despite her written requests to the party authorities.

10 In the summer of 1969 Vasyl Ryvak, a research officer at the Institute of Social Sciences, was arrested in Lvov. Ten years ago Ryvak, a staunch communist, returned to the Soviet Union from America. When he became disillusioned with the nationalities policy pursued in the U.S.S.R., Ryvak wrote and sent to *Pravda* an article about linguistic inequality and the forced assimilation of Ukrainians. After this article had been confiscated from someone during a customs inspection at the border, Ryvak was arrested. The investigation is being conducted by the Lvov K.G.B. A charge has been brought under article 62 of the Ukrainian Criminal Code. [In 1970, however, it was dropped.]

On November 5th, 1968,[39] Vasyl Omelyanovych Makukha, a 6
teacher from Dnepropetrovsk Region, aged fifty and the father
of two children, once a prisoner in Stalin's camps, committed
suicide in Kiev by self-immolation on Kreshchatik [Kiev's
main street]. When people ran up and began to put out the
flames, he shouted, 'Long live a free Ukraine!' The burns
he received proved fatal and he died in the October Hospital in
Kiev.

On February 10th, 1969, Mykola Breslavsky,[40] a 45-year-old 8
teacher from Berdyansk [S.E. Ukraine], father of three children
and ex-inmate of Stalin's camps, attempted to burn himself to
death outside the Kiev University building. Holding up
placards protesting against Russification, he set himself alight,
but at this point was arrested and put in a prison cell of the
Ukrainian K.G.B. A charge was entered against him under
article 62 of the Ukrainian Criminal Code, equivalent to
article 70 of the Russian Code.

On March 19th the Deputy Chairman of the Ukrainian
K.G.B., General Shulzhenko,[41] delivered a lecture to students
and staff of Kiev University on the subject 'Some problems of
the ideological struggle'. At one point he said roughly this:
'Some madman or other took it into his head to burn himself to
a frizzle, and came to Kiev University to do it. "Why didn't you
go to the bazaar?" we asked him, and he answered: "I wanted
to be with the young people. I mean, there's a university here,
isn't there?".' Shulzhenko lectured in Ukrainian. Admission
was unrestricted. His ironical remarks about Breslavsky, whom
he did not mention by name, were greeted with laughter in the
hall.

The republican K.G.B. organs are conducting an investigation into the Breslavsky case. In March a search was made of
the Dnepropetrovsk flat of his schoolfriend, the journalist
Volodymyr Sirenko.[42] Then Sirenko was summoned to Kiev for
interrogation, where the authorities tried to force him to sign a
deposition in which the investigator imputed to Sirenko a
testimony against Breslavsky: Breslavsky, according to the
investigator, had uttered anti-Soviet statements. Sirenko
refused to sign the deposition.

On May 28th, 1969, Mykola Oleksandrovych Breslavsky [...]

was sentenced to two and a half years in strict-régime camps under article 62 of the Ukrainian Criminal Code. The case was heard in closed session.

10 On June 20th the 37-year-old Stepan Bedrylo, a research officer of the Ukrainian Agricultural Academy, was arrested in Kiev. Bedrylo had completed his graduate course and was to have defended his Master's thesis in the summer. After his arrest he was sent to Lvov. He has been charged under article 62 of the Ukrainian Criminal Code, equivalent to article 70 of the Russian Code. The investigation is being conducted by the Lvov K.G.B. under investigator Malykhin.

Bedrylo has been accused of reading Ukrainian *samizdat* documents, particularly articles on V. Makukha's self-immolation in Kiev on November 5th, 1968, in protest against the policy of Russification, and on the attempted self-immolation of M. Breslavsky in February 1969.

During its investigation, the K.G.B. has been searching energetically for films of material on the position of political prisoners in Mordovia. The house of Bedrylo's mother and sister, in a village near Lvov, has been searched three times for films, but nothing was found. The mother and sister were questioned. According to rumours, two students of Lvov Agricultural Institute have also been arrested in connection with this case.

No. 11 having announced that 'the trial of the economist Bedrylo will take place in Lvov in January 1970', No. 12 reported that the four-year sentence then imposed had been reduced to two years at a closed appeal hearing in February.[43]

To conclude, clearly the Chronicle *has paid full attention to the Democratic Movement's Ukrainian wing, and the latter has reciprocated by supplying a constant stream of accurate information. None of this — given the Ukraine's status as the second largest Soviet republic, with a population of some 50 million and a comparatively Westward orientation due to its position and history — is surprising. A more intriguing point is some of the terminology concerned. Practically none of the literature referred to in this chapter uses the word nationalist: that word still implies—not only to officials but also to most dissenters—a non-democratic, extremist orientation. Maybe this situation will change as regards dissenters, but for the moment phrases like 'national movement' and 'equal national rights' are respectable to democrats in both Kiev and Moscow, while the words nationalist and nationalism are not.*

Nor are most of the Ukrainian dissenters narrow or self-absorbed in their national feelings. Many sympathetic references to the position of the Jews, the Belorussians, the Armenians and the Crimean Tatars[44] are to be found in the writings of Dzyuba, Karavansky, Moroz, Chornovil and others.

But notwithstanding all this, the need was nevertheless felt in 1970 to start an autonomous Ukrainian equivalent of the Chronicle: *the* Ukrainian Herald. *The first number of this remarkable journal appeared in January 1970,[45] the second in May,[46] the third in October and the fourth in January 1971. At the same time, the amount of Ukrainian material in the* Chronicle *declined somewhat, as Ukrainian energies were diverted elsewhere. It would, however, be surprising—also seriously damaging to the unity of the Democratic Movement—if future relations between the two journals were other than close and basically friendly.[47]*

15. THE JEWS

I am a Jew. I want to live in the Jewish state. That is my right, just as a Ukrainian has the right to live in the Ukraine, a Russian to live in Russia, a Georgian to live in Georgia ... I want my children to go to a Jewish school. I want to read Jewish papers, I want to go to Jewish theatres ... Is it really slander to say that in the multi-national Soviet state only the Jewish people cannot educate their children in their own national schools? Is it really slander to say that in the U.S.S.R. there are no Jewish theatres? Is it really slander to say that in the U.S.S.R. there are no Jewish papers? In fact no one denies all this ...

I want to live in Israel. My wish does not conflict with Soviet laws. I have been invited by relatives, all the formalities have been observed. So why on earth are you starting a criminal case against me? ... If you succeed in convicting me, then nonetheless—if I survive until my release—I shall still want to leave, on foot if need be, for the land of my fathers.

Boris Kochubiyevsky to Brezhnev, November 1968[1]

In 1968 the 'Jews of silence'[2] finally lost their patience. The Jewish community of the U.S.S.R. began to speak. In two short years it was shouting. By 1970, indeed, its protests had become more militant than those of any other dissenting group. The timing derived largely from the Arab–Israeli war: its repercussions made Soviet Jews' lives that little bit worse which tipped the balance. Another factor was the example presented by the mainstream radicals. The exceptional militancy, on the other hand, stemmed at least in part from something largely denied to other groups: a significant and tangible, if severely limited, degree of a commodity rare in the Democratic Movement—success.

The three million Soviet Jews have always been especially vulnerable to the tacit official nationalities policy of promoting the assimilation of all minorities into the Russian nation, never having had—because of their scattered areas of settlement—a national republic of their own. This fact facilitated Stalin's forcible suppression of virtually all Jewish educational and cultural institutions, a process very helpful to the policy clearly enunciated under Khrushchev of bringing the Soviet nations nearer and nearer together until their 'complete unity' (all as Russians, tacitly), with a common culture and language, could be achieved.[3]

This policy not surprisingly assisted the reappearance, after a break in the mid-1950s, of the often overt anti-semitism of the last two decades of

298

Stalinism, coinciding as it did with the anti-Israel Soviet line after the Suez crisis of 1956 and with Khrushchev's drive of 1958–64 against all religions, including Judaism. Hence various attacks on the latter—notably T. K. Kichko's book Judaism without Embellishments, *published in Kiev in 1963—easily became vehicles for crude anti-semitism. Simultaneously the number of open synagogues was reduced from about 450 in 1956 to 92 in 1964, and the baking of matzos was for a few years forbidden.*[4]

Public acts of opposition to the prevailing line came from the writers Victor Nekrasov and Evgeny Evtushenko,[5] *even more notably from the Ukrainian critic Ivan Dzyuba in his moving speech of 1966 at Baby Yar, which called for Ukrainian–Jewish reconciliation and mutual help.*[6] *But no such acts by Jews in the period up to late 1968 became known at the time, and only a very few have done since. Thus an admirable symposium,* The Jews in Soviet Russia 1917–67,[7] *could appear in 1970, containing an excellent chapter—'After the Six-Day War'—without one reference in it to opposition by Jews on Jewish matters.*

It was, in fact, only on October 30th, 1968—sixteen months after the war—that the outside world got hard documentary evidence that the dam was beginning to burst. On that day extracts from a remarkable letter by twenty-six Lithuanian Jews appeared in the American press.[8] *Written in February, the letter expressed the authors' anxiety at 'the rising wave of anti-semitism in Soviet Lithuania'. It was 'impossible to overlook the fact that ... the anti-Israel propaganda, especially the cartoons in the central press, are regenerating in a certain part of the Lithuanian (and not only Lithuanian) people, anti-semitic passions.' Examples followed, together with detailed criticism of discrimination against Jews in the political, professional and educational fields, and of the arbitrary destruction of Jewish monuments and cemeteries : 'In the whole period of the occupation even the Hitlerites did not touch the Jewish cemeteries in Lithuania. In East Prussia, in Sovetsk (formerly Tilsit) and Chernyakhovsk (formerly Insterburg), the Jewish cemeteries lay untouched for all the thirteen years of Hitlerite rule. Only now have they been completely destroyed, and not a trace remains. Just recently, without any warning, the Jewish cemetery in Ionava was destroyed.'*

Admittedly, 'only one bloody pogrom has occurred in the post-war period, in Plunge in 1958,' but in view of the post-Six-Day-War atmosphere a large percentage of Lithuanian Jews would like to leave if given the chance. However, 'a paradoxical situation exists. Here they do not want us, they persecute us in all sorts of ways, forcibly assimilate us and even insult us publicly in the press, but at the same time they forcibly hold us here. As in the well-known saying : "He does the beating, he also does the crying".' The authors end by calling on the Lithuanian authorities to take measures to prevent the otherwise likely drift towards pogroms.

Further evidence existed in 1968, apart from this document and the ominous contents of the Soviet press, to show that the Jews' position was deteriorating. Academician Sakharov, for example, deplored in his essay of summer 1968 a new 'backsliding into anti-semitism in our appointments policies'.[9] A year later the Chronicle *confirmed the trend :*

9 During the last six to twelve months, a sharp increase in anti-semitism has been generally observed regarding selection for employment and for admission to colleges. It is difficult to back up this judgment with concrete examples, as Jews are formally speaking refused jobs not for being Jewish but on any convenient — or inconvenient — pretext, while if possible they are failed in their entrance exams.

Such was the background to the breaking of the dam of silence in 1969–70.

The documents which poured through the breaches quickly revealed three things. First, they came from a wide range of places : Moscow, Leningrad, Latvia, Lithuania, Minsk, Kiev, Kishinyov, Kharkov and Georgia. Second, most of the signatories had despaired of Soviet policies towards the Jews ever easing, and now wanted of the régime only one thing : to be let out to Israel. Third, the small minority for whom this was not the overwhelming concern attached its second loyalty to the Democratic Movement in general, not striving to obtain greater rights merely for the Jews.

Those Jews anxious only to reach Israel can, of course, scarcely be seen as part of the Democratic Movement proper. They have, however, already contributed to its development both by the force of their example regarding tactics, organization and general bravery, and by their success in compelling the régime to establish a solid body of precedent for the right to emigrate to a non-communist country, if only on the condition that a person's relatives live in that country and invite him to join them. This limited right, which before 1968 existed in practice only on a tiny scale, could clearly be revoked at any time, but the régime's lack of tough and consistent leadership since 1953 makes this much less likely to happen than before.

It is indeed the loss of the old ruthlessness which accounts, in the main, for the success of the Jews in establishing their precedent. The régime has reacted hesitantly to their emigration campaign, imprisoning some, harassing or merely ignoring others, and letting yet others go. It no longer has the stomach for all-out repression, especially when it knows the world is watching. Thus it just hopes, weakly, that the problem will go away if it lets most of the militants out, while imprisoning a few so as to intimidate the less determined.

The Chronicle's *first reflection of the Jewish problem concerned an imprisonment :*

THE CASE OF BORIS KOCHUBIYEVSKY   6

At the beginning of December 1968 a thirty-year-old radio engineer, Boris Kochubiyevsky [see plate 57], was arrested in Kiev.

In 1967 he spoke at a lecture on the international situation given at the radio factory where he worked, argued with the lecturer, and expressed his disagreement with the description of Israel's actions in the Six-Day War as being aggression.[10] Afterwards his case was discussed by the factory committee of the trade union and they proposed that he should leave 'of his own free will'. He refused, and it was only after nearly a year, in which they tried every means to 'persuade' him, that he left in May 1968. In June 1968 he married a student in her fourth year at a pedagogical institute and in August he applied for permission to leave for Israel. In September a similar application was submitted by his wife, who is of Russian nationality. His application was rejected because of 'the non-existence of diplomatic relations', and hers because she had 'ageing parents' in Kiev. Later Larissa Kochubiyevskaya was expelled from the Young Communist League for 'Zionism'. She was not immediately expelled from the institute: for a long time they tried to persuade her to get a divorce, using arguments that would have done the Black Hundreds [Russian chauvinists of the early 1900s] proud. For example, to the young woman's sole and sincere argument ('I love him'), the deputy dean, Groza, replied almost word for word as follows: 'I know a girl who's married to a Jew, and she says all Jews stink. You love him — that's nothing; where you're going, the whole country will stink.'[11] Larissa's parents (her father is a K.G.B. official, her mother a respected teacher) have renounced her.

On September 29th an official meeting was held at Baby Yar near Kiev. The *Chronicle* has already reported [see p. 288] the way in which the Kiev authorities replaced the traditional meeting by the Shevchenko monument with an official festival. In exactly the same way [in 1968] they replaced the traditional annual meeting at Baby Yar with an official one.[12] The official speakers were principally concerned with condemning Israeli aggression, but they also used the usual stock phrases about the fascists who had killed Soviet people, without mentioning that the majority of those killed were Jews. An acquaintance came up to Boris Kochubiyevsky and told him about a conversation he had just overheard there:

MAN. What's going on here?
WOMAN. Here the Germans killed a hundred thousand Jews.
MAN. That wasn't enough.

Boris flared up, declaring that people talked like that because, on that very day and in that very place, Israeli aggression had been condemned from the official platform and no mention made of the facts that Jews had been killed here. Straight away a man came up to him, wishing to argue, and said that not only Jews had been killed here. Boris objected that Jews had been killed just because they were Jews. He began saying that he was not allowed to emigrate to Israel, and related the history of his family. One of his relatives had served in the Jewish Ministry under the Central Rada and had been shot as a follower of Petlyura.[13] Another had been a commissar at the end of the 'thirties and had been shot 'as a Trotskyite'. A third, an admiral, had been shot at the same time, as a result of one of the military trials. Boris's grandparents were wiped out by a gang of nationalists in Zvenigorod after the withdrawal of Soviet troops and before the arrival of the Germans. His mother and father were killed by the Germans, perhaps even here in Baby Yar.[14] 'In this country,' said Boris, 'I belong to no one. I want to go somewhere where I shall belong.'

In November Boris and Larissa Kochubiyevsky were given permission to leave for Israel. On November 28th they were due to go to the passport and visa office with their documents. That morning their flat was searched and they signed a statement that they would not leave. The report on the search stated that it had been carried out 'to remove documents, letters, etc.', without any reference to the content of the documents. In the search only copies of letters that Kochubiyevsky had written to official departments were removed. On or about December 7th Boris Kochubiyevsky was arrested on a charge of spreading by word of mouth deliberately misleading fabrications which defamed the Soviet political and social system, under Article 187–1 of the Ukrainian Criminal Code. Held against him are his address at the lecture on the international situation, his appearance before the radio factory committee, his statements at Baby Yar and the 'speeches'(?) he delivered at the passport and visa office.

On January 20th the investigation was completed and the case handed over to the court. But the court has returned the case for further investigation because of the lack of evidence of any intention to spread his views.

One of the principal witnesses in the case is that same unknown person who approached Kochubiyevsky at Baby Yar and provoked him into an argument. In addition evidence against Kochubiyevsky was given by a number of Jewish witnesses, including two victims of Baby Yar who figure in Anatoly Kuznetsov's book *Baby Yar*.[15] Many of those who were present at Kochubiyevsky's 'addresses', and could appear as defence witnesses, are themselves applying for permission to emigrate to Israel and do not wish to prejudice their chances.

THE TRIAL OF BORIS KOCHUBIYEVSKY   8

On May 13th–16th, 1969, the Kiev Regional Court examined the case of Boris Kochubiyevsky, accused under article 187–1 of the Ukrainian Criminal Code, which corresponds to article 190–1 of the Russian. Kochubiyevsky was charged with making statements on the position of the Jews in the U.S.S.R. Of the charges described in *Chronicle* No. 6 the speech Kochubiyevsky made at the lecture on Israel's 'aggression' in the Six-Day War did not figure in the indictment. The court found him guilty, and Kochubiyevsky was sentenced to three years in ordinary-régime camps.

Kochubiyevsky pleaded not guilty. He denied that his statements had been untrue, and said that even if some of them might be found to be untrue, they were not deliberate untruth, since he had been convinced of the truth of his words when he spoke them. The Procurator objected on this point: 'You have received higher education, passed graduate examinations in philosophy, you are acquainted with the Constitution of the U.S.S.R., and therefore you could not fail to know that in our country none of the things you spoke about can exist.' This formula, in almost identical wording, was included in the verdict as proof of the deliberate untruth of Kochubiyevsky's statements.

On one of the main charges in the indictment, concerning Baby Yar, eight witnesses appeared, only three of whom reinforced the prosecution's case. Kochubiyevsky asked one of the three, Rabinovich, how he came to be in Baby Yar. Rabinovich replied that he had been looking for a shop and arrived there accidentally. The court rejected the evidence of the defence witnesses, stating that all five of them were friends of the accused and had without exception supported the accused's 'Zionist views'[16] in court.

Both Judge and Procurator constantly used the clichés 'Zionist' and 'Zionist views', in spite of the fact that Kochubiyevsky categorically objected to this. To take a specific example, the Procurator asked: 'And have you thought what you've done to your wife? You've infected this sweet young Russian girl with your Zionist views.'

Here are two more examples of the logic of the prosecution:

PROCURATOR. You know what we were fighting against?
KOCHUBIYEVSKY. Fascism.
P. And what were we fighting for? Was it freedom?
K. Yes.
P. Did we win?
K. Yes.
P. Well, there you are, then, we have freedom.
JUDGE (or PROCURATOR) I know you will claim there is anti-semitism here, in view of the fact that there are 200,000 Jews in the Ukraine, but no Jewish schools, newspapers or theatres.
KOCHUBIYEVSKY. Yes, and that too.
J. But you know very well that here they don't all live together, they are scattered.
K. But in Canada there is a smaller Ukrainian population, yet they have their own papers, schools and theatres.

J. But what comparisons are you making? I mean, they live in a bourgeois state, they still have to win their freedom!

It is not an accident that no one could remember if it was the Judge or the Procurator who conducted this dialogue. The Judge on the whole behaved more like a spokesman for the prosecution; his manner was much more aggressive than that of the relatively mild Procurator. He kept interrupting the accused, and mocking him; he whipped up the unsympathetic elements among the public to make hostile remarks, and all the while he did not once call the public to order. All he did was to drop a gentle hint at one point to the effect that he disapproved of comments from the public benches.

Present in the courtroom were the relatives of the accused, and, after giving evidence, the witnesses. The remaining seats were occupied by the 'public', amongst whom several K.G.B. men were spotted. When people asked the policemen and the escorts why the public were not being admitted to the courtroom, they replied—besides giving the traditional answer 'full up'—that 'the K.G.B. won't allow it'. A policeman asked one of the K.G.B. men: 'Hey, Chief, which are your men here?' Without the permission of the 'Chief', the audience was not allowed out for a smoke during breaks. This 'Chief', who at one point gave his name to someone as Yury Pavlovich Nikiforov, stood behind Vitaly Kochubiyevsky, brother of the accused, and from time to time repeated quietly 'And you're a Yid, you're a Yid.'

Many members of the public were not allowed into the courtroom, although they had arrived long before the start of the proceedings and long before the appearance of the 'public' in the court. They sent a declaration to the Chairman of the Court, and later a protest to the Kiev City Procurator,[17] but without result. The only thing that everyone managed to hear was the sentence. Among those who protested at not being allowed into the courtroom was the daughter of an active witness for the prosecution, Rudenko.

In the second half of June the appeal in the Kochubiyevsky case was examined by the Ukrainian Supreme Court, and the sentence passed by the Kiev Regional Court was confirmed.

In August the Chronicle *reported the appearance in* samizdat *of a
'Record of the Trial of Boris Kochubiyevsky'* :[18]

9 The record is extremely interesting despite its fragmentary
nature. Some of the information is already familiar to readers of
the *Chronicle*, but a few details may be added which were not
mentioned in No. 8. The speech of the defence lawyer is an
example of the kind of address which the public has not heard
in recent years: describing the content of his client's real or
supposed statements, the lawyer does his utmost to blacken the
picture, and, incidentally, he believes not his client, who denies
ever having made many of these statements, but those witnesses who assert that Kochubiyevsky did indeed make them.
The only point made by the lawyer as a defence is a denial of
the *deliberate* falseness of the accused's statements, 'the sincerity
of his delusions'. It should be noted that 'deliberate falseness' is
an essential feature of a criminal offence under Article 187-1 of
the Ukrainian Criminal Code, and a defence can be con-
structed on this point alone; there is no need to sympathize with
the accused's opinions, nor, for that matter, to abuse them, nor
to declare his convictions harmful and slanderous, or his
testimony in court false.

*Three months after the trial, vicious articles against Kochubiyevsky—
carefully commissioned from Jewish journalists—appeared in the local
press.*[19] *By this time he was in his camp at Belichi in Kiev Region, where,
No. 12 later reported,*[20] *he was both beaten up by the criminal prisoners
for being a Jew and subjected to strong K.G.B. pressures to renounce the
Promised Land.*

*It would be wrong to think that the year 1968 saw the beginning of the
imprisonment of Jews for Zionism, or of resistance to the closing of
synagogues, or of other 'undesirable' Jewish activities. Even in the post-
Stalin period a trickle of Jews sentenced on such charges had helped to
keep the camps in business. One pre-1968 case recorded by the* Chronicle
probably resulted from the Six-Day War:

8 In the autumn of 1968 David Naidis, a native of Odessa,
formerly a fourth-year correspondence student of the Kiev

University Faculty of Journalism, was released from a camp. Naidis is the author of an essay on the likelihood of a Stalinist revival, which was not discovered during searches. He was arrested in mid-1967 on charges of printing leaflets on the Jewish question, and sentenced in 1968. Naidis has not been reinstated at the university.

Another case, which, as No. 12 later reported,[21] *began with the police discovery of writings about anti-semitism and with their author's participation in 'nationalist gatherings', was this one :*

In February 1967 Valentin Prussakov, a student of the Institute of Railway Engineers, was arrested in Moscow. During a search it was mainly his verses which were confiscated. He was charged under article 70 of the Russian Criminal Code. In February 1968 a trial was fixed but not held, and in March, after being kept for thirteen months in custody (in Lefortovo Prison), Prussakov was released and the case closed for lack of a *corpus delicti*.

Prussakov had in fact been persecuted in various ways since 1964, so in 1969 he decided to try emigration to Israel. In response to his application the K.G.B. men were direct : 'We won't let you out ... Your place is behind barbed wire.' Nevertheless, he began writing appeals to the authorities,[22] *and also showed his concern for the Democratic Movement by signing an open letter about the imprisonment of the biologist Medvedev.*[23] *In early 1971 he had yet to reach Israel.*

Responsible estimates in 1970 of the number of Jews similarly frustrated ranged, if families were accounted for, from about 100,000 to 500,000. At the same time, in 1968–70 — before the spurt of early 1971 — only some thousand a year appeared to have succeeded in getting out. Here is an episode in the life of one of those whose persistence at last got its reward in 1971 :

Iosif Kerler [see plate 59], the well-known Yiddish poet,[24] wrote a declaration of protest[25] on December 18th, 1969, against the forcible detention in the Soviet Union of Jewish citizens wishing to emigrate to Israel. The absence of any logical pattern in this detention is emphasized in the document: 'In the last two and a half years more Jews have been allowed to emigrate than in the period up to the Six-Day War.' Kerler points to the danger of a revival of Stalinist anti-semitism. He was prompted to write after reading an article (in *Izvestia*, No. 292)[26] by L. Berenshtein and M. Fridel, in which the authors, while recognizing the right of Jewish citizens to be reunited with their families or to emigrate ('whoever so desires'), at the same time pose a 'provocative alternative' ('Where exactly should the separated family be reunited—on capitalist or socialist soil?'). Kerler feels that this alternative gives full scope for arbitrary action and discrimination against Soviet Jews applying to emigrate to Israel, and insists that the desire to emigrate to Israel is not at variance with Soviet legislation.

This declaration is only one of many protests on the same subject.

Another such case[27] *concerned the household which consisted of a middle-aged woman, Udiya I. Kleizmer, and her young relatives Benedict I. Borukhovich and Boris L. Shlayen, whose collective letter to Mr Kosygin of June 25th, 1969,*[28] *the* Chronicle *summarized as follows:*

10 This letter raises the question of the free emigration of Jews to Israel from the U.S.S.R., to join their families and their people. The authors tell of their correspondence with a series of officials and organizations after they had applied on December 30th, 1968, to leave for Israel. Their request for permission to emigrate was motivated by the desire to join their relatives, and also by the impossibility of receiving a Jewish upbringing and education in the U.S.S.R. At the end of the letter there is a reference to the speech made by A. N. Kosygin in Paris in which he guaranteed free exit for Jews, and another reference to the [U.N.] Convention on the liquidation of all forms of racial and national discrimination.

Nor surprisingly, Kosygin's guarantee has been widely quoted in Jewish letters. His exact words, according to Pravda *of December 5th, 1966, were: 'As regards the uniting of families, if certain families want to meet up or want to leave the Soviet Union, then the door is open and no problem exists here.'*

But many problems[29] *arose for the three Moscow Jews—and several more letters had to be signed*[30] *— before in 1970 the door eventually opened. The* Chronicle *provides an illustration :*

Boris Leibovich Shlayen [was a] mechanic at a Moscow factory 11 which repairs calculating machines. After Shlayen had applied to the Department of Visas and Registration on December 30th, 1968, for permission to emigrate to Israel, he was given almost no more orders for work, with the result that his earnings fell roughly by half. The atmosphere of persecution later forced Shlayen to leave his job, on March 3rd, 1969, 'at his own request'.

Those Jews who have eventually achieved their goal of emigration have not always left the U.S.S.R. in comfort. In these two items the Chronicle *explains why :*

A CUSTOMS 'EXAMINATION' AT SHEREMETEVO   10
AIRPORT [MOSCOW]

In December 1968 the engineer David Khavkin, a former political prisoner in the Mordovian camps [see plate 32], applied to the appropriate authorities for permission to leave the U.S.S.R. for Israel. In August 1969 his application was refused. After sending in a second application through unofficial channels to Kosygin personally, the Khavkin family were granted permission to leave. David and Ester Khavkin and their nine-year-old son were due to fly to Vienna on September 29th, 1969. At Sheremetevo International Airport they were asked to undergo a customs examination an hour before departure, and this turned out to be a real 'body frisk' in classic camp style. Ester Khavkin was stripped naked, and subjected to a humiliating gynaecological examination. The search lasted more than three hours. The Khavkins missed their plane. When they tried to lodge a complaint, they were told quite openly: 'If you hadn't brought this mob here, we'd have let you go straight away'. (Some 186 people had come to see the Khavkins off [see plate 61].) They were refused tickets for the flight of September 30th, on the grounds that 'the Vienna flight on September 30th is for foreign currency passengers'.

On October 1st, after a five-minute customs inspection, the Khavkins flew off to Vienna.

11 There are reasons to suppose that customs examinations in the style of the 'body frisk' carried out in the camps have become the rule at Sheremetevo International Airport, at least for Jews emigrating to Israel.

On December 1st, two Jews from Novosibirsk were due to leave by air for Vienna. They were Israel Shmerler [see plate 61] and Moisei Mostkov. As in the case of David Khavkin they were searched until it was too late to embark. The only difference was that in their case the body search was carried out without using any especially humiliating methods. The airport manager Lemann openly connived with the customs officials and plainclothes men who conducted the 'examination'. He even attempted to take over the duties of a criminal investigation officer with regard to the indignant friends who were seeing the passengers off.

When the customs officials inspected their baggage, Marx's *Das Kapital*, among other things, was not allowed to pass through. On December 3rd, after another brief examination, Shmerler and Mostkov were able to leave for Vienna.

So far we have discussed people whose overriding goal has been Israel, and whose fates — with an unpredictability typical of many aspects of the Jewish situation — have taken very different paths. A somewhat different group is constituted by those Jews who have been closely involved not only in Zionist circles but also in the mainstream of the Democratic Movement. One such is Boris Tsukerman, the author of an excellent samizdat biography of General Grigorenko (see p. 136 and plate 24) and other documents, who was allowed to leave for Israel in January 1971. Another is an ex-Muscovite to whom the Chronicle has devoted several items, including the following. He fills out the first episode in his personal testimony written for this book (pp. 43-51).

7 On December 23rd, 1968, members of the K.G.B. searched the flat of the mathematician Julius Telesin [see plate 58]. He was forcibly detained in the street and taken home for the search. The search was made in connection with the Burmistrovich case [see pp. 67-70]. After a record consisting of only three

points had already been signed, the men who had carried out the search, using force, collected a number of books, poems, articles, letters and other papers, and, without making an inventory, took all this away in a briefcase belonging to Telesin. Apart from the papers a typewriter was also taken; it was returned about two weeks later. The witnesses—who according to the law (article 135 of the Russian Code of Criminal Procedure) must be 'citizens unassociated with the case'—were from among the people who took part in the detaining of Telesin and actively helped to search his flat. Ten days later, at an interrogation of Telesin at K.G.B. head-quarters, the investigator, Captain Solovyov, attempted to make him help in the compilation of an inventory of the property contained in the briefcase: naturally he refused. One of the 'witnesses' of the previous search also played the same role at this point.

On January 4th, 1969, Telesin sent a complaint to Major-General Volkov, the head of the K.G.B. investigation department. Having received no answer either when the statutory period of one month had expired, or later, Telesin wrote a statement to the U.S.S.R. Procuracy, in which he listed all the facts and also pointed out that members of the K.G.B.—Major Gulyayev, Captains Solovyov and Pustyakov, and Lieutenants Sergeyev and Fokin—as well as witnesses Koval and Khailov had carried out a blatant seizure of his personal property, an act defined as robbery in article 145 of the Russian Criminal Code.

At the beginning of March, clearly not wanting to produce a reply in written, documentary form, the K.G.B. rang Telesin up and proposed that he 'come to them for a reply'.

Julius Telesin, a mathematician at the Central Institute of 8 Mathematical Economics, has been dismissed by decision of the Academic Council, on the pretext of having failed to be re-elected in competition with other candidates.

The matter of Telesin's dismissal was examined in the absence of his supervisors: one was on a study trip, and the other was officially informed that the matter would not be raised on that day. This allowed the Deputy Director of the Institute, Yu. Oleinik, to make lying references to their negative opinion of Telesin, although the favourable report from Telesin's laboratory contradicted them. He also said that the subject of Telesin's research was 'old hat' — but there are other people engaged in identical research who are still continuing their work. After Telesin had exposed Oleinik's lies, the Director of the Institute, Fedorenko, declared that the Institute 'must liberate itself from certain persons'. Telesin was dismissed by eleven votes to six. The real reasons for his dismissal were the facts that he had signed several letters of protest[31] and that the K.G.B. were harassing him. According to a statement by the Procurator at the trial of Burmistrovich, the materials confiscated from Telesin were to be dealt with separately.

Doubtless the K.G.B. harassment had increased since Burmistrovich's trial in May 1969, as Telesin had been present and helped to compile the verbatim record.[32] Hence his swift dismissal and the threat to try him. Telesin's answer, however, was to start signing the Action Group's appeals to the U.N., to compile a samizdat anthology of unrepentant court speeches by defendants in political trials,[33] and, in March 1970, to sign a militant open letter by forty Moscow Jews.[34] The last act at once brought Izvestia[35] about Telesin's ears, and as seventy items of printed and other material had been confiscated from him in a new search only a few weeks earlier,[36] the outlook now seemed problematical. But instead of launching a trial, the K.G.B. suddenly decided to grant his request to emigrate. On May 7th the Western press[37] reported the emotional scenes as sixty friends saw him off at the airport, and the Chronicle, *in a rare tribute, praised Telesin — a 'mathematician and translator of poetry' — for the 'courage and persistence' with which he had defended various people's civil rights in the U.S.S.R.[38] The K.G.B. — by contrast — saw him as a persistent nuisance in two parts of the dissent movement at once, and therefore, on balance, better removed to Israel than Mordovia.*

Apart from the emigration question, the Chronicle *has also been concerned with Soviet — and even Polish[39] — anti-semitism in general. An aspect of this phenomenon has been the often viciously anti-semitic sentiments displayed in press cartoons,[40] articles and books — sentiments usually only thinly disguised beneath a mask of anti-Zionism. Two particularly notorious books, which blur the distinction between Zionists and other Jews, are discussed in these items:*

According to unconfirmed rumours, Yu. Ivanov, author of the **8**
much-discussed book *Beware, Zionism!*,[41] is the pseudonym of
the well-known journalist and international commentator
Valentin Zorin. Other sources give the name of the well-known
Soviet diplomat Valerian Zorin. The book *Judaism without
Embellishments* by T. Kichko, the publication of which caused a
big international scandal, has come out in a second edition in
the Ukraine.[42]

Rumours that Yu. Ivanov is the pseudonym of either Valentin **9**
or Valerian Zorin have turned out to be incorrect. Yury Ivanov
is a real person of about forty. It seems that he is a graduate of
the Institute of International Relations, and he knows English
well, but no other languages. Yury Ivanov works in the Central
Committee of the party. He was formerly employed in the
African department, but then he received a reprimand for
drunkenness, and although the normal practice in such cases is
to expel the culprit from the Central Committee apparatus,
Ivanov was transferred to the foreign travel department, where
the staff consists only of K.G.B. officials. At present Yury Ivanov
is the only expert on Israel working in the Central Committee.
He should not be confused with K. Ivanov (the pseudonym
under which the Deputy Minister of Foreign Affairs, [V. S.]
Semyonov, writes), who is one of the authors of the book *The
State of Israel*.[43]

*Apart from these publications, Kichko brought out in 1968 a new book of
similarly anti-semitic content,* Judaism and Zionism,[44] *and in 1969
Ivanov revealed a lot of his pseudonyms by publishing twelve articles in
book form,*[45] *as well as a long essay*[46] *in which he elevated Zionism to
'the most urgent problem of our times', an ideology which opposed everything progressive with black reaction. Thus the* Chronicle *was scarcely
overreacting by drawing attention to these anti-semitic propagandists.*

*In 1970 the anti-semitic campaign on the one hand, and the unintimidated
Jewish national revival on the other, produced a dangerous polarization of
the sort which, if continued, could lead to anti-Jewish violence at the local
level. Ominously, the* Chronicle *reported an increasing number of openly
anti-semitic incidents. Prior to 1970, however, many particular cases,
like the following, involved only a limited element of anti-semitism :*

9 Lilya Kosior, a director of cultural activity, and daughter of a
   former General-Secretary of the Central Committee of the
   Ukrainian Communist Party, Stanislav Kosior, has been dismissed 'at her own request' from her job at the Taxi-drivers'
   Club [in Moscow], after the administration had declared her
   production of Boris Gorbatov's play *The Youth of our Fathers*
   erroneous, and had also discovered from her personal documents
   that her mother was a Jewess.

10   THE CASE OF M. SH. RYZHIK

The case of Mikhail Shmerlevich Ryzhik has been in progress
for almost a year. He has been accused of refusing to undergo
military service.

   In 1961, as a third-year student at Kharkov University, M.
Sh. Ryzhik was called up into the Soviet Army, and after serv-
ing his term, was transferred to the reserve in 1964 as a Junior
Lieutenant in the Signals.

   In 1968 he graduated from the Moscow Institute of Steel and
Alloys, and then worked as an engineer at the 'Eksiton' factory
in the town of Pavlovsky-Posad [near Moscow].

   On November 14th, 1968, M. Sh. Ryzhik received his call-up
papers from the Pavlovsky-Posad military recruitment centre.
Larionov, the head of Department 3 of the recruitment centre,
informed Ryzhik that he was being called up for service in the
Soviet Army in accordance with article 61, paragraph b, of the
General Conscription Law, and should report for a medical
examination. In reply to this, Ryzhik declared that in his
opinion the law was being incorrectly applied in his case, and
that he would not report for a medical examination until he
had received an interpretation from the competent authorities
which would legally justify the compulsory peacetime call-up
of a man who had already served in the armed forces. Moreover, Ryzhik explained to Larionov and the military commissar
Kamendrovsky that it was irrational to use a specialist with
higher education in a Soviet Army post which would suit a man
with secondary school education. After that, Larionov and
Kamendrovsky asked Lebedev, an official of the recruitment
centre dressed in civilian clothes, into the room, and they drew
up a record of the proceedings. Everything Ryzhik had said was

entered in the record in a distorted form, and he refused to sign the document. The record was sent to the Pavlovsky-Posad Procuracy. Criminal proceedings were instituted. Meanwhile Ryzhik appealed to the Central Committee of the party and the Ministry of Defence, enquiring whether his conscription was legally justifiable; he received the reply that he was in fact liable for call-up. After that, Ryzhik informed the town recruitment centre that he was willing to serve in the Soviet Army. The recruitment centre, however, sent him back to the Procuracy.

In accordance with article 50 of the Russian Criminal Code, the case ought to have been closed at this point, but in spite of this the investigation continued. It was conducted by a grade-one lawyer, Kocherov, an investigator of the Pavlosky-Posad Procuracy, for whom objectivity was the least consideration. During his interrogations of Ryzhik, Kocherov was rude, refusing to include Ryzhik's additional statements and corrections in the record of the proceedings, and permitting himself anti-semitic insults. Ryzhik submitted a petition objecting to investigator Kocherov on the grounds that he was prejudiced. Ryzhik's petition was rejected, and investigator Kocherov, in reply to Ryzhik's complaint, declared: 'Of course you're not satisfied with your investigator. You wouldn't be satisfied with any investigator. You'd like your investigator to be ... Katsman, wouldn't you?' (There is no investigator by the name of Katsman in the Pavlovsky-Posad Procuracy.) Ryzhik's case was handed to the courts. He was charged under article 81 of the Russian Criminal Code—'refusal to obey a mobilization draft order'.

On February 3rd, 1969, at a session of the Pavlovsky-Posad town court chaired by Judge Sorokina, the accused Ryzhik was acquitted, since at the time of his summons to the military recruitment centre there had been no mobilization order from the Ministry of Defence. The Procurator Molodtsov appealed against the decision of the court. The investigation was resumed: this time criminal proceedings were instituted against Ryzhik under article 80 of the Russian Criminal Code—'refusal to obey a normal call-up order for military service'.

In April 1969 Ryzhik was tried a second time, in the [nearby] town of Noginsk, and once again the court acquitted him, on the grounds that he had undergone normal call-up in 1961–4, and that the new order was therefore not 'normal' in his case. The Pavlovsky-Posad Procurator, Junior Counsellor of Justice Fedonkin, appealed privately against the decision of the court. His appeal was granted by the Moscow Regional Court, and Ryzhik's case was reopened from the court investigation stage.

On October 13th, 1969, Ryzhik's case was given an open hearing in Noginsk. Judge Demskaya presided over the court. Procurator Molodtsov represented the prosecution, and Ryzhik's defence was conducted by lawyer Monakhov of the Moscow City Collegium of Lawyers.

During the hearing Judge Demskaya condemned young people who 'have learned to argue'. 'There's nothing to argue about! The order is given—obey it! Thinking won't get you anywhere!' she declared. She denounced Ryzhik's action as 'un-Soviet to the core'.

The testimony given at this trial by witnesses Lebedev, Larionov and Kamendrovsky, officials of the army recruitment centre, completely contradicted the testimony they gave at the pre-trial investigation—which had been written into the record of their interrogations—but the court disregarded this.

It is known for a fact that Ryzhik once informed the October District recruitment centre in Moscow of his wish to go to Vietnam as a volunteer. But the head of the October District recruitment centre, Lieutenant-Colonel Romanenko, and the chief of Department 3 of the same centre, Kalinin, supplied the court with a certificate (number 3/2287 of August 7th, 1969) which stated that M. Sh. Ryzhik 'has never been, and is not now, on the list of reserve officers at the October District recruitment centre, and has never made a written request to be sent to Vietnam as a volunteer'. The defence lawyer requested the court to examine M. Sh. Ryzhik's passport, in which there was a note that the passport had been issued after the holder had served his term in the Soviet Army, on the basis of a military identity card registered at the October District recruitment centre in Moscow, where Ryzhik was on the list from 1964 to 1968.

The unsubstantial and clumsily expressed accusations made by the Procurator were refuted by the defence arguments. The lawyer Monakhov stated that there was no law in the Criminal Code which specified that a man could be charged for refusing to do extra service, and that the application by analogy of article 80 of the Russian Criminal Code directly conflicted with the Criminal Code now in force and with the Basic Principles of Criminal Legislation in the U.S.S.R. The institution of analogy, which used to exist in Soviet criminal law, had been abolished in 1958 by the U.S.S.R. Supreme Soviet, when it adopted the Basic Principles of Criminal Legislation, and by the Russian Supreme Soviet in 1960 when it adopted the new Criminal Code. The abolition of the institution of analogy had been specifically emphasized at the session of the Supreme Soviet, and in the Soviet press, as an achievement of democracy. In conclusion the defence asked the court to find M. Sh. Ryzhik not guilty.

The court found Ryzhik guilty under article 80 of the Russian Criminal Code and sentenced him to one and a half years' imprisonment, his term to be served in a corrective labour colony of ordinary régime.

M. Sh. Ryzhik, who had been at liberty all this time, was taken into custody in the courtroom and interned in the prison of Noginsk.

This saga ended at last in November 1969, when the Russian Supreme Court changed the sentence to a suspended term of one year.[47] *A month later, to celebrate his liberty, Ryzhik signed a denunciation of the expulsion of Alexander Solzhenitsyn from the Union of Writers.*[48]

With the polarization of 1970, the Jewish national revival — led by its militant Zionist wing — not surprisingly gave birth to a journal. Its name, Exodus, was expressive. In 1970 it appeared three times, in April, July and November, and in putting the emphasis on the reproduction of documents lived up well to the Chronicle's *standards of accuracy and careful presentation.*[49] *As a Zionist journal, it was concerned with the struggle to leave for Israel rather than on efforts to improve the cultural and religious conditions of Jewish life in the U.S.S.R. Collective and individual appeals to emigrate therefore appeared in abundance, from Latvia, Lithuania, Belorussia, the Ukraine, Georgia, Leningrad, Moscow, and so on, as well as texts of semi-secret official documents about the necessary procedures for emigration.*

The régime's reactions to the new Jewish militancy of 1970 included not only an intensified anti-Zionist press campaign, but also a press conference of non-Zionist Jews, carefully stage-managed by the Ministry of Foreign Affairs on March 4th. This, however, by its denial of the existence of anti-semitism or any significant Zionist tendencies in the U.S.S.R., merely infuriated the Zionists and swelled their ranks. So desperate, indeed, did some of them become, that a group in Riga made plans to escape by hijacking an aeroplane to Sweden. On June 15th twelve people, including two Russians who wanted to emigrate because of persecution and imprisonment in the U.S.S.R., were arrested in Leningrad. Six months later two of them — Eduard Kuznetsov (see plate 56) and Mark Dymshits — received the death penalty, while their fellows got lengthy terms in camps. Only one, Mendel Bodnya, repented in full, and was rewarded with the light sentence of four years. Kuznetsov had been a dissenter and democrat as early as 1961, when he associated with Yury Galanskov and the contributors to the first Phoenix *and was given seven years for his pains. In 1968 the* Chronicle *reported his release from Mordovia.*[50]

Because the group had planned but not committed a hijacking, because they had carefully calculated it so that no harm should come to anyone else on the plane, and because of the repressive ban on their legal emigration which had driven them to such desperate measures in the first place, world opinion and the Democratic Movement were deeply shocked at the sentences. To halt the uproar of protest the appeal court sat with unprecedented speed only six days later — sooner than the law allowed — and commuted the death sentence to fifteen years.[51] *None the less, other group trials followed in the spring of 1971, the Jews concerned being accused of complicity in the hijack case and of illegal* samizdat *activity.*

But the official policy of letting some Zionists go while imprisoning those easiest to prosecute showed no signs in early 1971 of solving the problem. Several thousands were allowed to emigrate in the months before the 24th party congress in April — an attempt to reduce world-wide criticism and pressure — but these were mere drops in the ocean. Indeed, the eventual size of the exodus to Israel, how and when it would occur, and with what sacrifices for those released and those who would stay, all these questions remained, in 1971, matters impossible to predict.[52]

16. THE CHURCHES

In my fifty years, firm and clear convictions have formed in me; these are what I express in my articles. I write there the truth. You yourselves do not say that there is any untruth in them. I protest against the barbaric persecution of religion, which expresses itself in the destruction of churches and the humiliation of believers. I protest against a situation in which the Church has been reduced to scum, and comrade Trushin, who is present, is the dictator of the Moscow Church. He, an unbeliever and a communist, appoints and removes priests at whim. (The cause of this naturally lies not in him but in the existing system.) All this infringes every norm and even our Stalinist Constitution. Against all this I protest in my articles, which I have circulated, am circulating and will circulate, exercising my right to freedom of expression.

Anatoly Levitin, at a meeting with prominent atheists, May 1965[1]

All three Soviet constitutions to date proclaim as a cardinal principle the strict separation of Church and State. On the other hand, the Bolshevik ideology, the fanatical intolerance of Lenin personally towards religion,[2] and the close association of the Orthodox Church with the ancien régime all combined to make a live-and-let-live relationship impossible in practice. Almost immediately laws began to be passed undermining the separation principle, until, with the legislation of 1929, close state control of religious bodies was fully legalized in respect to everything except the supreme law, the Constitution.[3]

Apart from the developments on paper, religious groups often suffered much worse depredations 'in the field'. The fact that these started under Lenin, and were not just another aspect of the Stalinist terror, has interested the Chronicle. Here is how it commented on the appearance in samizdat of 'A Letter to the Members of the Politbureau':

This letter, dated March 19th, 1922,[4] is signed by Lenin and demands that *the most merciless measures* be taken to *crush* all opposition to the proposed confiscation of church treasures. The instructions contained in the letter do not conform to the principles of socialist legality. They are the product only of the political and tactical requirements of the moment: 'We must appropriate at all costs this source of several millions—or perhaps even milliards—of gold roubles'; 'suppress their (the clergy's) resistance so brutally that they will remember it for decades to come'; send a member of the All-Union Central Executive Committee of the Soviets (V.Ts.I.K.) to the town of Shuya [NE. of Moscow, where clashes had occurred], with 'verbal instructions' to arrest no less than several dozen representatives of the clergy, the middle classes and the bourgeoisie 'on suspicion of direct or indirect participation in violent resistance to the V.Ts.I.K. decree concerning the confiscation of church treasures'; 'on the basis of his report, the Politbureau will issue a detailed directive, also verbal to the judicial authorities, so that a trial of the rebels of Shuya for resisting the campaign to help the starving can be held as quickly as possible and can end, unfailingly, with the execution of a very large number of the most influential and dangerous Black Hundreders of Shuya, and if possible not only of Shuya, but of Moscow also, and several other ecclesiastical centres'; 'the more representatives of the reactionary bourgeoisie and the reactionary clergy we manage to execute on this suspicion, the better'. The famine appears consistently throughout the letter as providing a convenient set of circumstances in which the confiscation of church treasures can be carried out without fear of resistance from the peasantry. The millions or milliards of roubles are required not for famine relief, which admittedly might have justified repressions; they are necessary so that the Soviet team may feel itself a power at the Genoa conference [on European economic reconstruction of April-May 1922].

The letter is a top-secret document, and the channel through which it passed into *samizdat* is unlikely to be discovered. Therefore one should not regard the document as indisputably genuine: it would be wise to carry out a detailed textual analysis of the letter. Obviously official propaganda will not miss its opportunity to declare such a document a forgery. But in *samizdat*, where there is complete freedom of research, one should not rush to the opposite extreme: if the authenticity of the document is confirmed, then the profile of the first Chairman of the Council of People's Commissars will become more clear-cut in the mind of the public.

No. 15 duly reported that the letter's authenticity was confirmed by the appearance of a brief summary of it in Volume 45 of Lenin's Complete Works.[5] *Further confirmation lies in the fact that recorded events fit closely with the letter: a crowd at Shuya had been machine-gunned in clashes on March 15th, Izvestia recording four people killed, and forty-five priests and laymen later stood trial, twelve of whom were executed.[6]*

In the 1930s Stalin turned to the forcible closure of places of worship on a massive scale, with the aim of eradicating public religion completely. The war, however, prevented him completing his task: in order to gain believers' support he had to reopen the churches. After this, the next big onslaught did not follow until 1958–64, under Khrushchev, when at least half the religious buildings in the U.S.S.R. were closed by deception or force. The number of open Orthodox churches, for example, fell in this period from about 20,000 to some 10,000.[7] Since 1964 the situation has remained fairly static, but occasionally the Chronicle *has carried reports like this:*

In the town of Kolyvan[8] near Novosibirsk [in south-central 10 Siberia] the Orthodox church has been closed on the pretext of its not conforming with fire safety regulations. When the believers dug a pond to conform with the fire regulations, the local authorities filled it in again and prohibited church services, despite the fact that permission to hold services had been given by Moscow. Moreover the local authorities tore down the church's cupolas, killing a five-year-old child in the process. Instead of the church the believers have been given a small chapel which does not satisfy fire safety regulations.

THE ORTHODOX

Anatoly Levitin

No one in the Christian wing of the Democratic Movement has been more prominent than the colourful Anatoly Levitin (pen-name Krasnov — see plate 65), on whom much documentation is already available.[9] After the police came for him on September 12th, 1969, the Chronicle *drew on his extensive autobiographical[10] and other writings to compile this item:*

Levitin spent seven years — 1949–56 — in Stalin's camps. He 10 was later rehabilitated. Levitin's deep religious convictions, and his activities as an Orthodox writer, led [in 1958] to this

II

talented teacher and literary scholar being deprived of the right to teach in schools.

A. Krasnov is the author of a number of articles in the *Journal of the Moscow Patriarchate*.[11] Apart from this, he is the author of a three-volume history of the Living Church.[12]

Since 1959 Krasnov-Levitin has written a large number of works, in which he has spoken out in particular against violations of religious freedom in the Soviet Union: *Struggling for Light and Truth, The Brassy Clatter, The Fiery Chalice, The Drawn Bow-string, On Monasticism, The Free Church*, and others.[13] In recent years he has written two important philosophical works: *Stromati* and *Christ and the Master*, on which the *Chronicle* reported in No. 5. The journal *Science and Religion* has twice[14] written about Levitin-Krasnov (see Vasilev's article 'The Theologian-Inciter', 1966, No. 10,[15] and the section 'A Contemporary "Secular Theologian"' in N. Semenkin's article 'From Anathema to Vocation', 1969, No. 8).

Here we interrupt No. 10 so as to give No. 5's account of the samizdat *works just mentioned, and also of two others:*

5 *Christ and the Master* is an attempt to discuss several basic questions of Christian teaching through a literary and philosophical study of [Mikhail] Bulgakov's novel *The Master and Margarita*.[16] The thread of the argument is provided by the chapters in the novel about Christ. The book is written in a free, discursive manner with frequent digressions into the author's personal reminiscences and reflections.

The Greek word *stromati* literally means 'carpet', but in the figurative sense of 'miscellany' it was used by various ancient teachers of the Church as the title for their books. Written in the form of observations loosely tied together by the general theme of the part a Christian should play in society, Krasnov's book[17] deals with such questions as the moral responsibility of a Christian to society, the role of the Church in the life of society, and the collaboration of Christians with people of different views in the solution of common moral and political tasks. The author gives a brief survey of the various political trends at the present time and states his attitude towards them. At the end of the book the author gives his political credo, which he defines as 'democratic humanism',[18] and calls on people of different persuasions to unite on this basis.

His letter on 'The situation of the Russian Orthodox Church'[19] is addressed to the Pope, and it gives an account, based mainly on the author's personal observations, of the attitude of different generations of Russians to religion and the Church, the way in which some young people are turning to the Church, and the relations between different faiths. He raises the need for an inner revival of the Russian Orthodox Church, and examines the difficulties in the way of this. The author speaks of the criticism which he and others have made of the Russian bishops,[20] and contends that such criticism is both justified and necessary. The question of uniting the Western and Eastern Churches is also touched upon in this letter.

The article 'A Drop under the Microscope'[21] is about the difficulties which have arisen at the parish level in the Russian Orthodox Church as a result of a change in the parish administration. This change consisted of taking the administration of parish affairs out of the hands of the priest and transferring it to the council of twenty laymen headed by a church elder. The author shows that this reform is in conflict with canonical tradition, and he points out the practical consequences which it entails in conditions of constant interference by the authorities in the life of the church: infringement of the rights of the priest, unchecked power for the elder, who is appointed by the state authorities, etc. As an illustration, the example of the Nikolo-Kuznetskaya church [in Moscow] is described in detail.[22] The author also treats the more general question of the way in which the Russian Orthodox Church has been denied its rights in the Soviet Union, and of the responsibility of the Church hierarchy itself for this state of affairs.

Now No. 10 continues:

During recent years Levitin-Krasnov has also spoken out con- 10 tinually in defence of civil rights, and in defence of people arrested and sentenced on political charges. His signature stands at the foot of numerous collective protests, including the letter to the Budapest meeting [see pp. 86–8]. He is a member of the Action Group for the Defence of Human Rights in the

Soviet Union. As a publicist he has commented on the arrest
[see p. 327] of B. V. Talantov (*Drama in Vyatka*[23]) and [see
p. 136] of P. G. Grigorenko (*Light in the Little Window*[24]).

On September 12th, the Procuracy investigator L. S.
Akimova carried out a search in Levitin's flat. During the
search, the following works of A. E. Levitin-Krasnov were
confiscated: *A History of the Living Church*, *On Monasticism*,
Stromati, a letter to the Pope, a letter to the Patriarch in
support of the letter from [Moscow] priests Gleb Yakunin and
Nikolai Eshliman,[25] *Light in the Little Window*, *Drama in Vyatka*,
Listening to the Radio,[26] *The Brassy Clatter*, and others. Also
confiscated were *samizdat* materials and a typewriter.

Just before the search of Levitin's flat, his friends Oleg
Vorobyov and Vadim Shavrov[27] had been there. The search
began as soon as they had left the house, while they themselves
were quickly detained by the police on suspicion of 'stealing
suitcases'. Shavrov was released from the police station after
the search was over and Levitin-Krasnov had been taken away.
Vorobyov was searched at the police station, without a warrant
for the search of his person being issued, and the letter 'To the
Members of the Politbureau' by V. I. Lenin (about the events
in Shuya) was taken from him. He was then sent to the violent
patients' section of psychiatric hospital No. 15, from which he
was not released until October 20th. Oleg Vorobyov [see plate
63] was among those who signed their names in support of the
Action Group's [first] appeal to the United Nations [and later
received a six-year sentence in Perm].[28]

For three days A. E. Levitin was held in a preventive
detention cell at the police station, and then he was transferred
to Butyrka prison. An investigation was begun by the Moscow
city Procuracy. (The investigator was Akimova, already well
known as chief investigator of the cases of the Pushkin Square
demonstration of January 22nd, 1967, of the Red Square
demonstration of August 25th, 1968, and of Irina Belogorodskaya.) A charge was brought against Levitin under article 142
of the Russian Criminal Code (violation of the laws on the
separation of Church and State) and also under article 190-1.
Witnesses are being questioned about Krasnov-Levitin's works,
mainly about *Stromati*.

On October 9th Levitin's case was suddenly handed over to

the Krasnodar Procuracy, and A. E. Levitin-Krasnov was sent off to Krasnodar [in the north Caucasus].

Soon after Levitin's arrest, a letter began to circulate in *samizdat*, entitled 'To Public Opinion in the Soviet Union and Abroad',[29] signed by thirty-two Soviet citizens, including six former political prisoners (Leonid Vasilev [see p. 120], Zinaida Grigorenko, Alexander Esenin-Volpin, Victor Krasin, Vadim Shavrov and Pyotr Yakir). The letter says that A. E. Levitin 'was becoming more and more worried by problems of civil freedom, since freedom is indivisible and there can be no religious freedom if basic human rights are being trampled upon. He was the first religious person in our country in the post-Stalin years to affirm this truth and to raise his voice in defence of civil rights and of those who have fallen victims in the fight for civil freedoms.'

A letter by six Christian believers on the subject of A. Levitin-Krasnov's church and religious activities[30] has been sent to the World Council of Churches, with copies to Patriarch Athenagoras, Pope Paul the Sixth and the International Committee for the Defence of Christian Culture. The letter says:

> We deeply deplore the fact that the Russian Orthodox Church finds its supporters amongst laymen and ordinary priests, and not among the bishops of the Russian Church, many of whom are barren fig-trees, completely under the control of the Council for Religious Affairs ... Anatoly Emmanuilovich was doing his duty as a Christian, and none of his activities, which were all in defence of the Christian faith, infringed Soviet laws ... We, Christian believers and citizens of the Soviet Union, are deeply disturbed by the arrest of the Orthodox writer A. Levitin-Krasnov and [see below] the teacher B. Talantov. We join with them in their protest against the abnormal relations which exist between Church and State, and we demand the opening of the forcibly closed churches, monasteries, seminaries and houses of prayer.

The letter was signed by: J. Vishnevskaya,[31] B. Dubovenko, V. Kokorev, V. Lashkova,[32] E. Stroyeva and Yu. Titov [see plates 40 and 60].[33]

For nearly a year Levitin sat in prison. No. 11 reported that the investigation was 'expected to be completed in January 1970'. It was. But then the Krasnodar Provincial Court 'refused to accept the case and remitted it for further investigation, on the grounds that the charge of libel against Levitin was too vague, and that it was impossible to see exactly what law had been violated as a result of Levitin's incitement and by whom'.[34] The Procuracy appealed angrily to the Supreme Court against this unusual show of independence. At the same time it searched Father Yakunin's flat in Moscow, confiscating works by Levitin,[35] and probably inspired the subsequent scurrilous attacks on Levitin, Yakunin, and Eshliman in the paper Trud.[36] *Nevertheless, the Supreme Court upheld the Krasnodar court's decision, and on August 11th Levitin was freed. Undeterred by the continuation of the investigation, he quickly penned a long and vivid essay about his prison experiences[37] before returning to jail with a three-year sentence in May 1971.*

THE CASE OF BORIS TALANTOV

Chronicle *readers first learnt of Boris Talantov (see plate 64) from a summary, in the* samizdat *section, of his 'Statement to the U.S.S.R. Procurator-General':*[38]

5 This contains protests against the persecution to which the author, who lives in the city of Kirov [in the western foothills of the Urals], is being subjected for his opposition to interference by the Soviet authorities in the affairs of the Russian Orthodox Church, and to the acquiescence in this interference by the Church hierarchy.

Talantov's opposition had been vigorous since the early 1960s. Indeed it is from his pen that we have the most remarkable, vivid, detailed and horrifying picture of the effects of Khrushchev's anti-religious campaign on a typical provincial area.[39] He has also written penetratingly on Church history,[40] politics,[41] and Metropolitan Nikodim,[42] and he organized strong support from the Kirov diocese in 1966[43] for the two Moscow priests' attempt to reduce state control over the Church's life. Through all his writings run a deep love of the Church and its beautiful buildings, and a strong desire to rid Christians of their status as third-class citizens. Time and again he protests against this status, stressing its generally illegal basis. He also shows, with his references to the

Baptists, his strong support for Pavel Litvinov and Larissa Daniel, and his condemnation of labour camp conditions, that, like Levitin, he understands the indivisibility of freedom, and that freedom for the Orthodox requires freedom for Baptists and intellectuals as well.

In the light of all this, the Chronicle's *subsequent items about Talantov cause little surprise:*

On June 12th, 1969, Boris Vladimirovich Talantov was arrested 8 in the town of Kirov. He is a 66-year-old teacher of mathematics, who for many years has been exposing the illegal treatment of the Church, and the connivance in this of Church leaders. Talantov has been charged under article 190–1 of the Russia Criminal Code. The inquiry is being conducted by the Kirov Regional Procuracy, under senior investigator Boyarinov.

The *Chronicle* has already reported[44] that the 66-year-old B. V. 10 Talantov, a teacher, was sentenced by a court in Kirov to two years in [ordinary-régime] camps. In this issue some details of his trial are given.

The trial opened on September 1st. A group of believers, who sympathized with the accused, tried to get into the courtroom, but the seats had, as usual, been filled in advance.

B. V. Talantov was charged under article 190–1 of the Russian Criminal Code with writing a number of articles of religious content, an article on the nature of the Soviet state,[45] and various draft notes, including comments in the margin of a speech by L. I. Brezhnev. [He pleaded not guilty (No. 9).] Altogether only four witnesses were summoned in court, among them Gleb Talantov, son of the accused, and Nikodim Kamenskikh, a former seminarist.[46] All the witnesses gave evidence in favour of the accused.

Besides the Procurator, a former pupil of Talantov's — who is now a teacher of dialectical materialism — spoke at the trial as a public prosecutor. Talantov's defence was conducted by the lawyer [V. Ya.] Shveisky.

The Procurator agreed with the defence lawyer that the draft notes should not be held against Talantov, but otherwise he upheld completely the charge laid against him, saying that he considered all Talantov's articles, including those of religious content, 'deliberately false statements defaming the Soviet political and social system'. The Procurator demanded three years in camps for Talantov. The defence completely refuted the charge relating to the articles of religious content. Concerning the article on the nature of the Soviet state, in which there were some sharp criticisms of the Soviet state, the defence lawyer, while he did not agree with the views expressed in the article, maintained that its author sincerely believed in the correctness of his statements, and consequently there was no element of deliberate falsification in the document.

In his final plea, B. V. Talantov reaffirmed his allegiance to his convictions, although he allowed that he might have shown a subjective approach in certain of his judgments. He said farewell to his relatives, since, in view of his age and the state of his health, he had no hopes of regaining his freedom.

On September 3rd the court pronounced him guilty.

A year later, on January 4th, 1971, Boris Talantov died in captivity. The Chronicle *honoured him with a long obituary.*[47]

The Chronicle *has also informed its readers of the man who provided the stimulus to the two Moscow priests by leading a delegation of eight bishops to complain to the Patriarch about Church administration in 1965 — Archbishop Ermogen (see plate 62). For doing this he was retired to a monastery. Here, however, he applied himself to writing with the same outstanding success that he had achieved as a pastoral bishop.*[48] *Thus the* Chronicle *could announce in 1968 the circulation in* samizdat *of two letters and a historical study:*

5 The first of the letters written by Archibishop Ermogen to the Patriarchate (in which he disputes the legal validity of his dismissal) was written in November 1967, and the second in February 1968.[49] In these letters he not only shows the illegality of his dismissal (brought about under pressure from the authorities as a reprisal for his staunch resistance to actions detrimental to the Church), but also attempts an analysis, from the point of view of both canon and secular law, of the whole question of relations between Church and State in the U.S.S.R.

There is an even more detailed study of this question in his article 'On the fiftieth anniversary of the re-establishment of the office of Patriarch' (December 25th, 1967)[50] which makes numerous references to the decisions of the Ecumenical and National Councils of the Orthodox Church (including the National Council of the Russian Church of 1917–18).

But despite the restrained and dignified style in which Ermogen made his points and discussed the correct historical procedure for the election of a new Patriarch, the Synod proved unable either to accept or to answer his criticisms. Instead, it simply ordered him to shut up.[51]

Another Orthodox writer to emerge into view—from the ancient Russian town of Pskov near the border with Estonia—has been the priest Sergei Zheludkov. Cultivated and intellectual, but also passionately concerned about the Christian's role in society, he is cast in many ways in the Levitin mould. His big samizdat *book* Why I too am a Christian[52] *reveals vividly his modern theological thinking. This is how the* Chronicle *comments on two of his letters:*

In a letter to Pavel Litvinov,[53] S. Zheludkov expresses his support for the appeal by Litvinov and Larissa Daniel, 'To world public opinion', and speaks of the aims shared by all 'people of goodwill' irrespectively of how they define their views.

The 'Letter on the Day of St Nicholas and Victory Day' (May 9th, 1968)[54] is addressed to the heads of various [foreign] churches. It was written after reading Marchenko's book *My Testimony*. Referring to this book, the author of the letter speaks of the grievous situation of political prisoners in the U.S.S.R. and calls on all Christians, and particularly their spiritual leaders, to speak up in their defence.

Before writing the second letter Zheludkov had already protested to his own rulers about the Soviet camps and mental hospitals. He had also generalized to them like this:

> *Even to me it is clear: the terrible decline of literature and art, the obvious failures in economic life, the mysterious apathy of our young people—all this is the result of the lack of creative freedom. No one is aiming to seize your power—govern, please, but let this be not so much a privilege as a responsibility. It cannot be that the fate of a great people now consists only of the negative results of the absurd phenomena produced by the suppression of freedom and the withering of the spirit.*[55]

11*

The Chronicle *also summarizes Zheludkov's samizdat essay 'Some Reflections on Intellectual Freedom: a Reply to Academician Sakharov'* [56] *(see pp. 354–5):*

7 The author gives his analysis of those absurdities to which society has succumbed as a result of Stalinism: fear, duplicity, apathy. Father Sergei studies the problem of intellectual freedom as a religious problem and states that 'man's freedom does not even belong to God', that 'freedom is man's absolute, holy right and his sacred duty'. But 'today', writes the author, 'all of us Russians, willingly or unwillingly, are involved in a momentous historical experiment on the following subject: What will happen to a great people if it is deprived of its intellectual freedom?'

THE BAPTISTS

More samizdat documents — over a hundred, in fact — are available in the West from the Baptists than from any other religious group. Many of these have appeared in translation with extensive commentaries. [57] *Yet until No. 16* [58] *the* Chronicle *had carried only two brief items on this denomination. That said, No. 16 eventually indicated the nature of the problem. The Baptist protests stem from a schism in the Church provoked by the official leadership. In 1960–61 the latter — doubtless under pressure from the authorities — attempted to impose tighter controls on Church life and to reduce evangelism almost to nil. A grass-roots rebellion at once occurred, and the schismatic group began to campaign for greater religious freedom. In 1965 it set up its own organization, which the State has ever since refused to recognize, thus leaving the schismatic communities outside the law. One of the schismatic leaders is the subject of the open letter from the Kiev community summarized here by the* Chronicle:

5 This letter is the latest in a series of similar ones of 1967 and is in defence of the Baptist preacher G. P. Vins, who was arrested in 1967 [in fact in 1966] and is being subjected to cruel treatment in a camp. The letter is signed by 176 members of the community in the name of 400 Kiev Baptists and Evangelical Christians. [59]

The only other Baptist mentioned in the first eleven Chronicles *is a man already noted (p. 206) as having taken part in a camp strike in 1968 with Yuly Daniel and others. The news in 1969 was:*

Boris Zdorovets, a Baptist from the Donbass, who has spent [7] seven years in a labour camp, has been exiled for five years[60] to Krasnoyarsk Province; at his place of exile the police are carrying out 'educative' work on him, demanding that he publicly renounce his religion.

The Baptists — with perhaps several million adherents — are much less numerous than the Orthodox, with their several tens of millions, yet the volume of Baptist dissent is clearly greater. The poor reflection of this in the Chronicle *doubtless stems from the fact that only a few Baptists come from the intellectual groups which mainly constitute* Chronicle *circles.*

THE UNIATES

An important extra dimension is added to our picture of dissent in the west Ukraine by the following two items. The first is entitled 'New Persecution of Uniate Priests':

In spite of the U.S.S.R. Constitution, which guarantees freedom [7] of conscience, the Greek-Catholic, or Uniate, Church was forcibly liquidated in 1944 [-46] by organs of the M.G.B. [now K.G.B.] in western Ukraine. Priests who did not adopt the Orthodox faith were sent to camps after false charges had been fabricated.[61] The Uniate Church continued to function underground. Its activity has come to life in recent years, and at the same time the number of Uniate priests detained and beaten up by the police has grown. On October 18th, 1968, ten Uniate priests had their homes searched: legally permitted religious objects were confiscated, including even the Holy Sacrament — all this representing a flagrant encroachment into the sphere of religious ritual. At the end of 1968, two Uniate priests were arrested: one in Kolomiya, Ivano-Frankovsk Region, the other in Lvov. In January 1969, an underground bishop of the Greek-Catholic Church, Velychkovsky, was arrested. Velychkovsky is about seventy, he is ill and now in a prison hospital,

where his condition is serious. The case is being conducted by
the Lvov Procuracy: the charge is unknown. At the beginning
of 1969 more searches were carried out in the homes of Uniate
priests.

8 Now the *Chronicle* is in a position to give the following clarifica-
tions and additional information.

On October 18th, 1968, searches were carried out at the
homes of ten priests of the former Lvov Greek-Catholic metro-
polinate, including Bishop Vasyl Velychkovsky, the priests Petro
Horodetsky, Mykola Ovsyanko, [Ihnaty] Tsehelsky, [Ivan]
Lopadchak, [Fylymon] Kurchava, [Mykola] Deyneka, [V.]
Sternyuk and others. Ritual objects (chalices, crosses, vest-
ments, Holy Sacraments) as well as religious books, cameras,
tape-recorders and money were taken away.

At the same time one of them, Petro Horodetsky, was arrested
and charged under articles 187–1 and 138 of the Ukrainian
Criminal Code, i.e. propagation of deliberate fabrications which
defame the Soviet political and social system, and violation of
the laws concerning the separation of Church and State. The
investigation of his case was completed in April, and now the
trial is awaited.

At the end of 1968 the aged Bishop Vasyl Velychkovsky was
arrested in Kolomiya. At present rumours have spread to the
effect that he has died in prison, but there is no official confirmation of this.

In the spring of 1969 all over the west Ukraine dozens of
searches were carried out among Greek-Catholic priests, also in
flats where former nuns were living. Again ritual objects, books,
etc., were taken away.

In 1968 in Pochayev there was a meeting of West Ukrainian
Orthodox priests—mainly those priests who went over to
Orthodoxy under pressure in 1946. Some priests at the meeting
complained that they were being interfered with by Greek-
Catholic priests who had not accepted Orthodoxy, and that
these priests were carrying on their religious activities underground; Metropolitan Filaret gave the Orthodox priests instructions to spy on the Uniates and report on them. He
promised to appeal to the party and government, and in person
to the First Secretary of the Ukrainian Communist Party,

Shelest, and to request him to put an end to the activity of the Greek-Catholic priests.

As the Uniates affirm, referring to information received from Orthodox priests, the court and Procuracy officials have been instructed to put a stop to the activity of the Greek Catholic Church by all possible means in the course of one year — by the centenary of the birth of V. I. Lenin [in April 1970]. It looks as if precisely this was the reason for the arrests and large-scale searches.

In 1970 the Chronicle *extended its range, reporting for the first time on the persecution of Roman Catholics,[62] Adventists,[63] Jehovah's Witnesses[64] and the sectarian Truly-Orthodox Church.[65] All this helps to remind us that despite persecution, some of it built into the law, the U.S.S.R. is a more religious country than many secularized Western societies. Quite apart from private religious observance, perhaps as much as a quarter of the population dares to practise its religion openly, the proportion being higher in the Muslim areas, where Islam is ridden on a relatively light rein, than elsewhere. Part of the reason for this religiosity lies in the failure of the aridly official Marxism-Leninist ideology to satisfy most Soviet citizens as a philosophy for living. While this failure worries the régime, what really alarms it is when the only legally and widely available alternative to Marxism-Leninism — religion, in one or another form — becomes an ideological basis for political opposition. To some extent this has begun to happen.[66] It may well do so increasingly in the future.*

Part V · Mainstream Publications

17. ALEXANDER SOLZHENITSYN

In 1964 the journal *Novy mir* signed a contract with the author to publish *The First Circle*. Now, in 1968, the *Literary Gazette* informs us that the novel is 'a malicious libel on our social system'. What has changed? The novel? No. The system? Again, no. Our past? That is unchangeable. It is the weather that has changed. A new, soundless command has been given: cloak the past in mist. The reader who has not caught the sound of the command will not understand why neither *Cancer Ward* nor *The First Circle* have been published to this day. Why the author's archive was confiscated from him two years ago and has still not been returned. Why libraries have stopped issuing *One Day in the Life of Ivan Denisovich* ... Why, year after year, on special instructions, malicious lies are circulated about Solzhenitsyn: that he co-operated with the Germans! He was a prisoner of war! A criminal and a thief! A schizophrenic!

You see, they have to invent a way of dealing with a writer who carries on exposing Stalinism *after* the command has been given to forget about it.

Lydia Chukovskaya, July 1968

For many Soviet dissenters the career of Alexander Solzhenitsyn has come to symbolize the resistance of uncompromising moral integrity to the forces of reaction. After serving with distinction in World War II, Solzhenitsyn was arrested shortly before the close of hostilities for expressing criticism of Stalin in a letter to a friend. He served eight years in labour camps and three in 'eternal' exile, before the 20th party congress and the subsequent policy of de-Stalinization brought about his release and, in 1957, his rehabilitation.

Solzhenitsyn's first published work, One Day in the Life of Ivan Denisovich, *appeared in 1962 in* Novy mir, *causing a sensation at home and abroad. This laconic account of life in a labour camp embodies an indictment of Stalin's terror which is devastating in its understatement. Published with the express approval of Khrushchev himself, the story retains a certain immunity even to the present day. No such aura attended the appearance in* Novy mir *of three further stories during 1963,* Matryona's House, Incident at Krechetovka Station *and* For the Good of the Cause. *As early as 1963 Solzhenitsyn was rebuked for laying disproportionate emphasis on negative aspects of*

335

Soviet reality. Increasingly hostile attacks were spearheaded by the journal October *and the weekly* Literary Gazette, *organs of the R.S.F.S.R. and U.S.S.R. Writers' Unions respectively, while Solzhenitsyn's supporters looked to the liberal* Novy mir *as their champion. In late 1963* Novy mir's *editorial board nominated* One Day in the Life of Ivan Denisovich *for a Lenin Prize in literature, but despite their active campaign the nomination was defeated in April 1964.*

From then onwards Solzhenitsyn's name virtually disappeared from the pages of the Soviet press. Novy mir *printed occasional statements in support of the author, but failed in its attempts to clear his novel* The First Circle *for publication. In the autumn of 1965 the manuscript was returned to Solzhenitsyn and immediately confiscated by the K.G.B. together with the contents of his personal literary archive.* Novy mir *did succeed in publishing a comparatively uncontroversial story,* Zakhar the Pouch, *in January 1966, but had to reject the first part of* Cancer Ward, *which was finished that summer. Subsequent official procrastination, even after a meeting of the Moscow Branch of the Writers' Union had resolved to support publication of* Cancer Ward, *was a major theme of Solzhenitsyn's letter to the fourth Writers' Congress in May 1967, together with the question of the seizure of his manuscripts.*

The Chronicle *takes up the story in 1968,[1] at the point where Solzhenitsyn's repeated warnings about the imminent danger that* Cancer Ward *might appear in the West have at last evoked a public response from* Literary Gazette, *but only after the appearance of the first Western edition of* Cancer Ward.

2   A leading article in the *Literary Gazette* of June 26th[2] and a letter printed in it from Alexander Solzhenitsyn[3] dated April 21st, 1968, raise for the first time in the pages of the Soviet press the question of what has happened to the unpublished writings of Solzhenitsyn. Among other things, the *Literary Gazette* fulminates against a number of Solzhenitsyn's letters, starting with his well-known letter to the Writers' Congress,[4] and against the open letter sent by Veniamin Kaverin to Konstantin Fedin,[5] without however giving the addressee's name. All these documents exist in *samizdat* form. Last year's letter to the congress is widely known. The *Chronicle* provides here a survey of subsequent documents circulated in 1968.

After the ban laid on the publication in *Novy mir* of the novel *Cancer Ward*, the writer Veniamin Kaverin wrote a letter to one of the initiators of the ban, Konstantin Fedin, the Chairman of the Writers' Union Board; as young men, they were both members of the well-known literary group 'The Serapion Brothers'.[6] The letter contains a warning that the unpublished novel would remain extant in thousands of typed copies and would be published abroad. 'Possibly', Kaverin writes, 'there are to be found among the leaders of the Writers' Union people who think that they will be punishing the writer by consigning him to literature published abroad. They will punish him with world fame, which will be utilized by our enemies for political ends. Or is it their hope that Solzhenitsyn "will mend his ways" and start to write differently? This is ridiculous in the case of a writer who constitutes a rare example, and who insistently reminds us that we are functioning in the literature of Chekhov and Tolstoy.'

In April chapters from *Cancer Ward* appeared in the literary supplement to the London *Times*.[7] Subsequently, announcements appeared about the forthcoming publication of this novel in a number of Western editions and, quite recently, of the novel *The First Circle* also.[8] After the *Times* publication Solzhenitsyn sent a letter to a number of the members of the Writers' Union to say that *Cancer Ward* had got abroad because of the Writers' Union Secretariat having prevented it being printed in *Novy mir*.[9] Four documents were appended to the letter: Solzhenitsyn's letter to all the Writers' Union secretaries dated September 12th, 1967;[10] an account of the Secretariat meeting of September 22nd, 1967;[11] a letter of November 25th, 1967, from K. Voronkov, a secretary of the Writer's Union;[12] and Solzhenitsyn's letter to the Secretariat of December 1st, 1967.[13] These documents demonstrate the attitude and the responsibility of the Secretariat of the Union in the matter of the publication of the novel and in the campaign of persecution and slander surrounding the writer's name.

In April Solzhenitsyn sent to *Novy mir*, the *Literary Gazette* and members of the Union a further letter in connection with a telegram sent by the editors of *Grani** to *Novy mir*.[14] The telegram says that the State Security Committee has sent to the West through Victor Louis a copy of *Cancer Ward* in order to

* *Grani* [*Facets*]—a Russian literary journal published quarterly in Frankfurt am Main, Germany.

provide a reason not to publish it in the Soviet Union. One of the questions which Solzhenitsyn asks is—who is Victor Louis? The following is what can be said about him: he is a correspondent of the London *Evening Star* [in fact, of the *Evening News*] and a Soviet citizen. At the end of the 1940s and beginning of the 1950s Louis was in a political corrective-labour camp and was already well known as a *provocateur*. In recent years he is said to have been involved in handing over to the West a number of writings not published in the Soviet Union, acting in so doing as a *provocateur*, as when he sold to the West German periodical *Stern* a doctored version of the memoirs of Svetlana Alliluyeva.

Solzhenitsyn concludes his letter with the words:

> This episode causes one to ponder on the strange and obscure channels through which the manuscripts of Soviet writers manage to reach the West. It is an urgent reminder to us that literature must not be reduced to a situation where literary works become a profitable commodity for any kind of operator who holds a travel visa. The works of our authors must be allowed publication in their own country and not be handed over for exploitation by foreign publishers.

It has become known that some readers of *Literary Gazette*, in reply to the article about Solzhenitsyn, have cancelled their subscription, notifying the post office thereof and returning their receipt to Alexander Chakovsky, the chief editor.

One such reader was the physicist Valery Turchin,[15] *whose letter*[16] *was subsequently summarized in the* Chronicle *and also included in the fiery samizdat anthology* Seven Letters to Chakovsky.[17] *The letter was:*

7 A response to the editorial about Solzhenitsyn in the *Literary Gazette*. Valery Turchin accuses the paper of publishing an article which, in the guise of criticism, contains libel and falsifications, while the 'criticized' novels of Solzhenitsyn remain unpublished and unknown to the general public, and while he himself is not allowed to express himself in print and deny the libel. Turchin, who has occasionally had articles printed in *Literary Gazette*, rejects all future collaboration with the news-

paper, and refuses to subscribe to it or buy it any more. The letter, written on June 28th, 1968, only recently became available in *samizdat*.

Another fierce protest[18] *came from Lydia Chukovskaya, daughter of the late dean of Soviet letters, Kornei Chukovsky, and a staunch ally of Solzhenitsyn in his struggle against the censorship. Her letter provides the epigraph to this chapter.*

Such letters, full of moral significance, achieved, however, no concrete results. The hitherto somewhat ambivalent official attitude towards Cancer Ward *hardened in the wake of its publication in the West and* Literary Gazette's *attack, and the change was reflected at the local level. The following two incidents—similar to the one in Odessa already noted (p. 71)—both took place in Gorky during 1969:*

V. Selin, a lecturer on the history of the Soviet Communist 10 Party at the Polytechnic Institute, has been dismissed from his post and expelled from the party for possessing A. I. Solzhenitsyn's novel *Cancer Ward*. His wife has also been dismissed from her job.

Artsimovich, a woman journalist from Gorky, has been dis- 11 missed from her job on the editorial staff of a newspaper for reading Solzhenitsyn's *Cancer Ward*.

Sporadic attacks on Solzhenitsyn had appeared in the Soviet press during the second half of 1968 and through into 1969. It was obvious that any publication of his works in the Soviet Union was for the moment out of the question. Yet his summary expulsion from the Writers' Union in November 1969 took the world by surprise. The precedence and space given to this event in the Chronicle[19] *emphasize once again the extent to which Soviet dissenters of all persuasions look to Solzhenitsyn for a moral example:*

THE EXPULSION OF SOLZHENITSYN FROM THE 11
WRITERS' UNION

On November 4th the great Russian writer A. I. Solzhenitsyn was expelled from the Writers' Union by the Ryazan branch of the Writers' Union of the Russian Republic. Of the seven members of the Ryazan branch, six were present at the meeting:

Vasily Matushkin (Ryazan), Sergei Baranov (Ryazan, chaired the meeting), Nikolai Rodin (Kasimov, brought specially from hospital to form a quorum), Nikolai Levchenko (Ryazan), Evgeny Markin (Ryazan) and Solzhenitsyn. The branch secretary Ernst Safonov was absent owing to an appendicitis operation. Others present were secretary of the Writers' Union of the Russian Republic Frants Taurin, propaganda secretary of Ryazan Regional Party Committee A. S. Kozhevnikov, publishing-house editor Povarenkin and three other persons from regional organizations. There was only one item on the agenda: a report by secretary of the Writers' Union Taurin concerning the resolution passed by the Secretariat of the Union, 'On measures to intensify ideological-educative work among writers.'

The speakers accused Solzhenitsyn of not speaking at pre-election meetings; he had not taken part in the discussion of new writers' works, and had not reviewed their manuscripts; he had behaved superciliously towards Ryazan writers and their 'modest achievements in literature'; his Ivan Denisovich was an uninspiring character; his *Matryona's House* was painted entirely in black; his most recent works (although the Ryazan writers actually confessed they had not read them) conflicted with theirs; he had not dissociated himself from the sensation his name was causing in the West; and foreign countries were using his writings as a weapon. Solzhenitsyn spoke in reply and demonstrated the groundlessness of the charges brought against him.

The following resolution was adopted by five votes to one: 'This meeting is of the opinion that Solzhenitsyn's behaviour is of an anti-social nature, and fundamentally conflicts with the aims and tasks of the U.S.S.R. Writers' Union. For his anti-social behaviour, which conflicts with the aims and tasks of the U.S.S.R. Writers' Union, and for his flagrant violation of the basic principles of the statutes of the Writers' Union, the writer Solzhenitsyn should be expelled from the ranks of the Writers' Union of the U.S.S.R. We ask the Secretariat to approve this resolution.'

A transcript of the minutes of this meeting, made by Solzhenitsyn, is circulating widely in *samizdat*.[20]

On November 12th the *Literary Gazette* carried a report[21] on the expulsion of Solzhenitsyn by the Ryazan writers' organization, and on the approval of the resolution by the Secretariat of the Board of the Russian Republic Writers' Union. There was no mention of any name (apart from Solzhenitsyn's), nor of any date.

On November 14th *Literary Russia* reprinted the report from the *Literary Gazette*, adding the surnames of the Ryazan writers and also the writers who were present at the meeting of the Secretariat of the Board of the Russian Republic Writers' Union: L. Sobolev, G. Markov, K. Voronkov, A. Barto, D. Granin, V. Zakrutkin, A. Keshokov, V. Pankov, L. Tatyanicheva, F. Taurin, V. Fyodorov, and S. Khakimov. Again no dates were given.

A group of Moscow writers—[S.] Antonov,[22] [G.] Baklanov, [V.] Voinovich,[23] [V.] Maksimov, [B.] Mozhayev, [V.] Tendryakov and [Yu.] Trifonov—paid a visit to the secretary of the Russian Republic Writers' Union, Voronkov. They expressed their disagreement with the expulsion from the Writers' Union of a writer as great as Solzhenitsyn by a group of obscure littérateurs from Ryazan. They demanded that in view of the especial importance of this affair, it should be discussed at a Plenum of the Writers' Union in conditions of maximum publicity. They requested that this opinion, which was not only theirs but the opinion of many writers who had not presented themselves for official interviews, should be made known to all the secretaries of the Writers' Union and also to the party Central Committee. Voronkov assured them that he would pass it on. After this, some people (party members) were summoned to their district party committees, where they were worked over by their first secretaries and also by Yu. Verchenko, head of the Culture Department in the Moscow city party committee.

Soon there began to circulate very widely in *samidat* an Open Letter from A. Solzhenitsyn to the Secretariat of the Russian Republic Writers' Union.[24] It is worth quoting in full here:

Shamelessly trampling underfoot your own statutes, you have expelled me in my absence, as at the sound of a fire-alarm, without even sending me a summons by telegram, without even giving me the four hours I needed to come from Ryazan and be present at the meeting. You have shown openly that the RESOLUTION preceded the 'discussion'. Was it less awkward for you to invent new charges in my absence? Were you afraid of being obliged to grant me ten minutes for my answer? I am compelled to substitute this letter for those ten minutes.

Blow the dust off the clock. Your watches are behind the times. Throw open the heavy curtains which are so dear to you—you do not even suspect that the day has already dawned outside. It is no longer that stifled, that sombre, irrevocable time when you expelled Akhmatova[25] in the same servile manner. It is not even that timid, frosty period when you expelled Pasternak,[26] whining abuse at him. Was this shame not enough for you? Do you want to make it greater? But the time is near when each one of you will seek to erase his signature from today's resolution.

Blind leading the blind! You do not even notice that you are wandering in the opposite direction from the one you yourselves have announced. At this time of crisis you are incapable of suggesting anything constructive, anything good for our society, which is gravely sick—only your hatred, your vigilance, your 'hold on and don't let go'.

Your clumsy articles fall apart; your vacant minds stir feebly—but you have no arguments. You have only your voting and your administration. And that is why neither Sholokhov[27] nor any of you, of the whole lot of you, dared reply to the famous letter of Lydia Chukovskaya,[28] who is the pride of Russian publicistic writing. But the administrative pincers are ready for her: how could she allow people to read her book [*The Deserted House*][29] when it has not been published? Once the AUTHORITIES have made up their minds not to publish you—then stifle yourself, choke yourself, cease to exist, and don't give your stuff to anyone to read!

They are also threatening to expel Lev Kopelev, the front-line veteran, who has already served ten years in prison although he was completely innocent.[30] Today he is guilty: he intercedes for the persecuted, he revealed the hallowed secrets of his conversation with an influential person, he disclosed an OFFICIAL SECRET. But why do you hold conversations like these which have to be concealed from the people? Were we not promised fifty years ago that never again would there be any secret diplomacy, secret talks, secret and incomprehensible appointments and transfers, that the masses would be informed of all matters and would discuss them openly?

'The enemy will overhear'—that is your excuse. The eternal, omnipresent 'enemies' are a convenient justification for your functions and your very existence. As if there were no enemies when you promised immediate openness. But what would you do without 'enemies'? You could not live without 'enemies'; hatred, a hatred no better than racial hatred, has become your sterile atmosphere. But in this way a sense of our single, common humanity is lost and its doom accelerated. Should the Antarctic ice melt tomorrow, we would all become a sea of drowning humanity, and into whose heads would you then be drilling your concepts of 'class struggle'? Not to speak of the time when the few surviving bipeds will be wandering over a radioactive earth, dying.

It is high time to remember that we belong first and foremost to humanity. And that man has distinguished himself from the animal world by THOUGHT and SPEECH. And these, naturally, should be FREE. If they are put in chains, we shall return to the state of animals.

OPENNESS, honest and complete OPENNESS—that is the first condition of health in all societies, including our own. And he who does not want this openness for our country cares nothing for his fatherland and thinks only of his own interest. He who does not wish this openness for his fatherland does not want to purify it of its diseases, but only to drive them inwards, there to fester.

November 12th, 1969   A. SOLZHENITSYN

On November 26th, the *Literary Gazette* carried a special article, 'From the Secretariat of the Board of the Russian Republic Writers' Union'. It stated that the expulsion of Solzhenitsyn 'was supported by broad sections of the literary public in our country', that 'in his works and his statements' Solzhenitsyn 'had in fact allied himself with those people who speak out against the Soviet social system'. Isolated phrases are quoted from Solzhenitsyn's latest letter (the one cited here) as proof that he 'represents conceptions alien to our people and its literature'. There are also some other, less important allegations, and they too do not correspond to the truth. For instance, the Open Letter is dated November 14th instead of 12th. The article concludes by saying that if Solzhenitsyn should wish to leave the country he will not be prevented from doing so. The article was reprinted in full in *Literary Russia* on November 28th.

The National Committee of French Writers has issued a statement[31] saying that the expulsion of Solzhenitsyn was 'a terrible mistake which is damaging to the Soviet Union'. The authors of the declaration think that such actions are obviously intended 'to frighten not only all writers, but—more widely—the whole of the intelligentsia, to discourage them from their attempts to be more than just soldiers marching impeccably in step.' The statement says: 'Would anyone have thought that today in the motherland of triumphant socialism the fate that even Nicholas II did not inflict upon Chekhov—who was free to publish his *Sakhalin**—would become the lot of Alexander Solzhenitsyn, the most talented writer to continue the great Russian tradition, the victim of Stalinist terror whose chief crime is that he has survived it!' The statement is signed by, in particular, such well-known people as Triolet, Vercors, Aragon and Sartre. In the last few days dozens more Western progressive artists and cultural figures have added their signatures to this statement, among them Pablo Picasso.

On December 3rd the *Literary Gazette* published an item about a meeting of the Secretariat of the Board of the Moscow writers' organization which heard Sobolev and Voronkov speak in connection with the resolution of the Writers' Union Secretariat on the expulsion of Solzhenitsyn. As the paper puts it: 'All the speakers discussed the behaviour of, and the position adopted by, A. Solzhenitsyn, and unanimously approved the resolution passed by the Secretariat of the Writers' Union of the Russian Republic.' A list of those present at the discussion is given: A. Aleksin, G. Beryozko, A. Vasilev, S. Vasilev, S. Mikhalkov,

---

* An island off the Far Eastern coast of the Soviet Union, visited by Chekhov in 1890. His impressions of the forced labour camps and exiles' settlements located there are recorded in *Sakhalin Island* (first published 1893–4).

G. Radov, I. Rink, K. Pozdnyayev, A. Samsoniya, I. Sobolev, L. Fomenko, Ya. Tsvetov, Yu. Chepurin and L. Yakimenko.

In the same issue the paper carried a report of a meeting of the party organization of the Leningrad branch of the Russian Republic Writers' Union, at which a resolution was unanimously passed, stating among other things: 'The communists of the Leningrad writers' organization unanimously approve the resolution of the Ryazan writers' organization and the Secretariat of the Board of the Russian Republic Writers' Union concerning the expulsion of A. Solzhenitsyn from the ranks of Soviet writers as a man who has adopted a blatantly anti-Soviet position and thus gone over to the enemy camp.' Present: R. Nazarov, Yu. Ritkheu, Vyach. Kuznetsov, D. Granin, Yu. Pomozov, A. Shevtsov, V. Infantev, G. Kondrashev, V. Dyagilev, A. Barten, V. Dmitrevsky, A. Shagalov, E. Serebrovskaya, M. Demidenko, F. Abramov.

A week later Sergei Mikhalkov, speaking at a plenum of the Moscow branch of the Writers' Union, referred to Solzhenitsyn as (and the papers printed it)[32] 'a gifted writer in the professional sense' who is a 'talented enemy of socialism'.

A number of collective and individual letters are circulating in *samizdat* from Soviet citizens, addressed to the Writers' Union in protest at the expulsion of Solzhenitsyn:

1. *Letter of the 39*.[33] The expulsion of Solzhenitsyn is called 'shameful for our literature and, above all, for our writers, who acquiesced in it either by their silence or vocally'. The main reason for his expulsion was Solzhenitsyn's consistent exposure of Stalinist arbitrariness. An artist's place in the company of his colleagues should be determined above all by his talent and his craftsmanship, and Solzhenitsyn's talent, artistic significance and world-wide reputation are unquestionable.

2. *Letter of the 14 (December 19th)*.[34] ' ... the tragic campaign of slander has been crowned with the farce of public execution,' but it is not Solzhenitsyn who has been excommunicated from the great Russian tradition, rather 'the whole of the Writers' Union hiding behind the backs of the immoral quintet from Ryazan'. Criticizing the attitude of 'judicious silence', the authors draw a parallel with the recent past, 'when the best and most honest writers were hounded in exactly the same way, while some writers hooted their approval and others kept silent.

But those were the days when one writer's defence of another was called mutual covering-up, and informing was considered proof of reliability. In those days even silence could be heroism. Today it cannot even have the appearance of heroism.'

3. *Open Letter from Zhores Medvedev*[35] (*November 21st*). 'Solzhenitsyn was expelled because his talent as a writer, his humanism, his creative depiction and analysis of reality had overstepped the boundaries of the Ryazan Region and were beyond the control of a department of the Ryazan regional party committee. They had overstepped the boundaries of the Russian Republic and ceased to conform with the obscure and constantly changing instructions of the secret censorship. Alexander Solzhenitsyn has deservedly acquired in the U.S.S.R. and the whole world the reputation of a patriot and a fighter for the real truth. He has not betrayed that truth, those humanitarian ideas, he has not betrayed his conscience, or his principles, and he has not betrayed his people now that, in defiance of all logic and common sense, the arbitrary rule of the Stalin era has begun to reappear in disguised form and the threat of lawlessness and violence has come to hang once more over the land. And it was for this that they expelled him from the Union ... '

On the charge brought against Solzhenitsyn of having his books published in the West, the author writes of the 'piratical' practice of Soviet publishing-houses in publishing foreign authors and reproducing their works, all without their permission. This is the reason why our state refuses to sign the convention on the international defence of authors' rights, thereby putting Soviet authors too in a defenceless position.* On the charge that Solzhenitsyn's works were written 'from a different ideological standpoint', the author writes:

> The publication of *One Day in the Life of Ivan Denisovich* was approved by the Presidium of the Central Committee of the Soviet Communist Party. This story was acclaimed by the whole of the Soviet press and nominated for a Lenin Prize. Why then are you now hurling abuse even at this story? It means that *your* 'ideological standpoint' has changed, not that of Solzhenitsyn. It means that the

---

* The U.S.S.R. is not a signatory of any international copyright convention.

instructions to Glavlit [the censorship] have changed, and not the writer's creative style ... The expulsion of Solzhenitsyn from the Soviet Writers' Union grieves me as an indication of deeply regrettable changes in the way of running the Union and in the standpoint of those circles which are accustomed to consider the Union as merely a branch of the [party's] Ideological Commission. The expulsion of Solzhenitsyn is a unique event. It came about as a logical result of the new line of cautious repressions being directed against the intelligentsia. The aim is to instil into them the inertia of fear, the same fear that Stalin and his obedient minions created, who did not shrink from the destruction of millions of innocent citizens.

4. *Letter from Julian A. Vronsky*[36] (former investigator of the Moscow Regional Procuracy, address and telephone number given), December 2nd.

The author refers to Solzhenitsyn as 'a highly talented writer, a gallant fighter and a humanist', and sees his expulsion from the Writers' Union as a particular example of the Stalinist tendencies in the development of our country: political trials and the forcible confinement of dissenters in psychiatric hospitals, police shadowing, eavesdropping, the reading of mail by X-ray methods, provocation, illegal arrests, dismissals and expulsions from the party, the official lie, and the hounding of the most progressive writers. The author thinks that the initiative in Solzhenitsyn's expulsion came from the party and government leadership. He concludes as follows: 'I appeal to the conscience of those upon whom the fate of the writer depends—to however small a degree—I call upon them to remember once again their duty to Russia and to history, to the people and to mankind, to remember the best democratic traditions of our country's past; in the name of the future I call upon you to give all the encouragement and help you can to this most talented writer, for his tragedy is our tragedy, the tragedy of our country.'

At a meeting of the prose section of the Moscow branch of the Writers' Union, twenty-two people voted against the resolution approving the expulsion of Solzhenitsyn.

A telegram from L. K. Chukovskaya to the Writers' Union:
'Chukovskaya considers the expulsion of Solzhenitsyn from the
Writers' Union a national disgrace for Russia.'

On December 18th the London paper *The Times* published a
letter from a group of writers:

> The treatment of Soviet writers in their own country has
> become an international scandal. We now learn with dis-
> may of the expulsion from the Soviet Writers' Union of
> Alexander Solzhenitsyn, the one writer in Russia who, in
> the words of Arthur Miller, 'is unanimously regarded as a
> classic'. The two great poets who were previously so
> expelled were Anna Akhmatova and Boris Pasternak. One
> understands Solzhenitsyn's bitter exclamation: 'Was this
> shame not enough for you?'
> The silencing of a writer of Solzhenitsyn's stature is in
> itself a crime against civilization. We do not know whether
> any other steps are contemplated in this new witch-hunt.
> We can only hope that there is no repetition of the
> Sinyavsky-Daniel trial.
> Judging by experience, verbal protests do not sufficiently
> impress the Soviet authorities. We appeal to them, how-
> ever, to stop persecuting Solzhenitsyn.
> Should this appeal fail we shall see no other way but to
> call upon the writers and artists of the world to conduct an
> international boycott of a country which chooses to put
> itself beyond the pale of civilization until such time as it
> abandons the barbaric treatment of its writers and artists.

Amongst the signatories are: Arthur Miller, the American
playwright; Auden, the English poet; Rolf Hochhuth, the
German writer; Günter Grass; Julian Huxley; Mary
McCarthy; Graham Greene; Pierre Emmanuel, the French
poet and President of the P.E.N. Club; A. Toynbee, the
historian.
Altogether there are thirty-one signatures.[37]

Since the end of 1969 the Chronicle *has continued to follow Solzhenitsyn's fate with the closest interest.*[38] *His Nobel Prize, the circumstances*

surrounding his decision not to risk travelling to Stockholm to accept it, the protests on his behalf, the compilation of samizdat *collections of documents about him,*[39] *his honorary membership of Academician Sakharov's Human Rights Committee — these were the main themes in 1970. Of exceptional interest was the last step, which — for the first time — identified him fully with the Democratic Movement. No longer was he just a lone writer who obviously sympathized with the movement but carefully avoided any collective enterprise. Now he was irreversibly committed. The stakes, in fact, had risen still higher, both for Solzhenitsyn and for the régime. The latter especially — long uncertain how to deal with such a doughty critic — clearly had to reconsider whether or not to activate a scenario carefully fabricated and prepared since about 1965, and, using trumped-up charges, to imprison him.*

One of the greatest obstacles to such a course was the weight of pro-Solzhenitsyn opinion at home and abroad. Thus it is not surprising that the Chronicle *has often added to that weight by, in particular, giving good coverage to the less accessible foreign opinion. Not only have protests been reported, but also translated articles circulating in* samizdat.[40] *The following example — about a problem which more than any other has animated Solzhenitsyn's life and works — makes a good note on which to conclude the chapter:*

Heinrich Böll: 'World in bondage.' An article by one of the most important writers of our time (published in *Merkur* No. 5 [May 1969], pp. 474–83), on Solzhenitsyn's novel *The First Circle.* In this brief article the author gives a glowing appraisal of Solzhenitsyn's novel and can find nothing in the past decades of Western literature to equal it. Böll concentrates on the way in which the problem of freedom and bondage is resolved in the novel. There is no freedom for anyone in an enslaved society, but prisoners are sometimes freer than their gaolers and executioners. He cites the dialogue between the formidable minister Abakumov, who trembles with fear in the presence of his patron [Stalin], and the courageous prisoner Bobynin.

Böll thinks that the content of the novel goes beyond the theme of Stalinism, and gives profound expression to the basic features of the twentieth century, which, whatever other distinctions it may have, is above all 'the century of camps, prisoners and captives'.

18. THE WORLD OF *SAMIZDAT*

[In the mid-1960s] a new force emerged from within the Cultural Opposition, a force which stood not only against official culture but also against many aspects of the ideology and practice of the régime. It emerged as a result of the collision of two opposing trends: the striving of society to obtain greater information about politics and society, and the efforts of the régime to control even more completely every aspect of the information given to the public. This force came to be known as *samizdat* ...

Naturally the régime recognized *samizdat* as potentially more dangerous than the Cultural Opposition, and therefore it fights it with even greater vigour ... Nevertheless, *samizdat* ... has gradually given birth to a new, independent force, which can already be regarded as a real political opposition, or at least as a political opposition in embryo.

Andrei Amalrik,[1] April–June 1969

5   A REVIEW OF *SAMIZDAT* IN 1968

Samizdat is a specific medium for exercising freedom of expression in our country. During the last few years *samizdat* has evolved from a predominant concern with poetry and fiction towards an ever greater emphasis on journalistic and documentary writing. This is particularly true of 1968. In this year *samizdat* has not been enriched by a single major prose work, as it was in past years by such works as the novels of Solzhenitsyn, the memoirs of Evgenia Ginzburg,[2] the collections of stories by Shalamov,[3] and the novels by Chukovskaya,[4] Maksimov[5] and others; during the year no literary miscellany such as *Syntax* or *Phoenix* has appeared. On the other hand the readers of *samizdat* (they are also its volunteer publishers) have received during the year a regular flow of documents, open letters, speeches, commentaries, articles, news items, etc. In other words *samizdat*, in addition to its role as a supplier of books, has begun to carry out the functions of a newspaper. The following survey will probably not be a full one. Furthermore, the notes on some of the materials are too brief—but this is due to force of circumstances, and does not mean that they are of lesser importance. Consistency has not always been shown in deciding whether to include various materials of 1967 which were circulated mainly in 1968. The *Chronicle* feels, however, that the task of giving

readers a survey of the *samizdat* now in circulation is so important that it does not wish to restrict itself by considerations of a
formal bibliographical nature.

No. 5's lengthy review has—like its counterparts in Nos. 6–11—been
split up. The separate items appear at the most relevant points throughout
the book. This chapter, then, focuses on members of the Democratic
Movement who are known mainly for their samizdat work, and also on
translated samizdat material and discussions of samizdat per se. As
for the thin belles-lettres section, the following is the only item not
included in other contexts :

In 1968 there were three new collections of verse: Alexander 5
Galich, *Book of Songs*,[6] Natalya Gorbanevskaya, *The Wooden Angel*
(verse of 1967);[7] and Yuly Daniel, *Verse of 1965–7*. Apart from
these there are, as usual, many individual poems circulating in
samizdat—they include 'Farewell to Bukovsky' by Vadim
Delone, and several poems by unknown authors written under
the impact of the Soviet invasion of Czechoslovakia.

To turn now to an important discussion of samizdat, this item elicits
some revealing comments from the Chronicle :

A. ANTIPOV: 'FROM INTELLECTUAL CHAOS TO THE 7
   COORDINATION OF INTELLECTS'[8]

In essence the author puts forward a systematized programme
for *samizdat*, although he does not employ this particular term,
preferring to use 'uncensored literature' or 'literature circulated
in typescript'. The author considers that the current development of society into an intellectual phase demands an intensive
exchange of ideas:

> We need statistical material of good quality, basic
> research on the economic, political, social, legal, moral,
> cultural and psychological problems of our society, and
> objective works on its history. We also need translations of
> foreign specialists' work. We must fearlessly carry out
> research into our social organism—such is the essential
> task which can be undertaken only by a common effort and
> and in conditions of lively, free discussion. We have
> mastered speech—now it is time to learn to write.

A. Antipov considers that uncensored literature has achieved two things: it has removed the 'inner censor', which weighs upon an author during the process of creation, and it has created a new type of reader. 'We will not make a fuss' — so ends this short document — 'we will not fight for freedom of the press; we will create it.'

It should be noted first that the programme presented by A. Antipov as entirely new is already in fact being carried out in many respects by *samizdat*; and secondly, the creation of a free press in the form of uncensored literature does not exclude a *struggle* by society for this freedom — as well as for all the other freedoms and human rights — and partly through the medium of *samizdat*.

ANDREI AMALRIK

11 Andrei Alekseyevich Amalrik is thirty-one and lives in Moscow [see plate 66]. He is the author of the following books: *The Normans and Kievan Russia*,[9] *Involuntary Journey to Siberia*,[10] and *Will the U.S.S.R. survive until 1984?*",[11] and of a collection of poems and five plays,[12] one of which, *East and West*, is now playing at the Globus theatre in Amsterdam.

Thus wrote the Chronicle *in late 1969. But Amalrik had been known to the world at large earlier, ever since, on July 16th, 1968, he and his wife had demonstrated with placards outside the British Embassy against Britain's (and the U.S.S.R.'s) supply of arms to the federal side in the Nigerian civil war.*[13] *Moreover, as he reveals in his autobiographical* Involuntary Journey, *he had known members of Moscow's foreign colony since the early 1960s, a fact which accounts in part for the period of Siberian exile (1965–6) described in that remarkable book. Later, in January 1968, he provided moral and practical support to relatives of the condemned Galanskov and Ginzburg,*[14] *and in October the* Chronicle *reported:*

4 On the night of October 16th–17th Andrei Amalrik was detained by the police on a Moscow street. The suitcase he was carrying 'appeared suspicious' to the policemen. In the suitcase they discovered a typewriter and typewritten copies of some letters, all of which they confiscated on the pretext of checking whether the typewriter had been stolen. They refused to make an official record. Amalrik was also interrogated by K.G.B. men.

ladimir Gershuni,
w stonemason, before his
in 1969 (see pp. 169–70).

ladimir Bonsov of
grad, *c.* 1968 (see pp.

45. (*left*) Ilya Rips, Latvian Jewish student, before his attempted self-immolation in 1969 (see pp. 243–4).

46. (*right*) Gomer Bayev, Crimean Tatar engineer from Simferopol, before his arrest in 1969 (see pp. 266–8).

47. (*left*) Rollan Kadiyev, Tatar physicist from Samarkand, before his arrest in 1968 (see pp. 259 ff).

48. (*right*) Izzet Khairov, Tatar engineer from Tashkent, before his arrest in 1968 (see pp. 259 ff).

49 and 50. The breaking-up by the police of the Crimean Tatar festival in Chirchik, April 21st, 1968 (see pp. 250–51).

51. Crimean Tatar families, dumped on the station at Ust-Labinsk after their expulsion from the Crimea (see p. 268).

52. One of the families in front of its boarded-up house, after making its way back to the Crimea (see p. 268).

53. Vyacheslav Chornovil, Ukrainian journalist (see pp. 285 ff).

54. Valentyn Moroz, Ukrainian historian (see 286–7).

55. Ivan Dzyuba, Ukra critic and historian (see

56. Eduard Kuznetsov, 'hijacker' from Riga, ab 1969 (see p. 318).

59. Iosif Kerler, Yiddi Moscow, 1971 (see p.

57. Boris Kochubiyevsky, Jewish engineer from Kiev (see pp. 301 ff).

58. Julius Telesin, Jewish mathematician (see pp. 43 ff and 310 ff).

After Amalrik had made persistent complaints to the Procuracy everything that had been taken from him was returned.

The above all serves as background to the Chronicle's *first large item on one of* samizdat's *bravest and most individual exponents. This is a summary of Amalrik's 'Open Letter to Anatoly Kuznetsov',*[15] *written shortly after the latter — a writer widely published, if in censored form, in the U.S.S.R. — had defected to Britain:*

Amalrik decided to write to Kuznetsov after hearing his 'Appeal 11 to all people' on the radio and reading his article, 'The Russian writer and the K.G.B.'.[16] Kuznetsov makes frequent reference to the absence of freedom in the U.S.S.R., but, as Amalrik points out, the prerequisite for 'freedom round about us' is 'inner freedom ... The authorities may do a great deal to a man who has this but they are powerless to deprive him of his moral values'. Kuznetsov avoids this problem. 'You keep writing,' Amalrik continues, ' "I was summoned ... I was ordered ... the censorship always forced me to my knees" ... and so on. It seems to me that if you constantly made compromises and did things which, in your heart, you condemned, then you did not deserve any better treatment from the K.G.B. or the censorship.'

Amalrik's aim is not so much to reproach Kuznetsov personally, as to condemn 'the philosophy of impotence and self-justification'. He writes:

> No form of coercion can be effective without those who are prepared to submit to it. Sometimes it seems to me that the 'creative intelligentsia' in the Soviet Union, i.e. those people who are accustomed to think one thing, say another and do yet another, represents a phenomenon that is on the whole even more unpleasant than the régime which gave birth to it ...
>
> In general it is better to keep silent than to tell lies, better to refuse to have one of your books published than to let it appear saying the opposite to what you originally wrote, better to refuse trips abroad than to turn informer for the sake of going on them or to 'report' in the form of a facetious poem,[17] better to refuse to attend a press conference than to state publicly that creative freedom exists in our country.

12

Amalrik notes that the state of dependence on the K.G.B., in which Kuznetsov had placed himself, had made him exaggerate the might of that organization and its ability to crush any kind of protest. In particular, Amalrik rejects Kuznetsov's assertion that the K.G.B. could stamp out *samizdat* in two hours and is merely playing with it like a well-fed cat with a mouse. 'Perhaps the K.G.B. could arrest dozens of those who are circulating *samizdat* in the space of just two hours ... but the fact that the K.G.B. does not do this is indicative of the uncertain situation in which the K.G.B. and the régime as a whole find themselves.'

Amalrik does not consider that Kuznetsov, by remaining abroad, is letting his colleagues in Russia down. 'I do not think that the position has worsened. The trouble is not that they will not publish the latest pseudo-liberal doggerel or allow its author to travel abroad, but that many talented writers are completely deprived of the possibility of proving their worth. Some of them give up writing altogether, others take the path of pathetic conformism. As far as this is concerned your failure to return will not change anything, either for better, or for worse.'

The letter is dated November 1st, 1969. On November 24th it was reproduced in full[18] in the *Daily Telegraph* (London) and excerpts were later printed in other Western newspapers and magazines.

Throughout Nos. 12 to 17 Amalrik features prominently, now in the samizdat *section,*[19] *now giving a filmed interview to an American TV company,*[20] *now being arrested and defended by his friends, and finally, in November 1970, receiving three years at a trial in Sverdlovsk, after he had calmly denounced the court as illegal.*

ANDREI SAKHAROV, VALERY CHALIDZE, GRIGORY POMERANTS, ALEXANDER ESENIN-VOLPIN

A notable event in the samizdat *world was the circulation in June 1968 of Andrei Sakharov's 'Thoughts on Progress, Peaceful Coexistence and Intellectual Freedom'.*[21] *The* Chronicle *summarized thus:*

5 The author of this study, an academician and 'Father of the H-bomb', attempts a scientific approach to world problems. He shows that the world is threatened by a number of dangers:

thermo-nuclear destruction, famine for half of mankind, uncontrolled changes in the environment, threats to intellectual freedom, the growth of racism and nationalism, and the emergence of dictatorial régimes. In Sakharov's opinion the only solution is to be found in overcoming the divisions in mankind, attempts to bring the two economic systems closer to each other, a scientific and democratic approach to the formulation of internal and foreign policies, intellectual freedom, help to underdeveloped countries through a drastic reduction of military expenditure, and the observance of geo-hygiene. In line with these basic propositions Academician Sakharov makes concrete recommendations to the leaders of our country.

That these were not appreciated soon became apparent, No. 7 reporting:

The Ministry of Medium Machine Building, at which Sakharov 7 was a consultant, has dispensed with his services. Now Sakharov holds a post only at his own [Lebedev] institute, where no security pass is required.

In reply the 49-year-old physicist stepped up his activities in 1970, first addressing another memorandum,[22] with two colleagues, to the Soviet leaders. The authors argued that the Soviet economy would lag disastrously unless liberal economic and political reforms — which they spelt out — were quickly introduced. Sakharov also began to frequent courtrooms, gaining access to the trial of the mathematician Dr R. I. Pimenov[23] and also the appeal hearing of the Jewish 'hijackers'.[24] Even more interesting, in November he formed with his physicist colleagues Valery Chalidze (see plate 67) and Andrei Tverdokhlebov[25] a Human Rights Committee, whose aims were to study problems of rights and to help the authorities to introduce desirable reforms.[26]

Meanwhile both these colleagues had responded — like Father Zheludkov (p. 330), the group of technical intelligentsia in Estonia (p. 172), and others[27] — to the original memorandum, Chalidze gave his reply the same title, and the Chronicle *commented briefly:*

The author discusses the problem of the relation of Soviet state 9 law to the dualism of the party and state hierarchies, the dangers of departing from formalism in legal procedure, and other questions.

Evidence of Chalidze's enormous energy soon became a familiar feature of the Chronicle.[28] *Apart from analysing the Czechoslovak situation (pp. 373–4), he wrote* Class Discrimination in Soviet Law, *'a history of the appearance in Soviet law of restrictions according to class affiliation, and of their removal' (No. 11), and also* On the Civil Rights of Man:

8 This work is devoted to a historical and legal analysis of the theme indicated in the title. Besides general theoretical propositions, the book analyses United Nations documents on civil rights and contains reflections on the Soviet Constitution and its application in practice.

Most significant of all, however, was probably this item:

10 AN ANTHOLOGY OF SELECTED *SAMIZDAT* TEXTS ON SOCIAL PROBLEMS: COMPILED BY V. N. CHALIDZE. ISSUE NO. 1

Judging by the first issue, this anthology deals with problems from a theoretical standpoint. The texts have been chosen 'taking into account the topicality of the subject-matter, the qualifications of the author and the constructiveness of the text'. The anthology has a section called 'Documents', for the publication of historical and legal documents, and another section, 'Discussion', which includes reviews, comments and criticism of works published in *samizdat*. The contents of the first issue are as follows: A. Volpin, 'To all thinking people' [see p. 358]; B. Tsukerman, 'Letter to a B.B.C. editor', 'Letter to the editor of *Izvestia*'; V. Chalidze, 'On the optional clause: the optional clause to the International Treaty on Civil and Political Rights'; A. Tverdokhlebov, 'In support of Sakharov's letter'; V. Chalidze, 'Reflections on progress' [see above].

By the end of 1970 eight issues of this impressive forum for the free study of legal matters had appeared,[29] its name shortened by now to just Social Problems. *As for No. 2:*

11 The issue includes G. Pomerants's article, 'The moral make-up of historical personality':[30] 'There exists not only a continuity of events but also a continuity in the transmission of moral values, which is essential to any tradition.' The author goes on to examine the historical process which, by tearing the masses

away from their patriarchal environment, makes semi-educated boors of them. ' "A boor" is a man with a smattering of education—enough not to be afraid of breaking taboos, but not enough to enable him, through reason and experience, to arrive at moral truths.' The author shows how Stalin's dictatorship grew from the social soil of boorishness, how Stalin exploited the 'Asiatic' psychology of the backward masses, who desired not freedom of the individual, something unknown to them, but 'a master and law-and-order', how Stalin played upon the unconscious religious feeling of people who until recently had been peasants by setting himself in the place of the abolished god. 'To restore respect now for Stalin means to introduce respect for denunciations, torture and executions.'

Grigory Pomerants, No. 2 wrote after the Galanskov–Ginzburg trial,

is a philosopher and specialist on India, who works at [Moscow's] Fundamental Library of the Social Sciences, was an inmate of Stalin's camps, was rehabilitated, and is the author of several articles circulating in *samizdat*, two of which were printed in the almanac *Phoenix–66*.[31] He signed the letter of the 170. The defence of his thesis at the Institute for the Peoples of Asia has been postponed indefinitely. 2

This prolific writer of brilliant essays[32] *on the history and nature of human culture stands somewhat apart from the other* samizdat *authors in this section. He is more concerned, as we have seen, to provide lessons for the present by illuminating the past than—like the other three—to put his main efforts into trying to apply such lessons through social action. The* Chronicle *has also summarized his works 'Three Levels of Being' and 'Man of Air' :*[33]

The first article is about the roots of religious feelings in man. The author examines the various levels of being which arise with the awakening of different layers of the human psyche. The author concludes that there is an 'amorphous' mystical sense of religion, which is outside the Church and is not limited to its dogmas and Holy Scriptures. 5

The second article is about the concept of 'the people'. The author concludes that the concept has no real content.

Alexander Esenin-Volpin (see plate 69) — like, for example, the artist Yury Ivanov or the communist Sergei Pisarev — has been a fearless dissenter since Stalin's day. A son of the poet Esenin and a brilliant logician,[34] *he sent abroad in 1959 a philosophical treatise and a collection of his poems.*[35] *In 1965 he was one of the founders of the now traditional Constitution Day demonstrations (see p. 71); in 1966 he wrote about the Sinyavsky-Daniel trial;*[36] *and in 1967 he gave evidence at Bukovsky's trial.*[37] *At intervals since 1949 he has suffered internment in mental hospitals. The last time, however, as we have seen (pp. 80–83), a phalanx of high-powered mathematicians came to their colleague's defence and secured his quick release. Since then he has appeared regularly in the* Chronicle's *'Samizdat News' section, often as a contributor to Chalidze's journal, has interceded for General Grigorenko*[38] *and others,*[39] *and has also become a legal consultant to Sakharov's Human Rights Committee.*[40] *This is how the* Chronicle *summarizes five of his works of 1968–9:*

9   (a) 'To all Thinking People'. The author welcomes the great news that man has reached the moon, and muses on the future of space travel. Has mankind reached the stage where he will not need to resort in space to 'the age-old way of resolving problems on earth, by violence — problems which, if we had reached a higher level of moral development, we would solve only by peaceful means'? Volpin writes of the tragic spread of violence in the world, of the 'inertia which reinforces the corrupt traditions of servility and fear'. His conclusion is that mankind must use the time it has left before interplanetary flight becomes a commonplace, to achieve not only scientific and technological but also moral progress. In his postscript, the author declares: 'Being in Moscow, and enjoying the freedom of which my fellow freethinkers A. Marchenko, P. Grigorenko, I. Gabai, A. Sinyavsky, Yu. Daniel, Yu. Galanskov, A. Ginzburg, V. Bukovsky, L. Bogoraz-Brukhman [L. Daniel's maiden name], P. Litvinov and many others have been deprived, I consider it my pleasant duty to proclaim their absolute right to express their admiration for this unparalleled achievement of human intellect and courage. These people will not shame our planet.'

9   (b) 'An Open Letter to the U.S.S.R. Procurator-General, R. A. Rudenko'. The author shows that the trials of persons

charged with spreading deliberately false (libellous) fabrications which defame the Soviet social and political system, appear to thinking people more like a means of intimidating freethinkers than a method of fighting the spread of anti-social libel. Volpin draws the logical conclusion that if judicial investigation organs are really worried by the spread of such fabrications, then they should above all be concerned to refute information which has already been spread. According to article 7 of the Principles of Civil Legislation, any public or state organization, and the state itself—through the agency of the Supreme Soviet—has the right to bring a civil action against a person who has libelled it. That person will then be obliged either to prove the truth of his information, or publicly to refute it. The court decision and other trial materials can be published, and then criminal prosecution will not be necessary. Criminal proceedings create martyrs, and do not allow the validity or invalidity of the information spread to be satisfactorily determined.

(c) 'A Letter to the Editor of *Izvestia*'. The letter concerns an 8 article by M. Sturua entitled 'Time to Throw out This Dirt'.[41] Sturua suggests that a number of non-governmental organizations at the United Nations, which are concerned with human rights, should be 'chucked out of' the U.N. The author of the letter refutes Sturua's arguments as being based on omissions and misrepresentation of facts. He suggests that *Izvestia* turn its attention to the problem of civil rights, and, in particular, to corrective labour law. 'Perhaps at this very moment,' writes A. Volpin on the subject of the prisoner's right to unimpeded correspondence, 'there is an innocent man sitting in some Soviet prison, being subjected to unlawful persecution, and unable to inform your newspaper about it. And your paper, more than any international organization, would be able to put a stop to these abuses of the law! When I think of the possibility of there existing even one such case, I cannot understand why *Izvestia* ignores problems concerning the observance of the Code of Criminal Procedure and the Corrective Labour Code, preferring to print Sturua's ignorant attacks on non-governmental human rights organizations.'

(d) 'A Legal Memorandum for Those Faced with Interroga- 6 tion'.[42] Anyone may be faced with interrogation—sometimes it is enough for one's telephone number to be found in a notebook removed during a search. But few people know either their rights or the limits to the rights of the investigator conducting the interrogation. Volpin's 'memorandum', although written in the author's characteristic and complex style, contains a great deal of legal information which is indispensable to anyone under interrogation who wishes to avoid either a possible violation of legality or becoming an unknowing accomplice to such a violation.

11   (e) 'Soviet Legislation and the Pact on Civil and Political Rights'.[43] Two extracts from an unpublished manuscript. The author contrasts the pact of the title with Soviet legislation and practice.

Finally — in this law-oriented section which sheds so much light on the intellectual basis of the Democratic Movement's daily tactics — the Chronicle *summarizes a revealing book by Boris Tsukerman called 'Debates about Law' :*[44]

8   A collection of correspondence with officials, in ten parts. The subjects of the correspondence are fundamental problems of law: the right to marry; freedom of movement; freedom of the press; prohibition of discrimination against students for their convictions; the presumption of innocence; the ratification of international agreements on human rights; freedom of international postal correspondence; the length of time a man can be kept in detention without trial; and so on. The leitmotif of all the statements and complaints is their appeal for the consistent observation of Soviet laws.

STEALING AND SOCIETY

Turning to lighter matters, let us look now at an item which nevertheless raises acutely a lot of economic, legal and political issues. This is an unusual work by the Moscow radio-engineer and journalist Vikenty Gerasimchuk.[45] *The* Chronicle *reports:*

11   'Simplicity is worse than theft' is a pamphlet about how in our country 'an enormous number of conscientious citizens steal things in one way or another, some a little at a time, others by the wagon-load; they steal primitively or with miraculous ingenuity, for friends or for themselves, to get rich or to get

drunk. They steal meat and butter, instruments and medicines, planks, semi-conductors, engines, paper, young currant-bushes and cement, bricks and slate and anything under the sun ... ' In the first part of the pamphlet, however, only thefts from industrial enterprises, institutes and laboratories are examined in detail. The methods of stealing public property are classified: concealment in the pockets, next to the stomach, in the groin (the author advises caution in employing this method: 'a case is known where a man's scrotum was caught up in the line-control mechanism from a television set'), concealment down the back or by wrapping around the body. The methods of stealing 'non-portable' objects are also examined. And the reasons for all this thievery? 'People steal because it is much simpler, more convenient and more profitable to do so than to go mad trying to push one's way through crowds of fellow-shoppers, all driven frantic by the constant shortage of one commodity or another. People steal because while it is still considered shameful to steal private property, it is an amusing game to take what belongs to the State.' This is the way the lower strata of society think. And what example of moral behaviour is offered from above? The second part of the pamphlet deals with this. 'The ruling élite insatiably gobbles up all the tastiest morsels of the common cake ... High-ranking officials and their families suffer no pangs of conscience in exploiting everything they have ordered for themselves in accordance with their position on the party's secret table of precedence.' The author examines the various grades of privilege. 'There are many privileges, desirable and varied. But distinctions are strictly adhered to: no vulgar equality here ... One man gets his groceries at half price, another even more cheaply, one gets personal use of a car, another can use his only for business. Some even get one for the family, for the wife, mother-in-law and kids.' And so, the following of the slogan 'Grab what you can' 'merely leads to a more just distribution of the national income.'

RECENT HISTORY

Samizdat*'s historical items sometimes concern the fate of an individual, as with Elena Olitskaya's My Memoirs.*[46] *This book is:*

12*

6 The reminiscences of a member of the Socialist Revolutionary Party about her first arrest in 1924 and her long years in the camps of Solovki and Kolyma.

Sometimes, though, the purpose is to illuminate an episode deliberately obscured or falsified by official historiography. Hence the need for: 'On the Question of the Signing of the Soviet–German Non-aggression Pact in August 1939':

10 This collection consists of six documents published in Part 7 of [the Western publication] 'Documents of the German Ministry of Foreign Affairs', including the correspondence between Hitler and Stalin of August 20th–21st, 1939, Hitler's speech at a military conference in Berlin on August 22nd, a short record of the conversation between Hitler and Ribbentrop after the signing of the Soviet-German Pact, compiled by a member of the German delegation, a secret supplementary report of August 23rd (printed here in shortened form – the complete text also exists in *samizdat*), a report from an official of the German Ministry of Foreign Affairs dated September 1st, 1939, and a secret telegram sent to Stalin on the same day. A seventh document in the collection is taken from the [Soviet] journal *Party Construction*, No. 20 (October 1939). It is an extract from Molotov's speech at the session of the Supreme Soviet on October 31st, 1939. All the documents clearly show that the Soviet-German Pact was frankly aimed against Poland, which only a week after the signing of the Pact became the victim of a new world war, and also against the Western democracies.

Or the subject can be a broad historical analysis, as with the anonymous 'Transformation of Bolshevism':

8 This book, which consists of five chapters, is a critique of the present political line of the party from the standpoint of revolutionary and pre-revolutionary bolshevism. It takes as its starting-point quotations from the classics of Marxism, and also resolutions and decisions passed at party congresses during the first years after the revolution. The first chapter is devoted to the views of socialist thinkers of the past about the State, which

they regarded as a manifest but necessary evil, and which would remain such even after the passing of power into the hands of the proletariat. The first chapter also shows how these views underwent a transformation at the hands of those who drew up the present party programme [of 1961].

The second chapter analyses the electoral system used in our country, and the statutes of the present-day Soviets are compared and contrasted with the Soviets of the first years after the revolution.

The third chapter describes the part of the Bolshevik programme dealing with the creation of a people's police and the distribution of arms to each member of the population. The idea was to liquidate the regular police force and the regular army, and extend armed policing duties to all able-bodied adults among the population. The author tries to show that the principle of a police force organized on a territorial administrative basis could pave the way to a significant democratization of the present social system.

The central chapter is the fourth, which deals with problems of economics and management. The author is of the opinion that Soviet progress in industrialization can be fully explained by the advantages and benefits which ensue when the means of production are monopolized and all control of the national economy concentrated in the hands of the relevant state organs. From this it follows that one can talk of State Monopolism, but certainly not necessarily of socialism. The sine qua non of socialism is not only state ownership of the means of production, but also local self-government on the widest possible scale.

The last chapter examines the patterns of, and reasons for, the Bolshevik party's departure from its initial positions, a departure which was, in the author's opinion, inevitable in view of historical factors such as social backwardness, the low level of popular culture in the country, the frustrated expectation of a socialist revolution in Western Europe, and so on.

Finally, samizdat *also goes in for historical reprints, as with Varfolomei Zaitsev's 'The Violent Lackey, or a Manifesto of Servility':*

Why has this pamphlet, first published in Geneva in 1877 in the 9 uncensored paper *Obshchee delo* [*Common Cause*], got into *samizdat*? Any random quotation will explain why: 'We have been chained up in the cramped kennel of the Committee on Press Affairs [the censorship], we are fed on the left-overs of the foreign press, which is sent to us with passages blacked out all over its columns, and, running up and down on our chain in an area five steps wide, we bark for days on end at the whole world, rightly believing it completely hostile to our owner; we bark at foreign nations, at our own young people, and at every passing thought which does not bear the mark of our master.' Or: 'The wisdom of humility! Are we not wise! If the authorities order it — as the poet Kukolnik told us — I'll become a midwife tomorrow.' 'If the authorities order it' — said the liberal officers in Poland in 1863 — 'we'll organize another uprising tomorrow.' 'The authorities give the order — we crush the Hungarians and Poles. The authorities give the order — we liberate the Bulgarians and the Karakalpaks. They order us to play the liberal — we play the liberal, we glorify English customs, we condemn feudal payments and serfdom the moment we abolish them, we sympathize with Garibaldi and Gambetta, we abuse MacMahon, and we fulminate against the Pope, Austria and Napoleon.'

ESSAYS BY FOREIGNERS

It is not difficult to see why these foreign items got into samizdat:

11 Aldous Huxley: 'Science, Freedom and Peace.' An essay by the famous English writer published in England in 1947. Huxley writes that science and its discoveries in the modern world are being turned into instruments of totalitarianism, and discusses possible ways of combating centralization and totalitarianism.

Bertrand Russell: 'The Family and the State.' An extract in translation from his book *Marriage and Morals*. Russell shows how the functions of bringing up and educating children are performed by the modern state, which, by inculcating in them a narrow, bureaucratic, limited patriotism, reinforces the disastrous division of the world.

10 Leszek Kolakowski: 'I'll tell you what socialism is ... '. This is an essay written in 1957, for the journal *Po prostu*, by a thirty-

year-old philosophy professor at Warsaw University. The journal was closed down, and the essay was not published in Poland. The Russian text of the essay which has come out in *samizdat* is a translation from the Czech translation by F. Jungwirt and I. Korzan in the journal *Sešity pro mladou literaturu*, No. 20 (April 1968). Kolakowski lists seventy-two definitions of what socialism is *not*. Here are a few examples: A society in which a man is in for a bad time if he speaks his mind, and will prosper if he does not speak his mind; a society in which the man who has the best life is the man who never *has* a mind of his own; a State in which there are more informers than nurses, and more people in prison than in hospital; a State which turns out superlative jet-planes and repulsive footwear; a State in which the defence and the prosecution generally hold identical opinions; a State which awards prizes to insincere writers, and understands more about painting than the artists themselves; a State which knows what its people want even before they have asked the State for it; a State in which philosophers and writers say the same things as generals and ministers, but always after them; or a State which doesn't like its citizens to read old newspapers. The essay ends with the following words: 'That was the first part. And now—your attention please! I'll tell you what socialism *is*. Socialism—well, you know, it's a good thing!'

MATERIALS ON CZECHOSLOVAKIA

In the years 1968–9 by far the largest number of foreign samizdat items were translations from Czech or Slovak. Given the evidence in Chapter 4 of the Democratic Movement's support for the Czechoslovak Spring and outraged opposition at its suppression, this will cause no surprise. To start with, No. 5 made a survey of items circulated in 1968:

The first document to appear in this category was a speech made last year [1967] by Ludvik Vaculik at the fourth congress of Czechoslovak writers.[47] This speech gave a detailed account of the workings of a totalitarian régime. Attacking an undemocratic régime based on the triumph of 'mediocrities', Vaculik emphasized in the strongest terms that 'in criticizing the state power, I am not casting aspersions on the ideals of socialism, for I am not convinced that all that has happened in this country was inevitable and, furthermore, I do not identify the power in question with the idea of socialism ... '

In the spring and summer of 1968, a great variety of materials from Czech and Slovak newspapers and periodicals was circulated. Among them were interviews with the widows of Slansky and Clementis [the communist leaders executed in 1952], and other materials about the trials of the 'fifties; speeches by Dubček, Smrkovsky, Cisař and other leaders of the Czechoslovak Communist Party. Particularly important was the fact that *samizdat* made available the full text of the declaration known as 'Two Thousand Words',[48] which in the official Soviet press was described in a misleading way. *Samizdat* has also put into circulation an example of a truly free, non-totalitarian polemic: Joseph Smrkovsky's 'One Thousand Words in Reply to Two Thousand Words'.

The 'Czechoslovak Spring' was interrupted by brute force at the end of the summer. There are several *samizdat* documents relating to the first days of the occupation: leaflets addressed to Soviet soldiers, and messages to the population. 'On the third day of this treacherous aggression we are still free,' begins a message from the historians of Prague to their fellow-citizens: 'this brutal invasion has not brought our people to its knees'.[49]

In the months since the Moscow agreement [of August 26th] only very few Czechoslovak materials, unfortunately, have come into circulation via *samizdat*. The most important of these was the speech by Joseph Smrkovsky on August 29th, in which the President of the Czechoslovak National Assembly said outright that 'the country has suddenly been occupied by overwhelming military force'. He admitted that the Czechoslovak leaders in Moscow had been forced to accept a tragic compromise which had been dictated, however, not by cowardice but by a feeling of responsibility towards the population of the country. 'The talks and the decisions arrived at weigh heavily on our shoulders,' Smrkovsky said in conclusion. 'We are obliged to conduct this debate in the shadow of the tanks and aircraft that have occupied our country. The only way out of these difficulties is through the unity of the people and the government, through obedience to the call: "we are with you, as you must be with us".'

Of the later documents one may mention the appeal of the Czech writers of October 31st and the 'Ten Points' of the Students' Union of Bohemia and Moravia which formed the political basis of the student strike of November 18th–20th. The Ten Points are an expression of complete support for the 'action programme' of the Czechoslovak Communist Party;[50] they condemn any return to press censorship and government by an inner caucus, and demand guarantees of civil rights and liberties.

The steady stream of samizdat items which followed No. 5's review are now presented in chronological order of their composition:

MILAN KUNDERA: THE CZECH FATE   7

One of the most important representatives of the younger generation of Czech writers, discussing the significance of the post-January policies in an article published in the weekly journal *Listy* on December 19th, 1968, refuses to view the August days as a national catastrophe:

> What took place could not have been foreseen by anyone: the new policies have survived this terrible conflict. Although they have given some ground, they have not disintegrated or collapsed. They have not involved the return of a police régime, nor have they permitted a doctrinaire suppression of spiritual life; they have not betrayed themselves, nor denied their own principles, nor betrayed their authors; and not only have they not lost the support of public opinion, but precisely at the moment of mortal danger they have welded together the whole people, which has proved itself inwardly stronger than before August.

Posing the question 'What if the new government retreats so far that the new policies gradually turn back into the old ones?' Kundera places his hopes on Czech criticalness—not the kind which 'automatically discards all hope and easily resigns itself to hopelessness' and creates 'an ideal climate for the breeding of defeat', but 'genuine criticalness, which is the enemy of psychoses and knows that pessimism is as one-sided as optimism; this kind of criticalness is able to destroy illusions and false confidence, but remains itself at the same time full of confidence.' This criticalness 'gave birth to the Czechoslovak Spring, and in the autumn fought off the onslaught of falsehood and irrationality'.

7   PAVEL KOHOUT: SELF-CRITICISM

This short pamphlet, published on January 4th, 1969, in the newspaper *Prace*, parodies the opinions expressed by those who, under the guise of fighting against 'right extremists', act against the Czechoslovak people

THE SUICIDE BY FIRE OF JAN PALACH
[JANUARY 16TH, 1969]

Much varied material about this from Czechoslovak publications exists in *samizdat* form: reports on the suicide by fire of Jan Palach, on his death and funeral, and on the expressions of sympathy from Czechoslovak leaders and numerous organizations and individuals; also an article devoted to the memory of Jan Palach. Unfortunately, this material is circulated haphazardly and chaotically, without being collected into one volume.

8   DECLARATION OF CZECH ARTISTS, SCIENTISTS AND
JOURNALISTS, MAY 23RD, 1969

This declaration was signed by the Presidiums of the Czech unions of: writers; artists; composers; actors; architects; radio, cinema and television workers; scientific research workers; and cultural workers. Czech personalities in the world of culture, science and the arts make it known that they were resolutely determined to struggle for creative freedom, freedom in research and freedom of public opinion, and also for the freedom and independence of their people. In conditions of ever-increasing cultural repression, when the stifling of freedom of speech and freedom of the press is endangering all human rights and civil liberties, the authors of the declaration feel that their mission is to serve the truth. 'They can force us to be silent. But no one will ever succeed in making us say what we do not think.'

FRANTIŠEK KRIEGEL: SPEECH AT THE PLENUM OF 10
THE CENTRAL COMMITTEE OF THE CZECHOSLOVAK
COMMUNIST PARTY, MAY 30TH, 1969

Kriegel is the former Chairman of the Czechoslovak National
Front, and the only member of the Czechoslovak delegation
who refused to sign the Moscow agreement in August 1968,
after which he was removed from his post at the demand of the
Soviet government. As a deputy of the National Assembly, he
voted against 'the treaty on the temporary stationing of troops
in Czechoslovakia'. This fact was discussed at the plenum as a
disciplinary offence, for which it was proposed to expel Kriegel
from the Central Committee.

Kriegel declared that the treaty conflicted with the United
Nations Charter, the principles of international coexistence,
and the Statutes of the Warsaw Pact. It had been signed in an
atmosphere of political and military pressure, not with a pen
but with cannons and machine-guns, without consulting the
constitutional organs, and against the will of the Czechs and
Slovaks. Kriegel described the policy of the new party leadership as completely *alien* to the January 1968 course, despite all
the assurances of faithfulness to the post-January policies. The
party organs were being restructured, and the apparatus was
being drastically purged. The party was becoming isolated
from the people, and its leadership isolated from the mass of
party members. The party was being transformed from a guiding moral and political power into an organization which
wielded only force.

After this speech, Kriegel was expelled not only from the
Central Committee but from the party itself.

LETTER FROM PRAGUE, JUNE 1ST, 1969 8

The author of this letter demonstrates that in Czechoslovakia
there is taking place a 'total capitulation to Moscow'. Democratic socialism has been stifled—the natural result of the
deviation from principles which took place in Moscow at the
end of August [1968]. There was then only one course of action:
to insist, if only verbally, on the principle of sovereignty, on the
intolerability of the occupation, on freedom of speech, and to
rely on the international solidarity of the communist movement.
But this demanded unity of leadership, and a willingness to

take risks. Even as late as March it seemed that this course of action was still possible. But the leadership was no longer united, and when the second attack from outside came, it could not resist it. The author shows a flicker of optimism: 'It seems likely that August 21st will never be forgotten by the people. Nor by our [interventionist] "brothers", nor now by the party. Especially not by the young people who saw the tanks and the blood. And who see now on their television screens pathetic gatherings where people wear themselves hoarse chanting "Long Live the U.S.S.R.". And all in the presence of a smiling President and some of the January reformers.' The author concludes that democratic socialism is the alternative to totalitarian, Stalinist socialism. Western communists 'must defend our model which has been destroyed, campaign for it, study it and put it into practice themselves'. As for the socialist countries of Europe, if they do not realize in time that the only way of overcoming their economic backwardness in comparison with the West is through democratic socialism, then 'they will have only rockets and tanks left with which to oppose Western imperialism and Maoism'. To the question 'What *can* we do?' the author replies: insist on the principles of democratic socialism, preserve and develop its ideas, even if only underground.

9   KAREL KYNCL: SPEECH AT THE MEETING OF THE
PRAGUE CITY COMMITTEE OF THE CZECHOSLOVAK
COMMUNIST PARTY, JUNE 2ND, 1969

Karel Kyncl criticizes the speech made by Gustav Husak at the Praha-ČKD factory after the May Plenum of the Czechoslovak Communist Party Central Committee. Kyncl believes that Husak's assessment of developments which are immeasurably complex and, since August, frankly deformed in nature, was cheap, trivial and superficial. He had without question gone over to the side of the Warsaw letter,[51] with which ten months earlier he had fundamentally disagreed; and he had referred to the violent intervention of last August as nothing more than a misunderstanding. He had made crude attacks on leading figures in science and culture, and compared the weekly magazines *Reporter* and *Listy* with Radio Free Europe. Kyncl challenges Husak's assertion that not one man has been arrested or transferred to alternative work for political reasons: one could mention a long list of people, he says, from Hajek to Smrkovsky to dozens of journalists, who have been transferred to other jobs for exactly those reasons. Just before this issue of the *Chronicle* came out, Kyncl himself joined the list: the new management of Czech Television named him as one of the people with whom it would not co-operate, despite their excellent professional qualities, since they had 'taken part in hostile campaigns' — they would be replaced by other people. Also, when Kyncl made his speech, the wave of arrests had not yet begun: but now criminal proceedings have been instituted against several hundred people in Czechoslovakia on charges of 'distributing illegal publications'. A great many of the accused have been taken into custody. So that this assertion of Husak's too — that a return to the 'fifties is out of the question — has been disproved by reality.

INFORMATION ABOUT THE PRESENT SITUATION II
IN CZECHOSLOVAKIA

A number of articles have appeared in *samizdat* devoted to the present situation in Czechoslovakia.

1. 'Letter from a reader', published in the journal *Tvorba* of September 24th, 1969. The anonymous author of the letter, a worker and a communist, and a member of the People's Militia, states that the majority of the people condemn the pro-Moscow line adopted by the present government. The greater the pressure from outside, the stronger the people's resistance will become.

In their appended 'Reply' to the letter, the editors of *Tvorba* call the author a criminal who is insulting the citizens of Czechoslovakia and the brother-countries of the socialist camp. Noting that they are receiving large numbers of such letters, the editors of *Tvorba* suggest that their authors might like to carry on their polemic directly with the 'organs safeguarding the rights of citizens of the socialist state' (i.e. with the organs of state security).

2. Extracts from speeches made by A. Dubček and V. Bilak at the September 1969 Plenum of the Communist Party of Czechosolovakia, translated from the paper *Le Monde* of October 24th, 1969.

Dubček considers that Husak, in his speech, distorted the events of January to August 1968. He denies the existence in Czechoslovakia of a centre of counter-revolutionary activity supported by the forces of imperialism. He says that the policies pursued by the central committee headed by himself had enjoyed widespread popular support, and refers to the contents of negotiations with the Warsaw Pact allies which, he notes, made no mention at all of the possibility of outside interference in the affairs of Czechoslovakia.

Bilak accuses Dubček of political indecisiveness, and of diverging from firm commitments to the Soviet government. According to Bilak, the Soviet representatives had stated that under no circumstances would Czechoslovakia be allowed to leave the Socialist camp.

3. 'Letter from Czechoslovakia', written anonymously by a communist who left the party after the events of 1968. It tells of the present situation in Czechoslovakia, and of mounting extra-judicial persecution of citizens of the republic who protested against the troops of the Warsaw Pact being sent in. The letter mentions the circular put out by the Minister of Enlightenment, Jaromir Hrbek, which to all intents and purposes re-establishes the universal atmosphere of mutual denunciation. It further mentions the closure of journals and newspapers, the dismissal of scholars and journalists from their posts, and other symptoms of the revival of the methods of the Novotny period in Czechoslovakia. The letter analyses the present situation within the country. In particular, the author makes the following point:

There is no mass support for the régime established by the occupiers. The creative intelligentsia and the greater part of the scientific intelligentsia, together with the press, continue their opposition. Throughout our history there has never yet been a régime (except under Hacha's protectorate) which aroused so much revulsion. It has produced a new phenomenon — the emigration of anti-Stalinist communists. I imagine it was the fear that the numbers and intellectual strength of these emigrés would grow, and that they would form the nucleus of an opposition party centre abroad, which led to the closing of the frontier at this particular moment, when the progressives have been deprived of any influence at home. Also new is the disagreement of the Western communist parties with the policy of the Kremlin and with its interpretation of internationalism (this did not happen over Yugoslavia, Berlin, Poland and Hungary). Other new features are the unprecedented crisis in the international socialist and communist movements, and the fact that Soviet society thinks and reacts in a new way since the 20th party congress.

We know that we are not alone. This one factor lends us strength as well as bringing many obligations. I think that everyone in Czechoslovakia who asks himself the question 'Where do we go from here?' will come to the same conclusions.

VALERY CHALIDZE : LETTER TO THE FIRST 10
SECRETARY OF THE CENTRAL COMMITTEE OF THE
CZECHOSLOVAK COMMUNIST PARTY, G. HUSAK

The author of the letter says that for the last one and a half years Czechoslovakia has been the scene of a struggle of ideals — which have aroused his sympathy — against tendencies which are now represented by G. Husak. 'The outcome of this struggle is clear. Evidently using a wide spectrum of political methods and a theory of the evolution of the awareness of Czechoslovak society which I understand only imperfectly, you are gradually consolidating your victory and that of your political line.' Judging by the tone of the press and by historical experience, V. Chalidze comes to the conclusion that the personalities linked with the events of early 1968 may be subjected not only to party repression but to judicial repressions too. He shows that there are usually no difficulties involved in carrying out such measures 'in complete accordance with domestic notions of judicial procedure, the instigators of the measures having only to decide to what extent they should take into account the phenomenon generally known as world public opinion. The twentieth century has given us plenty of examples where this moral force has been disregarded ... ' The author expresses a certain amount of hope that the present Czechoslovak leadership will prefer to create a precedent of tolerance, and sounds a warning that if there are repressions, the reaction of 'every person of humanist inclinations in any country ... will be moral condemnation of the instigators of these repressions, to a degree comparable with the condemnation of the instigators of the best known political tragedies of our century.'

The Alexander Herzen Foundation

Finally, the Chronicle *draws the attention of* samizdat *authors to a possible foreign publisher of their works:*

11 The Alexander Herzen Foundation has been set up in Amsterdam, under the auspices of three Slavist scholars: Professor Dr J. V. Bezemer (chairman), Professor Dr K. R. van het Reve (secretary) and Dr P. Reddaway.[52] The Foundation's declared aim is not only the publication, in Russian and other languages, of Soviet authors, but the safeguarding of their copyright in all countries. The Foundation does this regardless of the political, religious or philosophical views expressed in the works; the sole criterion is their artistic or documentary merit. So far the Foundation has arranged the publication in the West of materials, most of which were circulating in *samizdat* prior to their publication. These include Academician A. D. Sakharov's treatise *Reflections on Progress [, Peaceful Coexistence and Intellectual Freedom]*; Anatoly Marchenko's *My Testimony*; *The Demonstration on Pushkin Square*;[53] *Letters and Telegrams to Pavel Litvinov*;[54] and Andrei Amalrik's *Involuntary Journey to Siberia*.

Part VI · Tributaries

19. LENINGRAD AND THE PROVINCES

> When a person is arrested, it provokes a sharp reaction in society.
> The reaction is especially strong in the capital, where an already
> well-formed public opinion exists. The provinces are another matter.
> There the reaction is muted and slower ... People are more timid
> than in Moscow, the authorities more tyrannical, their arbitrariness
> more cynical.
>
> Anatoly Levitin, June 1969[1]

Already the Chronicle *has taken us out of Moscow sufficiently often to
disperse any image of the Democratic Movement as a 'tiny, dwindling group
of dissidents in the capital'. Levitin's words notwithstanding, the provinces
have featured a lot. In Leningrad we have found much opposition, notably
to the Czechoslovak invasion, and been taken inside the notorious prison
hospital. In Estonia we have followed the fates of Soldatov and Gavrilov,
in Latvia those of Yakhimovich and Rips, in Kharkov those of Major
Altunyan and his colleagues. In Kiev the mathematician Plyushch, the
critic Dzyuba, the Jewish engineer Kochubiyevsky and the dissenting
Baptists have all had their activities brought into focus. In other parts
of the Ukraine we have learnt about the persecution of the historian
Moroz, the journalist Chornovil, the poet Sokulsky and various Uniate
priests. In the Crimea, Central Asia, Azerbaidzhan and Georgia we
have kept track of the peripatetic Crimean Tatars and Meskhetians.
General Grigorenko has been followed to Tashkent, Pavel Litvinov and
Larissa Daniel into Siberian exile. Reports have reached us from the jail
in Vladimir, the prison hospitals in Kazan and Chernyakhovsk, the
labour camps in Mordovia, Perm, Tyumen, Murmansk and Yakutia.
In Novosibirsk, Obninsk and Rostov we have found scientists voicing
their protests, likewise Orthodox writers in Kirov and Pskov. Nearer to
Moscow, we have watched the fate of the pro-Czech Lukanin in Roshal,
then the saga of the engineer Ryzhik in Pavlovsky-Posad. And finally, for
the ritualistic expulsion of Russia's greatest writer from official literature,
we have been taken — perhaps appropriately — to the medieval city of
Ryazan.*

But these episodes do not exhaust the Chronicle's *coverage of the*

375

provinces. Others—not tied to our earlier themes—abound, and they appear in this chapter under the appropriate area or city heading. We start in Leningrad—Russia's ex-capital and long a rebellious city²— then move clockwise round the country, ending up back in Moscow.

LENINGRAD

After Valery Ronkin's 'Union of Communards' (see Chap. 2, note 8) had been broken up in 1965, the next important Leningrad group to develop was:

THE ALL-RUSSIAN SOCIAL-CHRISTIAN UNION FOR THE LIBERATION OF THE PEOPLE

1 Between March 14th and April 5th [1968] seventeen Leningrad intellectuals were tried in the Leningrad City Court. Procurator Guseva and Judge Isakova (deputy chairman of Leningrad City Court) took part in the trial.

All the accused were charged under articles 70 and 72 of the Russian Criminal Code. The essence of the charge was participation in the All-Russian Social-Christian Union for the Liberation of the People.

BRIEF EXPOSITION OF THE UNION'S PROGRAMME

The establishment of a democratic system. The head of state is elected by the whole population and is accountable to Parliament. The upper chamber—a *Sobor* (representatives of the clergy)—has a right of veto vis-à-vis the head of state and Parliament.³ The land belongs to the State and is allocated to private people or collectives (exploitation forbidden); hired labour only permitted on a basis of equality. Enterprises are mostly owned by worker collectives, but the main industries—transport, electronics, etc.—to be state-owned. Basic principle of the economic system—personalism.⁴

STATUTES OF THE UNION

Strict conspiracy, members operating in 'groups of three'; each person knows the senior member of his 'three' and its second member. In addition, each person recruits new members, creating a new 'three' in which he becomes the senior. The head of the organization is not known to the members—in case of need they communicate with him in writing through the senior member of their 'three'.

In practice the organization engaged only in recruiting new members and distributing literature (the books and copies of books confiscated in searches included those of Djilas, Berdyayev, Vl. Solovyov,[5] [G. von] Rauch's *History of Soviet Russia*, Tibor Meray's *Thirteen Days that shook the Kremlin*—on Hungary in 1956, Gorky's *Untimely Thoughts*, etc., and even [Evgenia] Ginzburg's *Into the Whirlwind*).

The organization was formed in about 1964. By mid-1965 it had some ten members. By this time the Leningrad K.G.B. already knew it existed but did not stop its activities and allowed it to develop and expand (in court Alexander Gidoni appeared as a witness: he had denounced the organization to the K.G.B. in 1965 but was advised to continue to keep in touch with its members).

In February/March 1967 some sixty persons were arrested or detained (not only in Leningrad but also in Tomsk, Irkutsk, Petrozavodsk, etc.).

In November 1967 the Leningrad City Court tried four leaders of the organization (under articles 64, 70 and 72) and sentenced:

Igor[6] Ogurtsov (translator from Japanese, 30 years old) to 15 years of imprisonment; Mikhail Sado (orientalist, 30) to 13 years; Evgeny Vagin (literary critic from Pushkin House [a literary research institute], 30) to 10 years; and [Boris][7] Averochkin (jurist, 28) to 8 years—all to be served in strict-régime corrective-labour colonies.

The second trial lasted from March 14th to April 5th, 1968. The difference between the people brought into court as accused and those brought in as witnesses consisted basically in the fact that those on trial had engaged in recruiting people— even if only a single person—for the organization. All the accused admitted their guilt (evidently in the sense of admitting the facts of the charge) but not all of them recanted (particularly Ivoilov, Ivanov, Platonov and Borodin).

The following were sentenced (term of imprisonment shown after each entry in years, with term demanded by the Procurator in parentheses):

1. Vyacheslav Platonov, born 1941, orientalist — 7(7).
2. Nikolai Ivanov, born 1937, art critic, teacher in Leningrad University — 6(7).
3. Leonid Borodin, born 1938, school headmaster from the Luga District in Leningrad Region — 6(6).
4. Vladimir Ivoilov, economist (Tomsk), graduate of Leningrad University — 2(2) [in fact six years — see *Chronicle* 19].
5. Mikhail Kolosov,[8] born 1937, fitter employed in the Leningrad Gas organization, correspondence course student of the Gorky Literary Institute — 4(5).
6. Sergei Ustinovich, born 1938, Leningrad University graduate — $3\frac{1}{2}$(4).
7. Yury Buzin, born 1936, engineer, agricultural institute graduate — 3(4).
8. Valery Nagorny, born 1943, engineer in L.I.T.M.O. (Leningrad Institute of Precision Mechanics and Optics) — 3(4).
9. Alexander Miklashevich, born 1935, engineer (agricultural institute graduate) — 3(3).
10. Yury Baranov, born 1938, engineer (graduate of institute of cine-technicians) — 3(4).
11. Georgy[9] Bochevarov, born 1935, Leningrad University graduate — $2\frac{1}{2}$(3).
12. Anatoly Sudaryov, born 1939, translator, Leningrad University graduate — 2(2).
13. Anatoly Ivlev, born 1937, chemist, Leningrad University graduate — 2(3).
14. Vladimir Veretenov, born 1936, chemist, Leningrad University graduate — 2(3).
15. Olgerd Zobak, born 1941, L.I.T.M.O. mechanic — 14 months, the time already served while under pre-trial investigation (1 year).
16. Oleg Shuvalov, born 1938, L.I.T.M.O. — 14 months, the time already served (1 year).
17. Stanislav Konstantinov, librarian — 14 months, the time already served (1 year).

The trial was characterized by violations of legality similar to those in the Moscow trial [of Galanskov and Ginzburg]:

1. The terms of pre-trial detention exceeded the legal maximum in the case of some of the accused.

2. Admission was by permit to an 'open' trial (although the court was half empty).
3. Most witnesses were ejected from the courtroom immediately after testifying.

It is also not clear why the leaders of the organization were tried separately and why they were tried under article 64 (treason), as well as articles 70 and 72. Was the programme they had drawn up defined as 'a conspiracy aimed at seizing power'? If so, this was clearly illegal.[10] In the circumstances of the trial of the first group of four every kind of illegality could have been committed, since nothing was known of the trial until it was over and it was, apparently, completely closed.

It is reliably known that no one was charged with having connections with N.T.S., nor with engaging in currency transactions, nor with possessing arms.

This account of the two trials fits well with the only other substantial source yet available, an anonymous article of 1969 apparently written by a member of the Union.[11] This confirms that twenty-one people were sentenced, adding that twenty-nine in all stood trial and that the case materials filled over a hundred volumes. It also states that Union members were indeed charged with participation in 'a conspiracy aimed at seizing power', and that the Union's programme stood for armed revolution, although its activity had not reached the stage of acquiring any arms. The article provides a fascinating analysis of the Union's social composition, ideological development, programme and activities, and of the reasons for its betrayal. There is sufficient similarity between its programme and that of the 'Democrats of Russia, the Ukraine and the Baltic Lands' (see p. 173) to make it possible that the latter group includes people previously associated with the Union.

In any case, the next development was predictable enough:

In May and June 1968 the Russian Supreme Court considered the appeals of the Leningrad members of the All-Russian Social-Christian Union. The sentences on all those convicted were confirmed. Ogurtsov, sentenced to fifteen years' imprisonment, and Sado, sentenced to thirteen years' imprisonment, will, according to the sentence, spend the first five years of their terms under a prison régime. They are in the prison at Vladimir.

The other accused are now in camp 11 of the Mordovian camps: their address is: Mordovskaya A.S.S.R., st. Potma, p/o Yavas, p/ya ZhKh 385/11.

We have already met Ogurtsov, Sado, Platonov and Borodin in Vladimir prison and the camps (see pp. 207, 220). In addition, No. 9 recorded in 1969: 'Sado has been transferred from Vladimir prison to camp 3 of the Mordovian complex', but it did not explain why the transfer took place early. No. 10 then reported his further transfer to camp 17-a. This was where he became friends with a man of whom the Chronicle *wrote:*

10 Alexander Petrov (pseudonym Agatov), the Leningrad poet and author of the words of the song 'Dark Night' (from the film *The Two Warriors*), was convicted in Moscow in February 1969 under article 70 of the Russian Criminal Code for a book he had written (the title is unknown).

In a document written in Mordovia in late 1969 Petrov gives the date of his closed trial as January 7th–8th and the basis for his seven-year sentence as his 'poems about the tyranny of the Beria times, written in that period'.[12] Here he also describes Sado as 'a man with a wonderful heart, a fine mind and an unbreakable will', and in a later document he writes in detail of Sado's remarkable life-story.[13] In autumn 1970 Petrov was transferred to Vladimir for his pains, along with Borodin.[14] Earlier he had served over twenty years in camps, getting out in 1967, having a year of freedom and publishing a few works,[15] before returning.

The Case of Kvachevsky and Gendler
In earlier chapters we left Lev Kvachevsky on hunger-strike in Mordovia and his sister Dzhemma Kvachevskaya struggling to get her 'socially restive' husband Vladimir Borisov out of the Leningrad prison hospital. In 1965 brother and sister were both distantly connected with Ronkin's group.[16] In 1966–8 Kvachevsky and his friend Yury Gendler belonged to an informal circle which, among other things, became concerned about the trials of the Social-Christians. Gendler had once received some of the latter's material from Sado, and, with Kvachevsky and others, he tried in vain to gain admittance to both trials.[17] The group also joined in the Moscow campaign against the Galanskov–Ginzburg trial,[18] establishing friendly relations with Pavel Litvinov in the process.[19]

In April 1968 Kvachevsky was, like others,[20] *outraged by Alexander Chakovsky's libellous article in the* Literary Gazette *about the Moscow campaign, and wrote him an angry letter. Noting Chakovsky's annoyance that the intelligentsia's protest letters got abroad so quickly, he commented:*

> *Yes, it is indeed rather inconvenient. But for you the inconvenience consists solely in the fact that, like all children of darkness, you fear a pale ray of light, which, reflected back from 'the West', returns to its point of origin! ... You yourself write that the letters were sent to Soviet organizations, and 'the West' is merely informing Soviet citizens that such an act has taken place. The content of any such letter is hardly likely to be a secret. But why is it precisely the radio-stations of England, America and Germany which have become the communication link between our people and a part of the intelligentsia? (You do not, I trust, doubt that the broadcasts of these stations are listened to by millions of Soviet people.) Has the* Literary Gazette, *which always writes in such detail about trials, including those of fascist criminals, printed even one of the letters protesting against the judicial victimization of Ginzburg and Galanskov?*

Doubtless it was this letter which cost Kvachevsky his job two months later.[21]

Such is the background, then, to the Chronicle's *first reports on the Kvachevsky-Gendler case of 1968:*

Yury Gendler's flat was searched in a similar way [to Yakhimovich's—see p. 146] in Leningrad on August 1st. That evening a few Leningraders (eight or ten people) had gathered at his flat to draft a letter addressed to the citizens of Czechoslovakia. They were influenced in their decision by the letter Anatoly Marchenko had written to *Rude pravo, Prace,* and *Literarni listy.*[22] One may suppose that the young Leningraders wished to express their sympathy with the political developments in Czechoslovakia. On precisely the same evening the police came to search Gendler's flat. The search warrant alleged that 'Gendler, together with Tsal, had accepted bribes for the installation of telephones.' Suffice it to say that Yury Gendler is legal adviser to a soft-furnishing factory and can therefore have no connection with the installation of telephones. In addition, this was the first time that he had heard of the above-mentioned Tsal. Nevertheless there was not only a search of Gendler's flat but also a personal search of all those present, and a further search of all their flats. As a result of the searches several books and photocopies of books designated as 'anti-Soviet' were discovered. Consequently a number of people were detained for three days and a number arrested—this time not by the ordinary police but by the organs of state security.

5 THE LENINGRAD TRIAL OF DECEMBER 17TH–26TH, 1968

Issues No. 3 and 4 of the *Chronicle* gave news about the arrest of several people in Leningrad, and about the circumstances of their arrest. In October two of the accused in this case, Nikolai Danilov and Evgeny Shashenkov, were declared of unsound mind and the court ruled that they be confined for compulsory treatment in a mental hospital 'of special type' (i.e. in a prison hospital).

Nikolai Danilov, a lawyer by training, worked at the end of the 'fifties as a K.G.B. investigator in the Ukraine and on the island of Sakhalin [off the Pacific coast]; he then gave up this work and for a long time did ordinary manual labour; only recently did he begin to work as a legal consultant. He writes verse and has been doing a correspondence course at the Literary Institute. In April 1968, together with Yury Gendler, Lev Kvachevsky and Victor Fainberg, he wrote a letter to the U.S.S.R. Procurator-General about procedural irregularities at the trial [of the Social-Christians] in Leningrad last spring.[23] In June 1968 he was expelled from the Institute. He has a nine-year-old daughter.

Here we may insert a later and fuller biographical note:

9 In 1959 Danilov graduated from the Law Faculty at Rostov University. From 1960 to 1963 he worked in the Sakhalin regional Procuracy, where he dealt with the rehabilitation of victims of Stalinism. According to his account, by 1963 they had managed to rehabilitate only a quarter of all those who had perished. Since 1963 Danilov has been living in Leningrad. He has been employed as a worker and as a legal adviser. He published his poetry in the 'Young Leningrad' anthologies and

in the Leningrad 'Poetry Day' collection. The decision on his insanity and his internment in the severe conditions of a special psychiatric hospital were probably the result of his firm behaviour at the investigation, and also of the particular hatred of the K.G.B. organs for a former investigator who had voluntarily left his work in the investigation organs. At the moment Danilov is being given potent 'treatment'—insulin shocks, which have resulted in him genuinely being reduced to a serious condition.

No. 5 now resumes:

Evgeny Shashenkov is an engineer. In 1950, while a student at Leningrad University, he wrote a letter to Stalin as a result of which he was arrested and interrogated with all the brutality then prevalent, before being sent for the first time to a prison mental hospital. He was sent there a second time in 1963–4, and the same thing is now about to happen to him a third time. Nevertheless, as far as is known, Shashenkov has shown the greatest fortitude under interrogation, refusing to give any evidence.

There were thus three defendants[24] at the December trial: Yury Gendler, born in 1936, legal consultant, father of a five-year-old daughter; Lev Kvachevsky, born in 1939, chemical engineer, father of a six-year-old-son; and Anatoly Studenkov, born in 1935, physicist and engineer, father of a seven-year-old daughter. The Judge at the trial was the deputy chairman of the Leningrad City Court, Karlov; the prosecuting counsel was Procurator Dosugov; Gendler's defence counsel was Romm, and Studenkov's was Shafir. Lev Kvachevsky refused to have a lawyer and conducted his own defence.[25] His elder brother, Orion Kvachevsky, a geologist and former inmate of Stalin's concentration camps who was rehabilitated in 1956, wanted to appear for the defence, but was not allowed to, nor even to be present at the trial: the day before the trial he was sent off on a trip connected with his work.[26]

The defendants were accused of 'producing, harbouring and circulating' works 'of an anti-Soviet nature'. Among these were the following books and photocopies of books: [M.] Djilas, *The New Class*; [G. von] Rauch, *A History of Soviet Russia*;

[E. Stillman (ed.)], *Bitter Harvest*; [?], *The American Public*; the journal *Mosty*[27] [*Bridges*]; [N.] Sokolov, *The Murder of the Tsar and his Family*;[28] [Nikolai] Berdyayev, *The Origins and Meaning of Russian Communism*;[29] [Barry] Goldwater, *Why Not Victory?* and *The Conscience of a Conservative;* [A.] Avtorkhanov, *The Technology of Power*; [G.P.] Fedotov, *The New City*;[30] and others. Furthermore, they were charged both in the indictment and in the verdict with harbouring a number of typewritten *samizdat* materials, a precise list of which is not yet available. There is some evidence that the list even featured letters sent by Soviet citizens to high Soviet authorities. From the legal point of view the indictment and sentence sound odd when they speak of the accused having entered into 'criminal relations' with P. G. Grigorenko, V. A. Krasin, and P. M. Litvinov, from whom they had allegedly received material 'of an anti-Soviet nature'. Not one of these three was called as a witness at the trial. On the other hand, on the first day of the trial some unknown persons attacked Victor Krasin in Moscow, striking him on the face with a knuckle-duster.

Anatoly Studenkov, apart from being charged like the others under article 70, was also accused of illegally distilling vodka, forging documents, and petty larceny. It is clear that this circumstance played no small part in the full and 'sincere repentance' he made during the pre-trial investigation, and it was because of this repentance, as well as his full admission of guilt and the readiness with which he gave evidence under investigation and in court that, despite the four articles under which he was found guilty (articles 70, para. 1, 94, 158, para. 1, and 196, para. 1, of the Russian Criminal Code), Studenkov received the shortest sentence of all.

Yury Gendler pleaded guilty, but denied any anti-Soviet intent in his actions. He stated that he had been guided only by a wish to help in the democratization and liberalization of Soviet society on the lines laid down by the 20th and 22nd party congresses, and that it was only during the pre-trial investigation that he had 'realized the anti-Soviet nature of his actions'.

Lev Kvachevsky pleaded not guilty. He admitted most of the facts with which he was charged, but absolutely denied their criminal nature. In his speech in his own defence, and in his

60. Telesin's departure from Moscow's Sheremetevo Airport, May 6th, 1970.
Fifth from left, Iosif Kerler; 11th, Telesin; 12th, Yury Shikhanovich (see p. 91);
13th, Ivan Rudakov (pp. 197–8); 15th, Elena Stroyeva (pp. 325, 471–2); 16th,
Andrei Grigorenko (p. 131); 17th, Alexander Esenin-Volpin (pp. 81 ff and 358 ff);
18th Irina Belogorodskaya (pp. 197 ff); 21st, Irina Kristi (p. 86); 22nd, Yury Titov
(pp. 325, 471–2); 23rd, Volpin's wife Victoria (p. 444); 24th, Boris Tsukerman.

61. David Khavkin's departure from Sheremetevo, 1969 (see p. 309). Ester Khavkin
is standing first left in the front row, her husband David third left, and their son
Leonid is kneeling first left. Kneeling first right is Israel Shmerler (see p. 310), and
fourth right in the second row is Natalya Slepyan (see p. 469).

62. (*left*) Archbishop Ermogen, Orthodox pastor and scholar (see p. 328).

63. (*above*) Oleg Vorobyov, Orthodox believer from Perm (see p 324).

64. (*bottom left*) The late Boris Talantov (1903–71), Orthodox believer and mathematics lecturer from Kirov, 1968 (see pp. 326 ff).

65. (*below*) Anatoly Levitin, Orthodox writer from Moscow (see pp. 321 ff).

66. Andrei and Gyuzel Amalrik, Moscow, 1968 (see pp. 352 ff).

67. (*below left*) Historian Roy Medvedev (left) with his geneticist twin brother Zhores (see pp. 417, 421 and 413–14).

68. (*below right*) Valery Chalidze, Moscow physicist and legal expert, 1970 (see pp. 355 ff).

69. (*left*) Alexander Esenin Volpin, Moscow logician a legal expert, 1966 (see pp. 8 and 358 ff).

70. (*right*) Vladlen Pavlenl history lecturer from Gorky (see pp. 389 ff).

71. (*left*) Mikhail Kapranov, one of the four imprisoned Gorky students (see plates 72–4 and pp. 390 ff).

72. (*right*) Vladimir Zhiltsov.

73. (*left*) Vitaly Pomazov

74. (*right*) Sergei Ponoma

75. (*left*) The late Dr. Fritz Menders (1885–1971), Latvian social democrat from Riga (see p. 404).

76. (*right*) Moscow student Olga Iofe (see pp. 418 ff).

final plea, he reasserted his innocence and his right to read anything he wished.

The Procurator demanded imprisonment in strict-régime labour camps for all three defendants: six years for Kvachevsky, four for Gendler and eighteen months for Studenkov. Defence counsel for Gendler and Studenkov demanded that the indictment be reformulated under article 190–1 of the Criminal Code.

The court sentenced Kvachevsky to four years, Gendler to three and Studenkov to one—all in strict-régime camps.

On April 17th, 1969, the appeal hearing took place [...] The 7 sentence was left unaltered.

In addition to this account the Chronicle *reported a reprisal taken against one of the witnesses,[31] and also summarized[32] the* samizdat *item 'About the Trial of Kvachevsky (based on L. P. Nestor's record)'. Nestor's record is a long and unusually valuable document because of the extensive detail it gives both about the trial and about the mutual relationships of the different dissenting groups in Leningrad between 1965 and 1968. It adds to the* Chronicle's *account by, for example, revealing that Kvachevsky's letter to Chakovsky was among the charges against him, also that his brilliant speech in his self-defence drew some applause from an audience largely selected, of course, to be hostile to him. It also reports that Gendler's attitude in prison was for a long time uncompromising, and that it changed only at the last minute, after talks with some high officials who appear to have offered him a deal.*

But what of subsequent developments?

On August 25th [1969] Anatoly Studenkov [...] was released. In 9 his final plea he had begged the court to 'protect him from anti-sovietists' and not to send him to a camp. His request was granted: right to the end of his term ... he remained in a Leningrad prison.

Yury Gendler and Lev Kvachevsky [...] have still not been sent 8 to camps. They are being held in the Leningrad investigation prison as witnesses in some 'polytechnicians' case' about which the *Chronicle* has no information.

The case concerned may have been the subject of this 1969 item:

9 The trial was held in Leningrad this spring of two seventeen-year-old first-year students of the Polytechnic Institute, charged under article 190–1 of the Russian Criminal Code. The substance of the charge was the distribution of leaflets in the Institute. As minors they were each put on one year's probation. Both were expelled from the Institute along with about ten other students.

We soon learn the following, however:

9 The *Chronicle* report that Gendler and Kvachevsky were not sent to camps for some time because they were being held as witnesses in a new case was incorrect. Their departure was delayed because the decision of the appeal court took about one and a half months to reach Leningrad from Moscow.

   They have now been sent to the Mordovian camps, Gendler to camp 19 – Mordovskaya A.S.S.R., pos. Lesnoi, p/ya ZhKh 385/19 – and Kvachevsky at first to camp 3. Recently, however, according to unconfirmed reports, Kvachevsky was transferred to camp 17.

But:

10 The report that Lev Kvachevsky was transferred from camp 3 of the Mordovian complex to camp 17 has not been confirmed. Kvachevsky is still in camp 3, where he is working in his professional field as a chemical technologist ...

Eventually, however, the murder of a mentally defective prisoner by some guards provoked Kvachevsky (and others) beyond mere hunger-strikes to a categorical refusal to work. For this he was dispatched to Vladimir.[33]

Among the various Chronicle *reports of Leningraders paying a heavy penalty for their protests about trials*[34] *or neo-Stalinism,*[35] *or for distributing* samizdat,[36] *or for some other political offence, the following two are of particular interest:*

THE CASE OF VLADIMIR GOMELSKY

In January 1969 a Leningrad worker, Vladimir Gomelsky, 8 came out of a camp. His sentence of three years under article 190–1 of the Russian Criminal Code had been reduced to one and a half years under an amnesty. He had been charged with writing a letter of a critical nature to the 23rd congress [of the party in 1966]. In other words, his letter had been written before article 190–1 became law. At his trial it was maintained —without the slightest proof—that Gomelsky had been passing the letter around at a later date. The case against Gomelsky was begun after the party organizer of the All-Union Experimental Television Research Institute, Voinov, and the chairman of the local party committee, Pilts, sent a report to the Procuracy which included a distorted version of statements made by Gomelsky during a debate 'On Vulgarity', and also at party activist meetings in the Institute, and at an election campaign rally. Precisely these accusations were later withdrawn.

After returning from camp, Gomelsky cannot obtain a residence permit for Leningrad, although residence restrictions are not incurred by a charge under article 190–1. The Leningrad police have four times refused an application sent to the Leningrad Procurator, and have turned down three applications to the Procuracy of the Russian Republic. For half a year now Gomelsky has been without a permit and without work.

THE CASE OF YURY LEVIN

As reported in No. 8 of the *Chronicle*,[37] Yury Leonidovich Levin 9 has been arrested in Leningrad. On June 26th, 1969, he was summoned to appear before an investigator of the Leningrad Procuracy, Yu. M. Tumanov, and taken into custody. He was charged under article 190–1 of the Russian Criminal Code, and not, as stated in No. 8, under article 70.

In 1957 Levin was sentenced to ten years imprisonment under article 58–1a, but in 1964 he was amnestied after doing seven years of his term. The reason for his conviction was his attempt to emigrate. Since 1966 he has sent several letters by registered post to the 'Voice of America' radio-station. According to him, the letters did not contain anything political, but were 'innocent' and addressed to one of the lady announcers of the 'Voice of America'. However, they were obviously not reaching their destination, and Levin repeatedly complained to the Leningrad post office about this, but to no avail. Finally, said Levin, he decided to 'catch the K.G.B. out'. To this end, he sent a registered letter to the American Embassy in Moscow, stating that the sending of troops into Czechoslovakia was classified as a criminal offence under article 73 of the Russian Criminal Code. Levin assumed that the K.G.B. would take steps over this and thus unmask themselves as readers of private correspondence by X-ray-type techniques. The letter was sent on October 12th, 1968, and at the beginning of November of the same year Levin was put in a psychiatric hospital on the orders of Belyayev, the chief psychiatrist of Leningrad. Ten days later he was declared healthy and discharged.

In March 1969 Levin complained to the Procuracy that his letters were systematically going astray. On May 23rd, 1969, he was summoned to the district office of the K.G.B. on Vasilevsky Island, and had presented to him for signature the following statement: 'During a customs examination a letter written by Yu. L. Levin and addressed to the American Embassy in Moscow was found and confiscated, its contents being of a clearly anti-Soviet nature.' Here it may be recalled that according to the Russian Criminal Code interference in private correspondence is classified as a criminal offence. Nevertheless, a few days later [on June 5th — No. 8], the party activist group at the Institute of Mechanical Processing, where Levin was employed as a mechanic, discussed Levin's letter to the embassy in his presence, having been given the text by the K.G.B., then condemned him and passed a resolution: 'To request the Procuracy to institute criminal proceedings against Levin for libellous anti-Soviet statements sent to our enemies ...'

On June 24th, 1969, a search was made of Levin's flat and country cottage. He himself handed over all his correspondence with 'Voice of America', and also some tape-recordings of its transmissions, which he had managed to pick up in spite of the jamming. Apart from this, the search produced nothing significant. The next day Levin was arrested.

Finally, we may note that in the field of self-immolation Leningrad rivals Kiev. On January 22nd, 1970, a young worker, Gennady

Trifonov, made an unsuccessful attempt in front of the Smolny.[38] *And a few months earlier:*

At the end of September, at the foot of the Lenin statue on 10
Finland Station Square in Leningrad, an unknown citizen set
fire to himself. The *Chronicle* does not know his name, nor what
became of him.

GORKY

Striking east from Leningrad towards the Urals, we come, about halfway, to the ancient city of Nizhny Novgorod. Known for the last 40 of its 750 years as Gorky, it is strategically placed on the upper Volga and contains over a million inhabitants and much industry. Already we have seen (p. 339) what its authorities do to citizens found to be reading Solzhenitsyn. Here the Chronicle *reports on how they react to independent political action:*

EVENTS IN GORKY. In addition to the details given in 6
No. 5[39] the *Chronicle* is now able to report the following. In April
1968 leaflets appeared at the Polytechnic, Pedagogical and
Medical Institutes, and at the University of Gorky, calling on
people to 'follow the Czech example'. As a result students and
teachers of several higher educational establishments were
called to the Gorky K.G.B. in April and May. It was discovered
that they were not responsible for the leaflets; nevertheless a
number of them were subjected to various forms of repression.[40]
    As reported in No. 5, V. Pavlenkov [see plate 70] and S.
Pavlenkova, university teachers, Tavger, Head of the Department of Physics, and V. V. Pugachyov, Professor of History,
mistakenly described in No. 5 as Professor of Physics, were all
dismissed from their jobs.

In 1968 a number of university students studying under Pro- 10
fessor V. V. Pugachyov, a Doctor of Historical Science, were
arrested or subjected to interrogations by the K.G.B. When it
was found that they were behaving honourably at the interrogations, that they were aware of their rights, and that they
refused to be intimidated or to co-operate with the investigators,
the K.G.B. began demanding that they name 'the man who had

taught them' to behave in this way, and some of the students gave the name of Pugachyov. After this, Professor Pugachyov was put under pressure from party and administrative organs, and forced to leave the University where he had worked for many years.

6 A number of students have been expelled from the Komsomol for reading *samizdat*: in the history faculty, [V.] Buidin and Borisoglebsky, the latter a member of the faculty bureau of the Komsomol; in the physics faculty, Tartakovsky and Fishman, the latter a member of the university committee of the Komsomol; and three students from the Medical Institute.

The following have been expelled from both the Komsomol and the university: E. Kupchinov and I. Goldfarb, for distributing *samizdat* and refusing to give evidence, and V. Pomazov [see plate 73], for distributing *samizdat*, refusing to give evidence and participating in the writing and distribution of the essay, 'The State and Socialism'.[41] Two students were expelled from the Medical Institute for distributing *samizdat*. Several students were not admitted to their military departments.

In November 1968 Ternovsky, a student of the history faculty of the university and three students of the Polytechnic were expelled for distributing [the Czechoslovak liberals' manifesto] 'Two Thousand Words' [see p. 366].

In No. 5 it was reported that a student, whose last name was given incorrectly, had announced at a meeting of the Komsomol in the university that she was leaving the organization as a gesture of protest against the expulsion of students from it. According to more exact information the student who made the announcement was Klara Geldman.[42] She was not subjected to any immediate repression but in January 1969, having sat her final examinations and left for Kiev to write her diploma thesis, she received the news that she had been expelled from the university.

9 In Gorky two students of the university and two lecturers have been arrested on political charges.

10 This summer [1969] the following were arrested in Gorky: S. Ponomaryov, a graduate of the faculty of history and philo-

logy at Gorky University, and a contributor to the factory newspaper *Motor of the Revolution*; and Zhiltsov and M. Kapranov, fifth-year students of the faculty of history and philology. In October Vladlen Pavlenkov, a teacher at a technical college, was arrested. The reason for their arrest was the circulation of *samizdat* literature. V. Pavlenkov's wife, a teacher of foreign languages at the university, has been dismissed from her post.

Since the latest wave of arrests, an atmosphere of panic has overtaken the city of Gorky; it is particularly manifest in officials' fear of any sort of publicity.

It has become known that three graduates of Gorky University 11 will soon be brought to trial. They are: [Mikhail Sergeyevich] Kapranov, [Vladimir Ivanovich] Zhiltsov and [Sergei Mikhailovich] Ponomaryov, who have been charged under article 190–1 of the Russian Criminal Code with circulating leaflets opposing the revival of Stalinism.

A former history teacher at a technical school, Vladlen [Konstantinovich] Pavlenkov, has been arrested in connection with the same case. After a two-month investigation failed to establish Pavlenkov's complicity in the case of Kapranov and the others, the Gorky K.G.B. decided to send him for psychiatric examination.

The wife of Vladlen Pavlenkov, Svetlana, is the daughter of parents who underwent repression[43] during the years of the personality cult. She has been dismissed from her post as a lecturer at Gorky University, and is now alone with her nine-year-old son.

If her husband is adjudged of unsound mind, Svetlana Pavlenkova intends to set fire to herself in public.

Pavlenkov was, as a result perhaps, adjudged to be of sound mind, and eventually, in March and April 1970, the defendants' four-week closed trial took place. The long account in the Chronicle *reveals that the charges concerned pasting up leaflets, spreading* samizdat, *and plans to form an allegedly anti-Soviet organization, which, the* Chronicle *suggests, would in fact have been a human rights group. None of the four repented, each defending himself with vigour. Support came from some of the 96 witnesses. As a result, Pavlenkov and Kapranov (see plate 71) got seven years of strict régime, Ponomaryov five (see plate*

74), and Zhiltsov four (see plate 72).[44] *Savage reprisals, moreover, were taken against 22 of their friends and relatives.*[45] *Later the* Chronicle *showed its sympathy by printing the names, birth-dates and addresses of Pavlenkov's and Ponomaryov's young children.*[46] *It also reported the four-year sentence on Vitaly Pomazov for his authorship of 'The State and Socialism', passed in camera in February 1971.*[47]

PERM

If we now travel five hundred miles further east we reach Perm, the centre in Stalin's time of an enormous camp empire. Some of its establishments are still active, like the camps which have held Anatoly Marchenko in recent years. Here, in the Ural foothills, many of Stalin's political prisoners have settled, not allowed to leave the area since their release in the 1950s. Thus the residence here of an Action Group supporter and friend of Levitin's, Oleg Vorobyov (see p. 324), and the penetration of samizdat *to such a remote area, as shown in this item, are not as surprising as they might appear.*

7 Alexander and Ekaterina Lipelis, teachers at the Perm Pedagogical Institute, have been dismissed from work for possessing *samizdat* works; their dismissal was accompanied by a public inquiry, at which offensive and barbaric accusations were made; both were banned in future from teaching.

UFA

A short journey south brings us to the focal point of an exchange of letters which appeared in samizdat. *It casts revealing light on the already troublesome but potentially explosive issue of minority nationalism. A study of the complete text of the first letter*[48] *—full of examples of anti-Russian feeling among the minorities—shows that the author is a Russified Ukrainian and communist, who works in the Bashkir Agricultural Institute.*

10 'DEAR FRIEND'

This is a letter sent from the city of Ufa [capital of the Bashkir Autonomous Republic in the Urals] to a Central Committee official of the Soviet Communist Party, dated

June 5th, 1968, and signed 'Your friend'. The author—a representative of the Ukrainian national minority, as he calls himself—is disturbed by the growth of nationalism in various union and autonomous republics. Taking Bashkiria as an example, the author tells of the difficulties that normal high-level officials of Russian descent face in their everyday lives, and sees the root of this evil in the over-large number of officials of local nationality who occupy high positions. 'What is to become now of the great Russian people, the people which raised up the Tatars, the Bashkirs and all the other peoples out of darkness, slavery, lawlessness and such things? ... this phenomenon (nationalism) will accelerate in the future unless measures are taken immediately on a country-wide scale.' The author is worried and demands immediate preventive measures: 'there was no nationalism of this sort in Ufa before the war.'

'TO ROSSINANTE'

This is an answer to the letter 'Dear Friend'. The author, under the pseudonym 'Maloross' [little Russian, i.e. a Ukrainian], analyses the nature of nationality conflicts ('general animosity', 'enmity between different peoples'), and sees their cause in the bureaucratic 'Russification' effected by many representatives of national minorities (Ordzhonikidze, Dzhugashvili [i.e. Stalin], Dzerzhinsky, Zinoviev) and in 'the all-Russian chauvinism of the party'. The author sounds a warning: until the 'Russian empire is transformed into the Union of Soviet Socialist Republics—and each of these words must become a fact—animosity will increase'; 'the many-headed monster of nationalism' is only beginning to react to all the good works of the Moscow government.

SVERDLOVSK

Climbing the Urals and descending into west Siberia, we arrive at another great industrial city of a million inhabitants, Sverdlovsk. Up to the trial of Andrei Amalrik and his co-defendant Lev Ubozhko, a Sverdlovsk student, this city featured little in the Chronicle. *No. 5 revealed that 'Boris Feldman, a student at the Urals Polytechnic Institute, has been expelled for his involvement in* samizdat'*, but the only more substantial item was this:*

13*

5 Evgeny Goronkov, Master of Physical-Mathematical Sciences, works at the Urals Polytechnic Institute and is one of the leading members of its singing club. In May the club invited Yuly Kim* to come and sing in Sverdlovsk. Kim was met at the station by members of the volunteer police who told him to go back home. His performance was cancelled, but Kim sang some of his songs in the apartment of one of the people who had invited him. Two weeks later his host was arrested by the K.G.B., falsely accused of murder and intimidated into handing over all the tape-recordings made of the songs, and giving evidence of the sort required by the K.G.B.

Everyone holding office in the singing club was replaced, and Evgeny Goronkov was stopped on his way to Poland (on official business), and told to return home, where he was then dismissed from his job.

NOVOSIBIRSK

Almost a thousand miles further east we reach one of the freest-thinking communities in the country: the enormous concentration of scholarly talent in Novosibirsk, and especially in its science satellite-city Akademgorodok. The following episodes are therefore not surprising.

11 As has already been mentioned in the first issue of the *Chronicle*,[49] on the night of January 15th–16th, 1968, slogans protesting against the trial of Ginzburg, Galanskov and the others were painted in indelible red paint on the walls of numerous buildings in the Akademgorodok suburb. They read: THEIR CRIME WAS HONESTY, STOP CLOSED TRIALS — WE WANT TO KNOW THE TRUTH, ONLY FASCIST COUNTRIES HAVE ARTICLES LIKE 70 AND 190. An inquiry, undertaken by K.G.B. investigator Captain Lelyukov, Lieutenant Borisenko and an investigator from the District Police Station, Rakuta,

---

* No. 2 wrote of Kim after the Galanskov-Ginzburg trial: 'A teacher of Russian language and literature at the physics and mathematics boarding-school attached to Moscow University, an author and performer of well-known songs, a signatory of the letters of the 116, the 44 and the 170, of (with Ilya Gabai and Pyotr Yakir) the appeal "To Those Who Work in Science, Culture and the Arts", and of the appeal to the Budapest Conference [see pp. 79, 86–8], he has been sacked from his job "at his own request", all his singing appearances have been cancelled, and a contract to play the leading role in a film has been revoked.'

yielded no results. Oleg Petrik, a student at Novosibirsk State University who had been arrested on January 16th, 1968, had to be released. The case was closed.

In the summer of 1969 the inquiry was reopened (the investigator from the District Police Station was Goncharenko, and from the Novosibirsk Procuracy, Vyun). During the investigation three university students, Alexander Gorban, Leonid Popov and Yury Meshanin, confessed to direct involvement in painting the slogans; Galina Zhernovaya and Boris Kalnensky, also students at Novosibirsk University, confessed to being indirectly implicated.

The university authorities were informed that if Gorban, Popov and Meshanin were not expelled from the university, they would be put on trial.

In October a meeting of the Komsomol Committee of Novosibirsk University was held, with Boris Lukyanov in the chair. Present at the meeting were representatives of the Regional Komsomol Committee, a representative from the District Party Committee, almost the whole of Novosibirsk University's Party Committee, the secretary of the District Komsomol Committee and a representative of the Novosibirsk K.G.B. The meeting resolved to expel Gorban, Popov, Meshanin, Zhernovaya and Kalnensky from the Komsomol and to ask the university authorities to have them expelled from the university. In contravention of Komsomol statutes, the meeting was held before the matter had been discussed by Komsomol cells. It is interesting that, at the meeting, the K.G.B. representative expressed his surprise at the severity of the committee's decision.

The following resolutions were adopted at Komsomol meetings at the faculty level: that Meshanin be expelled from both the Komsomol and the university; that Popov be allowed to remain at the university (passed unanimously) and not be expelled from the Komsomol (the necessary two-thirds majority was not forthcoming); and that Zhernovaya and Kalnensky be expelled from the Komsomol but allowed to remain at the university. No Komsomol meeting at all was held in the Physics faculty where Gorban studied.

As things turned out, all five were expelled from the Komsomol. Gorban, Popov and Meshanin were expelled from the

university and refused the right to enter an institute of higher
education for a period of two years. The Procuracy has
evidently now closed the case.

*In many ways more serious, however, was the Novosibirsk protest-letter
of 'the 46'. This was noted in No. 1, along with the punishment of
one of its signatories, Yablonsky (see pp. 78–84). No. 2 followed up
with details of the reprisals taken against sixteen other signatories,[50]
and also with this more general report:*

2   In Novosibirsk, the central theme in the persecution campaign
has come to be the aim of purging the Akademgorodok—i.e.
the university and the institutes of the Siberian Section of
the Academy of Sciences [S.S.A.S.]—of those who signed the
Novosibirsk letter. This aim has found expression in many
forms: from more or less insistent suggestions that these people
should leave 'at their own request' (in return for which several
lecturers in the School of Physics and Mathematics have been
offered posts and flats in Novosibirsk—anywhere, in fact, but
in Akademgorodok) to outright threats. A 36-year-old corresponding member of the S.S.A.S., R. Sagdeyev, has said: 'They
should all be driven out of Akademgorodok—let them go and
load lead ingots.' Rumour has it that Academician Trofimuk,
corresponding members of the Academy Dmitry Belyayev and
Slinko, and the Pro-rector of the University, Evgeny Bichenkov,
are distinguishing themselves in the persecution campaign.
Because some of its lecturers had signed the letter, the Department of Mathematical Linguistics at Novosibirsk University
has been disbanded on the initiative of the Dean of the Humanities Faculty, corresponding-member Valentin Avrorin. The
continued existence of the Philology Department of the
Humanities Faculty, and of the Department of Northern
Languages and Siberian Literature in the S.S.A.S. Institute of
Philosophy, History and Literature, is threatened.

*In addition to all this, the central press weighed in,[51] and Akademgoro-
dok's famous art gallery was closed down. The permanent pictures were
taken to Moscow and buried in the basement of the Tretyakov Museum.
Novosibirsk's scholars were thus saved from contamination by the
gallery's imminent Chagall exhibition. Two years later its outstanding*

director, Mikhail Makarenko, stood trial. He got an eight-year sentence and the Chronicle *published a long account.*[52]

MAGADAN

A further 2,500 miles across Siberia brings us at last to the Pacific coast. Magadan, a port towards its northern end, was the centre of another of Stalin's vast death-camp complexes. At the time of the Galanskov–Ginzburg trial the occasional signature of someone from this city on a protest[53] *showed how far-flung were the Democratic Movement's outposts. So too does this item about the friend of a* samizdat *essayist and signatory of various protests:*

In the middle of March 1969, Ernst Makhnovetsky, a driver at the oil depot near the village of Khasyn in Magadan Region, was searched; personal papers, diaries, personal correspondence, a draft manuscript by his friend V. N. Gusarov, 'The desperate son of the Tambov provincial governor' (an essay on L. Trotsky), and extracts from a satirical story 'About Uncle and his Pals' were confiscated. Makhnovetsky was promised that everything not found to be incriminating would be returned after examination, and he was asked to write an explanation of why he had this material, which he did. Efforts were made to hush up the search, but, even before it was over, the inhabitants of the small village found out about it. 7

KARAGANDA

We now set off west again, but on a more southerly route. Passing Vladimir Dremlyuga in his Yakutian camp, Pavel Litvinov on the Manchurian border, Larissa Daniel just west of Lake Baikal, and finally a lot of Baptists in the camps of the Altai, we eventually arrive at the capital of another Stalinist camp empire — an area as large as France — Karaganda. Why we stop here becomes clear in this unusual item:

THE CASE OF M. P. YAKUBOVICH 10

Mikhail Petrovich Yakubovich was born in 1891. He is a great-grandson of the Decembrist A. I. Yakubovich[54] and a nephew of the poet and revolutionary P. F. Yakubovich.[55] From his youth he worked for the revolutionary movement in Russia.

He was first arrested while a schoolboy in the sixth class. At first he was a Bolshevik, but after the beginning of World War I he disagreed with the Bolsheviks on the question of the war, and joined the Menshevik fraction of the Russian Social-Democratic Workers' Party.

Yakubovich played an active part in the 1917 revolution, was elected the first Chairman of the Smolensk Soviet of workers' and soldiers' deputies, and was co-opted into the Petrograd Soviet as Representative of the Western Front. He was also elected a member of the All-Union Central Executive Committee of the Soviets (V.Ts.I.K.) of the First Convocation, and a member of the V.Ts.I.K. Bureau. At the time of Kornilov's putsch [September 1917], he arrested General Denikin,[56] acting as Commissar of the Provisional Government attached to the First Army. After the October Revolution Yakubovich occupied a leading position in the Menshevik fraction of the Russian Social-Democratic Workers' Party, and tried to persuade the Mensheviks to co-operate actively with the Bolsheviks and with the Soviet system. He himself was working then as a food-supply commissar for Smolensk Province — the only provincial commissar in Soviet Russia who was a Menshevik. When the attempted Menshevik-Bolshevik rapprochement failed in 1920, Yakubovich left the party and worked in executive posts in central Soviet institutions: Director of the State Funds Commission of the Council of Labour and Defence, Chief of the Manufactured Goods Administration of the U.S.S.R. People's Trade Commissariat, etc. Yakubovich was the author of a number of articles and larger works on economic policy and socialist construction.

In 1930 Yakubovich was arrested, and in 1931 sentenced to ten years at the trial of the 'Mensheviks' All-Union Bureau'. From 1931 to 1939 he was held in the political wing of Verkhneuralsk prison. In 1936 Zinoviev and Kamenev were in the same prison. In 1939 he was transferred to Oryol prison, and then to the Unzhlag camps (now Kostroma Region).

In 1941, soon after his term expired, while working as a free worker in the Unzhlag camps, he was re-arrested and sentenced in absentia to a further ten years by decision of the N.K.V.D.'s Special Conference.[57] In 1950 he was transferred to Spassk, near Karaganda, in the Peschlag camp complex. He later described his journey from the northern camps to those of Karaganda in an unpublished story, 'The Red Rose'.

After spending almost a quarter of a century in confinement, M. P. Yakubovich was only released in 1953, two years after his second term of imprisonment expired, and was sent to the Tikhonov home for invalids in Karaganda. Until 1955 he lived there as an exile. Yakubovich is still living there at the present time. He commands enormous respect and authority, and despite his advancing years leads an active public life as Chairman of the Culture Commission, which is in practice the organ of self-government for the invalids, through which they can defend their interests and rights before the administration. It is to a large extent through Yakubovich's efforts that the Tikhonov Home is notable for its relatively easy-going régime in comparison with other invalid homes.

In 1956 M. P. Yakubovich was rehabilitated in connection with his second case.

In 1961 he sent a letter to the 22nd congress of the party asking for a review of the 'All-Union Bureau' trial. The Procuracy-General answered that the guilt of Yakubovich and the others convicted with him had been proved by the pre-trial and court investigations, and also by the confessions of the accused themselves. Soon after that E. D. Stasova[58] sent a similar request to N. S. Khrushchev, but received no reply.

In 1966 M. P. Yakubovich was assigned a special pension of the sort given as an honour.

In 1967 he was summoned from Karaganda to Moscow, to the Procuracy-General. There he was questioned—in the form of an informal talk, with no written record—about the circumstances of the 'All-Union Bureau' trial, and then he was asked to put down everything he had related in written form. In his written explanation, addressed to the Procurator-General,[59] M. P. Yakubovich, the only surviving participant in one of the open political trials of the 'thirties, relates in detail how this trial was staged.

'No "Mensheviks' All-Union Bureau" ever existed,' writes Yakubovich, and he goes on to tell of how a 'sabotage organization' was fabricated by the O.G.P.U. The 'All-Union Bureau' was constituted by the investigation organs on the principle of departmental representation by well-known and influential

employees of the main economic organizations – the All-Union
National Economic Council, the People's Trade Commissariat,
the State Planning Commission and the Union of Consumers'
Co-operatives – people who were honest workers in the state
machinery, who had left the Menshevik party long ago, and
some of whom had never even belonged to it. By means of
promises, threats and tortures, applied on a strictly individual
basis according to the degree of resistance encountered, these
people were forced to 'confess' to counter-revolutionary
sabotage.

M. P. Yakubovich explains his behaviour at the trial by
saying that to have retracted the testimony he had given during
the investigation would in his opinion have wrecked the trial
and caused a world-wide scandal which could at that time have
damaged Soviet power and the communist party. Apart from
that, it would have meant condemning himself to a slow,
agonizing death by torture. If he had really been an enemy of
Soviet power and the communist party, he might possibly have
found the moral support to give him courage. But he was not an
enemy. On the eve of the trial the state prosecutor, Procurator
of the Russian Republic N. V. Krylenko, who had been a close
acquaintance of Yakubovich since before the revolution, tried
to persuade Yakubovich to confirm at the open trial the testimony he had given at the preliminary investigation, and said:
'I do not doubt that you personally are not guilty of anything.
We shall both be doing our duty to the party – I always considered you, and still do consider you, a communist ... '

During that same visit to Moscow in May 1967 Yakubovich
met A. I. Mikoyan, whose deputy he was on the eve of his
arrest.[60] During their conversation Mikoyan admitted that he
had never doubted Yakubovich's innocence, but there had been
nothing he could do for him at the time. On the possibility of
the 1931 trial being reviewed Mikoyan gave him to understand
that the question would ultimately be decided not by the
Procuracy-General but by some higher authority; however, at
present the latter considered it an unsuitable time to review
political trials and grant new rehabilitations.

Instead of the Procuracy-General sending a reply, the
journal *Problems of History* at the end of 1967 and the beginning
of 1968[61] published a series of articles by Senior Counsellor of

Justice D. L. Golinkov.[62] In a section called 'The Anti-Soviet Activities of the Mensheviks' (No. 2, 1968) the author, using among other things Yakubovich's testimony from the trial, writes about the 'All-Union Bureau' in the spirit of similar articles dating from the Stalin era.

While in the invalid home, Yakubovich has also occupied himself with literary work. Apart from the story mentioned above, 'The Red Rose', he has written the following: 'The Death of Boris Godunov', a historical-literary work in which he gives his reasons for believing that Godunov [1552–1605] was not implicated in the death of the Tsarevich Dmitry; 'Christianity and Hinduism', an essay on ethics and philosophy which attempts to prove the moral superiority of Hinduism; 'What is Time?', a philosophical analysis of the concept of time in Einstein's theory of relativity; 'Tolstoy's and Galsworthy's Attitudes to Death'; and 'Letters to a Stranger', a series of political character-sketches, written from a Leninist standpoint and based to a considerable extent on personal recollections and little-known facts: three works in this series—on Stalin, Kamenev and Trotsky—were completed in 1966–7, and a fourth, on Zinoviev, remains unfinished.

On April 24th, 1968, M. P. Yakubovich's room was searched, and all his manuscripts and letters taken away. At the same time the Karaganda K.G.B. began an investigation into the case of Yakubovich under the article of the Kazakh Criminal Code which corresponds to article 190–1 of the Russian Code. Two of his friends were also implicated in the case, accused of 'passing things around'. The behaviour of the investigator, Major Kovalenko, chief of the K.G.B. investigation department, was—at least as far as Yakubovich was concerned—proper in all respects. The interrogation records were a true reflection of Yakubovich's testimony. But the expert report on Yakubovich's writings was a complete contrast to the propriety of the investigation. The experts, Gorokhov and Mustafin, Professors of the Social Science Departments at Karaganda's Polytechnic Institute and Medical Institute respectively, and a third person whose name is not known, wrote their conclusions in the spirit of the worst examples of the Stalin period. Their report contained crude insults and abuse; distorting and falsifying the sense and content of

Yakubovich's writings, they accused him of provocation, counter-revolution, ideological subversion, propagation of Menshevik ideology, slander of Marxism-Leninism, and so on. All this related not only to his memoirs and political writings, but to his philosophical, literary and historical works as well.

Despite the experts' findings, the case was closed on instructions from Moscow on June 24th, when the two-month period allowed by law for the pre-trial investigation ended. The letters which had been removed during the search were returned, but all the manuscripts, the fruit of many years' labour, were kept by the K.G.B., 'attached to his criminal case'.

M. P. Yakubovich's address is: Kazakh S.S.R., Karaganda 1, Tikhonovsky dom invalidov.

UZBEKISTAN

Turning due south for 600 miles, we pass now through the wastes of Kazakhstan and enter Soviet Central Asia—an area rich in history, but Russian for only a century. Here, in Tashkent, in late April 1969, a riot took place outside the Pakhtakor football stadium after a match. According to a Soviet paper,[63] this led on June 2nd–3rd to the sentencing of some of those involved to long terms in strict-régime camps. Another source (a Crimean Tatar document of late May[64]) states that the Tashkent disturbances continued into early May and involved fighting between Russians and Uzbeks—the latter, like most of their neighbours, a Turkic people. By pointing out that none of those arrested was a Tatar, the document's author clearly hoped to counter the known desire of some of the authorities to shift the blame on to the Tatars. The latter were then in militant mood because of the imminent trial of ten of their leaders (pp. 257–62).

All this sets the scene for the first of these two items, and perhaps, indirectly, for the second as well:

8 In mid-May there were large-scale national disturbances in a number of places in Uzbekistan. They took the form of spontaneous meetings and rallies, under the slogan 'Russians, get out of Uzbekistan!'. The disturbances assumed such a violent character that troops were brought into Tashkent. About one hundred and fifty arrests were made in Tashkent and other towns. The majority were allowed to go free, but about thirty

people were given fifteen days in prison for 'petty hooliganism'. According to unconfirmed rumours, one of those kept under arrest was Rashidova, daughter of the First Secretary of the Central Committee of the Communist Party of Uzbekistan,[65] and another the son of one of the deputy chairmen of the Uzbek Council of Ministers.

In Uzbekistan disturbances are also going on among the 8 large Tadzhik population. When the identity cards of the many Tadzhiks living in Bukhara were reissued to them they contained the entry 'Uzbek' under the heading 'Nationality'. But the principle of 'divide and rule' did not work. The wrath of the Tadzhik population fell not upon the Uzbeks, but on the pioneers of the innovation—the Russian administrators. Their revenge for this insult to their national pride took a terrifying form: about eight murders were committed. The disturbances are continuing.

GROZNY

To reach the capital of the Chechen-Ingush Autonomous Republic in the north Caucasus we pass across wide deserts and skirt the Aral and Caspian seas. We find ourselves then in an area conquered by Russia— after fierce resistance—in the early nineteenth century. When subsequently, in 1941–3, the native Chechens and Ingushi showed too much sympathy for the Germans, Stalin deported them en bloc.[66] In 1957–8 they returned home, after—unlike the Tatars—being fully rehabilitated. Then, reportedly, they suffered a vicious pogrom at the hands of the hostile Russians of Grozny.[67]

Against this background the following item of 1969 becomes more understandable:

In the town of Grozny in May and July there were two attempts 9 to blow up the memorial statue of General Ermolov, 'the conqueror of the Caucasus'. The explosions were not very powerful. The first one blew off the General's head, but within twenty-four hours it had been replaced. The second one damaged part of the pedestal. It is well known that the local population wants to have, in the capital city of Checheno-Ingushetia, statues of their national heroes and not of tsarist colonizers.

LATVIA

Leaving behind the Meskhetians of Chapter 13, and traversing the Ukraine — familiar from Chapter 14 — in a north-westerly direction, we arrive after a 1,200-mile journey in Latvia. Here independence from Russia was proclaimed on November 18th, 1918, but lost again in 1940 after Stalin's deal with Hitler. Hence this item:

11 At the Latvian Cemetery[68] in Riga November 18th is [unofficially] observed as a day of remembrance. In Latvia it is virtually an established date. [In 1969] there was a meeting at the grave of a past president, J. Čakste [1859–1927]. Nearby graves were decorated with flowers — a row of red bouquets, a row of white ones, then red again, after the colours of the Latvian national flag. Candles were lit on the graves, a row of red, a row of white, then of red. The red-and-white striped flag was raised at President Čakste's graveside. People made speeches at the meeting, but their exact content is unknown to the *Chronicle*. The police detained about ten people at the cemetery, but released them eight days later.

A different aspect of Latvia's unhappy past is reflected in this report:

11 Information has reached the *Chronicle* about the arrest in Riga of the 84-year-old author of some memoirs published abroad, and about his trial. According to some reports, he was charged under article 65[69] of the Latvian Criminal Code, equivalent to article 70 of the Russian Code, and was sentenced to five years in a strict-régime camp. There is some speculation that the man is Fritz Menders (or Mendersh or Mende), one of the founders of the Latvian social-democratic party.

No. 17 later amended and clarified this item, pointing out first that the name's correct form in Russian is Mender, in Latvian Menders. A leading social-democrat, Dr Menders (see plate 75) was deported to Siberia in the mid-1940s, but had the luck to survive and to return home in 1955. His 1969 sentence was in fact five years of banishment from Riga, on the charge that he had allegedly given some materials to a foreign tourist. But no memoirs of his have yet been published abroad. In 1970 he was allowed to return to Riga, after a sharp decline in his health, and in April 1971 he died.

ESTONIA

Coming west into Estonia we are almost back in Leningrad. Here, however, apart from some opposition by Tartu students (pp. 101, 107) and the dramatic material on the Baltic Fleet officers in Chapter 8, the Chronicle *offers only a few brief flashes, all from late 1969 :*

A campaign against 'long-haired youths' has begun in Estonia. The journal *Noorus (Youth)* has published an article by Deputy Chairman of the Tallinn City Executive Committee Undusk, in which he writes that 'physical force' and 'violence' should be employed against 'long-haired youths'. Following this, letters of protest appeared from Estonian writers including P. E. Rummo. [11]

The prose-writer Teet Kallas was arrested in Tallinn in early November. He is twenty-seven. A search was made at the editorial offices of the magazine *Looming*, where Kallas worked, and some editorial material was removed.[70] [11]

Andres Ehin, assistant chief editor of the paper *Sirp ja Vasar*[71] has been dismissed from his post after manuscripts of his were confiscated from someone at the border. [11]

VLADIMIR

Although our 10,000-mile journey round the Soviet Union is now complete, we have yet, before returning to Moscow, to visit a few towns in the capital's environs. Our visit to Vladimir is of course a second one, as we saw inside its ancient prison in Chapter 10. Here we trace the unhappy fate of a man with the same name as Vladimir Borisov of Leningrad. But it was Borisov of Vladimir who founded :

THE UNION OF INDEPENDENT YOUTH 8

From two issues of the typescript information sheet 'Youth', it has become known that on December 16th, 1968, a Union of Independent Youth was organized in Vladimir, operating legally under article 126 of the Soviet Constitution. The organizers of the Union have applied to register it with the Executive Committee of the City Soviet.

According to its constitution, 'the Union of Independent Youth is a completely independent youth organization, run by the young people themselves, who guide all the Union's activities on their own initiative but within the bounds of Soviet law, and themselves direct these activities ... The basic aim of the Union of Independent Youth is to promote in every way possible the development of socialist democracy and social progress in our country.'

The Union demands: 'the introduction of truly free and democratic elections', 'real freedom of speech and of the press, freedom to gather, to hold meetings and demonstrations, and to form organizations *de facto*', 'an end to persecution of people for their convictions', 'the publication of all works written by Soviet authors', 'the liquidation of the illegal and anti-constitutional censorship', and 'the strengthening of the struggle against crime'.

Apart from information about the Union, the 'Youth' leaflets contain reports on events in Vladimir and other parts of the country.

The *Chronicle* quotes an extract from 'Youth' leaflet No. 2:

In Vladimir the K.G.B. are also carrying on the infamous 'traditions' of Stalinism. Employees of the Vladimir K.G.B. have several times threatened the President of the Union of Independent Youth, V. Borisov, with internment in a camp, and have spread malicious slanders about him.

The Vladimir K.G.B. men do not shrink from thieving. True, it wasn't they who did the actual thieving—they made a couple of cowards steal from V. Borisov two of his stories (one complete, the other unfinished).

Even among party workers the evil spirit of Stalinism still lives. For instance, Lapshin, the First Secretary of the city party committee, forbade V. Borisov, on behalf of the K.G.B. and the party authorities, and in the presence of Afanasev, the Secretary of the Chemical Works Party Committee, to make any political utterances whatsoever, threatened him with imprisonment in a concentration camp, and told him that the K.G.B. would follow him for the rest of his life.

The First Secretary of the Vladimir Regional Party Committee, [M.A.] Ponomaryov, refused to talk with V. Borisov after he learned that Borisov had described him as having fenced himself off from the people with a wall of policemen, so that he only saw the people through his car windows when he drove somewhere. So Ponomaryov has turned out to be rather touchy—he doesn't like it when people criticize him.

In May of this year, Vladimir Borisov, a worker, though a philologist by education, was searched, and then forcibly interned in the Vladimir city psychiatric hospital. After some time, leaflets appeared in the town describing the Union of Independent Youth and the fate of its president. This publicity had some effect. One of the Union's organizers was summoned to the City Executive Committee where he had a fairly peaceable discussion about the Union. Borisov's friends were allowed to visit him in hospital. During these visits they discovered that Borisov was being given some potent injections, although he had been put in hospital 'for investigation'. The hospital administration took fright when they learned that this had become known, and promised to release Borisov on June 30th. The *Chronicle* has no information on whether this promise was kept.

Due to the pressure of public opinion Vladimir Borisov, of the 9 town of Vladimir, was released from a psychiatric hospital at the beginning of July. His stay there was officially recorded as being for a medical examination on behalf of the military recruitment centre. Borisov has been declared healthy.

No. 10 expanded on this episode:

On May 31st, 1969, police-lieutenant Shary, accompanied by a 10 citizen in plain clothes, came to Vladimir Borisov's flat in the town of Vladimir, and, declaring that he had to report to the military recruitment centre, escorted him to a psychiatric hospital. The head of Department 9 of the hospital, Yu. A. Sokolov, gave Borisov injections of Aminazin by force, and reduced him to a state of shock. After he came out of hospital, Vladimir Borisov was summoned to V. I. Buzin at the K.G.B., who said: 'Stop thinking, or we'll put you away in prison.' A month after this threat Borisov was arrested.

11 The legal 'Union of Independent Youth' ... has now been dispersed. Its leader V. Borisov was arrested, and now, after two months' detention, he has been sent for psychiatric diagnosis so that he may then be confined in a psychiatric hospital prison.

Later the Chronicle *reported tersely: 'The diagnostic team decided that Borisov was of unsound mind. On May 19th, 1970, Vladimir Borisov hanged himself in the hospital wing of [Moscow's] Butyrka prison.'*[72]

ELEKTROSTAL

Moving into Moscow Region from the east, we reach a town where the Chronicle's *correspondence network did not prove able to clarify this single report:*

6 At the end of 1968 Bogdanov, a worker from Elektrostal, was sentenced under article 64 of the Russian Criminal Code, i.e. for 'betraying the fatherland'. From the extremely slender evidence available it seems that Bogdanov was drunk and got into conversation with some foreigners near one of the foreign embassies. He was photographed during the conversation and arrested immediately afterwards. The *Chronicle* hopes to provide fuller and more exact details later.

PUSHCHINO-on-the-OKA

Now we move round to the south of Moscow and enter an area well known for its high concentration of scientific research institutes. Near to the big centre of Serpukhov lies a small town on the River Oka called Pushchino. It was here that this indecisive but fascinating episode occurred:

8 At the end of May 1969 the decision was taken at a party meeting in the Academy of Sciences Institute of Biophysics to petition the Institute authorities for the dismissal of Abakumov and Dionisiyev from the Institute. The charge of political unreliability levelled at them was based on letters written by the inhabitants of certain [Siberian] villages on the River Enisei, where Abakumov and Dionisiyev had spent their holiday in the

summer of 1968. In the opinion of the letter-writers, Abakumov and Dionisiyev had held politically uninhibited conversations verging on anti-Soviet agitation. Their political unreliability was shown in particular by the fact that they had been listening to tape-recordings of the songs of Yuly Kim.[73] After the K.G.B.'s district office in Serpukhov had investigated the 'Abakumov and Dionisiyev affair' for over half a year, it handed the materials over to the Institute of Biophysics for internal handling.

The [Institute] participants in the party meeting offered friendly criticism of Abakumov's and Dionisiyev's conduct, but did not conclude that any change should be made in their status: the petition for their dismissal was added to the resolution at the suggestion of representatives of the district party committee.

The party meeting had been preceded by a meeting of the Institute's party activists, and by a session of the Academic Council where the affair was discussed in detail. Most of those who spoke at the activists' meeting were sharply critical of Abakumov and Dionisiyev, but no unanimous condemnation was forthcoming. Dubrovin, as the relevant laboratory head, reported favourably on Abakumov's and Dionisiyev's work and character. There were several speeches in defence of 'the accused'. These speakers were particularly indignant that Abakumov and Dionisiyev had not been invited to the activists' meeting. This is the explanation they were given in reply: 'Why are they needed here? All the circumstances of the case are clear as it is.' The head of one of the Institute laboratories, B. N. Veprintsev, called for caution in deciding such matters. He recalled the public condemnations of dissenters during Stalin's time, and the consequences of these.

At the session of the Academic Council, the Chairman L. P. Kayushin[74] informed his listeners that 'a crime has been committed by members of the Institute', and called upon the members of the Council to condemn them unanimously at a general meeting. Many of those who spoke sharply condemned Abakumov and Dionisiyev. B. N. Veprintsev protested against the idea of organizing such a meeting, and against carrying the campaign of censure any further. E. A. Liberman[75] declared that only a court could determine what was a crime according

to the law, and if his colleagues had been listening to songs—
well, that was their own private affair. Corresponding Member
of the Academy of Sciences Tikhomirov[76] declared that Soviet
scientists ought to feel gratitude to the government 'which
feeds them'. He said that he was surprised at some of the
speeches of those present, who were in effect justifying the
conduct of Abakumov and Dionisiyev. In his opinion, certain
intellectuals liked playing the liberal, and then, when they
went abroad, they 'behave badly there'. Liberman stressed
that he did not know any facts about the 'bad behaviour' of
'liberals' abroad. But the sort of people who liked making
demagogic speeches over here, such as Tikhomirov, whom they
had just heard, tended very often not to come back at all from
abroad. With this altercation between Tikhomirov and
Liberman the session of the Academic Council ended.

There is reason to believe that the 'letters from people resident
beside the Enisei' were organized by the local K.G.B. organs
there, who had followed the itinerary of Abakumov and Dionisiyev. This 'excursion' on the part of the K.G.B. detectives was
evidently occasioned by a private conversation Abakumov and
Dionisiyev had had with a local party worker whom they
happened to meet.

A footnote about the Stalin period was later added to this story:

10 The *Chronicle* has received some information on the role
Veprintsev played at that time.

Boris Nikolayevich Veprintsev was born in 1928. He is a
biologist, and recorded the famous set of gramophone records
'The Voices of Birds in their Natural Setting'.[77]

From January 1948 onwards Veprintsev was a secret
collaborator of the M.G.B. [the secret police]. He immediately
became active as a provocateur. This is confirmed by documentary evidence from the materials of the rehabilitation case
of a group of Moscow students who were arrested in 1950–51
as a result of Veprintsev's provocations. Veprintsev's success as
a provocateur was helped by his own anti-Stalinist views and
liberal statements, and also by the reputation he built for himself as a man who had suffered—his father had been imprisoned in the 'thirties.

In 1951 Veprintsev was arrested, thanks to the testimony of people who had suffered repressions as a result of his denunciations. In prison and in the camps Veprintsev continued to inform on his cellmates and fellow-prisoners.

OBNINSK

A little further west, and only fifty-odd miles from Moscow, lies Obninsk. Closed to foreigners, it is a centre for a vast colony of research scientists. In 1954 the first Soviet nuclear power station was built here. In 1965 Alexander Solzhenitsyn — a mathematician as well as a writer — bought an old cottage in the woods nearby. His wife, a chemist, had been elected to a research post at an Obninsk institute, only to be banned from taking it up by the authorities.[78] In the next years, as the censorship tightened and the Democratic Movement came into existence, a certain ferment clearly began to show among the privileged class of scientists which dominates the town. In September 1968 the paper Soviet Russia[79] *claimed that 'hostile plots' had been uncovered there, declaring: 'Certain people in Obninsk are allowed to spread non-communist ideas with impunity.' Moreover, no official political lectures had been given at the Scientists' Club for a long time. A leader of this club, whom we have met already, was Valery Pavlinchuk. Here the* Chronicle *writes of him and of various reprisals in Obninsk:*

Valery Alekseyevich Pavlinchuk was born in 1938, graduated 5 in physics at the Sverdlovsk Polytechnic Institute and then worked in the High-Energy Physics Institute at Obninsk, first as a senior laboratory assistant and then as a junior research officer. At the same time, he was taking an external degree at the Institute. He had been elected a member of the Council of the Scientists' Club, and helped, as an editor and translator, in bringing out the book *Physicists Joking*.[80]

[In spring 1968] he was expelled from the party for his *samizdat* 2 activities by the town party committee. The Kaluga regional committee then added to the reasons for his expulsion his signature to the letter of the 170 [see p. 77]. He was then deprived of his security pass and dismissed 'in connection with a reduction in staff'. The party organization of the department where Pavlinchuk had been a party organizer [and 'secretary of the party bureau' — No. 5] opposed the decision of the town committee as being a breach of the party rules, and in consequence it was dissolved.

5 The local press had written favourably about Pavlinchuk's work as a party member.

The sudden death of Pavlinchuk was reported in the third issue of the *Chronicle* [see p. 96]. Some details about the aftermath of his funeral in Obninsk have become available. Despite the fact that none of the people who spoke at his funeral went out of their way to mention the political side of his activity, those who came to honour his memory were nevertheless subjected to party and administrative sanctions. This was done on the initiative of the newly appointed Obninsk party secretary, Novikov, and the First Secretary of the Kaluga Regional Committee, Kondratenkov.

[In particular:]

R. Toshinsky, physicist, Master of Physical-Mathematical Sciences, has received a party reprimand.

R. Levit, economist, has been expelled from the party and sacked 'at his own request'. It was also held against Levit that he had once taken part in the publication of the well-known collection *Pages from Tarusa*.[81]

M. Yu. Lokhvitsky,[82] editor of the local newspaper, has been expelled from the party and dismissed from his post.

All these three were members of the Obninsk Town Party Committee. They were held responsible, in particular, for the presence at Pavlinchuk's funeral of the 'anti-Sovietists', Litvinov and Larissa Bogoraz.

Unjustified reprisals were also taken against Pavlinchuk's friend, A. G. Vasilev, head of a laboratory in the local branch of the Karpov Institute of Physical Chemistry. A. Vasilev is the author of fifty published works on physics. At the moment he has found work as a sanitary technician in the housing department of Obninsk. This happened after a session of the standing rules committee, headed by the branch director of the Institute, Nazarov, had passed a decision to deprive Vasilev of his permit for secret work. He was also, incidentally, accused of once having invited to the Scientists' Club (as a member of its council) the writers V. Kaverin [see p. 336] and A. Sharov, who, allegedly, gave anti-Soviet talks there.[83]

The sad Pavlinchuk saga was finally rounded off with this tragi-comic footnote:

The book *Physicists Continue Joking*[84] was delivered to the book- 6 shop at Obninsk in February 1969. One of the members of the editorial committee of this book was the late Valery Pavlinchuk. The first secretary of the town's party committee immediately appeared in the bookshop and forbade the sale of the book. When the manageress said she would complain to Kaluga, he replied: 'Complain wherever you want, but you won't sell it here.'

A prominent figure in Obninsk, whom we also met earlier, defending his friend Solzhenitsyn, was first mentioned by the Chronicle *in early 1969:*

At the Institute of Medical Radiology of the Academy of 6 Medical Sciences in Obninsk Zhores Medvedev [see plate 68], a Master of Biological Sciences, author of the well-known book *The Personality Cult of Stalin and Biological Science* and a member of the commission supervising the publication of the works of [the biologist] N. I. Vavilov, has been dismissed from his post 'for incompatibility with the requirements of his job'. This 'incompatibility' was arranged as follows: on the instigation of the Academy an order was issued reorganizing laboratories with fewer than four workers into groups, and the laboratory headed by Zhores Medvedev, which had seven members, was reorganized into a group 'compatible' with this order. Medvedev, who had formerly filled the competitive post of head of the laboratory, was transferred to the post of acting senior research officer—'acting', because he had naturally not competed for the post. And then he was sacked for 'incompatibility'. According to some reports his dismissal was connected not only with the general offensive of the Lysenko-ites but also with the impending publication of his book in an English translation in the United States.[85]

Although only forty-six, Medvedev had by 1970 published several books and over a hundred scholarly articles. Apart from his exposé of Lysenkoism mentioned above, two others of his books have not appeared in the

U.S.S.R.: Secrecy of Correspondence is Guaranteed by Law *and* The International Collaboration of Scholars and National Frontiers.[86] *The latter is summarized in No. 12, with this comment: 'Medvedev demonstrates in his new book the harm done to the country by the artificial isolation of our scientists from the scholarly world abroad.'*

In May–June 1970 the well-known episode of Medvedev's forcible confinement in the Kaluga Psychiatric Hospital occurred. But the K.G.B. had miscalculated. The protests of the scientific world both at home and abroad were so vociferous that after three weeks he had to be released.[87] In October, moreover, after nearly two years of being barred from any job, he landed one in the protein laboratory of the Institute for the Physiology and Biochemistry of Farm Animals, some twenty miles from Obninsk. Thus with his courage, sense of humour and immense popularity in the scientific community, he had—for the moment at least —won through.

MOSCOW

Finally, back to Moscow for two items unrelated to other chapters. The first shows a defence lawyer acting—in 1969—in Stalin-era fashion:

8 On June 20th the trial of Sergei Sarychev, a research fellow at the Institute of Oriental Studies,[88] took place in Moscow. He was sentenced to two and a half years in hard-régime camps, under article 206, para. 2—malicious hooliganism. The essence of the charge was 'flagrant violation of public order', in that Sarychev, having been detained in a state of intoxication in the Metropol restaurant, uttered 'hostile political statements' in a police room. The only witnesses of the affair were three policemen. The attitude of defence lawyer Korostylev to the case is surprising. He supported the Procurator's application for the case to be given a closed hearing; in his speech for the defence he regarded Sarychev's guilt as proved, and he approved the classification of his actions under article 206, para. 2, only requesting mitigation of the sentence in view of the absence of any previous convictions. The same lawyer Korostylev acted as defence for P. G. Grigorenko at his trial in 1964, when the decision was made to intern him in a psychiatric hospital, and did not once dispute either the medical diagnosis or the views of the prosecution.

The second item records an attempt to revive a dissenters' tradition of the period 1960–61:

On April 14th, 1969 – the anniversary of Vladimir Maya- 7
kovsky's death[89] some young people gathered in Mayakovsky
Square by the poet's statue. They read poems by Mayakovsky
in groups round the statue. From time to time policemen and
people in plain clothes pushed their way amongst the groups,
shouting: 'Disperse! Why have you gathered here? It's not
allowed! Read poetry at home!' Then, a little later, they simply
started quietly to grab the boys reciting poems and haul them
out of the crowd. In answer to their bewildered questions, they
rudely replied: 'Read Mayakovsky at home! It's forbidden to
form groups!' – 'Forbidden by whom?' – 'We know by whom!'
In one of the groups a youth was reading an extract from
[Mayakovsky's] poem 'Vladimir Ilich Lenin'. At the words
'Lenin is even now more alive than all the living, our knowledge, strength and weapon', a policeman pounced on him,
knocked off his glasses and began twisting his arms. The indignant young people put a stop to this violence and struck up the
Internationale. A policeman continued to repeat: 'It's not
allowed! Disperse!'

When the crowd at the statue had thinned out, some plainclothes men came up to the remainder and asked them to come
to police headquarters. These people did not have vigilante
armbands, and were asked who they were. One presented his
identity card: Yury Vladimirovich Vorobyov, commander of
a Komsomol security squad of Frunze District. At the police
headquarters, reports on the actions of the detained were made
on the basis of the Moscow Soviet's resolution of June 25th,
1966, 'On meetings'. The reports state that they disrupted
public order. The reports were drawn up by the above-
mentioned Vorobyov and a member of the security squad,
Burakov.

In 1970 the Chronicle *extended its correspondence network into more
and more provincial areas. Especially interesting are the substantial
reports from Armenia,[90] Moldavia[91] and Lithuania,[92] on which
Nos. 1–11 carry virtually nothing. One of the ways the net has spread,*

we should note, is through the personal links established in the camps and developed after prisoners' release. Levitin is doubtless right in saying that in the provinces people are generally more timid than in Moscow, the authorities more tyrannical. Nevertheless, much of the Democratic Movement's strength lies in its increasingly wide geographic base. No. 17 alone, for example, carries information from some thirty different cities or towns.

Part VII · Dams

20. STALIN, STALINISTS, FASCISTS AND CENSORS

Slowly but surely the process of restoring Stalinism goes on ... The name of Stalin has been cited from the highest platforms in a wholly positive context. The papers have written about the applause which has greeted the mention of his name. The papers have not written that this was often the applause of people with a servile hunger for a strong personality, people keen to justify their own conduct in the not too distant past, or people still infected with perverted nationalistic feelings. For how long was it necessary to pervert human nature so that it could applaud the murderer of hundreds of thousands of people, the organizer of tortures and torments?

Pyotr Yakir, Ilya Gabai and Yuly Kim, February 1968[1]

Part of the courage of the Soviet democrats lies in their recognition of the strong forces ranged against them. Opposed to their own values of tolerance, compromise, rationality and humanity lie, as they well know, not only a vast battery of vested interests intent on preserving the status quo, but also anti-democratic social and political traditions which permeate both the ruling class and many of the ruled. They see that the main source of a sense of legitimacy for the ruling class, at least, is Stalin, and so they fight consistently against his rehabilitation. Part of this fight involves telling — and defending — the truth about this period of dictatorship. As additions to the feats of Solzhenitsyn, Evgenia Ginsburg and others in this respect, we may note here two samizdat *items by Zhores Medvedev's twin brother Roy (see plate 68):*

Before the Court of History.[2] This book has long been known to a narrow circle but has only recently begun to circulate widely in *samizdat*. It is a three-volume study of the life and personality of J. V. Stalin, his administration and his crimes.

Svetlana Stalin and her 'Twenty Letters to a Friend'. In analysing Svetlana Alliluyeva's book, the author[3] charges her with insincerity, and with an attempt to justify Stalin and shift the blame on to Beria and the commander of Stalin's guard, General Vlasik.[4]

417

A belles-lettres depiction of Stalinism is this one by the actor and prolific
samizdat *writer Vladimir Gusarov :*[5]

11 *My Daddy Killed M.* The hero of this tale is the only son of a
high-ranking bureaucrat in the Stalin era. He grows up in an
atmosphere of lies and hypocrisy, where every word the
Generalissimo utters is proclaimed as a divine revelation, where
people have learnt to conceal their thoughts and hide their eyes.
The hero, disillusioned with it all and ignorant of the truth,
finishes up in Stalin's mincing machine: the Lubyanka, the
Serbsky Institute, the Kazan Special Psychiatric Hospital and
the Butyrka prison; people crippled by fate; brief meetings;
frank conversations. The tone is one of irony mingled with
grief; the author mocks bitterly the absurdity of such an
inhuman existence.

*But in addition to describing and analysing Stalinism, the Democratic
Movement has also consistently concerned itself with neo-Stalinism. The
latter became particularly marked in the winter of 1965–6, drawing from
twenty-five leading scientists and intellectuals a sharp warning against
any rehabilitation of the old tyrant.*[6] *It also provoked some of the acts
which underlie this report :*

11   ARRESTS OF MOSCOW STUDENTS

On November 20th, 1969, the K.G.B. arrested Vyacheslav
Bakhmin,[7] a fourth-year student of the physics and chemistry
department of the Moscow Institute of Physics Technology.
Bakhmin is twenty-two years old, and was a pupil at the
Kolmogorov boarding school (No. 18). He entered the Institute
in 1966. A search was made in the hostel where he was living;
Bakhmin himself was not present at the time, and his friends at
the hostel were told that he had gone away on a trip. (Now,
three weeks after his arrest, the Institute authorities want to
expel Bakhmin from the Institute for failing to attend classes.)
    The next day, December 1st, searches were made simul-
taneously in six Moscow flats and two girl students were
arrested: Irina Kaplun (a third-year student of Moscow University's Philological Faculty, in the department of structural
and applied linguistics), and Olga Iofe[8] (a second-year student
[see plate 76] taking evening courses at Moscow University's

Faculty of Economics). During the search, several items of *samizdat* were removed from Iofe, and also her own poetry and papers, verses by her father Yu. M. Iofe, and a typewriter. The search was made in Iofe's presence and after it she was taken for questioning under an escort of ten men. At nine o'clock that evening a warrant for her arrest was signed.

On the same day Irina Kaplun was taken for questioning. Earlier in the day, when she was still in the university building, she had been taken ill with heart trouble and had gone home. But she never reached her house. Evidently she was picked up on the way there and sent to the K.G.B. without being taken home for a search first. The search was made while she was being interrogated. Removed from her were *samizdat* items, verses and stories by herself, a home-made anthology of poems by Evtushenko and a typewriter.

Both girls are nineteen years old. Olga Iofe studied at physics and mathematics school No. 444, and Irina Kaplun at No. 16 special language school. In 1966 both girls, with nine other pupils of No. 16 special school, all under sixteen, pasted up leaflets, the contents of which was as follows: there must be no repetition of the Stalin period, everything depends on us. About three hundred of these leaflets were pasted up or put through letter-boxes of private dwellings in various districts of Moscow. Most of them were handed over to the K.G.B. by the recipients. The main question put later to the children was: tell us the names of the adults who organized this. The investigation was conducted by Major Eliseyev. School lessons alternated with interrogation sessions which lasted from four to six hours. At the interrogations, the girls were told: 'If you think that some things in our country are not quite as they should be, then you ought to come and see us at the K.G.B. and talk it over with us.' Irina Kaplun was told that 'she ought to be thankful that her uncle had been rehabilitated at all, they might well not have done it.' (Her uncle was a revolutionary who worked in the Profintern [the international trade union organization], the Communist International, and the Central Committee; he had been in prison under the Tsar; in 1938 he was executed and in 1956 rehabilitated.)

The case was not taken to court. After completion of the investigation, the school authorities took the matter up with the children. There were interviews and heart-to-heart talks with the district committee of the Komsomol. And it was always the same question: 'Surely you can tell me who were the adults involved?' Altogether two children were expelled from the Komsomol, one from the school, and all of them were given reprimands with entries in their personal files. Two teachers were deprived of their right to teach, the school head was relieved of his post, and the class teachers were given reprimands and relieved of their duties as directors of their classes.

It is assumed that the arrest at this stage of I. Kaplun and O. Iofe is connected with a protest which they were preparing against the celebrations for the ninetieth birthday of Stalin [see pp. 424–6].

On the same day, December 1st, a fourth-year student at the Moscow State Institute of Historical Archives, Tatyana Khromova, was subjected to a search and interrogation. During the search, personal letters and a file containing poems by O. Mandelshtam were removed. They wanted to carry off her icons, and were greatly interested in where she had obtained them, but after she had begged them at length, they agreed to leave them. They were interested to know if Khromova believed in God, and why there were so many religious poems in her flat.

For Bakhmin and Irina Kaplun the subsequent outcome was not so tragic: after ten months in prison the police dropped the case against them. But the fate of Olga Iofe was appalling: an inexplicable diagnosis of schizophrenia, a trial in her absence by a kangaroo court, then dispatch to the Kazan hospital prison. [9]

Neo-Stalinism gained a new impetus in 1967 from the fiftieth anniversary of Soviet rule and from the subsequent trial of Galanskov and Ginzburg. In response, however, came strong protests from the liberal intelligentsia, notably one of March 1968 by Lydia Chukovskaya:

5 'Not Executions, but Thought and the Word'.[10] This essay was written in connection with the fifteenth anniversary of Stalin's death, and speaks of the threat of the revival of Stalinist methods of ideological repression.

Another such document, of October 1968, was Nikolai Aleksandrov's 'Our Short Memory' :[11]

This is a pamphlet about historical 'forgetfulness', which is not 5 only an insult to the memory of millions of innocent victims, but also a real threat to the future of our people.

The next flurry of samizdat items against Stalin's rehabilitation came in March–April 1969, and for a particular reason :

Pyotr Yakir: 'A Letter to the Party Central Committee and the 6 Editors of the Journal *Kommunist*.'[12] The letter was prompted by the publication in Nos. 2 and 3 of *Kommunist*[13] of an article of apologetics on J. V. Stalin. The writer of the letter enumerates the crimes of Stalin in accordance with the current Criminal Code, citing a large number of little-known facts, such as the list of women shot as wives of 'enemies of the people', and a list of twenty-two Heroes of the Soviet Union, mainly pilots, heroes of the fighting in Spain, who were shot without trial in October 1941.

These same articles also provoked a letter from Leonid Petrovsky, the historian and grandson of G. I. Petrovsky, who lost his father during the era of the Stalinist repressions.[14]

No. 7 added a third reply :

Roy Medvedev: 'Is it Possible to Rehabilitate Stalin Today? 7 An Open Letter to the Editors of *Kommunist*'.[15] This is another letter on the articles of apologetics about Stalin which have appeared in *Kommunist*.

These lengthy, scholarly and pungently argued letters soon — and predictably — provoked reprisals :

Roy Medvedev, mathematician, historian and author of a 9 three-volume work on Stalin, has been expelled from the party 'for convictions incompatible with the title of party member'. His personal dossier was examined by the Lenin District party committee, no discussion taking place in his local party cell.

8 Leonid Petrovsky, a historian and official at the Lenin Museum, expelled from the party in the winter of 1968-9 for signing a letter protesting at the conviction of the demonstrators of August 25th,[16] and author of a recent letter to the editor of the journal *Kommunist* concerning articles advocating a revival of Stalinism, has been forced to resign from his job 'at his own request'.

A different but closely related aspect of the struggle against neo-Stalinism is shown in this samizdat *item:*

9 L. Anti-Tarasov:[17] 'On Certain Articles[18] by Former K.G.B. Colonel Lev Vasilevsky'. This work[19] is devoted to exposing the attempts of former K.G.B. Colonel L. Vasilevsky to libel in print the names of [the military leaders] F. F. Raskolnikov,[20] A. Eisner and others, who were libelled under Stalin and later rehabilitated as honourable men. Vasilevsky sometimes uses his real name, and sometimes writes under the pseudonym of L. Tarasov.

Resistance to Stalinist tendencies by party members using not samizdat, *but strictly intra-party methods, proved—probably—of more limited effect. The following story shows how the party reacted to a Leningrad member who (No. 7) 'wrote a number of letters to the Central Committee about a* Pravda *article called "The K.G.B.—Fifty Years of Defending Socialist Legality",[21] about Czechoslovakia, and about the signs of the rehabilitation of Stalin':*

9 No. 7 of the *Chronicle* reported the expulsion from the party of A. V. Gusev,[22] a senior research officer at the Academy of Sciences Zoological Institute, who fought in two wars and had been a party member since 1943. Several more details of his case have now come to light. The immediate reason for starting a case against him was a letter he sent to L. I. Brezhnev on August 26th, 1968, which contained a protest against the occupation of Czechoslovakia. In the opinion of the author of the letter, the decision to invade would damage the prestige of the Soviet Union and the building of a communist society. Instead of being answered, the letter was forwarded to his local party cell. During the investigation of his case, an earlier letter Gusev had sent to A. N. Kosygin, L. I. Brezhnev and the paper

Komsomolskaya pravda, about the plundering of the natural resources of Lake Baikal, Keret [on the White Sea] and other regions of natural beauty, was also held against him. Gusev indicated here that the irreparable damage caused by these activities was the result of the irresponsible attitude of top official bodies, which were acting with impunity. From Kosygin's secretariat, and from the editor of *Komsomolskaya pravda*, he received cautious but favourable replies; but Brezhnev's secretariat forwarded the letter to his local party cell for examination. Yet another letter, concerning matters of state and public life, and intended for dispatch to A. N. Kosygin, was stolen from Gusev's office desk by a commission investigating his case, led by O. S. Khmelevskaya, an instructor from the Vasilevsky Island District party committee. Stolen with it were letters of a personal nature, and these too were brought into the case. At an Institute party meeting chaired by O. A. Skarlato,[23] on December 8th, 1968, Gusev was expelled from the party; forty people voted for his expulsion, eleven against, and there was one abstention. A party member who knew of Gusev's letter about Lake Baikal and did not report it has had a case opened against him.

In October 1969 the Chronicle's *worries about the Stalin issue became especially acute. So too, as we have seen, did those of Bakhmin, Olga Iofe and Irina Kaplun. This item explains why:*

ON THE APPROACHING STALIN ANNIVERSARY   10

December 21st, 1969, will be the ninetieth anniversary of the birth of Stalin. According to reports, a meeting of the party Central Committee has been held, at which measures to be taken in honour of the forthcoming jubilee were discussed. It was decided to mark Stalin's ninetieth anniversary with articles in *Pravda* and *Izvestia*. Articles were to be prepared simultaneously for the journals *Kommunist* and *Problems of the History of the Party*, but the question of their publication would be decided separately. The Institute of Marxism-Leninism attached to the Central Committee had prepared a four-volume anthology of selected works by Stalin, which it was planned to publish in a mass edition. The articles on Stalin were to be prepared by a group of historians headed by Academician Pospelov.

The question of whether to hold a ceremonial meeting on the occasion of Stalin's ninetieth birthday has not yet been decided, but there have been suggestions that a meeting similar to that organized by the Institute of Marxism-Leninism a few years ago to mark the anniversary of A. A. Zhdanov should be held.

Several printing-works have received orders to manufacture placards carrying a portrait of Stalin, and art-studios have orders to produce sculptures of him.

In a new exhibition at the Central Lenin Museum a special section is to be devoted to the five-year plans and the Great Patriotic War, in which Stalin is to occupy a central position.

All the measures to be taken in connection with the Stalin anniversary celebrations are being directed by the Department of Science and Educational Establishments of the Central Committee, under S. P. Trapeznikov, who as early as September 1965 declared at a meeting of heads of social science departments, that he 'constantly turns to the works of Stalin even today, to get guidance and instruction from them'. 'I think', he said, 'that many of you do exactly the same thing, only you don't speak about it.'

The name of Trapeznikov was mentioned by Academician A. D. Sakharov in his famous treatise,[24] in connection with that election of members of the U.S.S.R. Academy of Sciences at which the scholars boycotted Trapeznikov's candidature, after his name had been submitted by the Central Committee for election to the Academy.

In the event — perhaps due in part to the Chronicle *raising the alarm — the editors' worst fears were not realized. Only* Pravda *carried an anniversary article, and this — while its very appearance must have encouraged the neo-Stalinists — avoided over-fulsome praise of their hero and even included some brief criticism. The Politbureau's balancing act was plain for all to see.*

Nevertheless, a confrontation almost occurred:

11 On December 21st, 1969 (the ninetieth anniversary of Stalin's birth), a group of people well known for their uncompromising attitude towards Stalinism went out on to Red Square, among them Zinaida Mikhailovna Grigorenko, Pyotr Yakir, Anatoly Yakobson and others. Their aim was to shame the Stalinists,

who, it was rumoured, were intending to go to Red Square on that day to express their love for the murderer of millions. (Indeed, according to some reports, the Stalinists did stage something akin to a demonstration: moving towards the Lenin mausoleum in the general flow of people, they turned aside towards the Kremlin wall and placed panegyrical obituaries and flowers on Stalin's grave. This half-concealed demonstration was noticed by few people apart from the security guards.)

One of the anti-Stalinists who was on Red Square describes the occasion thus:

Even before we got to Red Square we were warned by K.G.B. men, who were following our every footstep: 'Remember, no placards.' We came out on to Red Square from the Historical Museum side. The square was cordoned off on all sides with movable metal barriers and ringed with troops and policemen. A narrow gap had been left open for the queue of people going to the mausoleum. The cordons were swarming with plainclothes security men. A colonel of the M.V.D. turned to us and said: 'Clear off, there's nothing for you to do here, you won't succeed in carrying out your schemes.' We passed GUM [the State Universal Store] and, keeping together, came up to the cordon from the direction of Execution Place [in front of St Basil's Cathedral]. We stood there, hemmed in by a crowd of K.G.B. men. Convinced that in these conditions any unauthorized activity was inconceivable, and hence that any open demonstration by the Stalinists would be impossible, we decided to leave. At that moment one of our comrades dropped on the ground a portrait of Stalin with a black cross painted over it. (We had decided to hold this portrait up above our heads as a protest, should the Stalinists appear on Red Square, as expected, with pictures of their idol.) The dropped portrait fell by A. Yakobson's feet. Yakobson was instantly seized by K.G.B. agents, bundled into a car (there were vehicles standing at the ready) and driven away.

Yakobson was taken to police station No. 47, from which he was released after six hours' detention, having been searched

14*

and interviewed by an investigator with the rank of Major. Next day Yakobson was taken from his home by an agent of the criminal investigation department to police station No. 80, and there it was suggested that he sign a fantastic record, compiled who knows when, attributing to him actions he had never committed. Yakobson did not sign the 'record'. He was searched and then sent to police station No. 6, where, after another search, he was again put in a pre-trial detention cell, this time for the night.

On December 23rd, Yakobson was tried 'for petty hooliganism' by the Lenin District People's Court, and fined on a charge of violating public order.

Had the demonstration of December 21st got out of hand, or a confrontation taken place, the anti-Stalinists knew what sort of police action to expect. The Chronicle, *clearly basing its account on an official document, had already spelt out the possibilities :*

10 For certain troop battalions of the Ministry of Internal Affairs instructions exist about how to disperse demonstrations. This requires a platoon consisting of three units of ten men each, and an armoured carrier. The instructions provide for three courses of action :

1. Two grenade throwers, grenades with a depressive gas (code-named 'Cherry Tree'); the officers have pistols loaded with ampoules of the same gas; they advance in two columns, with two officers in front, while behind them is an armoured carrier, then two columns of soldiers, each column with a grenade-thrower. The columns fan out, cutting their way through the crowd.

2. Dispersal with the help of water-cannons. A vehicle with water-cannons is used, similar to the kind used to put out oil-fires. The crowd is dispersed by streams of water cutting through its ranks.

3. Dispersal by rifle-fire. In this method, shooting at women, children or mental defectives is forbidden.

Special vehicles are permanently on duty to keep order in contingencies of this sort, i.e. to prevent mass marches and other forms of demonstrations from taking place.

THE SOVIET EICHMANNS

Understandably enough, the Democratic Movement pays attention not only to neo-Stalinists like Trapeznikov, but also to notorious surviving Stalinists, like the subject of this item:

A SHORT BIOGRAPHY OF ANDREI SVERDLOV   7

This note is based on the *samizdat* document 'About the Unusual Fate of the Family and Relations of Ya. M. Sverdlov.'

Andrei Yakovlevich Sverdlov, only son of [Lenin's comrade] Yakov Mikhailovich Sverdlov, began to work when quite young—no more than twenty—for the N.K.V.D. Here he was quickly promoted for his pathological cruelty and coarseness. To start with, he had to deal mainly with the children of party and government officials, with whom he had been at school and whom he had known well since childhood. When Khanna Ganetskaya,[25] after refusing to give evidence, saw A. Sverdlov come into the investigator's room, she rushed towards him exclaiming: 'Adik!'[26] whereupon Sverdlov let out some coarse swear-words. In Moscow there live at least seven people whom Andrei Sverdlov personally interrogated, using torture and brutality. He took part also in the investigation of Elizaveta Drabkina,[27] who from 1918–19 was secretary to Ya. M. Sverdlov. At the latter's request she took away his son Andrei and daughter Vera from his flat a few hours before his death. Andrei Sverdlov knew quite well that Drabkina had not committed the crimes with which she was charged, but nevertheless he forced 'confessions' and 'recantations' out of her.

After a short time Andrei Sverdlov was arrested. But this arrest was only a show one. The N.K.V.D. accounts department continued paying his wages, and in prison he played the role of informer, taking advantage of the confidence which his name inspired. When his activity was discovered by the prisoners, he once more donned an N.K.V.D. uniform. After the shooting of Ezhov [1938], N.K.V.D. colonel A. Ya. Sverdlov became one of the prominent people in Beria's entourage. After Stalin's death, Andrei Sverdlov took up 'scientific work' at the Institute of Marxism-Leninism. In 1956 after the 20th congress he lived through a year of hardship in the Kremlin hospital, but afterwards he again returned to the

Institute, to the department of party history. Andrei Sverdlov was one of the first to raise a hue and cry over the discussion of Nekrich's book at the Institute of Marxism-Leninism.[28] The very same day he wrote a report on this discussion's organizers and participants to the party Control Committee attached to the Central Committee and to the party committee of the Institute, slanderously asserting that 'anti-Soviet' speeches had been made during the discussion.

Andrei Sverdlov's address is: ul. Serafimovicha 2, kv. 319 (the same Government House from the rooms of which so many victims were taken). Tel. no.: at home 231–94–97, at work 181–23–25.

Seven months later, coincidentally or otherwise, Andrei Sverdlov was dead: an obituary praising his work in the N.K.V.D. and the Institute of Marxism-Leninism appeared in the paper Soviet Russia.[29]

In any case, 1969 saw the birth of a new samizdat *bulletin,* Crime and Punishment, *about whose issue No. 3*[30] *the following summary appeared*:

9 The *Chronicle* is not in possession of any other issues. This publication is devoted to uncovering the crimes of the butchers of Stalin's time. It tells of the butchers, the sadists, the informers and those who committed crimes against humanity, where they are now and what they are doing. The 'monster-investigator' Stolbunsky[31] – he was described thus in the memoirs of Army general A. V. Gorbatov *Years and Wars*[32] – is living in Moscow and receives a high pension. Former commander of the Georgian N.K.V.D., Nadaraya,[33] whose speciality was supplying women and girls for Stalin and Beria, was sentenced to ten years, released in 1965, and now lives in Georgia. Retired K.G.B. colonel Monakhov now lives in a well-appointed country house outside Leningrad. At the beginning of the Soviet–Finnish war, an extermination brigade led by him annihilated several hundred foreign communists in the Solovki camps. They were lined up in a row, and one by one their heads were pierced through with lead-pointed sticks. When it was suggested that Monakhov should be expelled from the party, the first secretary of the Leningrad regional party committee, Tolstikov, intervened to prevent it.[34]

Alexander Vasilevich Sugak was deputy head of the Timir-yazev District K.G.B. in Moscow. In 1952 he became even more savage than usual when persecuting the Jewish doctors [who were falsely accused of plotting to poison top political leaders]. Now he resides in a villa outside Moscow, and is employed as deputy director of the Central Lenin Museum.

In 1966, Valentin Nikolayevich Astrov, writer of hundreds of denunciations, had a book published by 'Sovetsky Pisatel' — *The Steep Slope*[35] — in which he depicts — using pseudonyms — the people he previously libelled, and libels them yet again.

No. 3 of the journal also contains information about Andrei Yakovlevich Sverdlov, which will be familiar to readers of the *Chronicle*. An interesting extra detail is the information that A. Ya. Sverdlov writes detective stories for children under the pseudonym of A. Ya. Yakovlev.[36]

The only other issues listed by the Chronicle *are:*

CRIME AND PUNISHMENT NO. 5:   10
ACADEMICIANS OF CRIME

This issue contains the letter of the Marxist philosopher P. I. Shabalkin [b. 1904], who died in 1964 after [earlier] spending twenty years in prison, to N. S. Khrushchev. 'The culprits specifically and directly responsible for all my misfortunes', wrote Shabalkin, 'are Mitin, M. B., and Yudin, P. F., now members of the Academy, Professor F. B. Konstantinov, also now an Academician, and V. Beresnev.' Details are given of discussions held in the Institute of Red Professors in 1931–2, and of articles denouncing the above-named persons in the journal *Under the Banner of Marxism*. All the above-mentioned philosophers, apart from Yudin, who died recently, are successfully continuing their 'academic' activities.

CRIME AND PUNISHMENT NO. 7

This issue gives a detailed account of the criminal activities of L. M. Kaganovich during the Stalinist period, with references to various documents and facts. There are the facts about Kaganovich's slanderous campaign against Bukharin, about Kaganovich's activities while he held leading posts, and about his purging and annihilation of the best officials in the Soviet hierarchy. The issue reports that Kaganovich is receiving a large pension, has an excellent flat and a country house, and enjoys medical treatment in a special polyclinic.

What — ideally — should be done with the Soviet Eichmanns, of whom thousands are still alive and of whom none have been brought to justice (except for the handful sentenced in 1953–6,[37] when the party leadership was pre-empting the political threat from Beria's police apparatus)? Perhaps the Chronicle *hints at its own view by summarizing a samizdat item called 'On the Repression of 160 Soviet Children in 1938':*

10 This material is reprinted from the newspaper *Soviet Siberia* for February 17th and 21st–24th, 1939. It covers the progress of the open sessions of the Military Tribunal at which four high-ranking officials of the N.K.V.D. and the Procuracy in Leninsk-Kuznetsky [south-central Siberia] were convicted. The accused had arrested schoolchildren in the town, including young ones, and charged them with committing the gravest counter-revolutionary crimes.[38] The accused were given sentences of five to ten years 'without loss of their electoral rights'.

SOVIET FASCISTS

Just as the Democratic Movement has gradually come into being since the mid-1960s, so too — as part of the incipient politicization of Soviet society, of the trend away from passivity in politics towards a greater amount of independent activity — has a chauvinistic, quasi-fascist tendency. This takes visible form in the officially tolerated clubs called 'Rodina' (Motherland) or 'Rossiya' (Russia).[39] Some light is thrown on the phenomenon in the following episode:

8 In January 1968 there was a cultural evening for young people at the Leningrad House of Writers. After the evening, a group of members of the literary club Rossiya, made up of V. Shcherbakov, N. Utekhin and V. Smirnov, sent a letter to the regional party committee. It was a lengthy denunciation of the evening, full of slanderous fabrications and openly anti-semitic in character. The evening was called 'a Zionist rally'. On the basis of this denunciation, and without verification of any of the facts, the deputy director of the House of Writers, A. Z.

Shagalov, and a consultant of the Leningrad branch of the Writers' Union, S. S. Tkhorzhevsky,[40] were dismissed from their posts. Furthermore, plans to publish manuscripts by several writers who participated in the evening — Iosif Brodsky,[41] Maiya Danini[42] and Yakov Gordin[43] — were cancelled. Moreover, Yakov Gordin received a reprimand from the party group committee of the Leningrad branch of the Writers' Union, for having put his signature to a letter protesting against political trials,[44] and his contracts with the publishing-houses Sovetsky Pisatel and Detskaya Literatura were annulled.

In a few cases[45] *quasi-fascism has turned into full fascism:*

THE FETISOV GROUP   7

In March or April 1968, the economist A. Fetisov and the architects M. Antonov, V. Bykov and O. Smirnov were arrested in Moscow. Accused under article 70, all four were pronounced by a psychiatric diagnosis team to be not answerable for their actions, and at present they are in special mental hospitals in Leningrad[46] and Kazan.

The ideas of Fetisov and his followers are a critique of the Soviet political, economic and social system from an extreme totalitarian and chauvinistic position. Fetisov's work presents the historical development of mankind as having taken the form of a struggle between order and chaos, chaos having been embodied in the Jewish people, who created disorder in Europe for two thousand years, until the German and Slav principles — the totalitarian régimes of Hitler and Stalin — put a stop to this chaos. Fetisov and his supporters consider these régimes to have been historically inevitable and positive phenomena. The economic programme of the group includes, in particular, the de-industrialization of the European section of the U.S.S.R., the transfer of industry and a mass deportation of workers to Siberia, and the re-establishment of a system of patriarchally run communes on the territory of European Russia. This programme was embodied in the projects of the young architects: their building designs presupposed de-urbanization and a return to the agricultural commune. One of them based his thesis on this idea, and when the academic council of the Institute of the Theory and History of Architecture voted against him being given a degree, he stated that this was because 'only Jews' were on the academic council. A. Fetisov, too, is well known for his explicit pronouncemenets against the Jews and the intelligentsia. Incidentally, in 1968, not long before his arrest, Fetisov left the party in protest against the de-Stalinization of 1956 — exactly at the time when the whole of the democratic intelligentsia felt the danger of the re-emergence of Stalinism; but to Fetisov these attempts to restore the past must have seemed feeble and inconsistent.

Fetisov's ideas make an impression upon, and gain supporters among, a variety of circles: among some sections of the technical intelligentsia who plan to establish a technocracy with the aid of cybernetics, systems theory, and so on; among that section of the Slavophile-oriented intelligentsia in the humanities, whose Slavophilism merges into chauvinism; and among people with little education [who long for simple, strong methods for transforming the world.

But whatever these ideas may be, one must not forget that four people were sentenced under article 70 for what amounts to *their views* and are now experiencing the dreadful conditions of a special mental hospital, i.e. imprisonment with enforced treatment, *for their views*. In the light of this, the document 'He did not recognize his own', now being circulated in *samizdat*, is disturbing, and on this occasion the *Chronicle* will abandon its usual practice of not passing judgment.

The document is discreditable in two respects. *Firstly*, instead of presenting anything resembling a serious criticism, the author of the document confines himself to mocking the obvious stupidity of Fetisov's ideas which could be entertained only 'in virginally pure heads as yet incapable of thinking properly'. The *Chronicle* considers that such a radical anti-democratic programme demands an equally radical, but absolutely serious, scientific criticism which could shake those of Fetisov's supporters who have been attracted by one or another side of this programme but have not realized its general direction. *Secondly*, a polemic with imprisoned people, or rather with their ideas, which continue to spread and have an influence, can be considered ethical. But to express satisfaction over the fact that the authorities have sent your intellectual opponent to 'a nut house' is immoral. This involves becoming like Fetisov himself, who considered that Sinyavsky and Daniel should have been shot. The author of 'He did not recognize his own' has not given his name, and the result of his anonymity is that the document gives the impression of expressing the views of certain circles of the democratic intelligentsia. This, it must be hoped, is not the case.

CENSORS

As a free journal intent on reporting what the official press omits or distorts, the Chronicle *naturally takes a keen interest in matters of censorship.*[47] *The latter's severity is what stimulates* samizdat *: if it relaxed,* samizdat *would doubtless decline. But the post-1965 neo-Stalinist trends have of course tightened it. These items show how it decides what may or may not be written :*

The publishing-house Politizdat has issued a book by A. **10** Romanov about the spaceship designer Sergei Pavlovich Korolyov. The book is divided chronologically into chapters: 1907–17, 1917–27, 1927–37, 1937–47, 1947–57 and 1957–66. There is no mention of the fact that Korolyov was arrested and subjected to repressive measures, nor of what became of Korolyov's immediate teachers and closest friends. The book contains a great deal of interesting information about the construction of Soviet rockets, and the names of their first constructors are mentioned—Tikhomirov, Kleimenov, Langemak and others. All these people were annihilated at the end of the 'thirties during the Stalinist repressions. Of this too there is not a word.

S. REZNIK'S «NIKOLAI VAVILOV»   **6**

The publishing-house Molodaya Gvardiya was due to bring out a book by S. Reznik, *Nikolai Vavilov*, in its series 'The Lives of Outstanding People'. In the book the role of T. D. Lysenko in the tragedy of our biological science is described objectively and in detail.[48] On December 19th, 1968, the book was passed as fit for publication. But after a phone call 'from above' the whole edition was destroyed.

Nikolai Vavilov [...] is being reset. Even in its previous form the **7** publishers had cut out everything about the arrest and death of

N. I. Vavilov, but the book still contained an account of the debate with the Lysenko-ites. One may assume that the new cuts made concern precisely this theme.

10 *Nikolai Vavilov* [...] went on sale in the early autumn [of 1969]. It is a biography of the greatest Soviet horticulturalist and geneticist, who was arrested in 1940 and died of hunger in Saratov prison in 1943. It is said that during his years in prison N. I. Vavilov wrote a large scientific work, and that they burned the manuscript before his very eyes. The arrest and death of N. I. Vavilov are described in the book thus:

> On August 1st Vavilov and his companions left Lvov for Chernovtsy [in the south-west Ukraine]. On August 3rd and 4th they toured experimental stations in the region of Chernovtsy, collecting samples of crops, and studying the research being carried out. On August 5th, writes F. Kh. Bakhteyev, Vavilov spent the whole day 'visiting the university, meeting the few teachers who were still there, and its research workers, getting to know the museums, the Botanical Gardens and the town'. In the evening Vavilov gathered together the local specialists for a meeting, and asked them to help the expedition. They decided without further ado to set out next morning for the Carpathian mountains in the direction of Putila. 'There were many people who wanted to participate in the expedition,' recalls F. Kh. Bakhteyev. 'Two extra cars were added to Nikolai Ivanovich's, but even so there was one man without a seat. On N.I.'s advice, I had to drop out of the expedition in favour of one of the guests who had been at the meeting.' V. S. Lekhnovich recounts how the road to the Carpathians was covered with sharp pebbles and the cars had very old and worn tyres. They had one puncture after another. The car in which Lekhnovich was travelling was particularly unlucky. It fell a long way behind the others, and when they had used all their spare inner tubes, the driver turned back ... That was the last journey of Academician N. I. Vavilov. Two and a half years later he was no more ... Nikolai Vavilov's trip to the west Ukraine turned out to have been extremely productive, as were all

his expeditions. While sorting the contents of Vavilov's rucksack, F. Kh. Bakhteyev came across—among other things—samples of an ancient type of German wheat which, according to Vavilov's hypothesis, needed to be looked for in the Carpathian foothills, and whose existence the local scientists had never suspected.

At the end of the book there is a list of the 'Main dates in the life and work of N. I. Vavilov', and this is how his last years are described:

'July–August 1940: expedition to the west Ukraine. August 6th—F. Kh. Bakhteyev found in Vavilov's rucksack the last of the varieties of wheat he discovered. May 1942—elected Fellow of the Royal Society, London. 1943, January 26th—died at the age of fifty-five.'

Apart from giving other examples of this type of censorship,[49] *the* Chronicle *also shows an official going one step further, and trying actually to dictate to writers what they should write about:*

At a meeting of the board of the Lvov branch of the Writers' 8 Union, a propagandist of the Lvov Regional Party Committee, Podolchak, expressed his annoyance and alarm at the failure of the board to define the subjects which its writers should treat, and at its lack of control over what they were writing: why had all the writers become addicted to history instead of writing about present-day reality? He was also angered that a non-party critic should 'dare to point the way' to a poet who was a party member.

Another form of censorship is the prevention of people from reading certain publications. The following report of 1969 sheds some light on one of the mechanisms for achieving this:

This spring in Leningrad two graduate students of history at the 10 Herzen Pedagogical Institute were arrested for 'divulging material from the special collection'. The special collection is the department in a library where restricted books are kept and issued only on the application of scientific or other bodies. One of the students was writing a thesis on 'The Gnoseological Roots of Fascism', and he had been telling his acquaintances about the contents of the books he had been reading in the special collection. The names of these students, and their fate, are unknown.

ANATOLY KUZNETSOV

Both library censorship and the wider themes of this last chapter are well illustrated in the Chronicle's *coverage of a Soviet writer who decided to remain in Britain in July 1969.*

9 On August 7th a search was made in Tula [south of Moscow] of the flat of Anatoly Kuznetsov, the writer who has emigrated. The search[50] was carried out by Lieutenant-Colonel Zaitsev, head of the K.G.B. investigation department, and K.G.B. men Lieutenant Derevyanko and First Lieutenant Bychkov. The writer's wife Irina Marchenko and his private secretary Nadezhda Tsurkan were present during the search. Fifteen hundred pages of manuscript were removed, together with 22 photographic films, 14 tapes, and 168 letters, including letters from the Crimean Tatars asking Kuznetsov to appear as their public defence spokesman at the trial [of July–August— see pp. 257–62], and letters from Alexander Solzhenitsyn, Jan Prochazka, Alan Sillitoe, Graham Greene, and others. Among the manuscripts removed were early versions of Kuznetsov's novel *Baby Yar*. A search was also made of his private secretary's room. This was illegal, since no separate warrant was produced. Some *samizdat* was taken from her.

The next item reveals what sort of people are employed to shadow 'unreliable' Soviet citizens on foreign trips :

9 A certain Gogi Andzhaparidze went to London with Kuznetsov as his 'escort'. This young man persistently moved in 'liberal' circles, and was even a freelance reviewer for the journal *Novy mir*[51]—at least that is what he liked to claim.

He was expelled from the Faculty of Mathematical Linguistics at Moscow State University for his lack of aptitude, having failed several attempts to pass the mathematics examination set by the lecturer Shikhanovich. In the spring of last year, after Shikhanovich had signed the mathematicians' letter in support of Volpin, Gogi Andzhaparidze was the organizer of a 'students' declaration' demanding the dismissal of Shikhanovich as an unfair examiner.[52]

Finally, the neo-Stalinist essence of the Brezhnev–Kosygin régime — which still feels the need, at great cost, to turn a person who emigrates into an unperson — shows vividly in these paragraphs:

The Ministry of Culture has sent an order to libraries not to 9 issue the works of Anatoly Kuznetsov. Readers are being told that the books are on loan, but meanwhile Kuznetsov's name is disappearing from the catalogues. In the Lenin Library [in Moscow], for instance, all the cards for Kuznetsov's books have already been removed from the readers' catalogue.

At the end of August, No. 7 of the journal *Yunost* appeared in 10 'Soyuzpechat' kiosks. When it was first put on sale and went out to subscribers, the list of members of the editorial board on the back cover included the name A. V. Kuznetsov. After Anatoly Kuznetsov asked for political asylum in London, the remaining copies of the 2-million edition were sent back to the printers, and the back cover, reprinted without Kuznetsov's name, was substituted in all the unsold copies.

CONCLUSION

Throughout 1970 the slow but steady polarization between reactionary régime and Democratic Movement—begun in 1966—continued. A steady succession of political trials on the one hand, an impressive development of independent activities, especially samizdat, *on the other. Enormous physical strength on the one side, tremendous moral strength on the other.*

Where, then, if anywhere, was the strain beginning to show? In the régime ranks a liberal wing could hardly be seen, while, on the right, chauvinist and Stalinist elements seemed increasingly impatient with the indecisive policies of the leadership. Among dissenters the great majority continued to believe, however grim the immediate prospect, in the need for reformism, and for the civic education of the people—or at least the intelligentsia—through the media of samizdat *and the foreign radio-stations, while a tiny, more impatient minority showed signs of taking to underground conspiracy.*

Meanwhile, the Chronicle *maintained its strength, recording the confrontation with integrity, guiding discreetly its own 'side', and digging itself in for what would clearly be a long campaign.*

NOTES

The following abbreviations have been used:

NRS—Novoye Russkoye Slovo (New Russian Word), a daily paper edited at 243 West 56th Street, New York, N.Y. 10019.

RM—Russkaya Mysl (Russian Thought), a weekly paper edited at 91 rue du Faubourg Saint-Denis, Paris 10.

Vestnik RSKhD—Vestnik Russkogo Studencheskogo Khristianskogo Dvizheniya (Herald of the Russian Student Christian Movement), a quarterly edited at 91 rue Olivier de Serre, Paris 15.

Possev I—Possev: Pervyi spetsialnyi vypusk (Possev: First Special Issue), August 1969. Contains texts of *Chronicle* Nos. 1–6.

Possev II–VIII—Succeeding Special Issues: II (December 1969) contains *Chronicles* 7–9, III (April 1970) has 10–11, IV (June 1970) has 12–13, V (November 1970) has 14, VI (February 1971) has 15–16, VII (March 1971) has exclusively Jewish material, and VIII (June 1971) has 17–18. This publication is an irregular supplement to the monthly journal *Possev*, and is published by Possev-Verlag, D623 Frankfurt/M 80, Flurscheideweg 15, West Germany.

NZh—Novyi Zhurnal, a quarterly edited at 2700 Broadway, New York, N.Y. 10025.

PoC—Problems of Communism, bi-monthly, Washington, D.C.

As regards the English texts of the *Chronicle* from No. 12 on, the editor hopes to publish them in a future volume. Meanwhile, English texts of No. 16 on are available as individual booklets from Amnesty International Publications, Turnagain Lane, Farringdon Street, London E.C.4. These booklets are referred to below as 'Amnesty edition'.

INTRODUCTION (pp.15–40)

1. A. I. Herzen, *Selected Philosophical Works* (Moscow, 1956), p.561.
2. See p.53.
3. *Survey*, London, 74–5 (1970), p.111. Russian text in *Possev* IV, p.41.
4. See his essay, *Will the Soviet Union Survive Until 1984?* (Allen Lane, The Penguin Press, London, 1970).
5. The following frank passage by a high Soviet official has general relevance:
'Before me are issues of several provincial papers published on the same day. Above all one is struck by the papers' remarkable similarity. Like twins they can

hardly be distinguished from one another. If it were not for the masthead ... any one of the papers could be substituted for another and neither the reader nor the staff themselves would notice.' (M. Strepukhov in *Kommunist* 6 (1955), p.95.)

6. English versions of some of the poetry in these journals appear in K. Bosley (trans.), *Russia's Other Poets* (Longmans, London, 1968). The Russian texts of the journals are in *Grani*, Frankfurt, 52, 58, 59, 63, 64, 65, 67, 68, 69, 70, 75.

7. See Priscilla Johnson and Leopold Labedz, *Khrushchev and the Arts* (M.I.T. Press, Cambridge, Mass., 1965).

8. S. G. Bannikov and N. F. Chistyakov, appointed in October 1967.

9. The word may have existed in very narrow circles a little earlier. See a statement by Olga Kislina in *Possev* IV, p.56. In general, see an interesting article on *samizdat*'s evolution by L. Sergeyeva in *Possev* 10 (1969), pp.38–47.

10 See *Molodoi Kommunist* 1 (1969), p.59. See other mentions of the word in *Oktyabr* 1 (1969), p. 62, and in the *Literary Gazette* 5 (1970), p.4 (article by M. Alekseyev).

11. The Stalinist writer Vsevolod Kochetov, in his novel *What is it You Want, Then?*, based largely on real persons, describes a Moscow woman intellectual who 'listened to radio broadcasts from dozens of different countries' and obtained lots of foreign newspapers. 'She took down radio broadcasts in shorthand and carefully filed newspaper cuttings according to subject ... Scientists, specialists in literature and experts in international affairs needed this information ... Her address was confided only to the most trustworthy, reliable people ... At her place you could find shorthand records of, for example, confidential meetings of the Writers' Union ... the records of certain trials and even of conversations with people in top party circles.' See *Oktyabr* 11 (1969), p.125.

12. Letter of August 27th, 1888, quoted in Ronald Hingley, *Russian Writers and Society* (Hutchinson, London, 1967), p.238.

13. This analysis is based in part on the findings of A. Amalrik in his essay - see note 4.

14. See *Chronicle* 15, *Possev* VI, pp.8–10.

15. Russian text in *Possev* 4 (1968), pp.16–17.

16. See note 4.

17. See pp.213, 347, 84, and *Chronicle* 12, *Possev* IV, pp.11–12, which describes Fyodorov's case and a (separate?) one involving five Leningrad officials, one of them a senior procuracy investigator. Fyodorov received six years, the others from three to six years each.

18. See pp.92, 140 and *Chronicle* 12, *Possev* IV, pp.14–16.

19. See, respectively, pp.225 and 381, and *Possev* 8 (1970), p.5 (English text in *Survey* 77 [1970], p.145).

20. Stepniak, *Russia under the Tsars* (Ward and Downey, London, 1885), vol. II, p.285. Quoted in an as yet unpublished paper by Dr Barry Hollingsworth of Manchester University, 'The Society of Friends of Russian Freedom: English Liberals and Russian Socialists, 1890–1917'. I am much indebted to this paper.

21. Stepniak, *op. cit.*, vol. II, p. 69. Quoted in V. Moroz's brilliant essay, 'A Report from the Beria Reservation', in Michael Browne (ed.), *Ferment in the Ukraine* (Macmillan, London, 1971), p.140.

CHAPTER 1: THE *CHRONICLE* ABOUT ITSELF (pp.53–9)

1. The article appeared in *Vechernii Leningrad*, November 29th, 1963. On the Brodsky affair of 1963–4 see Victor Frank's note in *Encounter* (November 1964), pp.93–5, the abbreviated transcript of the trial in ibid. (September 1964), pp.84–91, the full transcript in Russian in R. N. Grynberg (ed.), *Vozdushnye puti—Almanakh IV* (Grynberg, New York, 1965), pp.279–303, and the intro-

duction by Georgy Stukov to Iosif Brodsky, *Stikhotvoreniya i poemy* (Inter-Language Literary Associates, New York, 1965).

2. No. 10 of the *Chronicle* later reported this item on the same case: 'Konstantin Azadovsky, son of the professor and folklore expert Mark Azadovsky who was imprisoned during the Stalin period, a teacher at the Herzen Pedagogical Institute in Leningrad, a specialist in German studies, a translator of Rilke and other German and Spanish poets, has been prevented from defending his thesis and dismissed from his job "for amoral conduct"—in reality, for his refusal to give testimony useful to the investigating organs in the Slavinsky case.'

3. Quite possibly the same journal as the monthly *Political Diary*. This began to appear in 1964, and some copies reached the West in 1971.

CHAPTER 2: THE CASE OF SINYAVSKY AND DANIEL (pp.61–71)

1. L. Labedz and M. Hayward (eds.), *On Trial: the Case of Sinyavsky (Tertz) and Daniel (Arzhak)* (Collins/Harvill, London, 1967), p.7.

2. A. Ginzburg, *Belaya kniga po delu A. Sinyavskogo i Yu. Danielya* (Possev-Verlag, Frankfurt, 1967). Most of the material here is in English in the book referred to in note 1, which, however, also contains additional material by Westerners which is not in Ginzburg's book.

3. An engineer, he also wrote a protest about the Galanskov-Ginzburg trial. Its Russian text is in *NRS*, October 24th, 1968, also P. Litvinov's *The Trial of the Four*, document IV–12. See Chap. 3, note 6.

4. See English translation in Labedz and Hayward, op. cit., pp.89–96.

5. No. 1 reported that 'It was recently suggested to Andrei Sinyavsky (Mordovskaya A.S.S.R., st. Potma, p/o Yavas, p/ya 385/11) that he should petition for clemency. Sinyavsky refused.' No. 2 corrected the timing of this: 'In some copies of the first number there was an unconfirmed report that Andrei Sinyavsky was recently asked if he would like to sign a plea for clemency. In fact this rumour was based on a suggestion made to him last year [1967] and not repeated since.' At the end of 1969 the writer Alexander Petrov-Agatov reported that he had met Sinyavsky in camp 11: 'He is a splendid Christian, a man of high culture and broad intellect, an honest citizen of his fatherland, a talented man of letters.' See *Possev* 6 (1970), p.11.

6. Russian text in *Grani* 77 (1970), pp.4–14.

7. Pall Mall, London, 1969, chapter 'Yuli Daniel', also pp.411–14.

8. A *samizdat* journal put out by a Leningrad group—the Union of Communards—in 1965. On other members of the group see p.455. In all, nine people were arrested, and Ronkin and Sergei Khakhayev, both chemical engineers, were the group's leaders. *The Bell* carried the epigraph 'From the dictatorship of the bureaucracy to the dictatorship of the proletariat'. Russian text of two numbers published in *Possev* 24 (1967), 4 (1968), pp.57–8, and 1 (1968), pp.11–13. English text in P. Reddaway's forthcoming book *Russia's Other Intellectuals* (Longmans, London). On Ronkin and Khakhayev see Galanskov's moving words in *Possev* 7 (1970), pp.31–4, also *Grani* 80 (1971), pp.157–60.

9. See the documents by her in *Atlas*, New York (December 1967), pp.22–6, and in C. R. Hill (ed.), *Rights and Wrongs: Some Essays on Human Rights* (Penguin, Harmondsworth, 1969), pp.108–10. For the Russian text of the latter document see *RM*, November 2nd, 1967.

10. English text in *The Times*, London, January 17th, 1970. Russian text in *Possev* 1 (1970), pp.15–16.

11. For the text of this and of the different articles see Pavel Litvinov, *The Demonstration on Pushkin Square* (Collins/Harvill, London, 1969), pp.15–16, 118.

12. Under the title *Pravosudiye ili rasprava? Delo o demonstratsii na Pushkinskoi ploshchadi 22 yanvarya 1967 goda.*

13. Litvinov, op. cit., pp.120–24.

14. *Possev* IV, p.18.

15. See his miniature stories in Michael Scammell (ed.), *Russia's Other Writers* (Longmans, London, 1970), Russian text in *Grani* 65 (1967).

16. See shortened text in No. 14, *Possev* V, p.9.

17. See full text in *Survey* 77 (1970), pp.139–45. Bukovsky also gave a newspaper interview to an A.P. correspondent, Holger Jensen, whose write-up was widely published. See, e.g., the *Daily Telegraph*, London, May 22nd, 1970.

18. His arrest was announced in No. 2, which included details not in No. 8: 'It is said that works by Sinyavsky and Daniel, a stenographic record of their trial, *Untimely Thoughts* by [Maxim] Gorky, and words by Tsvetayeva, Platonov, Kipling, Joyce and others were found in his flat.' No. 5 wrote that the investigation was 'nearing completion'.

19. For a bibliography of the two authors' works in English and Russian see Labedz and Hayward, op. cit., pp.382–4.

20. This fascinatingly detailed record appears with a letter of late May 1968 by Burmistrovich's wife Olga Kislina, in *Possev* IV, pp.43–61.

21. Amnesty edition pp.84.

22. *Chronicle* 11 indicates Omsk, but this was corrected to Odessa in No. 12.

23. See also, for 1970, *Chronicle* 17, Amnesty edition pp.81–2.

24. For neglected documents on this demonstration see Ginzburg, op. cit., pp.61–3.

CHAPTER 3: THE GALANSKOV–GINZBURG TRIAL (pp.72–94)

1. For some documents of his of 1961 see *RM*, April 25th, 1968, translated in P. Reddaway's forthcoming *Russia's Other Intellectuals* (Longman's, London, 1972). In 1965 he staged a one-man demonstration outside the U.S. Embassy in Moscow, in protest against the American intervention in the Dominican Republic.

2. In Russian, Narodno-Trudovoi Soyuz, full English name, Popular Labour Alliance of Russian Solidarists. Founded in 1930, the N.T.S. profited from the German occupation of the western U.S.S.R. in 1941–4 to spread propaganda there, and clearly a few of its members had pro-Nazi tendencies. Its 'third force' line of 'neither Stalin nor Hitler' eventually led, however, to most of its leaders being interned in German camps. Now based in Frankfurt, it appears— despite its tiny size and evidently very limited resources—to be considerably the most troublesome of the émigré groups from the K.G.B. viewpoint. This is probably because of its excellent channels for bringing news and manuscripts out of the Soviet Union and its generally responsible publication of these materials in the political monthly *Possev* and the literary-political quarterly *Grani*, both of which it effectively controls. Its ideology of solidarism—strongly oriented to Christianity—owes much to the philosopher Berdyayev, and stands ideally for a political democracy, the rule of law and a mixed, partially socialist, economy. All this is to be achieved in Russia after an inevitable revolution has removed the communists, the latter being seen as certain not to yield power voluntarily. The N.T.S. shows a tendency towards Russian nationalism and a lack of concern for the non-Russian peoples of the U.S.S.R.

3. On its reaction to the Soviet press attacks see, e.g. *Possev* 2 (1968), pp.22–4; 3 (1968), pp.22–3; 9 (1968), pp.15–18. See also *Possev* 4 (1968), pp.11–14.

4. No. 5: 'The main letters on this trial were listed in the first issue of the *Chronicle*. Apart from these, there are *samizdat* versions of the speeches by the defence

lawyers B. A. Zolotukhin and D. I. Kaminskaya, as well as of the final pleas of the defendants Alexander Ginzburg and Yury Galanskov, for whom they appeared. There is also the letter to the editors of *Literary Gazette* from Vadim Delone, in which he shows, from his knowledge of the preposterous evidence given by Dobrovolsky in the investigation of the case in which he (Delone) was implicated together with Bukovsky and Kushev [see p.66], that the sentences in the [Galanskov] trial were based on false evidence by Dobrovolsky. Also circulating in *samizdat* are letters sent by various people to Larissa Bogoraz and Pavel Litvinov after their statement [about the Galanskov trial] — the best known of these is the letter signed by twenty-four school children.' For this letter see K. van het Reve (ed.), *Letters and Telegrams to Pavel M. Litvinov* (Reidel, Dordrecht, Holland, 1969), which contains the English and Russian texts of 63 such communications, both favourable and hostile, and is of outstanding interest.

5. No. 6: 'Edited and annotated by Pavel Litvinov. This book, completed by Litvinov literally on the eve of his arrest [August 25th, 1968] contains a maximally complete collection of documents connected with the trial: a record of the trial itself and the appeal hearing, collective and individual letters written before and after the trial, and material from the Soviet press dealing with the trial and the letters about it.'

6. An English edition is due to be published in Britain by Longmans, Green in 1972, edited by Peter Reddaway. The Russian original, *Protsess chetyryokh*, has been published by the Alexander Herzen Foundation, Amsterdam, 1971. Additional material on the trial appears in an overlapping collection, *Protsess tsepnoi reaktsii* (Possev-Verlag, Frankfurt, 1971).

7. This contains some of his publicistic writing. It is published in *Grani* 63, 64, 65, 67, 68, 69, 70, 75. For some English translations of his articles see Abraham Brumberg (ed.), *In Quest of Justice: Protest and Dissent in the Soviet Union Today* (Pall Mall, London, 1970), documents 48 and 62.

8. Published in *Grani* 52 (1962). Translations of poems by Galanskov are in Brumberg, op. cit., and K. Bosley (ed.), *Russia's Other Poets* (Longmans, London, 1968).

9. Published in *Grani* 58 (1965), pp.95–193. Some translations in Bosley, op. cit.

10. Published in Russian in *Grani* 64 (1967), pp.194–201, in English in *PoC*, XVII, 5 (1968), pp.79–82.

11. No. 2 carried this clarification: 'The sentence about the material evidence which figured in the trial was misleadingly formulated. The main items were: a copy of the almanac *Phoenix-66*, confiscated during a search of Galanskov's apartment; a copy of the same almanac, confiscated during a search of Ginzburg's apartment; money, a hectograph, paper for cryptography, and N.T.S. pamphlets, confiscated during a search of Dobrovolsky's apartment; and typewriters confiscated during searches of various people's apartments. As for the "White Book", published in France in February [1967], and an issue of the journal *Grani*, published in March, both appeared after the defendants' arrest and quite naturally could not be, and were not, confiscated in the apartment of any of them.'

12. Published in Litvinov's book (doc. II–16): see note 6.

13. Many vivid accounts of the scene appeared in the world press during the trial. See also the one by the eminent Norwegian lawyer I. A. Soerheim, appendix II in Litvinov's book (see note 6). Soerheim tried to obtain access to the trial as an observer from the organization Amnesty International, but he was persistently barred.

14. This document, like most of the others mentioned in this chapter, appears in full in Litvinov's *The Trial of the Four* (doc. III–2), which will henceforth—with both Russian and English editions in mind—be designated simply *The Trial*. See English text also in Brumberg, op. cit., doc. 7, Russian text also in *Possev* 2 (1968), p.8.

15. The authors may have been encouraged to demand the admission of international observers by the presence outside the court of the lawyer I. A. Soerheim (see note 13).

16. All these are reproduced in *The Trial* (section V).

17. See text in *The Trial* (doc. IV–11). See English text also in Brumberg, op. cit., doc. 18, Russian text also in *NRS*, February 27th and March 7th, 1968.

18. As note 17 (doc. IV–17), but doc. 30 and *NRS*, March 10th, 1968.

19. As note 17 (doc. IV–22), but doc. 28 and van het Reve, op. cit., pp.140–41.

20. See text in *The Trial* (doc. IV–3). See Russian text also in *NRS*, October 27th, 1968.

21. As note 17 (doc. IV–21), but doc. 35 and *Possev* 8 (1968), pp.15–16.

22. As note 17 (doc. IV–23), but doc. 31 and *Possev* 7 (1968), pp.20–21.

23. See text in *The Trial* (doc. IV–28), English text also in Michael Browne (ed.), *Ferment in the Ukraine* (Macmillan, London, 1971), pp.191–6, Russian text also in *Possev* 12 (1968), p.58.

24. As note 17 (doc. V–33), but doc. 19 and *NRS*, June 1st, 1968.

25. As note 17 (doc. V–38), but doc. 21 and *NRS*, November 23rd, 1968.

26. As note 17 (doc. V–35), but doc. 20 and *NRS*, May 31st, 1968.

27. See text in *The Trial* (doc. V–37). Not published earlier.

28. As note 17 (doc. IV–4), but doc. 25 and *Possev* 3 (1968), pp.2–3.

29. As note 17 (doc. IV–9), but doc. 36 and *Possev* 8 (1968), p.2.

30. As note 27, but doc. IV–13.

31. As note 27, but doc. II–17. Only 42 signatures are listed in *The Trial*.

32. As note 17 (doc. II–18), but doc. 5 and *RM*, March 14th, 1968.

33. The non-repetitive passage here refers to 'the letter of the 44 demanding a public trial in the light of rumours then circulating that the trial would be officially closed to the public, and the letter of the 31 which expressed unease for the fate of Alexander Ginzburg under conditions of possible infringements of legality and of the absence of any publicity.'

34. As note 17 (doc. IV–10), but doc. 27 and *RM*, March 29th, 1968.

35. See text in *The Trial* (doc. IV–19). See Russian text also in *NRS*, October 27th, 1968.

36. As note 17 (doc. IV–7), but doc. 16 and *Possev* 3 (1968), pp.5–6.

37. See text in *The Trial* (doc. IV–24), Russian text also in *NRS*, December 8th, 1968.

38. As note 17 (doc. V–32), but doc. 15 and *Possev* 4 (1968), pp.7–8.

39. As note 17 (doc. V–34), but doc. 23 and *NRS*, June 9th, 1968.

40. See text in *The Trial* (doc. V–39), Russian text also in *Possev* 3 (1969), pp. 59–60.

41. On January 19th, they had tried to give a press conference about it, but the Western correspondents in Moscow obeyed an order by the Soviet authorities not to attend. See Andrei Amalrik's account, 'The press conference of L. I. Ginzburg and O. V. Timofeyeva which did not take place', appendix III in *The Trial*.

42. When, No. 2 reports, 'he was threatened with prosecution under article 190–1 of the Criminal Code'. No. 2 describes him as 'a physicist at the Institute of Precision Chemical Technology' who 'wrote a letter to Soviet and foreign communist papers about his "prophylactic chat" with the K.G.B. concerning

the trial of Vladimir Bukovsky, signed the letters of the 116 and the 44, the appeal (with Larissa Bogoraz) "To World Public Opinion" and the appeal to the Budapest conference [see pp.86–8], and was dismissed "for absenteeism" a few days before the January trial began and right after his first letter was published in the Western press.'

43. This letter, dated February 19th, is available, but has yet to be published.

44. English text in Brumberg, op. cit., doc. 33, Russian in *Possev* 4 (1968), pp.4–5. Subsequently 15 of the signatories sent to Radio Moscow a protest against the way the letter had gained publicity by reaching the West and being broadcast back to the U.S.S.R. Text in Brumberg, op. cit., doc. 34.

45. In Russian: *Zakonodatelstvo po zdravookhraneniyu.* Vol. 6 is virtually unobtainable.

46. No. 5 reported on the *samizdat* aspect of the Volpin and Gorbanevskaya cases as follows: "The confinement of Volpin in a mental home gave rise to a whole number of documents: the note which he left for his wife when he was taken from his home; a record of his conversations with the doctors; his appeal to his friends [Russian text, dated March 3rd, in *NRS*, October 6th, 1968]; a letter from his wife, Victoria, to the Minister of Health, B. V. Petrovsky; a letter from ninety-nine mathematicians in his defence [see note 44]; a note written by his wife and mother, about the conditions under which he was held in the hospital [Russian text, dated March 24th, in *NRS*, October 13th, 1968]; the text of the order by which he was forcibly confined, and other materials.

'The story of how Gorbanevskaya was sent to a mental hospital is told in her own account entitled "Free Medical Aid".' [Russian text, dated March 1968, in *Possev* 6 (1969), pp.43–54, English extracts in *The Times*, London, July 9th, 1970.]

47. 'As "professionally inadequate" ', according to No. 2, which adds that 'she has appealed to the courts'. She is 'an historian' and signed also 'the letter of the 116 and 44'. See also pp.134–192.

48. Also 'the letter of the 31', according to No. 2, which adds that he 'was demoted from full to candidate membership of the Moscow Section of the Union of Artists [M.S.U.A.].' No. 2 also reports that, presumably earlier, 'Three members of M.S.U.A.—Boris Birger, Yury Gerchuk and Igor Golomshtok—were discussed and condemned at a meeting, but only verbally, no sanctions being imposed. Then the board presidium was convened, no notice of this being given, however, either to those to be discussed or to the five presidium members who might have been expected to object to sanctions. Only by chance did Birger and these five people hear of the meeting and attend. Thanks to this the motion to expel the three men failed.'

No. 2 says elsewhere of Gerchuk, however, that he is 'a fine arts specialist at the Institute of the Theory and History of Architecture, signed the letters of the 116 and the 80, and was expelled in his absence from M.S.U.A. by its presidium'. No. 5 then reports his 'demotion at work', possibly for being a friend of Anatoly Marchenko (see p.192).

No. 2 describes Golomshtok as 'a fine arts specialist and signatory of the letters of the 116 and the 80' who 'was demoted in his absence from full to candidate membership of M.S.U.A. for a period of six months by its presidium'.

Gerchuk and Golomshtok both played prominent roles in the Sinyavsky-Daniel case. Golomshtok once co-authored a book with Sinyavsky.

All three artists were strongly attacked in the paper *Moskovskii Khudozhnik*, April 19th and May 24th, 1968, also Nikolai Andronov, whom No. 2 describes as 'an artist and signatory to the letter of the 120' who 'has received a severe party reprimand'. See texts of attacks in *The Trial.*

49. No. 2 adds that she was also 'dismissed from her job, but was readmitted to the party by the Party Control Committee, her expulsion being commuted to a severe reprimand'.

50. No. 2 adds that he was also 'dismissed from his job. His appeal for readmission to the party has not been upheld.' (This passage is omitted in error from the text in *Possev* I, p.17).

51. 'On the director's order and without a decision by the Academic Council', No. 2 adds.

52. 'A Pushkin specialist' (No. 2), he was later 'expelled from the Union of Journalists and his appeal for readmission to the party was rejected' (No. 5).

53. Correct name: 'Institute of Biochemistry of the Academy of Medical Sciences' (No. 2).

54. No. 2 adds that he also 'works in radio, was an inmate of Stalin's camps, was rehabilitated and readmitted to the party … he made an anti-Stalin speech at a meeting in memory of [the writer] Andrei Platonov.'

55. No. 2 adds that he also signed 'the letter of the 116 … was demoted at work, but has been readmitted to the party by the Party Control Committee, his expulsion being commuted to a severe reprimand.'

56. See text in *The Trial* (doc. IV–15). No. 2 refers to his wife as 'the philologist Anna Rappoport'.

57. 'And demoted to the position of workshop engineer' (No. 2).

58. 'By order of the director and without a decision by the Academic Council' (No. 2). He also signed 'the letter of the 116'.

59. No. 2 describes him as 'a chemist in the Institute of Catalysis of the Siberian section of the Academy of Sciences, a writer and performer of songs … An article by Yu. Shpakov violently attacking him has appeared in the paper *Soviet Russia* [May 28th, 1968].' See Novosibirsk section in Chap. 19.

60. This remarkable speech, also his speech at the appeal hearing, appear in *The Trial* (sections III and IV). English text of first speech also in Brumberg, op. cit., doc. 13.

61. 'And from the Collegium of Lawyers' presidium. Finally, in June, he was expelled from the Collegium itself, i.e. deprived of the right to appear for the defence. The reasons for his expulsion were that "he uttered careless, politically vague formulations which gave our political enemies the chance to use them to the detriment of the Soviet state and Soviet justice, and did not take measures to deny them". His appeal for readmission to the party, presented to the Party Control Committee, has not been upheld' (No. 2).

62. No. 2 adds that he is 'a Master of Philosophical Sciences … and a member of the Writers' Union', and that he was 'expelled in his absence by the Moscow city committee'. It also records that 'Boris Yampolsky, a prose writer and member of the Writers' Union, has received a severe party reprimand for an anti-Stalin speech read, though not by himself', at the same Platonov evening.

63. See English text in Brumberg, op. cit., doc. 61, Russian text in *Possev* 9 (1968), pp.55–8.

64. No. 2 reports that 'During a discussion in the Institute of the Russian Language concerning 11 research officers who had signed letters about the trial, a 32-year-old Master of philological sciences, Lev Skvortsov, distinguished himself by showing the greatest zeal in condemning them. This is approximately what he said: "I know that there is an anti-Soviet organization in Moscow and its centre is to be found in our Institute." Lev Skvortsov is known as a secret participant in the expert textual examination conducted in the Sinyavsky-Daniel case (the official expert was, as is well-known, Academician Victor Vinogradov). [Correction in No. 5: "In fact Skvortsov had nothing to do with

it and the work was actually done by Kostomarov, who is at present director of the Centre for Russian Language Teaching at Moscow University."]

'Skvortsov was also a consultant during the investigation into the case of Galanskov and the others, but the results of his textual analysis were not presented to the court for scrutiny because of their hypothetical nature. It is said that among his conclusions the "Letter to an Old Friend", for example, was pronounced to be the joint work of Galanskov and Ginzburg, although to an unbiased eye and without resorting to stylistic and textual study, it is evident that it was written by a person of another generation. Since the "Letter to an Old Friend" was pronounced an anti-Soviet document in the court's verdict, and had been presented as such in the indictment, the seriousness of an accusation of authorship may be well understood.'

65. 'By decision of the Academic Council,' according to No. 2, which adds that he is 'a linguist' and also signed 'the letter of the 31'.

66. Both 'dismissed "through a reduction in staff" ' (No. 2). Both then 'appealed to the courts' but were 'refused reinstatement'. Morozov is also 'a literary scholar'.

67. 'Dismissed "through a reduction in staff" ', 'a mathematician' who also signed 'the letter of the 116' (No. 2).

68. 'Dismissed "through a reduction in staff" ' from his directorship of 'the laboratory of computer mathematics' (No. 2).

69. The following list is alphabetical, the source being No. 2 — and the city concerned Moscow — unless otherwise indicated:

Alla Aleksandrova: a first-year student in the Historical and Philological Faculty of the Pedagogical Institute, signed the letters of the 116 and the 170, expelled from the Komsomol and the Institute.

[A. V.] Arkhangelsky: Doctor of Physical-Mathematical Sciences, professor at Moscow University, signed the letter of the 99, severe party reprimand.

Yury Davydov: Master of Philosophical Sciences at the Institute of the History of the Arts, signed the letter of the 80, severe party reprimand.

Mstislav Grabar: Master of Physical-Mathematical Sciences and senior lecturer at the Institute of Aviation Technology, signed the letters of the 116, the 80 and the 99, dismissed 'at his own request'.

A. Gurvich: Doctor of Biological Sciences at the Institute of Experimental Medicine, signed the letter of the 120, dismissed from the directorship of his laboratory.

Irina Kamyshanova: a typist and witness at the trial of Galanskov and the others, signed the witnesses' letter, dismissed from her job 'at her own request'.

Alexander Kon: physicist at the Institute of Atmospheric Physics, signed the letter of the 120, expelled from the Komsomol.

Lidia Kronrod: mathematician, lecturer at the Pedagogical Institute, signed the letter of the 99, dismissed by decision of the Academic Council.

Leonid Krysin: linguist, Master of Philological Sciences, Institute of the Russian Language, signed the letter of the 120, removed from the editorial board of the journal *The Russian Language in School* [from No. 4 (1968), onwards — the title, corrected here, is given wrongly in the *Chronicle*].

Sergei Larin: critic, translator of Polish prose, works on the journal *Soviet Literature* (published in foreign languages), signed the writers' letter, expelled from the Journalists' Union.

Vladimir Lebedev: on the staff of the magazine *The Tourist*, signed one of the letters on the trial, dismissed 'because of redundancy' (No. 5).

Vyacheslav Luchkov: a physiologist at the Institute of Psychology, signed the letter of the 170, expelled from the Komsomol by the Komsomol district committee.

Margarita Luchkova: engineer, signed the letter of the 170, expelled from the Komsomol.

Vadim Meniker: Master of Economic Sciences, Institute for the Economics of the World Socialist System, well known for his letter about the Sinyavsky-Daniel trial [see Chap. 2, notes 1 and 2], signed the letters of the 116 and the 80, dismissed by decision of the Academic Council.

Vladimir Miklashevich [or Miloshevich]: employee of the Weather Bureau, signed one of the letters on the trial, dismissed 'because of redundancy' (No. 5).

Yury Pilyar: prose-writer, member of the Writers' Union, an inmate of Mauthausen and then of Stalin's camps, rehabilitated, signed the writers' letter [then retracted his signature: see *Literary Gazette*, April 24th, 1968, *The Trial* (doc. V–17), Brumberg, op. cit., doc. 29], severe party reprimand.

Alexander Pyatigorsky: Master of Philological Sciences, specialist in Indian languages at the Institute of the Peoples of Asia, signed the letter of the 80, dismissed 'for absenteeism'. The absenteeism was provoked by the fact that he was not granted either leave or a business-trip in order to attend a conference in Estonia of which he was one of the organizers, and he went 'off his own bat'.

Irina Rapp: member of the quantum generators department of Kharkov University, signed the letter of the 170 concerning the trial of Galanskov, Ginzburg and the others, repeatedly summoned for interrogations about *samizdat* (No. 7).

Natalya Romanova: mathematician at the Institute of Atmospheric Physics, signed the letter of the 120, expelled from the Komsomol.

Dmitry Segal: linguist at the Institute of Slavonic Studies, signed the letters of the 31 and the 170, defence of his dissertation indefinitely postponed.

Victor Shakhsuvarov: engineer, signed the letter of the 170, dismissed 'because of redundancy'.

Georgy Shchedrovitsky: Master of Philosophical Sciences, signed the letter of the 170, expelled from the party.

Galina Shestopal: Master of Physical-Mathematical Sciences, teacher at the Pedagogical Institute, signed the letter of the 99, dismissed by decision of the Academic Council.

Natalya Ustinova: typist and witness at the trial of Galanskov and the others, signed the letters of the 116 and the 44 and the witnesses, dismissed 'at her own request'. [See her poems from *Phoenix-66* in *Grani* 70 (1969), pp.119–20.]

Nikolai Vilyams: mathematician and lecturer at the Institute of Precision Chemical Technology, former inmate of Stalin's camps then rehabilitated, signed the letters of the 80 and the 99, dismissed 'at his own request'.

Zoya Volotskaya: linguist at the Institute of Slavonic Studies, signed the letter of the 170, defence of her dissertation indefinitely postponed.

Isaac Yaglom: mathematician and Doctor of Pedagogical [or Physical-Mathematical?] Sciences at the Pedagogical Institute, dismissed by decision of the Academic Council.

Alexander Zholkovsky: linguist at the laboratory of machine translation of the First Moscow State Pedagogical Institute of Foreign Languages, signed the letter in defence of Ginzburg, defence of his thesis indefinitely postponed, under constant threat of dismissal from job (No. 5).

N. Zorkaya: Master of Fine Arts, at the Institute of the History of the Arts, signed one of the letters on the trial, expelled from the party and demoted for a year from senior to junior research officer (No. 5).

70. On April 24th, 1968. See text in *The Trial* (doc. V–17).

71. On May 1st, 1968. See text in *The Trial* (doc. V–21), also in Brumberg, op. cit., doc. 88.

72. 'Poet and member of the Writers' Union, signed the writers' letter, severe party reprimand' (No. 2).

73. No. 2 reported that Balter, a prose writer who 'signed the writers' letter, has received a severe party reprimand', and No. 5 that he had been 'expelled from the party by the Moscow city committee'.

74. 'A prose writer and playwright ... he signed the writers' letter. His two plays *I Want to be Honest* and *Two Comrades* have been taken out of the repertoire, the latter one having been in rehearsal in 36 theatres around the country but not performed' (No. 2). Later, however, No. 5 reported: 'The ban on the staging of plays by Vladimir Voinovich has recently been lifted.'

75. 'On the journal *Foreign Literature*, signed the letter of the 120, expelled from the party by his district committee, demoted at work' (No. 2).

76. 'Master of Philosophical Sciences, Institute of the History of the Arts, signed the letters of the 116 and the 31, severe party reprimand' (No. 2).

77. 'A prose writer ... signed the writers' letter, severe party reprimand' (No. 2).

78. No. 2 gave these extra details: '[Yu. A.] Shikhanovich: mathematician, Master of Pedagogical Sciences ... signed the letter of the 99, dismissed from his post.'

79. This episode is covered in depth in *The Trial* (appendix IV), where the full texts of the pamphlet and of the long account in *Izvestia*, June 21st, 1968, are given. See also much detail about both demonstrations and the groups concerned in *Possev* 7 (1968), pp.7–13.

80. In fact on February 17th.

81. These are Russell's original words in English. See the *Listener*, London, January 25th, 1968.

CHAPTER 4: THE INVASION OF CZECHOSLOVAKIA AND THE RED SQUARE DEMONSTRATION (pp.95–111)

1. From Yakobson's remarkable article in Natalya Gorbanevskaya, *Polden* (Possev-Verlag, Frankfurt, 1970), pp.495–7, English edition entitled *Red Square at Noon*, due in 1972 from André Deutsch, London.

2. See note 1.

3. *The Times* and the *New York Times* published it on August 29th.

4. In *Red Square* Gorbanevskaya suggests that these men are, on reflection, more likely to have belonged to the K.G.B. teams which constantly followed Litvinov and his friends wherever they went.

5. In addition No. 4 revealed the concealed authorship of a notorious Soviet work of propaganda: 'According to information from a reliable source the book *On the Events in Czechoslovakia* was put together by Felix Borovinsky and Boris Kozlov, who work in the department for socialist countries of the Novosti press agency.'

6. Prefaced in No. 6: 'To conclude this issue the *Chronicle* considers it essential to print the following document.'

7. Under which (No. 10) he 'has been charged'. The meaning of this addition is not clear, since No. 9 reports the trial as having already taken place.

8. See the *Daily Telegraph*, London, August 21st, 1969.

9. See Chap. 2, note 8.

10. See *Possev* IV, pp.17, 25.

11. See the press articles gathered together by Gorbanevskaya to form the first part of *Red Square*.

12. See *Possev* 2 (1969), pp.13–14, English text in A. Brumberg (ed.), *In Quest of Justice* (Pall Mall, London, 1970), doc. 81. Written around the beginning of October 1968.

13. See *Possev 12* (1968), pp.4–9. Dated September 30th, 1968, this stirring tract derives its title from the pseudonymous author's point that only a year separated the Munich agreement from September 1939.

14. See *RM*, July 3rd, 1969. Dated September 29th, 1968. In *Red Square* Gorbanevskaya writes that this document was not available to her because the last copy in the U.S.S.R. was confiscated from Grigorenko by the K.G.B.

15. See *Possev 2* (1969), pp.58–9. Dated October 24th, 1968. French text in *Samizdat 1: La Voix de l'Opposition Communiste en URSS* (Seuil, Paris, 1969), pp.583–7.

16. This phrase appears not in Kosterin's letter but in Marchenko's. See p.191–3.

CHAPTER 5: THE TRIAL OF THE DEMONSTRATORS (pp.112–26)

1. See *Red Square at Noon* (André Deutsch, London, 1972), and pp.369–89 in *Polden* (cf. Chap. 4, note 1).

2. See details in the *Guardian*, London, October 5th, 1968.

3. 'A student of the Institute of Historical Archives ... a few days later she was expelled' (No. 5). Bayeva was in fact the eighth participant in the demonstration, but she denied this to the police and only later decided to admit her role. See her lively account in *Red Square* and pp.77–82 in *Polden*.

4. See this man's full account in *Red Square* and pp.137–8 in *Polden*.

5. Correction in No. 5: 'In fact he was summoned to the Procuracy. Incidentally, the name of the witness is Rozanov and his photograph may be seen on the inside cover of the magazine *For Traffic Safety*, No. 11, 1968.'

6. For a full record of the three days' hearings see *Red Square* and pp.139–349 in *Polden*.

7. See *Red Square* and pp.363–8 in *Polden*.

8. See Chap. 4, note 1.

9. See Chap. 4, note 14.

10. For the letter of the seven and the attached letter of the 56, sent on October 9th to party leaders to demand an open trial, see *Red Square* and pp.126–8, 135–6, in *Polden*, also first publication in *NRS*, November 26th and October 31st, 1968, respectively. Two of the attached documents are omitted from Gorbanevskaya's book, but appeared in *NRS*, October 31st, 1968. They are: a telegram from Grigorenko to Shchelokov, the Minister of Internal Affairs, calling on him to put an end to the organized hooliganism; and a letter to Brezhnev to the same effect, signed by Grigorenko, Kirill Velikanov, Genrikh Altunyan and Leonid Plyushch. Both were sent on October 9th.

11. See *Red Square* and pp.393–7 in *Polden*, where the letter is followed by Gorbanevskaya's affectionate description of Lapin and an incident he was involved in outside the court. No 6 reports about Lapin, 'a poet and part-time literary adviser to the magazine *Pioneer*, in charge of the section devoted to children's work', that 'when his contract for part-time work expired no new contract was made'. No. 10 notes the appearance in *samizdat* of his *To my Readers: a Miscellany* (1969).

12. See *Red Square*, and pp.441–6 in *Polden*.

13. As note 12, but pp.324–32. Condensed versions appeared earlier: see Russian text in *Possev 11* (1968), pp.4–5, English in Brumberg (ed.), *In Quest of Justice* (Pall Mall, London, 1970), docs. 69 and 70.

14. As note 12, but pp.333–41. Russian text published earlier in *Possev 1* (1969), pp.3–5.

15. As note 12, but pp.310–23.

16. See shortened version on pp.227–31.

17. Also 'Victor Sokirko, engineer at a Moscow tube factory', who 'has been expelled from Moscow's Bauman Higher Technical Institute, where he was an

external graduate student, on the recommendation of a factory meeting. A record of this factory meeting is available in *samizdat*' (No. 7).

18. On the appeal hearing see *Red Square*, and pp.405–39 in *Polden*.

19. Nothing has become known about this work or its author.

20. This strong work is dedicated to the 23rd congress of the party. See text in *Possev* 3 (1969), pp.57–8.

21. See text in the collection *Kaznimye Sumasshestviem* (Possev-Verlag, Frankfurt, 1971).

22. See *Chronicle* 19.

CHAPTER 6: GENERAL GRIGORENKO AND HIS FRIENDS
(pp.127–49)

1. From 'Light in the Little Window' ('Svet v okontse'); see *Possev* 11 (1969), pp.37–41.

2. For four documents by Grigorenko relating to this period and written in 1966, see *Possev*, October 13th, 1967.

3. Available, but not yet published.

4. See p.81 and Chap. 3, note 43. No. 5 notes this long letter's circulation in *samizdat*.

5. Additional details noted in No. 2: 'recently worked as an engineer in a construction-assembly directorate ... signed the letter of the 116 and the 80 ... dismissed "because of redundancy" '.

6. According to B. I. Tsukerman's as yet unpublished biography Grigorenko's published articles number no less than 78.

7. See p.139 below and also Ilya Gabai's account of this episode. See Chap. 5, note 1.

8. See Grigorenko's speech at Kosterin's funeral, *Possev* 4 (1969), pp.54–5.

9. Ibid., p.54.

10. Ibid., pp.47–61. A French translation is in *Samizdat 1: La Voix de l'Opposition Communiste en U.R.S.S.* (Seuil, Paris, 1969), pp.437–80.

11. English translation in the *Listener*, London, May 15th, 1969.

12. See English text in Brumberg (ed.), *In Quest of Justice* (Pall Mall, London, 1970), doc. 40, Russian in *Possev* 6 (1968), pp.8–10.

13. See document referred to in Chap. 4, note 15.

14. *Possev* 4 (1969), p.55.

15. Text in *Grani* 68 (1968), pp.137–56; 69 (1968), pp.134–53. From Galanskov's *Phoenix 1966*. In his introduction Galanskov states that the authorship is uncertain. It has since been established that while the essay was found in Varga's archive he was not the author.

16. This may refer to his letter to the journal *Kommunist* concerning the controversy begun by the historian Nekrich about Stalin's responsibility for the Soviet defeats at the start of the war. See text in *NZh* 96 (1969), pp.221–63.

17. The confiscated items and the search are described by Grigorenko at some length in his letter of December 4th, 1968, to Procurator-General Rudenko. See Brumberg, op. cit., doc. 83, *Possev* 1 (1969), pp.6–10.

18. This letter was for some reason never dispatched. None the less the K.G.B. obtained a copy, with the following sort of result: 'Maria Petrenko, a geologist at the All-Union Research Institute for Nuclear Geophysics and Geochemistry, was interviewed by the Institute's "triumvirate" [the secretaries of the Party Bureau, the Trade Union and the Komsomol bureau] on the subject of her signing the letter. The following questions were asked: Why did you sign the letter? Are you its author? Where did you sign the letter?' (No. 8).

19. Not yet available. It may have been for this letter that Mrs Grigorenko 'was expelled from the party (in her absence) by her district party committee,

without her case being discussed by her local party cell. She had been a party member since 1930' (No. 8).

20. See note 1.

21. Available but not yet published.

22. See Chap. 3, note 34.

23. No. 2, issued on June 30th, 1968, has these extra details: 'a teacher of history and literature, recently an editor in the Institute of the Peoples of Asia ... signed the letters of the 44 and the 170 ... and the appeal to the Budapest conference, dismissed from his temporary job on March 1st, one month earlier than agreed, signed himself up in May for a geological expedition, but was turned down at the last moment on the direct instructions of the K.G.B.'

24. Published, with a moving introduction signed 'Friends', in *NZh* 97 (1969), pp.145–9. No. 10 records the appearance of his 'Selected Poems' in *samizdat*. These are probably the same poems as those published in *Grani* 76 (1970), pp.3–15. Other poems are in *Grani* 77 (1970), pp.49–53.

25. A copy did, however, reach the West. See *NRS*, March 23rd, 1969. Translated excerpts in the *Observer*, London, May 11th, 1969.

26. Genuine volunteer police (*druzhinniki*) are not normally controlled by the K.G.B. Outside political trials K.G.B. agents pose as *druzhinniki*, but, so as to keep maximum freedom of manoeuvre, do not wear armbands.

27. *Chronicle* 13, *Possev* IV, p.38.

28. For extensive detail on this demonstration see *Possev* 10 (1969), pp.2–3; 11 (1969), pp.22–3; 12 (1969), pp.18–20.

19. Full text in *Possev* 4 (1970), pp.2–11, condensed text in *Chronicle* 12, *Possev* IV, pp.4–7. English translation of the latter in Survey 77 (1970), pp.181–6.

30. See *Chronicle* 12, *Possev* IV, pp.7–8.

31. See ibid., pp.8–9.

32. Character in Chekhov's story of the same name about a provincial doctor.

33. October 30th, 1964. English text in *PoC* XVII, 4 (1968), pp.49–52.

34. See Chap. 3, note 36.

35. 'By the district party committee in his absence' (No. 2).

36. 'After he had gone away to take some exams' (No. 2).

37. *NRS*, August 31st, 1969.

38. English text in Brumberg, op. cit., doc. 81, Russian in *Possev* 2 (1969), pp.13–14.

39. See note 16.

40. English text in Brumberg, op. cit., doc. 82, Russian in *RM*, May 29th, 1969.

41. 'Of Russian language and literature in the "Jauna Gvarde" collective farm school: she has been dismissed' (No. 2).

42. Two versions are available, the earlier one with 18 signatures, the later with 25. See *Possev* 5 (1969), p.2, and *NRS*, August 31st, 1969.

43. *Possev* IV, p.30. In May 1971 Yakhimovich was released.

CHAPTER 7: THE ACTION GROUP FOR THE DEFENCE OF CIVIL RIGHTS (pp. 150–70)

1. Russian and English texts in *For Human Rights — Za prava cheloveka* (Possev-Verlag, Frankfurt, 1969), pp.5–15. Russian also in *Possev* 7 (1969), pp.2–4, English also in the *New York Review of Books*, August 21st, 1969, and A. Brumberg (ed.), *In Quest of Justice* (Pall Mall, London, 1970), pp.458–61.

2. Text in *Possev* 10 (1969), pp.4–5, partial English translation in A. Marchenko, *My Testimony* (Penguin, Harmondsworth, 1971), pp.426–7.

3. 'They are: Genrikh Altunyan (engineer and communist); Zinaida Mikhailovna Grigorenko (pensioner and communist); Ilya Gabai (teacher, at present in a

Tashkent prison cell); Reshat Dzhemilev (worker, Krasnodar Region); Irma Kosterina (office worker); Anatoly Levitin-Krasnov (religious writer); Leonid Petrovsky (historian and communist); Sergei Pisarev (pensioner and communist); Leonid Plyushch (mathematician, Kiev); Pyotr Yakir (historian)' (No. 8).

4. Dated June 1st, text in *Possev* 7 (1969), p.7, where in addition a description is given of the problem involved in handing it over.

5. Russian text in *Possev* 11 (1969), pp.2–3, English in the *Observer*, London, October 19th, 1969.

6. Four documents in all. Russian texts in *Possev* 11 (1969), pp.3–6.

7. See *Possev* IV, p.21, and *The Times*, London, January 19th, 1970. The full text, as with the fourth letter, has yet to be published.

8. Written in May 1970, this reached the West six months later. See Russian text in *Possev* 11 (1970), pp.8–9.

9. The *Chronicle* reports elsewhere about him: 'A geophysicist at the Institute of Terrestrial Physics, he has had the defence of his dissertation postponed after signing the letter in defence of P. G. Grigorenko' (No. 8). See also his penetrating letter about the Galanskov–Ginzburg trial in Litvinov's *The Trial*, doc. IV–5.

10. See documents about his vain efforts to emigrate in 1966–8 in *Possev* III, pp.56–61, and *NZh* 90 and 93 (1968).

11. As No. 11 reported, he was duly released.

12. One of these, 'Romantic Poetry in the Twenties', has appeared in *samizdat*. It is: 'An essay in literary criticism, which examines the moral aspect of the ideology of so called revolutionary romanticism. The author bases his arguments on the work of young poets of the post-revolutionary years—Bagritsky, Svetlov, Altauzen, Golodny, etc. He comes to the conclusion that the prettification of violence cannot be morally justified.' (No. 8.) This work has reached the West.

See also the role of Yakobson and other Action Group people in the extra-ordinary manoeuvring between Stalinists and anti-Stalinists on Red Square on the ninetieth anniversary of Stalin's birth (pp.424–7).

13. No. 5 had earlier reported: 'The mathematician Leonid Plyushch has been expelled "on account of redundancy" from the Institute of Cybernetics: not only did he sign the collective [Ukrainian] letter [of the 139], but also wrote one of his own about the trial in Moscow last winter' (see Chap. 3, note 40).

14. A student born in 1947. Sentenced in April 1970 to three years. See *Possev* IV, p.30.

15. No. 5 earlier gave these extra details: 'Economist at the Central Economics and Mathematics Institute, signatory of one of the letters on the [Galanskov] trial, of the appeal to the Budapest meeting, and of the appeal by the friends of Marchenko—dismissed "at his own request".'

16. See Chap. 3, note 46.

17. One of the greatest modern Russian poets (1888–1966). Her long poem *Requiem*, about the tragedy of Stalinism, has not been printed in the U.S.S.R. It was published as a booklet by Possev-Verlag, Frankfurt, in 1964, with a German translation.

18. See Introduction, note 14.

19. Available but not yet published. Marked 'November 1968, Tashkent'.

20. In the published Russian text—*Possev* II, p.42—a line is omitted here in error.

21. The U.S.S.R. Procurator-General.

22. *Possev* IV, pp.8–9.

23. No. 5 refers to 'August 9th' and 'ten' citizens. 'Altunyan's flat was searched a second time' (No. 7).

24. No. 5 adds: 'in violation of the law'.

25. 'At the end of March [1969] Altunyan's expulsion from the party was

confirmed at a meeting of the Party Commission of the Main Intelligence Directorate of the High Command, in the presence of a group of generals' (No. 7).

26. See Chap. 5, note 10.
27. See Chap. 6, note 42.
28. This unique document is in *Possev* V, pp.45–8.
29. Text in *Possev* 11 (1969), pp.4–5, also *Possev* V, pp.49–50.
30. See text in *Socialist Commentary*, London, October 1965.
31. See note 4.
32. See *Possev* IV, pp.27–9.
33. 'A worker in the Likhachyov car factory [...] an inmate of Stalin's camps, rehabilitated, signed the letters of the 116, the 44 and the 170, dismissed "because of redundancy" ' (No. 2).
34. A mainly peasant, populist party founded in 1902 and suppressed in 1922.
35. Earlier name for K.G.B.
36. No. 10 describes this episode as 'a provocation': 'His person was searched without a warrant being produced, and then he was allowed to go.' The plainclothes men directed 'policemen of the underground station "Kievskaya" '.
37. See Chap. 6, note 10.
38. *Possev* IV, p.24.
39. *Chronicle* 17, Amnesty edition, pp.84–5.

CHAPTER 8: THE CASE OF THE BALTIC FLEET OFFICERS (pp.171–83)

1. The Russian text of this open letter, written under the pseudonym Alekseyev, is in Possev 1 (1969), pp.53–60, French text in *Samizdat 1* (Seuil, Paris, 1969), pp.564–82.
2. Russian text in *Possev* 1 (1969), pp.17–20, English in *Studies in Comparative Communism*, Los Angeles, III, 2 (1970), pp.145–8.
3. Published as *Programma Demokraticheskogo Dvizheniya Sovetskogo Soyuza* (Alexander Herzen Foundation, Amsterdam, 1970).
4. *Sochineniya* (Geneva, 1875–9), V, p.131.
5. See *Chronicles* 14, *Possev* V, pp.21–2, and 17, Amnesty edition, p.88, and extracts from the second document, whose full 15,000 words are due to be published by Possev-Verlag, in *Possev* 4 (1971), pp.38–44.
6. A story-writer and critic, especially well known for his frank article 'On Sincerity in Literature', published in *Novy Mir* soon after the death of Stalin. He died in 1971.
7. 'Full title: Baltic Fleet, Twice decorated with the Order of the Red Banner' (*Chronicle*'s note).
8. Possibly a reference to Lieut. Ilin's assassination attempt of five months earlier.
9. See *Chronicle* 14, *Possev* V, pp.15–16.
10. See *Chronicle* 12, *Possev* IV, p.16.
11. See *Chronicle* 15, *Possev* VI, p.16, and the supplement to *Chronicle* 17. The *samizdat* 'Register of People Sentenced in the 1960s' adds that while Gavrilov and Kosyrev were officers, Paramonov was a petty officer first class. Gavrilov was also a party member, and his wife, Galina Vasilevna, and child live in Paldiski in Estonia (ul. Sadima 22, kv. 18). Finally the Register states that the arrests took place on June 10th–11th, 1969.

CHAPTER 9: THE CASE OF ANATOLY MARCHENKO (pp.185–202)

1. See her open letter in A. Marchenko, *Moi pokazaniya* (Possev-Verlag, Frankfurt, 1969), p.378. English text in his *My Testimony*, paperback edition (Penguin, Harmondsworth, 1971), pp.398–401.

2. This took place in Teheran in June 1968. Mr Kosygin sent a telegram to wish it success in its work.
3. *My Testimony* (Pall Mall, London, 1969), paperback edition with many added documents on Marchenko's case (Penguin, Harmondsworth, 1971). The best Russian edition, containing similar documents as appendices, is that referred to in note 1.
4. *My Testimony* (1969 edition), p.3.
5. See also pp.222–3.
6. Both these and the 'Regulations on Camps and Prisons' are semi-secret documents which have never been published. See a discussion of them by P. Reddaway in C. R. Hill (ed.), *Rights and Wrongs* (Penguin, Harmondsworth, 1969), pp.96–7.
7. *My Testimony* (1971 edition), pp.392–8, and A. Brumberg (ed.), *In Quest of Justice* (Pall Mall, London, 1970), doc. 63, Russian text in *Moi pokazaniya*, pp.368–75, and *RM*, July 10th, 1969.
8. *My Testimony* (1971), pp.401–5, *Moi pokazaniya*, pp. 380–85.Two other appeals were also circulated: see texts in Brumberg, op. cit., docs. 64 (also in *My Testimony* [1971 edition] pp.405–6) and 65, and *NRS*, September 18th, 1968.
9. *Possev* I, p.29, erroneously transcribes the original as 'four'.
10. See note 1.
11. Dated July 4th. Text in *RM*, July 17th, 1969, and *My Testimony* (1971 edition), p.389.
12. No. 5 wrote: 'Marchenko's book, which gives an account of the life of Soviet political prisoners during the current decade, came into circulation in 1967. One can form a partial idea of it from the letter by Marchenko included in the second issue of the *Chronicle*. This letter, together with a number of other documents, forms part of an appendix to the book compiled in the autumn of 1968, when Marchenko was sentenced for infringement of the identity-card regulations and sent to a strict-régime camp in the north of the Perm Region. The appendix includes: Marchenko's letter to A. Chakovsky, editor of *Literary Gazette*, in reply to a sentence in the latter's article, "Answer to a Reader", about political prisoners being kept "at public expense"; Marchenko's open letter to the President of the Soviet Red Cross and to a number of other officials about the situation of political prisoners; the reply to this letter from the Vice-President of the Soviet Red Cross Executive Committee, F. Zakharov; Marchenko's open letter to the Czechoslovak newspapers; a statement by eight friends of Marchenko concerning his arrest; Larissa Bogoraz's letter, "On the arrest of Anatoly Marchenko"; and a statement by the same author in connection with the arrest of Irina Belogorodskaya.' The last item has not reached the West, but all the others are in *Moi pokazaniya* and *My Testimony* (1971 edition).
13. Not yet published in Russian. English extract in *My Testimony* (1971 edition), pp.406–9. The other signatories are Gabai, Kim, Yakir, Krasin, Krasnov-Levitin, Z. Asanova, A. Kaplan, V. Kozharinov and J. Telesin.
14. See *Possev* 10 (1969), pp.4–5, and *My Testimony* (1971 edition), pp.426–7.
15. No. 9's brief report included the following points not in No. 10: 'The witnesses consisted of prisoners convicted for serious crimes or as recidivists, and camp administration workers ... Marchenko pleaded not guilty ... At present Marchenko is in the transfer prison at Solikamsk. Another exhausting journey is in store for him, in an unknown direction.'
16. Text in *Moi pokazaniya*, pp.379–80, dated August 12th, 1968.
17. Ibid., pp.387–9, dated January 12th, 1969.
18. Ibid., pp.390–417, translated and slightly abbreviated in *My Testimony* (1971 edition), pp.409–25.

19. See the document protesting against this, signed by eleven people, in *Moi pokazaniya*, pp.385-7.

CHAPTER 10: THE CAMPS AND PRISONS (pp.203-26)

1. See full text in *Possev* 6 (1970), pp.12-14.
2. I. V. Shmarov, F. T. Kuznetsov and P. E. Podymov, *Effektivnost deyatelnosti ispravitelno-trudovykh uchrezhdenii* (Moscow, 1968), p.153.
3. See the list of 233 Baptist prisoners as of August 1968 in Rosemary Harris and Xenia Howard-Johnston (eds.), *Christian Appeals from Russia* (Hodder, London, 1969), pp.92-143, from which material was used for the list of camps in *Possev* 3 (1969), pp.3-4. A list of 176 prisoners, as of November 1969, giving many new camp addresses, and another of October 1970 listing 168, have since reached the West.
4. See also the article by P. Reddaway in the *Observer*, London, January 3rd, 1971.
5. Another Soviet source gives a figure of 500,000, but without any supporting evidence. See the booklet by S. Zorin and N. Alekseyev, *Vremya ne zhdyot* (Frankfurt, 1970), p.42.
6. *Pravda*, January 28th, 1959, p.9, col. 3.
7. Document as yet unpublished; summarized in *The Times* and the *New York Times*, February 22nd, 1968.
8. The numbering of camps is a complex matter. A corrective-labour colony (*ispravitelno-trudovaya koloniya* or *I.T.K.*), more normally called a 'camp department' (*lagotdeleniye*), can contain a physically separate camp called a 'camp-point' (*lagpunkt*). Thus 'camp department' 17 includes 'camp-point' 17a. 'Camp department' 5 similarly has a camp-point, but this is simply called camp-point 5. It contained in 1969 some 200 foreign prisoners, political and criminal, while the main camp held some 2,000 Soviet citizens.
9. On the journalist Kalniňš, Shukhevych and Zdorovets see pp. 212, 214 and 331 respectively. As for Moshkov, No. 8 later reported: 'On June 12th, 1969, the Leningraders Vadim Gayenko and Sergei Moshkov came out of the Mordovian strict-régime camps. They had served four years under articles 70 and 72 of the Russian Criminal Code for their part in the affair of the journal *The Bell* and in an illegal Marxist circle [see Chap. 2, note 8].' No. 2 had earlier reported: 'In Mordovian camp No. 11 a lathe has torn the fingers off one of the hands of Vadim Gayenko.' It also reported that the Leningraders Veniamin Iofe and Valery Smolkin, from the same group, had served their 3-year terms and been 'released from the Mordovian political camps in late 1967–early 1968', at the same time as 'En Tarto, from the city of Tartu, and Alexander Potapov from Lipetsk, formerly the secretary of the town Komsomol committee, sentenced to five years under article 70 for composing anti-Khrushchev leaflets.' On Potapov see Marchenko, *My Testimony* (1969 edition), pp.285-8, and on Tarto see *Chronicle* 15, *Possev* VI, pp.5, 6, 10. Tarto (b. 1938) was sentenced to 5½ years in 1962 under article 70.
10. The prison within each Soviet labour camp is usually a damp building of concrete (not wood, like most of the other buildings), and is officially called a 'punishment isolator' (*shtrafnoi izolyator* or *shizo* for short). The general colloquial term is either *shizo* or *kartser*. The prisoners are kept in cells, on specially low rations, which are even lower if they do not go out to work. The B.I.R. (*barak usilennogo rezhima* or *B.U.R.* in Russian) is a particular form of *kartser*, where prisoners are kept in cells but normally let out each day to do manual work. Here they often spend periods of up to 6 months, in contrast to the 15-day terms which are the norm in an ordinary *kartser*.
11. No. 2 reported: 'Since the investigation [of Ginzburg's case] began, Irina

Zholkovskaya has been actively soliciting the registration of her marriage to Ginzburg. The K.G.B. replied that the question of her marrying Ginzburg would be decided by the court which would try him. On February 19th [1968] she was received by Judge Mironov who told her that he was not responsible as the matter had gone on appeal to the Russian Supreme Court.'

12. See note 9.

13. Dated March 1969, Russian text in the remarkable *samizdat* collection on this hunger-strike, *Istoriya odnoi golodovki* (Possev-Verlag, Frankfurt, 1971), English extracts in the *Observer*, London, June 29th, 1969, French extracts in *Samizdat 1* (Seuil, Paris, 1969), pp.523-5.

14. See this Lithuanian's portrait by Yury Ivanov in *Possev* 2 (1971), p.5.

15. See p.214 and also Marchenko, op. cit. (1969 edition), p.35.

16. Kvachevsky, Aidov and Tarnavsky took part in further strikes in 1970. See *Chronicle* 14 and 15, *Possev* V, p.18, VI, p.19. Aidov and Berg were sentenced in 1968 to three and seven years respectively. *Chronicle* 17 (Amnesty edition, p.84) gives the address in Kishinyov of Aidov's little daughter: ul. Lenina 64, kv. 87. Tarnavsky (b. 1940), a Ukrainian teacher, was sentenced to seven years in 1964 in Kishinyov as one of a group of six.

17. No. 4 reported: 'In recent months, the following people have been freed from the Mordovian political camps:

'Vladimir Osipov, sentenced to 7 years under article 70 in the first *Phoenix* case.

'Vladimir Ershov, from Latvia, who was sentenced twice and had served more than 17 years under article 58, paras. 9, 10, 11 and 12.

'Eduard Kuznetsov, who had served the same term on the same charge as Osipov, has also been released, in this case from the prison at Vladimir.'

On Osipov and Kuznetsov see the documents of 1961 in *RM*, April 20th, 1968. See also Osipov's letter of March 1962 in *RM*, April 25th, 1968, his documentary essays of 1970 in *Possev* 1 (1971), pp.44-50, and *Grani* 80 (1971), his statement of 1971 about his *samizdat* journal *Veche* in *Possev* 5 (1971), pp.7-8, and *Chronicle* 18's comments on this journal's neo-Slavophile orientation. On Kuznetsov see also p.318. The first *Phoenix* appeared in *Grani* 52 (December 1962).

No. 7 reported the release from Mordovia in 1968 of 'Anatoly Futman, sentenced under article 70 of the Russian Code. He got this political sentence while in a camp for ordinary criminals. Now, after his release, he has been placed under surveillance.' On him see Marchenko, op. cit. (1969 edition), pp.375-9, 411-12.

See ibid., pp.313-19, 357-8, concerning the subject of this item from No. 11: 'In the autumn of 1969 G. A. Krivtsov was released from the Mordovian camps, having served two terms, a total of twenty-one years. He was first arrested in 1948 in Czechoslovakia, where he had married a Czech girl and deserted from the army; soon after leaving the camp, he was arrested a second time, for "anti-Soviet propaganda". Krivtsov spent eight years in Vladimir prison and appears as one of the characters in Marchenko's book *My Testimony.*'

And finally—except for items included in other chapters, especially Chap. 14 on the Ukraine—No. 11 reported: 'In July 1969 Vilho Forsel, a Finn, was released from Vladimir prison. A graduate of Petrozavodsk University and a translator, he had served ten years, in effect because of his refusal to collaborate with the K.G.B.' On Forsel see doc. 11, by Valentyn Moroz, in M. Browne (ed.), *Ferment in the Ukraine* (Macmillan, London, 1971), p.149, and *Chronicle* 15, Possev VI, pp.5, 6, 10.

18. English text in *The Ukrainian Quarterly*, New York, 3 (1968), pp.206-11, Ukrainian text in *U pivstolittya radyans'koi vlady* (P.I.U.F., Paris, 1968), pp.47-53.

19. On these four people see Browne, op. cit., doc. 6 (by Ivan Kandyba), pp.71-2, and *Chronicle* 15, *Possev* VI, p.20. For Soroka's portrait see *Possev* 6 (1970), p.7.

20. This may be the same Belov mentioned by Marchenko, op. cit. (1969 edition), p.382.
21. See Chap. 3, note 2.
22. No. 9: 'In Dubrovlag (the Mordovian strict-régime camps), camp No. 11, which hitherto had the largest number of inmates, has been broken up. Instead of it, new strict-régime camp zones for political prisoners have been organized at camp No. 3 (Barashevo station), camp No. 17 (Ozerny settlement), and camp No. 19 (Lesnoi settlement). A new camp 17 has been organized to replace the women's ordinary-régime zone, and it has not been amalgamated with camp 17a, which contains only a small number of prisoners. Among the latter are Yury Galanskov and Alexander Ginzburg; Vyacheslav Platonov and Leonid Borodin, convicted at the social-christians' trial; and several men convicted at so-called "nationalist" trials, Victor Kalninš (sentenced to 10 years), Janis Kapicinš (15 years), Dmytro Verkholyak (25 years), Mykhaylo Soroka (25 years), and others There are also some sentenced Baptists.'
   For a portrait of Kapicinš, who died in January 1970 at the age of 52, see *Possev* 6 (1970), p.11.
23. Near Irkutsk in central Siberia.
24. On the south-west side of the Urals.
25. '*Nerazmennyi chervonets*'.
26. On the methods used at Saransk see *Chronicle* 13, *Possev* IV, pp.38–9.
27. See *Possev* 6 (1970), pp.3–11, 2 (1971), p.5, 3 (1971), p.9. See also his remarkable essay on Vladimir prison in *Vestnik RSKhD* 99 (1971), pp.122–35.
28. See Marchenko, op. cit. (1969 edition), pp.131–8.
29. On these three, Varenkov and Pronin, and (below) Nakashidze and Golub, see ibid., pp.396–7.
30. No. 4 records that he has 'been freed in recent months'.
31. See attack on him in *Komsomolskaya pravda*, October 30th, 1963.
32. At a big press conference in Moscow on April 18th, 1962, reported in the world press the next day. Aleksei Golub defected on October 10th, 1961, and returned home on March 27th, 1962.
33. See p.220, also Marchenko, op. cit. (1969 edition), pp.316–19, 357–8.
34. Ibid., pp.390–7.
35. 'To the list ... the name of Georg Gladko, who attempted to escape from East to West Germany, can be added. Gladko is now in Vladimir prison' (No. 9).
36. See V. Chornovil, *The Chornovil Papers* (McGraw-Hill, New York, 1968), pp.138–49, and Masyutko's very important letter of 1967 in Browne, op. cit., doc. 8.
37. See ibid., docs. 9 and 10, and Chornovil, op. cit., pp.103–16.
38. On their case see Browne, op. cit., docs. 1–7, nos. 2 and 7 of which are by Lukyanenko and no. 6 by Kandyba.
39. In fact 15 years and in the same case as Lukyanenko. See note 38. See also the appeal to the U.N. by these two and Mykhaylo Horyn from the Potma camps, June 1969, alleging deliberate poisoning of their food and describing in detail the symptoms produced. Ukrainian text in *Suchasnist* 10 (1969), pp.104–5, English in Browne, op. cit., doc. 31. See also Kandyba's long appeal of October 1969 to the U.N. in *Ukrains'ky samostiynyk*, Munich, 161 (January 1971), pp.2–6.
40. The *Chronicle* here misspelt Dyak as Lyak. On the case of these three—respectively a headmaster (b. 1937), a teacher and writer (b. 1928), and a police officer (b. 1939)—see Chronicle 17, Amnesty edition, pp.64–6.
41. See note 35.
42. i.e. concerning anti-Ukrainian bias. See Chornovil, op. cit., pp.170–80 and, on Karavansky in general, pp.166–221.

43. See preceding item, also docs. 8–11 in Browne, op. cit.
44. No. 11 recapitulates, with one slight inaccuracy, Karavansky's career, adding about the period 1960–65 that he 'returned to Odessa, where he studied and worked as a journalist. In 1965 he sent to *Izvestia* an article criticizing the nationality policy in the Ukraine.'
45. *Possev* IV, p.29.
46. See Marchenko, op. cit. (1969 edition), p.409.
47. See Chap. 9, note 1. See also V. Osipov's essay in *Possev* 1 (1971) and A. Amalrik, *Involuntary Journey to Siberia* (Collins/Harvill, London, 1970), pp.83–5, 246, 281.
48. In an important but as yet unpublished document of February 20th, 1968, addressed to President Podgorny.
49. Russian text in *NRS*, June 28th, 1969, English extracts in the *Daily Telegraph*, London, June 2nd, 1969.
50. Marchenko calls these for short the 'Regulations for Camps and Prisons'. See the brief summary of them in *Vedomosti Verkhovnogo Soveta R.S.F.S.R.*, 37 (1961), p.556, also the discussion of these problems by P. Reddaway in C. R. Hill (ed.), *Rights and Wrongs* (Penguin, Harmondsworth, 1969), pp.95–7.
51. See note 1.
52. The last is a theatre producer, the first six are writers.
53. Text in *Possev* 7 (1970), pp.28–35.

CHAPTER 11: THE PRISON MENTAL HOSPITALS (pp.227–47)

1. Part of a denunciation of the committal of Zh. Medvedev to a mental hospital. See English text in L. Labedz, ed., *Solzhenitsyn* (see Chap. 17, note 1). Russian text in *RM*, July 2nd, 1970 and *Chronicle* 14, *Possev* V, p.8.
2. *Chronicle*'s preface: 'In her book *Midday*, Natalya Gorbanevskaya includes the following account ... which is published here in abbreviated form.' See full text in *Polden* (Frankfurt, 1970), pp.461–73, and in English in *Red Square at Noon* (André Deutsch, London, 1971).
3. Pre-revolutionary figures. Professor V. P. Serbsky (1858–1917) died too early to prevent his name being used for the Serbsky Institute.
4. According to Grigorenko's full account the investigator said: 'Pyotr Grigorevich ... You're an absolutely normal person. I have no doubts about that, but in your medical record there's a note about some bruises, and in such cases a psychiatric diagnosis is obligatory. Without it the court won't accept the case.'
5. See *My Testimony* (Pall Mall, London, 1969), especially chapter 'The Mentally Sick', pp.192–4.
6. According to Grigorenko's full account: Volodya (i.e. Vladimir) Pantin.
7. Russian text (and attached documents) in *Possev* V, pp.35–44, English in *Survey* 77 (1970), pp.175–81.
8. *K novoi zhizni*, Moscow 5 (1970), p.22, quoted in *Chronicle* 14, *Possev* V, p.18.
9. In Russian: *detskii priyomnik-raspredelitel*.
10. See pp.81–2. Both here and in P. Reddaway's chapter in C. R. Hill (ed.), *Rights and Wrongs* (Penguin, Harmondsworth, 1969), p.93, it is wrongly stated that the 1961 instruction conflicts with articles 58–60 of the Russian Criminal Code. This is not so, the instruction being part of civil, not criminal law. For detailed treatment of these matters see Esenin-Volpin's open letter to Solzhenitsyn, of July 1970, about Grigorenko and about Solzhenitsyn's comparison of the prison-hospitals with the Nazi gas chambers. Russian text in *Possev* 9 (1970), pp.24–30, English extracts in *The Times*, August 26th, 1970.
11. See Hill, loc. cit.

12. See, respectively, pp.148–9; *Possev* IV, pp.7–8, and Kallistratova's long petition in *Possev* V, pp.39–44; and pp.241–2.
13. Collins/Harvill, London, 1965. Russian text in *Grani* 57, January 1965.
14. See p.87.
15. See *Chronicle* 14, *Possev* V, pp.6–8, and R. and Zh. Medvedev, *A Question of Madness* (Macmillan, London, 1971).
16. See Chap. 2, note 17. Here Bukovsky describes a form of punishment additional to the drug-tortures mentioned in this chapter. This involves wrapping a prisoner in a piece of wet canvas, which almost suffocates him as it dries and shrinks.
17. On Baptists see Hill, op. cit., p.118, and on Orthodox see M. Bourdeaux, *Patriarch and Prophets: Persecution of the Russian Orthodox Church Today* (Macmillan, London, 1970), pp.103, 105, 107.
18. See note 10, last sentence.
19. Such, in Moscow, appear to be No. 1 Kashchenko Psycho-Neurological Hospital, No. 3 Psycho-Neurological Hospital (known colloquially as 'the Sailor's Rest' after the street it is on), No. 4 Gannushkin Psychiatric Hospital, No. 5 Psychiatric Hospital at Stolbovaya Station forty miles from Moscow, No. 8 Solovyov Psychiatric Hospital, and No. 13 Psycho-Neurological Hospital in the suburb of Lyublino.
20. Grigorenko gives 1951 and says the building was formerly a women's prison. See Gorbanevskaya, *Polden* (Frankfurt, 1970), pp.467–8. Pisarev may still be right, however, to say that the Leningrad prison-hospital dates from the Ezhov period. For Esenin-Volpin served a term of compulsory treatment in 1949–50 in Leningrad's 'Prison No. 2 (Psychiatric Hospital)', which suggests that the prison-hospital was earlier situated there. See A. S. Yesenin-Volpin, *A Leaf of Spring* (Thames & Hudson, London, 1961), p.62. Grigorenko also reports (pp.462–3) that in 1964–5 many of the material—as opposed to moral—aspects of the Leningrad hospital conditions were good.
21. Formerly the East Prussian city of Insterburg.
22. Soviet brand names. Aminazin appears to be a form of largactil, Sulfazin a 1 per cent sterile solution of purified sulphur in peach oil. For their effects see p.239, also Bukovsky in *Survey* 77 (1970), p.142.
23. Signed the letter of the 31 denouncing the internment of Zh. Medvedev, Summary in *Chronicle* 14. See *Chronicle* 18, Amnesty edition, pp.142–4, for his obituary.
24. See pp.382–3. Shashenkov was still there, No. 18 reports, in early 1971.
25. One of the Fetisov group of fascists, he was still there in early 1971. See pp.431–3.
26. This ship berthed in Formosa in the mid-1950s and many of its crew asked for asylum.
27. See his wife's vigorous protest against this. English text in Hill, op. cit., pp.119–120, Russian in *Possev*, May 12th, 1967.
28. See pp.286–7.
29. See Chap. 6, note 15.
30. Some of these details had already appeared in No. 8. In January 1971, No. 18 reported, a psychiatric commission's recommendation of his release was rejected by the Moscow Regional Court.
31. The inaccuracies—in No. 7—were that his placard read 'Freedom for Czechoslovakia', that he was already 21, and that his name was spelt Reps. The report that he had been transferred to Moscow after arrest may possibly also have been an error.
32. No. 11 later reported: 'Professor Plotkin, Doctor of Physical-Mathematical

Sciences, head of the Algebra Department at the University of Latvia and academic supervisor to Ilya Rips, has been dismissed from the university.'

33. No. 9 reported the appearance in *samizdat* of ' "Ilya Rips — Biographical Documents": Reproductions of diplomas awarded to Ilya Rips for his victories in schools' mathematical, physico-mathematical and physics Olympiads; character references; a Diploma for first place in the Republican competition for the best piece of student work; and brief articles from the newspaper *Rigas Balss* [*The Voice of Riga*]. Finally two published papers by Ilya Rips are listed. The second of them was printed in *Papers of the U.S.S.R. Academy of Sciences*, Vol. 186, No. 2, 1969, not long before his attempted self-immolation.' Published in *Vestnik RSKhD* 99 (1971).

34. No. 6 reveals that Kvachevskaya is also 'the sister of Lev Kvachevsky and a student in her fifth year at the Medical Institute', from which she was expelled in 1965 in connection with the affair of *The Bell* [see Chap. 2, note 8] and then reinstated. She has now been expelled for a second time in connection with the judicial persecution of her brother [see pp.380–86], although the official phrase is: 'for actions incompatible with the title of Soviet student'. No. 9 adds that she 'has been deprived of her residence permit for Leningrad. Moreover, the administration of the Leningrad Medical Institute, from which she was expelled — in reality for refusing to repent and to condemn her brother — refuses to give her an academic reference, and because of this Dzhemma Kvachevskaya is deprived of the opportunity to complete her education.'

35. No. 8 recorded the June 12th episode and added: 'Kvachevskaya has been told that if she does not cease her efforts to obtain his release the same will be done to her.'

36. No. 9 reported, with reference to about this time: 'The doctors are saying quite openly: "He's perfectly healthy, of course, but orders is orders".'

37. In Russian: '*Sotsialno-bespokoinyi*'.

38. See *Chronicle* 14, *Possev* V, p.18.

39. See the case of the Baptist V. P. Kolesnik in Hill, op. cit., p.118.

40. Published in the massive collection *Kaznimye sumasshesviem* (Possev-Verlag, Frankfurt, 1971), extracts in *Possev* 3 (1971), pp.2–7. English text of Bukovsky's appeal in *The Times*, London, March 12th, 1971.

41. September 16th, 1971.

CHAPTER 12: THE CRIMEAN TATARS (pp.249–69)

1. From the draft for his intended speech at the Tashkent 'trial of the ten'. Text in *NRS*, September 19th–20th and 22nd, 1969, extracts in *Possev* 9 (1969), pp.6–7.

2. The figure given in almost all other Tatar sources is 46 per cent.

3. The latter three were then, respectively, secretary of the Supreme Soviet Presidium, head of the K.G.B., and Minister for the Preservation of Public Order.

4. No. 2 of the *Chronicle* noted: 'Quite recently three Crimean Tatars arrested on April 21st in Chirchik — Sadi Abkhairov, Reshat Alimov and Refat Izmailov — were, after a trial, sentenced to terms of 2 to 3 years.' No. 4 added: 'Between October 22nd and 28th in Tashkent members of the Crimean Tatar movement were tried on a charge of making "deliberately false statements which defamed the Soviet social and political system". The basis of the charge was the 66th issue of their information bulletin, which recounted an appeal to figures in the cultural field and the events in Chirchik on April 21st, 1968. [Dated April 23rd and signed by 16 Tatars. English text in *PoC*, XVII, 4 (1968), pp.92–3, Russian in *Possev* 6 (1968), pp.10–11. See, for the only photos of such events yet to reach the West, figs 49, 50, and others in the *Observer*, London, March 30th, 1969,

Possev 5 (1969), pp.3–4.] All the accused were sentenced to terms of imprisonment. Lyuman Umerov, Idris Kasymov, Shevket Seitablayev received one year, but all three were released as they had already served this term in their period of pre-trial detention. Lennara Guseinova and Yusuf Rasinov were given suspended sentences of one year.'

5. No. 2 noted: 'Yury Osmanov, Enver Memetov, Seidamet Memetov and Sabri Osmanov have been sentenced in Tashkent on charges of having disseminated slanderous fabrications discrediting the Soviet social and political system (article of the Uzbek Criminal Code corresponding to article 190–1 of the Russian Code). Their real offence was to have taken an active part in the fight for the restoration of national autonomy and for the return of the people to the Crimea. The defendants were sentenced to imprisonment for terms of six months to two and a half years.' Yury Osmanov is a young physicist, author of two important documents. See one, written in prison in 1968, in *Possev* 6 (1969), pp.7–8. The other, of December 1967, is as yet unpublished.

6. See also pp.88, 131, 254–5.

7. For complete list see A. Brumberg (ed.), *In Quest of Justice* (Pall Mall, London, 1970), doc. 39.

8. *The Nation Killers* (Macmillan, London, 1970). See *passim*, and, on recent events, Chap. 14. A closer study is *The Crimean Tatars and Volga Germans*, prepared by Ann Sheehy for the Minority Rights Group, 36 Craven St, London W.C.2, 1971.

9. On Dzhemilev see also *NZh* 97 (1969), pp.207–10.

10. See pp.310–12. In fact Telesin is a mathematician.

11. Western reporters present duly fell for this, as revealed in the world press the next day.

12. See her speech, *Possev* 4 (1969), pp.58–9.

13. See ibid., pp. 47–61, his speech p.53.

14. See Chap. 6, note 42.

15. No. 8: 'On June 8th, 1969, Niara Khalilov and Rustem Veliulayev arrived in Moscow as mandated spokesmen for the Crimean Tatar people, bearing letters addressed to the Central Committee of the Communist Party. They were detained by the police at the Kazan Station [in Moscow] and forcibly sent back to Tashkent.

'On June 14th the people's representative Reshat Osmanov, an armless invalid, was deported from Moscow by the police to his place of residence in Krymsk, in Krasnodar Province. In Krymsk the police took his passport from him and are now demanding that he leave the territory of Krasnodar Province.

'During these same June days about ten more Crimean Tatar representatives were deported from Moscow.'

16. In addition to No. 10's listing of an item 'Crimean Tatar Poems in Translation', No. 5 carried these two paragraphs:

' "Information Bulletins Issued by Representatives of the Crimean Tatars in Moscow": As in past years, these bulletins continued in 1968 to describe the activities of the Crimean Tatars' representatives in Moscow and to provide information about the persecution of individual members of the movement as well as about large-scale acts of repression (such as the events at Chirchik on April 21st and in Moscow on May 16th–17th). The bulletins also contain various appeals by the Crimean Tatars' representatives to cultural figures and to world public opinion. [See, e.g., No. 82, issued for the 1969 New Year, English text in the *Observer*, March 30th, 1969, Russian in *Possev* 4 (1969), pp.6–7.]

' "Crimean Tatars on Trial": This anonymous pamphlet describes the tragic expulsion of the Tatars from the Crimea, the struggle waged by them for their rehabilitation, and recent repressive court proceedings in which "every document containing information about the national movement ... is regarded by the local authorities as being anti-Soviet", and peaceful demonstrations and meetings ... are described as "mass disorders". The author of the pamphlet recalls the events in Chirchik, the police raids in Moscow and the Crimea, and the suppression of the national movement for justice for the Crimean Tatars.' [This document was later signed 'Russian Friends of the Crimean Tatars' and dated January 1969. See Chap. 6, note 25. Russian text also in *NZh* 97 (1969), pp.172–8.]

17. First arrests reported briefly in No. 4, which gave three names. No. 6 gave a fourth name, reporting that the total to be tried was ten, and also that an eleventh, 'a hero of the partisan fighting in the Crimea, Ramazan, has already been sentenced by the Tashkent City Court to one year's imprisonment.' No. 8 gave the full list of ten names and announced that the trial would begin on July 1st.

18. Reported in No. 5. Details of the subsequent three postponements of the trial are given in an as yet unpublished document of May 22nd, 1969, written anonymously in Tashkent.

19. The document described in note 1.

20. This important document of some 80 pages is available but has yet to be published.

21. No. 8 names 'Mourning Information No. 69' (a long, as yet unpublished document of June 1st, 1968, with 115 signatures), 'Call the Chirchik Thugs to Account' and 'Bloody Sunday' (the document referred to in note 4).

22. On Kadiyev's prowess as a physicist see *Survey* 72 (1969), pp.162–3, and Grigorenko in *Possev* 6 (1969), p.3.

23. Here the *Chronicle* mistakenly puts 'Turkmen'.

24. A copy of this typescript, some 300 pages long, is in the possession of the Alexander Herzen Foundation, Amstel 268, Amsterdam-C.

25. The last point appears to be inaccurate. For a careful discussion of all available statistics see Conquest, op. cit., pp.160–63, also Grigorenko's document in *Possev* 6 (1969), pp.3–6.

26. An available but unpublished document, written in about September 1968.

27. In addition No. 11 reported, 'Reports on events in the Crimea between October 10th and December 10th, 1969, tell of the arbitrariness of the local authorities and of police raids on the homes of Crimean Tatars (a small number of Crimean Tatars have returned to their homeland in recent years despite the obstacles put in their way by the authorities). The families of Crimean Tatars who have returned are being thrown out of the Crimea; people are being subjected to outrages, beatings and arrest; their homes are being confiscated and their belongings plundered. And all this even after the Decree [...] concerning the "rehabilitation" of the Crimean Tatar people. The reports quote protests made by Russian and Ukrainian workers on collective farms in the Crimea, against the inhuman persecution of their Tatar neighbours.'

28. A fifty-page document of about February 1969. Extracts in *NZh* 97 (1969), pp.202–17.

29. No. 6 had briefly reported the trial in preparation.

30. This probably refers to Nina Senichkina, a research worker at the Institute of Marxism-Leninism of the Central Committee of the party, and her article, 'A Fraternal Union of Free Nations'. See *Kommunist Tadzhikistana*, Dushanbe, December 30th, 1967, p.2.

31. No. 8 reported the appearance of the speech in *samizdat*: 'This speech, made at his trial on April 30th, 1969, is devoted to the fate of the Crimean Tatar people, and the persecutions to which they are being subjected,'

32. See the six appeals to the U.N. and other bodies in *Possev* VI, pp.45–56.
33. Taras Franko and Maria Lysenko. See summary in *Chronicle* 13, *Possev* IV, p.35. On recent developments see also No. 18.

CHAPTER 13: THE MESKHETIANS (pp.270–79)

1. From a still unpublished letter, 'Respected Comrades!', written in mid-February 1968 to the Budapest conference of communist parties.
2. Writing about Kosterin's funeral Grigorenko reports: 'Very few Volga Germans were present. But then their situation is even worse than that of the Crimean Tatars. Appreciating this, we express our admiration at the courage of those who made the journey for the funeral, but record neither their names nor the speech of their spokesman.' See *Possev* 4 (1969), p.48. Also, materials on the Volga German movement were confiscated from Grigorenko. See p.132.
3. See his article 'Russia's Meskhetians – a lost people', in *The Times*, August 5th, 1970. For an analysis of the Meskhetians in the context of the other deported peoples see Conquest's *The Nation Killers* (Macmillan, London, 1970), *passim*.
4. No 7's text – 'decree of October 31st, 1956' – has been corrected here in the way indicated by No. 18.
5. See obituary in *Zarya vostoka*, Tbilisi, September 24th, 1963.
6. See full text in Conquest, op. cit., pp.188–9.
7. Corrected as described in note 4.
8. It is not yet clear whether the correct spelling is Khozravanadze or Khozre-vanadze.

CHAPTER 14: THE UKRAINIANS (pp.280–97)

1. See Moroz's essay in M. Browne (ed.), *Ferment in the Ukraine* (Macmillan, London, 1971), p.145. For a broad picture of the post-Stalin period see Julian Birch, 'The Ukrainian Nationalist Movement in the U.S.S.R. since 1956', in the *Ukrainian Review*, London, 4 (1970), pp.2–47.
2. See Chap. 3, note 23.
3. No. 2: 'Mykhaylo Biletsky, a mathematician of Kiev, has been dismissed "at his own request". Yury Tsekhmistrenko, Master of Physical-Mathematical Sciences, Kiev, has been expelled from the party.' Correction in No. 5: 'Tsekhmistrenko … in fact received a severe reprimand.'
4. No. 5: 'I. H. Zaslavska, Master of Physical-Mathematical Sciences and research worker of the Institute of Semi-Conductors (prior to her dismissal the party bureau expressed its lack of political confidence in her).
   'L. Yashchenko, research worker at the Institute of Folklore and Art History, member of the Composers' Union of the Ukraine and composer of such well-known songs as "Verkhovyna" and others.
   'L. N. Kovalenko, a member of the Academy's Institute of Literature, received a "strict reprimand" as a party member.
   'Doctor of Chemistry H. Dvorko, of the Institute of Physical Chemistry, was expelled from the party.
   'The Academic Council and the Assembly of the Institute of Linguistics took a decision to dismiss Z. T. Franko.'
   No. 8 added later: Zynoviya Franko, granddaughter of Ivan Franko [an eminent Ukrainian writer and scholar, 1856–1916], has been dismissed from the Academy of Sciences Institute of Language Studies, in effect for carrying on a correspondence with a friend in Canada. A letter in which she described various sorts of discrimination in the Ukraine did not reach its destination. The letter was opened, kept, and later read out at a closed party meeting at the Institute.

'A. L. Put, Master of Biological Sciences and senior research officer, and H. F. Matviyenko, junior research officer, have been dismissed from the Institute of Zoology of the Ukrainian Academy of Sciences, for signing the letter (of the 139) from the intelligentsia of the Ukraine. The dismissal of H. O. Bachynsky from the same Institute has already been reported in the *Chronicle* [No. 5 — also his dismissal "from another post which he took up later"]. The man behind all the dismissals is the Institute's Director, Academician I. H. Podoplichko, who at the end of the 'forties publicly renounced his student son, who had been arrested and sentenced to ten years for "Ukrainian nationalism".'

5. For Drach's statement of November 1966 in New York see Browne, op. cit., doc. 18. His expulsion was later annulled.

6. Other reprisals listed in Nos. 5 and 7: 'A meeting of the Institute of Mathematics recommended that Corresponding Members of the Ukrainian Academy of Sciences, Yu. M. Berezansky and A. V. Skorokhod, should not be allowed to teach in the University.

'L. V. Zaboi, a fifth-year woman student, has been expelled from the Kiev Institute of Fine Arts.

'The schoolmistress L. Orel has twice been dismissed from different schools' (No. 5).

'In November 1968 a search was made, at Irpen in the Ukraine [Kiev Region], of the flat of the translator Hryhoriy Kochur [b. 1908], who at the beginning of 1968 signed the Ukrainian protest letter against illegal trials in Moscow and the Ukraine. Apart from A. D. Sakharov's essay [see pp.354–5] and some other Ukrainian *samizdat* works, during the search a leaflet was confiscated which Kochur had never seen until that moment. Those carrying out the search discovered this leaflet with suspicious rapidity: it was taken out of a book on a shelf. The subject of the search is convinced that the leaflet was planted on him in advance.

'In Lvov at the beginning of 1969, Yaroslav Kendzor was searched "so that the slanderous work of Chornovil might be confiscated". The search led only to the confiscating of an old edition of a novel by the Ukrainian classical writer Panteleimon Kulish [1819–97] *The Black Council* [*Chorna Rada*]. At the very time of the search a new edition of this book was issued by the Dnipro publishing house' (No. 7).

7. No. 7 reported, for example: 'A poem ["Churches"] by the poet Ihor Kalynets was published [on September 29th, 1968, in Munich] in the Ukrainian émigré newspaper *Khrystyyansky Holos* (*The Christian Voice*). A meeting was organized to criticize him in the Lvov regional archives where he works, and the secretary of the Lvov region's party committee, Chugayev, spoke of "the subversive activity" of Kalynets in several speeches to the Lvov intelligentsia. It should be pointed out that the poem was not of a political nature and, in addition, Kalynets knew nothing about its publication.'

8. Svitlychny — imprisoned without trial from September 1965 to April 1966 — is the author of doc. 1 and co-author of doc. 14 in Browne, op. cit.

9. 'A Kievan signatory to the Ukrainian letter, she has been dismissed from her job' (No. 2). Also a signatory of doc. 14 in Browne, op. cit.

10. A. Avtorkhanov, *Tekhnologiya vlasti* (Possev-Verlag, Frankfurt, 1959), published in English as *Stalin and the Soviet Communist Party* (Munich, 1959).

11. First published in English (Weidenfeld & Nicolson, London, June 1968), then in Ukrainian (Suchasnist, Munich, July 1968). The second English edition (October 1970) contains a long postscript (pp. 233–50) describing in detail Soviet reactions to the book's appearance and the ensuing 'Dzyuba affair'. This involved, among other things, the publication in Ukrainian and English in Kiev

of a 200-page book—*What I. Dzyuba Stands For, and How He Does it* (*Once more about the book 'Internationalism or Russification?'*) by Bohdan Stanchuk—aimed at countering Dzyuba's arguments.

12. For an anti-liberal article by Vasyl Kozachenko see Browne, op. cit., doc. 26

13. On this whole expulsion-reinstatement episode see the second English edition of Dzyuba's book, pp.247–50, also *Chronicle* 12, *Possev* IV, pp. 17–18.

14. The other—by Dzyuba, Mykhaylyna Kotsyubynska, Lina Kostenko, Yevhen Sverstyuk and Victor Nekrasov—is doc. 30 in Browne, op. cit.

15. For the full text in Ukrainian see *Suchasnist*, Munich, 4 (1969), pp.76–81, and in English, the *Ukrainian Review*, 4 (1969), pp.61–5.

16. Published on July 16th, 1968. See English text in Browne, op. cit., doc. 29. The correct title is 'Whom are certain "humanists" protecting?'.

17. i.e. Mykhaylo Masyutko and Mykhaylo Horyn.

18. In addition, No. 4 reported the release from Mordovia in autumn 1968 of 'Yaroslav Hevrych, sentenced to 3 years for "anti-Soviet agitation and propaganda" in one of the so-called "nationalist" cases of 1965', and No. 7 wrote: 'At the end of 1968 the following were released from the Mordovian strict-régime camps after serving their sentence:

'Ivan Hel from Lvov, sentenced under article 62 of the Ukrainian Criminal Code to three years for distributing Ukrainian *samizdat* works; after his return he was not given permission to live in Lvov, and was not reinstated at Lvov University, from which, in his last year of study, he had been expelled after his arrest.

'Bohdan Horyn from Lvov, an art critic who worked in the Museum of Ukrainian Art before his arrest, was sentenced under article 62 to three years for distributing Ukrainian *samizdat* works; after his return he was not allowed to live in Lvov, and he now works as a carpenter on a building-site in Lvov Region.'

19. Dates here corrected in the way indicated in No. 7. No. 5 mistakenly put 'May 30th to June 17th.'

20. For important material about Chornovil's case, including his final speech at his trial, see Browne, op. cit., docs. 12–15.

21. 'Woe from Wit' is a literal translation of Chornovil's Ukrainian title *Lykho z rozumu*. The Ukrainian edition appeared under this title in Paris (publishers P.I.U.F., 3 rue du Sabot) in 1967, soon followed in 1968 in New York by the English edition, *The Chornovil Papers* (McGraw-Hill), which contains additional material. The book contains extensive personal details on all twenty intellectuals. Further important documentation about the 1966 trials is available in the anonymously edited *samizdat* collection *Ukrains'ka inteligentsiya pid sudom K.G.B.* (Munich, 1970). On this book see Browne, op. cit., pp. 212–14. The material of the book documents Chornovil's introductory essay (pp.2–73) in *The Chornovil Papers*.

22. On Osadchy see Chornovil, *The Chornovil Papers*, pp.153–61, also Browne, op. cit., *passim*, but especially pp. 150, 153. Osadchy's book was in fact destroyed just before its release, after his arrest.

23. Full text in Browne, op. cit., pp.119–53. On Moroz see also doc. 10 in ibid. and Chornovil, op. cit., pp.150–52. A *samizdat* translation of Moroz's original Ukrainian text into Russian has appeared in *Novy Zhurnal*, 93 (1968), pp.172–203, but—regrettably—with some brief passages criticizing Russian chauvinism excised.

24. *Chronicle* 14, *Possev* V, p.16.

25. Published in Ukrainian (Western translation from a Russian *samizdat* translation of the Ukrainian original) in *Ukrains'ky samostiynyk*, Munich, 158 (October 1970), pp.2–16, and in English by Ukrainian Congress Committee of America, New York, 1971.

26. Levko is a familiar form of Lev. On Lukyanenko see p.220.

27. In April 1970. See *Chronicle* 13, *Possev* IV, p.29.

28. No. 5 carried another item of this sort: 'H. Minyailo has been dismissed from his work in the Kiev Institute of Micro-Instruments after organizing a discussion club (with the permission of the Komsomol Central Committee).'

29. Also, Volodymyr Komashkov, one of the 139, 'appeared as a witness in the case' (No. 8). No. 7 had reported that 'Komashkov, a worker at the Kiev hydro-electric station and an evening student of the Kiev University faculty of philology, was expelled from the university the day before defending his graduation thesis, after taking his state exams.'

No. 7 also wrote: 'In March 1969, the appeal hearing in the case of Nazarenko and the others took place in the Ukrainian Supreme Court. The defence lawyers demanded a redefinition of the offence under article 187-1 instead of article 62 of the Ukrainian Code. One of the arguments was that the defendants had been adjudged guilty under article 62 for distributing Chornovil's book, whereas Chornovil himself had been tried under article 187-1. The sentence was left unaltered.' The *samizdat* 'Register of People sentenced in the 1960s' adds that Karpenko (b. 1938) and Kondryukov (b. 1936) were party members, but that Nazarenko (b. 1930) was not.

The witness Sheremetyeva, discussed below, wrote a letter with Chornovil and P. Skochok in defence of Dzyuba in 1966. See text in both Chornovil, *Lykho zrozumu*, pp.309–20, and *Suchasnist* 11 (1967).

30. No. 7 reported the release from the Mordovian strict-régime camps in 1968 of: '[I. V.] Strutynsky from Lvov Region, sentenced under article 56 of the Ukrainian Code (equivalent to article 64 of the Russian Code) to 10 years', and 'Myroslava Tershivska from Drogobych [in Lvov Region], sentenced to 3 years under article 62 of the Ukrainian Code for preparing and distributing hand-written leaflets with her husband, Dyky; after the camp she has now been exiled for 3 years to Krasnoyarsk Province; her husband is in camp 11 of the Mordovian complex, having been sentenced to 5 years in a camp and 3 years of exile.'

On Strutynsky and his case see Browne, op. cit., p.69.

No. 8 reported the release in June 1969 from the same camps of 'the Ukrainian Roman Duzhynsky, four year term, national movement, article 62 of the Ukrainian Code.'

31. No. 9: 'A young man by the name of Hai has been arrested in Chernovtsy [SW Ukraine]. He is accused of "connections with Ukrainian nationalists".'

No. 10: 'In Ternopol [W Ukraine] this September [1969] there was a trial under article 62 of the Ukrainian Code, equivalent to article 70 of the Russian Code. The accused, numbering about ten, were charged with circulating *samizdat* writings on the nationalities question and on the events in Czechoslovakia.'

32. This important and detailed letter, addressed to the Central Committee in Moscow, is in *Possev* VIII, pp.61–3.

33. A reference to the impostor Khlestakov, the central character in Gogol's play *The Inspector General*.

34. *Sobor u ryshtovanni* (P.I.U.F., Paris, Smoloskyp, Baltimore, 1970), English extracts in the *Ukrainian Review*, 3 (1970), pp.22–48.

35. See Ukrainian text in *Suchasnist*, Munich, 2 (1969), pp.78–85, English in the *Ukrainian Review*, 3 (1969), pp.46–52.

36. Other details from No. 7:

'I. P. Opanasenko, from Dnepropetrovsk, employed by the newspaper *Zorya*, has been dismissed from work.

'Ryma Stepanenko, director of the Ukrainian Shevchenko Theatre in

Dnepropetrovsk, has been expelled from the party and dismissed from work for the production of a play by M. Stelmakh called *The King's Pal*.

'S. Levenets, secretary of the Dnepropetrovsk section of the Ukrainian theatrical society, has been dismissed from work.

'V. Chemerys, writer, employee of the Dnepropetrovsk publishing-house "Promin", has been dismissed from work.

'B. Karapysh, writer, employee of the Dnepropetrovsk publishing-house, "Promin", has been given a severe reprimand by the party.'

37. According to a vicious attack on the letter and those connected with it in *Zorya*, February 7th, 1970, Skoryk is stated to have been co-author with I. Sokulsky. See translation in the *Current Digest of the Soviet Ukrainian Press*, Munich, XIV, 10 (October 1970), pp.1–5.
38. *Possev* IV, p. 10.
39. Date as corrected in No. 10. No. 6 put 'December 5th'.
40. Name as corrected in No. 10. No. 8 put 'Berislavsky'.
41. On Shulzhenko see Moroz in Browne, op. cit., p.127.
42. The Dnepropetrovsk appeal (see note 35) records Sirenko's dismissal from his job. This was just the latest in a series of persecutions over the previous few years, ever since Sirenko began to write in Ukrainian.
43. *Possev* IV, p.17.
44. See especially the account of a *samizdat* document by the philologist Taras Franko and the biologist Maria Lysenko which calls for the return home of the Tatars and the cession of the Crimea by the Ukraine. In this way the Crimea could resume its status as an autonomous republic. *Chronicle* 13, *Possev* IV, p.35.
45. See *Chronicle* 13, *Possev* IV, p.36.
46. These two issues are published in book form under the title *Ukrains'ky visnyk*. *Vypusk I-II* (P.I.U.F., Paris; Smoloskyp, Baltimore, 1971), but became available too late to be used in this chapter. Issues 1–4 are due to appear as a book in English.
47. *Chronicle* 18 carried material from Nos. 1–3 of the *Herald*.

CHAPTER 15: THE JEWS (pp.298–318)

1. Russian text in M. Decter (ed.), *A Hero for our Time* (Conference on the Status of Soviet Jews, New York, 1970), p.37. English text in ibid., p.13, also *Jews in Eastern Europe*, London, IV, 2 (July 1969), pp.57–8. Decter's book contains eleven documents in English on Kochubiyevsky and his trial, nine of which are also in *Jews in Eastern Europe*, IV, 3 (January 1970), pp.11–29.
2. *The Jews of Silence* is the title of a moving book by Elie Wiesel (New York, 1966), which records his meetings with Soviet Jews, particularly at the Simchat Torah celebrations in Moscow. On the 1970 celebrations see No. 16, Amnesty edition, p.26.
3. See *Programme of the Communist Party of the Soviet Union* (Moscow, 1961), pp.102–5.
4. See 'The Jews as a Religious Minority' by Cornelia Gerstenmaier in *Religious Minorities in the Soviet Union (1960–1970)* (Minority Rights Group, Report No. 1, London, 1970).
5. Both writers called for a monument to the victims of Baby Yar.
6. English text in A. Brumberg, *In Quest of Justice* (Pall Mall, London, 1970), doc. 38, and V. Chornovil, *The Chornovil Papers* (McGraw-Hill, New York, 1968), pp.222–6.
7. Lionel Kochan (ed.), *The Jews in Soviet Russia, 1917-67* (Oxford University Press, London, 1970).
8. In the *Washington Post* and the *New York Times*. Full Russian text (translation from the original Lithuanian) in *NRS*, May 10th, 1969, slightly condensed English text in *Jews in Eastern Europe* IV, 2 (July 1969), pp.51–5.

9. Andrei Sakharov, *Progress, Coexistence and Intellectual Freedom* (André Deutsch, London, 1968), pp.65–6

10. A fascinating eye-witness account of this meeting appears in an interview given by a Jew who later emigrated, printed in the *Jewish Chronicle*, London, October 30th, 1970.

11. No. 8 commented later: 'One of the witnesses for the prosecution was Deputy-Dean Groza, who had said "Jews stink". This was corroborated at the trial. However, according to Groza she had not been stating it as a fact, but asking if it were true.'

12. On the different meetings of 1968–70 see *Chronicle* 16, Amnesty edition, p.29.

13. The Central Rada was the Ukrainian legislature in 1917–18. S. Petlyura, a socialist, commanded the Ukrainian nationalist forces and briefly headed the Ukrainian Directory, the government which functioned in 1918–19.

14. Correction in No. 8: 'In fact it was only his father who perished then; his mother died of natural causes a few years ago.'

15. No. 8 added after the trial: 'Davydov, a figure in Anatoly Kuznetsov's novel *Baby Yar* [uncensored English text, *Babi Yar* (Cape, London, 1970)], did not speak at the trial, but he did make a statement to various people, including an investigator, saying that he had written a denunciation of Kochubiyevsky while drunk. The content of the denunciation was not used to incriminate Kochubiyevsky.'

16. A very interesting document, 'Why I am a Zionist', written not later than June 1968 and almost certainly by Kochubiyevsky, appears in Decter, op. cit., pp.33–5.

17. English text in ibid., p.16.

18. An English text of part of this is in ibid., pp.18–24. It includes transcripts of Kiev Procurator Surkov's main speech and of Kochubiyevsky's final speech, but the defence lawyer's speech is missing. Extracts first appeared in the *New York Times*, June 5th, 1969.

19. See *Vechirniy Kyiv*, August 9th and September 4th, 1969, English texts in Decter, op. cit., pp.25–33.

20. *Possev* IV, p.17.

21. Ibid., p.12.

22. Ibid., loc. cit., also *Chronicle* 14 in *Possev* V, p.21.

23. Dated June 20th, 1970, summarized in *Chronicle* 14, but not yet published.

24. Kerler was born in 1918. For his biography see the *Kratkaya Literaturnaya Entsiklopediya*, vol. 3, and *NRS*, January 16th, 1790. See also the collection of his poems, translated into Russian, *Khochu byt dobrym* (Moscow, 1965), and the English text of his letter to the singer Nehama Lifshits, who was allowed to emigrate in March 1969, in M. Decter (ed.), *Redemption: Jewish Freedom Letters from Russia* (American Jewish Conference on Soviet Jewry, New York, May 1970), pp.53–5. In this letter Kerler writes that he has not published a line since 1965.

25. English extracts in *Jews in Eastern Europe*, IV, 5 (August 1970) pp.90–92, Russian text in *Iskhod* I, *Possev* VII, pp.18–21.

26. i.e. of December 14th, 1969. See condensed English text in *Jews in Eastern Europe*, IV, 5, pp.94–5.

27. Yet another which eventually turned out well had this earlier chapter: 'On November 13th [1969], at an enlarged session of the Komsomol Committee of the Moscow Institute of Electrical Engineering, Natalya Slepyan [see plate 61] was expelled from the Komsomol "in view of the incompatibility of her views with membership of the Komsomol". The reason for this was Slepyan's request for a reference to submit to the Department of Visas in connection with her intention to emigrate to Israel' (No. 11).

28. Russian text available but not yet published.
29. See the vicious attack on Shlayen by B. Lesnov in *Izvestia*, March 12th, 1970.
30. E.g. the letter of the 25 Moscow Jews to Angie Brooks of about December 31st, 1969, handed to her by the Israeli Ambassador to the U.N. on January 26th, 1970. Russian text in *Iskhod* 1, *Possev* VII, pp.6–7, English extracts in the American *Jewish Exponent*, January 30th, 1970.
31. e.g. three concerning the Galanskov-Ginzburg trial. See P. Litvinov, *The Trial of the Four*, documents II–16, IV–11, IV–17.
32. Text in *Possev* IV, pp.43–61.
33. See *Chronicle* 12 in *Possev* IV, p.20. *Chronicle* 17 reveals that Telesin was the compiler.
34. Often referred to as the 'Letter of the 39', as one signature, Telesin's, was added late. Its English text (condensed) appears in *Jews in Eastern Europe*, IV, 5, pp.16–18, and its Russian text (part of *Iskhod* 1) in *Possev* VII, pp.10–12.
35. Article by B. Lesnov of March 12th, 1970.
36. *Chronicle* 12 in *Possev* IV, p.16.
37. See, e.g., the *Daily Telegraph*, London. Other papers carried a Reuter dispatch.
38. *Chronicle* 14, in *Possev* V, p.19.
39. No. 10 reported the circulation in *samizdat* of a translation of Claude Erial's *Anti-Semitism in Poland*: 'In this article, contemporary Polish anti-semitism is analysed in detail, together with its significance—in the author's opinion, a dominant one—in the struggle for power during the political crisis of 1967–8.'
40. The whole of *Jews in Eastern Europe*, IV, 4 (July 1970), is devoted to reproductions of such cartoons. In almost every issue this journal translates anti-semitic and anti-Zionist items from the Soviet press.
41. *Ostorozhno, sionizm!* (Moscow, 1969) printed in an edition of 75,000 copies. The book is summarized in *Jews in Eastern Europe*, IV, 2 (July 1969), pp.10–22. pp.22–5 summarize its unreserved endorsement by the Soviet press.
42. Here the *Chronicle* confuses *Iudaizm bez prykras* (Ukrainian Academy of Sciences, Kiev, 1963), with Kichko's other book (see note 44). The almost medieval anti-semitism of the first book, which sees the Jews manoeuvring everywhere to dominate the world, caused such an uproar outside the U.S.S.R in March 1964 that a month later the Ideological Commission of the Party Central Committee in Moscow condemned the book and supposedly withdrew it. But it was not banned. See *Soviet Jewish Affairs*, No. 1 (London, 1971), pp.109–13.
43. K. Ivanov, Z. Sheinis, *Gosudarstvo Izrail* (Moscow, 1958; expanded edition, 1959).
44. *Iudaizm i sionizm* (Kiev), summarized in *Jews in Eastern Europe*, IV, 1 (January 1969), pp.17–20.
45. *Komu oni sluzhat?* (Moscow), printed in an edition of 100,000 copies.
46. Printed in *Molodoi kommunist*, Moscow, 6 (1969), and summarized in *Jews in Eastern Europe*, IV, 3, pp.56–65.
47. *Chronicle* 14 in *Possev* V, p.18.
48. See L. Labedz (ed.), *Solzhenitsyn: a Documentary Record* (Allen Lane, The Penguin Press, London, 1970), pp.169–70.
49. Russian text of Nos. 1 and 2 in *Possev* VII, which also contains other Jewish documents. Nos. 2 and 4 (No. 4 is wholly devoted to the 'hijack trial') have been published in English by the Institute of Jewish Affairs, 13–16 Jacob's Well Mews, George Street, London W.I.
50. See Chap. 10, note 17.
51. See on this trial *Chronicle* 17 and *Exodus* 4.
52. One of the most dispassionate analyses on which to base a study of these questions is 'The Jewish Question in the U.S.S.R.', some penetrating *samizdat*

'theses'. See Russian text in *Possev* 12 (1970), pp.57–60. The theses are anonymous and appear to have been written in late 1969.

CHAPTER 16: THE CHURCHES (pp.319–33)

1. English text of a transcript of the meeting in A. Brumberg (ed.), *In Quest of Justice* (Pall Mall, London, 1970), document 46, Russian text in Arkhiepiskop Ioann San-Frantsisskii (ed.), *Zashchita very v S.S.S.R.* (Ikhthus, Paris, 1966), pp.88–101.

2. Documented with great thoroughness by Bohdan Bociurkiw in Leonard Schapiro and Peter Reddaway (eds.), *Lenin: the Man, the Theorist, the Leader* (Pall Mall, London, 1967), Chap. 6.

3. For the development of Soviet legislation on religion see B. Bociurkiw's chapter in Max Hayward and W. C. Fletcher (eds.), *Religion and the Soviet State: a Dilemma of Power* (Pall Mall, London, 1969).

4. No. 9 reads 'February', but No. 15 corrected this to March.

5. *Polnoe sobraniye sochinenii* (5-oe izdaniye, Moscow), vol. 45, pp.666–7.

6. Nikita Struve, *Christians in Contemporary Russia* (Collins/Harvill, London, 1967), p.35.

7. See Michael Bourdeaux, *Patriarch and Prophets: Persecution of the Russian Orthodox Church Today* (Macmillan, London, 1969), p.31, also *Religious Minorities in the Soviet Union (1960–70)*; Minority Rights Group, 36 Craven Street, London, W.C.2, Report No. 1 (December 1970), p.13.

8. 'Kolyancha' appears in the original, but is probably a mistyping of Kolyvan.

9. See especially the two collections of his articles, *Zashchita very* (see note 1) and *Dialog s tserkovnoi Rossiei* (same editor and publisher, 1967), also English translations and commentaries in Bourdeaux, op. cit., Chap. 7 and elsewhere, Peter Reddaway's contribution to Brumberg, op. cit., pp.63–4, 232–40, German translations in Levitin's *Kampf des Glaubens* (Schweizerisches Ost-Institut, Bern, 1967), and Italian translations in Chiesa e Società 4, *U.R.S.S.: Dibattito nella Communità Cristiana* (Jaca Book, Milan, 1968). A moving sketch of Levitin by a friend 'A.I.' is in *Vestnik RSKhD*, 95–6 (1970), pp.69–74. See also his introduction to the collection of poems by his friend Evgeny Kushev, *Ogryzkom karandasha* (Possev-Verlag, Frankfurt, 1971).

10. See especially the autobiographical article in Bourdeaux, op. cit., pp.255–63.

11. About forty, written under various names in the period 1957–8.

12. One volume of this work, *Ocherki po istorii russkoi tserkovnoi smuty*, in fact written jointly with Vadim Shavrov, has appeared in *NZh* 85–8 (December 1966–September 1967). Unfortunately the text is somewhat condensed and has proved, on comparison with a *samizdat* copy of the original, to contain systematic omissions by the *Novy Zhurnal* editors of sentences considered too sympathetic to the Living Church or too critical of the Patriarch. The Living Church was the schismatic Orthodox group which, co-operating with the régime, existed for some twenty years from the early 1920s, and to which Levitin belonged until 1944.

13. These are the names of *samizdat* collections of articles. *On Monasticism* forms the core of *Zashchita very* (see note 1).

14. In fact three times. See also the article attacking Levitin in No. 5 (1960), pp.32–7, to which he replied with characteristic vigour; text in *Dialog* ..., pp.43–69.

15. English text in Bourdeaux, op. cit., pp.272–5.

16. Completed in 1938, this novel was first published, in censored form, in the U.S.S.R. in 1966. The uncensored text appeared in English in 1967 (Collins/Harvill, London), and in Russian in 1968 (Y.M.C.A. Press, Paris). Levitin's long essay is in *Grani* 71, 72, 73, 1969.

17. *Stromati*, which started to circulate in 1968 and is due to appear from Possev-Verlag in 1971, consists of ten essays, whose titles are given in *Possev* 7 (1969), p.35. The text of one — 'Orlinnaya pesnya' — is in ibid., pp.35–42, and of another — 'Slovo khristianina' — in *Possev* 12 (1969), and 1 and 2 (1970).

18. Elsewhere he calls himself a democratic socialist. See, e.g., Bourdeaux, op. cit., pp.262–3.

19. Written in about October 1967. Russian text in *Vestnik RSKhD*, 95–6 (1970), pp.74–92, English text in *Religion in Communist Dominated Areas (R.C.D.A.)*, New York, IX, 19–20 (October 1970), pp.151–7.

20. See, e.g., Bourdeaux, op. cit., pp.275–303.

21. See English text in ibid., pp.307–15.

22. On this Church's tribulations see Chap. 8 of ibid., 'Archpriest Shpiller and his Parish', also for a fuller text of one document, *PoC*, XVII, 4 (1968), pp.102–4.

23. Noted in *samizdat* section of No. 8, Russian text in *Possev* 10 (1969), pp.6–7.

24. Russian text in *Possev* 11 (1969), pp.37–41.

25. Probably the article 'With Love and Anger' of May 1966, much of which is addressed directly to the Patriarch. English text in Bourdeaux, op. cit., pp.275–288. The English text of the two Moscow priests' letter to the Patriarch of December 1965 is in ibid., pp.194–223. For details of the priests' lives and an evaluation of the effects of their letter from the perspective of 1970, see the *samizdat* article in *Vestnik RSKhD*, 95–96 (1970), pp. 99–108.

26. Dated August 1966, English text in Bourdeaux, op. cit., pp.288–303.

27. Born 1924. See note 12, also his essay on how he became a Christian in *Grani* 63 (1967), pp.97–110.

28. Vorobyov, born 1939, 'a worker from Perm' (No. 11) and a former Moscow University student, also signed other protests, e.g. that of the 39 against Solzhenitsyn's expulsion from the Writers' Union (see Chap. 15, note 48). On September 24th, 1970, he was arrested and charged under article 70, and, in early 1971, sentenced together with R. Vedeneyev. See No. 16, Amnesty edition, pp.23–4, and No. 18, also *Possev* VI, p. 43.

29. Dated September 26th, 1969, Russian text in *Possev* 11 (1969), pp. 3–4.

30. Dated September 1969, Russian text in ibid., pp.5–6.

31. Julia Vishnevskaya, born 1949, is an accomplished poet. See her poems in *Grani* 59, 61, 70. *Chronicle* No. 10 announced the appearance in *samizdat* of her *Poems: an Anthology, 1969*. In December 1965 she was arrested and put in a mental hospital for a brief spell, after taking part in the demonstration demanding an open trial for Sinyavsky and Daniel. In 1969–70 she signed the appeals of the Action Group to the U.N. On July 7th, 1970, she was attacked by a policeman outside the court where Natalya Gorbanevskaya was being tried. Arrested and put in the Serbsky Institute, she was diagnosed as having 'mild chronic schizophrenia', but released on October 12th. See *Chronicles* 15, 16, 17, in *Possev* VI and VIII. In March 1971 she was again forcibly hospitalized.

32. Vera Lashkova: see Chap. 3 for her trial. She also signed the letter of the 32 about Levitin.

33. The artist Yury Titov and the editor Elena Stroyeva, a married couple, have signed various documents, including the letter of the 32 about Levitin and the third appeal of the Action Group to the U.N. See also reproductions of Titov's work in Gervis Frere-Cook (ed.), *The Decorative Arts of the Christian Church* (Cassell, London, 1971). In March 1971 Titov and Stroyeva were arrested and 'hospitalized', having earlier suffered a vicious press attack for their *samizdat* activity. See *Sovetskaya Litva*, Vilnius, June 26th, 1970, quoted in *Possev* 1 (1971), p.52.

34. No. 15, *Possev* VI.

35. See Nos. 12 and 13, *Possev* IV, pp.16, 39.

36. *Trud*, March 20th, 1970, article by A. Belov and A. Drugov. Drugov is the pseudonym of a K.G.B. official who specializes in Church affairs, A. Shelkov. See *Possev* IV, p.39.

37. The Russian text—*Moyo vozvrashcheniye*—is in *Grani* 79 (1971). On Levitin's case (and attitudes) as of December 1970 see the document in *Possev* VI, pp.43-4.

38. Russian text in *Possev* 11 (1968), pp.53-60, English extracts in Bourdeaux, op. cit., pp.332-9, and Brumberg, op. cit., pp.240-44.

39. English text in Bourdeaux, op. cit., pp.125-52.

40. See ibid., pp.330-31.

41. See his article 'Soviet society' in *Possev* 9 (1969), pp.35-41.

42. See Bourdeaux, op. cit., pp.153-4.

43. Russian text in *Vestnik RSKhD* 82 (1966), pp.3-20, English extracts in Bourdeaux, op. cit., pp.60-61, 237-8.

44. Brief note in No. 9.

45. See note 41.

46. For important documents on how Kamenskikh was expelled from the Odessa Seminary see *Vestnik RSKhD* 89-90 (1968), pp.68-76. Kamenskikh signed the letter referred to in note 43, on which see also Bourdeaux, p.334.

47. See No. 18, Amnesty edition, p.131.

48. On Ermogen see Bourdeaux, op. cit., *passim*, and Reddaway in Brumberg, op. cit., pp.67-8.

49. English texts in Bourdeaux, op. cit., pp.239-44, 248-54.

50. English extracts in ibid., pp. 244-7, full text in *R.C.D.A.*, VII, 9-10 (1968), full Russian text in *Vestnik RSKhD* 86 (1967), pp.66-80.

51. See item in *Zhurnal Moskovskoi Patriarkhii*, Moscow (April 1969), reported in *Possev* 6 (1969), p.19.

52. *Pochemu i ya khristianin* (Possev-Verlag, Frankfurt, 1971). Zheludkov has also written an open letter to Alexander Solzhenitsyn concerning philosophical and theological matters, but it is still unpublished. See the reply to it by an anonymous priest, a friend, in *Vestnik RSKhD* 93 (1969), pp.16-25.

53. English and Russian texts in K. van het Reve (ed.), *Letters and Telegrams to Pavel M. Litvinov* (Reidel, Dordrecht, Holland, 1969), pp.154-63, English extracts in Bourdeaux, op. cit., pp.339-41.

54. Text in Pavel Litvinov, *The Trial of the Four*, doc. IV-29. Russian text also in *Possev* 11, 1968, pp.10-11.

55. Written in about March or April 1968. Russian text in *NRS*, December 2nd, 1968.

56. Russian text, dated March 12th, 1969, in *Vestnik RSKhD* 94, 1969, pp.46-57.

57. See especially: M. Bourdeaux, *Religious Ferment in Russia: Protestant Opposition to Soviet Religious Policy* (Macmillan, London, 1968), and *Faith on Trial in Russia* (Hodder, London, 1971); his and P. Reddaway's 'State and Church and Schism: the Recent History of the Soviet Baptists' in Hayward and Fletcher, op. cit., pp.105-42; and Rosemary Harris and Xenia Howard-Johnston (eds.), *Christian Appeals from Russia* (Hodder, London, 1969).

58. No. 16, Amnesty edition, pp.15-17.

59. Dated February 25th, 1968, English text in Brumberg, op. cit., doc. 43.

60. The list of 205 Baptist prisoners given in Harris and Howard-Johnston, op. cit., gives an exile term of 3 years, as do subsequent lists. See pp.120-21 for this and other details on Zdorovets.

61. On these episodes see, e.g., Struve, op. cit., pp.260-64. On the Uniates generally see W. Mykula, 'The Gun and the Faith: Religion and Church in the Ukraine', in the *Ukrainian Review*, 3 (1969), pp.24-34.

62. In Nos. 15, 16 and 17. See an important R.C. document in *Studies in Comparative Communism*, Los Angeles, III, 2 (1970), pp.141–5.

63. In No. 14, *Possev* V, pp.12–13.

64. In No. 15, *Possev* VI, p.20.

65. As note 64.

66. In addition to this chapter, see pp.378–80 on the Leningrad Social Christians, also P. Reddaway's discussion of these questions in Brumberg, op. cit., pp.69–72.

CHAPTER 17: ALEXANDER SOLZHENITSYN (pp.335–49)

1. For details of the story prior to 1968 (and up to 1970) see especially: in English, Leopold Labedz (ed.), *Solzhenitsyn: a Documentary Record* (Allen Lane, The Penguin Press, London, 1970); in Russian, vol. 6 ('*Delo Solzhenitsyna*'. *O tvorchestve A. Solzhenitsyna*, 1970) of Aleksandr Solzhenitsyn, *Sobranie sochinenii* (Possev-Verlag, Frankfurt). More generally, see Michael Scammell's forthcoming *Solzhenitsyn: a Biographical and Critical Study* (Praeger, New York, 1972).

2. English text in Labedz, op. cit., pp.133–41.

3. English text in ibid., p.122.

4. The letter is dated May 16th, 1967. English text in ibid., pp.64–9, Russian in vol. 6 (see note 1), pp.7–13. See also the support for the letter from about a hundred writers. Texts in the same books, pp.69–80 in the first, and 14–30 and 389–98 in the second.

5. Dated January 25th, 1968. Russian text in ibid., pp.94–6, English in Labedz, op. cit., pp.114–16.

6. A loosely-knit group of 12 young writers, formed in 1921 under the patronage of Maxim Gorky and Evgeny Zamyatin.

7. *Times Literary Supplement*, April 11th, 1968.

8. For a good account of these developments see the American periodical, *Publishers' Weekly*, New York, particularly May 27th, 1968, pp.34–5, and June 17th, 1968, pp.45–6.

9. The letter is dated April 16th, 1968. Russian text in vol. 6 (see note 1), pp.97–8, English in Labedz, op. cit., p.117.

10. Russian text in vol. 6, pp.31–2, English in Labedz, op. cit., pp.80–81.

11. English text in ibid., pp.82–101, Russian in vol. 6, pp.33–57.

12. Russian text in vol. 6, p.61, English in Labedz, op. cit., p.103.

13. Russian text in vol. 6, pp.62–3, English in Labedz, op. cit., pp.103–4.

14. The letter is dated April 18th, 1968. Russian text in vol. 6, pp.99–100, English in Labedz, op. cit., pp.120–21. See also the subsequent statement by *Grani*, Russian text in vol. 6, pp.102–3, English in Labedz, op. cit., p.123.

15. Valery Fyodorovich Turchin is a physicist of considerable stature (see, e.g., *Novy Mir*, 6 (1970), p.276) and the author of a well-known *samizdat* essay, 'The Inertia of Fear', described by No. 6 as 'a philosophical examination of some problems of contemporary society'. It has not yet appeared in the West. He is also co-author with Academician Sakharov and Roy Medvedev of an 'Appeal to the Party and Government Leaders of the U.S.S.R.', dated March 19th, 1970, and summarized in No. 13. Full Russian text in *Possev* 7 (1970), pp.36–42, English in *Survey*, London, 76 (1970), pp.160–70.

16. English text in Labedz, op. cit., pp.145–7, Russian in vol. 6, pp. 116–21.

17. Listed in No. 9: 'A collection of letters sent to A. Chakovsky, [the first six] about his article "Reply to a Reader" and [the last] about the slanderous campaign against Solzhenitsyn in the pages of *Literary Gazette*. The authors of the letters are: 1. film-worker L. S. Kogan; 2. loader and former political prisoner A. Marchenko (now imprisoned again); 3. B. I. Tsukerman; 4. chemical engineer (now political prisoner) Lev Kvachevsky; 5. sailor L. N. Tymchuk; 6. turner V.

N. Kryukov; 7. V. F. Turchin.' The collection, edited by 'P.S.' and dated August 1969, has not yet been published in the West. However, items 1, 2, 4, 5 and 6 are documents V-41 to V-44 in Pavel Litvinov, *The Trial of the Four* (Longmans, London, 1972). On item 2 see also Chap. 9, note 12.

18. Surprisingly, the *Chronicle* only recorded its title—'The Responsibility of a Writer and the Irresponsibility of *Literary Gazette*'—and that it 'is concerned with Solzhenitsyn, his readers and his critics' (No. 5). The English text (condensed) is in Labedz, op. cit., pp.142–5, the Russian in vol. 6, pp.122–34.

19. See No. 12 for much revealing detail of the machinations surrounding the expulsion. Russian text in *Possev* IV, p.13, English in Labedz, op. cit., pp.165–6.

20. Full English text in ibid., pp.148–58, Russian (with a few missing passages) in vol. 6, pp.135–46.

21. English text in Labedz, op. cit., p.159, Russian in vol. 6, p.147.

22. See his letter of 1967 supporting Solzhenitsyn; English text (extracts) in Labedz, op. cit., pp.73–4, full Russian text in vol. 6, pp.396–8.

23. See his telegram of 1967 supporting Solzhenitsyn; texts in the same books, pp.71 and 391 respectively.

24. A slightly different version of the Russian text is in *Possev* 12 (1969), p.5.

25. Anna Akhmatova (1888–1966), the outstanding Russian poet who was expelled from the Writers' Union in 1946 after scurrilous attacks on her by Zhdanov and others.

26. Boris Pasternak (1890–1960) was expelled from the Writers' Union in 1958 for having his novel *Doctor Zhivago* published abroad. See on this: Robert Conquest, *Courage of Genius: the Pasternak Affair* (Collins/Harvill, London, 1961).

27. Mikhail Sholokhov (b. 1905): author of *And Quiet Flows the Don*, but now an extreme conservative in literary and political matters.

28. Chukovskaya's letter to Sholokhov of April 1966 attacked him ferociously for his reactionary speech at the 23rd Party Congress. English text in L. Labedz and M. Hayward (eds.), *On Trial* (Collins/Harvill, London, 1967), pp.292–6, Russian in *Grani* 62 (1966), pp.131–5.

29. *The Deserted House* (Barrie and Rockliff, London, 1967). Russian edition: *Opustelyi dom* (Librairie des Cinq Continents, Paris, 1965). Under the title *Sofya Petrovna* the story also appeared in *NZh* 83 and 84 (1966). It was written 'for the drawer' in 1939–40.

30. No. 2 wrote of Kopelev (b. 1912) after the Galanskov-Ginzburg trial: 'a critic and specialist in German literature, Master of Philological Sciences, member of the Writers' Union, former inmate of Stalin's camps, rehabilitated and reinstated in the party, works at the [Moscow] Institute of Art History, signed the letter of the 120 and a personal letter about the trial [document IV-25 in Pavel Litvinov, *The Trial of the Four*], and wrote [in late 1967] the article "Why the Rehabilitation of Stalin is Impossible", printed in the Austrian communist journal *Tagebuch* [Vienna, no. for January-February 1968; Russian text in *NRS*, April 19th, 1968, English in A. Brumberg, *In Quest of Justice* (Pall Mall, London, 1970), doc. 74]. He has now been expelled from the party by his district committee, books and articles of his already accepted for publication have been cancelled, and he has been sacked from his job by order of the director, without any decision by the Academic Council.'

31. French text in *Le Monde*, November 19th, 1969, Russian in vol. 6, pp.189–92, English in Labedz, op. cit., pp.162–3. See also other foreign protests in ibid., pp.161–3.

32. See, e.g. *Literary Russia*, December 19th, 1969, p.4.

33. English text in Labedz, op. cit., pp.169–70, Russian in *Possev* 1 (1970), pp.10–11.

34. Full text not yet available.
35. Full text not yet available. Medvedev is a personal friend of Solzhenitsyn. See, e.g. his book *The Medvedev Papers* (Macmillan, London, 1971), pp.35–43 and *passim*. When he was forcibly interned in a mental hospital in May–June 1970 Solzhenitsyn wrote a devastating protest on his behalf, reproduced in *Chronicle* 14. See English text in Labedz, op. cit., pp.171–2.
36. Full text not yet available. Vronsky was one of the hundred members of the Writers' Union who supported Solzhenitsyn in 1967. See ibid., pp.69–70.
37. For the full list see ibid., p.164. The text given here is as in *The Times*, not a re-translation.
38. See especially Nos. 12, 14, 16 and 17.
39. Summarized in the *samizdat* section of Nos. 16 and 17, these are entitled, respectively, *The Word Forces its Way Through* and *He was Sent by the God of Anger and Sorrow*. The former is in the possession of the Y.M.C.A. Press, Paris.
40. See also the articles by Pierre Emmanuel and Gabriel Laub in No. 12, *Possev* IV, pp.13–14, English text in Labedz, op. cit., pp.166–7.

CHAPTER 18: THE WORLD OF *SAMIZDAT* (pp.350–73)

1. From his *Will the Soviet Union Survive until 1984?* (Allen Lane, The Penguin Press, London, 1970), pp.7–9. The Russian edition, *Prosushchestvuyet li Sovetskii Soyuz do 1984 goda?*, appeared in 1969 in Amsterdam.
2. i.e. her *Into the Whirlwind* (Collins/Harvill, London, 1967). Russian text in *Grani* 64–8.
3. Russian texts of Varlam Shalamov's stories are in *NZh* 85, 86, 89, 91, 96, 98, 100 (1966–70), and *Grani* 76 and 77 (1970); two English translations are in Michael Scammell (ed.), *Russia's Other Writers* (Longmans, London, 1970). See also the vivid account of a speech by Shalamov at an evening in memory of the poet Mandelshtam, *Grani* 77, pp.86–8.
4. See Chap. 17, note 29.
5. Russian text of a section of Vladimir Maksimov's novel, entitled *Dvornik Lashkov*, in *Grani* 64 (1967); English, entitled *House in the Clouds*, in Scammell, op. cit. The whole novel, *7 dnei tvoreniya*, is due to be published by Possev-Verlag, Frankfurt.
6. Published in his *Pesni* (Possev-Verlag, Frankfurt, 1969). In 1970 Galich was elected to Academician Sakharov's Human Rights Committee. See No. 17, Amnesty edition, p.47.
7. Text in her *Stikhi* (Possev-Verlag, Frankfurt, 1969), pp.117–38.
8. Russian text in *Vestnik RSKhD* 93 (1969), pp.89–92. Antipov is probably a pseudonym. See also a summary of an article by Antipov on Solzhenitsyn's expulsion from the Writers' Union in *Possev* IV, p. 20.
9. A typescript is in the possession of the Alexander Herzen Foundation, Amsterdam.
10. Collins/Harvill, London, 1970. Russian edition: *Nezhelannoye puteshestviye v Sibir* (Harcourt, Brace & World, New York, 1970).
11. See note 1.
12. These five, plus Amalrik's adaptation of Gogol's story *The Nose*, were published as *Pesy* (Amsterdam, 1970).
13. See text of the leaflets they handed out, *Possev* 6 (1969), p.12, also a photo of their demonstration on the jacket of the U.S. edition of *Will the Soviet Union …* (Harper & Row, New York, 1970).
14. See his contribution in Pavel Litvinov, *The Trial of the Four*, appendix III.
15. English text in *Will the Soviet Union …* (London), pp.93–105, and in *Survey* 74–5 (1970), both of which contain other important documents by and about Amalrik.

16. Published in, e.g. the *Sunday Telegraph*, London, August 10th, 1969.
17. Probably a reference to a practice of the poet Evgeny Evtushenko.
18. An error: in fact in unfortunately chosen extracts, which made Amalrik seem much less sympathetic to Kuznetsov than does the full text.
19. e.g. with his article 'The Foreign Correspondents in Moscow', English text in the *New York Review of Books*, March 25th, 1971, Russian in *Possev* 11 (1970), pp.42–8. Here he criticizes certain journalists for being intimidated by the K.G.B. and failing to do their journalistic duty.
20. See full text of this interview with C.B.S., shown in the U.S. on July 28th, 1970, in *Survey* 77 (1970), pp.128–36.
21. English edition, *Progress, Coexistence and Intellectual Freedom* (André Deutsch, London, 1968). Russian edition: *Memorandum akademika Sakharova: Tekst, otkliki, diskussiya* (Possev-Verlag, Frankfurt, 1970). On the evolution and publication of the essay see Zh. Medvedev, *The Medvedev Papers* (Macmillan, London, 1971), pp.387–8. For two collective protests signed by Sakharov in 1966 see P. Litvinov, *The Demonstration on Pushkin Square* (Collins/Harvill, London, 1969), pp.15–16, and *Possev*, September 16th, 1966. For details on his publications see *Possev* 1 (1969), p.23.
22. See Chap. 17, note 15.
23. See *Chronicle* 16, Amnesty edition, p.8.
24. See *Ishkod (Exodus)*, No. 4.
25. At least until 1968 he worked at the Institute of Theoretical and Experimental Physics attached to the government's State Committee on the Uses of Atomic Energy. With V. B. Kopeliovich he published an article in *Yadernaya fizika* vol. 8, No. 2, (August 1968), pp.371–8, translated in *Soviet Journal of Nuclear Physics*, vol. 8, No. 2 (February 1969), pp.212–16.
26. See the committee's 'Principles' in No. 17, Amnesty edition, pp.45–6.
27. See the responses of foreign scientists, collected together in V. Poremsky's useful article in *Grani* 72 (1969), pp.192–212, reprinted in *Memorandum* ... (see note 21).
28. See also his practical actions in defending, e.g., both Pimenov and Amalrik (No. 16). These intercessions may well have cost him his leadership of the polymer physics group at Moscow's Plastics Research Institute, from which he was demoted in autumn 1970 'for political reasons' (No. 16).
29. See summaries in Nos. 13, 14, 16, 17 (*samizdat* news sections). The journal is due to be published in the West by René Cassin's Institute for the Rights of Man.
30. This essay was included in *Phoenix-66*. See English text in A. Brumberg (ed.), *In Quest of Justice* (Pall Mall, London, 1970), doc. 75, Russian in *Grani* 67 (1968).
31. On one of them see note 30. The Russian text of the other—'Kvadrilon'— is in *Grani* 64 (1967), and the English text will appear in P. Reddaway's forthcoming *Russia's Other Intellectuals* (Longmans, London, 1972).
32. No. 12 announced the *samizdat* circulation of a collection of twenty of his essays. This is soon to be published by Possev-Verlag. No. 13 reported that Chalidze's journal (No. 4) included an essay by Pomerants on the Russian national spirit. A long essay—*Chelovek bez prilagatelnogo*—has appeared in *Grani* 77 (1970): its original title was *Man of Air*.
33. The first of these two is included in the collection mentioned in note 32. The second is the essay named in note 32.
34. He is a junior research officer at Moscow's All-Union Research Institute for Scientific and Technical Information (V.I.N.I.T.I.), where he has given lectures on semiotics. His publications are numerous. See, e.g. his article 'The Contemporary Situation as Regards the Basis of the Theory of Aggregates

(mnozhestv)' in S. G. Mikhlin and others (eds.), *Trudy chetvertogo Vsesoyuznogo matematicheskogo sezda. Leningrad, 3-12 iyulya 1961,* (Leningrad, 1964), t. 2. See also about him *Possev* 3 (1968), pp.12-13.

(5. Published as A. S. Yesenin-Volpin, *A Leaf of Spring* (Thames & Hudson, London, 1961). The book contains parallel Russian and English texts.

36. See A. Ginzburg, *Belaya kniga* (Possev-Verlag, Frankfurt, 1967), pp.399-405.

37. See Pavel Litvinov, op. cit., pp.70-73, also 98.

38. See Chap. 11, note 10.

39. See his letter to the Supreme Soviet's Presidium, written jointly with Sakharov, Chalidze and Pyotr Yakir, which thanks the Presidium for quashing a case against two young dissenters and then appeals for similar action in other cases. *Possev* 11 (1970), p.62.

40. See No. 17, Amnesty edition, p.47.

41. Melor Georgiyevich Sturua's article is in *Izvestia* of April 9th, 1969, p.2.

42. Text in *Possev* IV, pp.59-63.

43. Text in *Possev* VI, pp.59-62. Included in *Social Problems*, No. 2.

44. This book is due to be published in the West. Its section on international postal correspondence forms the basis of pp.440-50 in Medvedev, op. cit. See also p.437.

45. Text in *Possev* 7 (1970), pp.49-53. Gerasimchuk has published numerous articles in journals like *Znaniye — sila* and *Tekhnika — molodyozhi.*

46. Published by Possev-Verlag: *Moi vospominaniya,* 1971.

47. See English text (extracts) in Z. A. B. Zeman, *Prague Spring* (Penguin, Harmondsworth, 1969). pp.61-5.

48. See English text in ibid., pp.152-5. First published in *Literarni listy,* June 27th, 1968.

49. On the first week of the invasion see Robert Littell (ed.), *The Czech Black Book* (Pall Mall, London, 1969). The book was prepared by members of the History Institute of the Czechoslovak Academy of Sciences and sent to the West.

50. See Chap. 7, 'The April Action Programme', in Zeman, op. cit.

51. Letter sent by the Soviet, East German, Polish, Hungarian and Bulgarian parties to the Czechoslovak party on July 15th, 1968, as an ultimatum against further liberalization. See English text in *Studies in Comparative Communism,* Los Angeles, I, 1-2 (1968), pp.257-62. This issue has 160 pages of documentation covering the period up to October 1968. An excellent analysis of high-level politics up to early 1969 by Pavel Tigrid is in *Survey* 73 and 74-5.

52. The *Chronicle* errs: P. Reddaway is not 'Dr'. The Foundation's address is Amstel 268, Amsterdam-C.

53. Edited by P. Litvinov (English edition, Collins/Harvill, London, 1969).

54. Edited by K. van het Reve (Reidel, Dordrecht, Holland, 1969).

CHAPTER 19: LENINGRAD AND THE PROVINCES (pp.375-416)

1. From Levitin's essay about Talantov: *Possev* 10 (1969), pp.6-7.

2. For details of some of the oppositional activities in Leningrad from 1958 to 1967, see *Possev* 1 (1968), pp.9-13, and in the mid-1960s, see the big article by L. P. Nestor in *Possev* V, pp.23-34.

3. Only in fact in ethically complex matters. See *Possev* 1 (1971), pp.39-40.

4. For a fuller explanation see ibid., p.40.

5. Vladimir Solovyov (1853-1900), a Christian philosopher and poet of the first rank.

6. Wrongly recorded as Vladimir in No. 1. Corrected in No. 2.

7. The Christian name Boris is given by Vladimir Osipov in his essay in *Grani* 80 (1971).

8. Konosov, according to No. 1. However, A. Petrov-Agatov gives Kolosov, which is more likely, adding that he is a poet. Petrov-Agatov also gives patronymics for Ogurtsov, Sado, Vagin, Ivanov and Bochevarov. These are, respectively, Vyacheslavovich, Yukhanovich, Alexandrovich, Viktorovich and Nikolayevich. See *Possev* 6 (1970), pp.10–12.

9. First name added in No. 2.

10. The exact meaning of this sentence is not clear. Several meanings seem possible.

11. See *Possev* 1 (1971), pp.38–43.

12. See ref. in note 8.

13. See text in *Possev* 3 (1971), where Petrov also draws an admiring portrait of Borodin.

14. See *Chronicle* 17. See also his poems in *Possev* 5 (1971) and *Grani* 80 (1971).

15. See his poems in *Prostor* 10 (1967), and *Neva* 3 (1968), and his essay 'The Secret of the Old Catholic Church' in *Neva* 8 (1968).

16. See L. P. Nestor's article in *Possev* V, pp.25, 27, 29, 31.

17. See ibid., p.25, also Kvachevsky's letter in Pavel Litvinov, *The Trial of the Four*, doc. V-42.

18. See the letter signed by ten of them in ibid., doc. IV-3.

19. See *Possev* V, p.27, and Gendler's letters to Litvinov in K. van het Reve (ed.), *Letters and Telegrams* ... , docs. 16 and 58.

20. See the *samizdat* collection of replies described in Chap. 17, note 17. Chakovsky's article is doc. V-11 in Litvinov, op. cit., and Kvachevsky's reply is V-42.

21. No. 2 reported: 'Kvachevsky ... a signatory to the letters of the 170 and the ten Leningraders, has been sacked "in connection with a reduction of staff".'

22. See pp.110, 193.

23. Although this text is not available, a probably slightly earlier letter from Danilov and Gendler to the Procurator-General is. Dated April 3rd, 1968, when the trial was nearly over, it asks carefully formulated questions about how to gain access, in view of the authors' failure to do so. It has not yet been published.

24. No. 4 had previously reported the charging under article 70 of these three plus Danilov and Shashenkov.

25. Kvachevsky may have been tricked into this. See *Possev* V, pp.23, 34.

26. See ibid., pp.28, 34. See also his letter in Litvinov, op. cit., doc. IV-24.

27. Published in Munich.

28. *Ubiistvo tsarskoi semi*, published in the West by Judge Sokolov after his investigation of 1919. His conclusions are challenged in Guy Richards, *The Hunt for the Czar* (Peter Davies, London, 1971).

29. *Istoki i smysl russkogo kommunizma* (Y.M.C.A. Press, Paris, 1955).

30. *Novyi grad* (Chekhov Press, New York, 1952).

31. No. 6: 'Yury Lyubarsky, a mathematician at the Institute of Telegraphy [...] who gave evidence in court in favour of the defendants, having renounced part of the evidence he had given at the pre-trial investigation, has been sacked from his job.' For details on his role see *Possev* V, p.27, where his name is spelt — probably wrongly — as Lyubansky.

32. No. 10: 'It includes the interrogation of the witnesses and the accused, the Procurator's speech, and speeches of the defence, the final pleas of the defendants, and the sentence. Violations of legality are indicated, and the background of the trial is described. There is a short transcript of the appeal hearing.' The last item is missing in *Possev* V, pp.23–34, which is simply Nestor's record, dated January 10th, 1969.

33. See *Chronicles* 14 and 15, *Possev* V, p.18, and VI, p.19.

34. No. 8: 'Irina Muravyova has been expelled from the Union of Journalists, and the writer Boris Ivanov has been expelled from the party and dismissed from

his job, both for signing letters of protest.' For an interesting essay by Muravyova, see the almanac *Molodoi Leningrad* (1964), pp.84–103. No. 11: 'On November 5th B. O. Mityashin was arrested in Leningrad. For one and a half years he had been writing letters under his own name to Soviet journals and papers, condemning acts of political repression (the trial of the demonstrators of August 25th, 1968, and the trial of Ginzburg et al.). All the letters have turned out to be in the possession of the investigating organs (Porukov being the investigator). Mityashin had been summoned to the K.G.B. on more than one occasion and ordered to make a signed statement to the effect that he would cease his "activities". Mityashin is charged under article 70 of the Russian Criminal Code.'

35. No. 11: 'On August 12th, 1969, Boris [Lvovich] Shilkrot, a student at the Leningrad Electro-technical Institute, was arrested in Leningrad. During a search of his flat, a large number of *samizdat* manuscripts were seized.

'In April 1968 Shilkrot had written and circulated in the lecture-halls of the Institute an appeal calling on students not to tolerate manifestations of Stalinism and to fight for the democratic transformation of our society.

'In mid-December Shilkrot was in a Leningrad special psychiatric hospital for diagnosis. His trial is expected soon.'

No. 14 gives details of the confiscated *samizdat*, also of his closed trial in January 1970, at which he received three years of strict régime. See *Possev* V, p.17. The *samizdat* 'Register of People Sentenced in the 1960s' adds that he is a Jew and a bachelor, was born in 1946, and has the home address of Leningrad, ul. Skorokhodova, d. 30, kv. 10, where his sister and brother live.

36. No. 9: 'Berger (not Bergel, as reported in *Chronicle* [No. 8], Braun [son of the poet Nikolai Braun—No. 8], Malchevsky and Vodopyanov, arrested [in May] in Leningrad, have been charged under article 70 of the Russian Criminal Code. Their trial is expected in September or October [1969]. They have been accused of circulating *samizdat* and books published abroad.' The 'Register of People Sentenced in the 1960s' indicates that Nikolai Nikolayevich Braun (b. 1938) and Sergei Andreyevich Malchevsky (b. 1935) received seven years in camps plus two in exile, and Anatoly Solomonovich Berger (b. 1938) four and two years respectively. Their Leningrad addresses are, respectively, ul. Lenina, d. 34, kv. 57; Vasilevsky Ostrov, 13-aya liniya, d. 16, kv. 15; and ul. Podvodnika Kuzmina, d. 48, kv. 22. Braun is a poet, Malchevsky a taxi-driver, and Berger a publishing administrator and poet.

37. No. 8's report adds to No. 9 only that Levin 'is a senior technician at the Experimental Research Institute for the Mechanical Processing of Mineral Resources'.

38. See *Chronicle* 14, *Possev* V, pp.18–19.

39. The only additional information in No. 5 is that five students including Pomazov, Kupchinov and Buidin were drafted into the army after their expulsion, and that the dismissal of the four teachers followed the circulation of 'The State and Socialism' and other *samizdat* materials, also searches of their homes.

40. Perhaps including the subject of this item: 'Valentina Yurkina of Gorky, who typed out works of *samizdat*, was expelled from the Komsomol in the spring of 1968, and in February 1969 sacked from her job "for unworthy behaviour".' (No. 7).

41. 'A Marxist analysis of our state. The work of history students at Gorky University.' (No. 6: '*Samizdat* news').

42. Described as 'a student of the Department of Mathematic Linguistics' in No. 5, which wrongly called her 'I. Goldfarb'.

43. The word repression signifies in Russian, with reference to the Stalin period, either death or imprisonment in a concentration camp. Mrs Pavlenkov's father

died in a camp and her mother spent many years in one. See *Chronicle* 15, *Possev* V, p.26.

44. See *Chronicles* 12 and 13, *Possev* IV, pp.11, 25–7. They were born in 1929, 1943, 1945 and 1946 respectively.

45. See *Chronicle* 14, *Possev* V, pp.14–15.

46. See *Chronicle* 17, Amnesty edition, p.85. The 'Register of People Sentenced in the 1960s' adds that Kapranov's wife Galina and their sons live in Central Asia: Uz.S.S.R., Andizhanskaya obl., Chustsky raion, pos. Kassansai, and Zhiltsov's mother at: Ryazanskaya obl., Rybatsky poselok Elatma, ul. Proletarskaya 10.

47. Vitaly Vasilevich Pomazov (in some sources, Pomozov), born 1947, was arrested in October 1970 after his return from the army. See *Chronicles* 16 and 18, *Possev* VI, p.39, and VIII, p51.

48. See Russian text and Ukrainian translation in *Biblioteka 'Vilna dumka'*, Paris, 5 (1969), pp.1–7. The text of the second letter is not yet available.

49. Not in the copy received in the West.

50. No. 2 is the source except where otherwise indicated.

'Igor Alekseyev, a philosophy lecturer at Novosibirsk University [N.U.], has received a severe party reprimand.'

'Raisa Berg, Doctor of Biological Science, geneticist at the S.S.A.S. Institute of Molecular Biology, has been dismissed "at her own request".'

'Lyudmila Borisova, a sociologist, has received a severe party reprimand.'

'Maiya Cheremisina, a linguist and Master of Philological Sciences at N.U., has been dismissed "because of staff reductions", in connection with the closure of the Department of Mathematical Linguistics.'

'Felix Dreizin, a linguist at N.U. and Master of Philological Sciences, has been dismissed "at his own request".'

'Abram Fet, a Doctor of Physical-Mathematical Sciences at the S.S.A.S. Institute of Mathematics, has been demoted by the Academic Council to junior research fellow.' 'Abram Fet has been dismissed from his job' (No. 5).

'Aleksei Gladsky, Doctor of Physical-Mathematical Sciences, who works at the S.S.A.S. Institute of Mathematics and at N.U., has been dismissed "because of staff reductions" from N.U., in connection with the closure of the Department of Mathematical Linguistics.'

'Iosif Goldenberg, a literary scholar and teacher at N.U., has been banned from teaching' (No. 5). He also signed the 'letter of the 170'.

'M. M. Gromyko, Doctor of History, who works at the S.S.A.S. Institute of History, Literature and Philosophy and is a [woman] Professor of N.U., has been banned from teaching at the university' (No. 5).

'Kirill Ilichyov, a physicist at the S.S.A.S. Institute of Kinetics, has been expelled from the Komsomol by its district committee.'

'Vladimir Konev, a lecturer in philosophy at N.U., has received a severe party reprimand.'

'Esfir Kositsyna, a school-teacher of English at the S.S.A.S. Physics and Mathematics School [P.M.S.], has been expelled from the party and dismissed from her job "at her own request".'

'Boris Naidorf, a physics teacher at the S.S.A.S. P.M.S., has been dismissed "at his own request".'

'Vladimir Pertsovsky, a literature teacher at the S.S.A.S. P.M.S., has been dismissed from his job.'

'Svetlana Rozhnova, a historian and graduate student at N.U., has been expelled from the party.'

'[E.] Shtengel, of the S.S.A.S. Institute of Automation, has been dismissed "because of staff reductions".'

51. See Chap. 3, note 59.

52. See *Chronicle* 16, *Possev* VI, pp.35–6, Amnesty edition, pp.17–19, also *Possev* I (1971), pp.10–12.

53. See, e.g., the architect S. D. Albanov's signature on doc. IV-17 in Litvinov, *The Trial of the Four*.

54. Lived 1792–1845, exiled to Siberia for his part in the abortive officers' revolt of December 1825.

55. Lived 1860–1911, a leading member of the populist, revolutionary underground organization Narodnaya Volya (The People's Will).

56. A. I. Denikin (1872–1947) was implicated in General L. G. Kornilov's attempted putsch against Kerensky's Provisional Government. Later he commanded a White Army in south Russia during the Civil War.

57. A police tribunal established in 1934 with extensive powers of punishment.

58. Elena Stasova (1873–1966) was a member of the party from 1898, worked in its secretariat after 1917, faded from view under Stalin, but re-emerged in 1956.

59. This long and important document, dated May 5th, 1967, is available but has not yet been published.

60. Mikoyan was then People's Commissar of Foreign and Domestic Trade.

61. i.e. *Voprosy istorii* 12 (1967), and 1 and 2 (1968).

62. David Lvovich Golinkov is an 'investigator of especially important cases attached to the U.S.S.R. Procuracy-General and the R.S.F.S.R. Procuracy.' He has done police work for over thirty years.

63. The Turkic language *Sovet Uzbekistoni*, Tashkent, June 10th, 1969, named three people sentenced to five years each.

64. Available but as yet unpublished.

65. i.e. Sh. R. Rashidov, also a candidate member of the party Politbureau in Moscow.

66. See Robert Conquest, *The Nation Killers* (Macmillan, London, 1970), *passim*.

67. According to the Ukrainian Mykhaylo Masyutko, the pogrom took place on July 27th, 28th and 29th, 1958, many Chechens being killed and 2,500 Russians punished for their involvement. See Michael Browne (ed.), *Ferment in the Ukraine* (Macmillan, London, 1971), p.104. Masyutko's account clearly needs confirmation. If true, it probably explains why a top Soviet leader, N. G. Ignatov, attended a party meeting in Grozny in August 1958, at which 'sharp criticism' was levelled at the local officials and the 'isolation of many party and Soviet organs from the masses' was deplored. See Conquest, op. cit., p.156, and *Pravda*, September 2nd, 1958.

68. i.e. the Brethren's Cemetery just outside Riga.

69. The *Chronicle*'s slip of putting 'article 67' has been corrected.

70. In its list of people arrested or tried in 1969 No. 11 indicated that Kallas had been charged under article 70. No. 12 corrected the date of arrest to October 16th and reported that a court had adjudged him of unsound mind in January 1970. *Possev* IV, p.17. *Looming* (*Creation*) appears in Tallinn monthly.

71. *Sickle and Hammer*, a Tallinn weekly.

72. *Chronicle* 14, *Possev* V, p.18.

73. On Kim see p.394.

74. The co-author of articles in (a) *Problema nervnoi trofiki v teorii i praktike meditsiny* (*The Problem of Nerve Nutrition in Medical Theory and Practice*), a conference record published by the Academy of Medical Sciences, Moscow, 1963, and (b) *Vodorodnaya svyaz* (*Hydrogen Bonding*), a collection published by the Institute of Chemical Physics, Moscow, 1964.

75. A doctor of biology, Liberman has published widely. See, e.g., his article,

'Methods of Studying the Effect of Ionizing Radiation on the Functions of the Nerve Cell', in *Biofizika* (1958), III, 2.

76. V. V. Tikhomirov, a specialist in radio technology, became in 1963 the head of the department for automation in biological experiments at the Institute of Biological Physics. See the article, 'The Scientific Centre of Biological Research in Pushchino', in *Vestnik AN S.S.S.R.* 11 (1968), pp.9–18.

77. Among Veprintsev's writings see his and V. I. Markov's book *Metodika i tekhnika zapisi golosov zhivotnykh v polevykh usloviyakh* (Moscow, 1963).

78. See Zh. Medvedev's account of all the manoeuvres in his *The Medvedev Papers* (Macmillan, London, 1971), pp.35–43.

79. September 11th, 1968.

80. *Fiziki shutyat*. A co-editor was Valery Turchin. On Pavlinchuk's activities, deception by a provocateur, and death, see Medvedev, op. cit., pp.404–5, 464–7.

81. *Tarusskiye stranitsy* (Kaluga, 1961), edited in English by Andrew Field as *Pages from Tarusa* (Little, Brown, Boston, 1963).

82. See praise of him in Medvedev, op. cit., p.400.

83. On these episodes see ibid., pp.404–5.

84. *Fiziki prodolzhayut shutit*.

85. Published as *The Rise and Fall of T. D. Lysenko* (Columbia University Press, New York and London, 1969). The Russian text of an earlier and incomplete draft appears in *Grani* 70 and 71 (1969). On the book see Medvedev, op. cit., pp.42–3, 389, and on Medvedev's dismissal see pp.397–407.

86. These appear together in *The Medvedev Papers*, and also in a Russian edition due out in London in 1971.

87. See the long account of all this, based partly on his twin brother Roy's record, in *Chronicle* 14, Possev V, pp.6–8. A book on the subject by the twins is to be published by Macmillan in 1971, *A Question of Madness*.

88. S. S. Sarychev is a specialist on the history of Persian and Afghan philosophy. See, e.g., his contributions to the Institute of Philosophy's *History of Philosophy*. In vol. 4 (1959) he wrote Chap. 3 on the philosophical thought of the Central Asian peoples, and in vol. 5 (1961) Chap. 8 on the philosophy of the peoples of Tadzhikistan.

89. Mayakovsky committed suicide, partly in disillusionment with the Soviet system, on April 14th, 1930.

90. See No. 16, *Possev* VI, pp.32–3.

91. See especially items in ibid, pp.38–9, and in No. 17.

92. See especially the items in No. 17.

CHAPTER 20: STALIN, STALINISTS, FASCISTS AND CENSORS (pp.417–37)

1. See Chap. 3, note 34.

2. This 1,400-page typescript is due to be published in the U.S. On its evolution see Zh. Medvedev, *The Medvedev Papers* (Macmillan, London, 1971), pp.388–9.

3. Said by No. 6 to be anonymous, but corrected in No. 7.

4. In her second book, *Only One Year* (Hutchinson, London, 1969), Miss Alliluyeva agrees that she drew an over-favourable picture of her father in her first book, which she wrote in Moscow in 1963 and published in the West after her defection (Hutchinson, London, 1967).

5. Only one of his essays has so far appeared in the West: 'And Shepilov Who Joined Them', *RM* Nos. 28 34–6 (1971). Six others essays have been listed by the *Chronicle*. Gusarov was forcibly interned in a psychiatric hospital in March–May 1971.

6. Russian text in *Possev*, September 16th, 1966.

7. Mistyped in No. 11 as Vakhmin, but corrected here.

8. Misspelt in No. 11 as Ioffe, but corrected here.

9. See *Chronicles* 14, 15 and 16, *Possev* V, pp.16–17, and VI, pp.12–14, 37.

10. This stinging essay is doc. 73 in A. Brumberg (ed.), *In Quest of Justice* (Pall Mall, London, 1970), Russian text in *Possev* 8 (1968), pp.47–9.

11. Russian text in *Vestnik RSKhD* 94 (1969), pp.62–5. Aleksandrov is probably a pseudonym.

12. English text in *Survey* 70–71 (1969), pp.261–9, Russian in *Possev* 5 (1969), pp.57–60. Both texts in the booklet *Za prava cheloveka* (Possev-Verlag, Frankfurt, 1969).

13. i.e. the review by E. Boltin in No. 2 and the article by V. Golikov, S. Murashov, I. Chkhikvishvili, N. Shatagin and S. Shaumyan in No. 3.

14. English and Russian texts in *Za prava cheloveka*, pp.45–98. G. I. Petrovsky (1878–1958) occupied high political posts from 1917 to 1939, when he was disgraced. On his subsequent fortunes see Robert Conquest, *The Great Terror* (Macmillan, London, 1968), pp.469–70.

15. Russian text in *Possev* 6 (1969), pp.25–31, and 7 (1969), pp.25–34. French text in Roy Medvedev, *Faut-il réhabiliter Staline?* (Paris, 1969).

16. See p.122.

17. Textual analysis suggests that this is a pseudonym of Lev Petrovsky.

18. See *Ogonyok* 7, 8 and 9 (1966), under L. Tarasov, and *Literary Russia*, December 5th, 1968, under Vasilevsky.

19. Russian text in *Possev* V, pp.51–8.

20. See the French text of Raskolnikov's famous letter of 1939 in *Samizdat I* (Seuil, Paris, 1969), pp.93–101

21. i.e. a speech by the K.G.B. chief Andropov in *Pravda*, December 21st, 1967.

22. An ichthyologist with various publications to his credit.

23. Co-author of an article on marine biology in *Okeanologiya* (1964), IV, 4, pp.707–719.

24. See his *Progress, Coexistence and Intellectual Freedom* (André Deutsch, London, 1968), pp.56–7, 125–6.

25. Her father Yakov Ganetsky, Director of the Museum of the Revolution, was purged and shot in the late 'thirties.

26. A familiar form of Andrei.

27. See her 'Zimnii pereval' in *Novyi mir* 10 (1968), attacked in *Soviet Russia*, July 13th, 1969.

28. A long transcript of this meeting appears in Russia in *Possev*, January 13th, 1967, and in English in *Survey* 63 (1967), and in Vladimir Petrov, *Soviet Historians and the German Invasion* (Columbia, South Carolina, 1968).

29. Issue of November 25th, 1969, reprinted in *Possev* II, p.63.

30. A typescript copy marked No. 2 has appeared in *Possev* VI, pp.57–8. As it contains some of the material described by the *Chronicle* as being in No. 3, it seems possible that No. 3 is an expanded version of No. 2. It is also possible, however, that a mistake has occurred in the numbering, and that the typescript published in *Possev* VI reached the West in incomplete form.

31. Misspelt in the *Chronicle* copy received in the West as Solunsky.

32. Russian text in *Novyi mir* nos. 3–5 (1964), English: *Years Off My Life* (Constable, London, 1964).

33. Misspelt in the *Chronicle* as Nadraya. On his trial see Robert Conquest, *Power and Policy in the U.S.S.R.* (Macmillan, London, 1961), pp.449–51.

34. Trouble threatened Monakhov after the 22nd Congress of 1961, but Tolstikov averted it after Khrushchev's fall. See *Possev* VI, p.58.

35. *Krucha.*

36. e.g. *Tonkaya nit*, written with Ya. Naumov, 1965.

37. On some of those not executed—mentioned in Marchenko's *My Testimony*—see *Chronicle* 17, Amnesty edition, p.76.

38. Leonid Petrovsky writes that torture was used, and gives other details. See *Za prava cheloveka*, pp.53, 80.

39. On this subject see A. Amalrik, *Will the Soviet Union* ... (Allen Lane, The Penguin Press, London, 1970), pp.36–7.

40. See a biography of him in *Pisateli Leningrada* (Leningrad, 1964), p.281.

41. On Brodsky see p.56 and Chap. 1, note 1, also his big collection of poems *Ostanovka v pustyne* (Chekhov Press, New York, 1970).

42. See her collection of stories *Zhivye dengi* (Leningrad, 1967), and her essay in *Molodoi Leningrad 1964*, pp.36–46.

43. See his articles of literary criticism in *Novyi mir* 9 (1967), pp.264–9, and *Prostor* 4 (1969), pp.75–9.

44. This letter is not available.

45. See also the item 'Word of the Nation' in No. 17's *'Samizdat News'*. More difficult to evaluate is this report from No. 7: 'According to rumours, three students from the economics faculty of Moscow University have been arrested, the children of highly placed persons: one of them is the son of the editor of *The Economic Gazette*, [A. F.] Rumyantsev. According to the same, as yet unconfirmed, rumours, they were the members of a group of pro-Chinese tendency.'

46. See the reference to Oleg Smirnov on p.238.

47. See, e.g. the very long summary of a *samizdat* book on early Soviet censorship in No. 14, *Possev* V, pp.13–14.

48. As also by Zh. Medvedev (see Chap. 19, note 85) and, in some degree, by Mark Popovsky in his *Tysyacha dnei Akademika Vavilova*, serialized in *Prostor*, Alma-Ata, in the summer of 1966. A monument to Vavilov was opened in Saratov in 1970, to the annoyance of the authorities. See *Chronicle* 17, Amnesty edition, p.78.

49. No. 7: 'The head of the literature department of the publishing-house 'Prosveshcheniye' has been dismissed from his job because the book *Three Centuries of Russian Poetry* [compiler Nikolai Bannikov, 1968] includes poems by Nikolai Gumilyov and Osip Mandelshtam.'
No. 7: 'The publishing-house "Molodaya Gvardiya" has cut an essay on the students of the 1920s by Evgenia Ginzburg, author of *Into the Whirlwind*, out of the almanac *Prometheus* [*Prometei: istoriko-biograficheskii almanakh*], which was ready for the press.'
No. 9's *'Samizdat* News'': 'Alexander Tvardovsky: "By Right of Memory". This is a lyrical narrative poem, a few parts of which have been published in *Novyi mir*. The full text of the poem was set up and printed, but the censor removed it from the page proofs.' See a long but not full text in *Possev* 10 (1969), pp.52–5, also Tvardovsky's protest at this publication in the *Literary Gazette*, February 11th, 1970.

50. For the writer's comments on this account of the search, which includes some apparent inaccuracies, see *Possev* II, p.63. He considers that 'the K.G.B. only wasted time on the search'.

51. See, at any rate, his articles in the *Literary Gazette*, March 10th, 1971, and *Vestnik Moskovskogo universiteta: Filologiya*, 1 (1967), pp.51–62.

52. On this episode see p.91. Shikhanovich has written the text-book *Vvedenie v sovremennuyu matematiku* (Moscow, 1965).

INDEX OF PROPER NAMES

Entries in bold figures refer to plate numbers